Seconds

Seconds

Bryan Lee O'Malley

with

Jason Fischer	Drawing Assistant
Dustin Harbin	Lettering
Nathan Fairbairn	Color

SELF
MADE
HERO

Over and Over
Words and music by Christine McVie
© Copyright 1979 Fleetwood Mac Music.
Universal Music Publishing International MGB Limited.
All rights reserved. International Copyright secured.

Published by arrangement with Ballantine Books, an imprint of Random House, a division of Random House LLC, New York, NY USA. All rights reserved.

First published in the UK 2014
by SelfMadeHero
139–141 Pancras Road
London NW1 1UN
www.selfmadehero.com

Publishing Assistant: Guillaume Rater
Editorial and Production Manager: Lizzie Kaye
Marketing Manager: Sam Humphrey
Publishing Director: Emma Hayley

A CIP record for this book is available from the British Library

ISBN: 978-1-906838-88-1

10 9 8 7 6 5 4

Printed in Slovenia

I felt a kind of vertigo, as if
I were merely plunging from
one world to another, and in
each I arrived shortly after
the end of the world had
taken place

—Italo Calvino,
If on a winter's night a traveler

And I said
Could it be me?
Could it really, really be?
Over and over

—Fleetwood Mac

Seconds

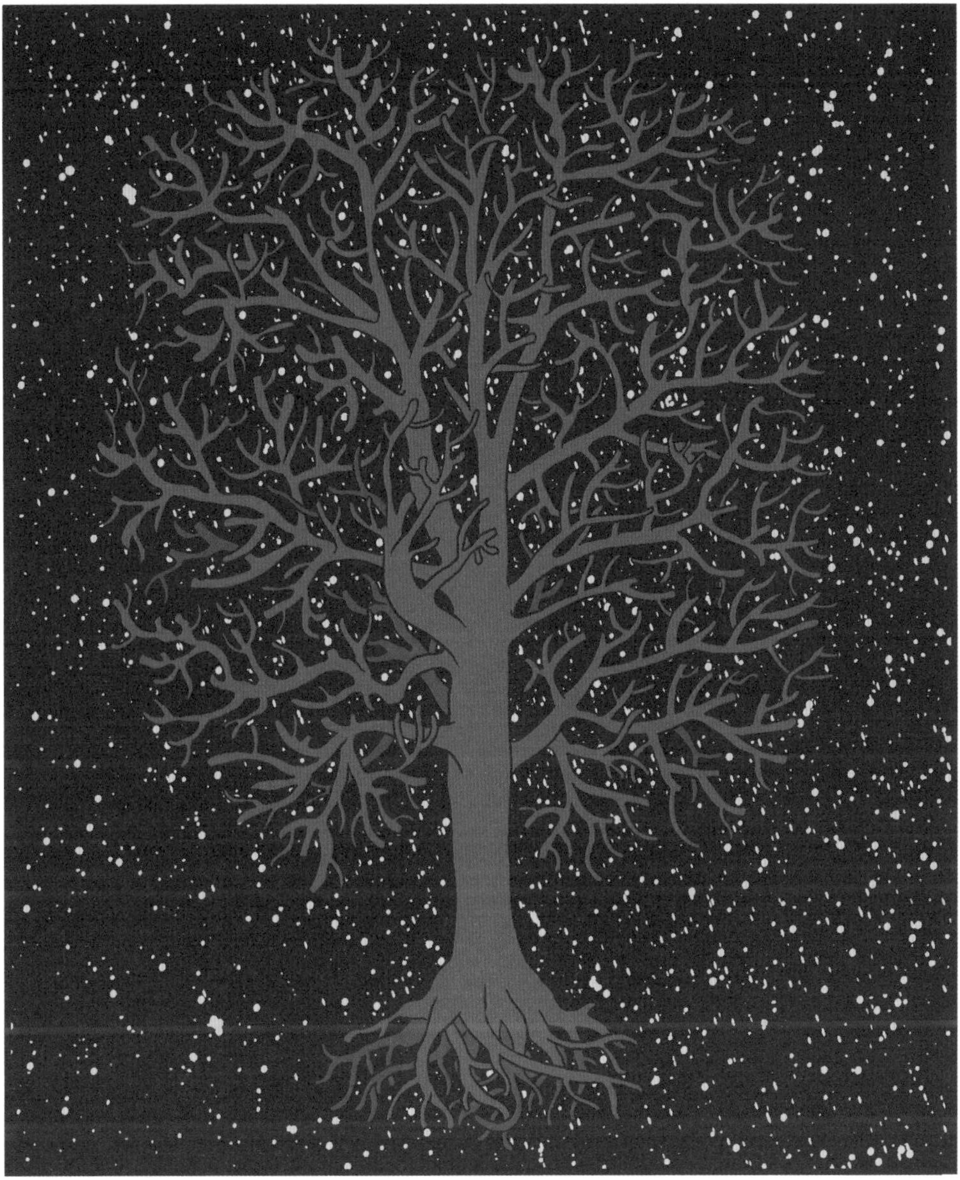

She
woke
up,

and
there
was a
glow.

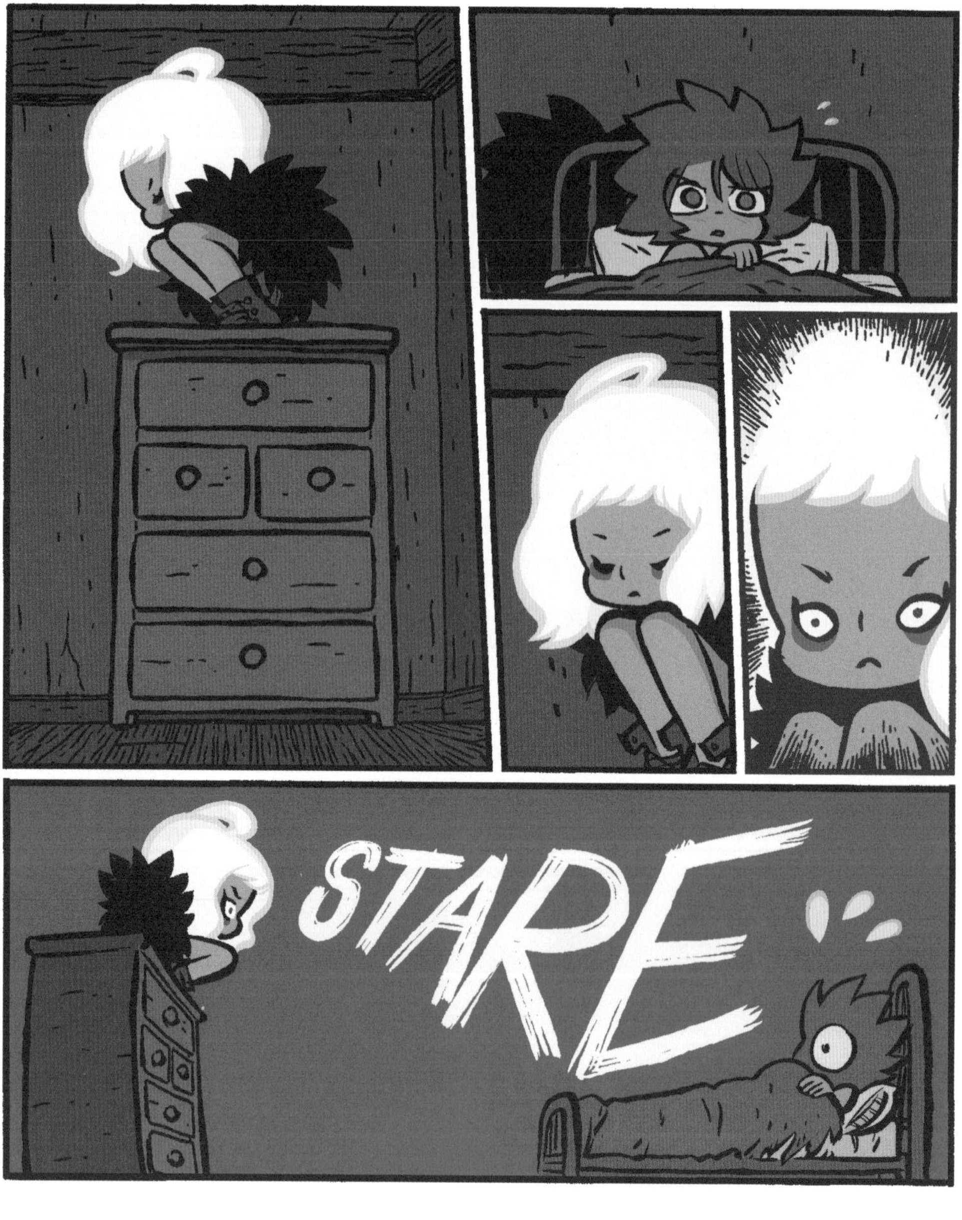
STARE

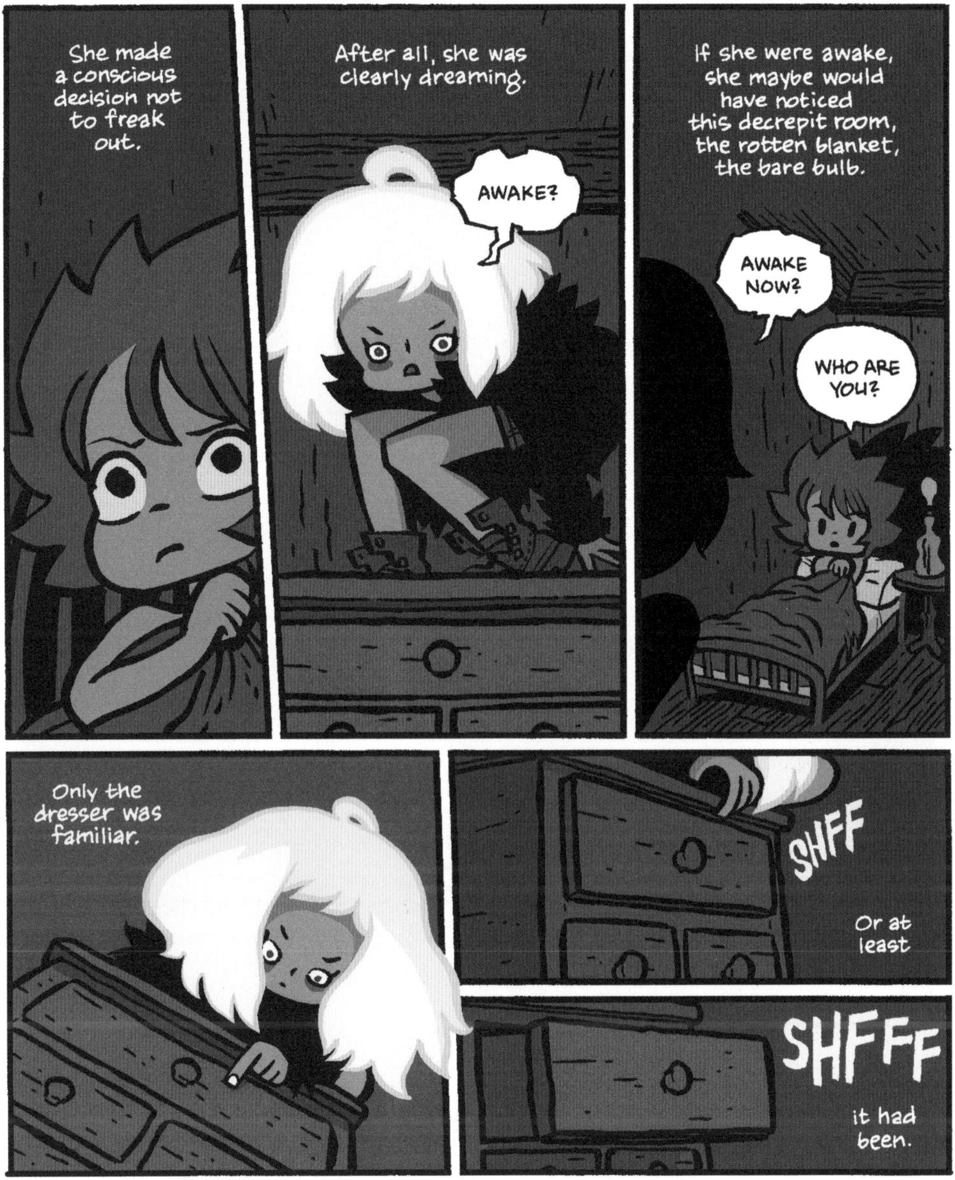
She made a conscious decision not to freak out.
After all, she was clearly dreaming.
AWAKE?
If she were awake, she maybe would have noticed this decrepit room, the rotten blanket, the bare bulb.
AWAKE NOW?
WHO ARE YOU?
Only the dresser was familiar.
SHFF
Or at least
SHFFF
it had been.

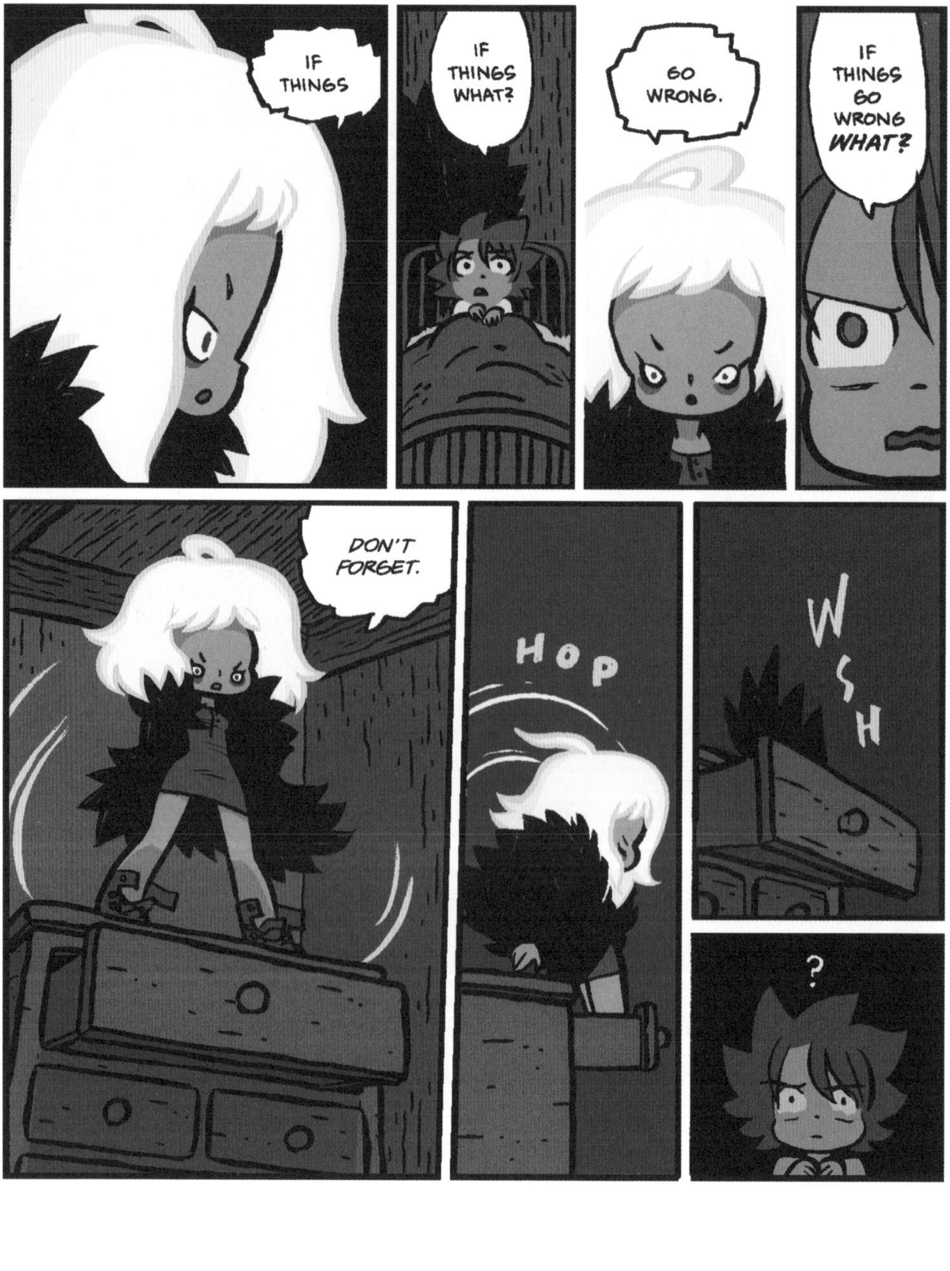
IF THINGS
IF THINGS WHAT?
GO WRONG.
IF THINGS GO WRONG *WHAT?*
DON'T FORGET.
HOP
WSH
?

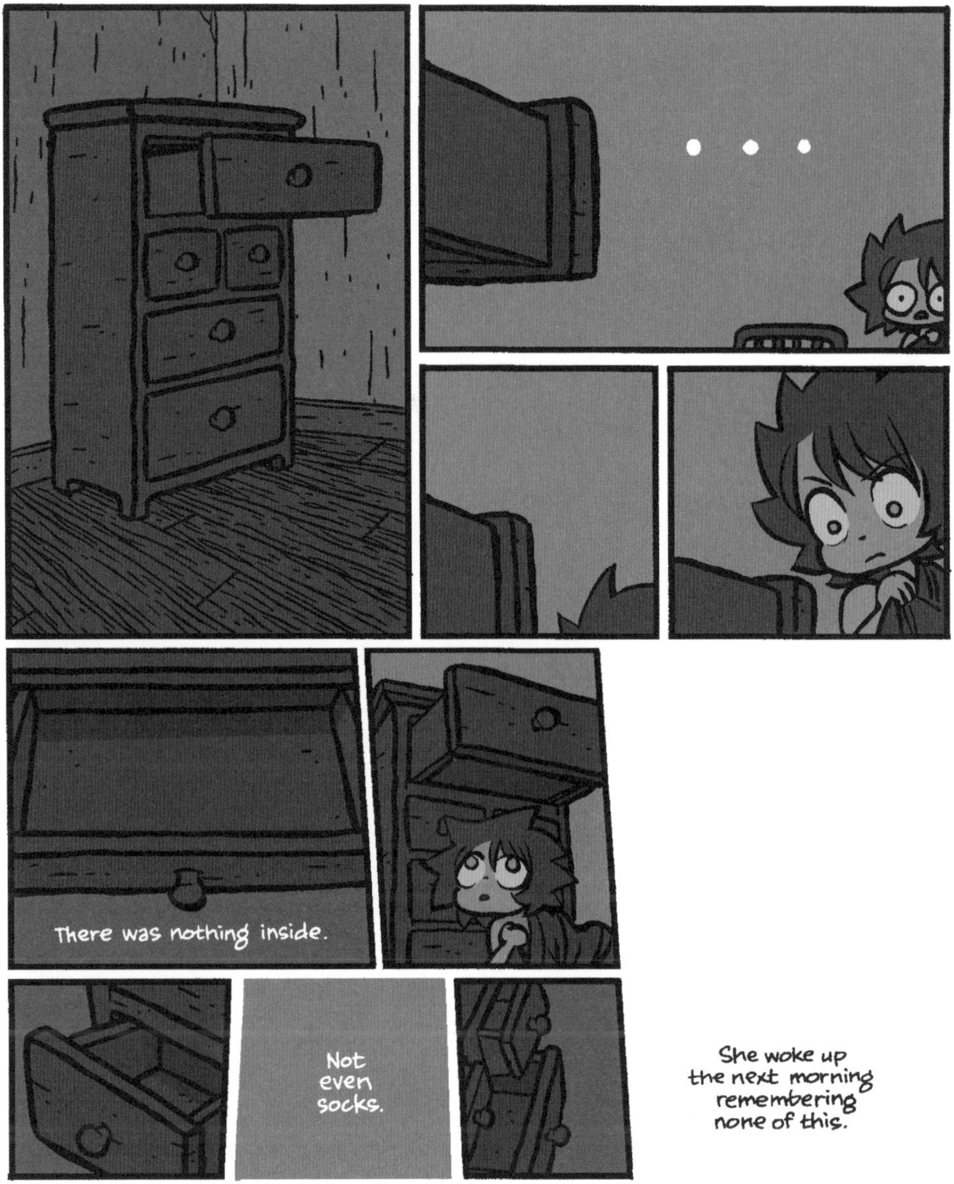
. . .
There was nothing inside.
Not even socks.
She woke up the next morning remembering none of this.

1

Katie

Katie was stressed out.

I'M PERFECTLY FINE.

She was sleeping too little, worrying too much, feeling old.

SHE WAS IN HER TWENTIES AND YOUNG AND TOTALLY GREAT.

At 29, she felt like everything was slipping away.

UM, NO.

...and she was talking to herself more than usual.

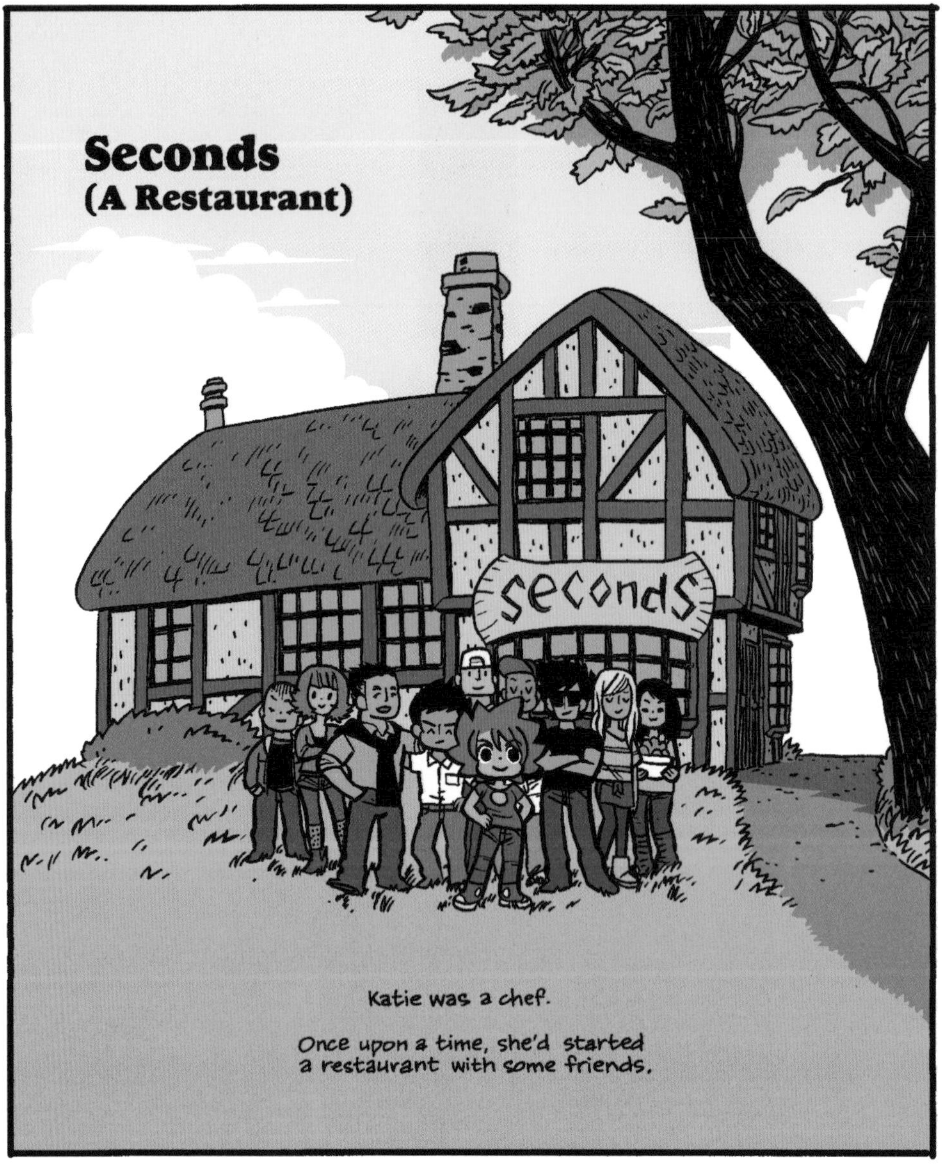
Seconds
(A Restaurant)
seconds
Katie was a chef.
Once upon a time, she'd started a restaurant with some friends.

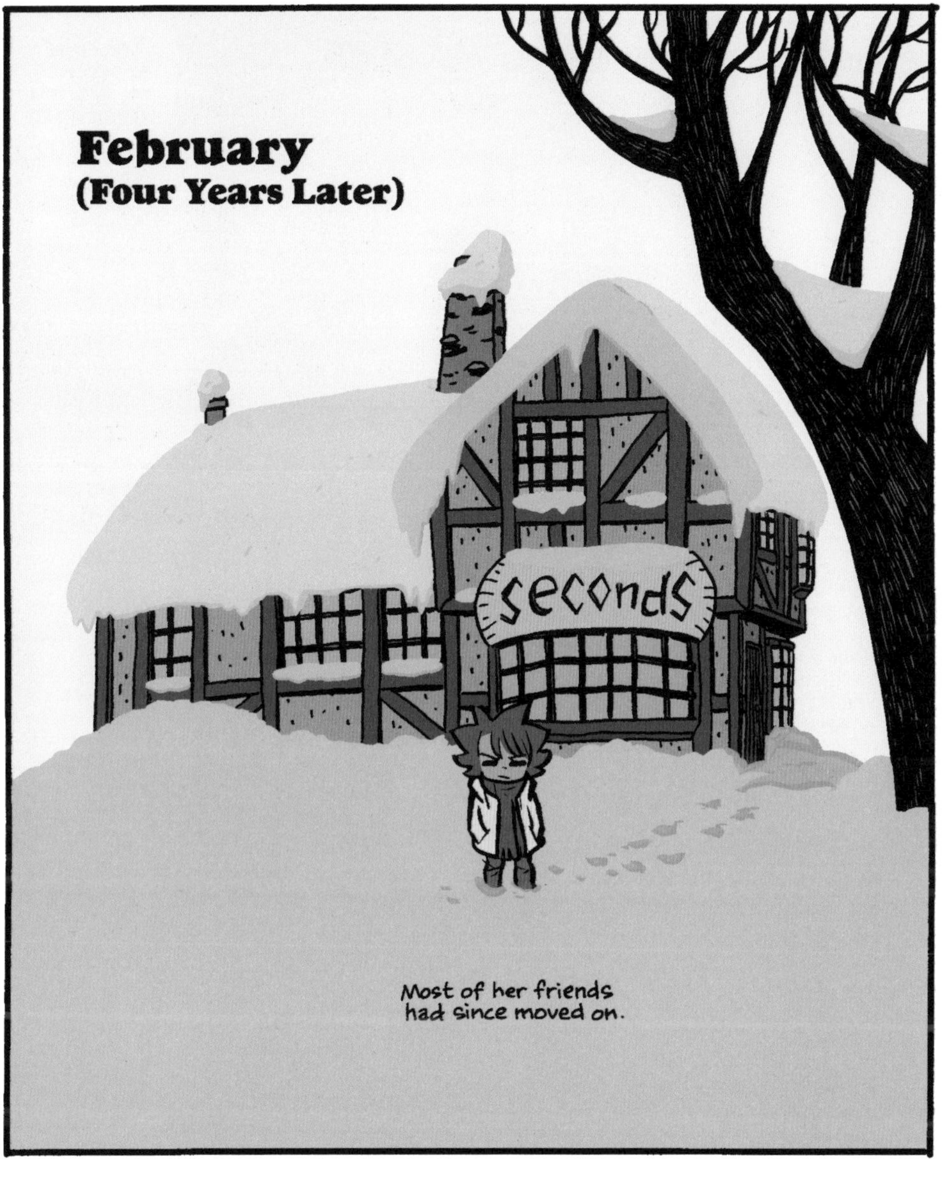
February
(Four Years Later)
seconds
Most of her friends had since moved on.

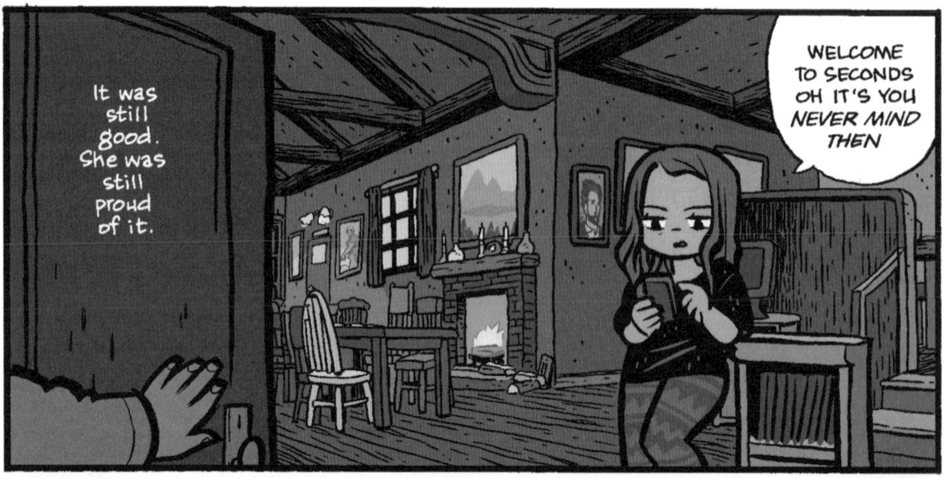
It was still good. She was still proud of it.
WELCOME TO SECONDS OH IT'S YOU NEVER MIND THEN

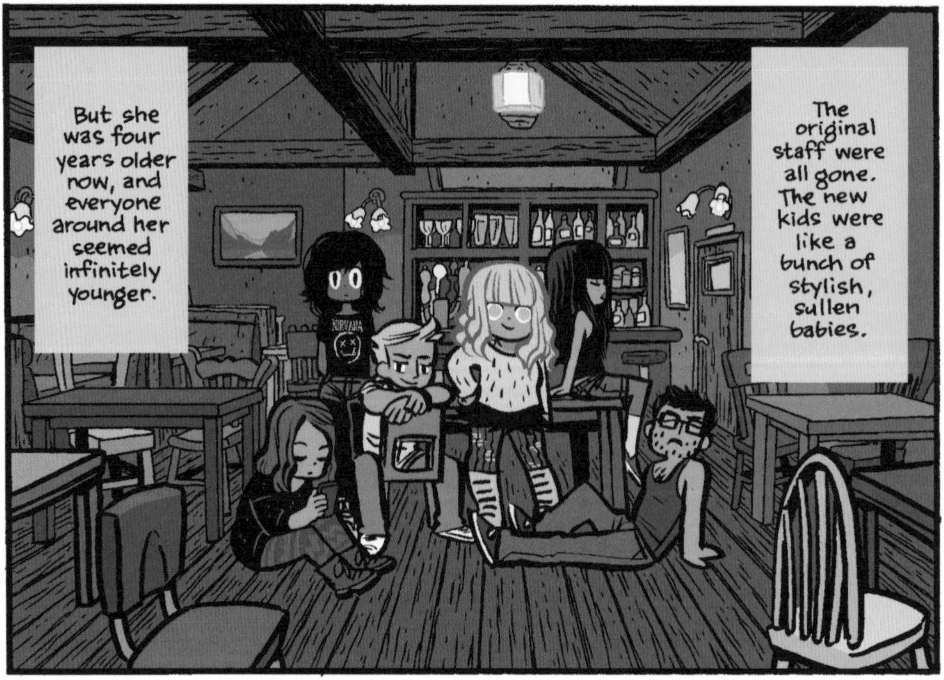
But she was four years older now, and everyone around her seemed infinitely younger.
The original staff were all gone. The new kids were like a bunch of stylish, sullen babies.

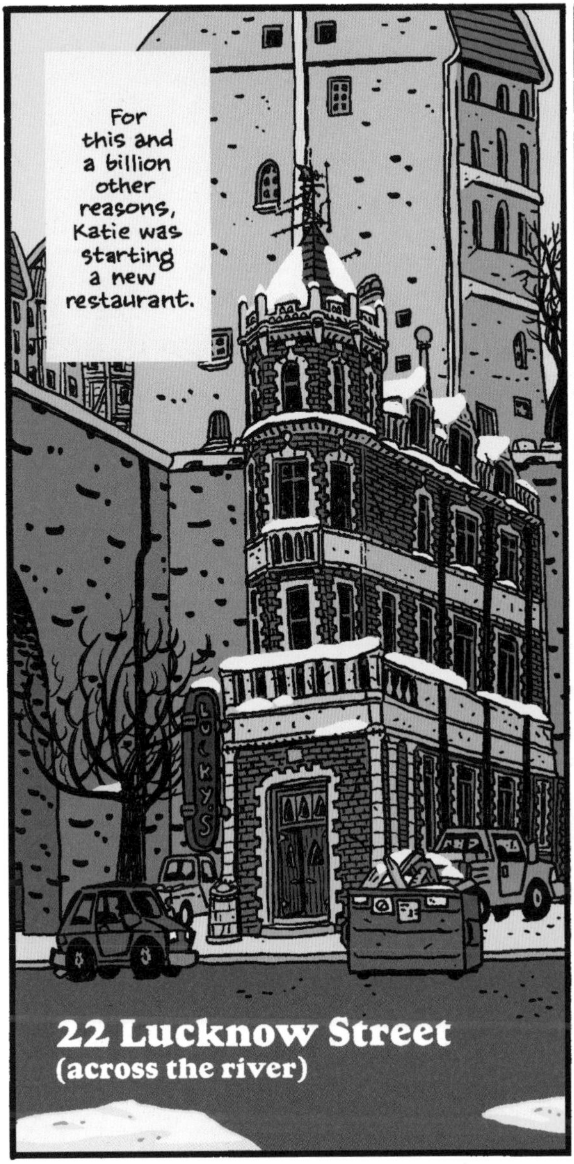
For this and a billion other reasons, Katie was starting a new restaurant.
LUCKY'S
22 Lucknow Street
(across the river)

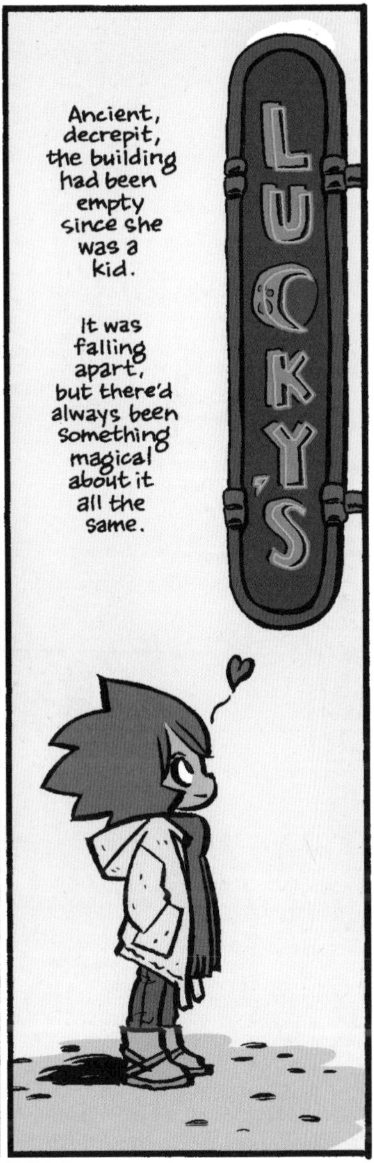
Ancient, decrepit, the building had been empty since she was a kid.
It was falling apart, but there'd always been something magical about it all the same.
LUCKY'S

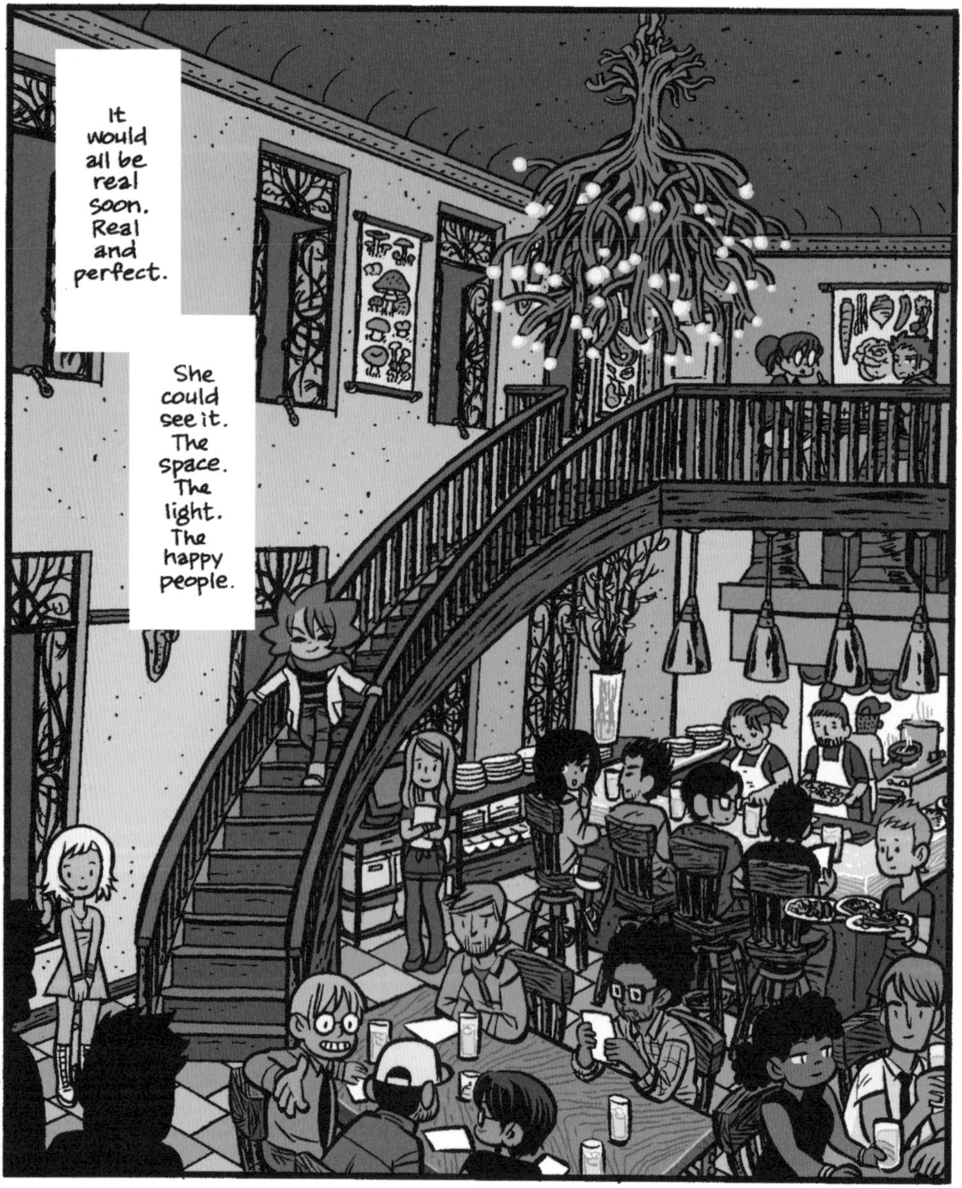
It would all be real soon. Real and perfect.
She could see it. The space. The light. The happy people.

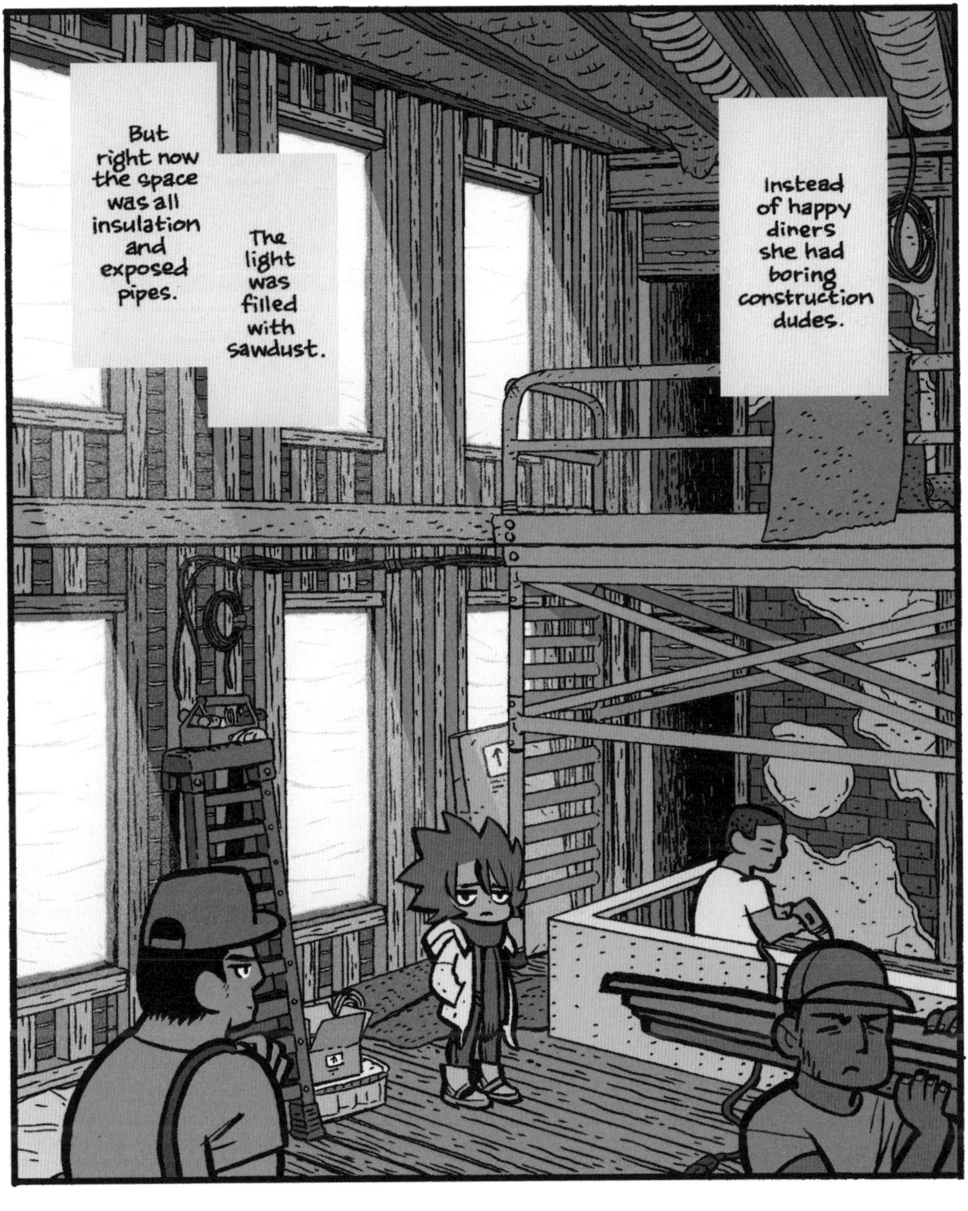
But right now the space was all insulation and exposed pipes.
The light was filled with sawdust.
Instead of happy diners she had boring construction dudes.

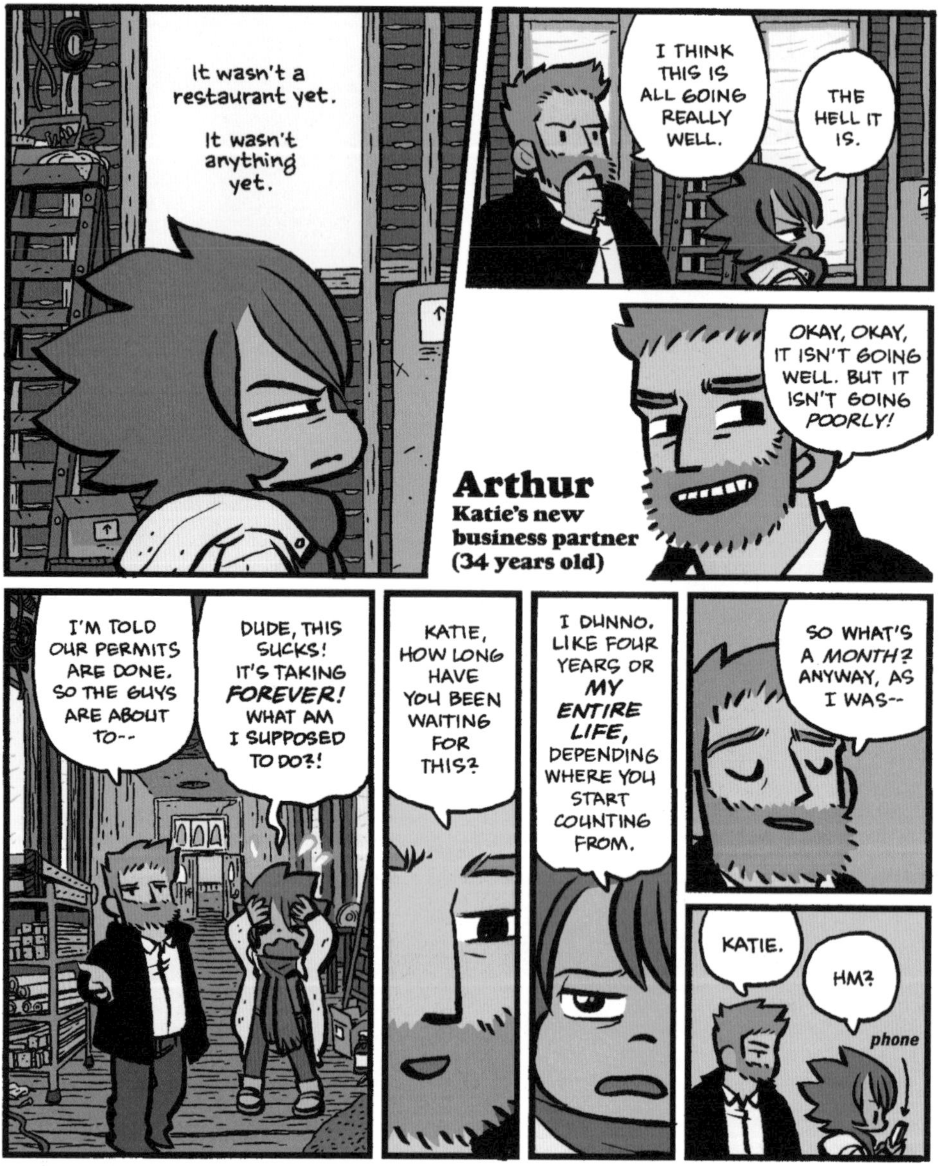
It wasn't a restaurant yet.
It wasn't anything yet.
I THINK THIS IS ALL GOING REALLY WELL.
THE HELL IT IS.
OKAY, OKAY, IT ISN'T GOING WELL. BUT IT ISN'T GOING *POORLY!*
Arthur
Katie's new business partner (34 years old)
I'M TOLD OUR PERMITS ARE DONE. SO THE GUYS ARE ABOUT TO--
DUDE, THIS SUCKS! IT'S TAKING *FOREVER!* WHAT AM I SUPPOSED TO DO?!
KATIE, HOW LONG HAVE YOU BEEN WAITING FOR THIS?
I DUNNO. LIKE FOUR YEARS OR *MY ENTIRE LIFE,* DEPENDING WHERE YOU START COUNTING FROM.
SO WHAT'S A *MONTH*? ANYWAY, AS I WAS--
KATIE.
HM?
phone

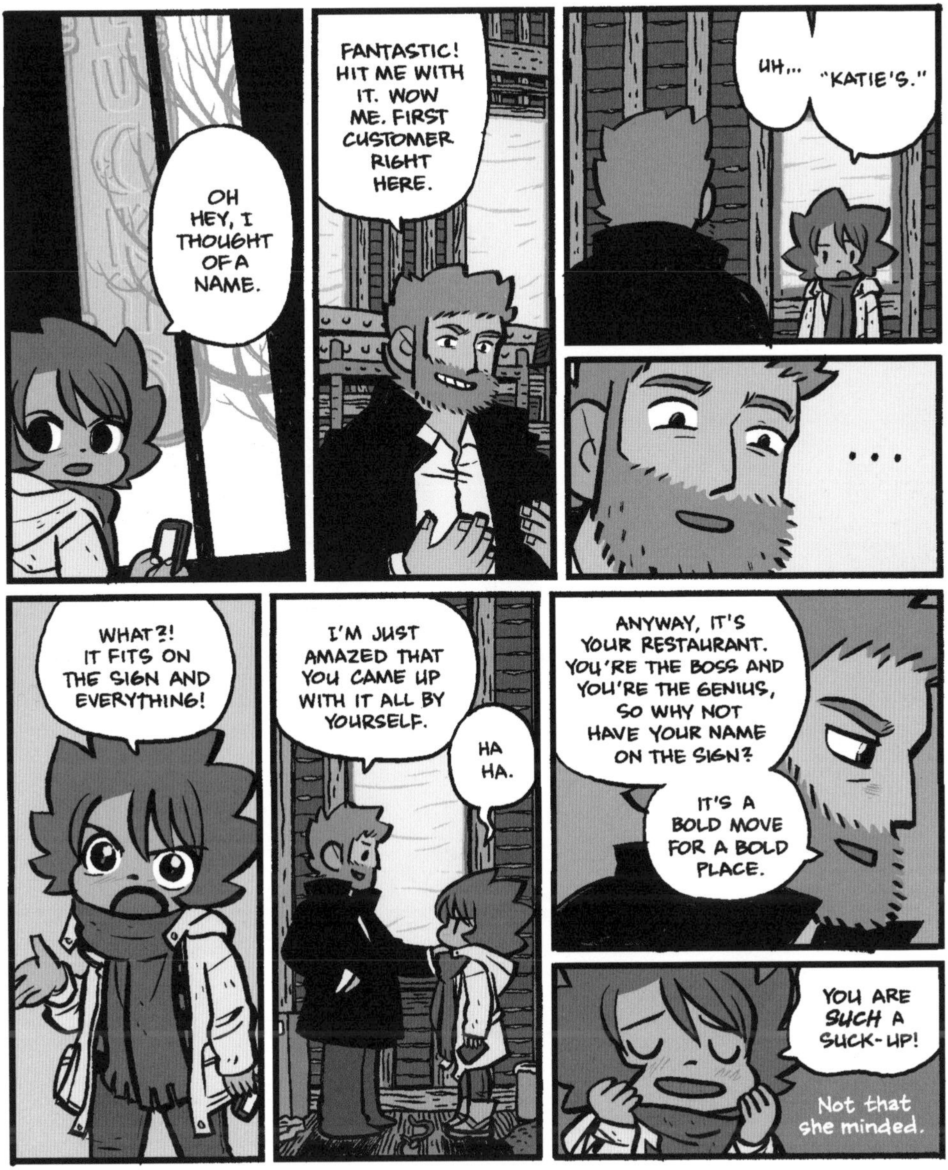
OH HEY, I THOUGHT OF A NAME.
FANTASTIC! HIT ME WITH IT. WOW ME. FIRST CUSTOMER RIGHT HERE.
UH...
"KATIE'S."
...
WHAT?! IT FITS ON THE SIGN AND EVERYTHING!
I'M JUST AMAZED THAT YOU CAME UP WITH IT ALL BY YOURSELF.
HA HA.
ANYWAY, IT'S YOUR RESTAURANT. YOU'RE THE BOSS AND YOU'RE THE GENIUS, SO WHY NOT HAVE YOUR NAME ON THE SIGN?
IT'S A BOLD MOVE FOR A BOLD PLACE.
YOU ARE SUCH A SUCK-UP!
Not that she minded.

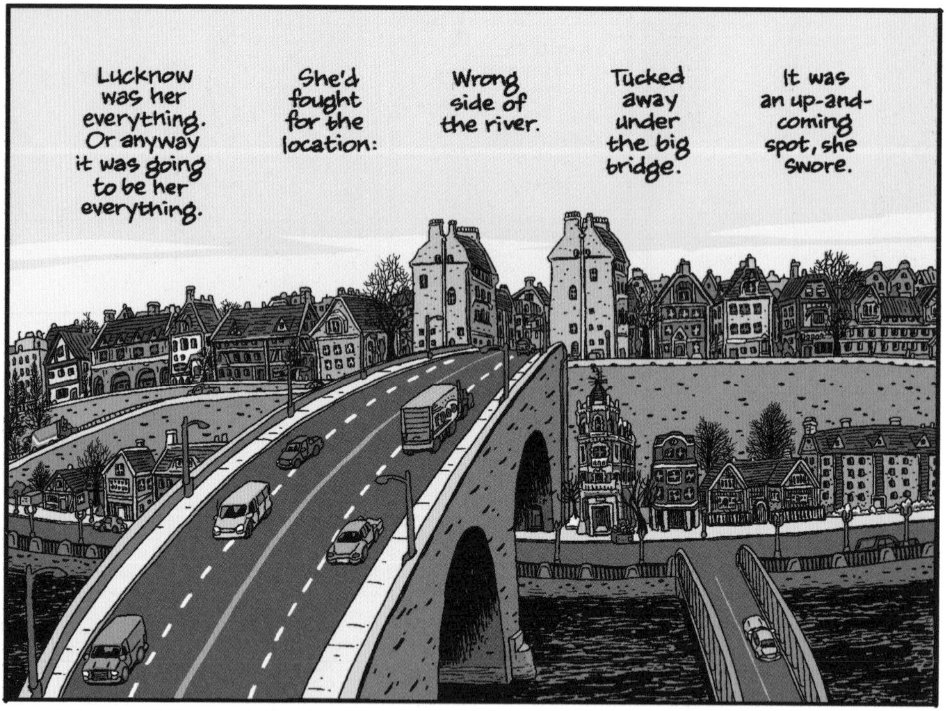
Lucknow was her everything. Or anyway it was going to be her everything.
She'd fought for the location:
Wrong side of the river.
Tucked away under the big bridge.
It was an up-and-coming spot, she swore.

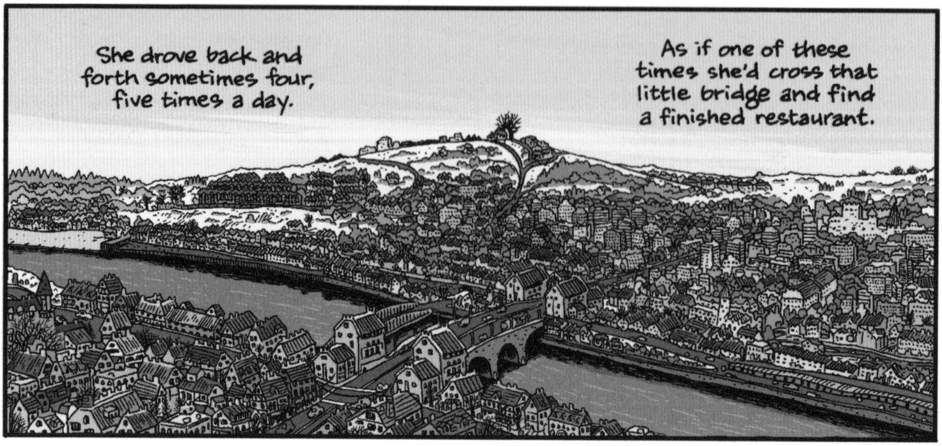
She drove back and forth sometimes four, five times a day.
As if one of these times she'd cross that little bridge and find a finished restaurant.

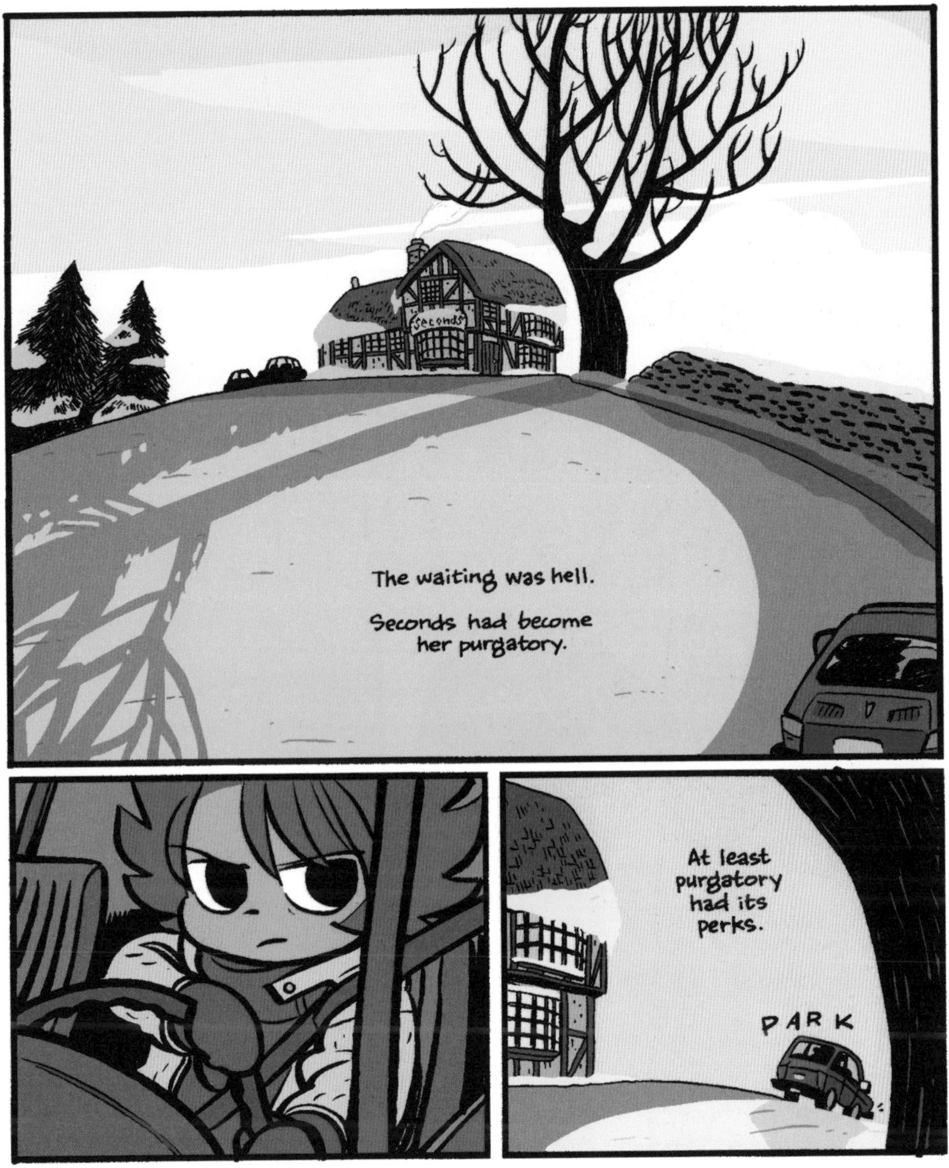

Seconds
The waiting was hell.
Seconds had become her purgatory.
At least purgatory had its perks.
PARK

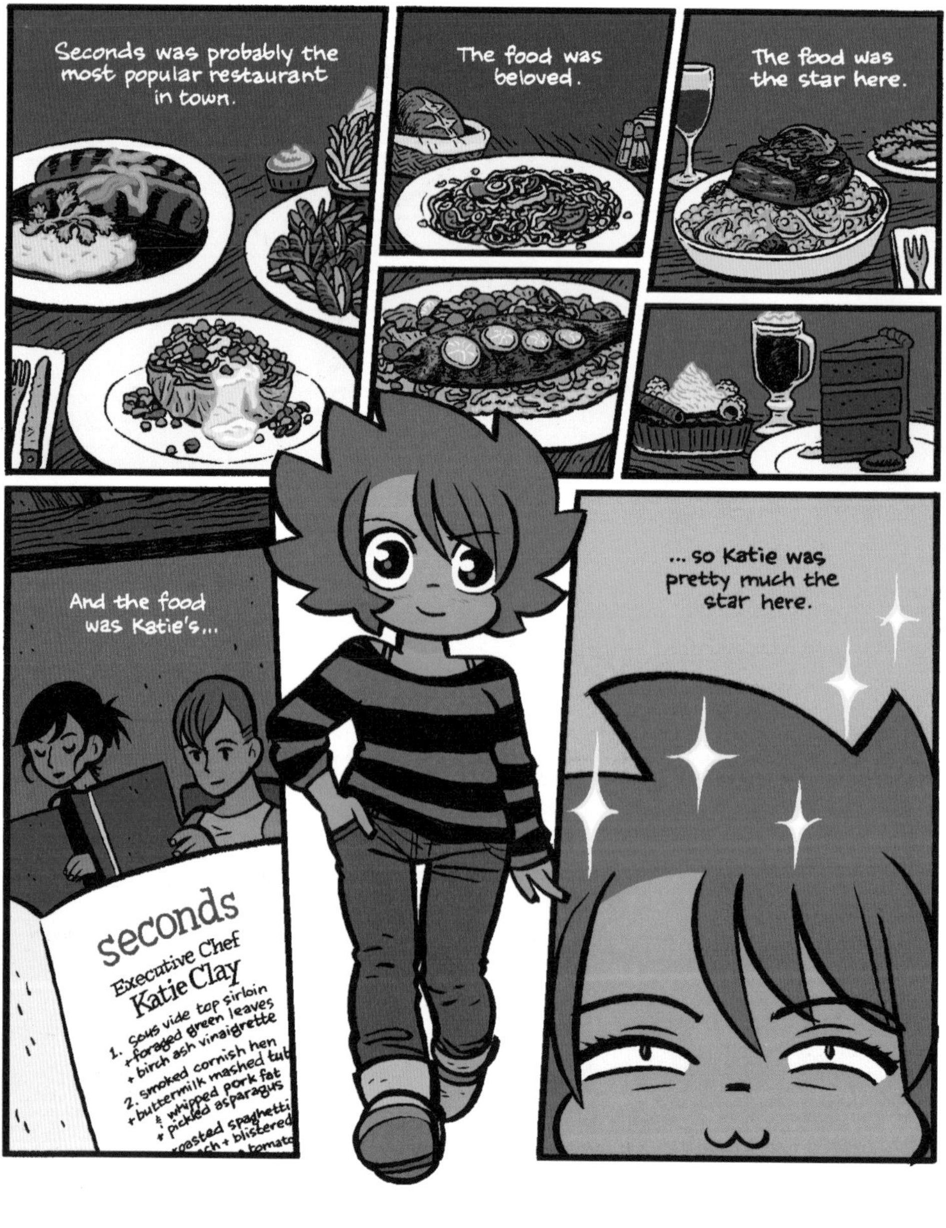
Seconds was probably the most popular restaurant in town.
The food was beloved.
The food was the star here.
And the food was Katie's...
seconds
Executive Chef
Katie Clay
1. sous vide top sirloin
+ foraged green leaves
+ birch ash vinaigrette
2. smoked cornish hen
+ buttermilk mashed tub
+ whipped pork fat
& pickled asparagus
...so Katie was pretty much the star here.

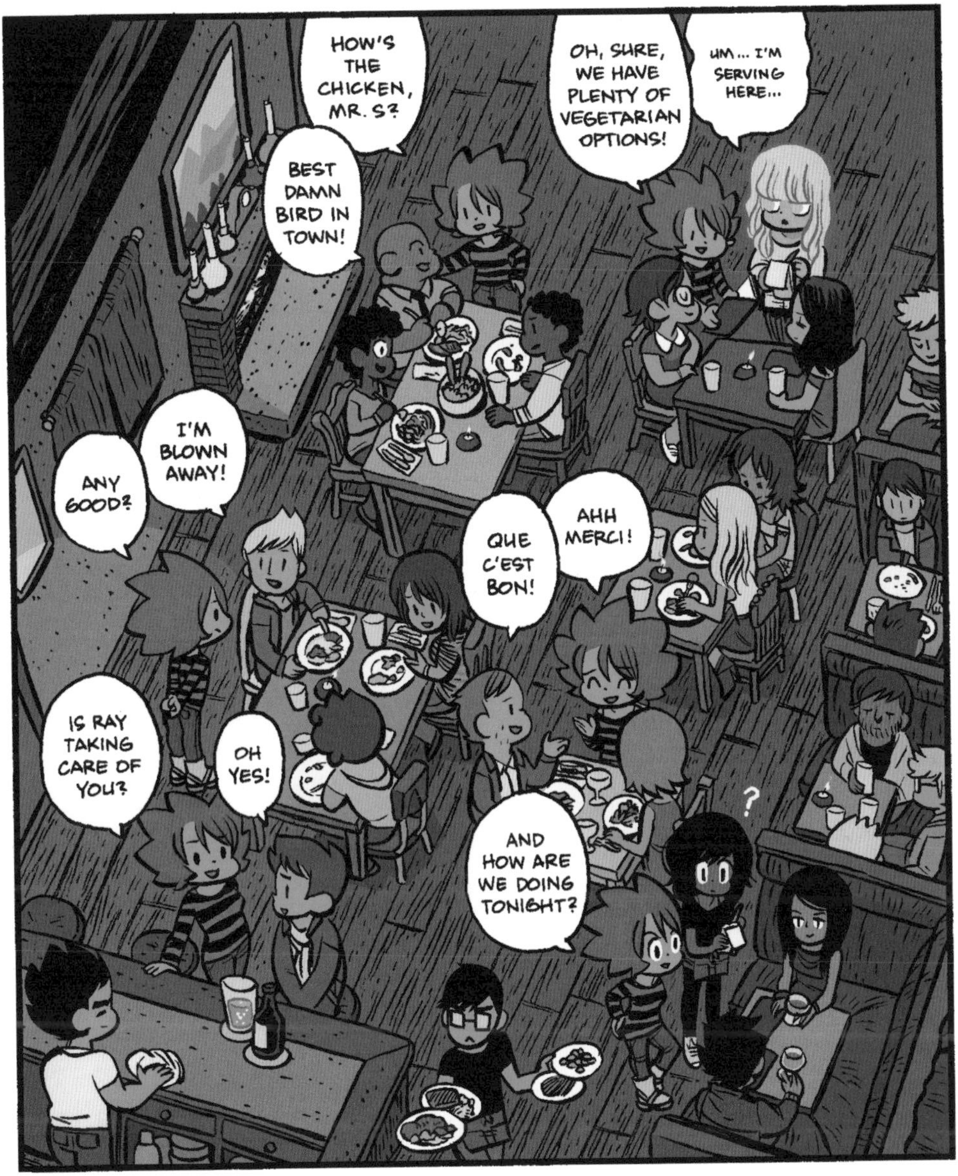
HOW'S THE CHICKEN, MR. S?
BEST DAMN BIRD IN TOWN!
OH, SURE, WE HAVE PLENTY OF VEGETARIAN OPTIONS!
UM... I'M SERVING HERE...
ANY GOOD?
I'M BLOWN AWAY!
QUE C'EST BON!
AHH MERCI!
IS RAY TAKING CARE OF YOU?
OH YES!
AND HOW ARE WE DOING TONIGHT?
?

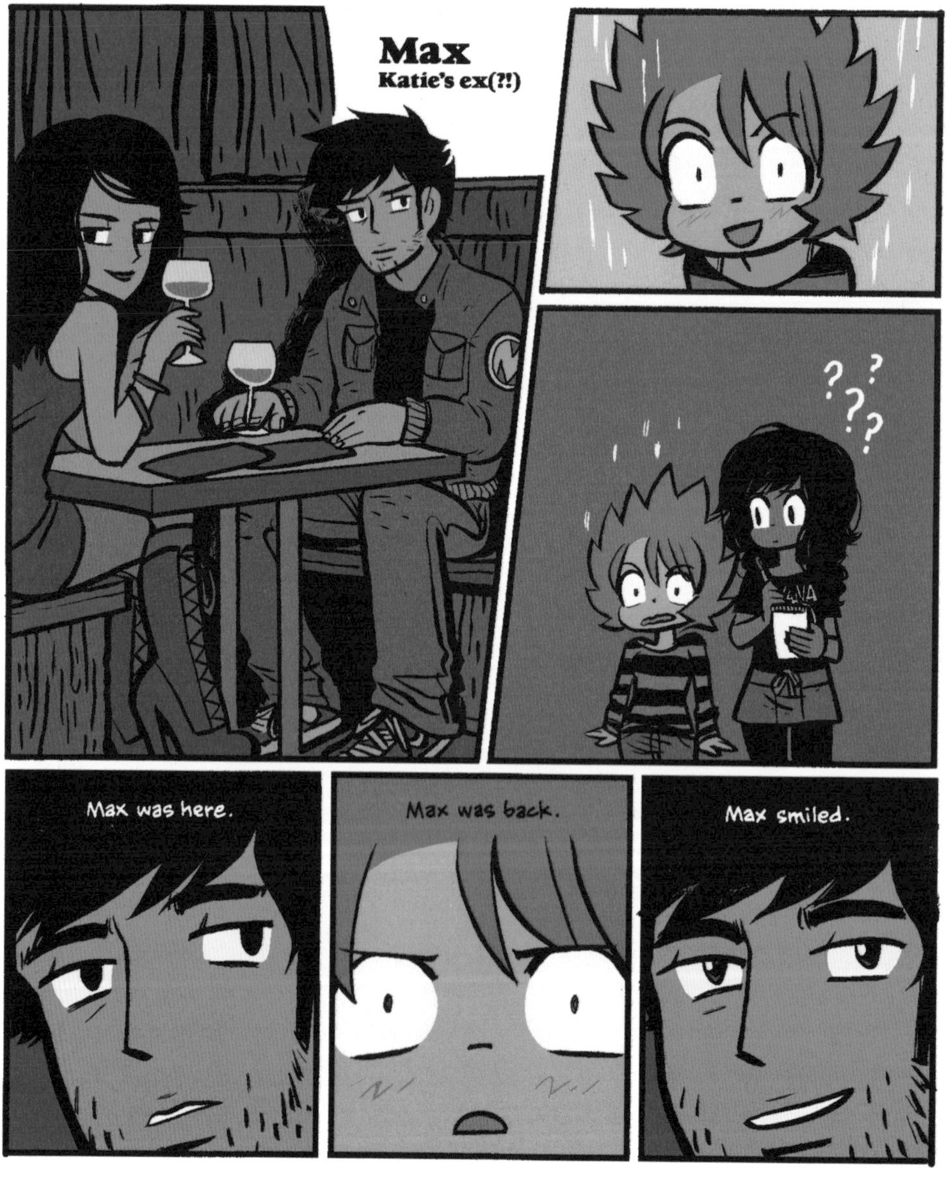
Max
Katie's ex(?!)
? ? ? ? ?
Max was here.
Max was back.
Max smiled.

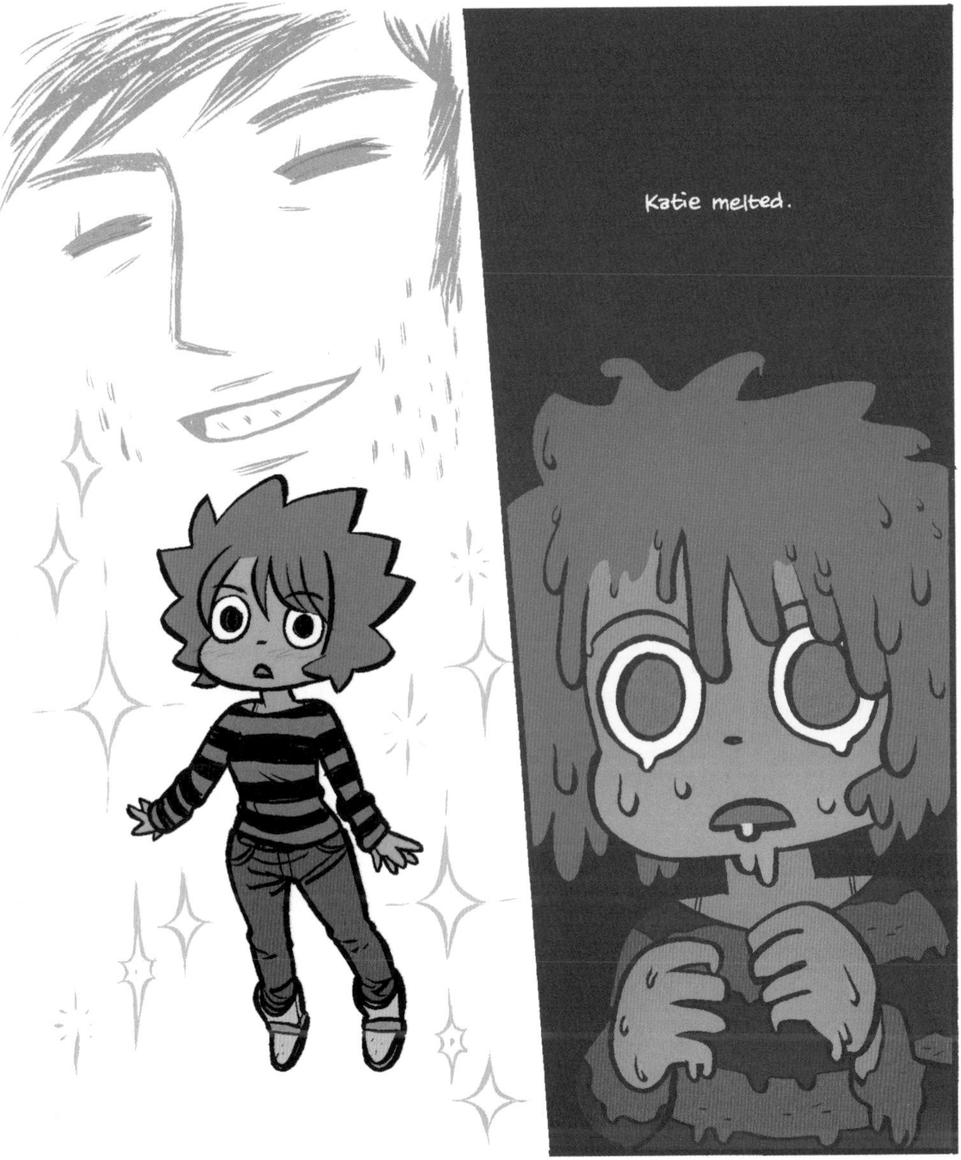
Katie melted.

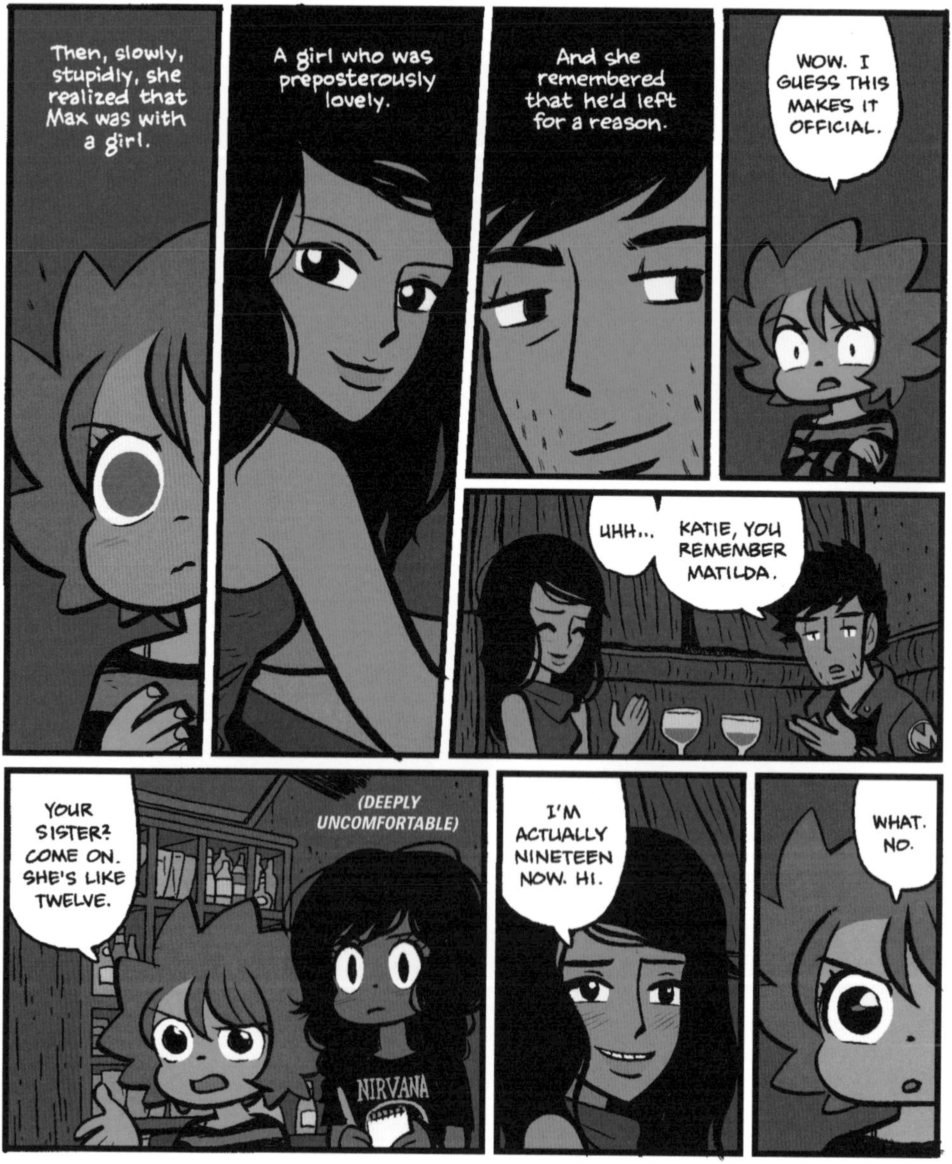
Then, slowly, stupidly, she realized that Max was with a girl.
A girl who was preposterously lovely.
And she remembered that he'd left for a reason.
WOW. I GUESS THIS MAKES IT OFFICIAL.
UHH...
KATIE, YOU REMEMBER MATILDA.
YOUR SISTER? COME ON. SHE'S LIKE TWELVE.
(DEEPLY UNCOMFORTABLE)
NIRVANA
I'M ACTUALLY NINETEEN NOW. HI.
WHAT. NO.

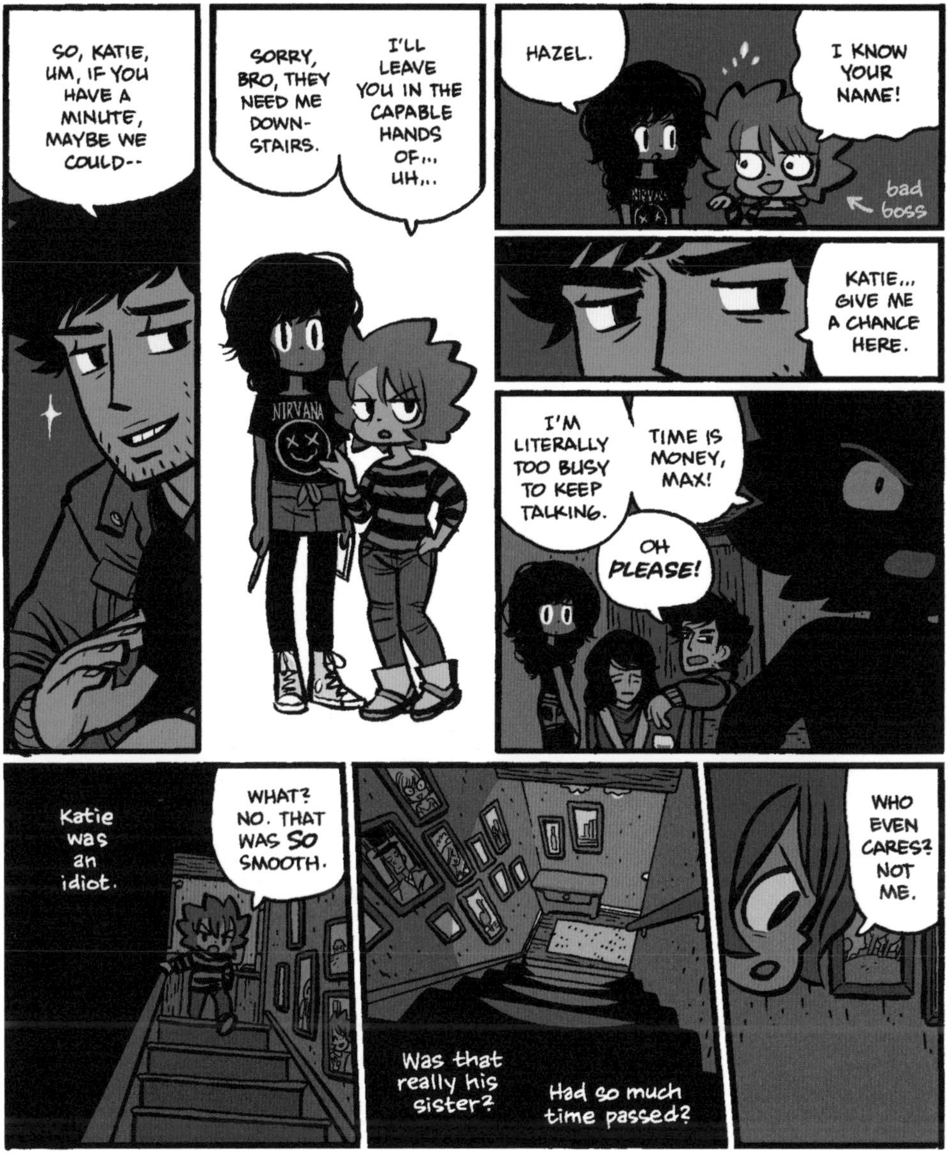
SO, KATIE, UM, IF YOU HAVE A MINUTE, MAYBE WE COULD--
SORRY, BRO, THEY NEED ME DOWN-STAIRS.
I'LL LEAVE YOU IN THE CAPABLE HANDS OF... UH...
HAZEL.
I KNOW YOUR NAME!
bad boss
NIRVANA
KATIE... GIVE ME A CHANCE HERE.
I'M LITERALLY TOO BUSY TO KEEP TALKING.
TIME IS MONEY, MAX!
OH PLEASE!
Katie was an idiot.
WHAT? NO. THAT WAS SO SMOOTH.
Was that really his sister?
Had so much time passed?
WHO EVEN CARES? NOT ME.

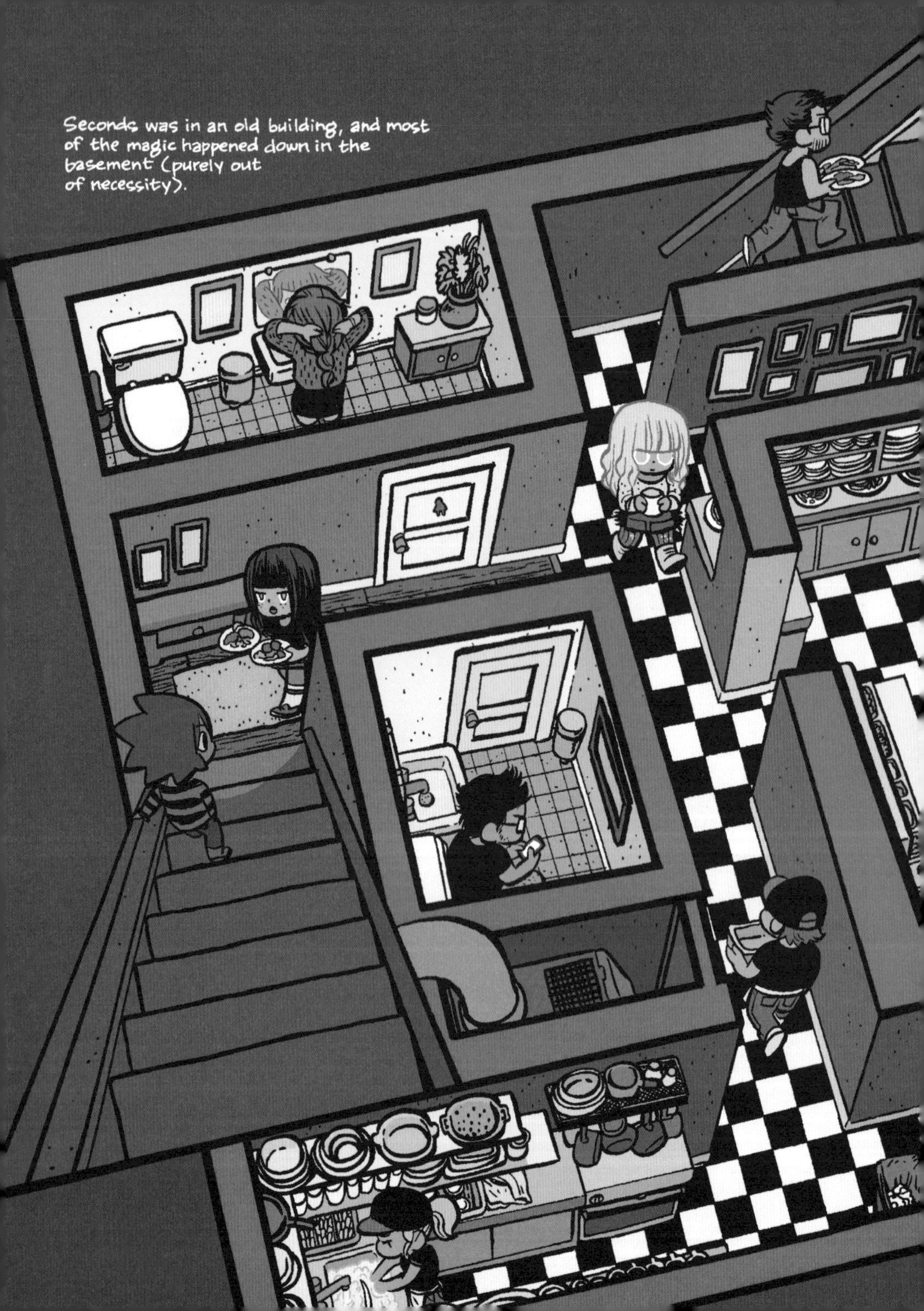
Seconds was in an old building, and most of the magic happened down in the basement (purely out of necessity).

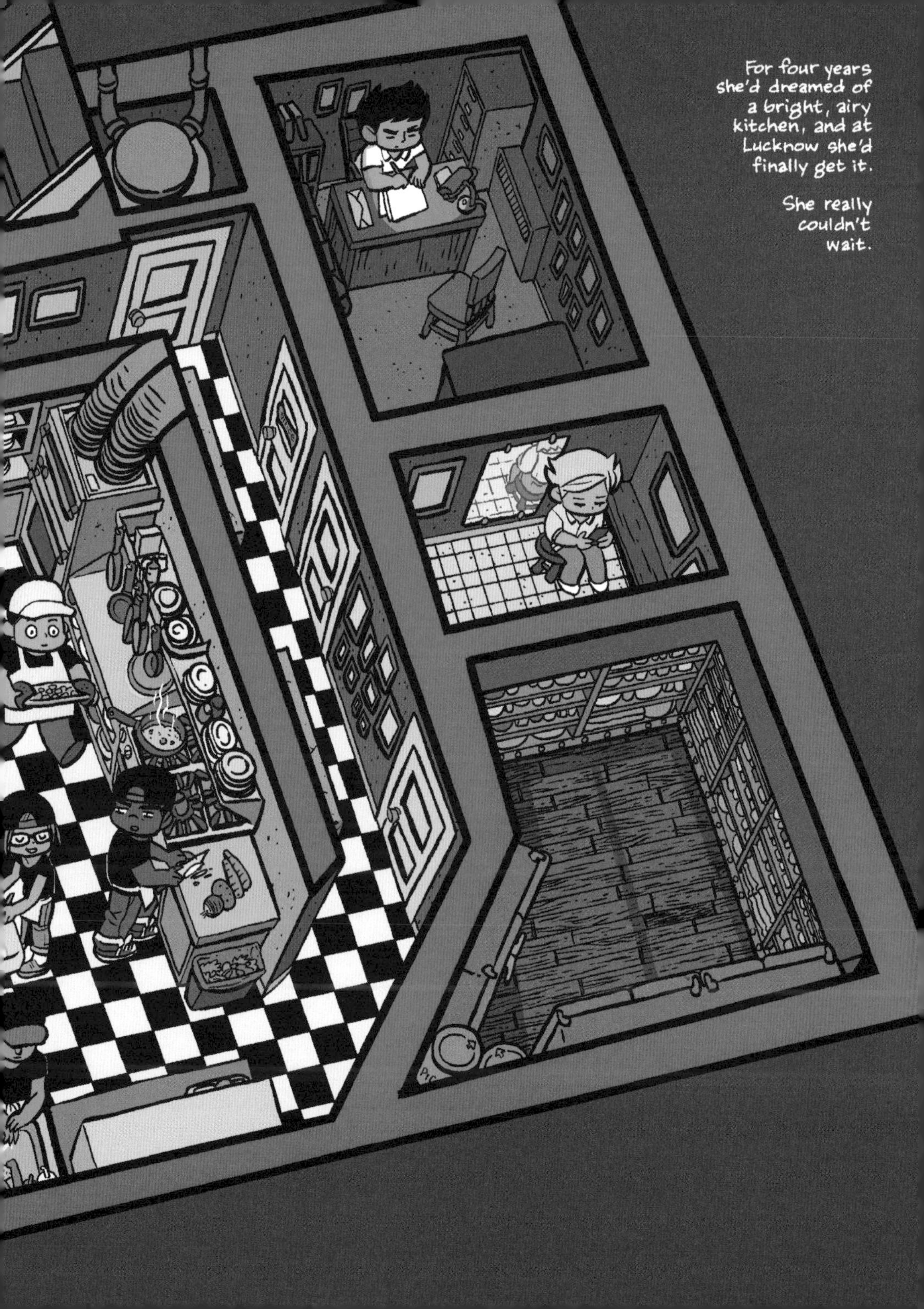
For four years she'd dreamed of a bright, airy kitchen, and at Lucknow she'd finally get it.
She really couldn't wait.

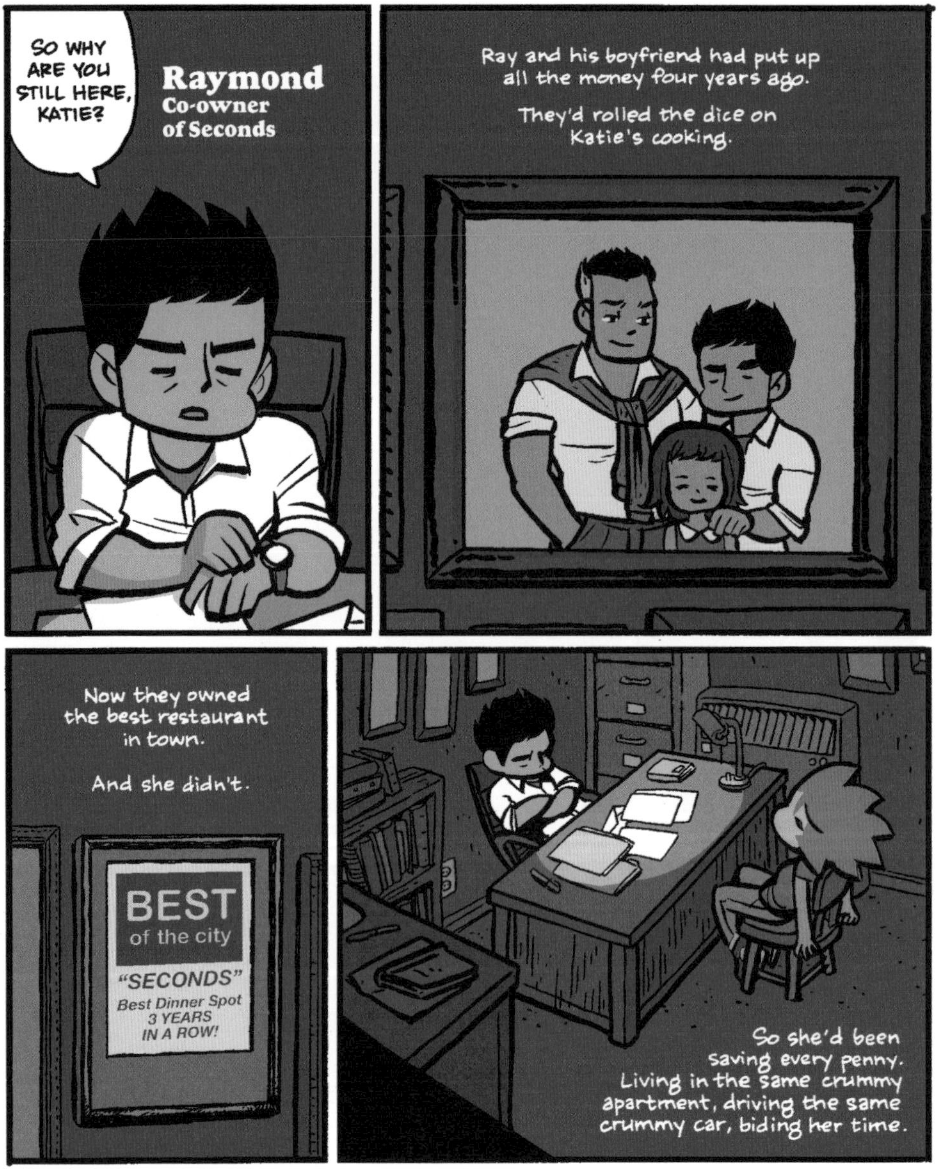
SO WHY ARE YOU STILL HERE, KATIE?
Raymond
Co-owner of Seconds
Ray and his boyfriend had put up all the money four years ago.
They'd rolled the dice on Katie's cooking.
Now they owned the best restaurant in town.
And she didn't.
BEST
of the city
"SECONDS"
Best Dinner Spot
3 YEARS
IN A ROW!
So she'd been saving every penny.
Living in the same crummy apartment, driving the same crummy car, biding her time.

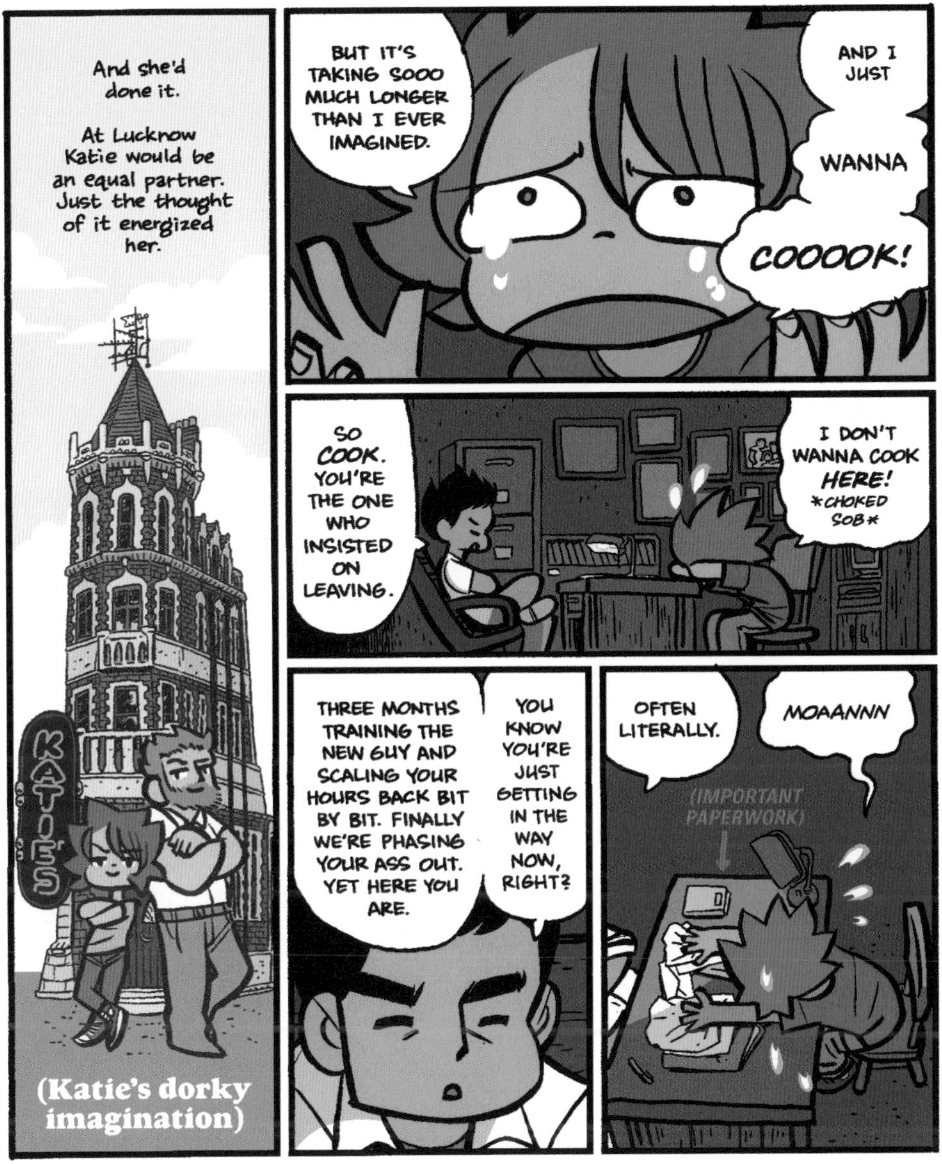
And she'd done it.
At Lucknow Katie would be an equal partner. Just the thought of it energized her.
KATIE'S
(Katie's dorky imagination)
BUT IT'S TAKING SOOO MUCH LONGER THAN I EVER IMAGINED.
AND I JUST
WANNA
COOOOK!
SO COOK. YOU'RE THE ONE WHO INSISTED ON LEAVING.
I DON'T WANNA COOK HERE! *CHOKED SOB*
THREE MONTHS TRAINING THE NEW GUY AND SCALING YOUR HOURS BACK BIT BY BIT. FINALLY WE'RE PHASING YOUR ASS OUT. YET HERE YOU ARE.
YOU KNOW YOU'RE JUST GETTING IN THE WAY NOW, RIGHT?
OFTEN LITERALLY.
MOAANNN
(IMPORTANT PAPERWORK)

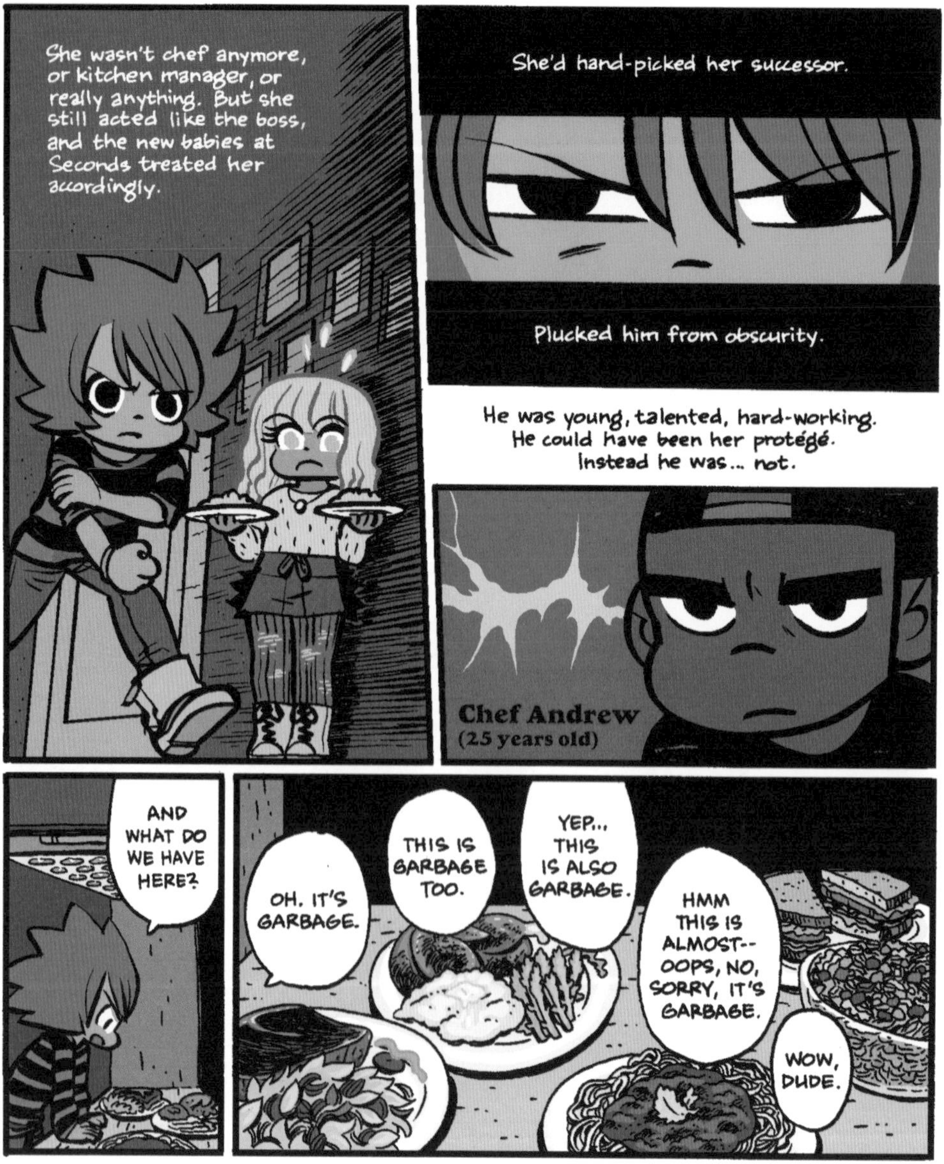

She wasn't chef anymore, or kitchen manager, or really anything. But she still acted like the boss, and the new babies at Seconds treated her accordingly.
She'd hand-picked her successor.
Plucked him from obscurity.
He was young, talented, hard-working. He could have been her protégé. Instead he was... not.
Chef Andrew
(25 years old)
AND WHAT DO WE HAVE HERE?
OH. IT'S GARBAGE.
THIS IS GARBAGE TOO.
YEP... THIS IS ALSO GARBAGE.
HMM THIS IS ALMOST-- OOPS, NO, SORRY, IT'S GARBAGE.
WOW, DUDE.

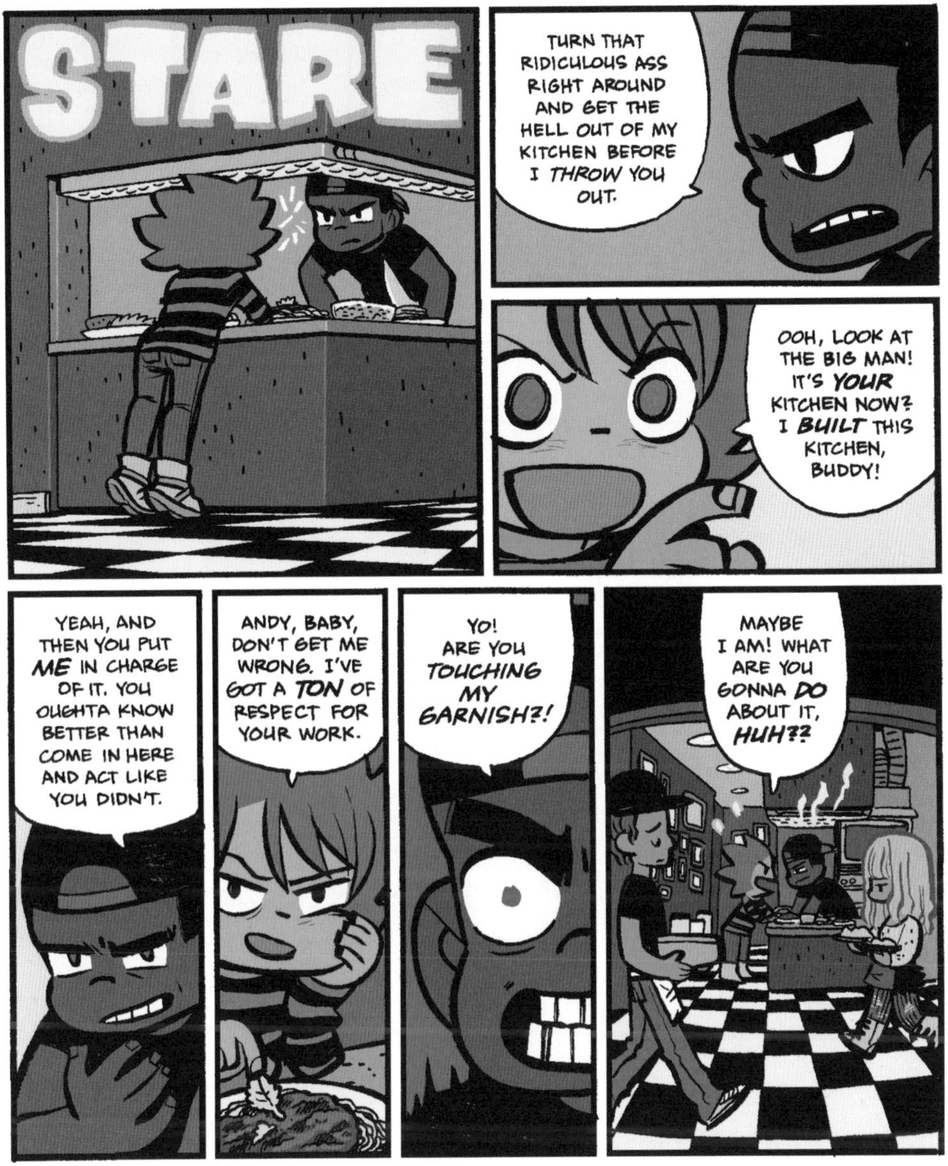
STARE
TURN THAT RIDICULOUS ASS RIGHT AROUND AND GET THE HELL OUT OF MY KITCHEN BEFORE I *THROW* YOU OUT.
OOH, LOOK AT THE BIG MAN! IT'S ***YOUR*** KITCHEN NOW? I ***BUILT*** THIS KITCHEN, BUDDY!
YEAH, AND THEN YOU PUT ***ME*** IN CHARGE OF IT. YOU OUGHTA KNOW BETTER THAN COME IN HERE AND ACT LIKE YOU DIDN'T.
ANDY, BABY, DON'T GET ME WRONG. I'VE GOT A ***TON*** OF RESPECT FOR YOUR WORK.
YO! ARE YOU *TOUCHING MY GARNISH?!*
MAYBE I AM! WHAT ARE YOU GONNA ***DO*** ABOUT IT, ***HUH??***

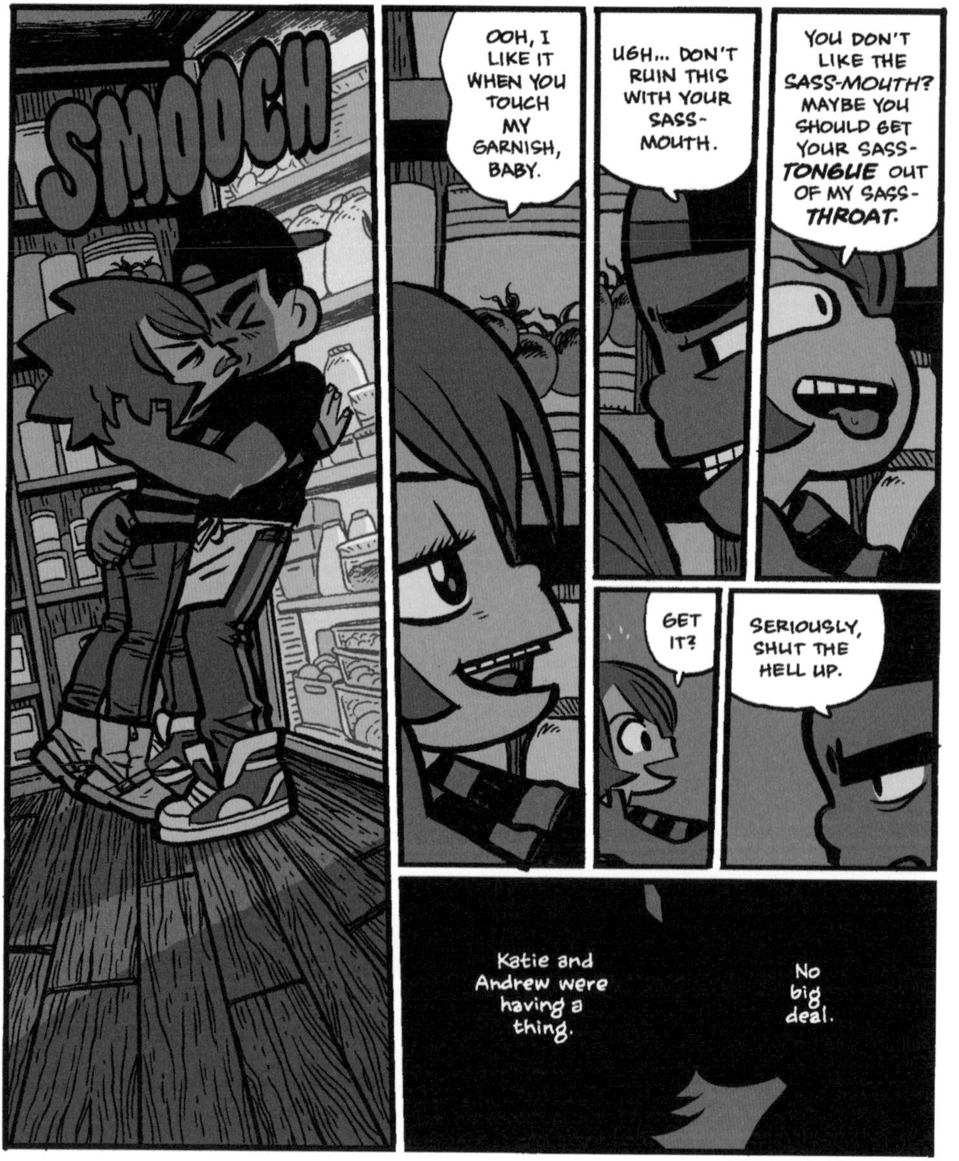
SMOOCH
OOH, I LIKE IT WHEN YOU TOUCH MY GARNISH, BABY.
UGH... DON'T RUIN THIS WITH YOUR SASS-MOUTH.
YOU DON'T LIKE THE SASS-MOUTH? MAYBE YOU SHOULD GET YOUR SASS-TONGUE OUT OF MY SASS-THROAT.
GET IT?
SERIOUSLY, SHUT THE HELL UP.
Katie and Andrew were having a thing.
No big deal.

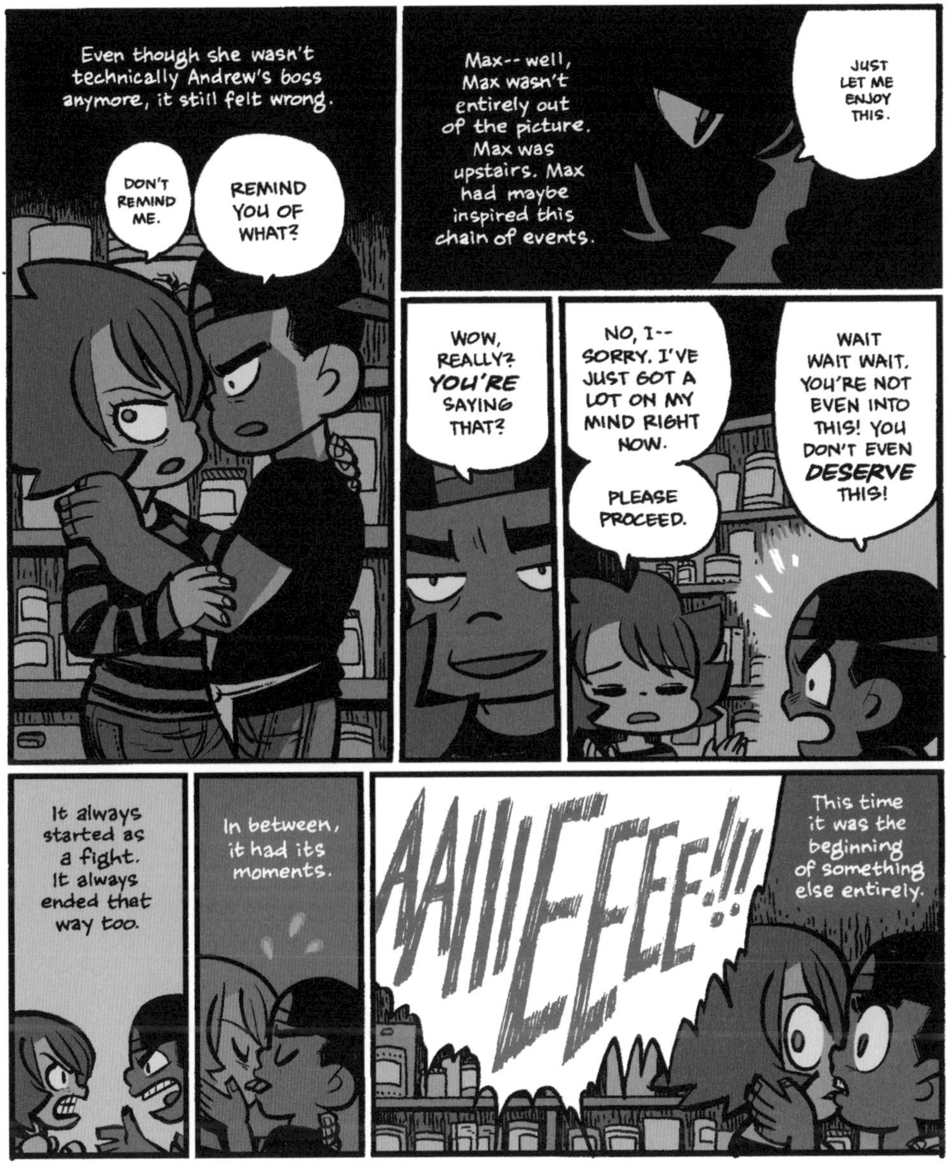
Even though she wasn't technically Andrew's boss anymore, it still felt wrong.
DON'T REMIND ME.
REMIND YOU OF WHAT?
Max-- well, Max wasn't entirely out of the picture. Max was upstairs. Max had maybe inspired this chain of events.
JUST LET ME ENJOY THIS.
WOW, REALLY? *YOU'RE* SAYING THAT?
NO, I-- SORRY. I'VE JUST GOT A LOT ON MY MIND RIGHT NOW.
PLEASE PROCEED.
WAIT WAIT WAIT. YOU'RE NOT EVEN INTO THIS! YOU DON'T EVEN *DESERVE* THIS!
It always started as a fight. It always ended that way too.
In between, it had its moments.
AAIIIEEEE!!!
This time it was the beginning of something else entirely.

Hazel
(21 years old)

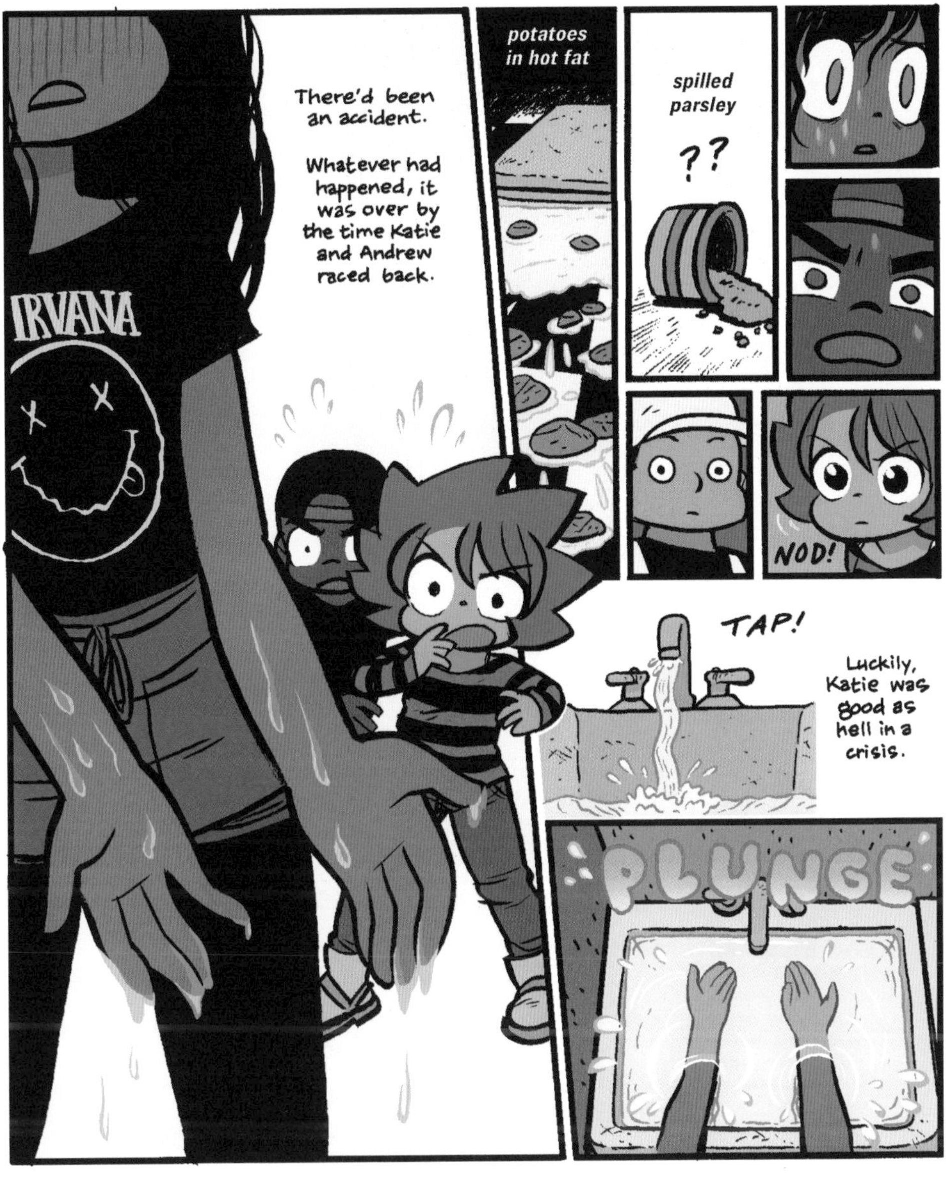
IRVANA
There'd been an accident.
Whatever had happened, it was over by the time Katie and Andrew raced back.
potatoes in hot fat
spilled parsley
??
NOD!
TAP!
Luckily, Katie was good as hell in a crisis.
PLUNGE

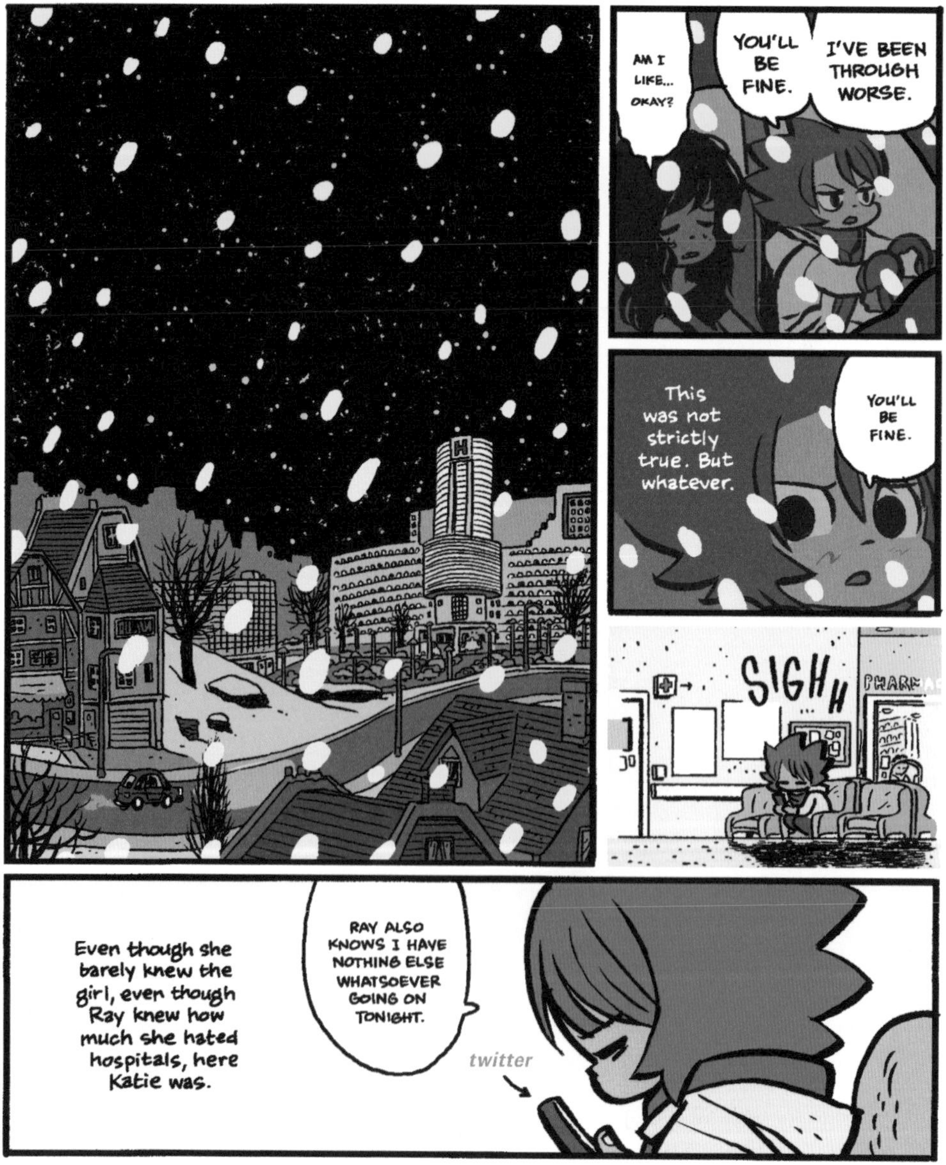
AM I LIKE... OKAY?
YOU'LL BE FINE.
I'VE BEEN THROUGH WORSE.
This was not strictly true. But whatever.
YOU'LL BE FINE.
SIGHH
...
Even though she barely knew the girl, even though Ray knew how much she hated hospitals, here Katie was.
RAY ALSO KNOWS I HAVE NOTHING ELSE WHATSOEVER GOING ON TONIGHT.
twitter

Apparently what had happened was this:

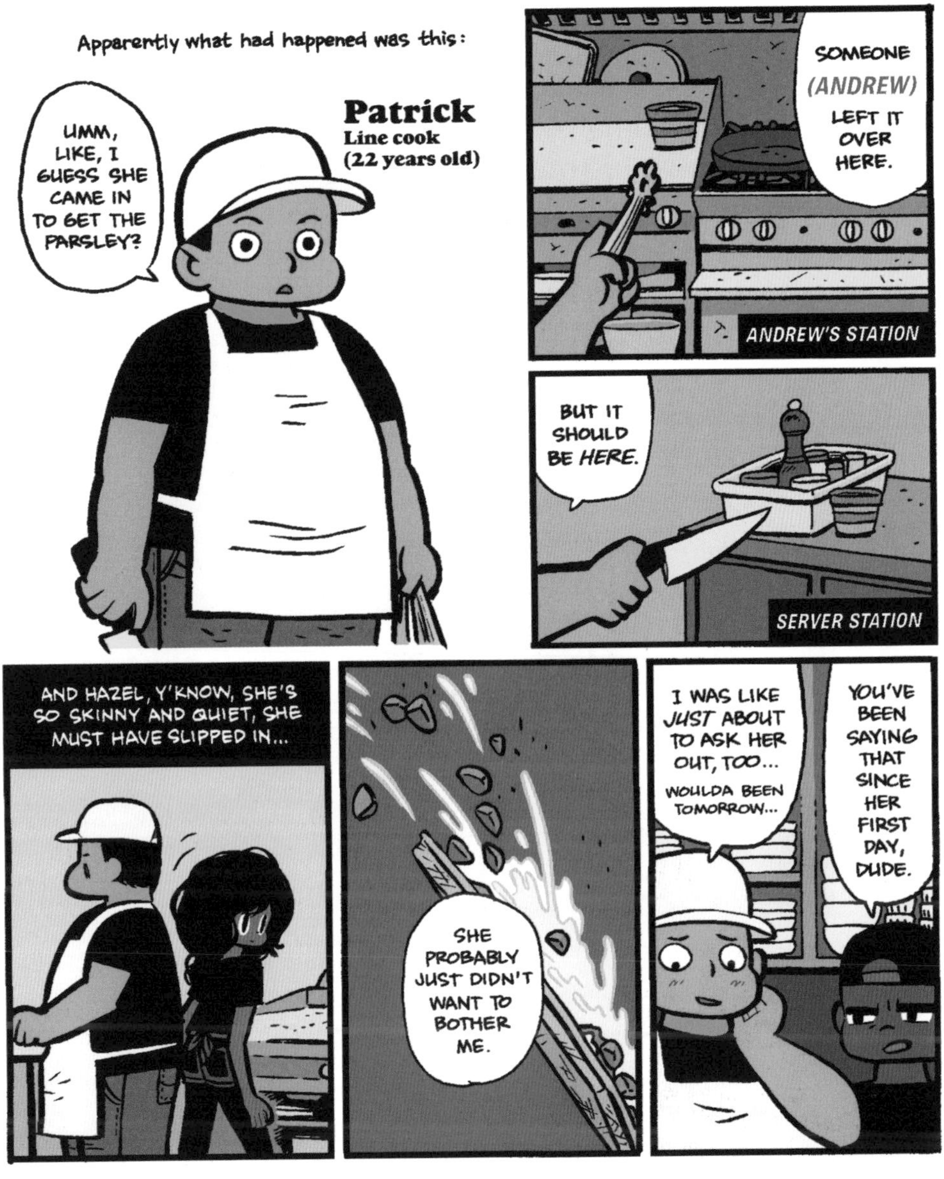

Patrick
Line cook
(22 years old)
UMM, LIKE, I GUESS SHE CAME IN TO GET THE PARSLEY?
SOMEONE (ANDREW) LEFT IT OVER HERE.
ANDREW'S STATION
BUT IT SHOULD BE *HERE*.
SERVER STATION
AND HAZEL, Y'KNOW, SHE'S SO SKINNY AND QUIET, SHE MUST HAVE SLIPPED IN...
SHE PROBABLY JUST DIDN'T WANT TO BOTHER ME.
I WAS LIKE *JUST* ABOUT TO ASK HER OUT, TOO...
WOULDA BEEN TOMORROW...
YOU'VE BEEN SAYING THAT SINCE HER FIRST DAY, DUDE.

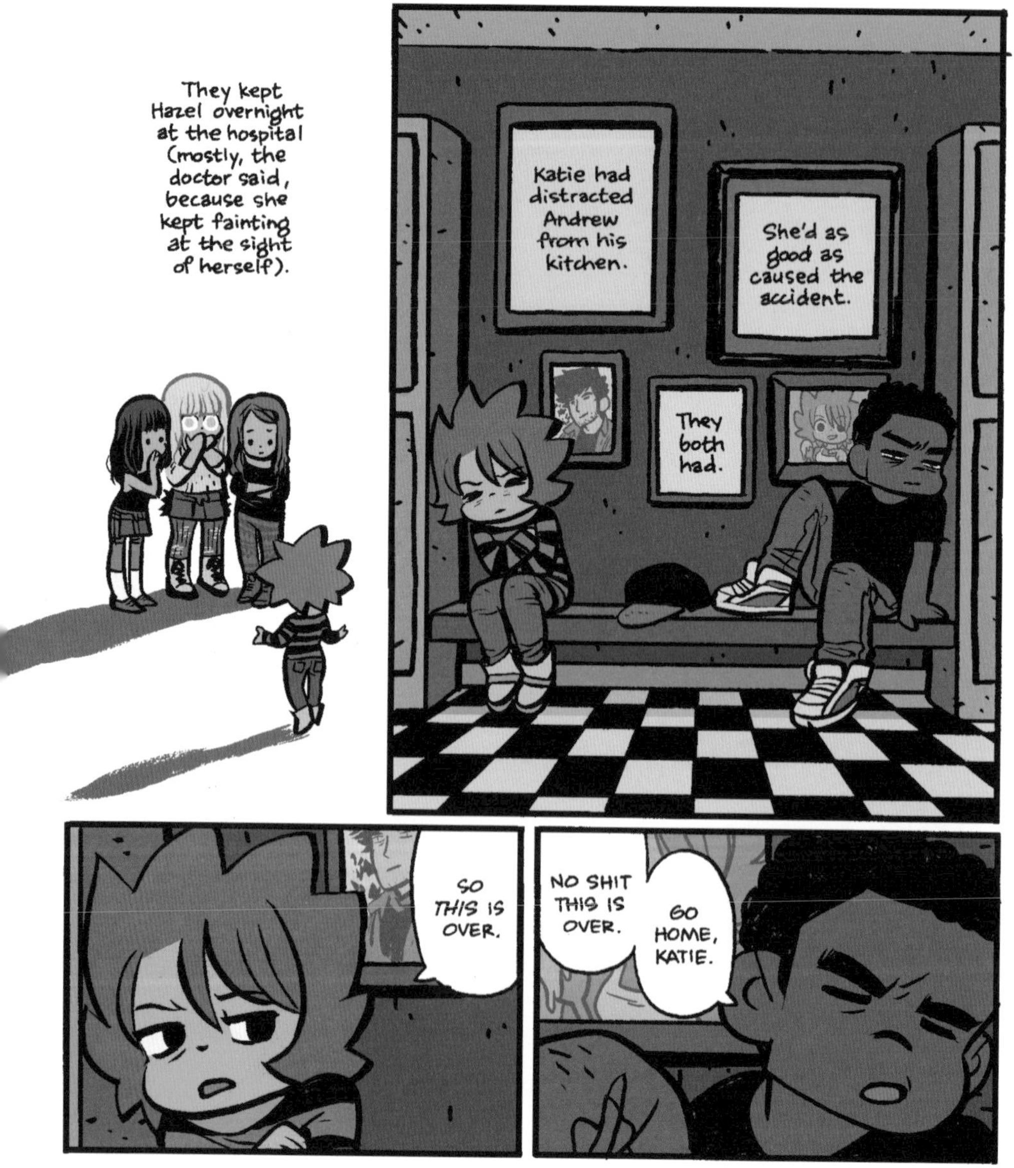
They kept Hazel overnight at the hospital (mostly, the doctor said, because she kept fainting at the sight of herself).
Katie had distracted Andrew from his kitchen.
She'd as good as caused the accident.
They both had.
SO THIS IS OVER.
NO SHIT THIS IS OVER.
GO HOME, KATIE.

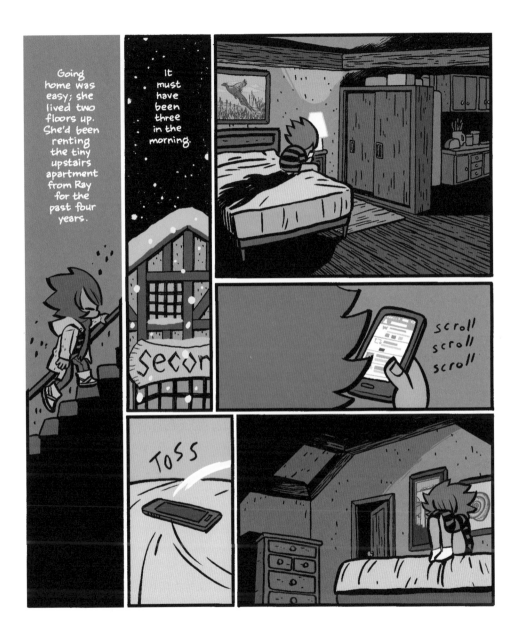

Going home was easy; she lived two floors up. She'd been renting the tiny upstairs apartment from Ray for the past four years.

It must have been three in the morning.

scroll
scroll
scroll

TOSS

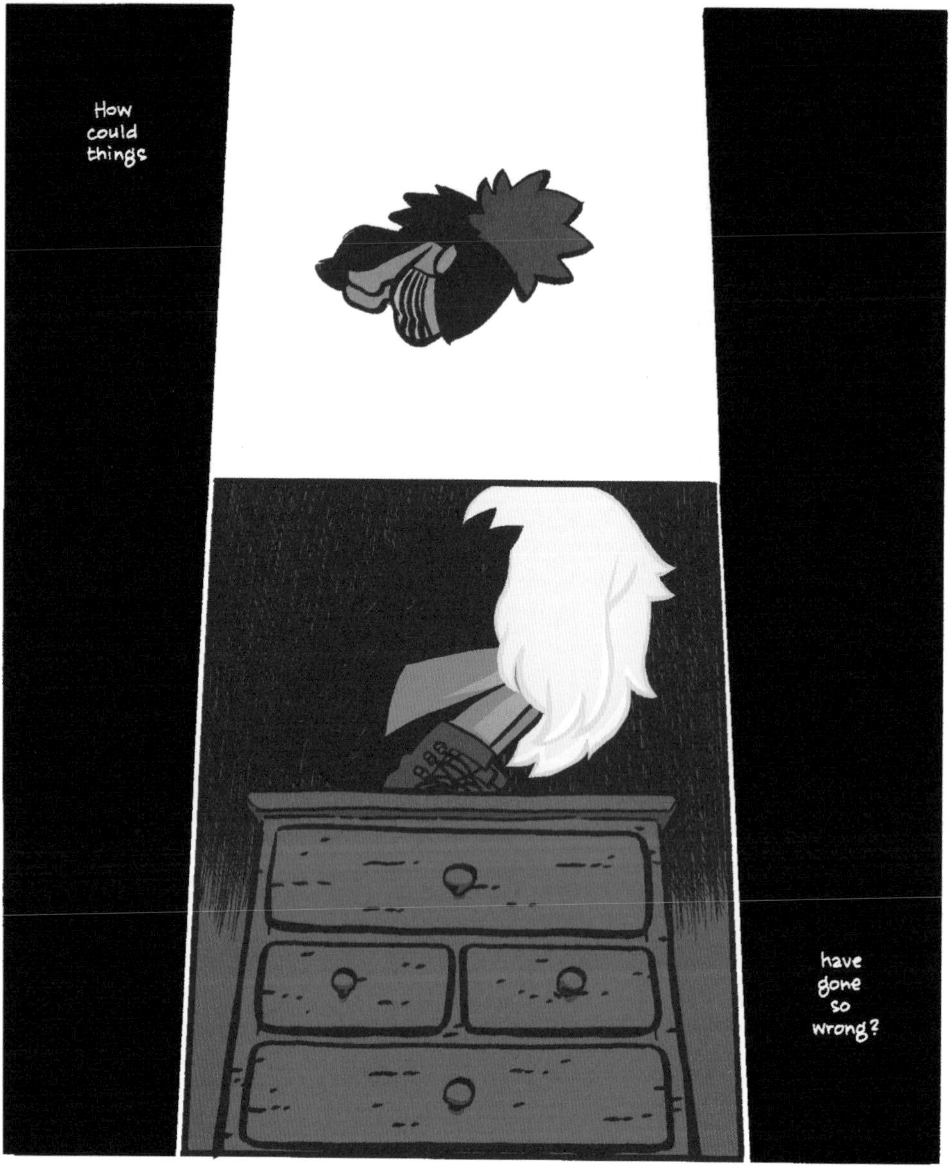
How could things
have gone so wrong?

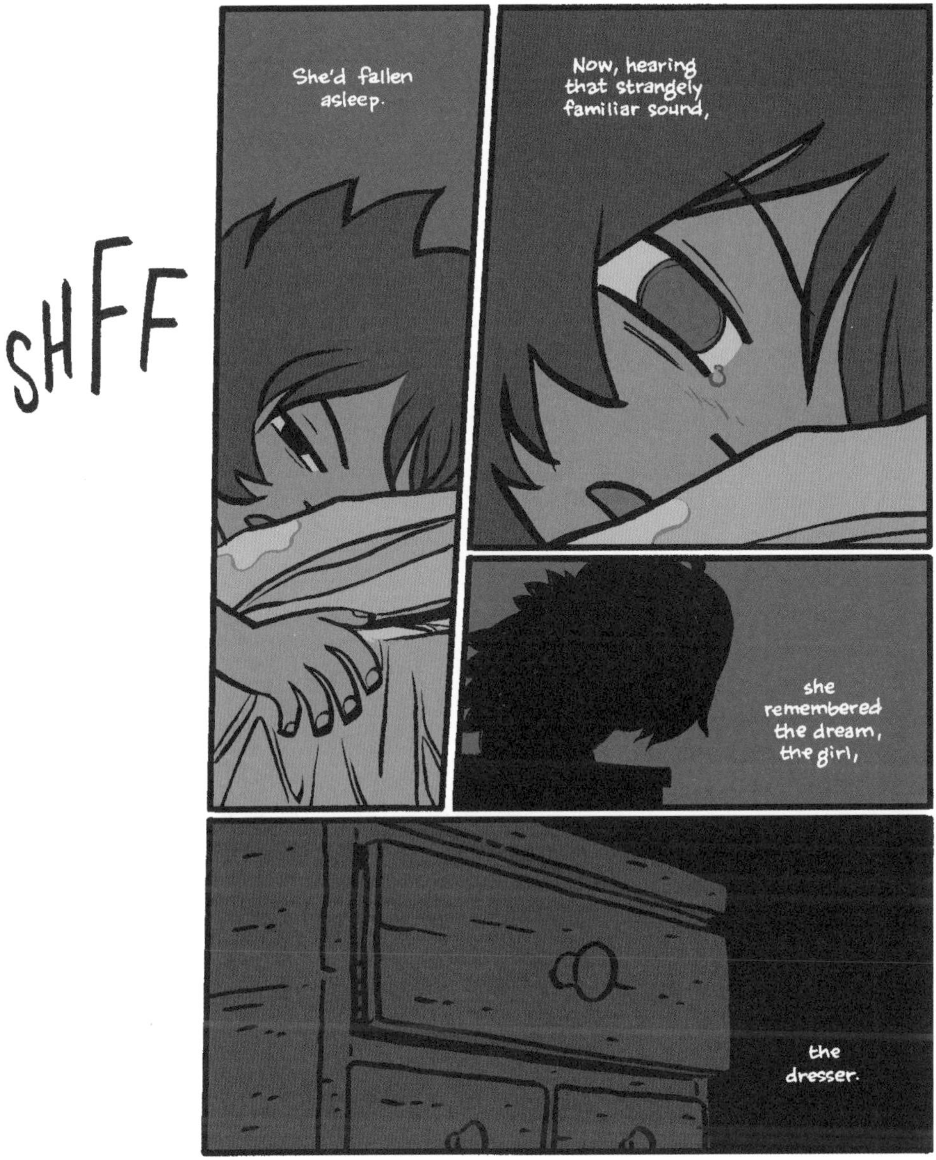
SHFF
She'd fallen asleep.
Now, hearing that strangely familiar sound,
she remembered the dream, the girl,
the dresser.

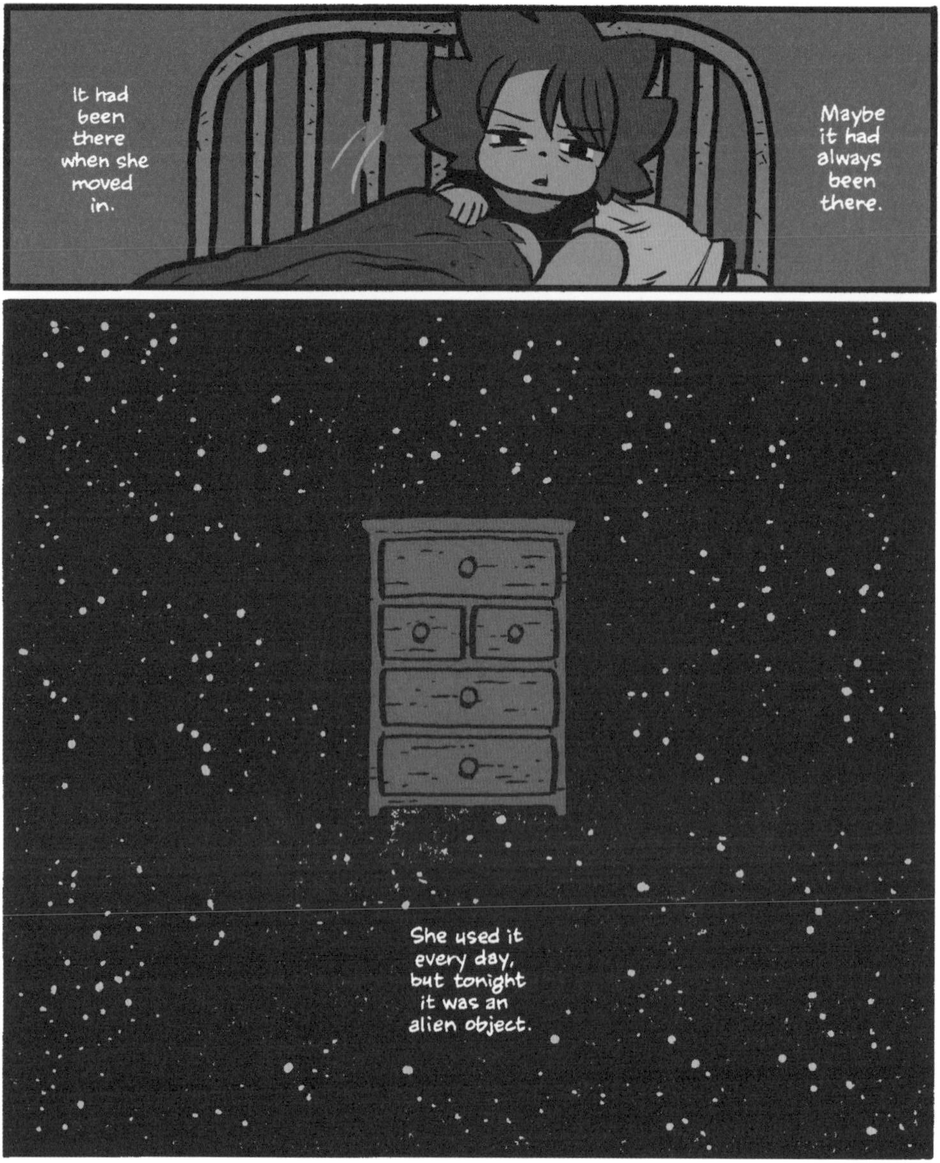
It had been there when she moved in.
Maybe it had always been there.
She used it every day, but tonight it was an alien object.

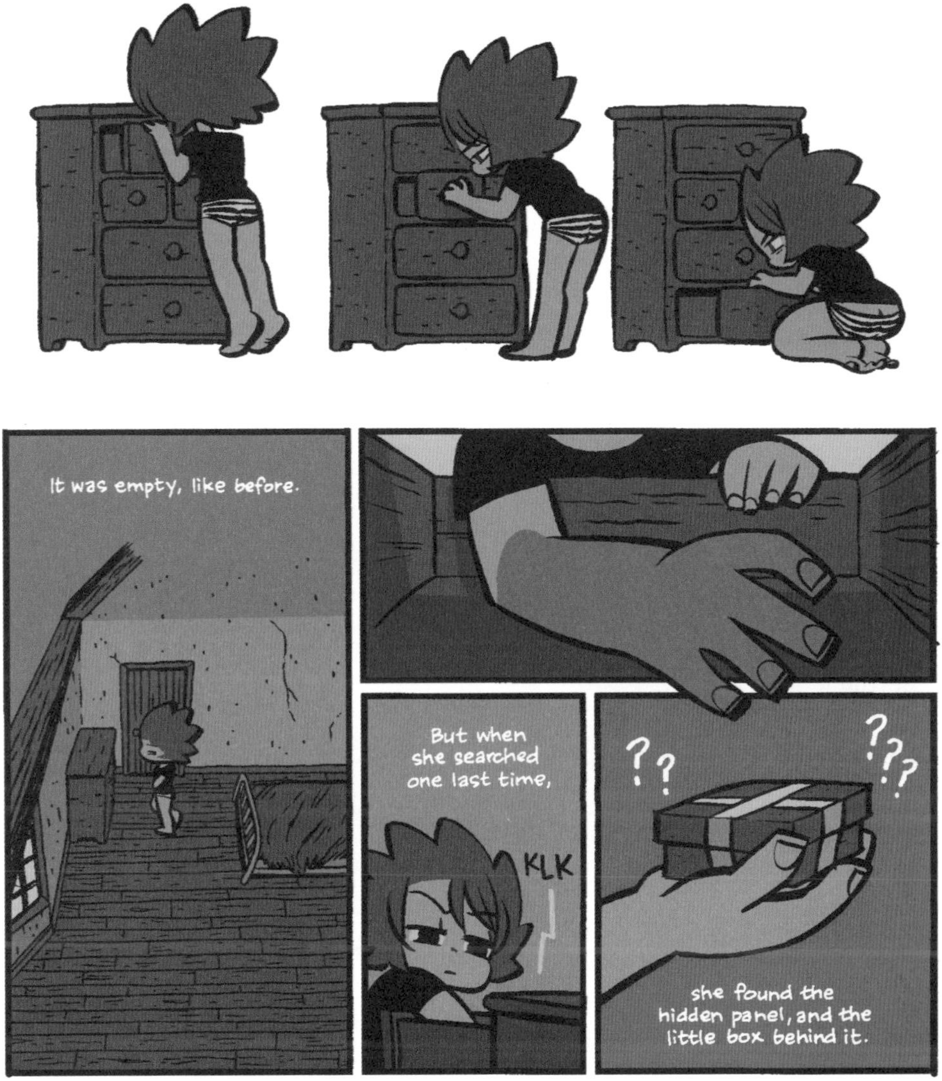
It was empty, like before.
But when she searched one last time,
KLK
??
???
she found the hidden panel, and the little box behind it.

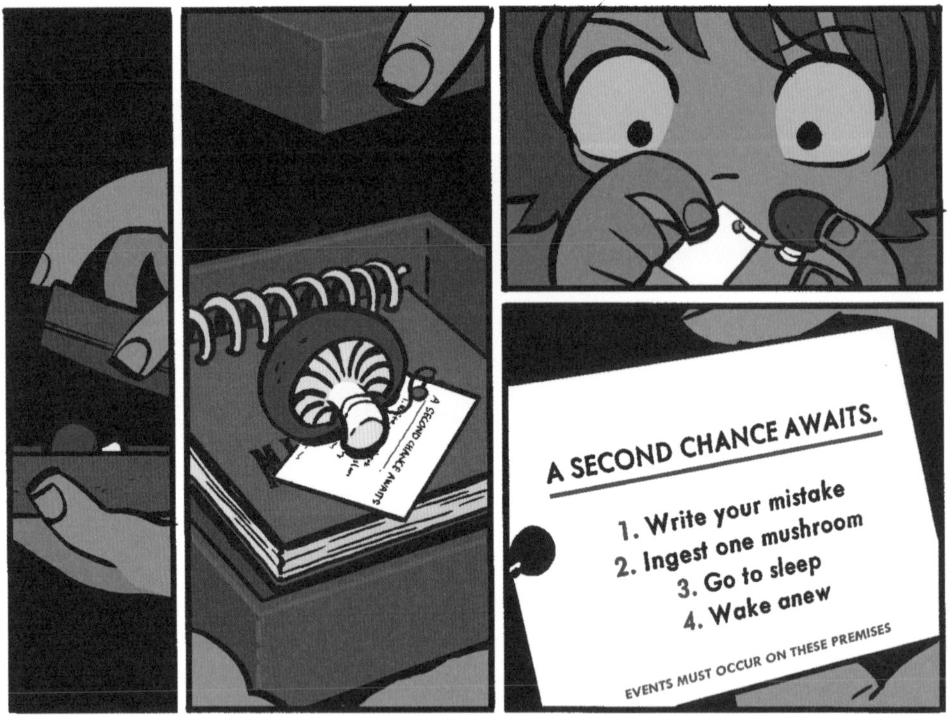
A SECOND CHANCE AWAITS.
1. Write your mistake
2. Ingest one mushroom
3. Go to sleep
4. Wake anew
EVENTS MUST OCCUR ON THESE PREMISES

Contents of the little box:

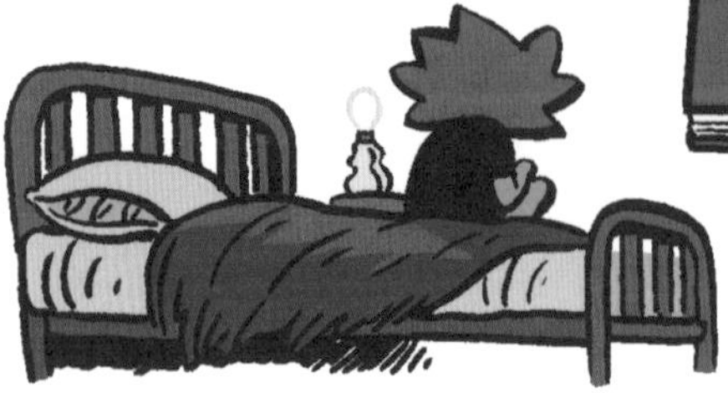

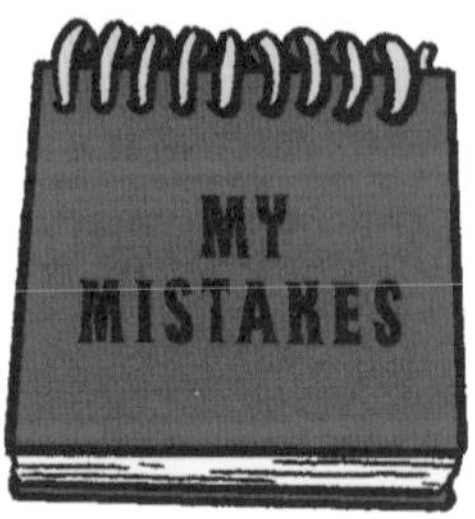
MY MISTAKES

notebook titled "MY MISTAKES"

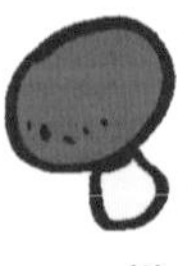

one (1) mysterious red-capped mushroom

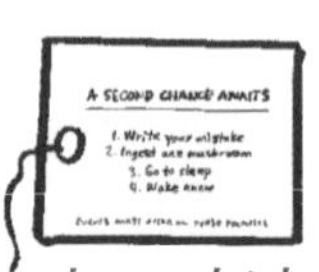
A SECOND CHANCE AWAITS

immaculately printed instruction card

FLIP

The notebook felt old, like something from an earlier era.

Judging by the heft of it, some of its pages had been removed at some point in the past.

She'd need a pen. And one was there.

SNIC

Her favorite pen. So familiar in her hand. She hadn't seen it since the third day of high school.

My Mistake
by Katie Clay
I shouldn't of fooled around W/ ANDREW! Workplace canoodling IS NO GOOD!

FLIP

MY MISTAKES

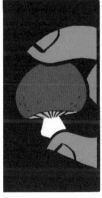

REVISION #1

Max
smiled
again.
Katie
melted
again.
THIS IS MY SISTER.
Everything
GUH BLUH
was happening
... ARE YOU OK?
again.
HM?

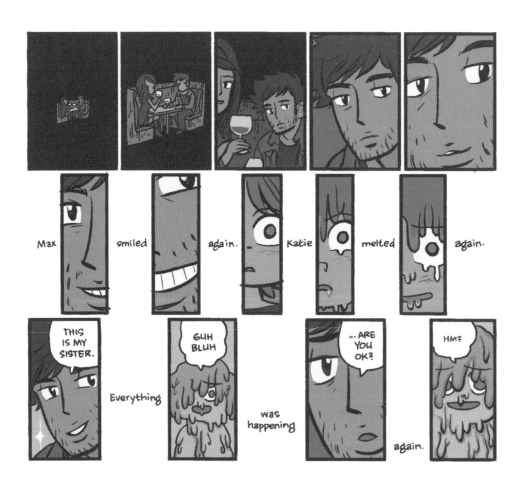

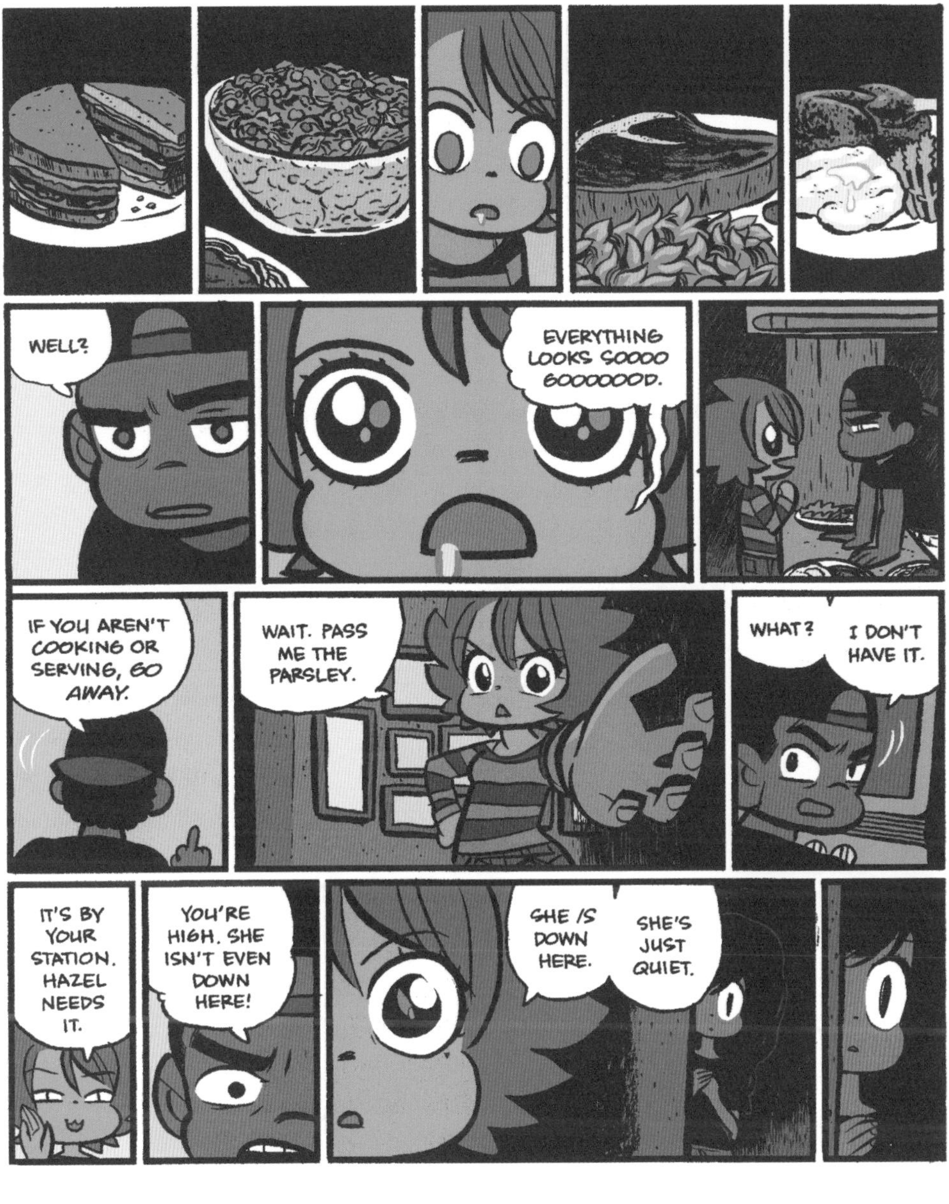
WELL?
EVERYTHING LOOKS SOOOO GOOOOOOD.
IF YOU AREN'T COOKING OR SERVING, GO AWAY.
WAIT. PASS ME THE PARSLEY.
WHAT?
I DON'T HAVE IT.
IT'S BY YOUR STATION. HAZEL NEEDS IT.
YOU'RE HIGH. SHE ISN'T EVEN DOWN HERE!
SHE IS DOWN HERE.
SHE'S JUST QUIET.

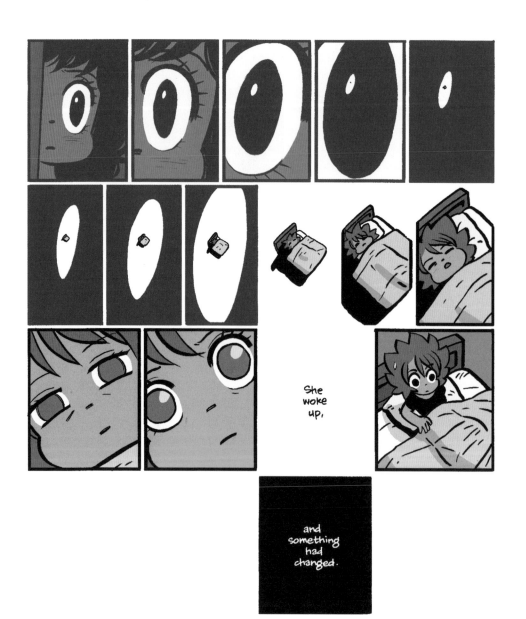

She woke up,

and something had changed.

2

Hazel

That morning, the girl wasn't at the hospital.

Katie found the girl's address in a three-month-old unread work email (re: new staff).

HAZEL.

HER NAME'S HAZEL.

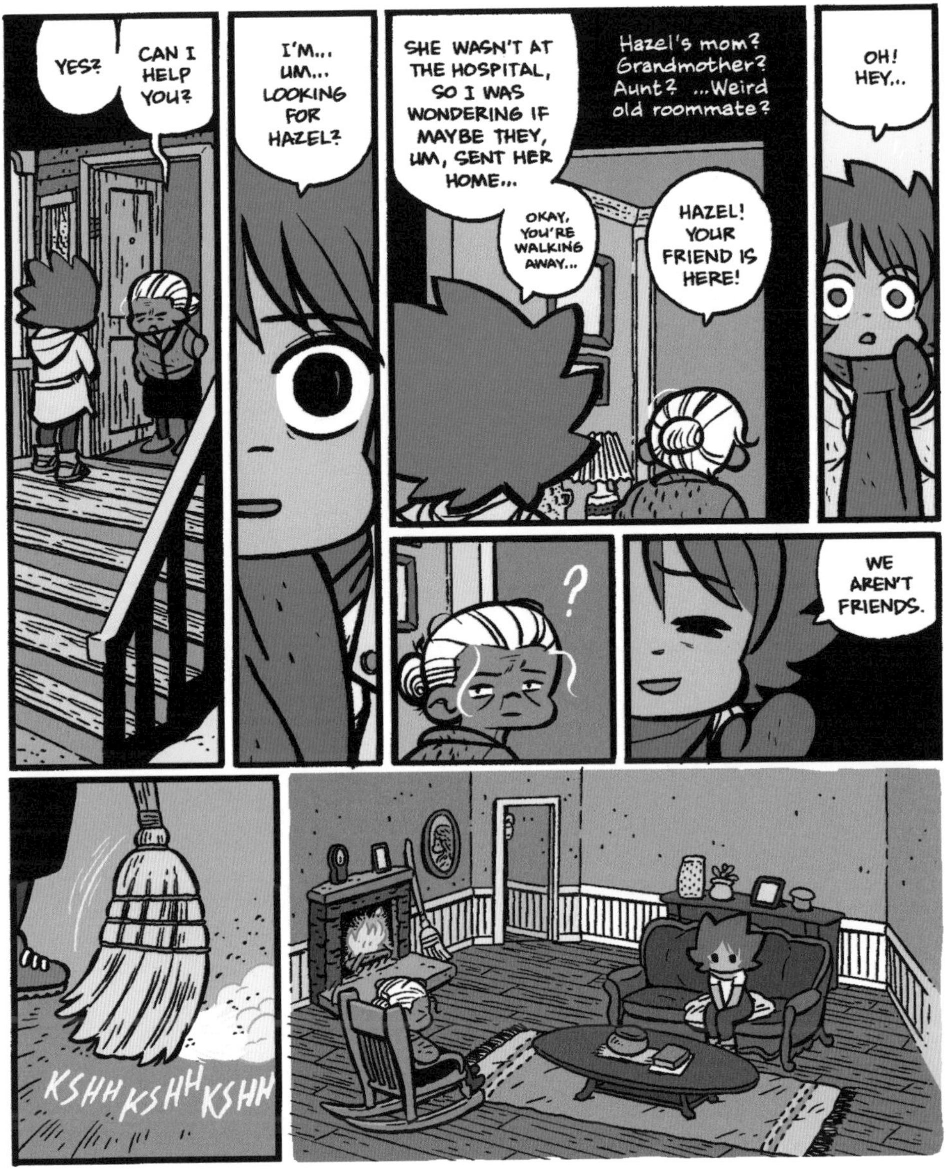
YES?
CAN I HELP YOU?
I'M... UM... LOOKING FOR HAZEL?
SHE WASN'T AT THE HOSPITAL, SO I WAS WONDERING IF MAYBE THEY, UM, SENT HER HOME...
Hazel's mom? Grandmother? Aunt? ...Weird old roommate?
OKAY, YOU'RE WALKING AWAY...
HAZEL! YOUR FRIEND IS HERE!
OH! HEY...
?
WE AREN'T FRIENDS.
KSHH KSHH KSHH

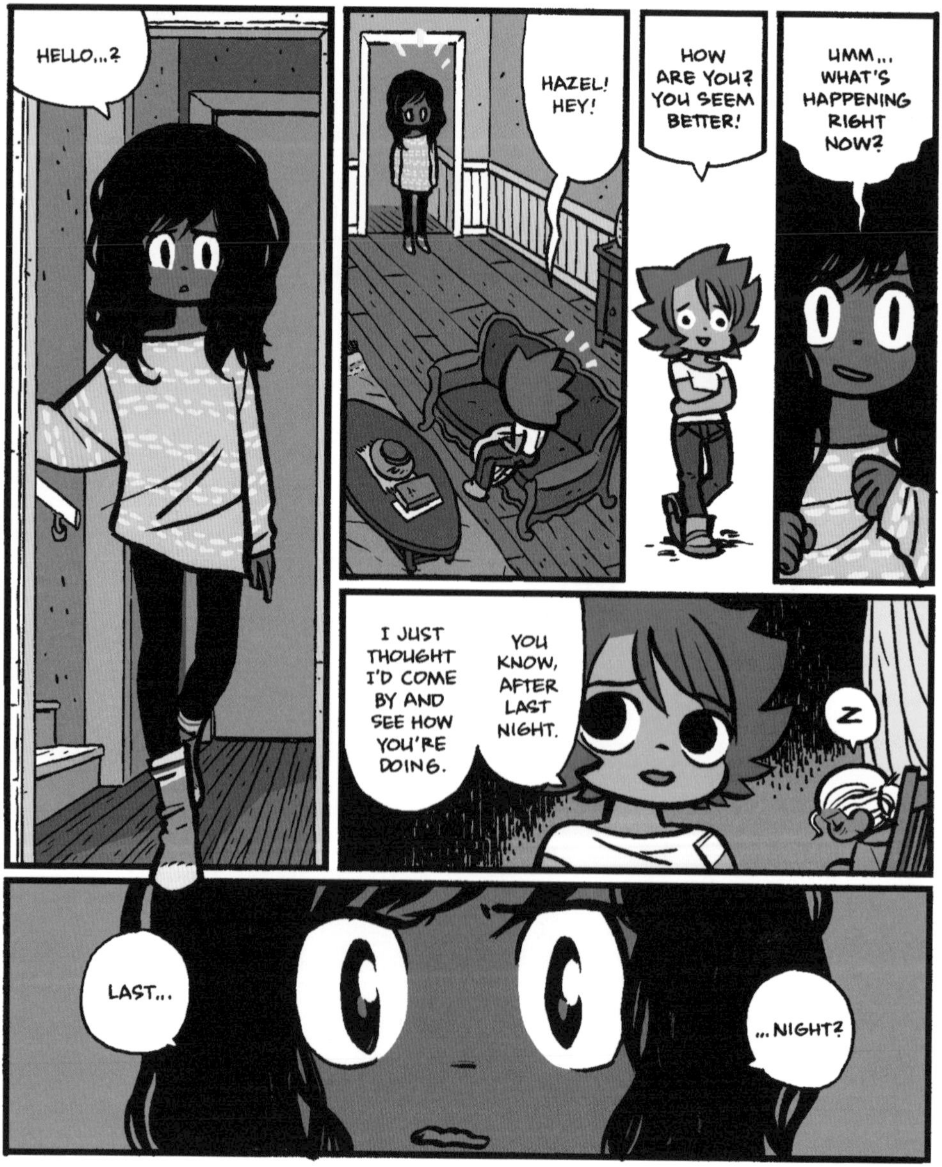

HELLO...?
HAZEL! HEY!
HOW ARE YOU? YOU SEEM BETTER!
UMM... WHAT'S HAPPENING RIGHT NOW?
I JUST THOUGHT I'D COME BY AND SEE HOW YOU'RE DOING.
YOU KNOW, AFTER LAST NIGHT.
Z
LAST...
...NIGHT?

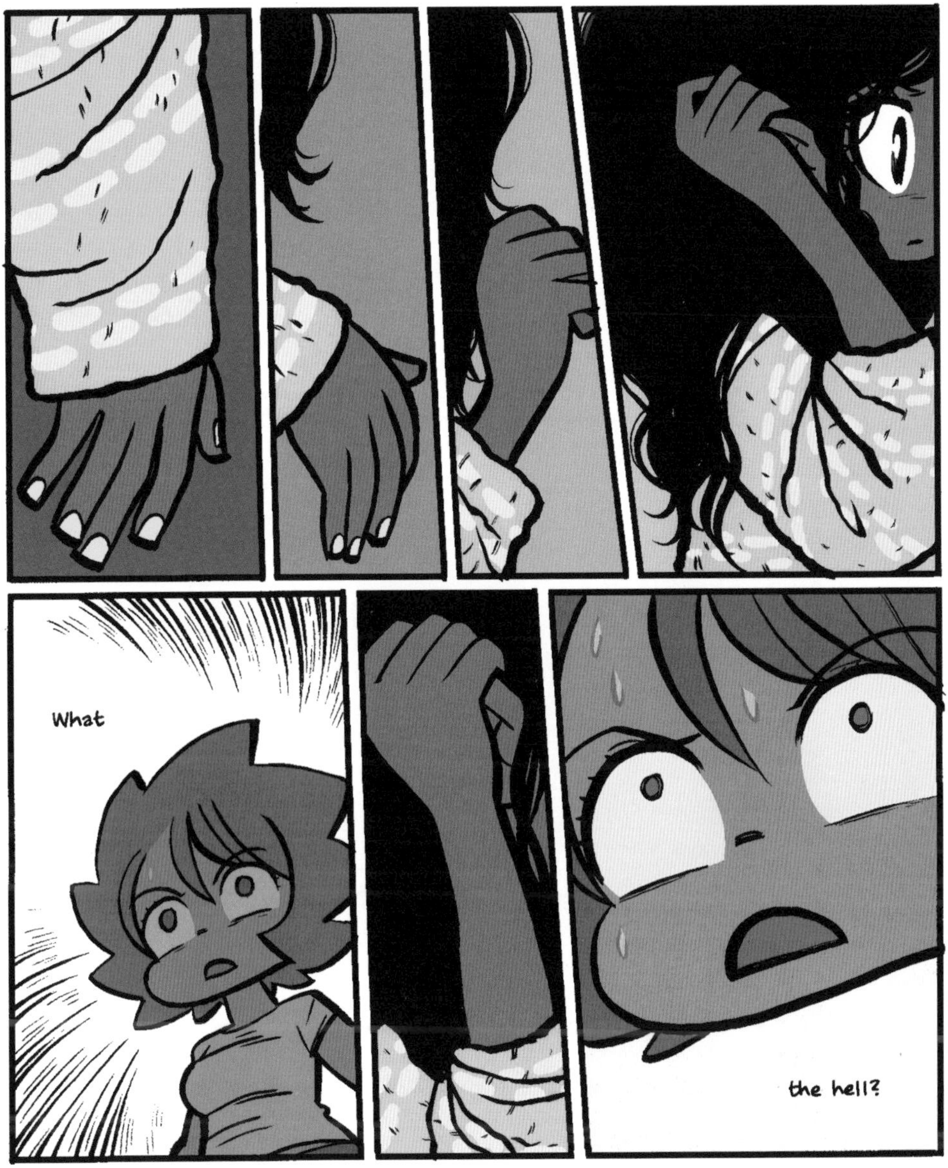
What
the hell?

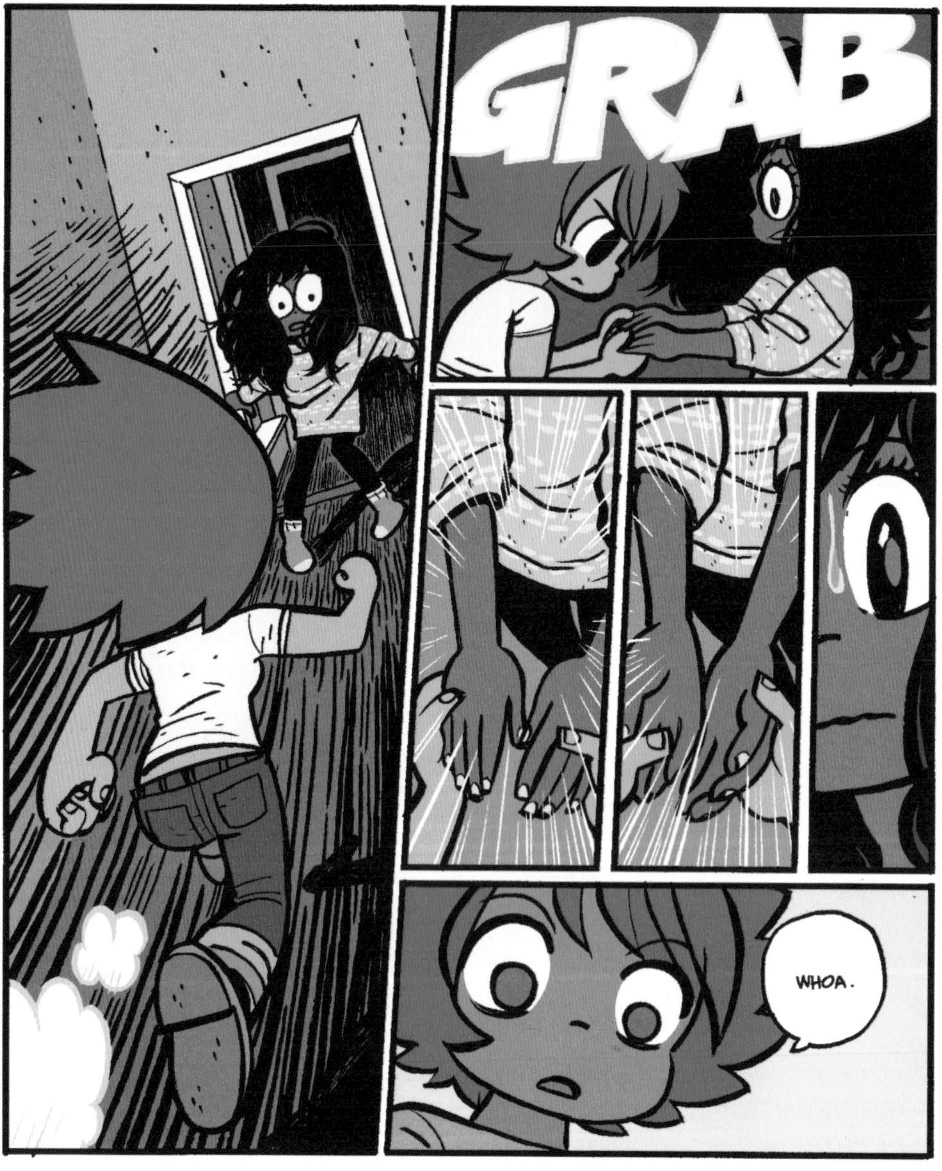
GRAB
WHOA.

Katie's heart wouldn't stop racing.

Was her memory meaningless? Her experience insubstantial?

Was she losing her grip on reality?

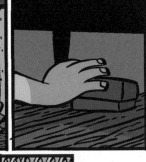

MY MISTAKES

y Mistak
y Katie Cl
shouldn't of
oled around
ANDREW
orkplace
anoodling

Was she even awake?

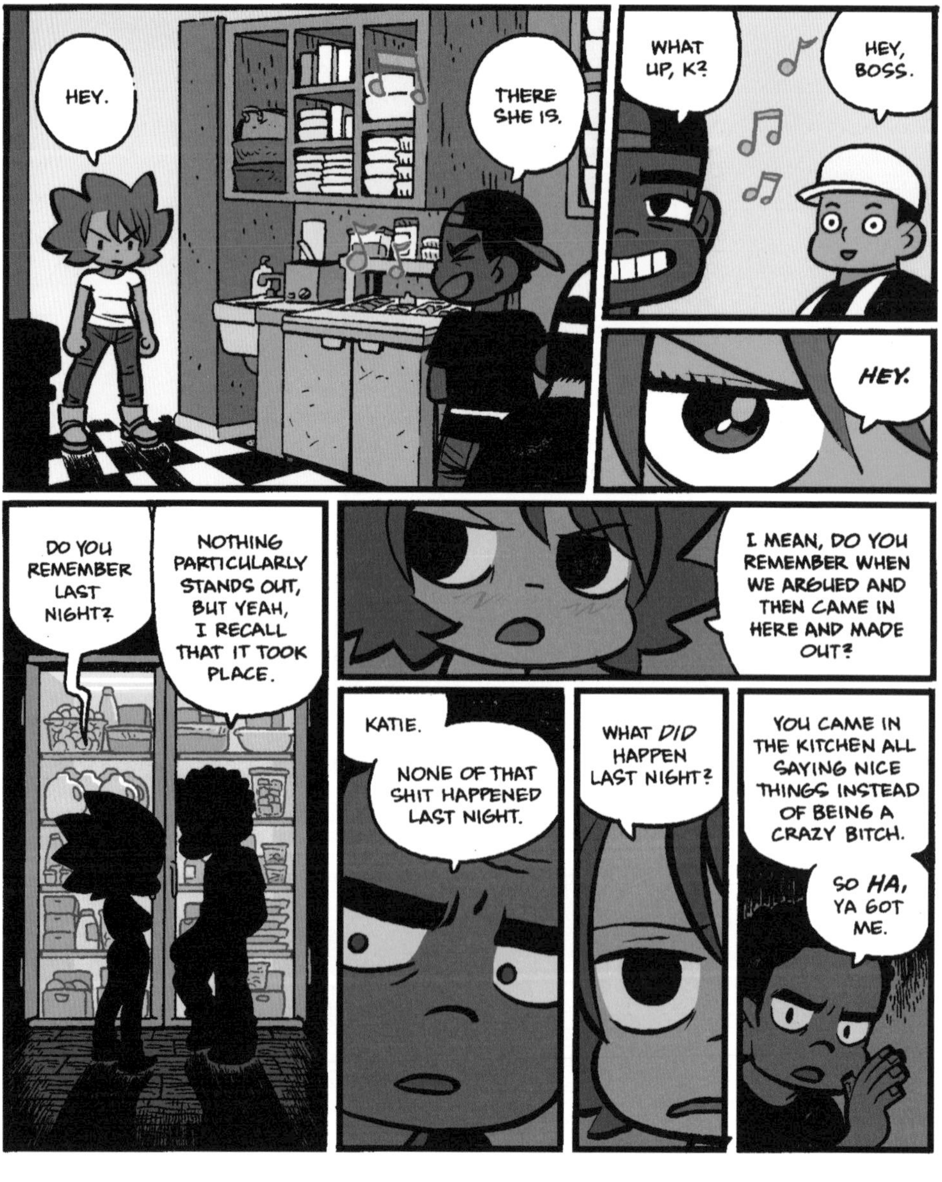
HEY.
THERE SHE IS.
WHAT UP, K?
HEY, BOSS.
HEY.
DO YOU REMEMBER LAST NIGHT?
NOTHING PARTICULARLY STANDS OUT, BUT YEAH, I RECALL THAT IT TOOK PLACE.
I MEAN, DO YOU REMEMBER WHEN WE ARGUED AND THEN CAME IN HERE AND MADE OUT?
KATIE.
NONE OF THAT SHIT HAPPENED LAST NIGHT.
WHAT DID HAPPEN LAST NIGHT?
YOU CAME IN THE KITCHEN ALL SAYING NICE THINGS INSTEAD OF BEING A CRAZY BITCH.
SO HA, YA GOT ME.

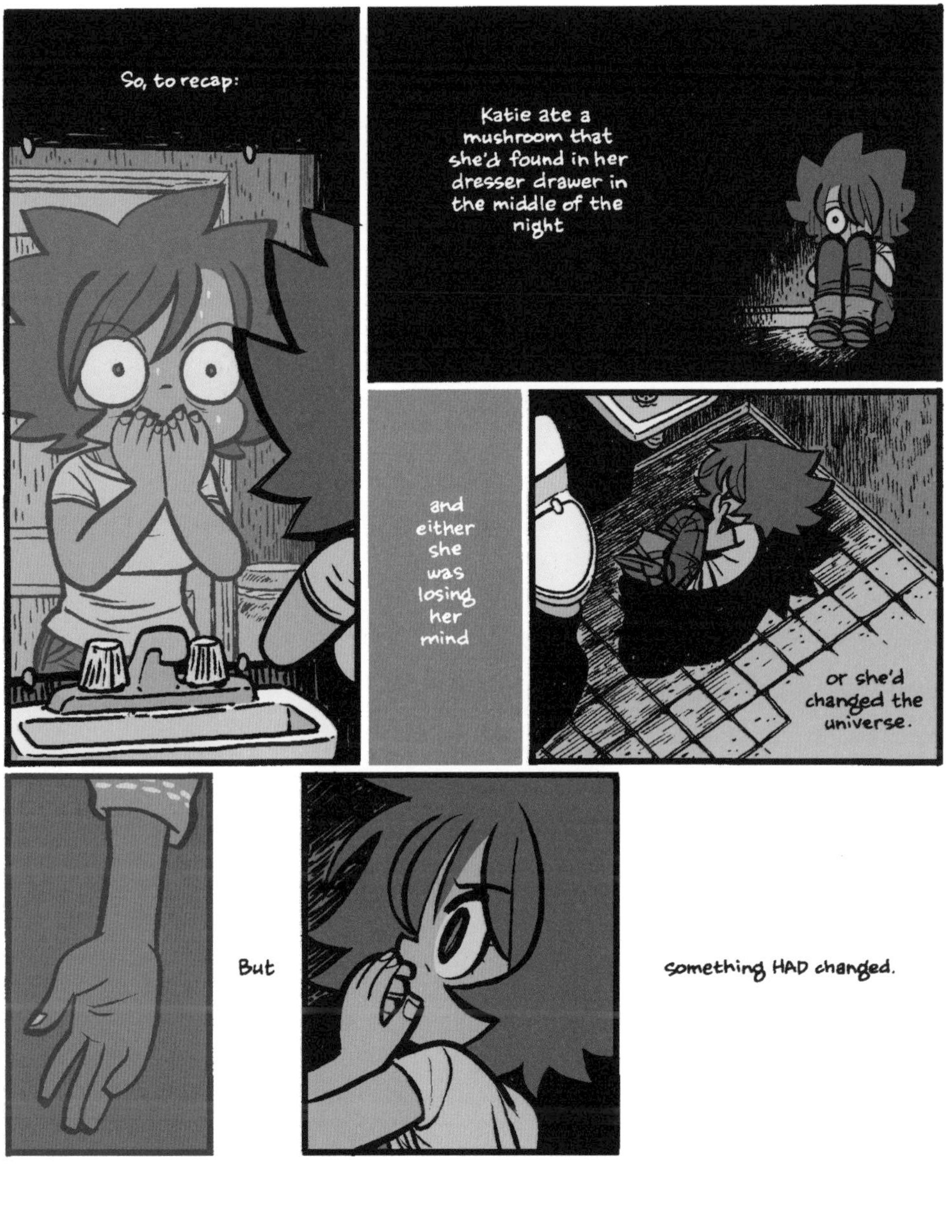

So, to recap:
Katie ate a mushroom that she'd found in her dresser drawer in the middle of the night
and either she was losing her mind
or she'd changed the universe.
But
something HAD changed.

THE ACCIDENT *DID* HAPPEN. I *KNOW* IT DID.

The sickening smell of it

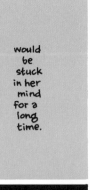

would be stuck in her mind for a long time.

And if the smell was real, the accident was real.

Hazel had burned,

and then she hadn't.

It had been Katie's fault.

BUT NOW IT'S NO-ONE'S FAULT!

Katie had *fixed* it.

She had been given a second chance.

And it seemed like she was the only one who knew.

60

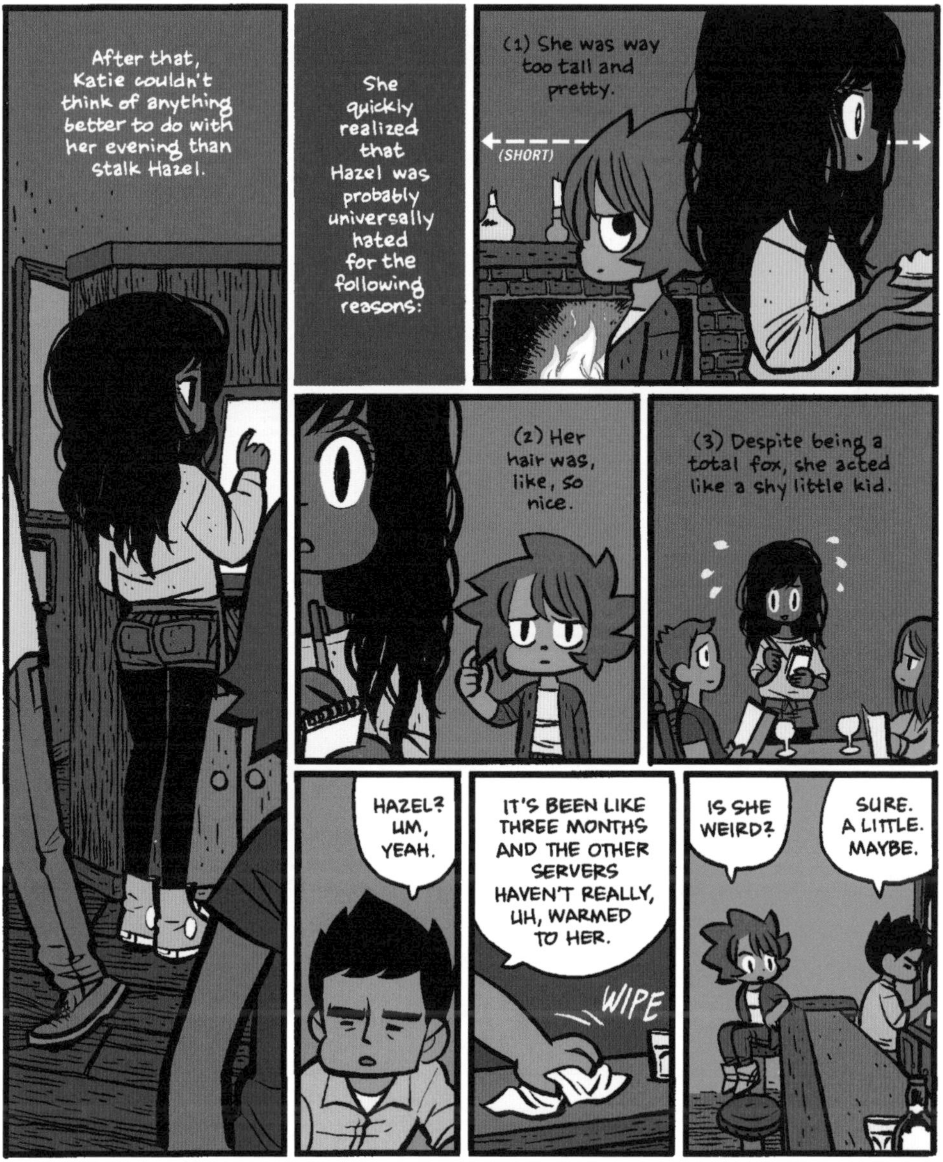
After that, Katie couldn't think of anything better to do with her evening than stalk Hazel.
She quickly realized that Hazel was probably universally hated for the following reasons:
(1) She was way too tall and pretty.
(SHORT)
(2) Her hair was, like, so nice.
(3) Despite being a total fox, she acted like a shy little kid.
HAZEL? UM, YEAH.
IT'S BEEN LIKE THREE MONTHS AND THE OTHER SERVERS HAVEN'T REALLY, UH, WARMED TO HER.
WIPE
IS SHE WEIRD?
SURE. A LITTLE. MAYBE.

COMPARE & CONTRAST:

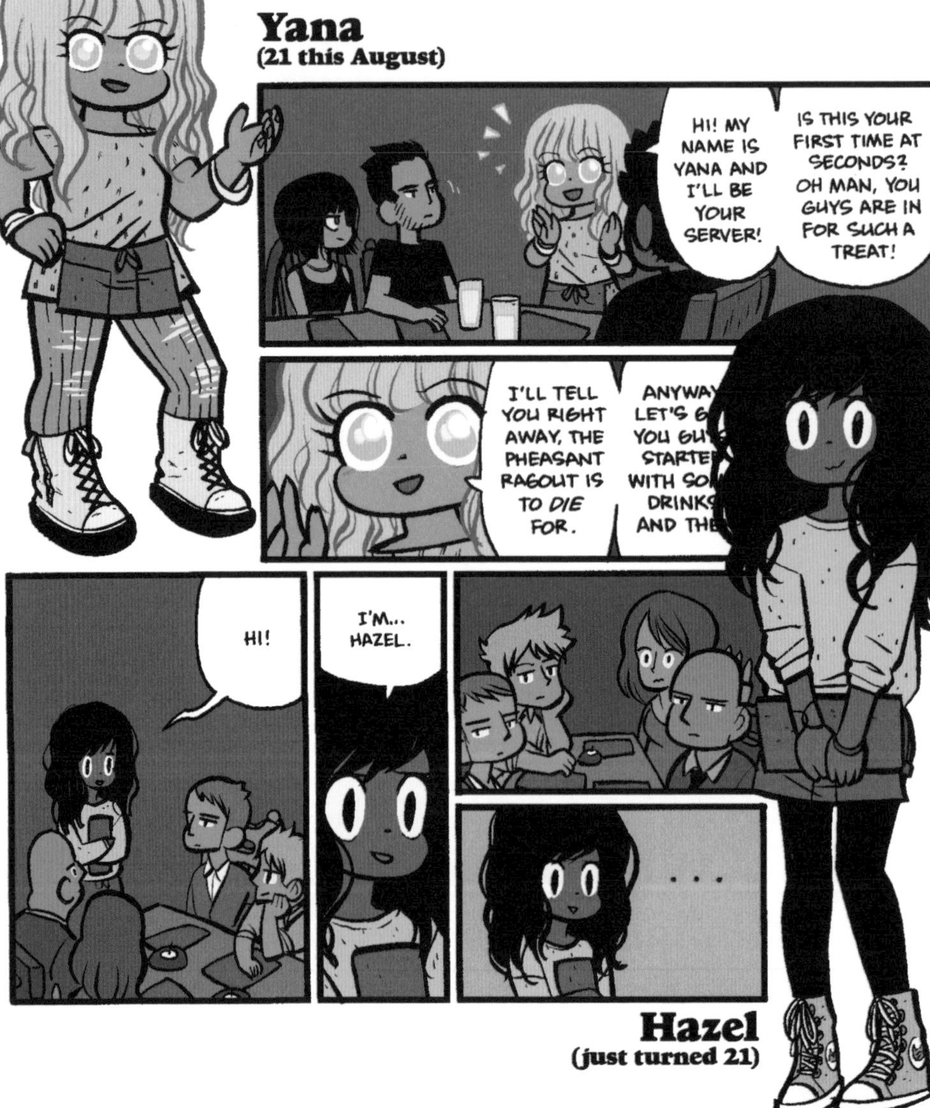
Yana
(21 this August)
HI! MY NAME IS YANA AND I'LL BE YOUR SERVER!
IS THIS YOUR FIRST TIME AT SECONDS? OH MAN, YOU GUYS ARE IN FOR SUCH A TREAT!
I'LL TELL YOU RIGHT AWAY, THE PHEASANT RAGOUT IS TO *DIE* FOR.
ANYWA LET'S G YOU GU STARTE WITH SO DRINKS AND THE
HI!
I'M... HAZEL.
. . .
Hazel
(just turned 21)

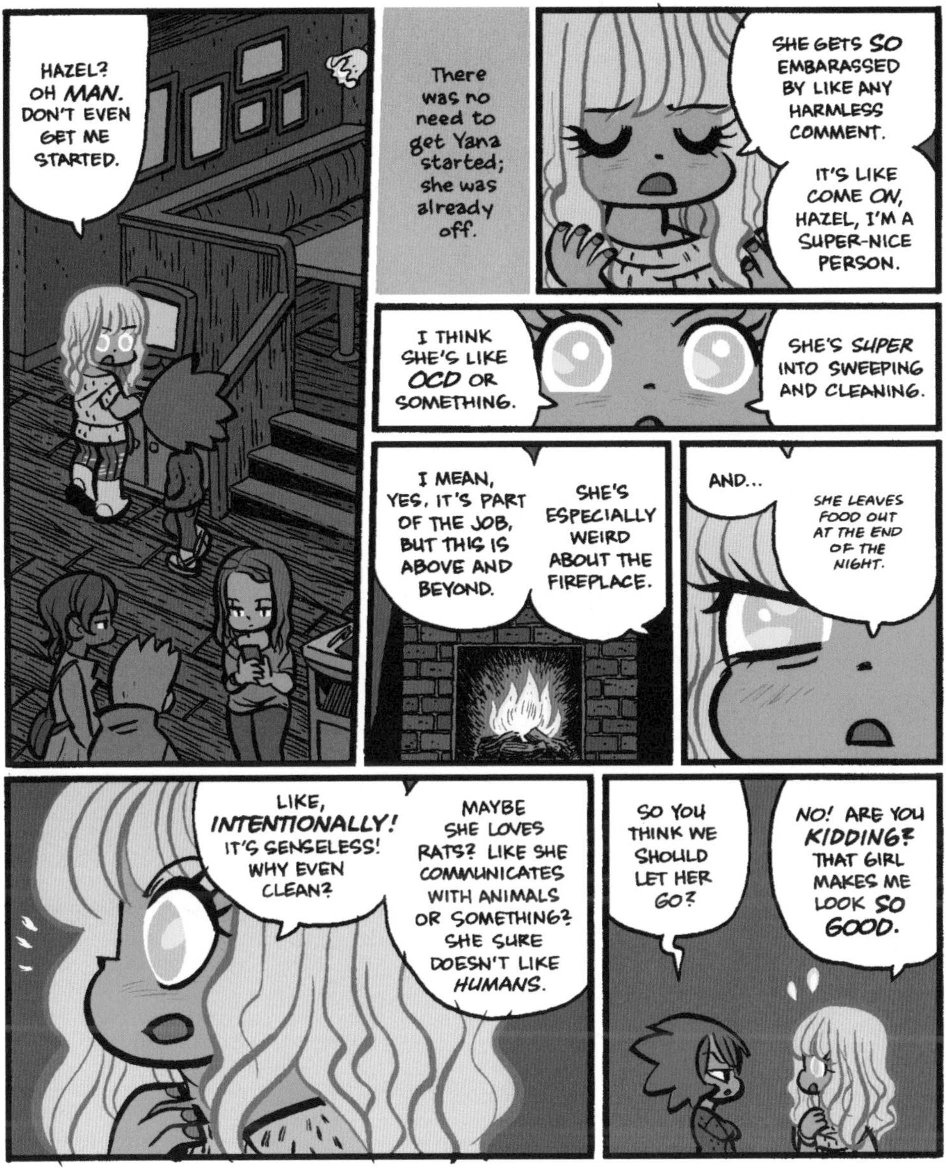
HAZEL? OH MAN. DON'T EVEN GET ME STARTED.
There was no need to get Yana started; she was already off.
SHE GETS SO EMBARASSED BY LIKE ANY HARMLESS COMMENT.
IT'S LIKE COME ON, HAZEL, I'M A SUPER-NICE PERSON.
I THINK SHE'S LIKE OCD OR SOMETHING.
SHE'S SUPER INTO SWEEPING AND CLEANING.
I MEAN, YES, IT'S PART OF THE JOB, BUT THIS IS ABOVE AND BEYOND.
SHE'S ESPECIALLY WEIRD ABOUT THE FIREPLACE.
AND...
SHE LEAVES FOOD OUT AT THE END OF THE NIGHT.
LIKE, INTENTIONALLY! IT'S SENSELESS! WHY EVEN CLEAN?
MAYBE SHE LOVES RATS? LIKE SHE COMMUNICATES WITH ANIMALS OR SOMETHING? SHE SURE DOESN'T LIKE HUMANS.
SO YOU THINK WE SHOULD LET HER GO?
NO! ARE YOU KIDDING? THAT GIRL MAKES ME LOOK SO GOOD.

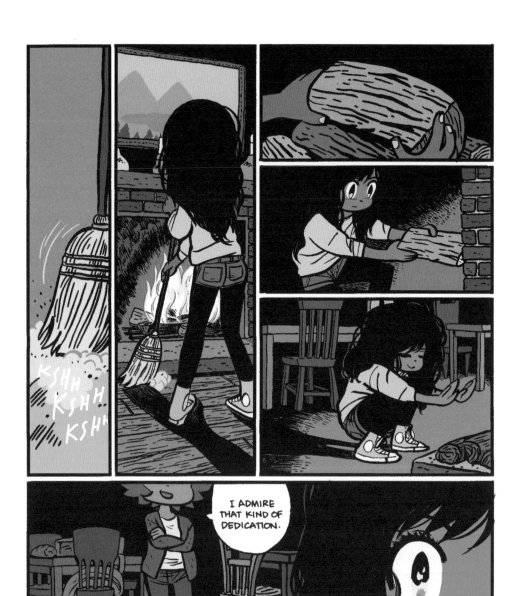

I ADMIRE THAT KIND OF DEDICATION.

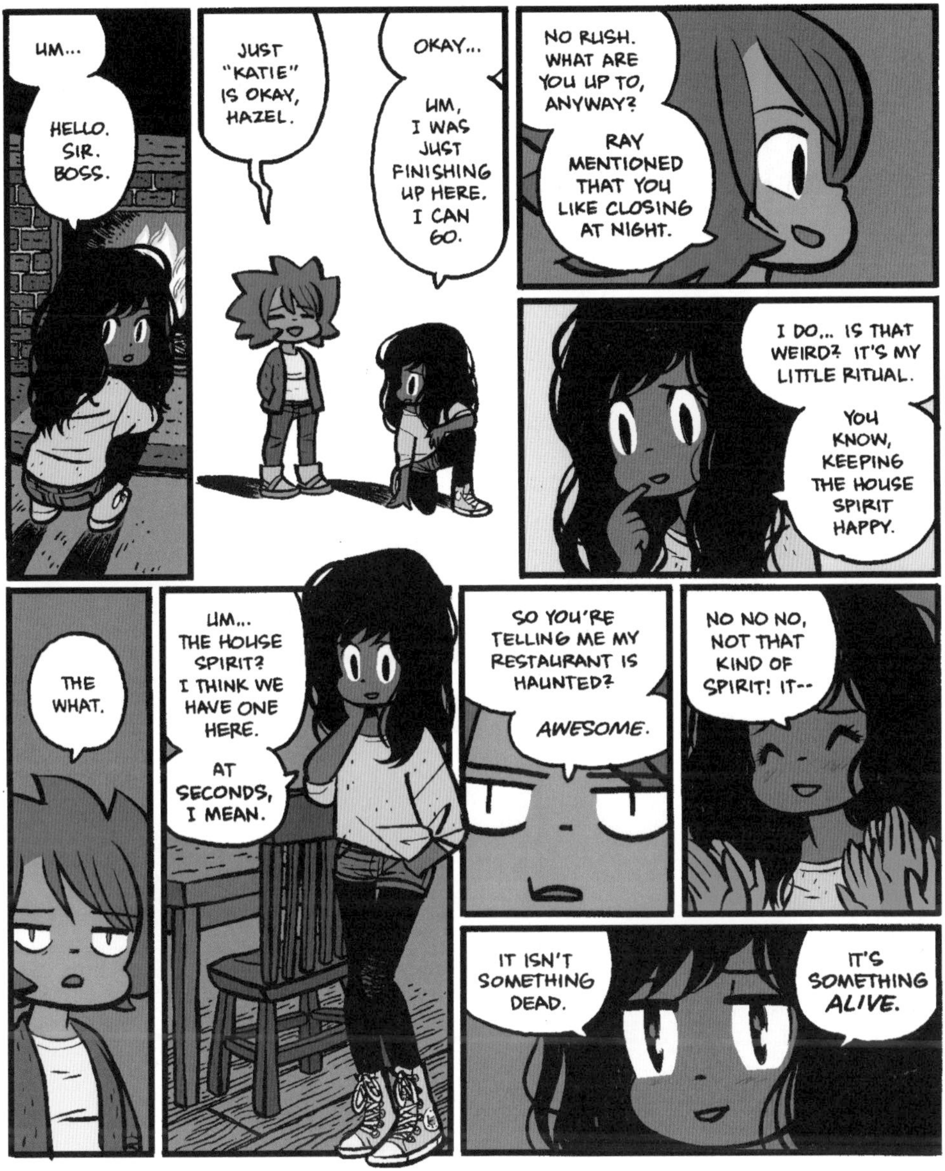
UM...
HELLO. SIR. BOSS.
JUST "KATIE" IS OKAY, HAZEL.
OKAY...
UM, I WAS JUST FINISHING UP HERE. I CAN GO.
NO RUSH. WHAT ARE YOU UP TO, ANYWAY?
RAY MENTIONED THAT YOU LIKE CLOSING AT NIGHT.
I DO... IS THAT WEIRD? IT'S MY LITTLE RITUAL.
YOU KNOW, KEEPING THE HOUSE SPIRIT HAPPY.
THE WHAT.
UM... THE HOUSE SPIRIT? I THINK WE HAVE ONE HERE.
AT SECONDS, I MEAN.
SO YOU'RE TELLING ME MY RESTAURANT IS HAUNTED?
AWESOME.
NO NO NO, NOT THAT KIND OF SPIRIT! IT--
IT ISN'T SOMETHING DEAD.
IT'S SOMETHING ALIVE.

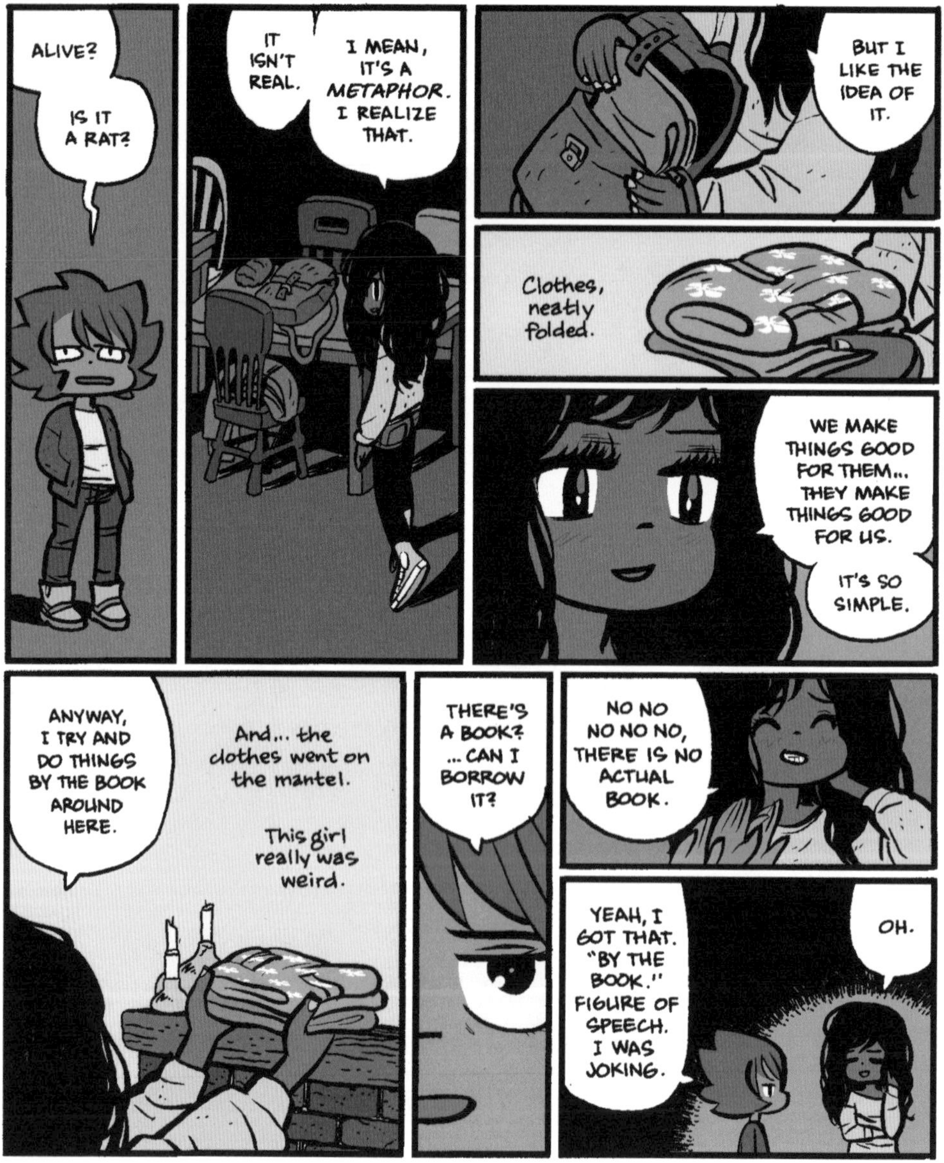
ALIVE?
IS IT A RAT?
IT ISN'T REAL.
I MEAN, IT'S A *METAPHOR*. I REALIZE THAT.
BUT I LIKE THE IDEA OF IT.
Clothes, neatly folded.
WE MAKE THINGS GOOD FOR THEM... THEY MAKE THINGS GOOD FOR US.
IT'S SO SIMPLE.
ANYWAY, I TRY AND DO THINGS BY THE BOOK AROUND HERE.
And... the clothes went on the mantel.
This girl really was weird.
THERE'S A BOOK? ...CAN I BORROW IT?
NO NO NO NO NO, THERE IS NO ACTUAL BOOK.
YEAH, I GOT THAT. "BY THE BOOK." FIGURE OF SPEECH. I WAS JOKING.
OH.

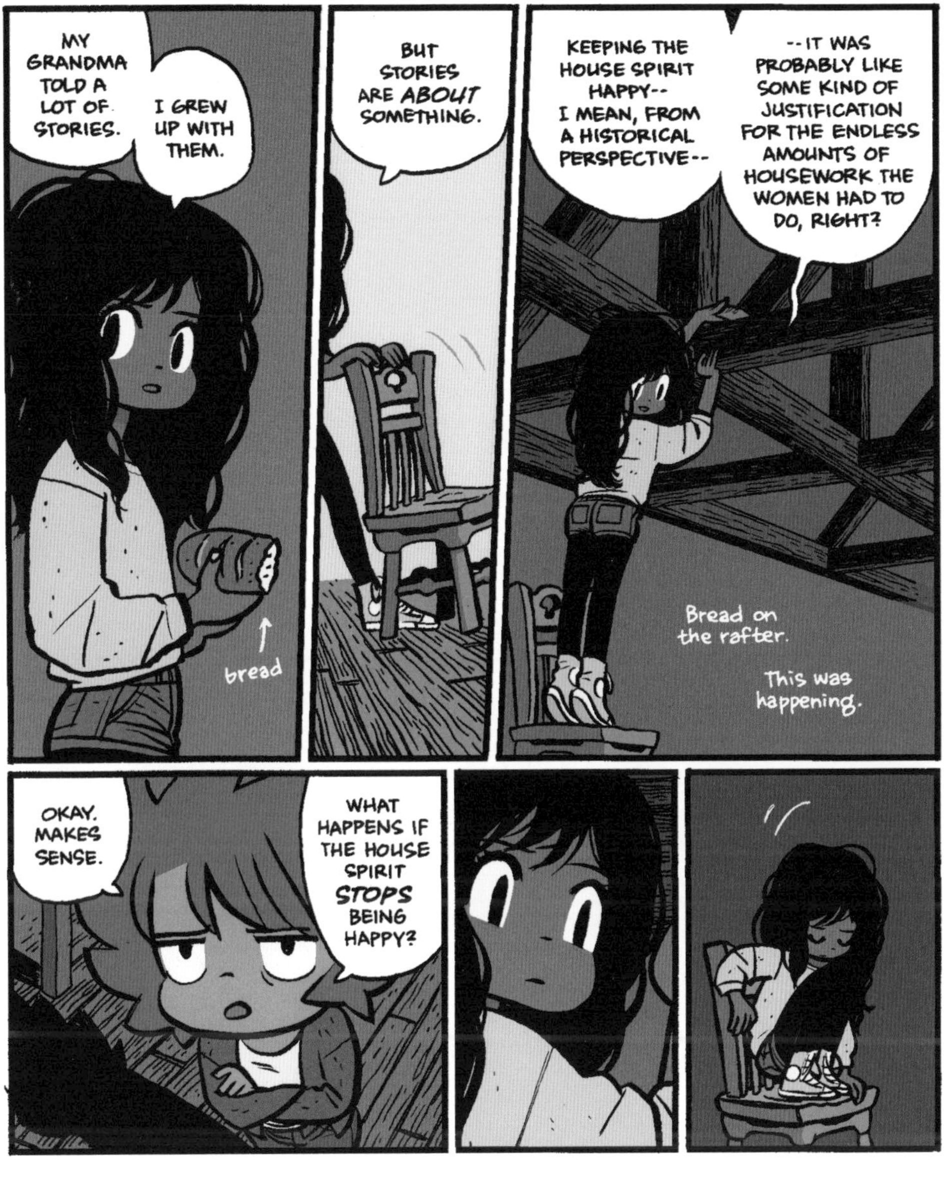

MY GRANDMA TOLD A LOT OF STORIES.
I GREW UP WITH THEM.
bread
BUT STORIES ARE *ABOUT* SOMETHING.
KEEPING THE HOUSE SPIRIT HAPPY-- I MEAN, FROM A HISTORICAL PERSPECTIVE--
--IT WAS PROBABLY LIKE SOME KIND OF JUSTIFICATION FOR THE ENDLESS AMOUNTS OF HOUSEWORK THE WOMEN HAD TO DO, RIGHT?
Bread on the rafter.
This was happening.
OKAY. MAKES SENSE.
WHAT HAPPENS IF THE HOUSE SPIRIT **STOPS** BEING HAPPY?

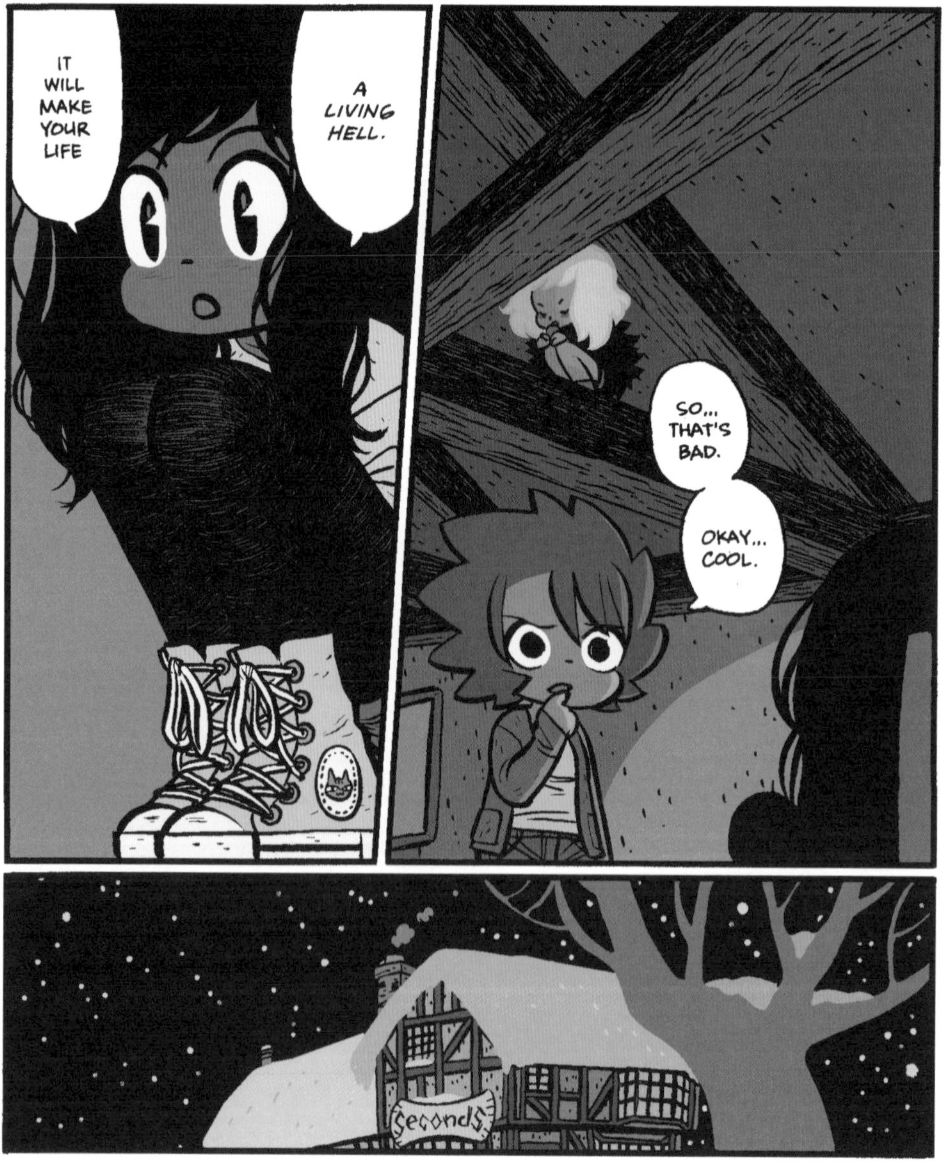
IT WILL MAKE YOUR LIFE
A LIVING HELL.
SO... THAT'S BAD.
OKAY... COOL.
SECONDS

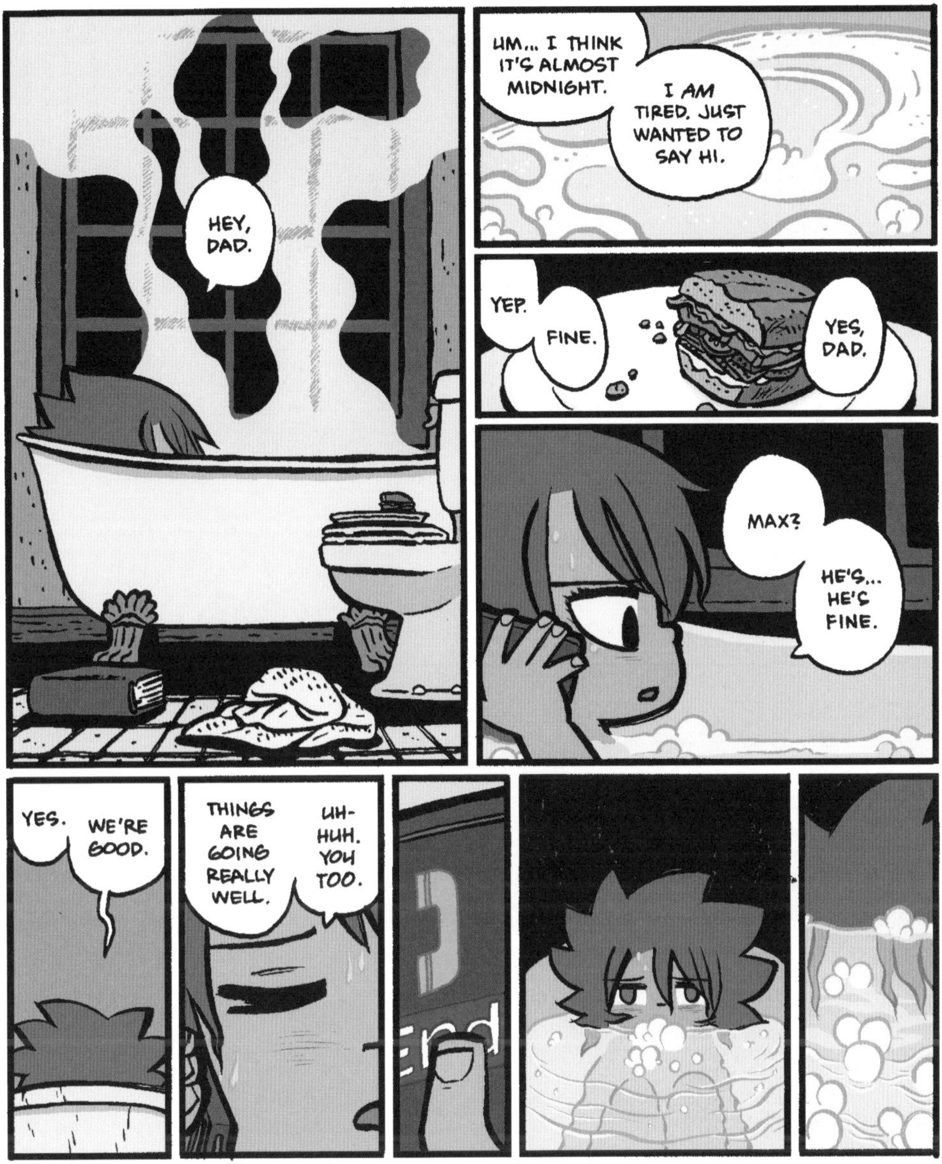
HEY, DAD.
UM... I THINK IT'S ALMOST MIDNIGHT.
I AM TIRED. JUST WANTED TO SAY HI.
YEP.
FINE.
YES, DAD.
MAX?
HE'S... HE'S FINE.
YES.
WE'RE GOOD.
THINGS ARE GOING REALLY WELL.
UH-HUH. YOU TOO.
End

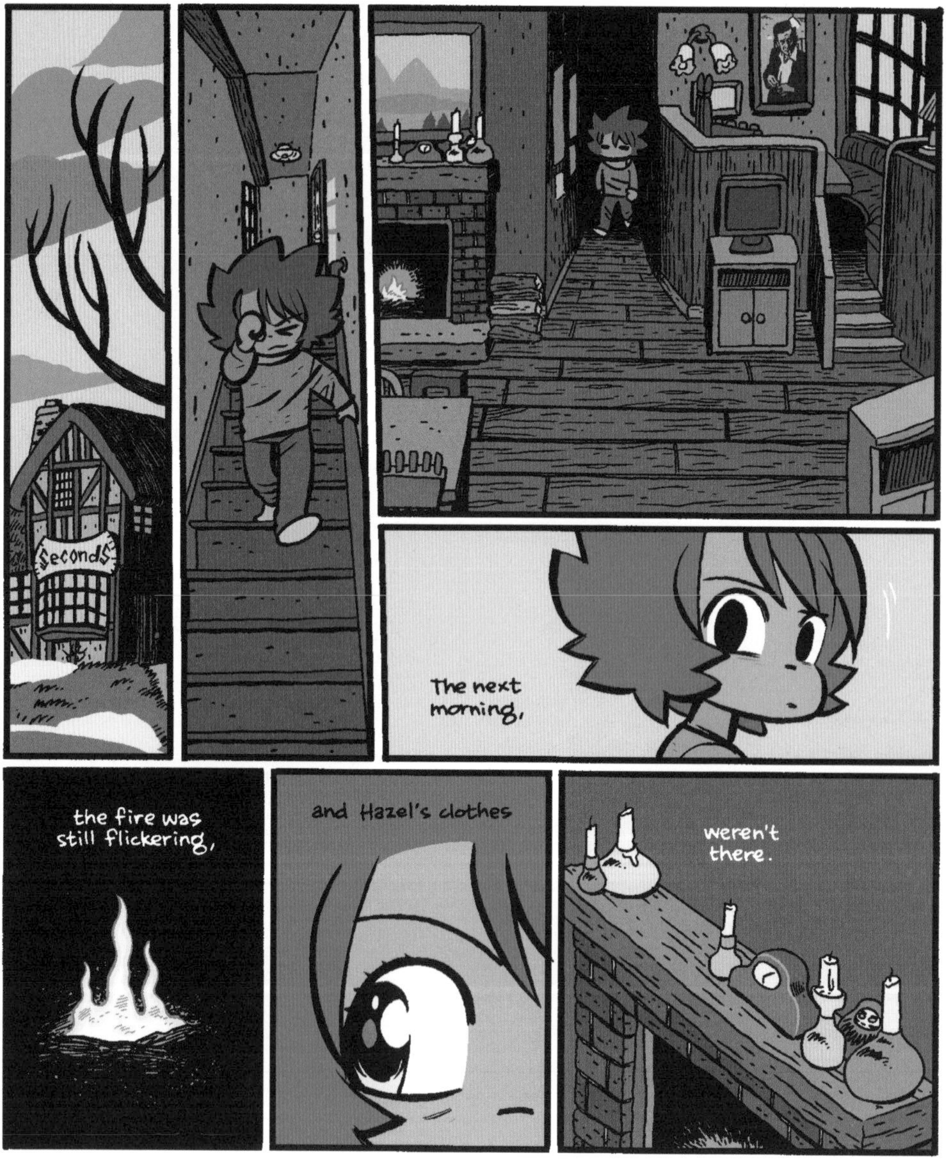
Seconds
The next morning,
the fire was still flickering,
and Hazel's clothes
weren't there.

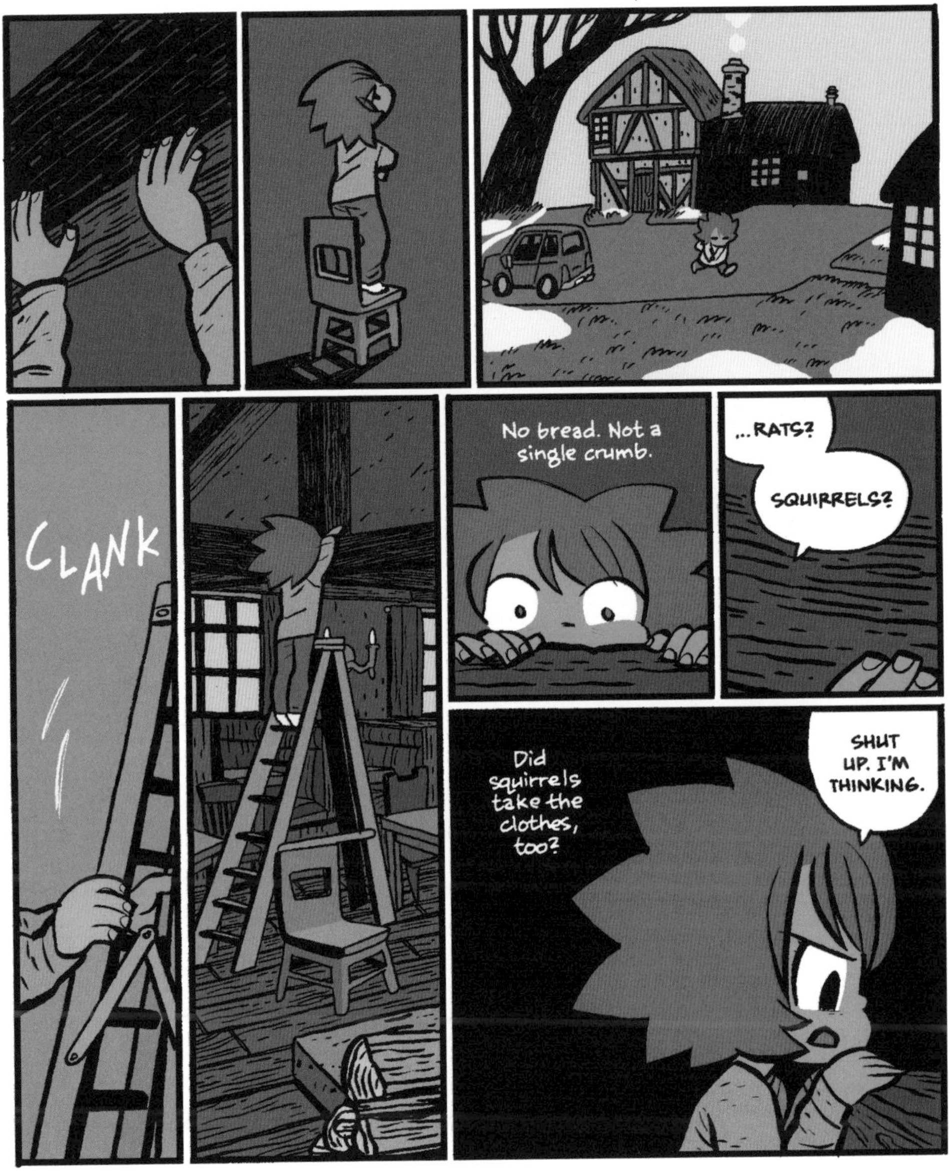
CLANK
No bread. Not a single crumb.
...RATS?
SQUIRRELS?
Did squirrels take the clothes, too?
SHUT UP. I'M THINKING.

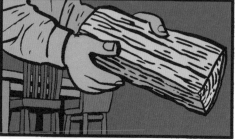

3
Lis

It felt like she hadn't seen Arthur in a week, which was unusual.

HEY.

WHERE AAARE YOU, DUDE?

I TOLD YOU LIKE FIFTY TIMES.

I KNOW. SORRY. BRAIN BAD.

She suddenly remembered, but only after it was too late.

...FUNERAL.

I... UM... I'M SORRY FOR YOUR... I MEAN... YOU KNOW...

IT IS WHAT IT IS, KATIE. ENOUGH ABOUT ME. I'M FINE. ARE YOU ALRIGHT?

OH... SURE... YEAH. THINGS ARE OKAY...

GREAT. LISTEN, JUST LEAVE THE SITE TO ME, KATIE. EVERYTHING'S FINE. THERE'S NOTHING TO GET ALARMED ABOUT. I'M TAKING CARE OF IT.

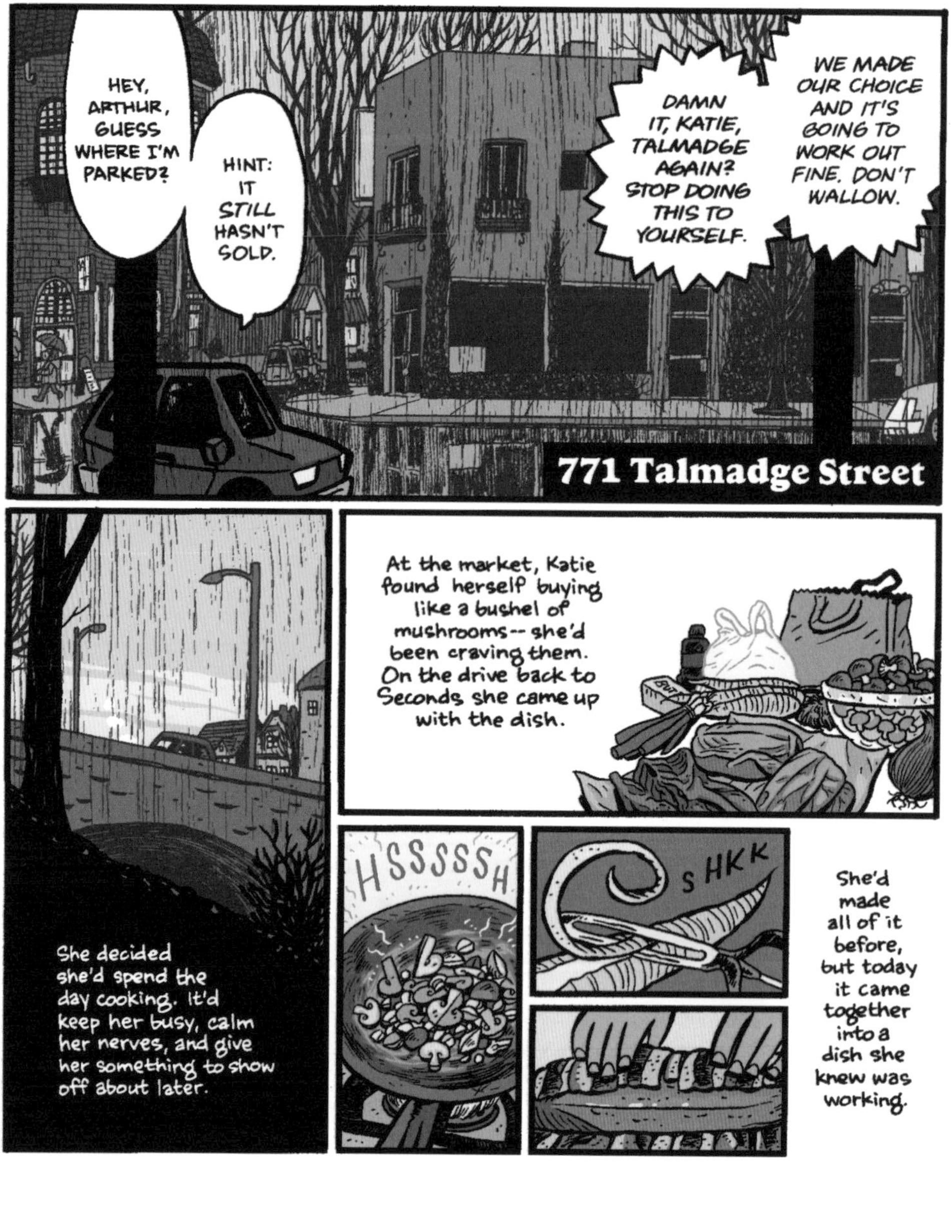
HEY, ARTHUR, GUESS WHERE I'M PARKED?
HINT: IT STILL HASN'T SOLD.
DAMN IT, KATIE, TALMADGE AGAIN? STOP DOING THIS TO YOURSELF.
WE MADE OUR CHOICE AND IT'S GOING TO WORK OUT FINE. DON'T WALLOW.
771 Talmadge Street
She decided she'd spend the day cooking. It'd keep her busy, calm her nerves, and give her something to show off about later.
At the market, Katie found herself buying like a bushel of mushrooms-- she'd been craving them. On the drive back to Seconds she came up with the dish.
HSSSSSH
SHKK
She'd made all of it before, but today it came together into a dish she knew was working.

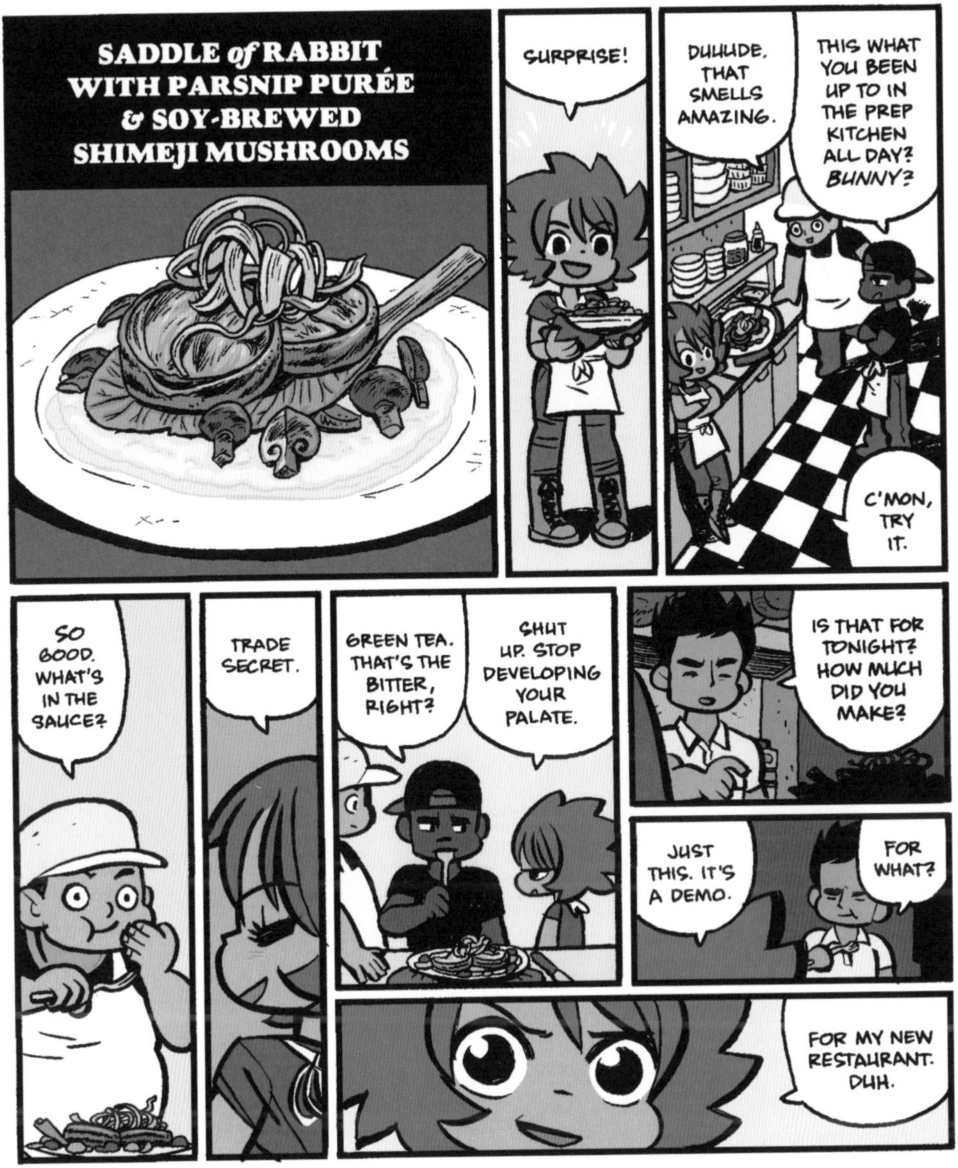
SADDLE of RABBIT WITH PARSNIP PURÉE & SOY-BREWED SHIMEJI MUSHROOMS
SURPRISE!
DUUUDE. THAT SMELLS AMAZING.
THIS WHAT YOU BEEN UP TO IN THE PREP KITCHEN ALL DAY? BUNNY?
C'MON, TRY IT.
SO GOOD. WHAT'S IN THE SAUCE?
TRADE SECRET.
GREEN TEA. THAT'S THE BITTER, RIGHT?
SHUT UP. STOP DEVELOPING YOUR PALATE.
IS THAT FOR TONIGHT? HOW MUCH DID YOU MAKE?
JUST THIS. IT'S A DEMO.
FOR WHAT?
FOR MY NEW RESTAURANT. DUH.

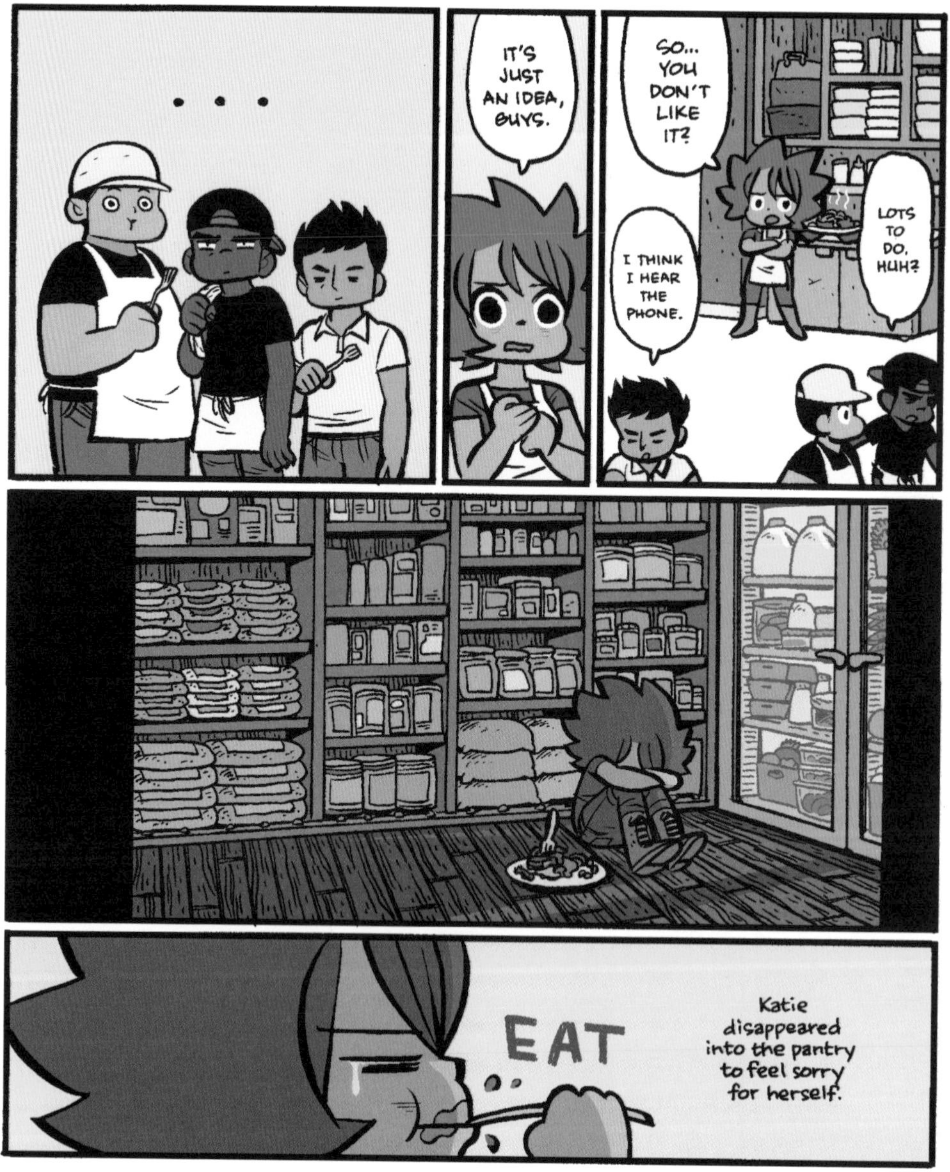
• • •
IT'S JUST AN IDEA, GUYS.
SO... YOU DON'T LIKE IT?
LOTS TO DO, HUH?
I THINK I HEAR THE PHONE.
EAT
Katie disappeared into the pantry to feel sorry for herself.

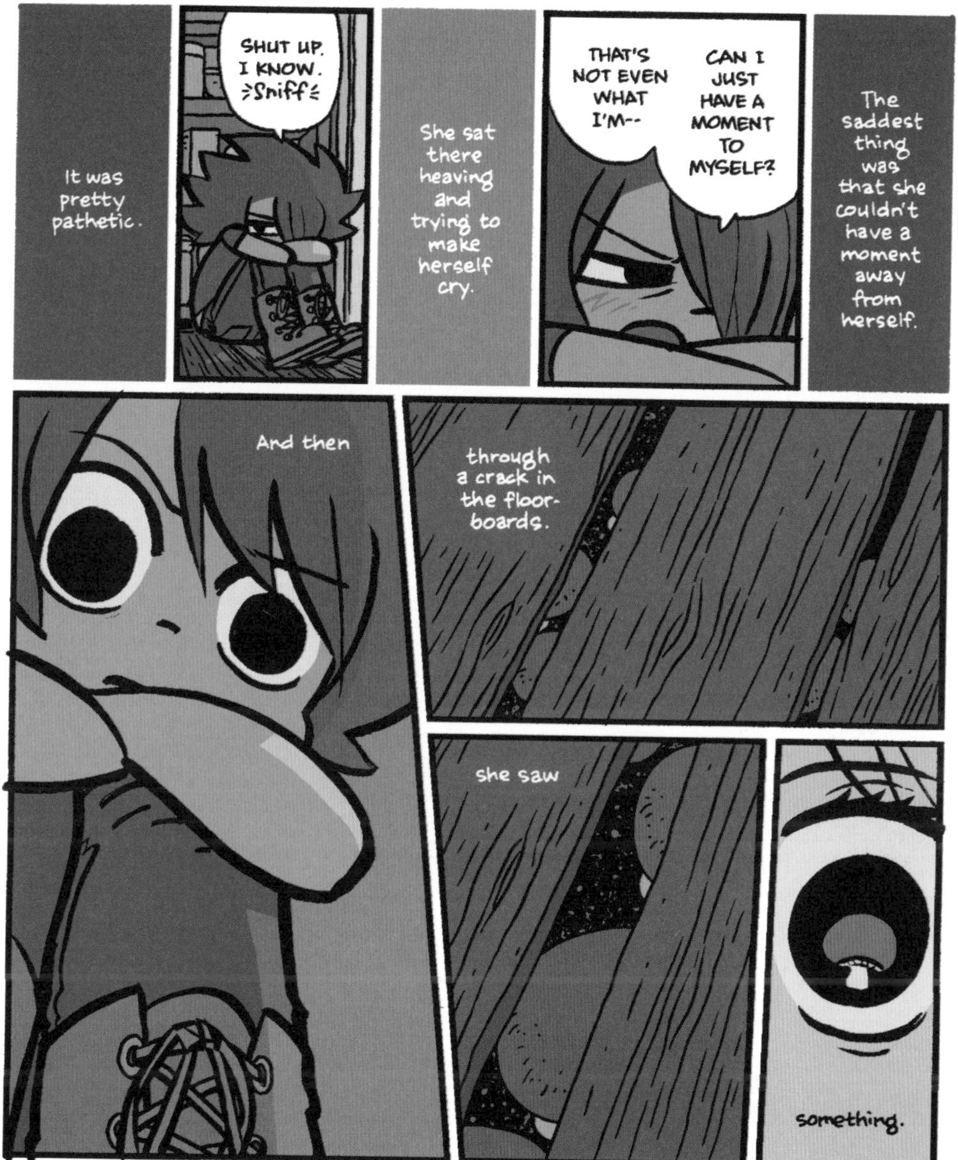
It was pretty pathetic.
SHUT UP. I KNOW. ≥Sniff≤
She sat there heaving and trying to make herself cry.
THAT'S NOT EVEN WHAT I'M--
CAN I JUST HAVE A MOMENT TO MYSELF?
The saddest thing was that she couldn't have a moment away from herself.
And then
through a crack in the floor-boards.
she saw
something.

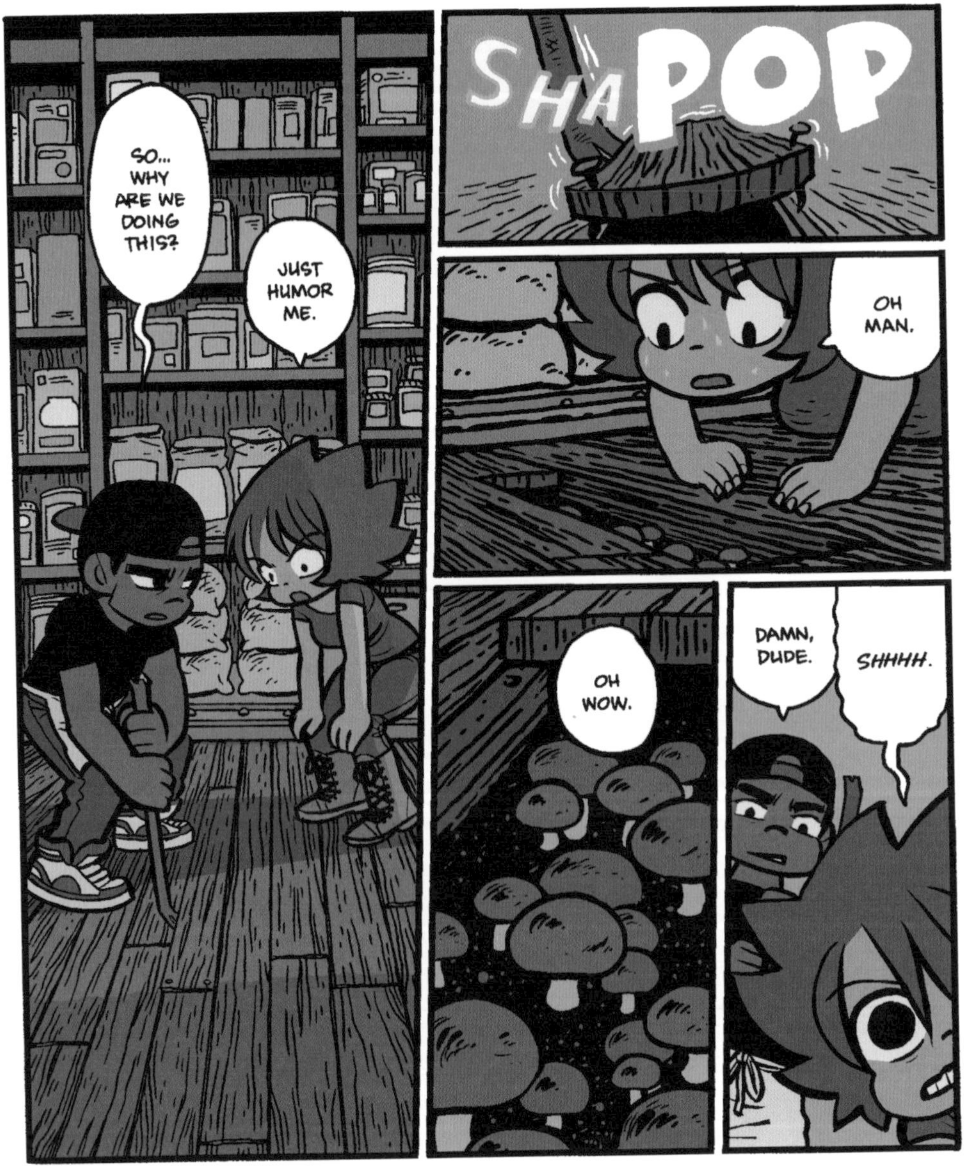
SO... WHY ARE WE DOING THIS?
JUST HUMOR ME.
SHAPOP
OH MAN.
OH WOW.
DAMN, DUDE.
SHHHH.

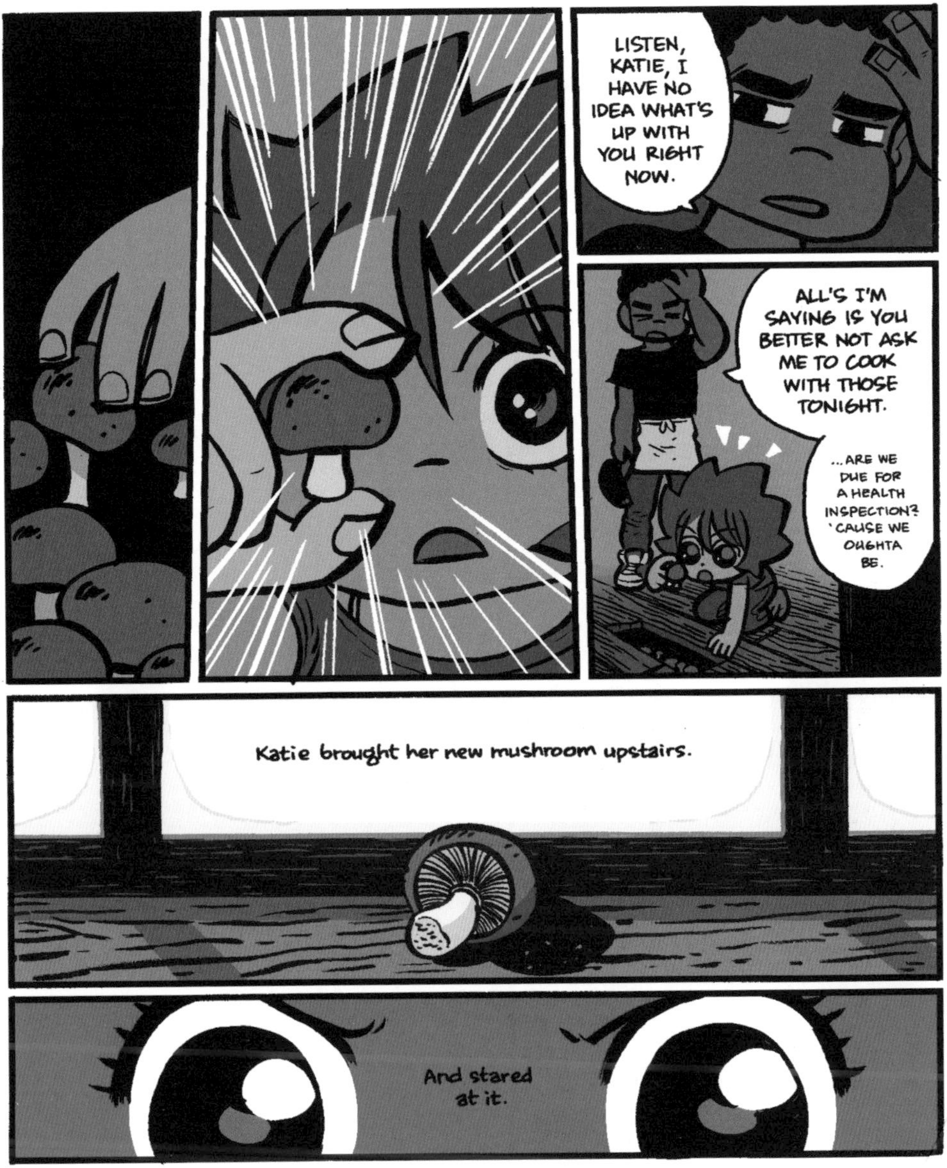
LISTEN, KATIE, I HAVE NO IDEA WHAT'S UP WITH YOU RIGHT NOW.
ALL'S I'M SAYING IS YOU BETTER NOT ASK ME TO COOK WITH THOSE TONIGHT.
...ARE WE DUE FOR A HEALTH INSPECTION? 'CAUSE WE OUGHTA BE.
Katie brought her new mushroom upstairs.
And stared at it.

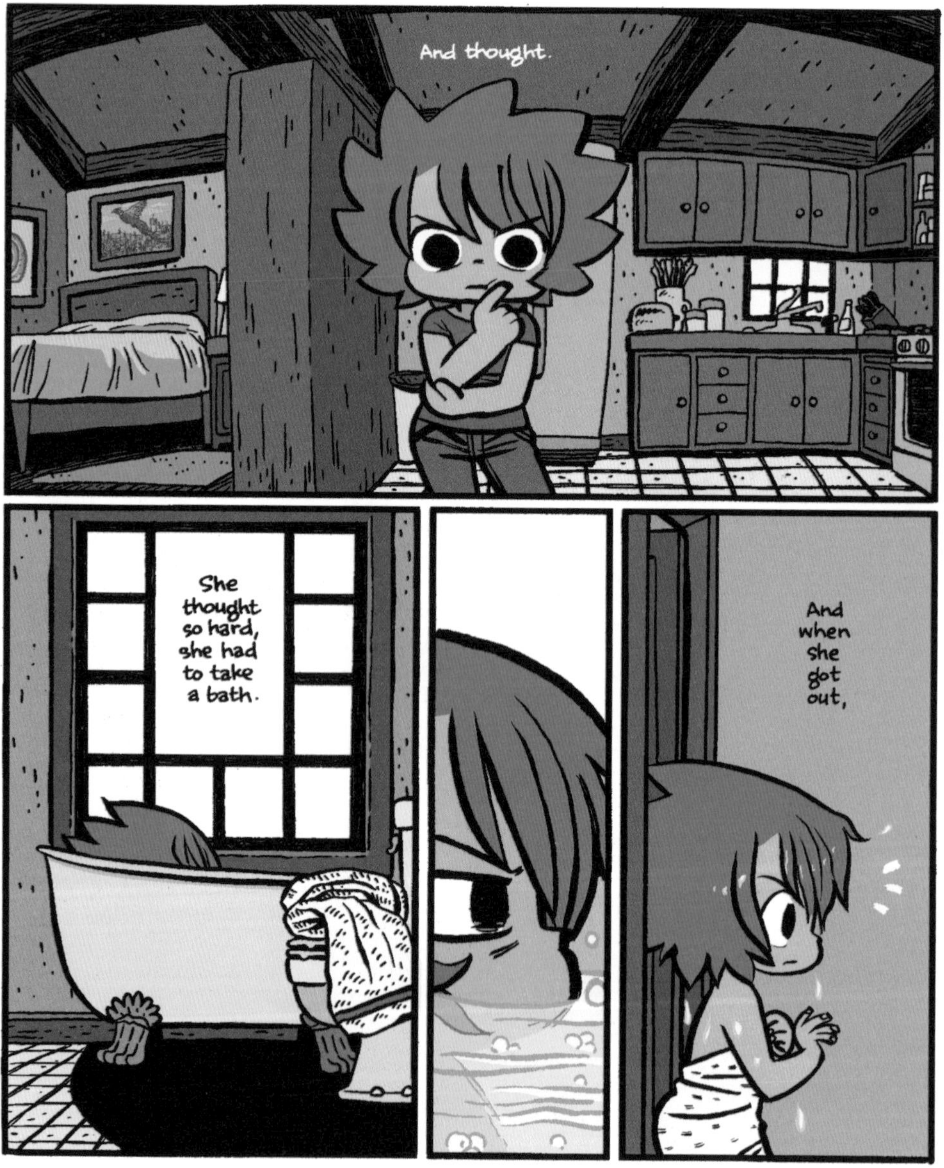
And thought.
She thought so hard, she had to take a bath.
And when she got out,

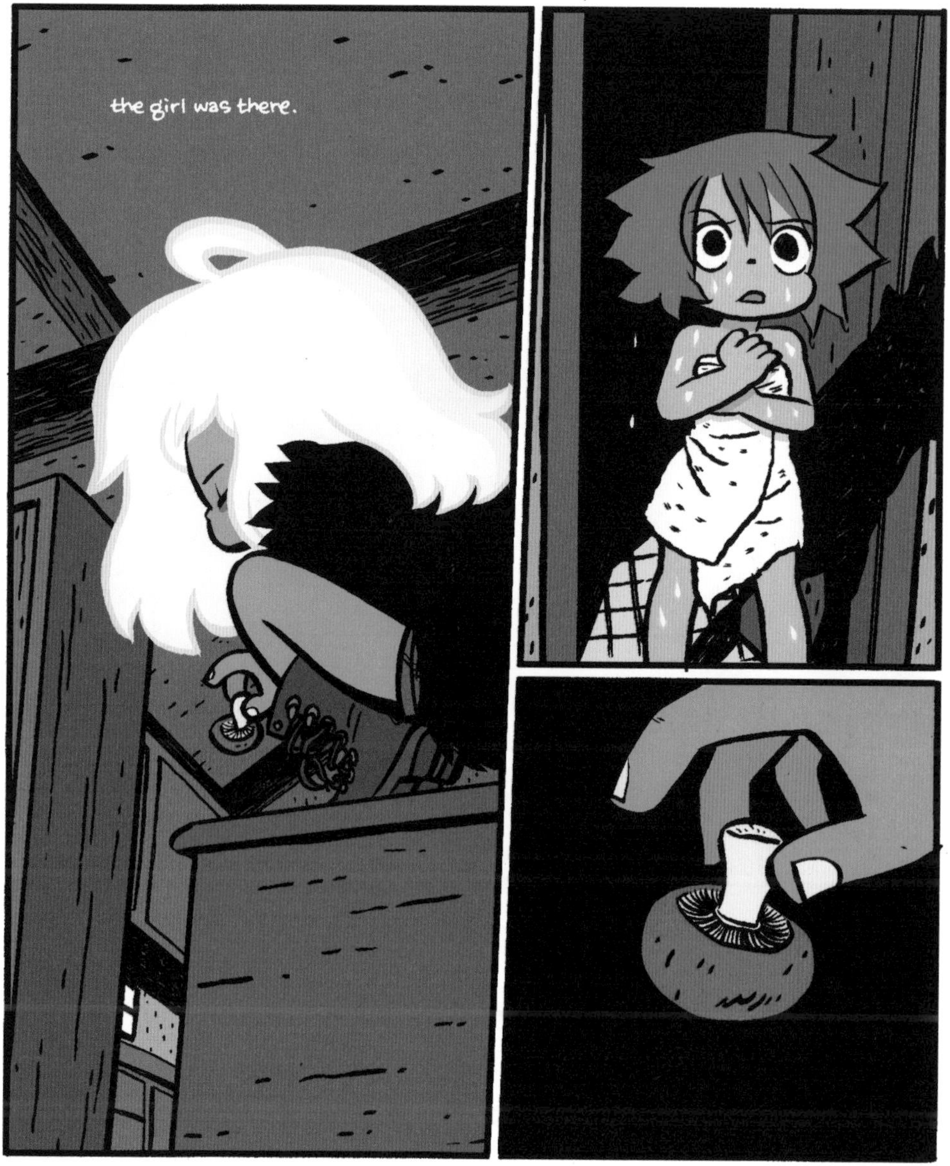
the girl was there.

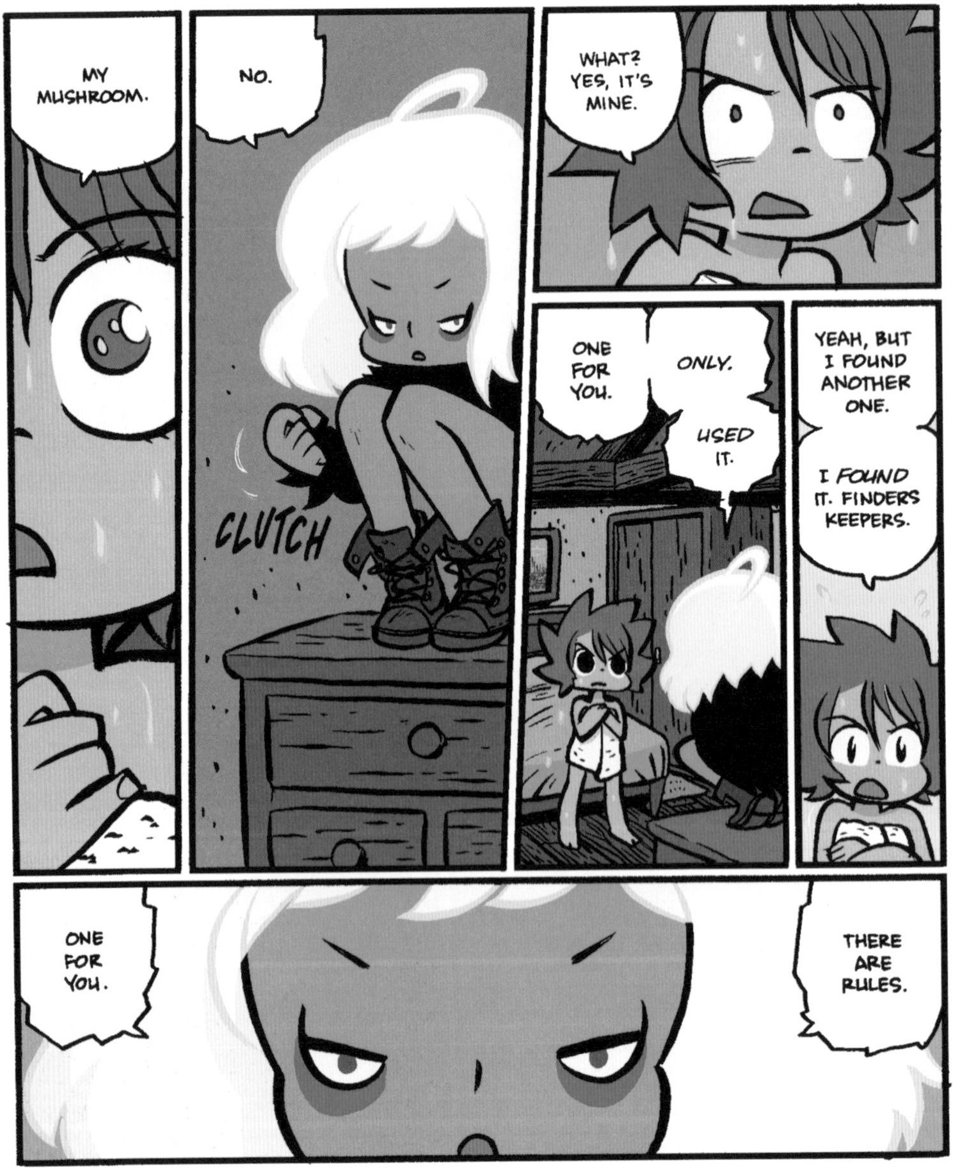
MY MUSHROOM.
NO.
CLUTCH
WHAT? YES, IT'S MINE.
ONE FOR YOU.
ONLY.
USED IT.
YEAH, BUT I FOUND ANOTHER ONE.
I *FOUND* IT. FINDERS KEEPERS.
ONE FOR YOU.
THERE ARE RULES.

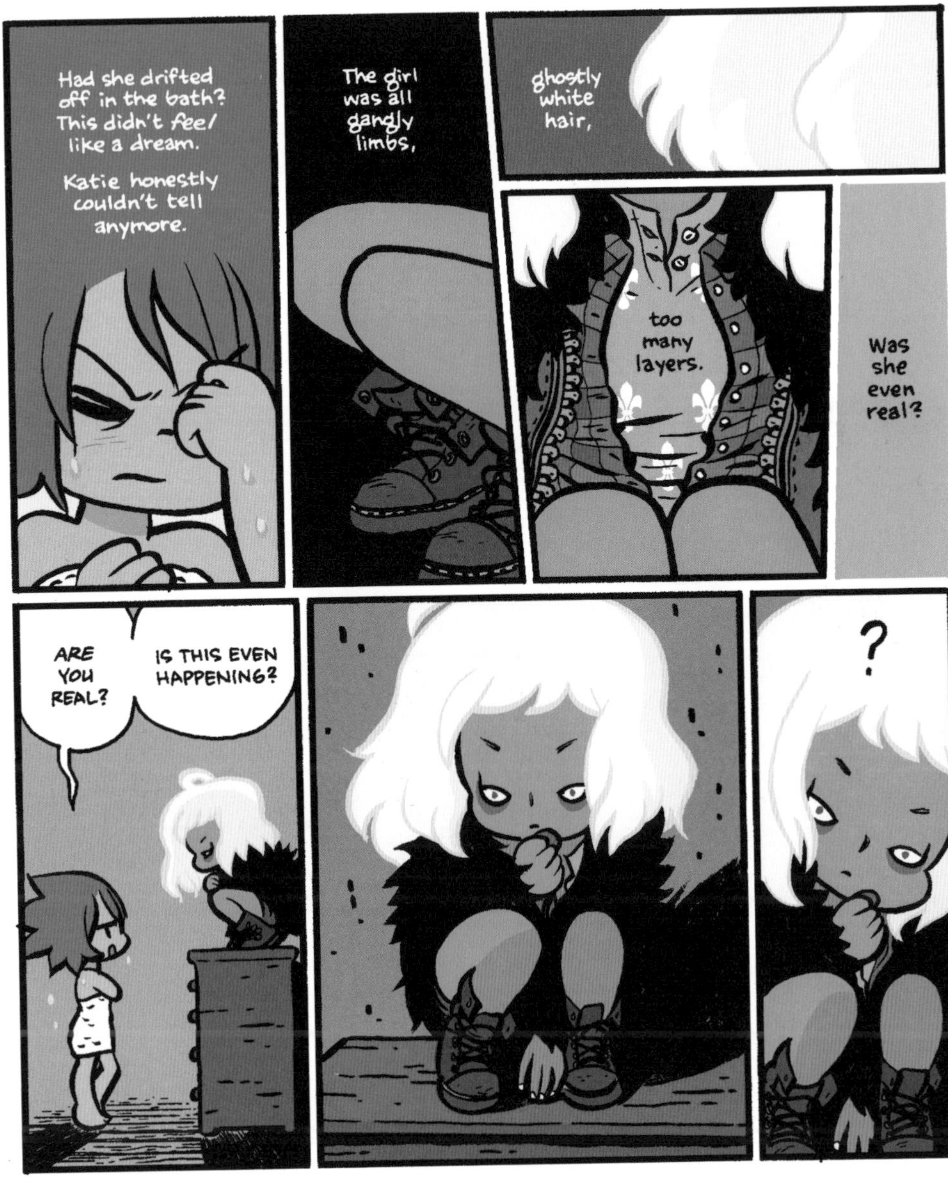
Had she drifted off in the bath? This didn't feel like a dream.
Katie honestly couldn't tell anymore.
The girl was all gangly limbs,
ghostly white hair,
too many layers.
Was she even real?
ARE YOU REAL?
IS THIS EVEN HAPPENING?
?

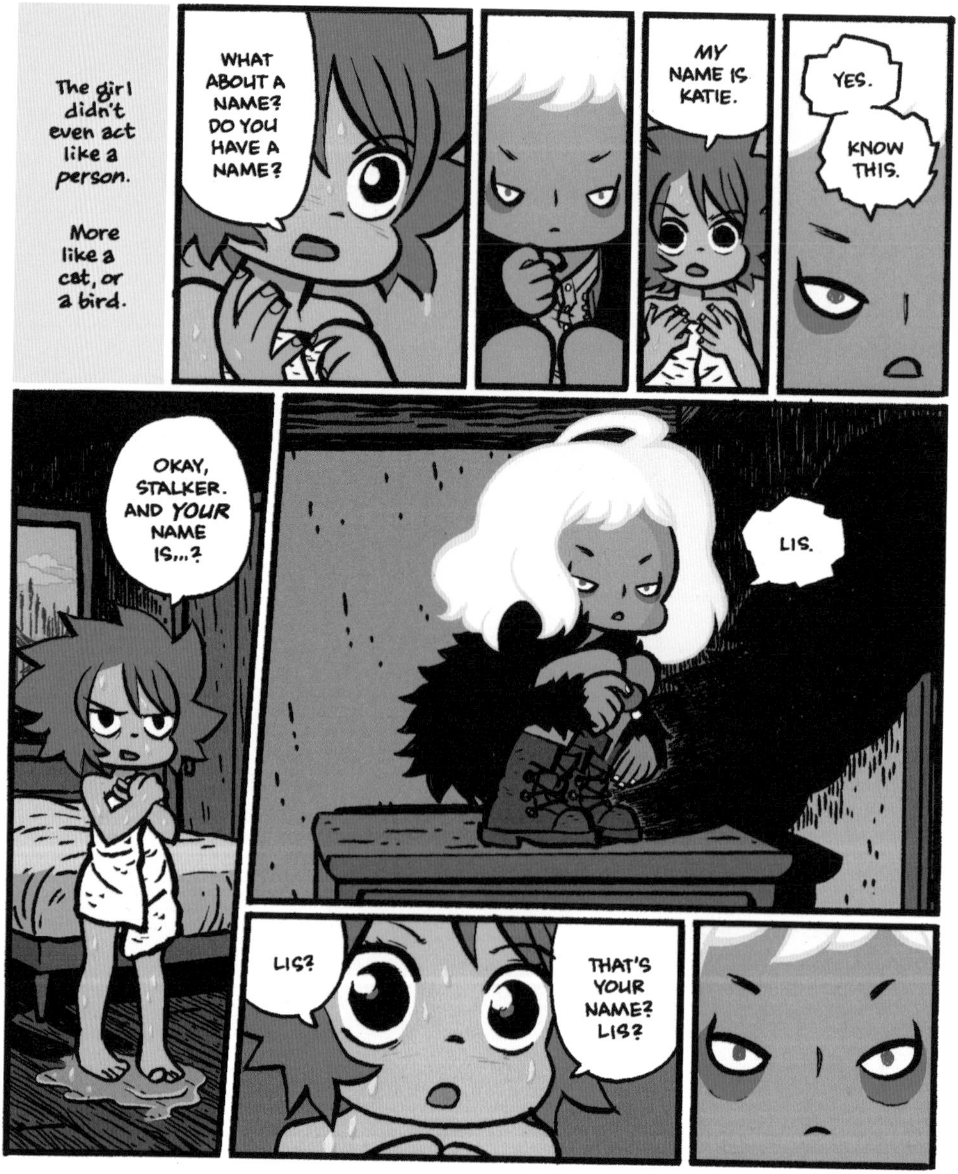
The girl didn't even act like a *person*.
More like a cat, or a bird.
WHAT ABOUT A NAME? DO YOU HAVE A NAME?
MY NAME IS KATIE.
YES.
KNOW THIS.
OKAY, STALKER. AND *YOUR* NAME IS...?
LIS.
LIS?
THAT'S YOUR NAME? LIS?

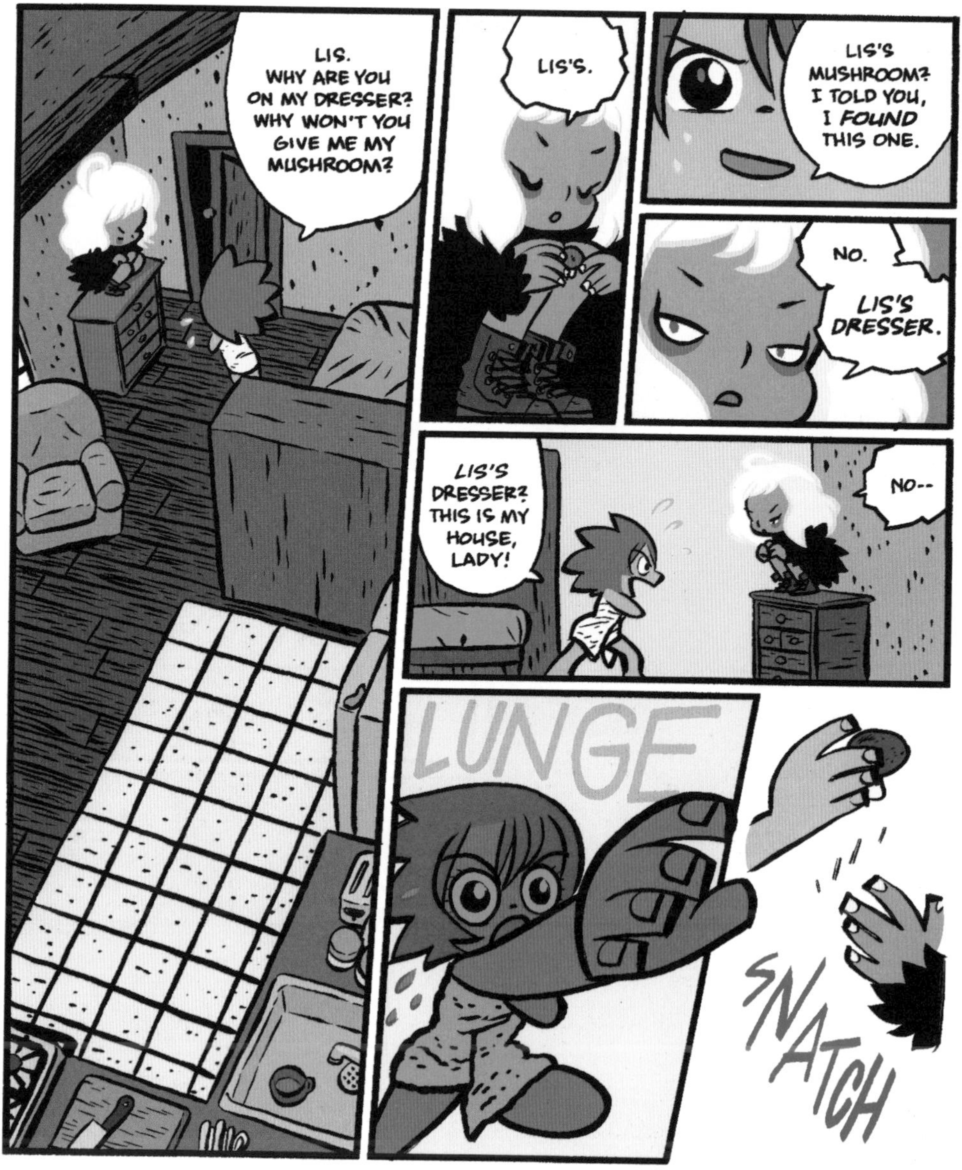
LIS.
WHY ARE YOU ON MY DRESSER? WHY WON'T YOU GIVE ME MY MUSHROOM?
LIS'S.
LIS'S MUSHROOM? I TOLD YOU, I *FOUND* THIS ONE.
NO.
LIS'S DRESSER.
LIS'S DRESSER? THIS IS MY HOUSE, LADY!
NO--
LUNGE
SNATCH

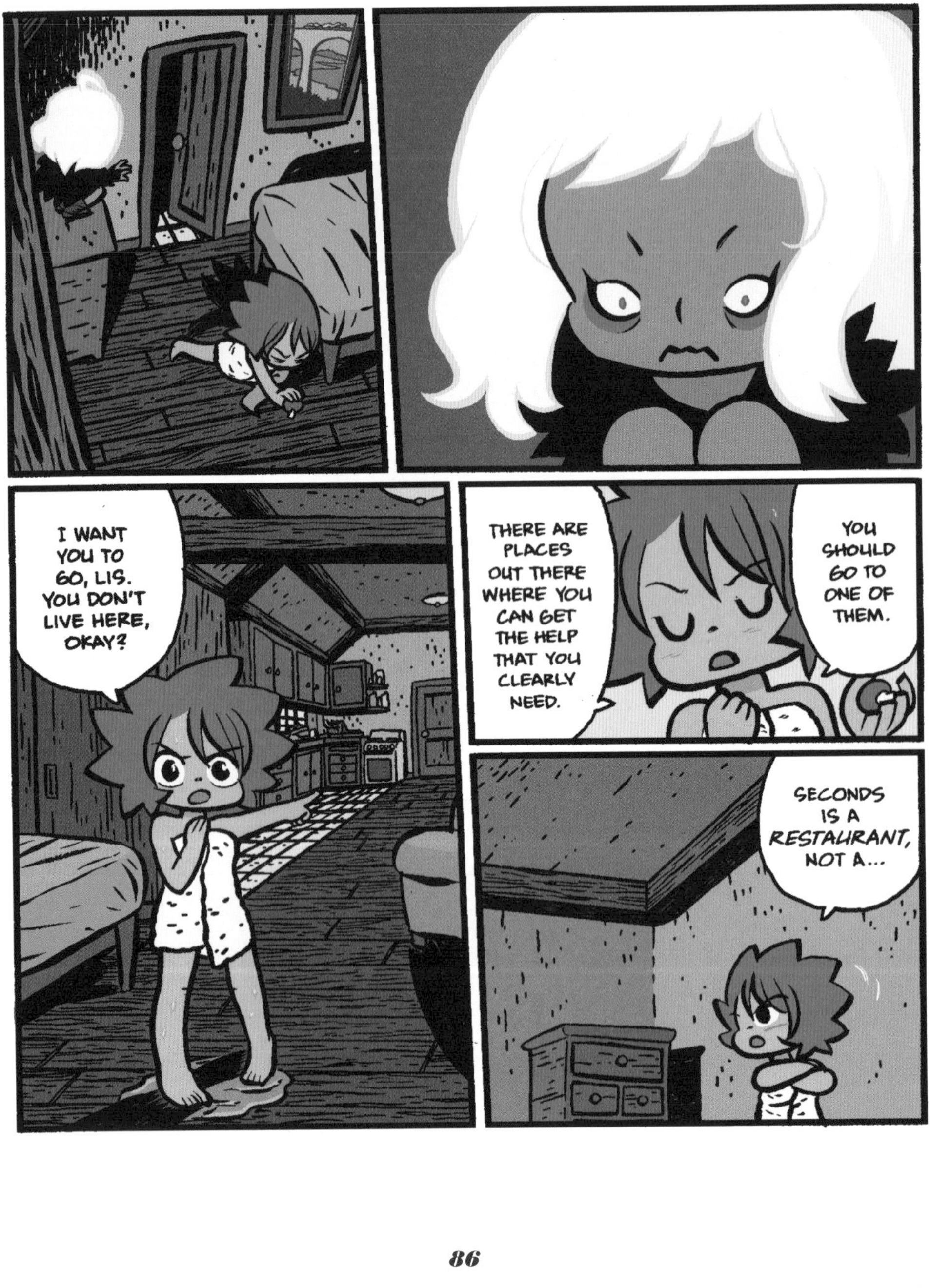
I WANT YOU TO GO, LIS. YOU DON'T LIVE HERE, OKAY?
THERE ARE PLACES OUT THERE WHERE YOU CAN GET THE HELP THAT YOU CLEARLY NEED.
YOU SHOULD GO TO ONE OF THEM.
SECONDS IS A *RESTAURANT*, NOT A...

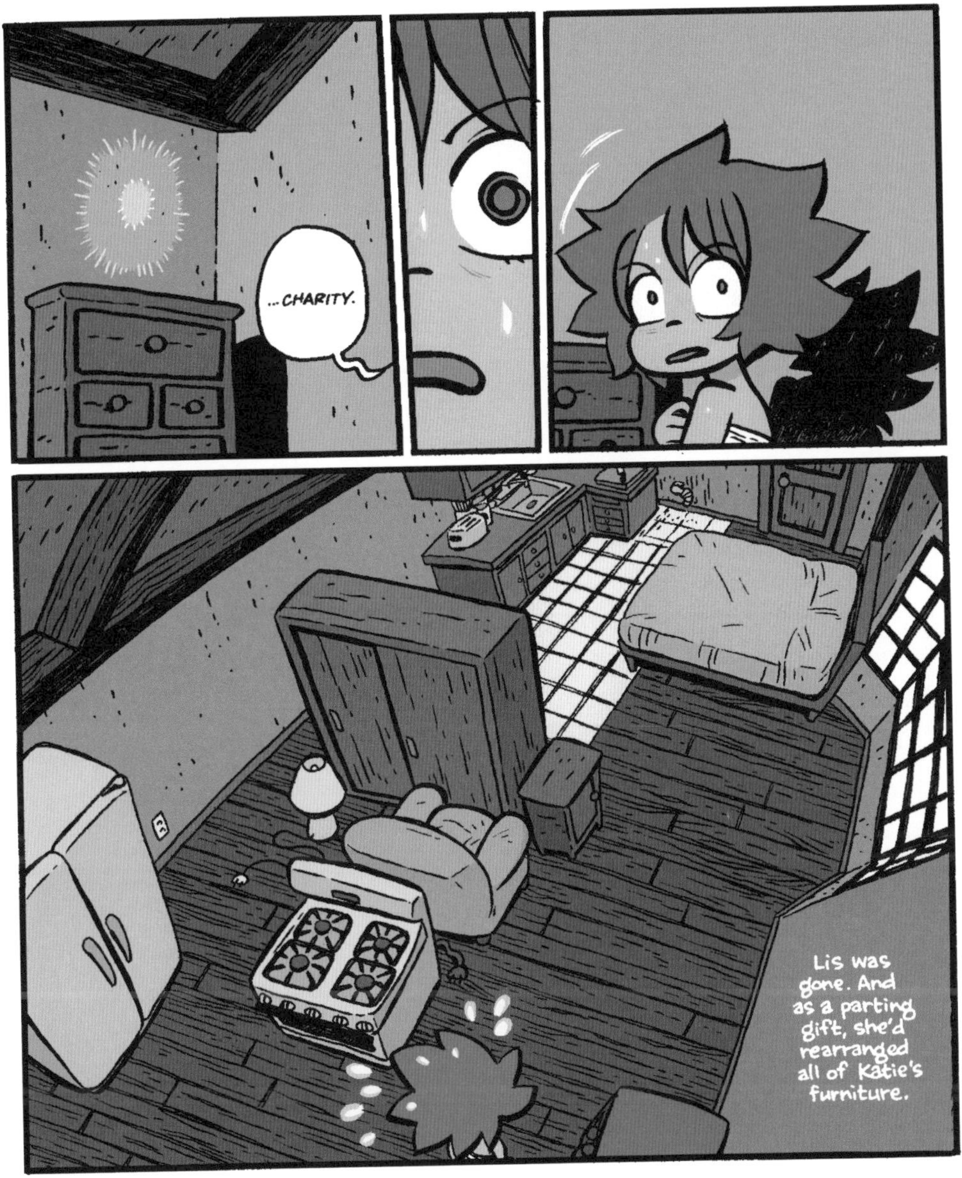
...CHARITY.
Lis was gone. And as a parting gift, she'd rearranged all of Katie's furniture.

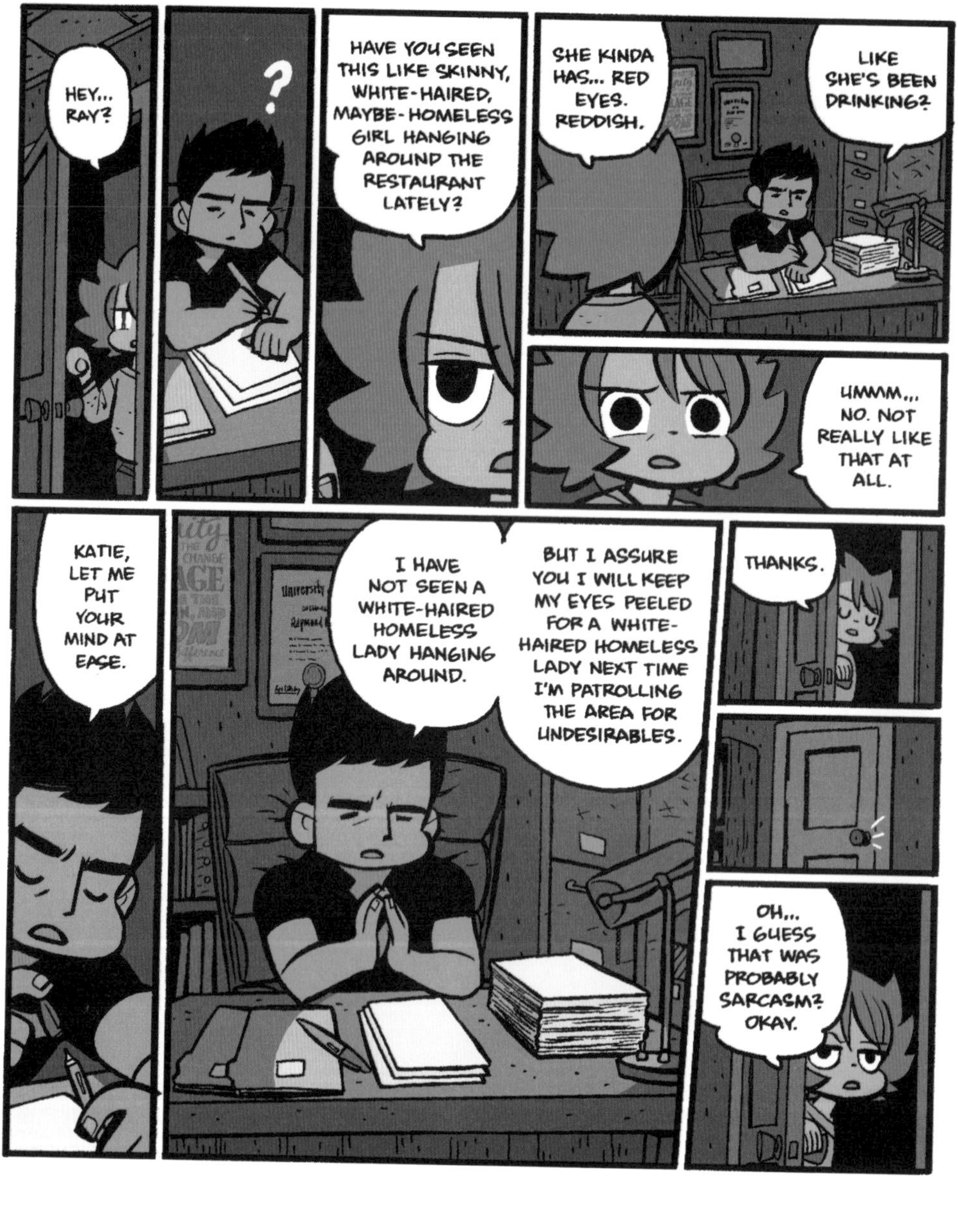
HEY... RAY?
HAVE YOU SEEN THIS LIKE SKINNY, WHITE-HAIRED, MAYBE-HOMELESS GIRL HANGING AROUND THE RESTAURANT LATELY?
SHE KINDA HAS... RED EYES. REDDISH.
LIKE SHE'S BEEN DRINKING?
UMMM... NO. NOT REALLY LIKE THAT AT ALL.
KATIE, LET ME PUT YOUR MIND AT EASE.
I HAVE NOT SEEN A WHITE-HAIRED HOMELESS LADY HANGING AROUND.
BUT I ASSURE YOU I WILL KEEP MY EYES PEELED FOR A WHITE-HAIRED HOMELESS LADY NEXT TIME I'M PATROLLING THE AREA FOR UNDESIRABLES.
THANKS.
OH... I GUESS THAT WAS PROBABLY SARCASM? OKAY.

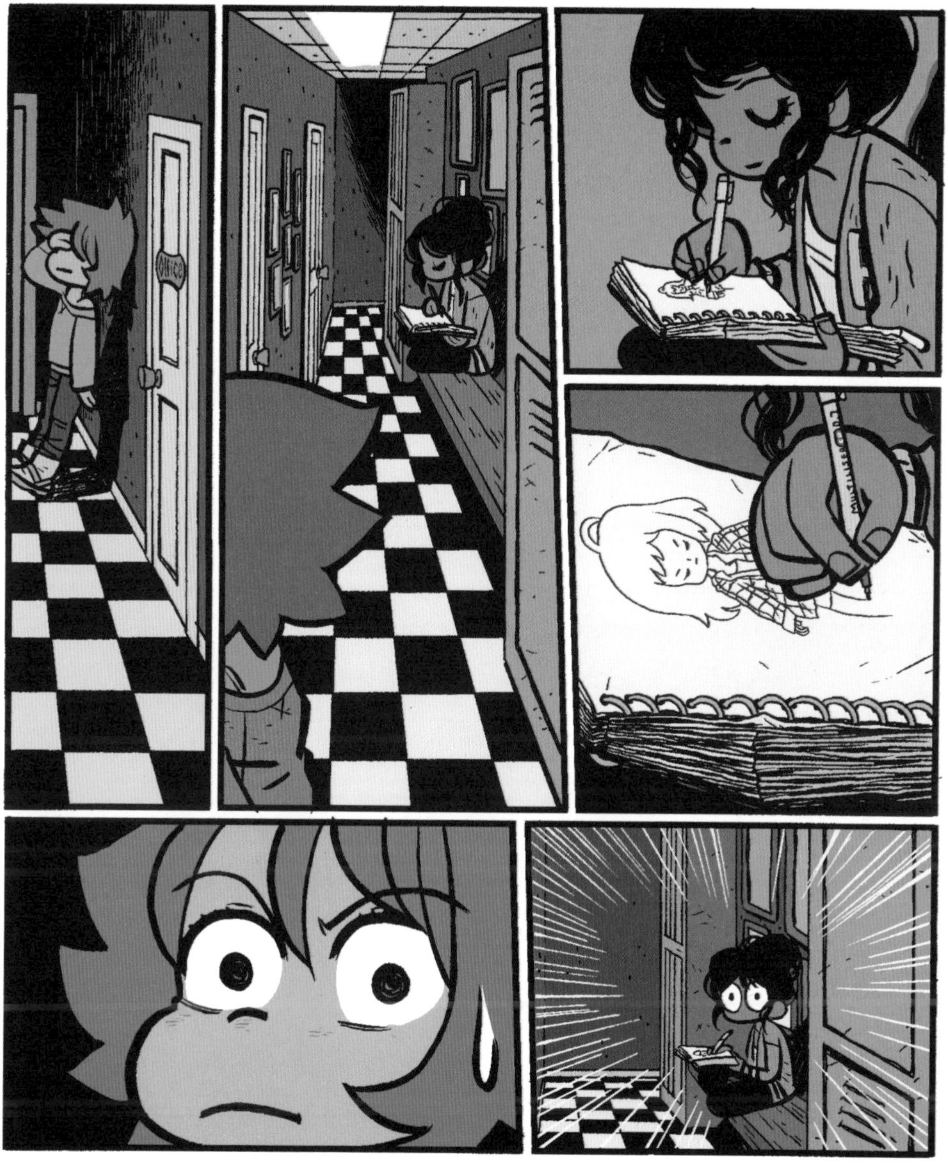

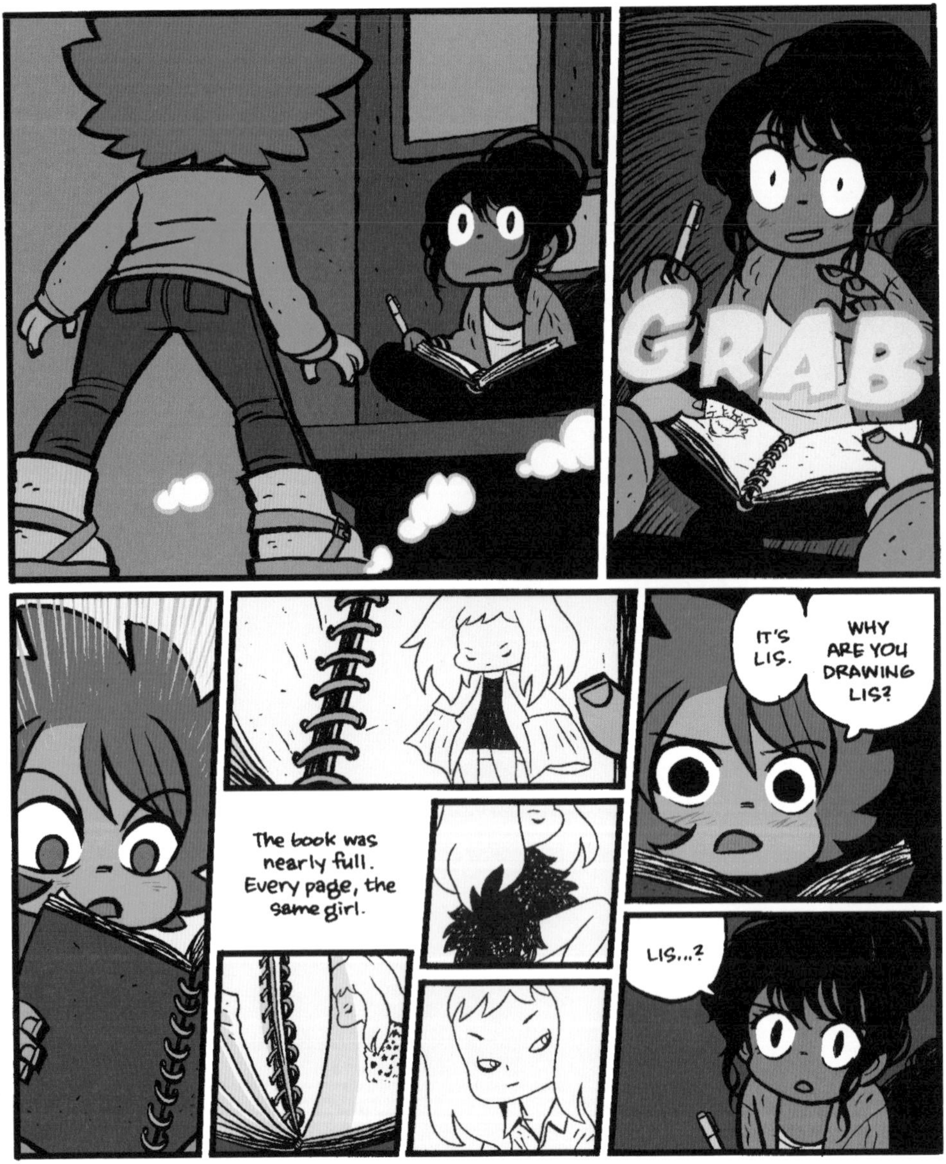
GRAB
IT'S LIS.
WHY ARE YOU DRAWING LIS?
The book was nearly full. Every page, the same girl.
LIS...?

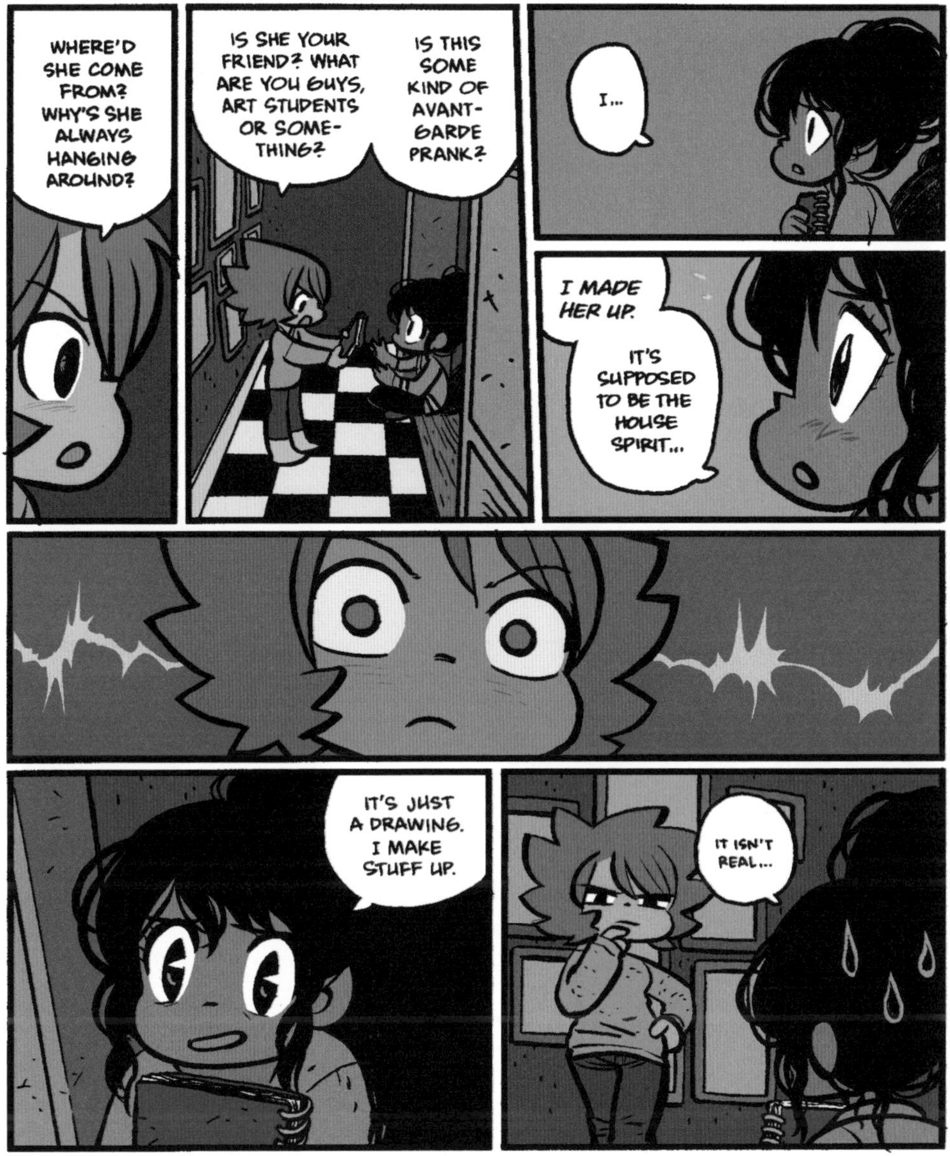
WHERE'D SHE COME FROM? WHY'S SHE ALWAYS HANGING AROUND?
IS SHE YOUR FRIEND? WHAT ARE YOU GUYS, ART STUDENTS OR SOME-THING?
IS THIS SOME KIND OF AVANT-GARDE PRANK?
I...
I MADE HER UP.
IT'S SUPPOSED TO BE THE HOUSE SPIRIT...
IT'S JUST A DRAWING. I MAKE STUFF UP.
IT ISN'T REAL...

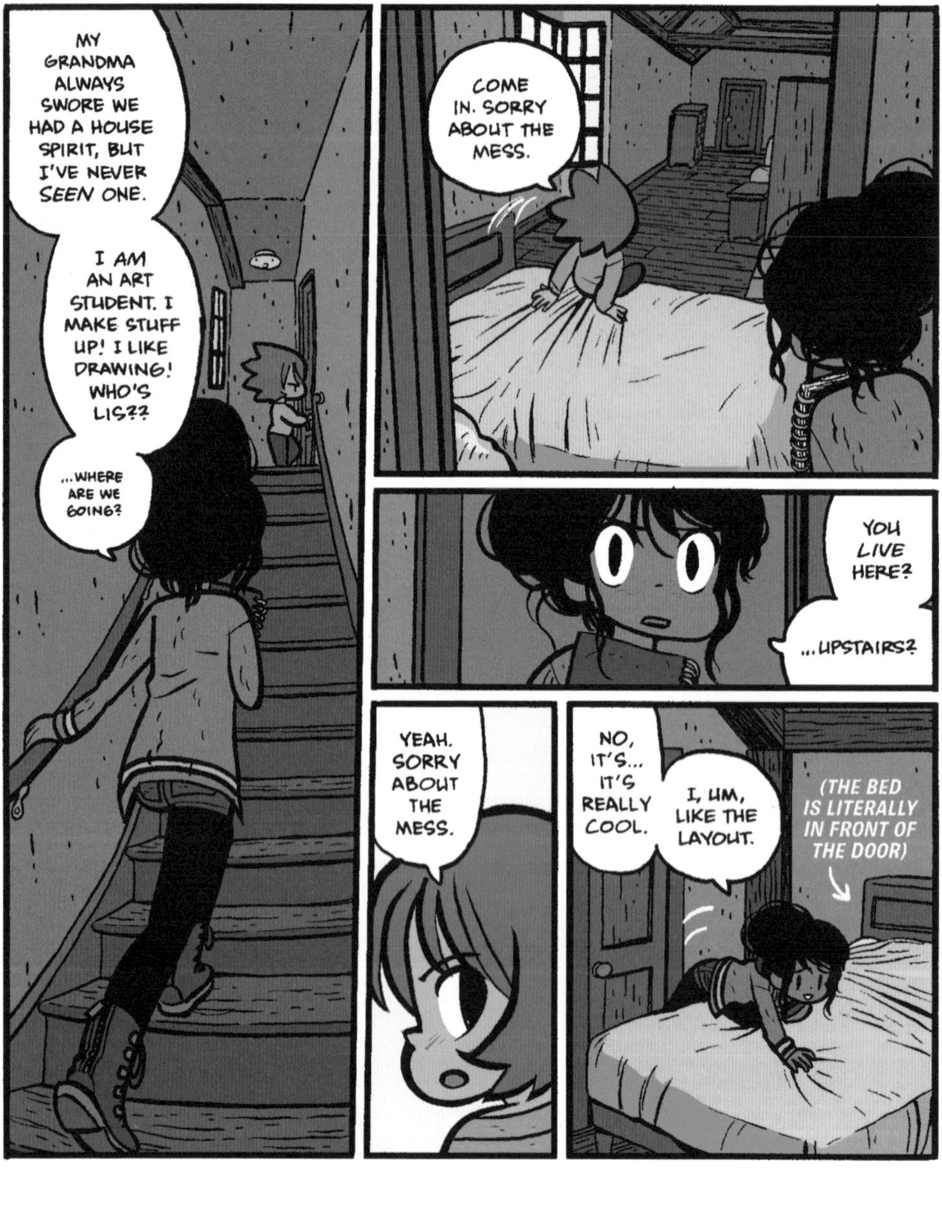
MY GRANDMA ALWAYS SWORE WE HAD A HOUSE SPIRIT, BUT I'VE NEVER SEEN ONE.
I AM AN ART STUDENT. I MAKE STUFF UP! I LIKE DRAWING! WHO'S LIS??
...WHERE ARE WE GOING?
COME IN. SORRY ABOUT THE MESS.
YOU LIVE HERE?
...UPSTAIRS?
YEAH. SORRY ABOUT THE MESS.
NO, IT'S... IT'S REALLY COOL.
I, UM, LIKE THE LAYOUT.
(THE BED IS LITERALLY IN FRONT OF THE DOOR)

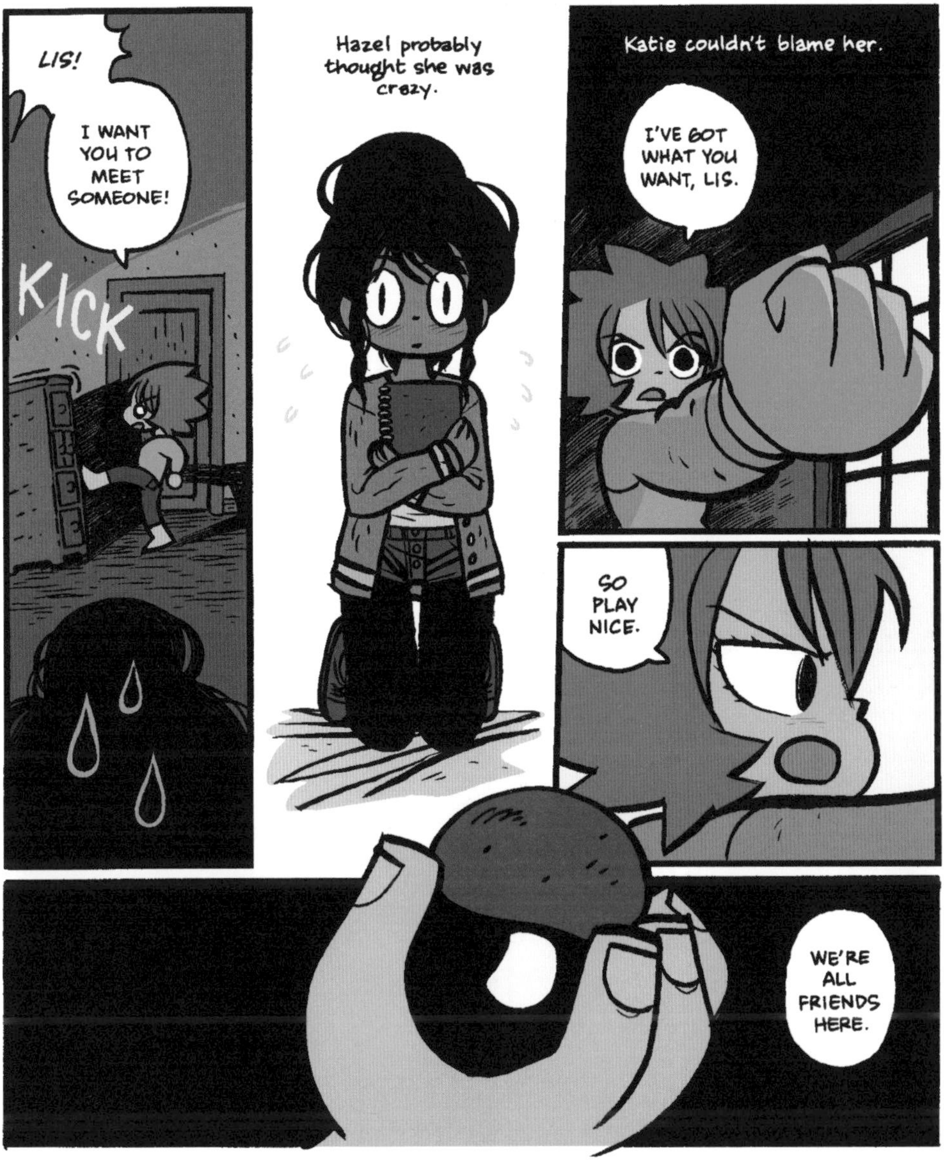
LIS!
I WANT YOU TO MEET SOMEONE!
KICK
Hazel probably thought she was crazy.
Katie couldn't blame her.
I'VE GOT WHAT YOU WANT, LIS.
SO PLAY NICE.
WE'RE ALL FRIENDS HERE.

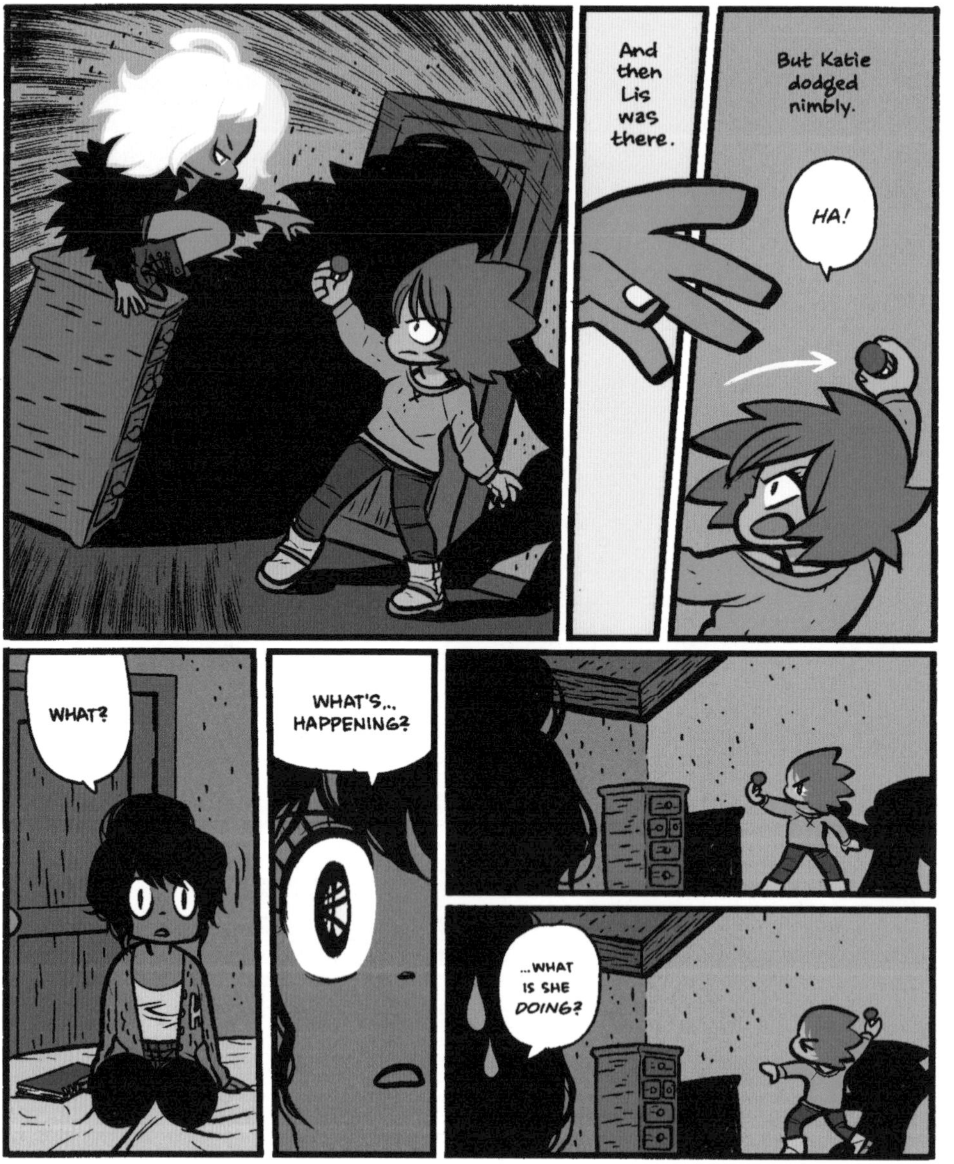
And then Lis was there.
But Katie dodged nimbly.
HA!
WHAT?
WHAT'S... HAPPENING?
...WHAT IS SHE DOING?

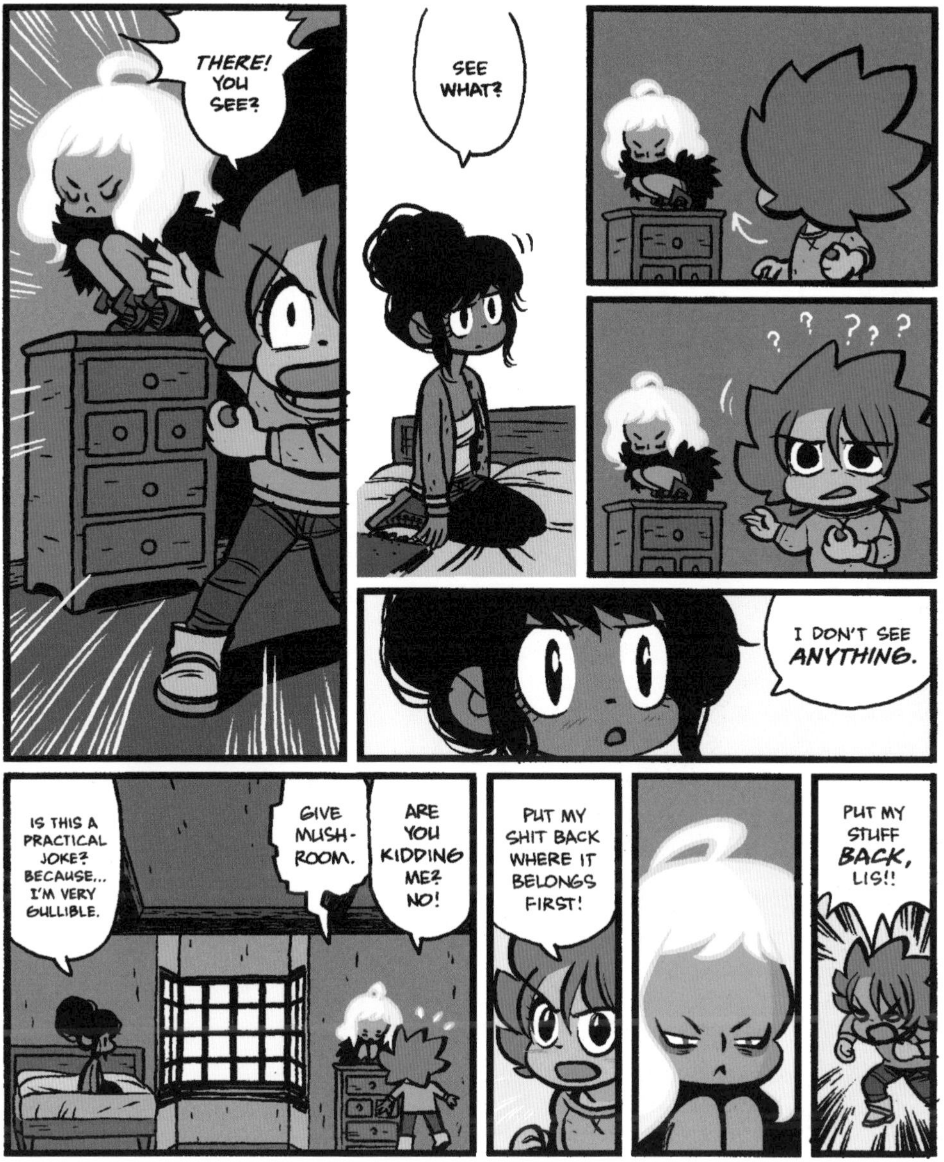
THERE! YOU SEE?
SEE WHAT?
? ? ??? ?
I DON'T SEE ANYTHING.
IS THIS A PRACTICAL JOKE? BECAUSE... I'M VERY GULLIBLE.
GIVE MUSH-ROOM.
ARE YOU KIDDING ME? NO!
PUT MY SHIT BACK WHERE IT BELONGS FIRST!
PUT MY STUFF BACK, LIS!!

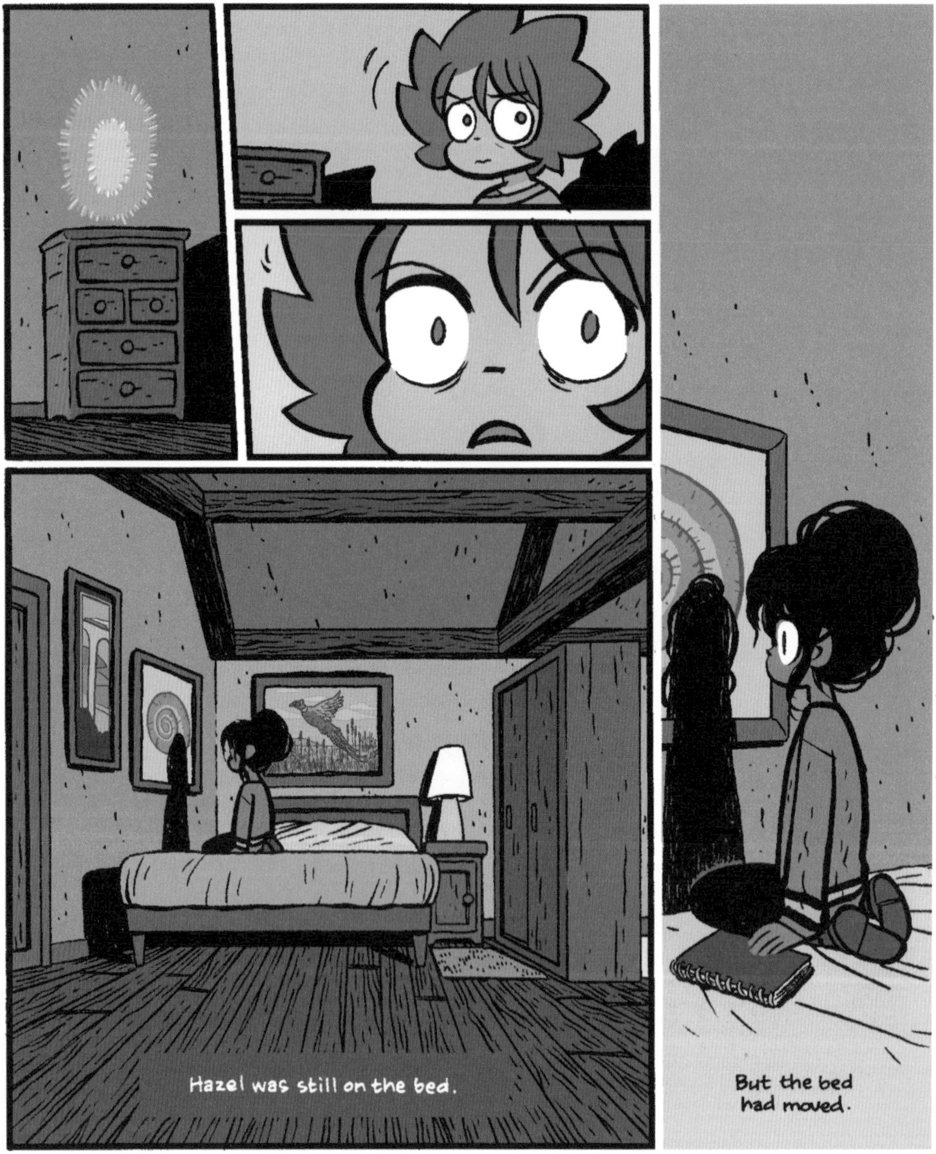
Hazel was still on the bed.
But the bed had moved.

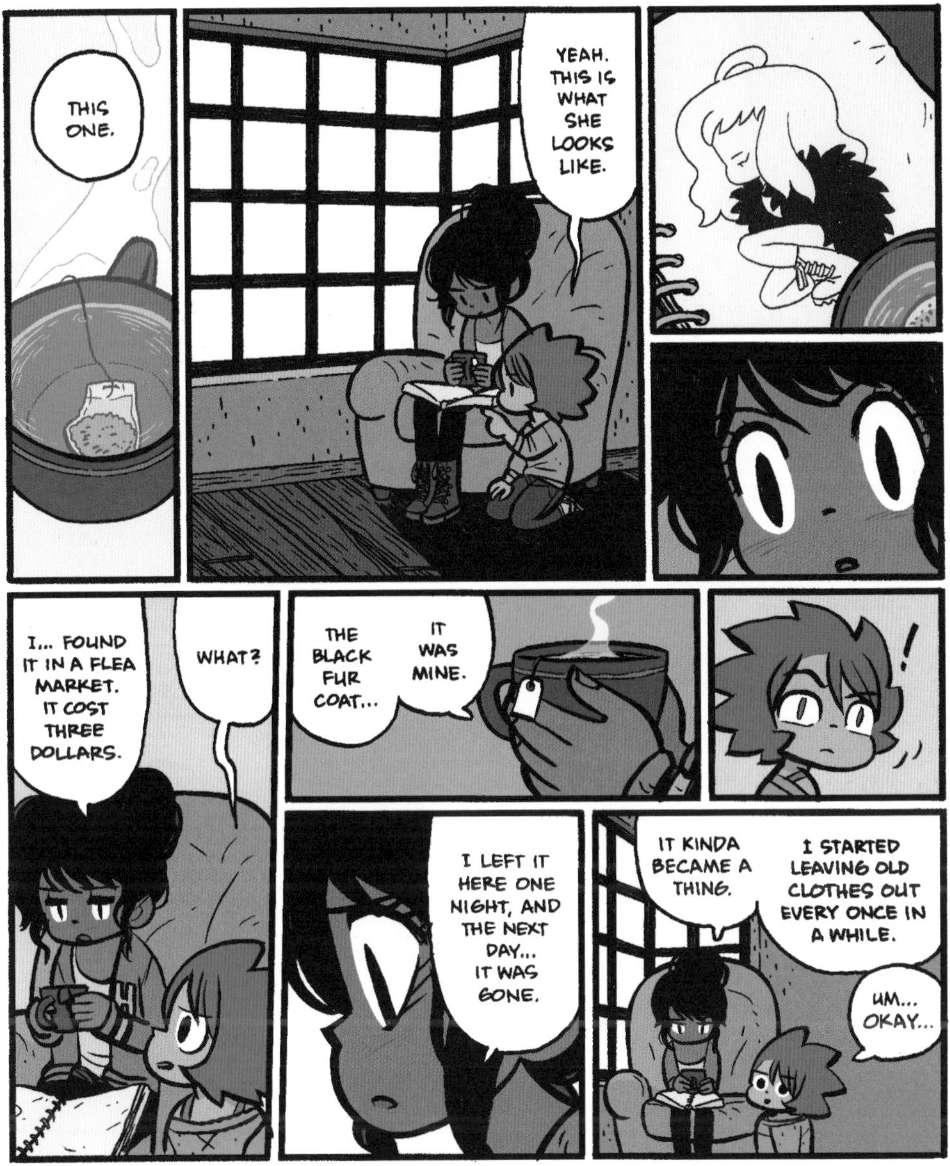

THIS ONE.
YEAH. THIS IS WHAT SHE LOOKS LIKE.
I... FOUND IT IN A FLEA MARKET. IT COST THREE DOLLARS.
WHAT?
THE BLACK FUR COAT...
IT WAS MINE.
!
I LEFT IT HERE ONE NIGHT, AND THE NEXT DAY... IT WAS GONE.
IT KINDA BECAME A THING.
I STARTED LEAVING OLD CLOTHES OUT EVERY ONCE IN A WHILE.
UM... OKAY...

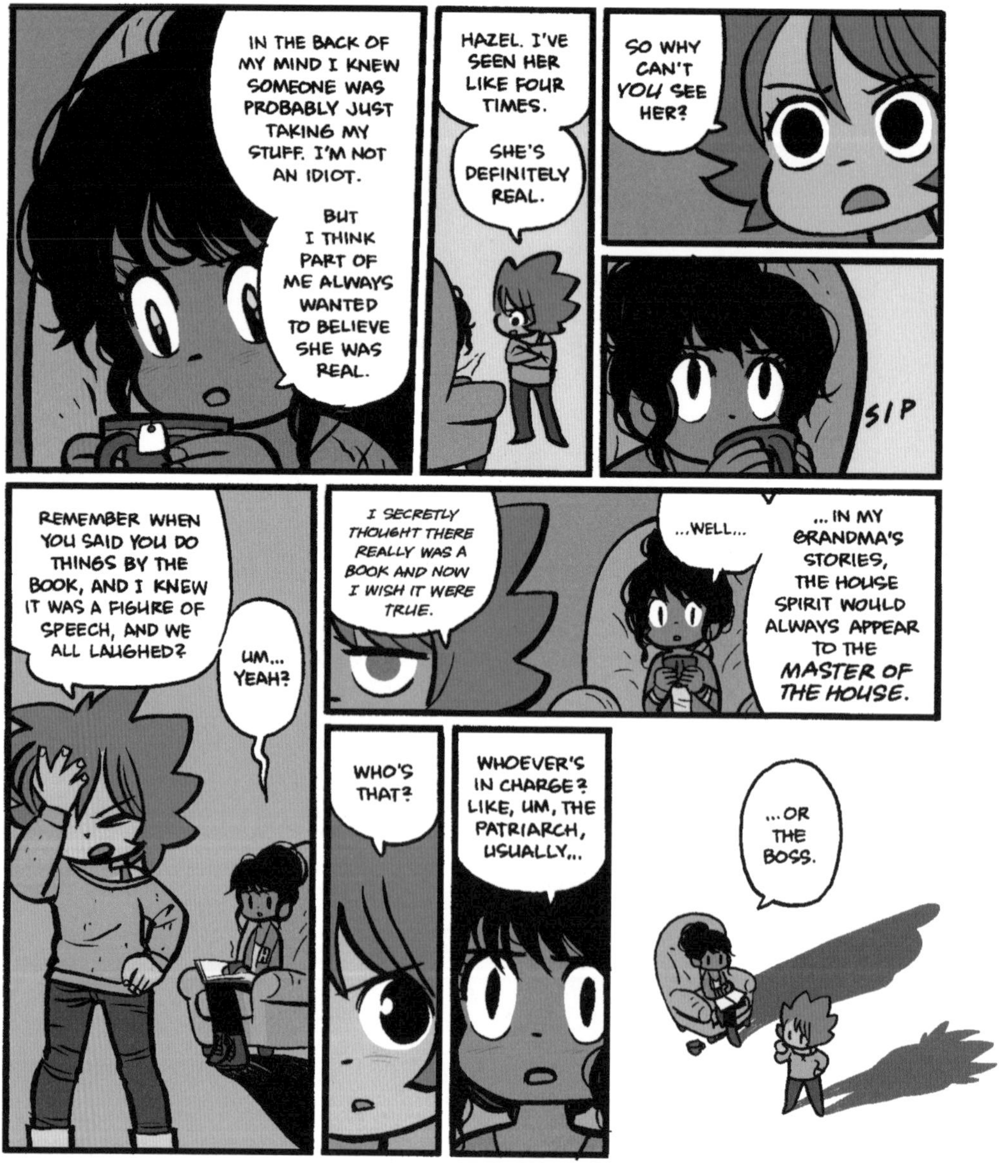
IN THE BACK OF MY MIND I KNEW SOMEONE WAS PROBABLY JUST TAKING MY STUFF. I'M NOT AN IDIOT.
BUT I THINK PART OF ME ALWAYS WANTED TO BELIEVE SHE WAS REAL.
HAZEL. I'VE SEEN HER LIKE FOUR TIMES.
SHE'S DEFINITELY REAL.
SO WHY CAN'T *YOU* SEE HER?
SIP
REMEMBER WHEN YOU SAID YOU DO THINGS BY THE BOOK, AND I KNEW IT WAS A FIGURE OF SPEECH, AND WE ALL LAUGHED?
UM... YEAH?
I SECRETLY THOUGHT THERE REALLY WAS A BOOK AND NOW I WISH IT WERE TRUE.
...WELL...
...IN MY GRANDMA'S STORIES, THE HOUSE SPIRIT WOULD ALWAYS APPEAR TO THE *MASTER OF THE HOUSE*.
WHO'S THAT?
WHOEVER'S IN CHARGE? LIKE, UM, THE PATRIARCH, USUALLY...
...OR THE BOSS.

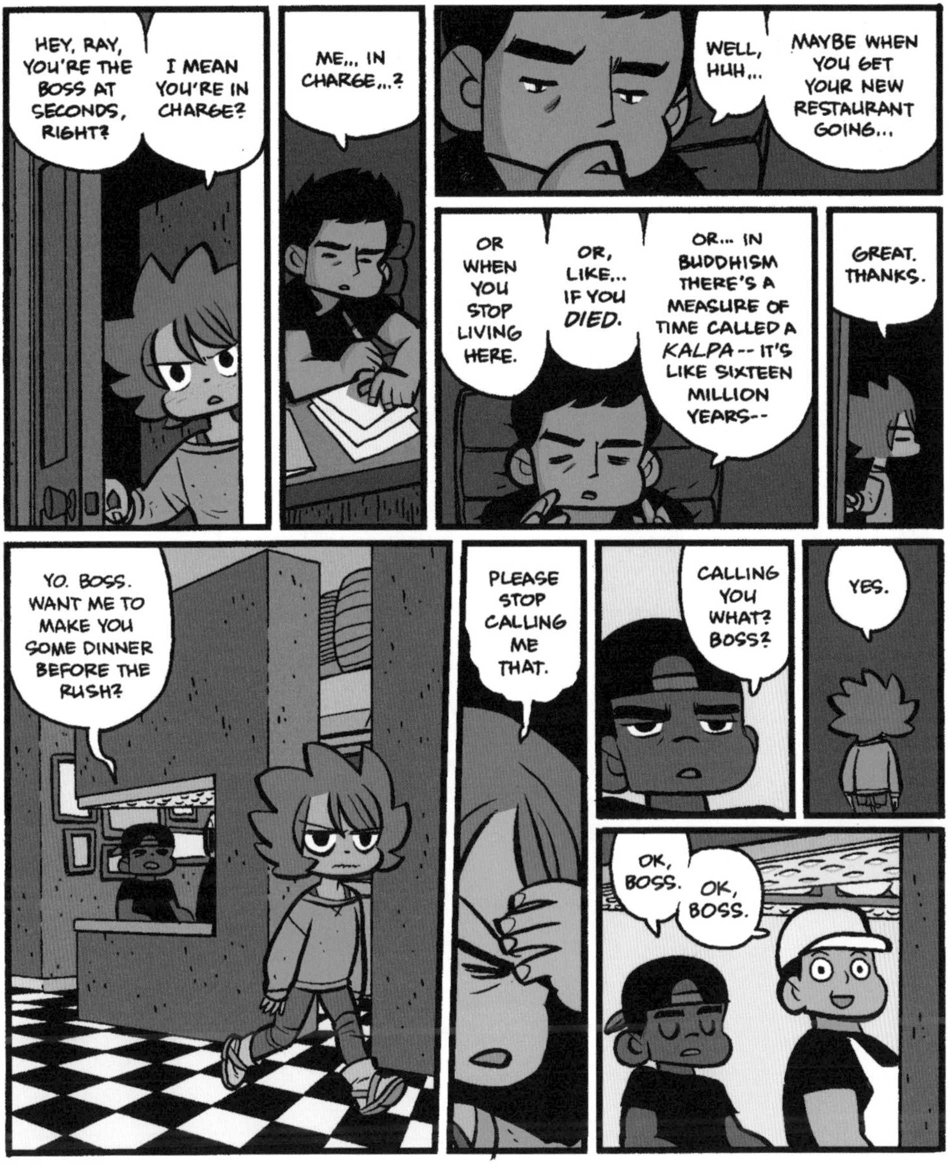
HEY, RAY, YOU'RE THE BOSS AT SECONDS, RIGHT?
I MEAN YOU'RE IN CHARGE?
ME... IN CHARGE...?
WELL, HUH...
MAYBE WHEN YOU GET YOUR NEW RESTAURANT GOING...
OR WHEN YOU STOP LIVING HERE.
OR, LIKE... IF YOU *DIED.*
OR... IN BUDDHISM THERE'S A MEASURE OF TIME CALLED A *KALPA* -- IT'S LIKE SIXTEEN MILLION YEARS--
GREAT. THANKS.
YO. BOSS. WANT ME TO MAKE YOU SOME DINNER BEFORE THE RUSH?
PLEASE STOP CALLING ME THAT.
CALLING YOU WHAT? BOSS?
YES.
OK, BOSS.
OK, BOSS.

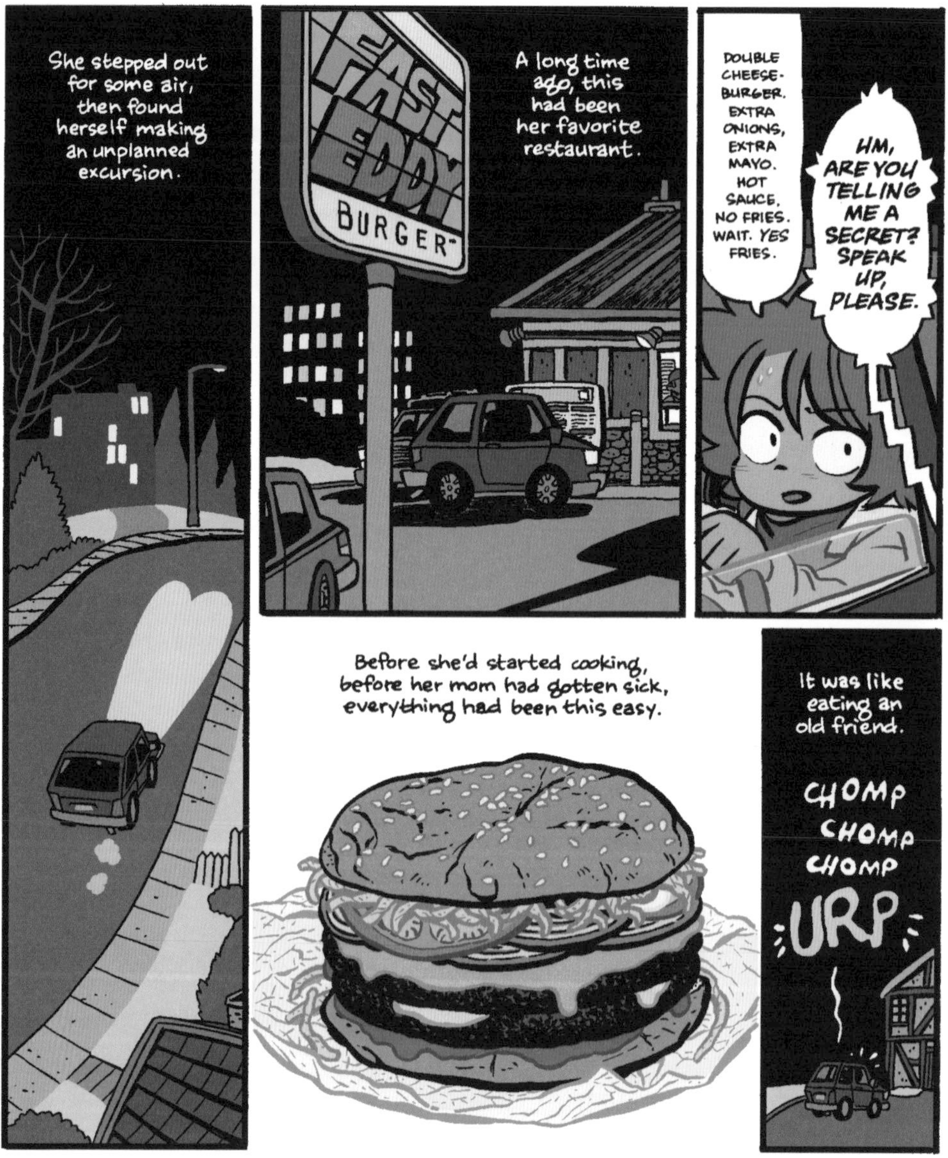
She stepped out for some air, then found herself making an unplanned excursion.
FAST EDDY BURGER™
A long time ago, this had been her favorite restaurant.
DOUBLE CHEESE-BURGER. EXTRA ONIONS, EXTRA MAYO. HOT SAUCE, NO FRIES. WAIT. YES FRIES.
UM, ARE YOU TELLING ME A SECRET? SPEAK UP, PLEASE.
Before she'd started cooking, before her mom had gotten sick, everything had been this easy.
It was like eating an old friend.
CHOMP
CHOMP
CHOMP
URP

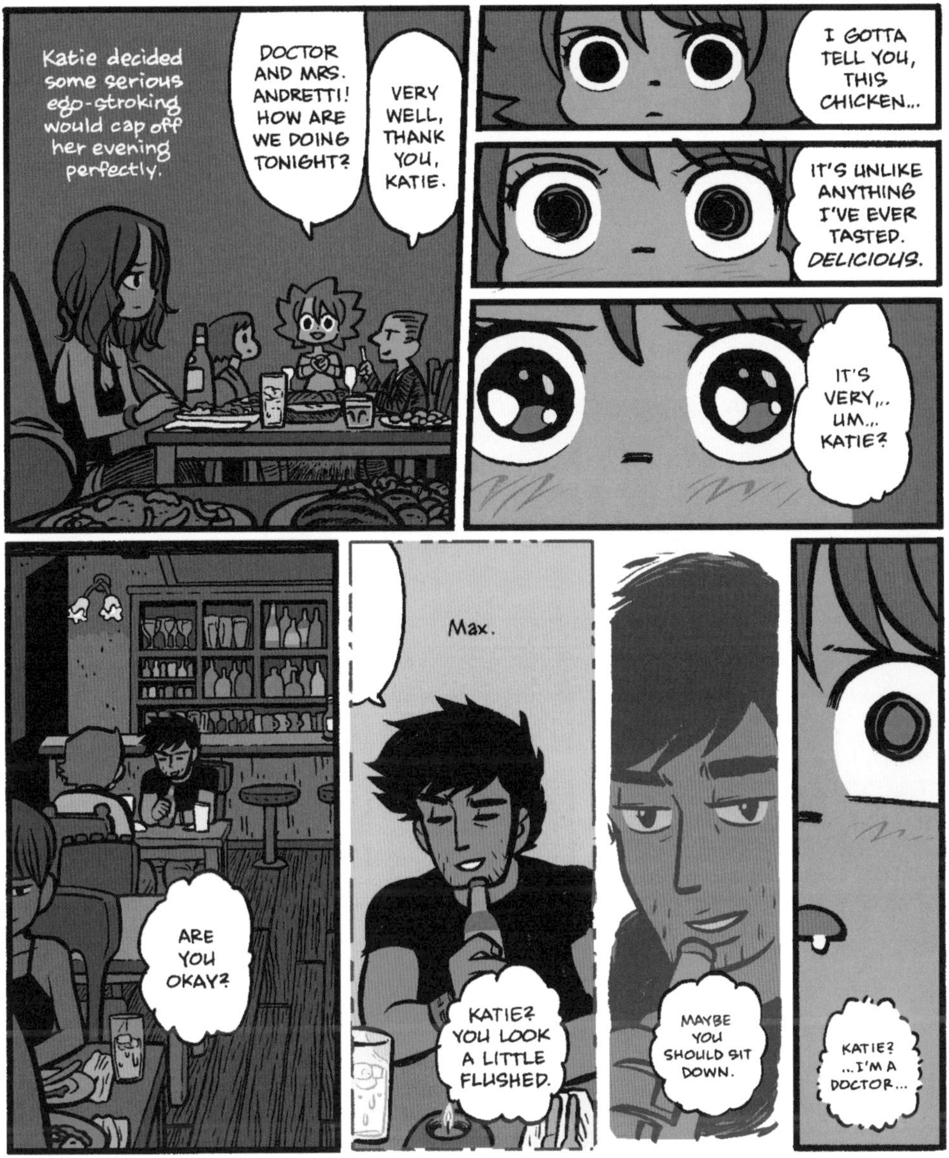
Katie decided some serious ego-stroking would cap off her evening perfectly.
DOCTOR AND MRS. ANDRETTI! HOW ARE WE DOING TONIGHT?
VERY WELL, THANK YOU, KATIE.
I GOTTA TELL YOU, THIS CHICKEN...
IT'S UNLIKE ANYTHING I'VE EVER TASTED. DELICIOUS.
IT'S VERY,.. UM... KATIE?
ARE YOU OKAY?
Max.
KATIE? YOU LOOK A LITTLE FLUSHED.
MAYBE YOU SHOULD SIT DOWN.
KATIE? ...I'M A DOCTOR...

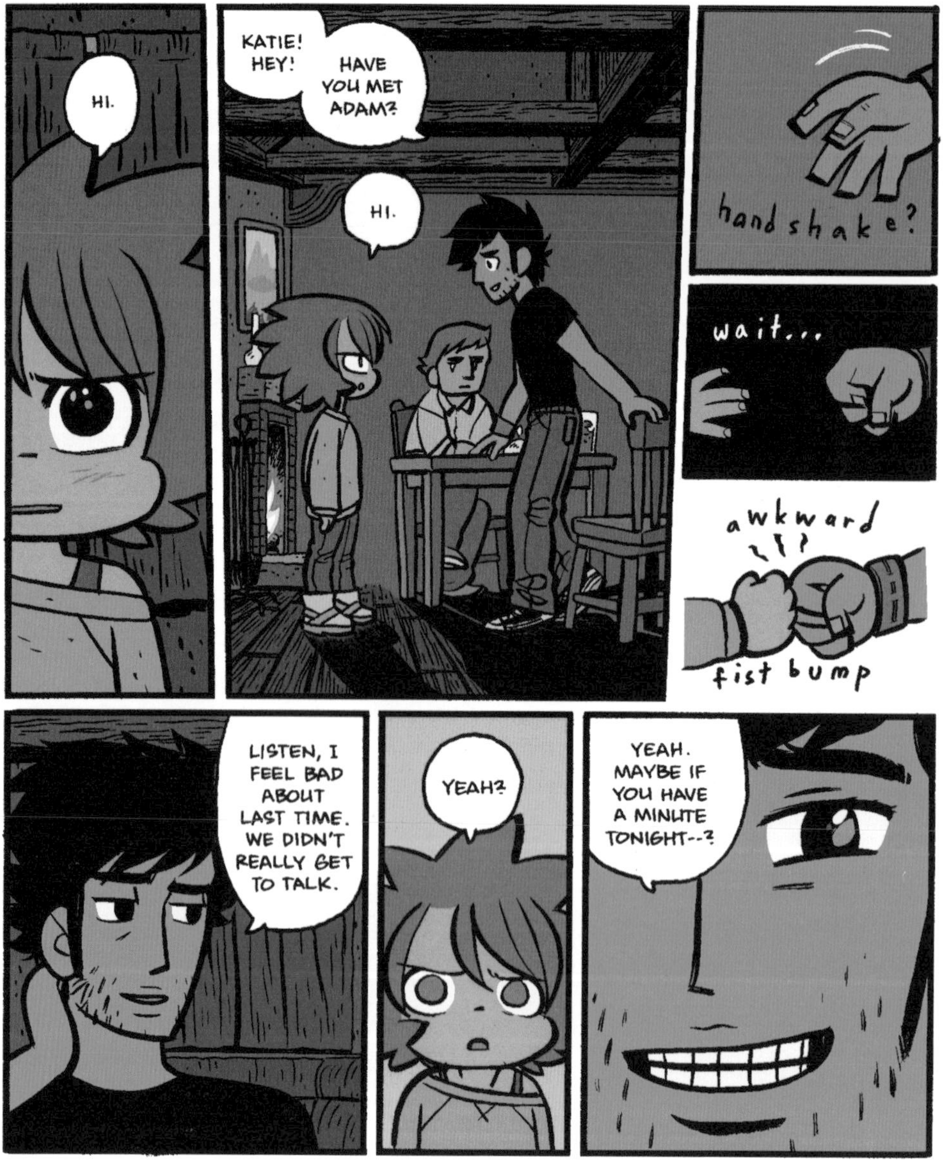
HI.
KATIE! HEY!
HAVE YOU MET ADAM?
HI.
handshake?
wait...
awkward
fist bump
LISTEN, I FEEL BAD ABOUT LAST TIME. WE DIDN'T REALLY GET TO TALK.
YEAH?
YEAH. MAYBE IF YOU HAVE A MINUTE TONIGHT--?

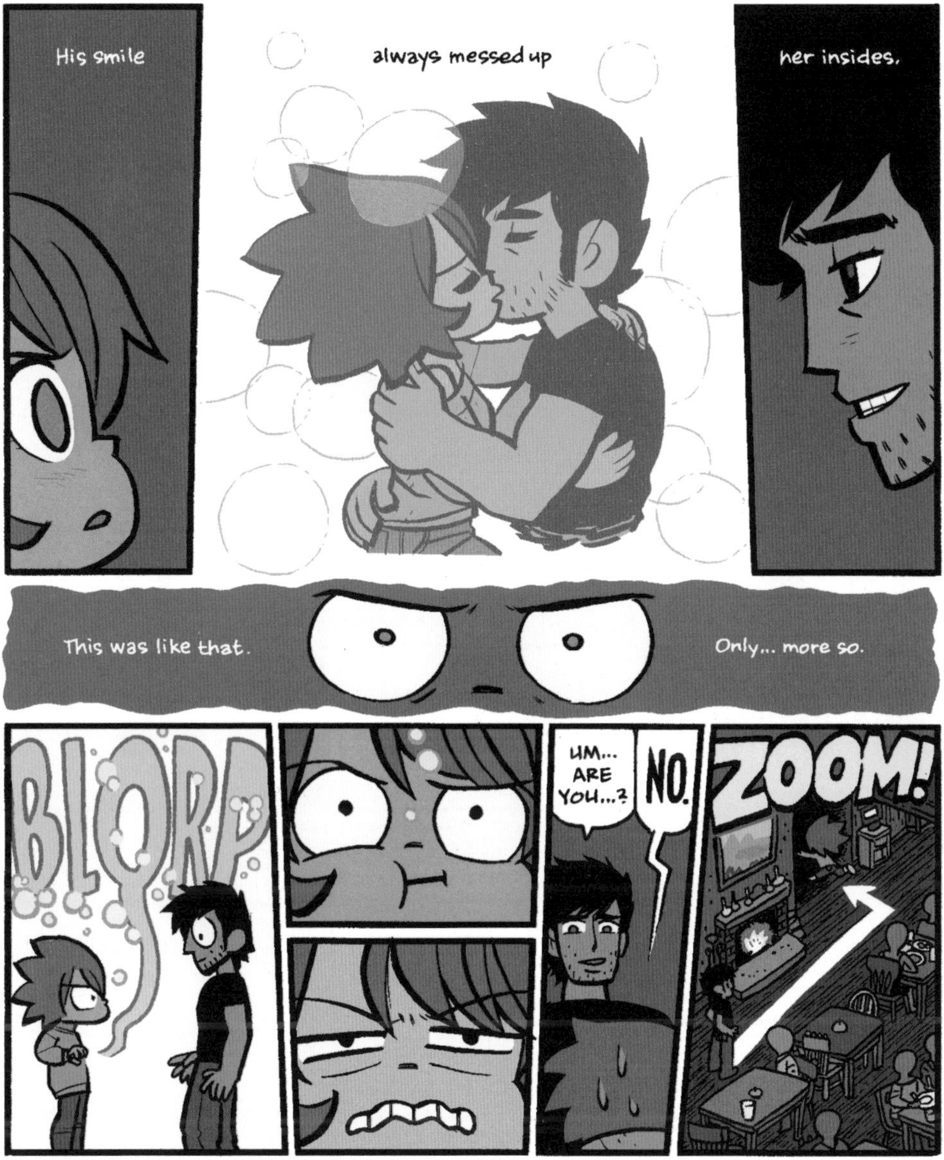

His smile
always messed up
her insides.
This was like that.
Only... more so.
BLORP
UM... ARE YOU...?
NO.
ZOOM!

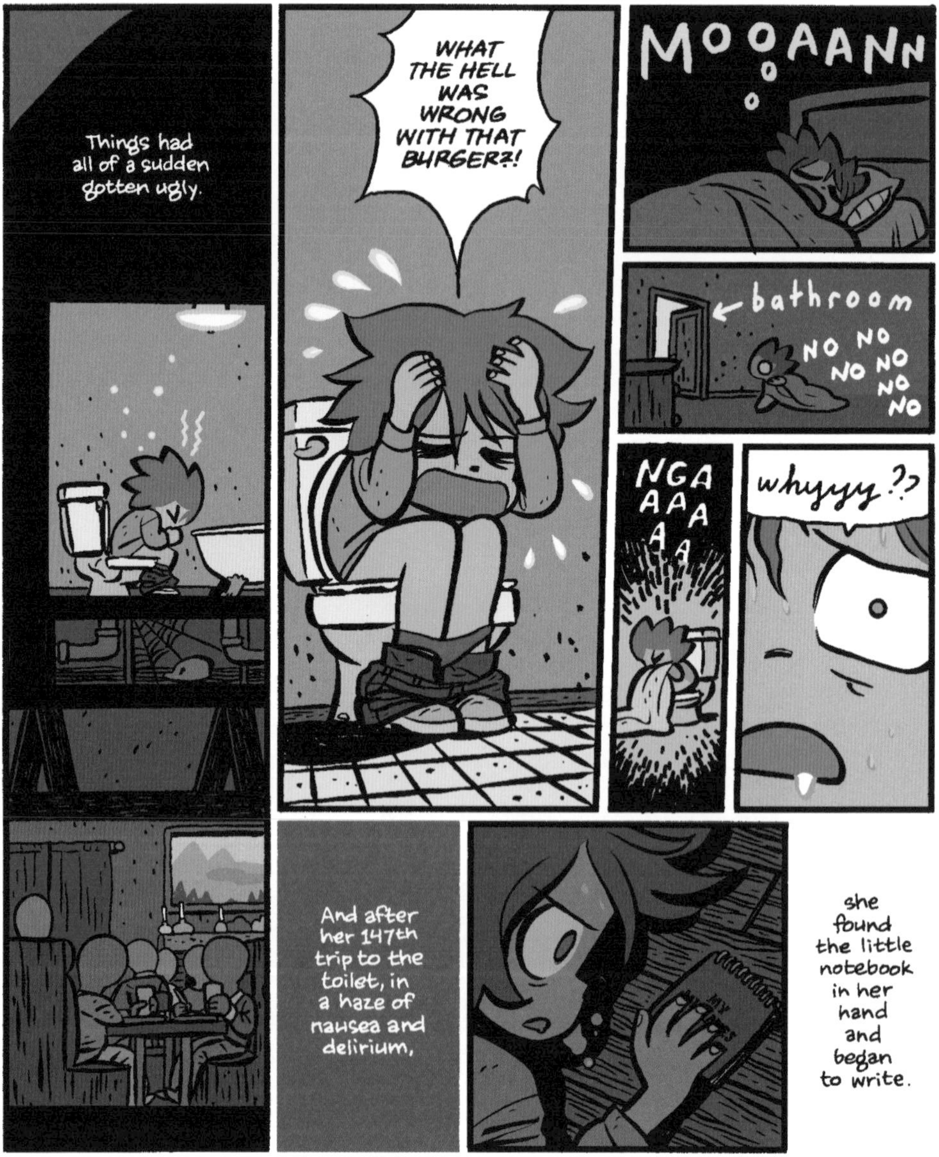
Things had all of a sudden gotten ugly.
WHAT THE HELL WAS WRONG WITH THAT BURGER?!
MOOAANN
bathroom
NO NO NO NO NO NO
NGA AAA AA
whyyy??
And after her 147th trip to the toilet, in a haze of nausea and delirium,
she found the little notebook in her hand and began to write.

REVISION #2

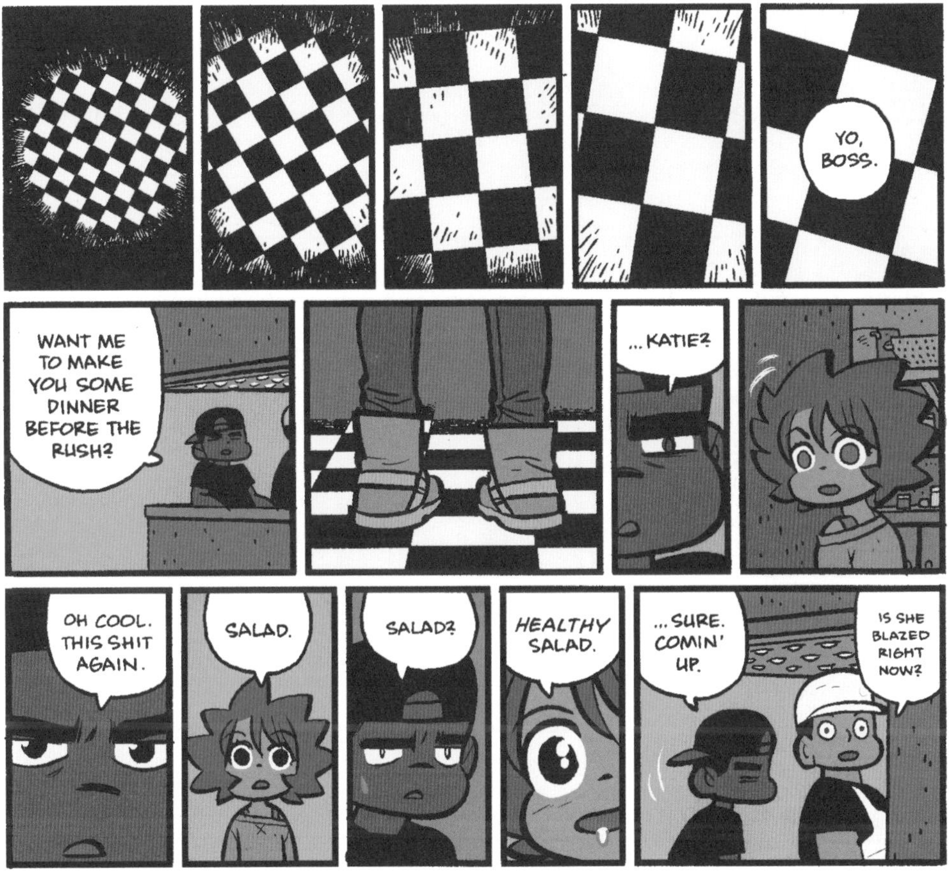

YO, BOSS.
WANT ME TO MAKE YOU SOME DINNER BEFORE THE RUSH?
...KATIE?
OH COOL. THIS SHIT AGAIN.
SALAD.
SALAD?
HEALTHY SALAD.
...SURE. COMIN' UP.
IS SHE BLAZED RIGHT NOW?

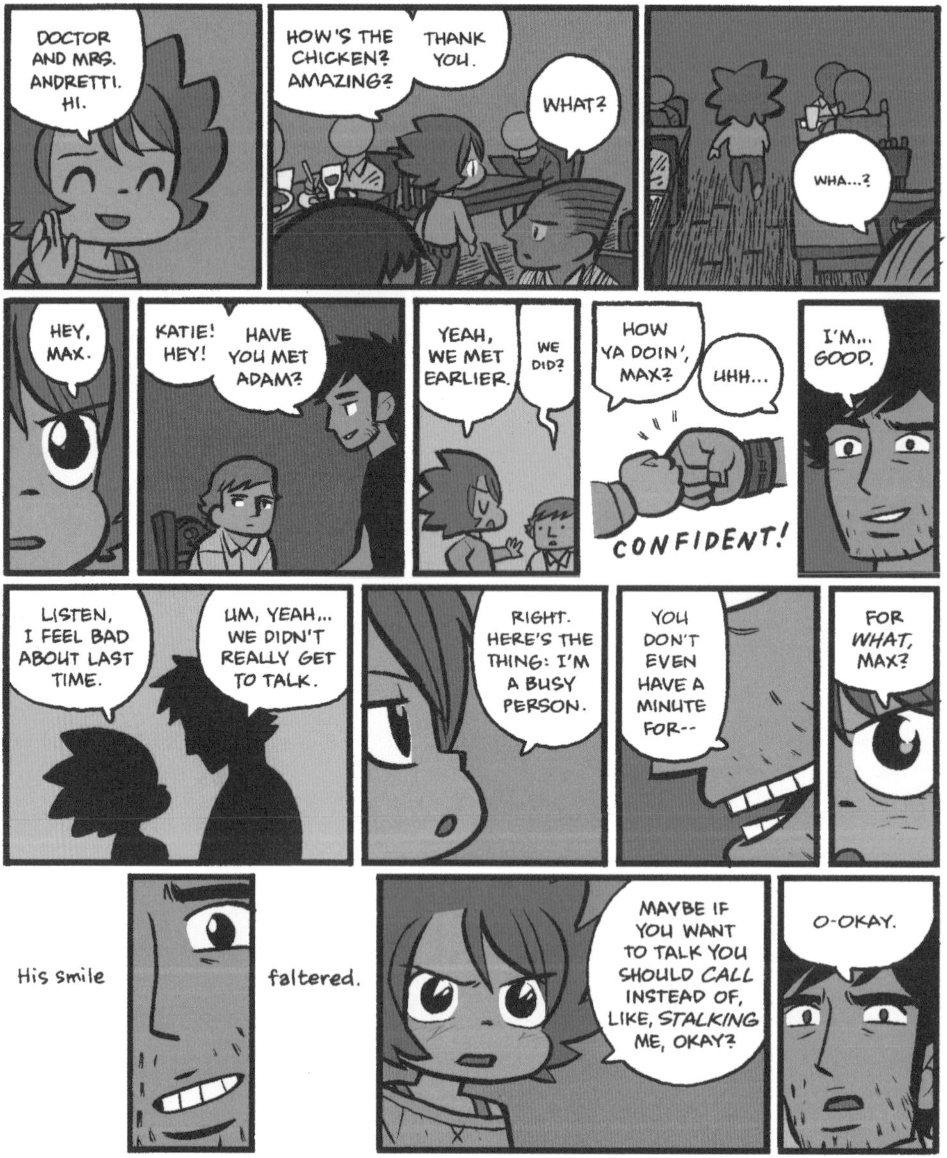
DOCTOR AND MRS. ANDRETTI. HI.
HOW'S THE CHICKEN? AMAZING?
THANK YOU.
WHAT?
WHA...?
HEY, MAX.
KATIE! HEY!
HAVE YOU MET ADAM?
YEAH, WE MET EARLIER.
WE DID?
HOW YA DOIN', MAX?
UHH...
CONFIDENT!
I'M... GOOD.
LISTEN, I FEEL BAD ABOUT LAST TIME.
UM, YEAH... WE DIDN'T REALLY GET TO TALK.
RIGHT. HERE'S THE THING: I'M A BUSY PERSON.
YOU DON'T EVEN HAVE A MINUTE FOR--
FOR WHAT, MAX?
His smile
faltered.
MAYBE IF YOU WANT TO TALK YOU SHOULD CALL INSTEAD OF, LIKE, STALKING ME, OKAY?
O-OKAY.

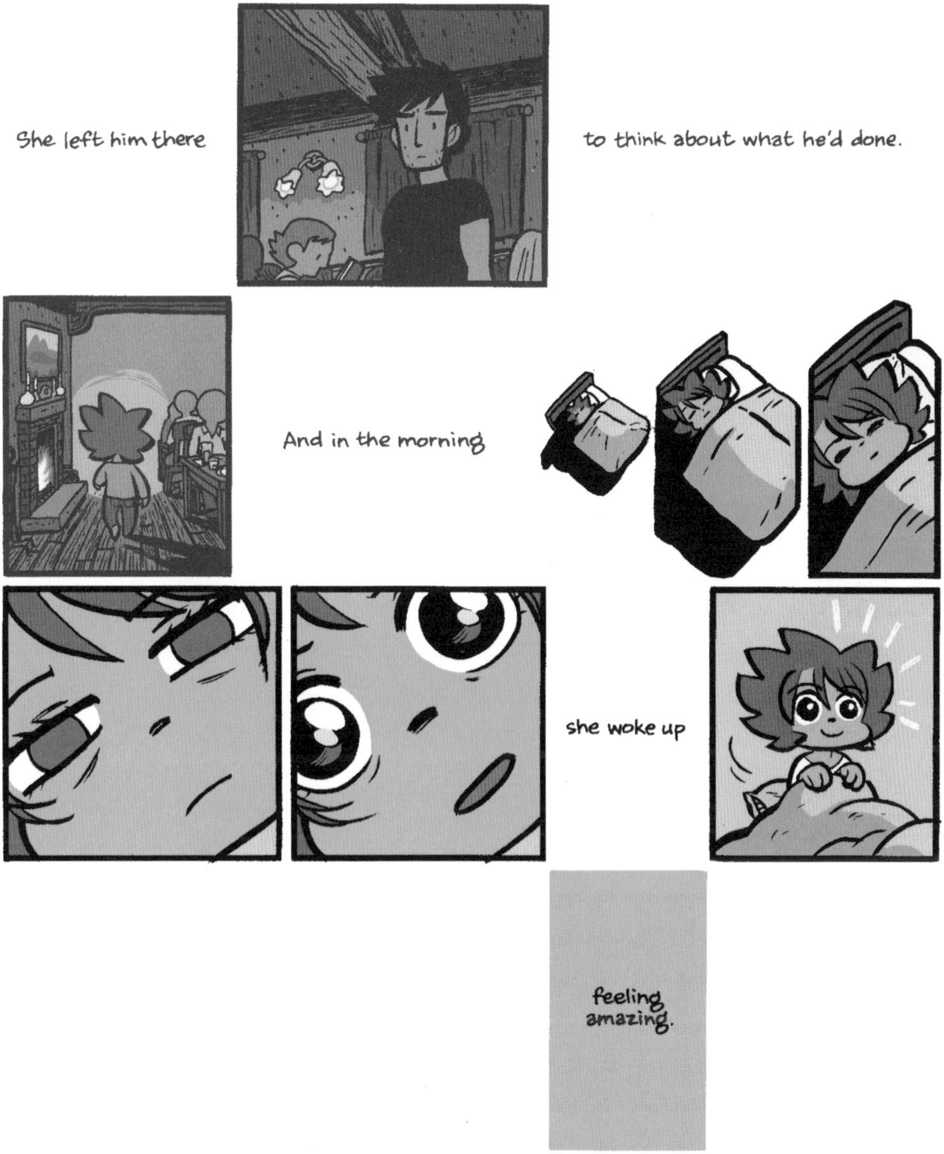
She left him there
to think about what he'd done.
And in the morning
she woke up
feeling amazing.

4

Rules

Arthur called as Katie was getting dressed.

HOW ARE THINGS?

THINGS ARE GREAT! AND WEIRD. ...THEY'RE WEIRD.

EXCELLENT. SO, YES, PERMITS HAVE BEEN DELAYED, THE CONTRACTOR IS BEING A PETULANT CHILD...

...BUT WHEN YOU GO IN THERE, PLEASE DON'T FREAK OUT ON HIM.

NOT YET, HA HA.

ARTHUR, I KNOW YOU JUST DID A FUNERAL AND YOU'RE PROBABLY MEGA BUMMED RIGHT NOW.

BUT THIS IS ALL GONNA WORK OUT. I HAVE A STRONG FEELING.

YEAH. YOU'RE RIGHT.

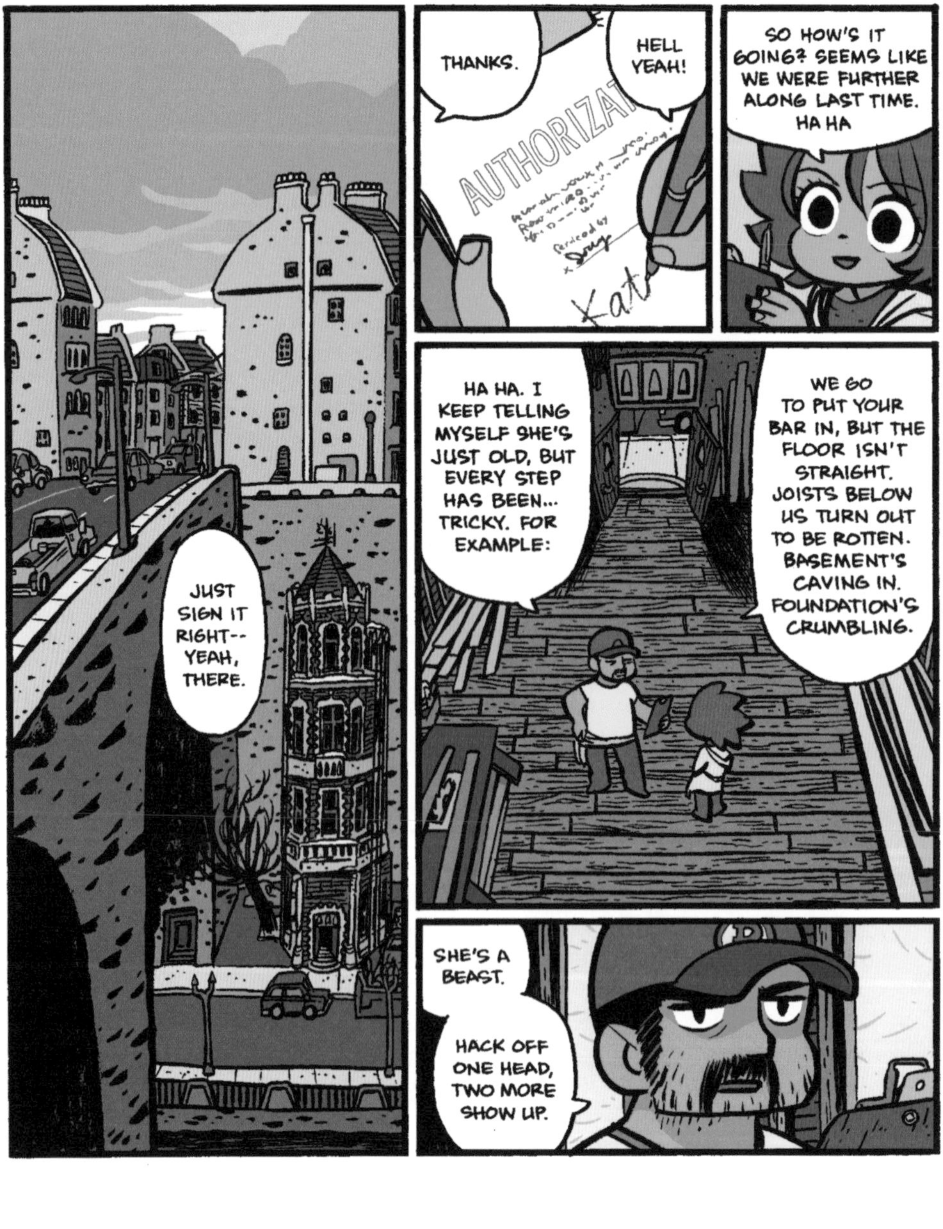
JUST SIGN IT RIGHT-- YEAH, THERE.
THANKS.
HELL YEAH!
AUTHORIZAT
SO HOW'S IT GOING? SEEMS LIKE WE WERE FURTHER ALONG LAST TIME. HA HA
HA HA. I KEEP TELLING MYSELF SHE'S JUST OLD, BUT EVERY STEP HAS BEEN... TRICKY. FOR EXAMPLE:
WE GO TO PUT YOUR BAR IN, BUT THE FLOOR ISN'T STRAIGHT. JOISTS BELOW US TURN OUT TO BE ROTTEN. BASEMENT'S CAVING IN. FOUNDATION'S CRUMBLING.
SHE'S A BEAST.
HACK OFF ONE HEAD, TWO MORE SHOW UP.

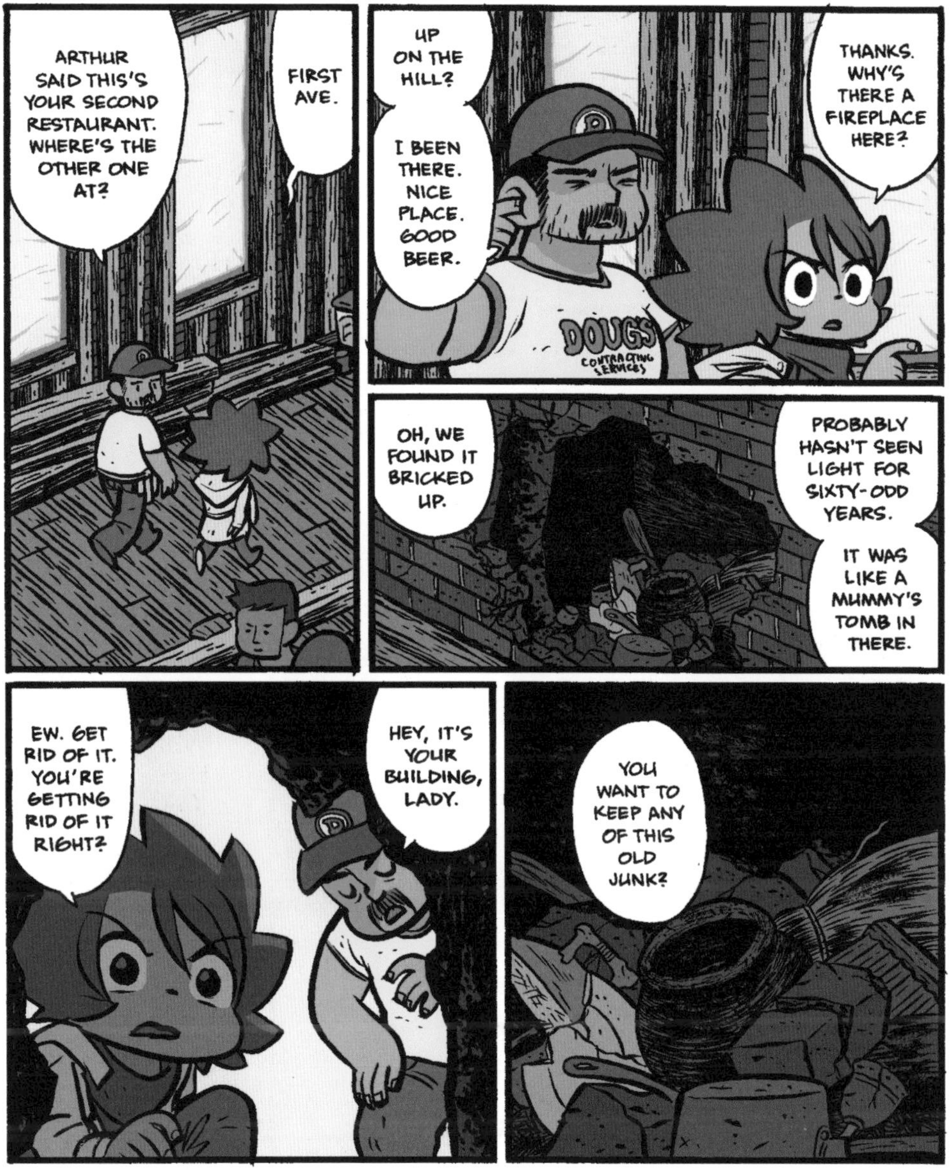
ARTHUR SAID THIS'S YOUR SECOND RESTAURANT. WHERE'S THE OTHER ONE AT?
FIRST AVE.
UP ON THE HILL?
I BEEN THERE. NICE PLACE. GOOD BEER.
THANKS. WHY'S THERE A FIREPLACE HERE?
DOUGS CONTRACTING SERVICES
OH, WE FOUND IT BRICKED UP.
PROBABLY HASN'T SEEN LIGHT FOR SIXTY-ODD YEARS.
IT WAS LIKE A MUMMY'S TOMB IN THERE.
EW. GET RID OF IT. YOU'RE GETTING RID OF IT RIGHT?
HEY, IT'S YOUR BUILDING, LADY.
YOU WANT TO KEEP ANY OF THIS OLD JUNK?

And so Katie claimed a treasure from the ancient pile before they dumpstered the whole thing.

It didn't look sixty-odd years old. It looked a *thousand* years old.

Back at Seconds, she went downstairs to show off a little.

..A MUMMY'S TOMB?? WICKED!

WHAT IS THIS THING? A POT?

THE WORD I'D USE IS *CAULDRON.* PRETTY COOL, HUH?

WHAT'S A CAULDRON?

YO, DUMMY. IT'S LIKE AN OLD POT THAT BELONGS TO A WITCH.

.. WHAT?

112

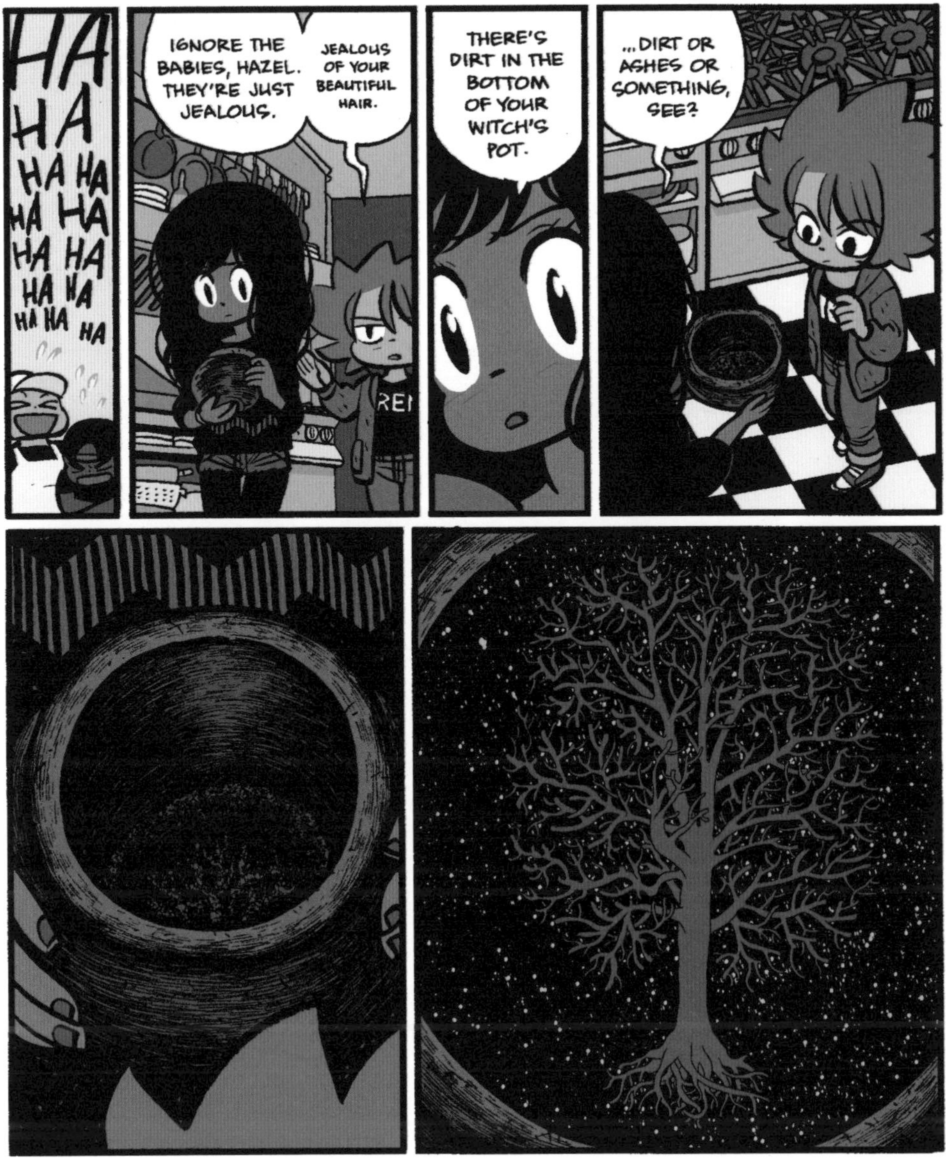
HA HA HA HA HA HA HA HA HA HA HA HA HA HA HA
IGNORE THE BABIES, HAZEL. THEY'RE JUST JEALOUS.
JEALOUS OF YOUR BEAUTIFUL HAIR.
THERE'S DIRT IN THE BOTTOM OF YOUR WITCH'S POT.
...DIRT OR ASHES OR SOMETHING, SEE?

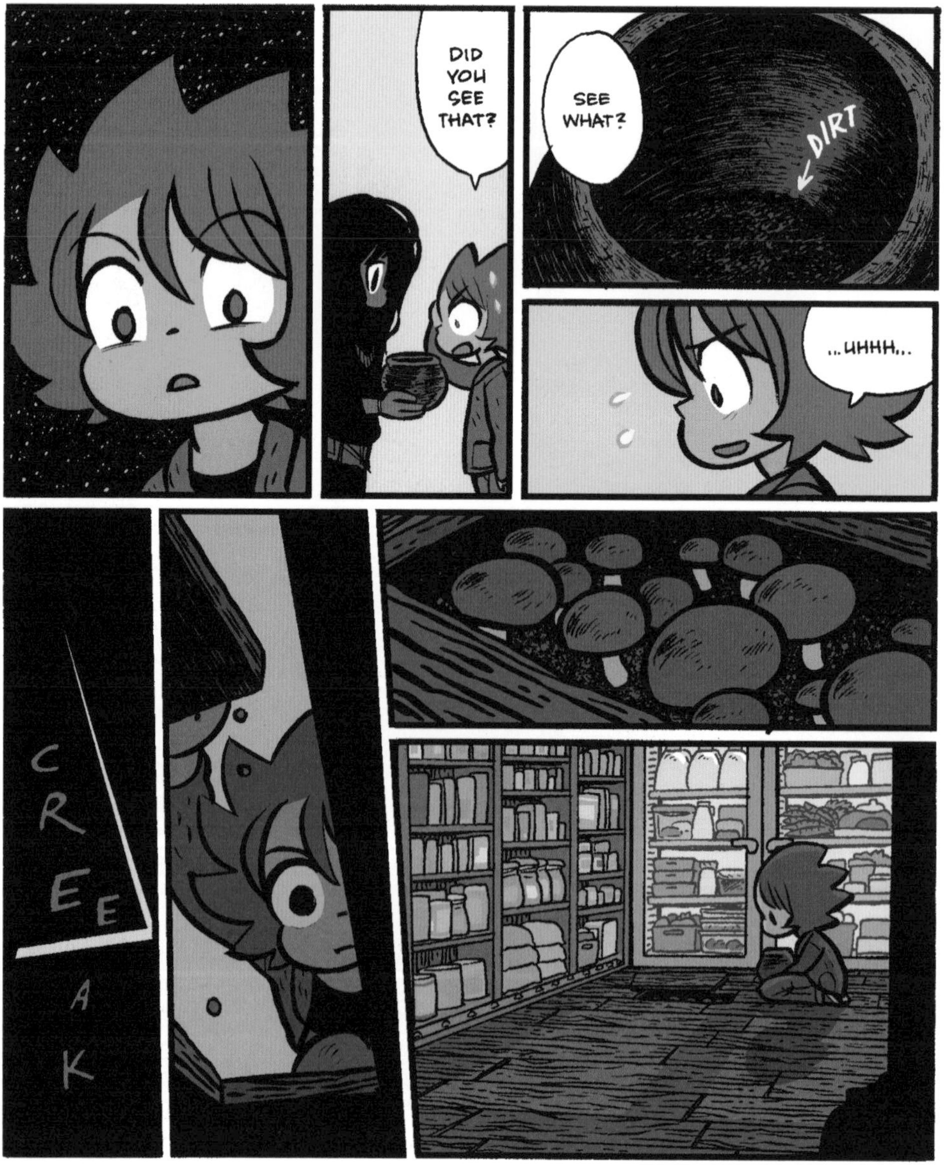
DID YOU SEE THAT?
SEE WHAT?
DIRT
...UHHH...
CREEAK

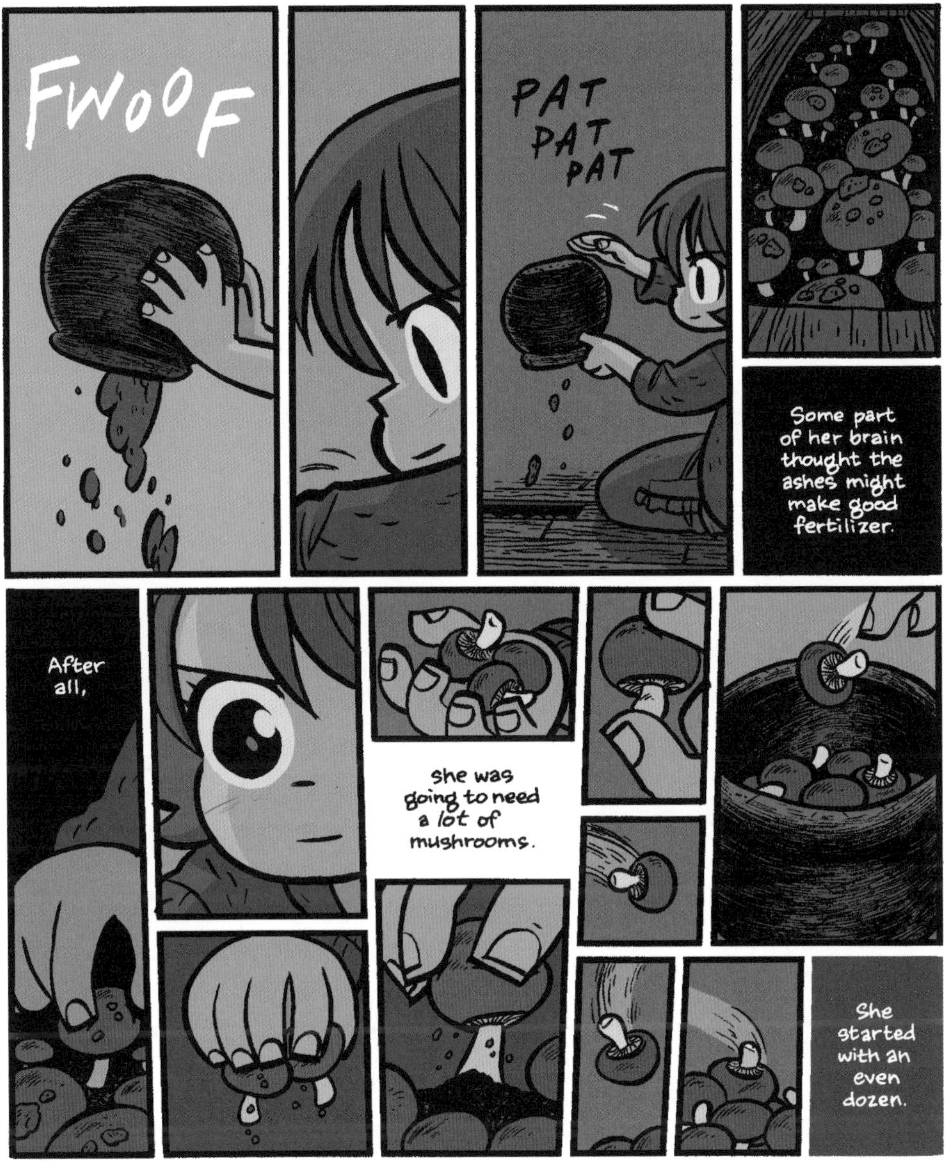
FWOOF
PAT PAT PAT
Some part of her brain thought the ashes might make good fertilizer.
After all,
she was going to need a *lot* of mushrooms.
She started with an even dozen.

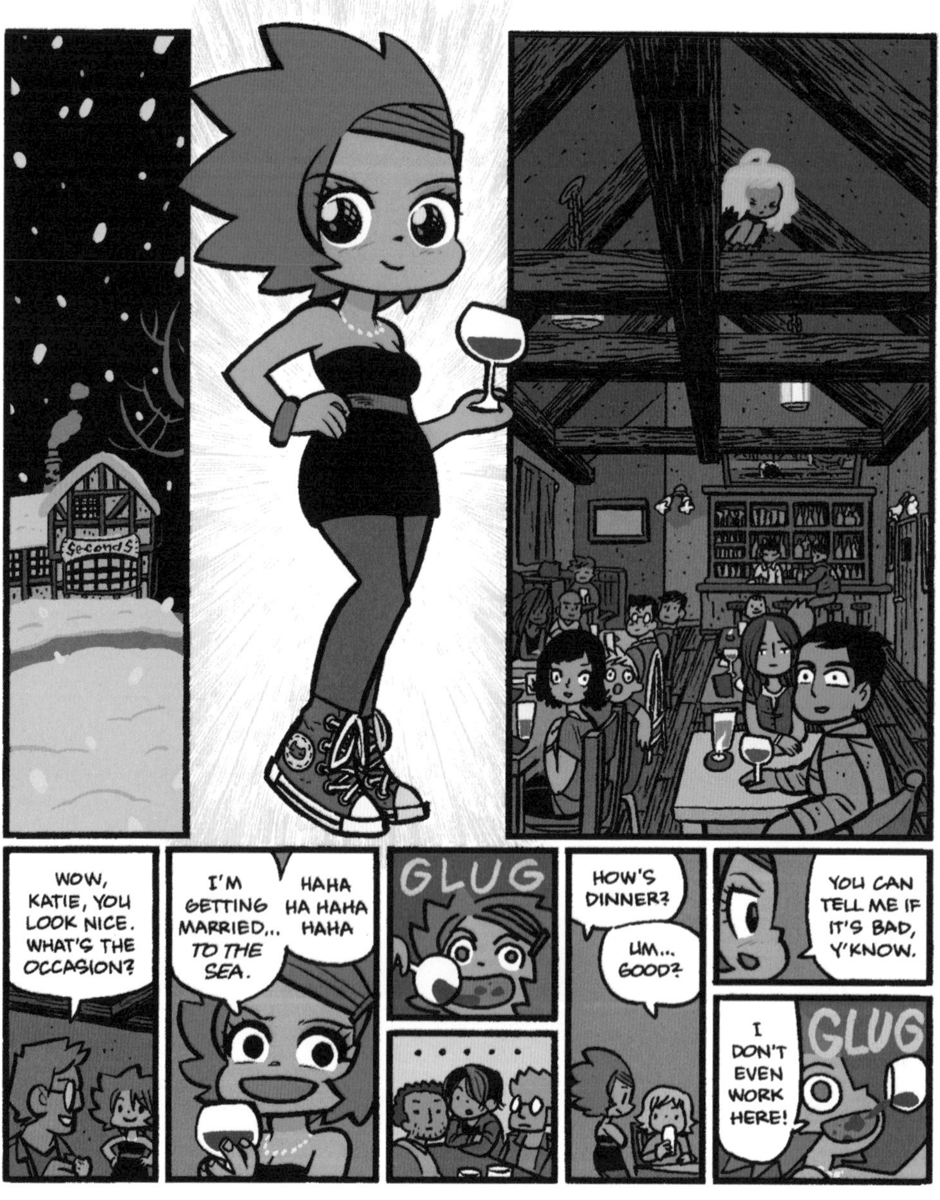

Seconds
WOW, KATIE, YOU LOOK NICE. WHAT'S THE OCCASION?
I'M GETTING MARRIED... TO THE SEA.
HAHA HA HAHA HAHA
GLUG
• • • • •
HOW'S DINNER?
UM... GOOD?
YOU CAN TELL ME IF IT'S BAD, Y'KNOW.
I DON'T EVEN WORK HERE!
GLUG

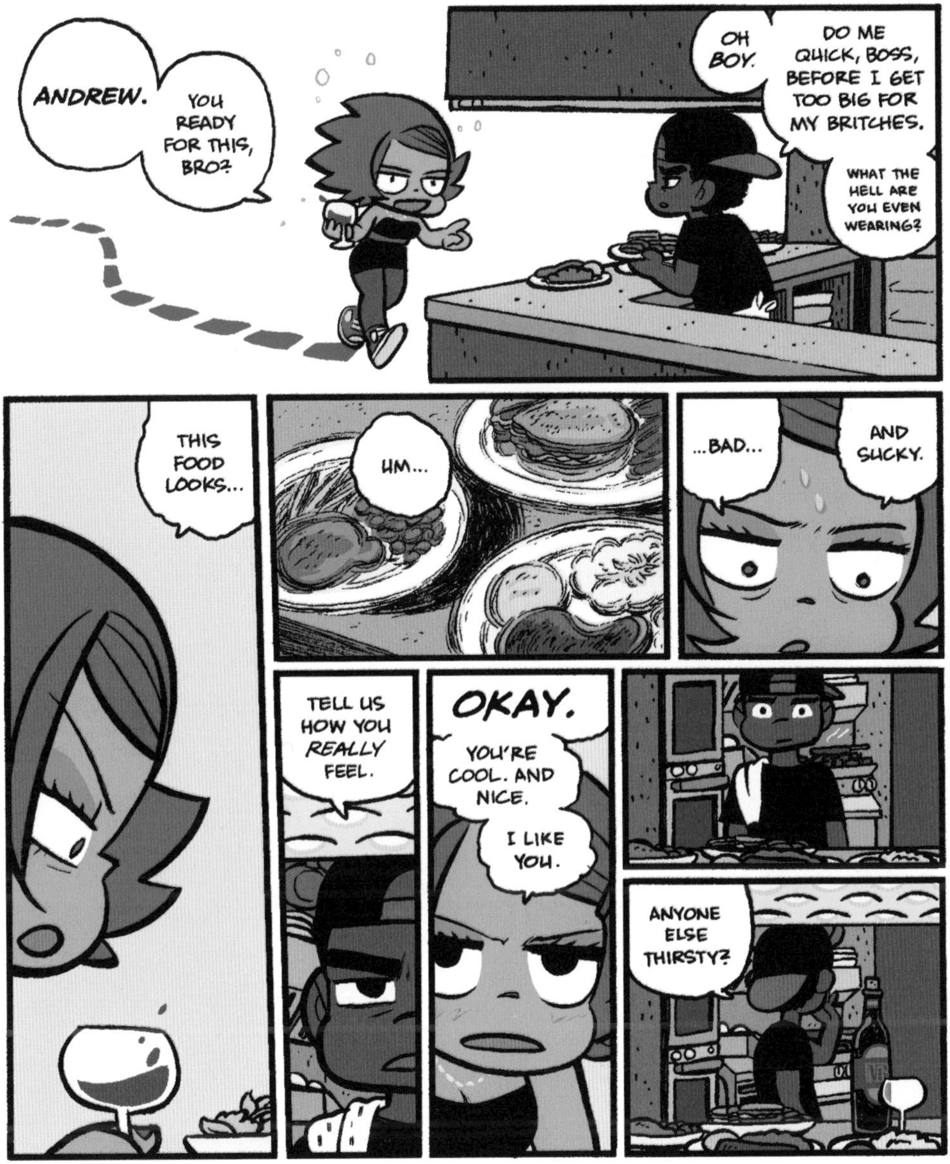
ANDREW.
YOU READY FOR THIS, BRO?
OH BOY.
DO ME QUICK, BOSS, BEFORE I GET TOO BIG FOR MY BRITCHES.
WHAT THE HELL ARE YOU EVEN WEARING?
THIS FOOD LOOKS...
UM...
...BAD...
AND SUCKY.
TELL US HOW YOU *REALLY* FEEL.
OKAY.
YOU'RE COOL. AND NICE.
I LIKE YOU.
ANYONE ELSE THIRSTY?

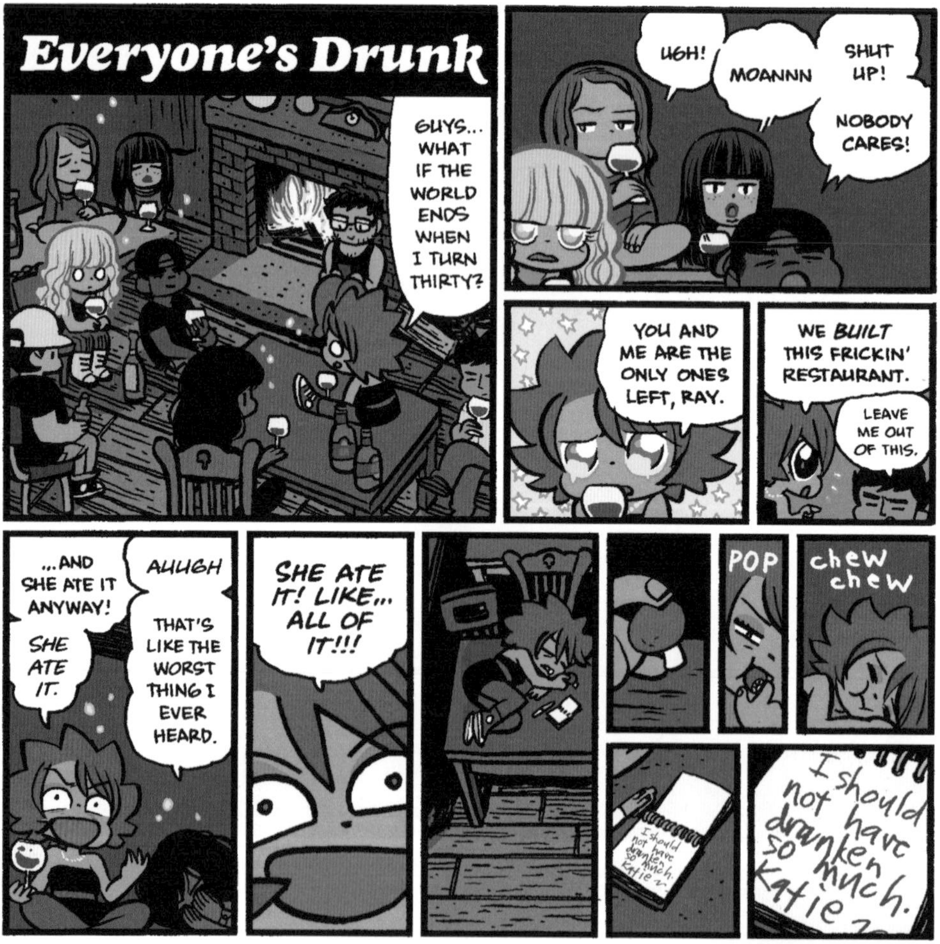
Everyone's Drunk
GUYS... WHAT IF THE WORLD ENDS WHEN I TURN THIRTY?
UGH!
MOANNN
SHUT UP!
NOBODY CARES!
YOU AND ME ARE THE ONLY ONES LEFT, RAY.
WE BUILT THIS FRICKIN' RESTAURANT.
LEAVE ME OUT OF THIS.
...AND SHE ATE IT ANYWAY!
SHE ATE IT.
AUUGH
THAT'S LIKE THE WORST THING I EVER HEARD.
SHE ATE IT! LIKE... ALL OF IT!!!
POP
chew chew
I should not have dranken so much. Katie

REVISION #3

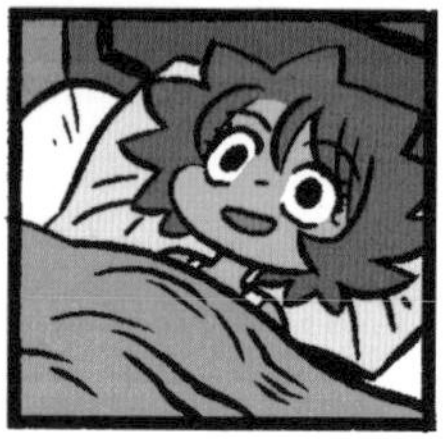

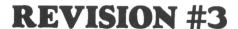

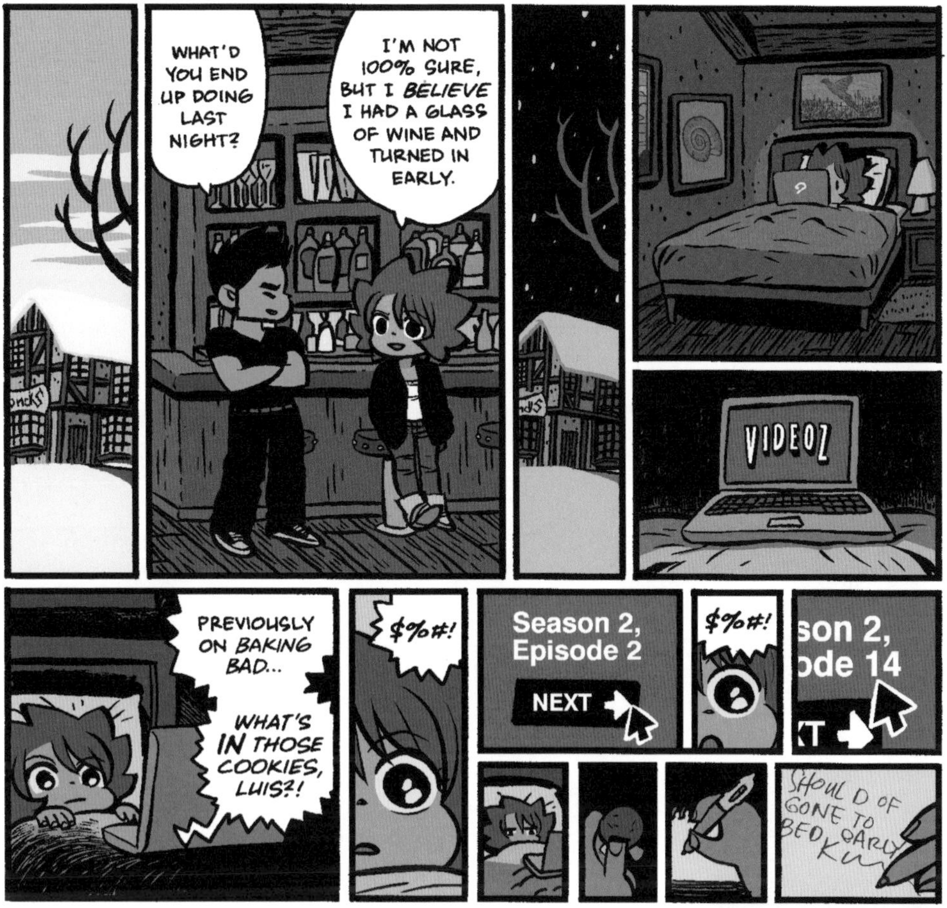
WHAT'D YOU END UP DOING LAST NIGHT?
I'M NOT 100% SURE, BUT I BELIEVE I HAD A GLASS OF WINE AND TURNED IN EARLY.
VIDEOZ
PREVIOUSLY ON BAKING BAD...
WHAT'S IN THOSE COOKIES, LUIS?!
$%#!
Season 2, Episode 2
NEXT
$%#!
son 2, ode 14
SHOUL D OF GONE TO BED EARLY

REVISION #4

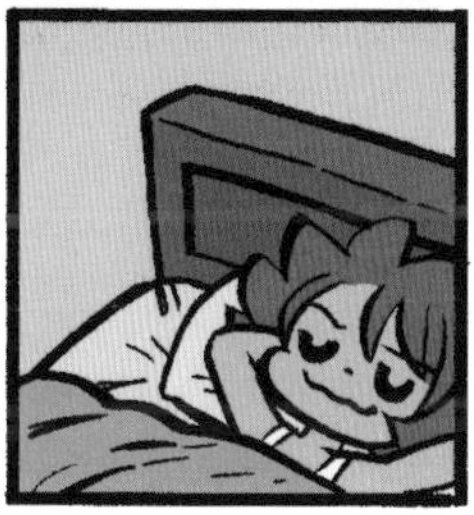

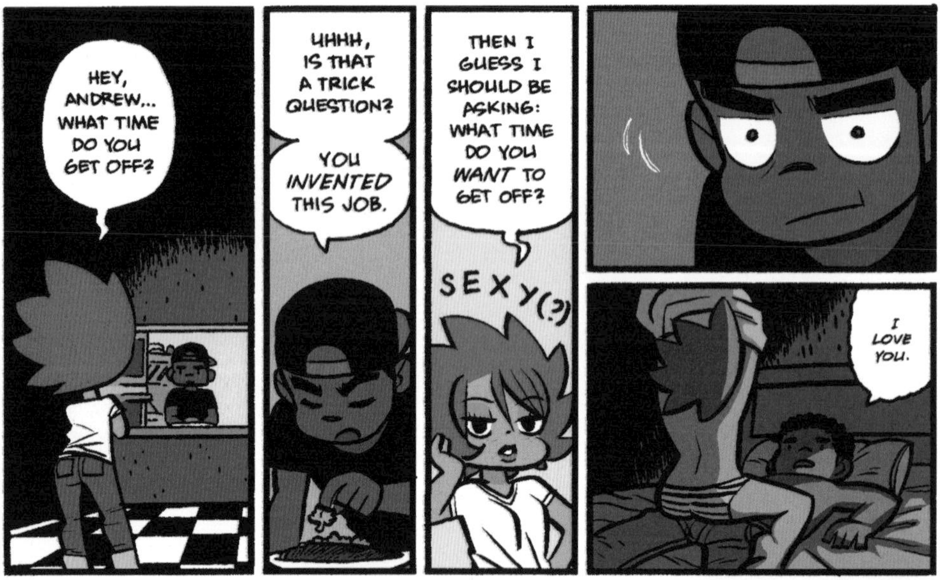
HEY, ANDREW... WHAT TIME DO YOU GET OFF?
UHHH, IS THAT A TRICK QUESTION?
YOU *INVENTED* THIS JOB.
THEN I GUESS I SHOULD BE ASKING: WHAT TIME DO YOU *WANT* TO GET OFF?
SEXY(?)
I LOVE YOU.

REVISION #5

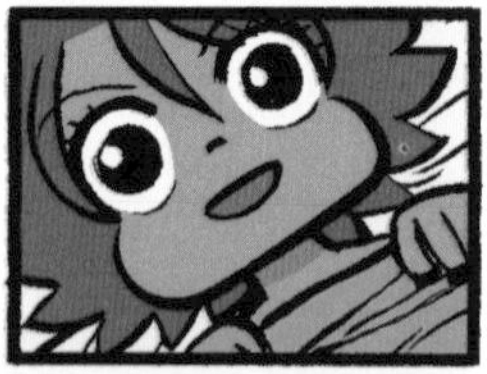

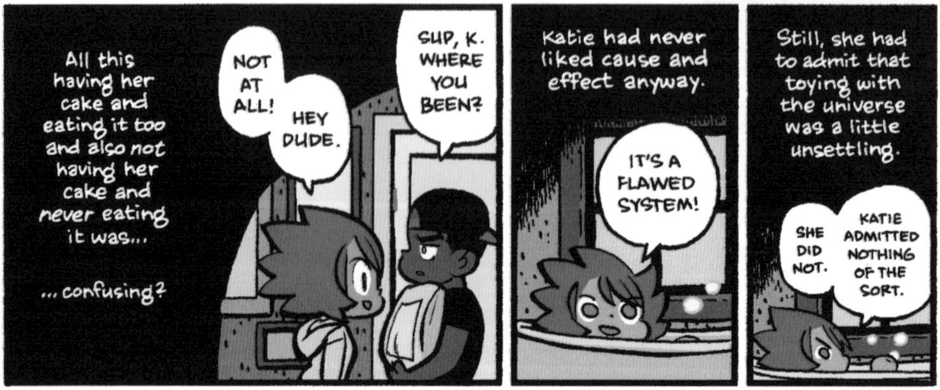
All this having her cake and eating it too and also *not* having her cake and *never* eating it was...
...confusing?
NOT AT ALL!
HEY DUDE.
SUP, K. WHERE YOU BEEN?
Katie had never liked cause and effect anyway.
IT'S A FLAWED SYSTEM!
Still, she had to admit that toying with the universe was a little unsettling.
SHE DID NOT.
KATIE ADMITTED NOTHING OF THE SORT.

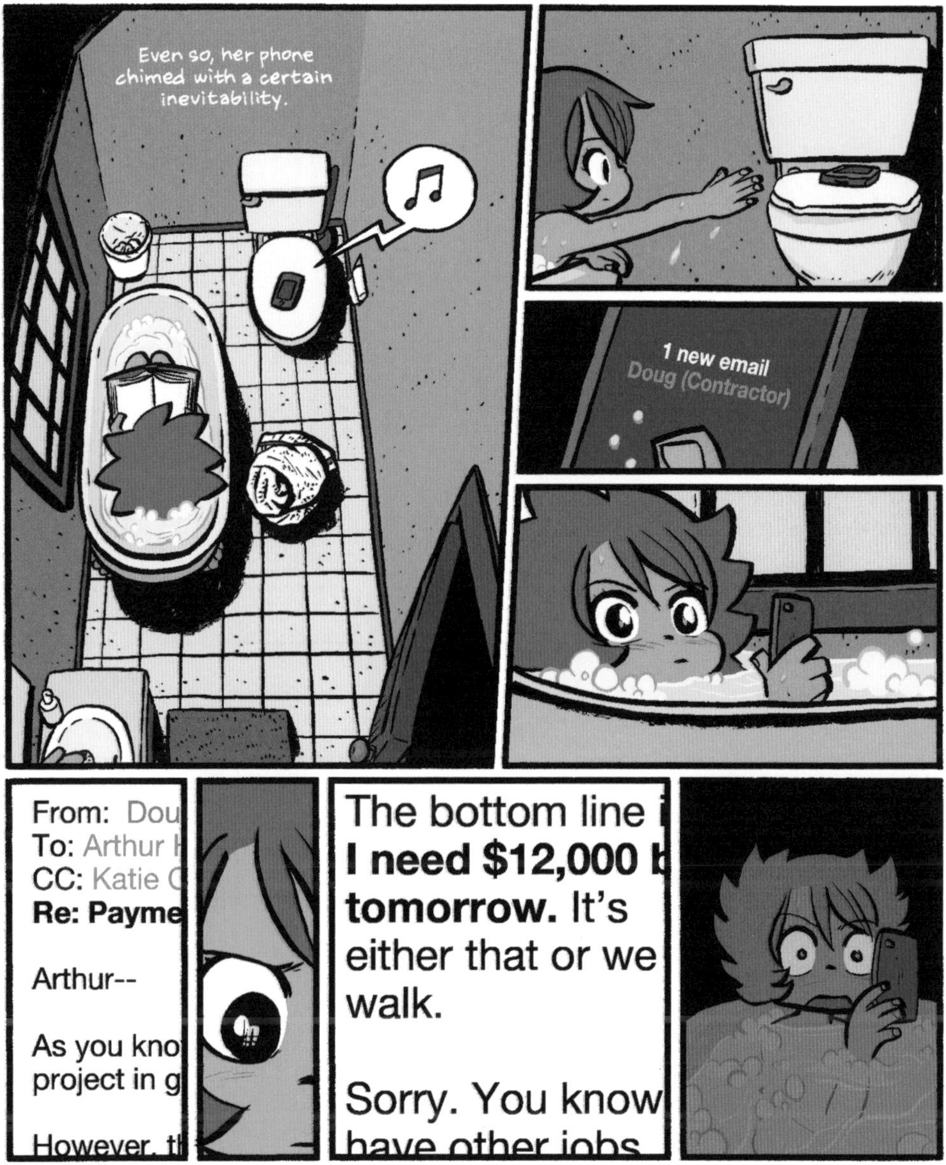
Even so, her phone chimed with a certain inevitability.
1 new email
Doug (Contractor)
From: Dou
To: Arthur H
CC: Katie C
Re: Payme
Arthur--
As you kno
project in g
However, th
The bottom line i
I need $12,000 b
tomorrow. It's
either that or we
walk.
Sorry. You know
have other jobs

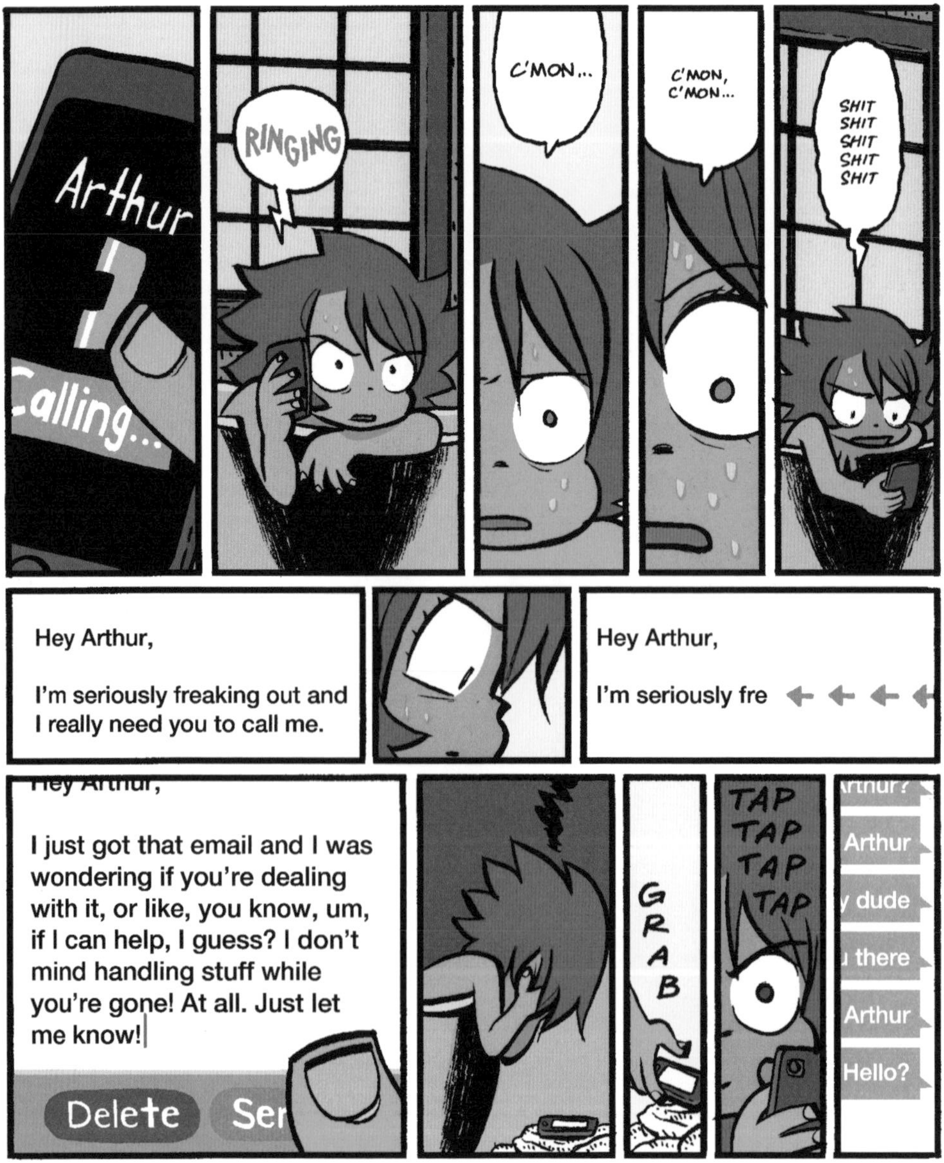
Arthur
Calling...
RINGING
C'MON...
C'MON, C'MON...
SHIT SHIT SHIT SHIT SHIT
Hey Arthur,
I'm seriously freaking out and I really need you to call me.
Hey Arthur,
I'm seriously fre
I just got that email and I was wondering if you're dealing with it, or like, you know, um, if I can help, I guess? I don't mind handling stuff while you're gone! At all. Just let me know!
Delete
GRAB
TAP TAP TAP TAP
Arthur
Arthur
Hello?

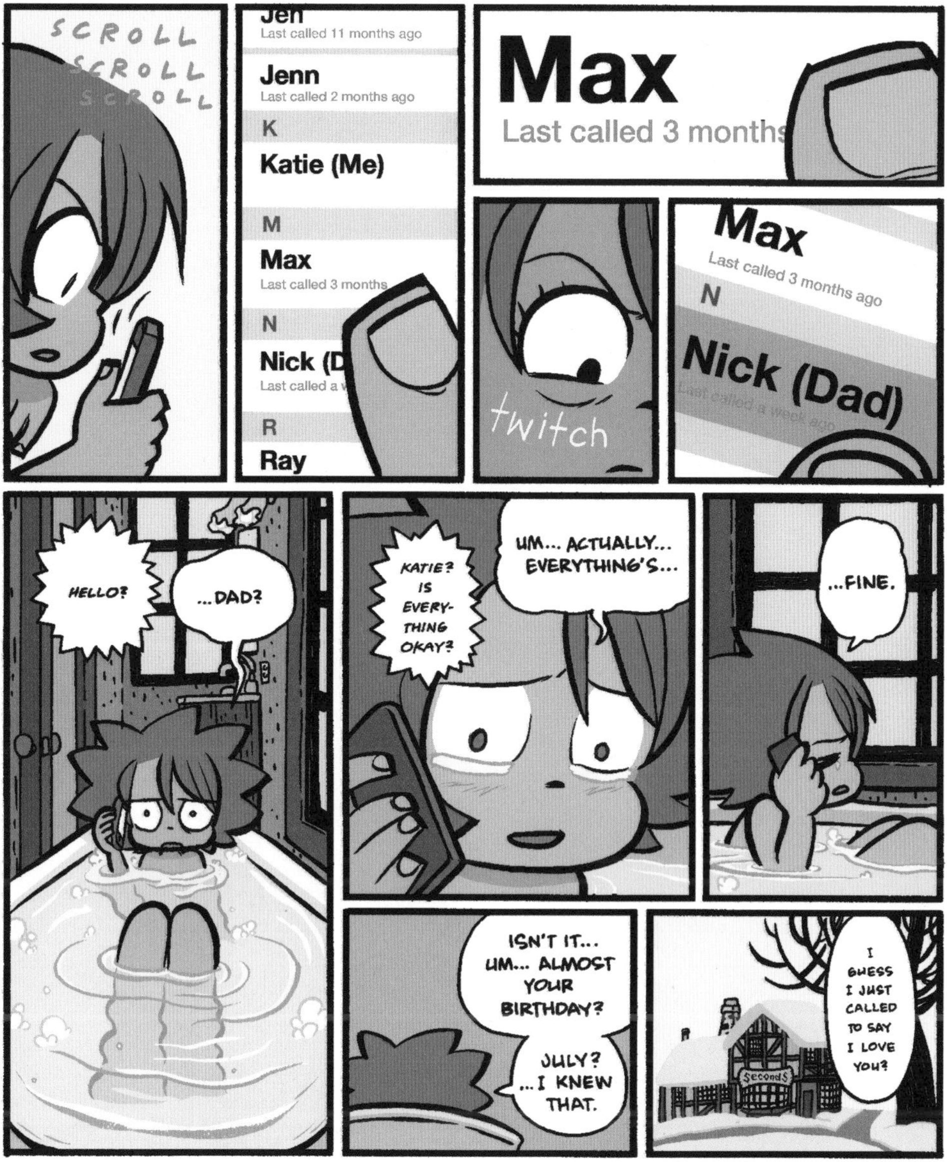
SCROLL
SCROLL
SCROLL
Jen
Last called 11 months ago
Jenn
Last called 2 months ago
K
Katie (Me)
M
Max
Last called 3 months
N
Nick (D
Last called a w
R
Ray
Max
Last called 3 months
twitch
Max
Last called 3 months ago
N
Nick (Dad)
HELLO?
...DAD?
KATIE? IS EVERYTHING OKAY?
UM... ACTUALLY... EVERYTHING'S...
...FINE.
ISN'T IT... UM... ALMOST YOUR BIRTHDAY?
JULY? ...I KNEW THAT.
Seconds
I GUESS I JUST CALLED TO SAY I LOVE YOU?

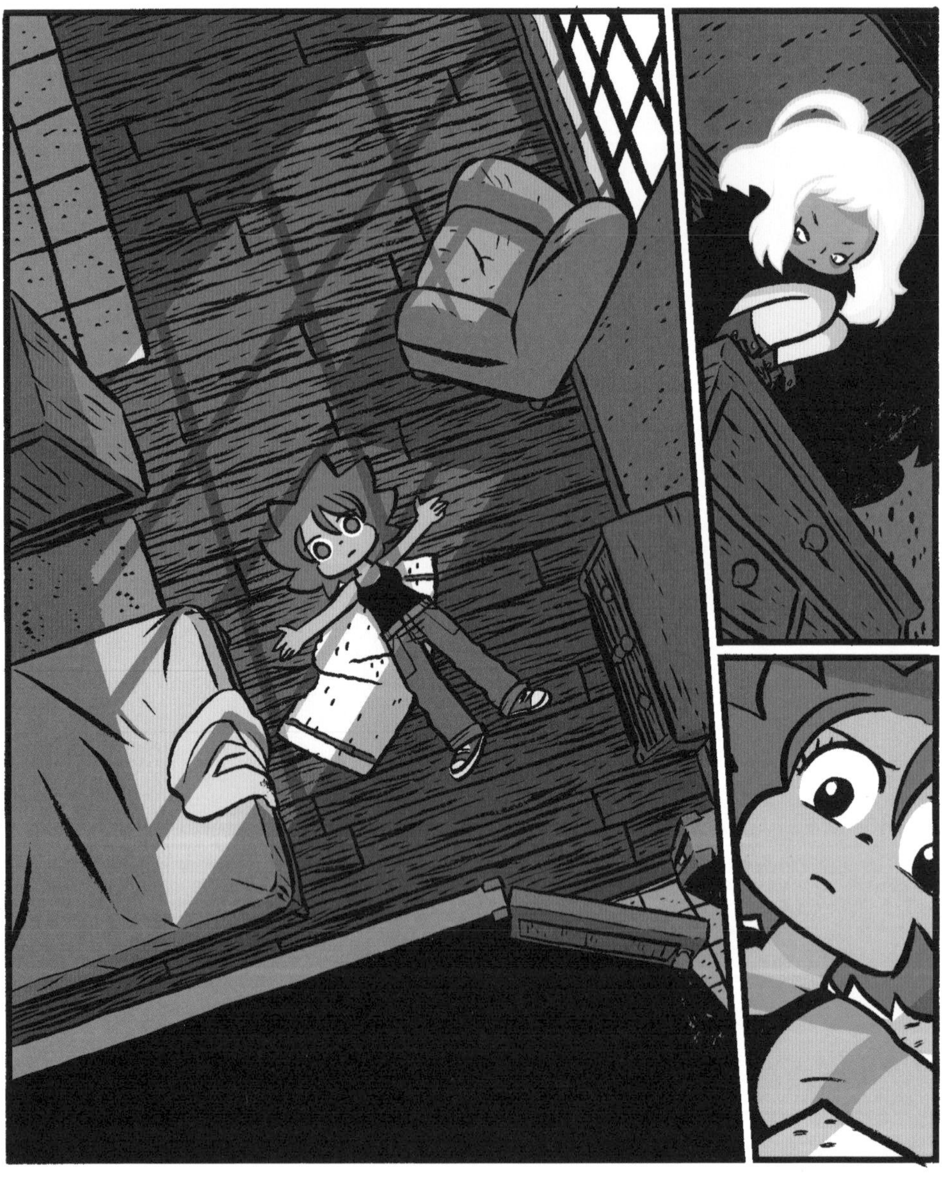

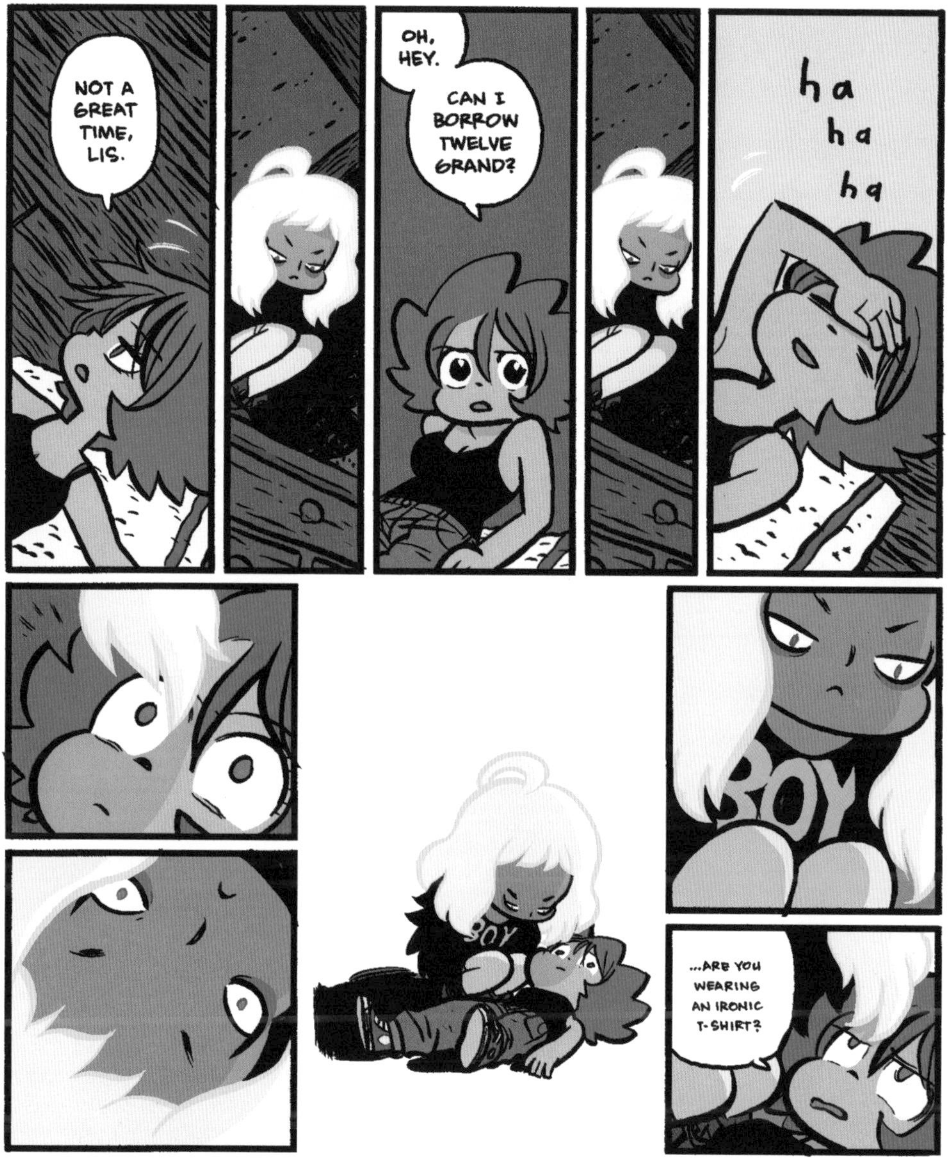
NOT A GREAT TIME, LIS.
OH, HEY.
CAN I BORROW TWELVE GRAND?
ha ha ha
...ARE YOU WEARING AN IRONIC T-SHIRT?
BOY

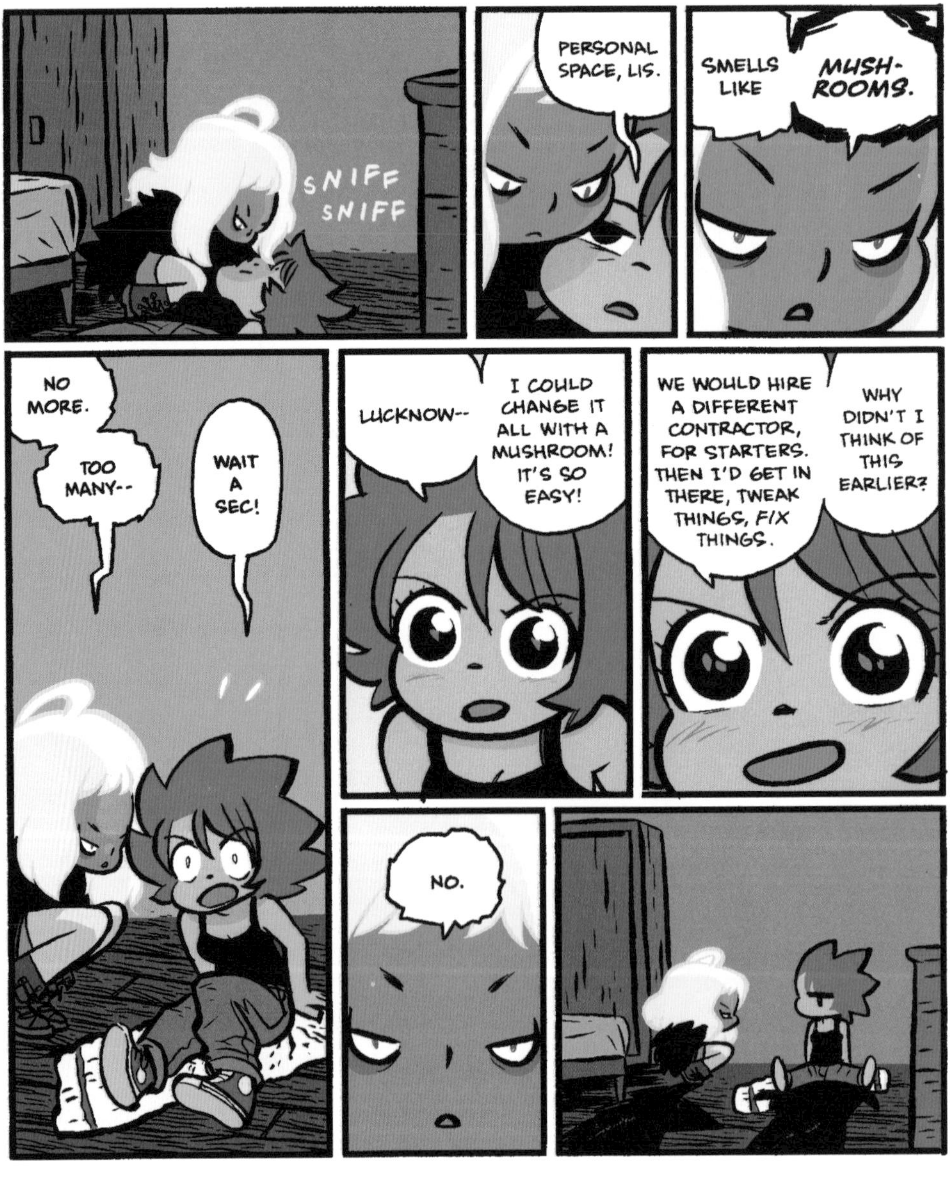
SNIFF SNIFF
PERSONAL SPACE, LIS.
SMELLS LIKE
MUSH-ROOMS.
NO MORE.
TOO MANY--
WAIT A SEC!
LUCKNOW--
I COULD CHANGE IT ALL WITH A MUSHROOM! IT'S SO EASY!
WE WOULD HIRE A DIFFERENT CONTRACTOR, FOR STARTERS. THEN I'D GET IN THERE, TWEAK THINGS, FIX THINGS.
WHY DIDN'T I THINK OF THIS EARLIER?
NO.

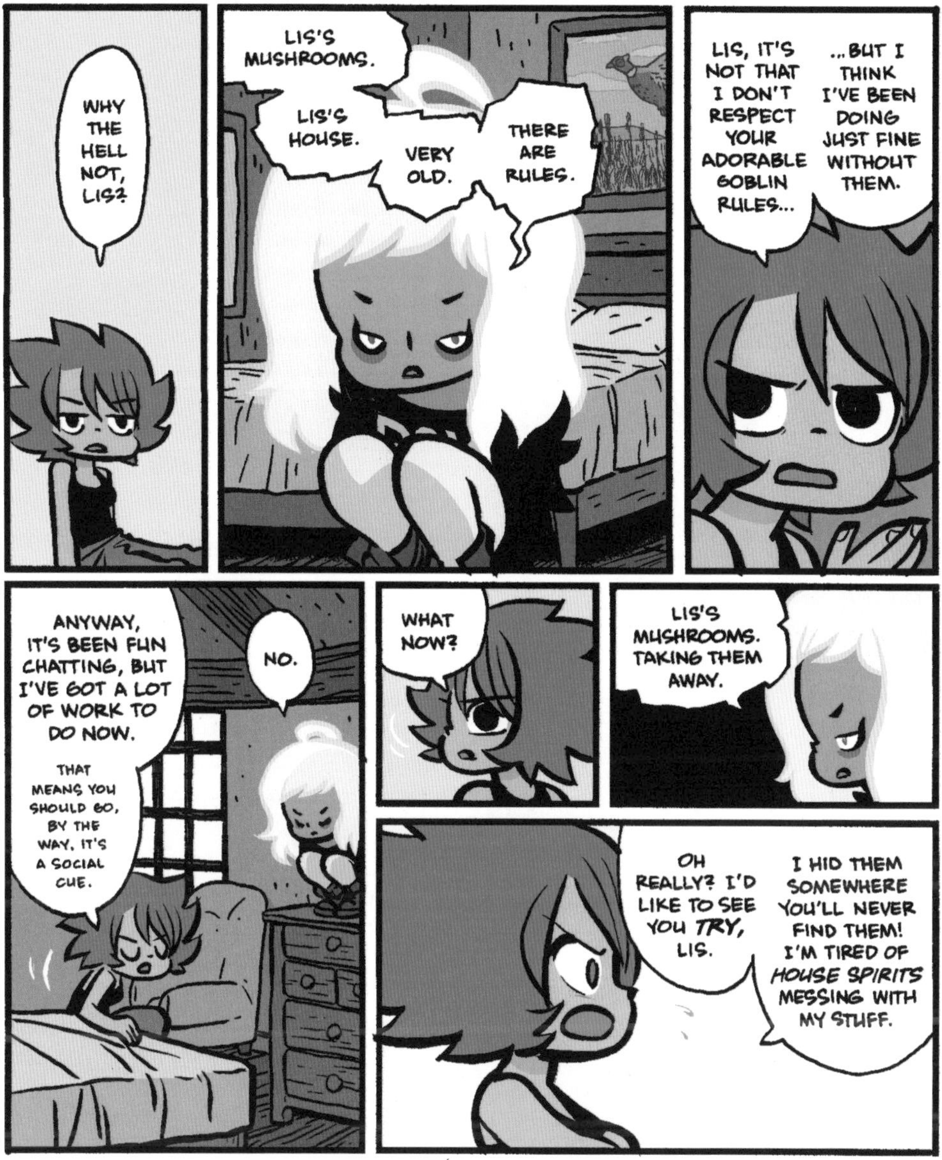
WHY THE HELL NOT, LIS?
LIS'S MUSHROOMS.
LIS'S HOUSE.
VERY OLD.
THERE ARE RULES.
LIS, IT'S NOT THAT I DON'T RESPECT YOUR ADORABLE GOBLIN RULES...
...BUT I THINK I'VE BEEN DOING JUST FINE WITHOUT THEM.
ANYWAY, IT'S BEEN FUN CHATTING, BUT I'VE GOT A LOT OF WORK TO DO NOW.
THAT MEANS YOU SHOULD GO, BY THE WAY. IT'S A SOCIAL CUE.
NO.
WHAT NOW?
LIS'S MUSHROOMS. TAKING THEM AWAY.
OH REALLY? I'D LIKE TO SEE YOU *TRY*, LIS.
I HID THEM SOMEWHERE YOU'LL NEVER FIND THEM! I'M TIRED OF *HOUSE SPIRITS* MESSING WITH MY STUFF.

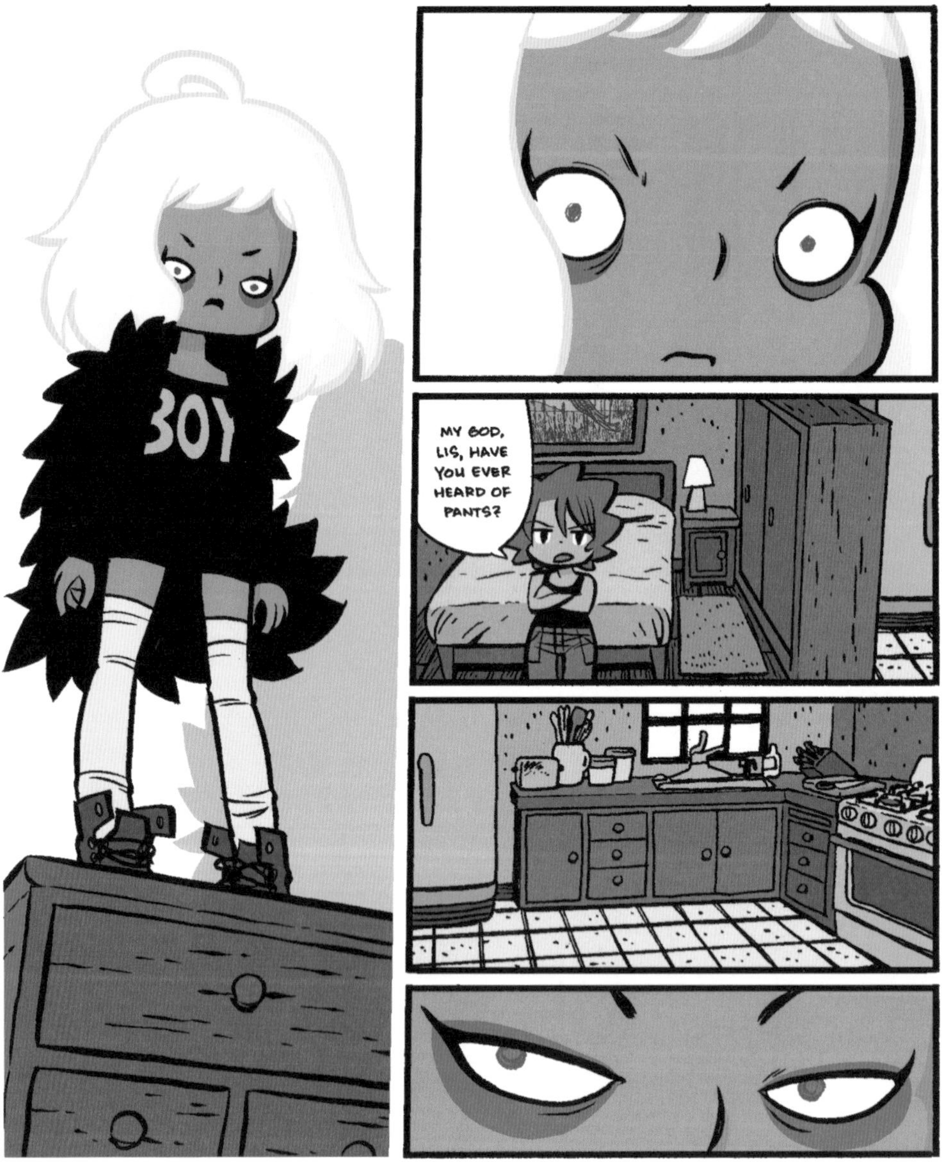
BOY
MY GOD, LIS, HAVE YOU EVER HEARD OF PANTS?

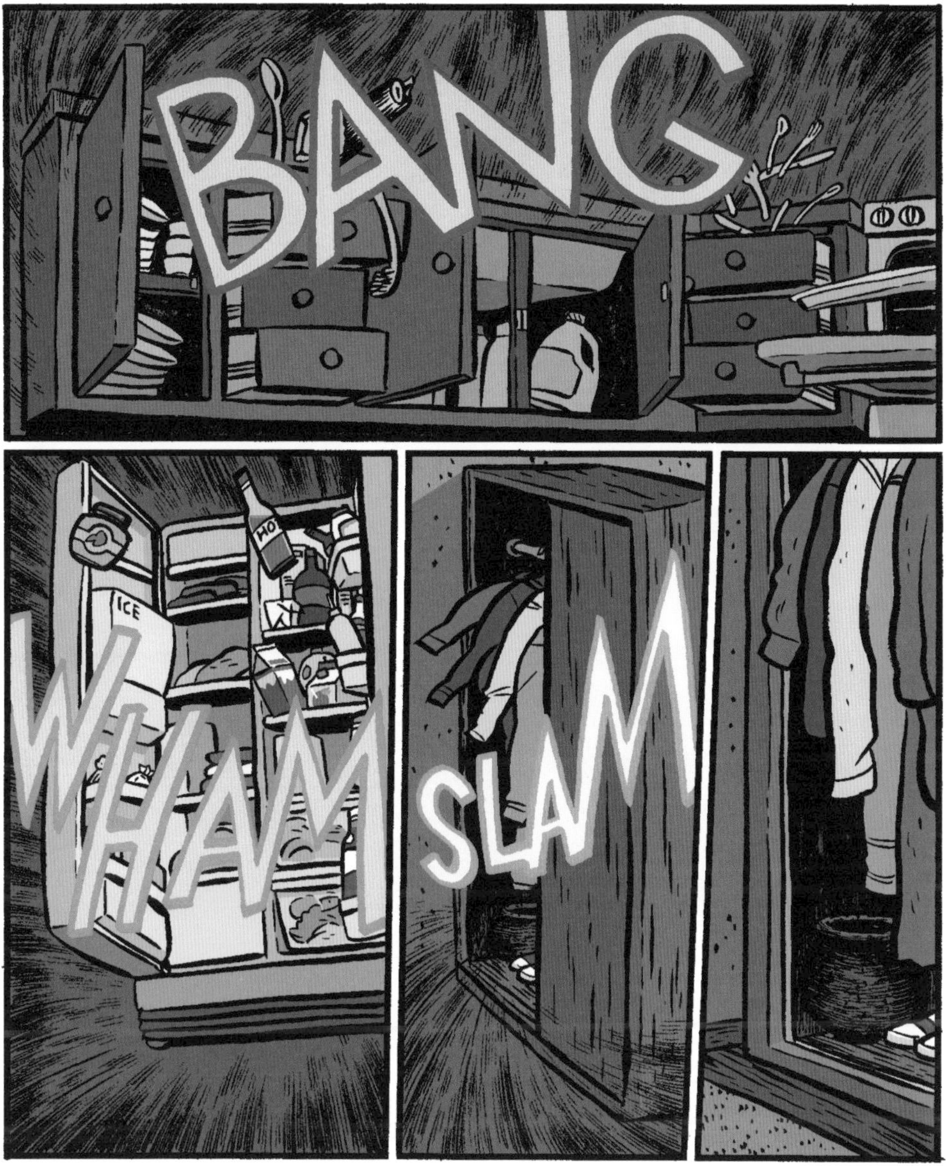
BANG
ICE
WHAM
SLAM

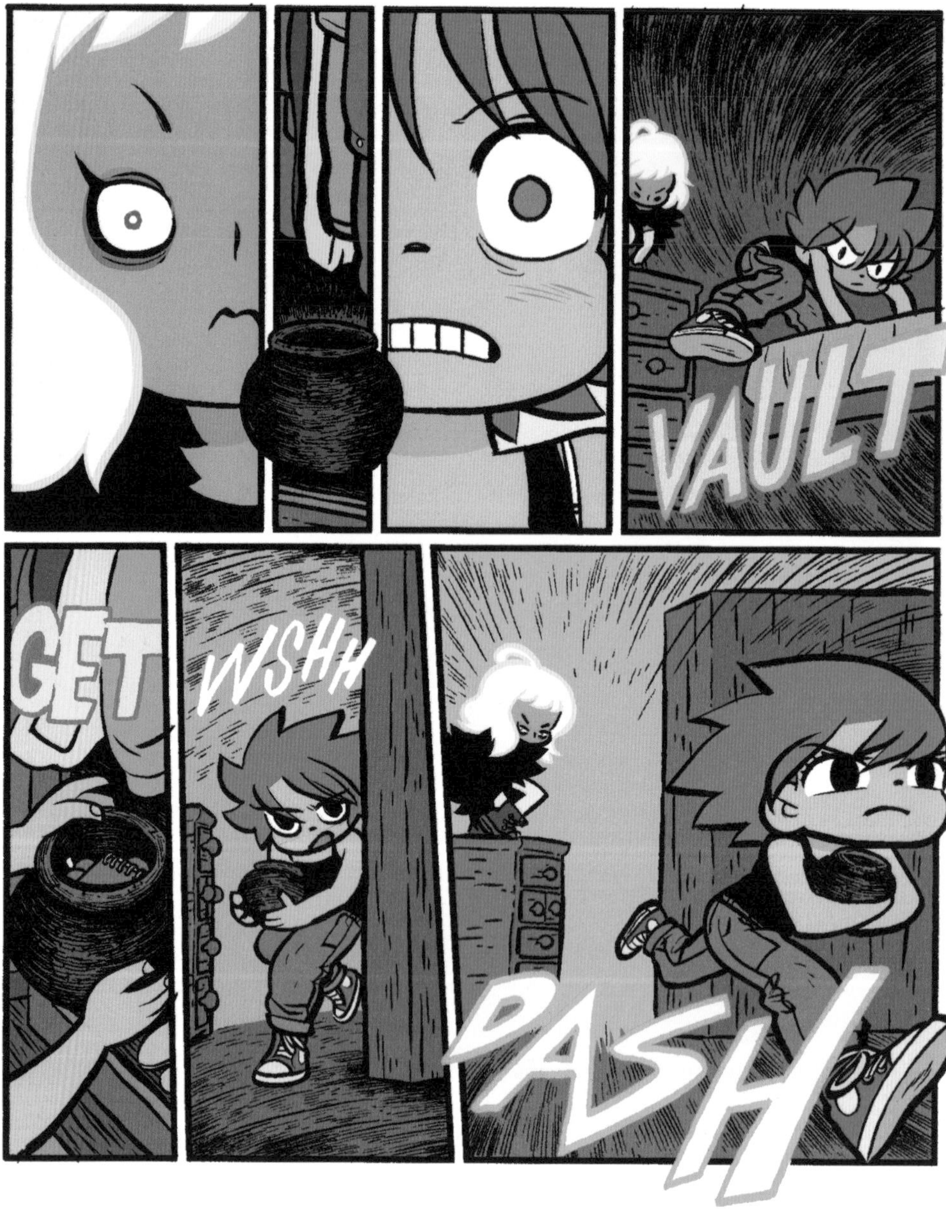
VAULT
GET
WSHH
DASH

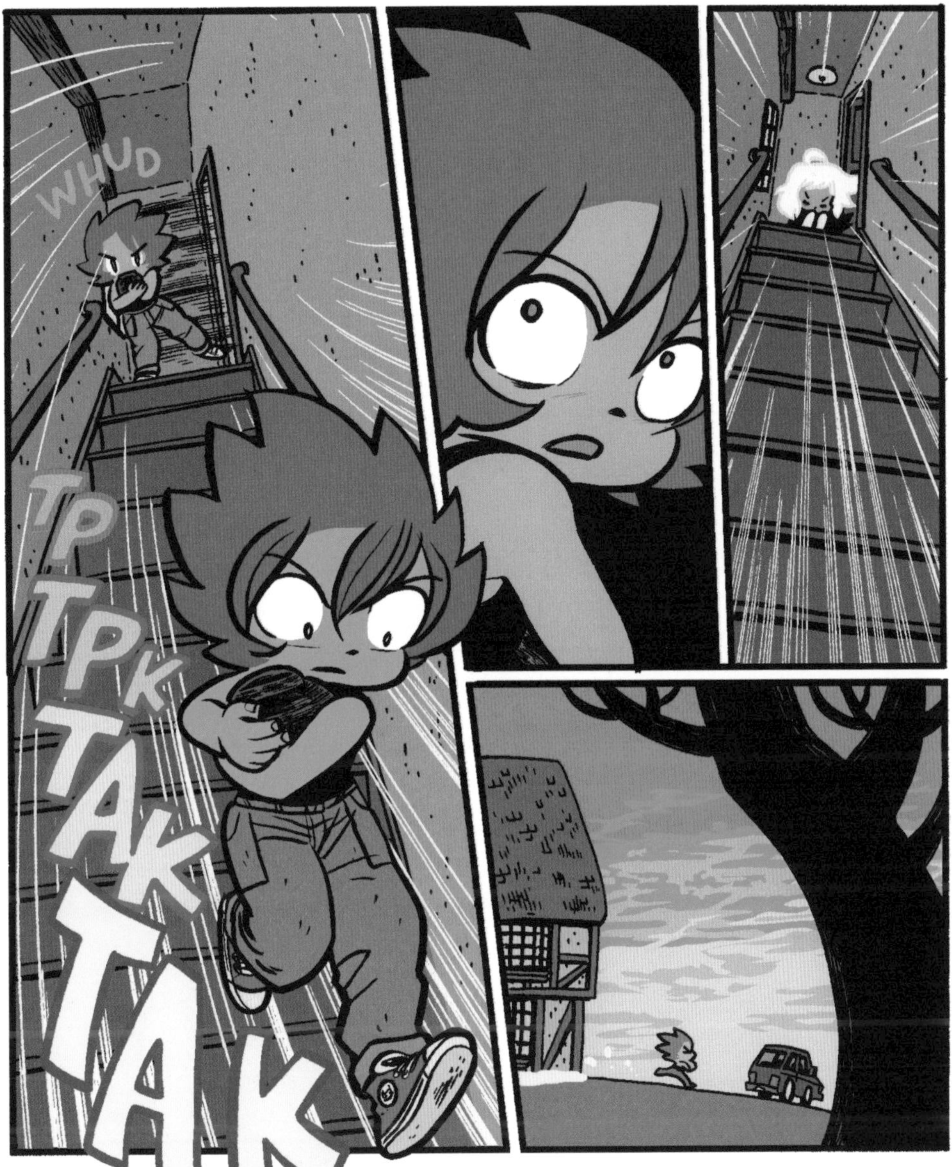
WHUD
TP
TP
TPK
TAK
TAK
TAK

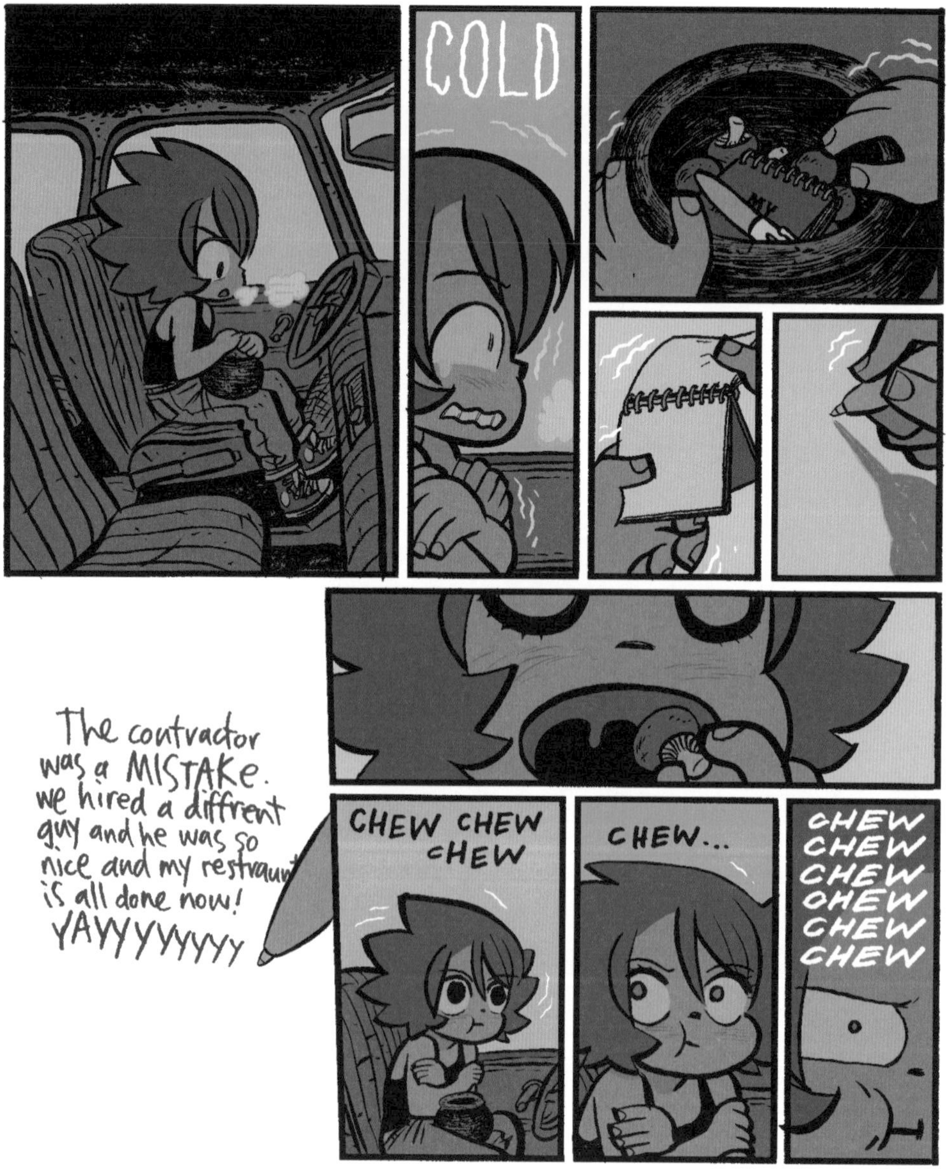
COLD
MY
The contractor was a MISTAKE. we hired a diffrent guy and he was so nice and my restraunt is all done now! YAYYYYYYYY
CHEW CHEW CHEW
CHEW...
CHEW CHEW CHEW CHEW CHEW CHEW

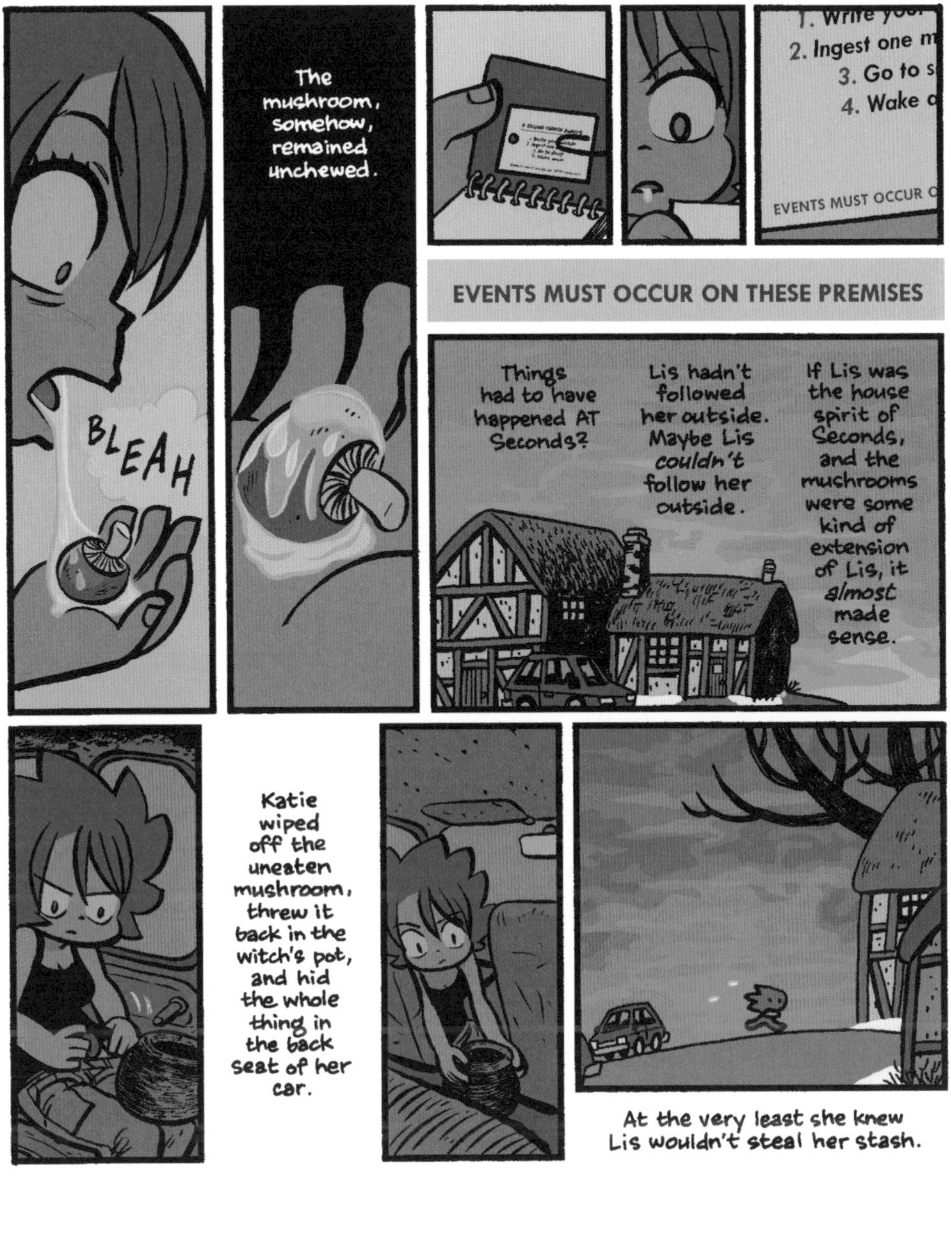
BLEAH
The mushroom, somehow, remained unchewed.
1. Write your
2. Ingest one m
3. Go to s
4. Wake u
EVENTS MUST OCCUR O
EVENTS MUST OCCUR ON THESE PREMISES
Things had to have happened AT Seconds?
Lis hadn't followed her outside. Maybe Lis *couldn't* follow her outside.
If Lis was the house spirit of Seconds, and the mushrooms were some kind of extension of Lis, it *almost* made sense.
Katie wiped off the uneaten mushroom, threw it back in the witch's pot, and hid the whole thing in the back seat of her car.
At the very least she knew Lis wouldn't steal her stash.

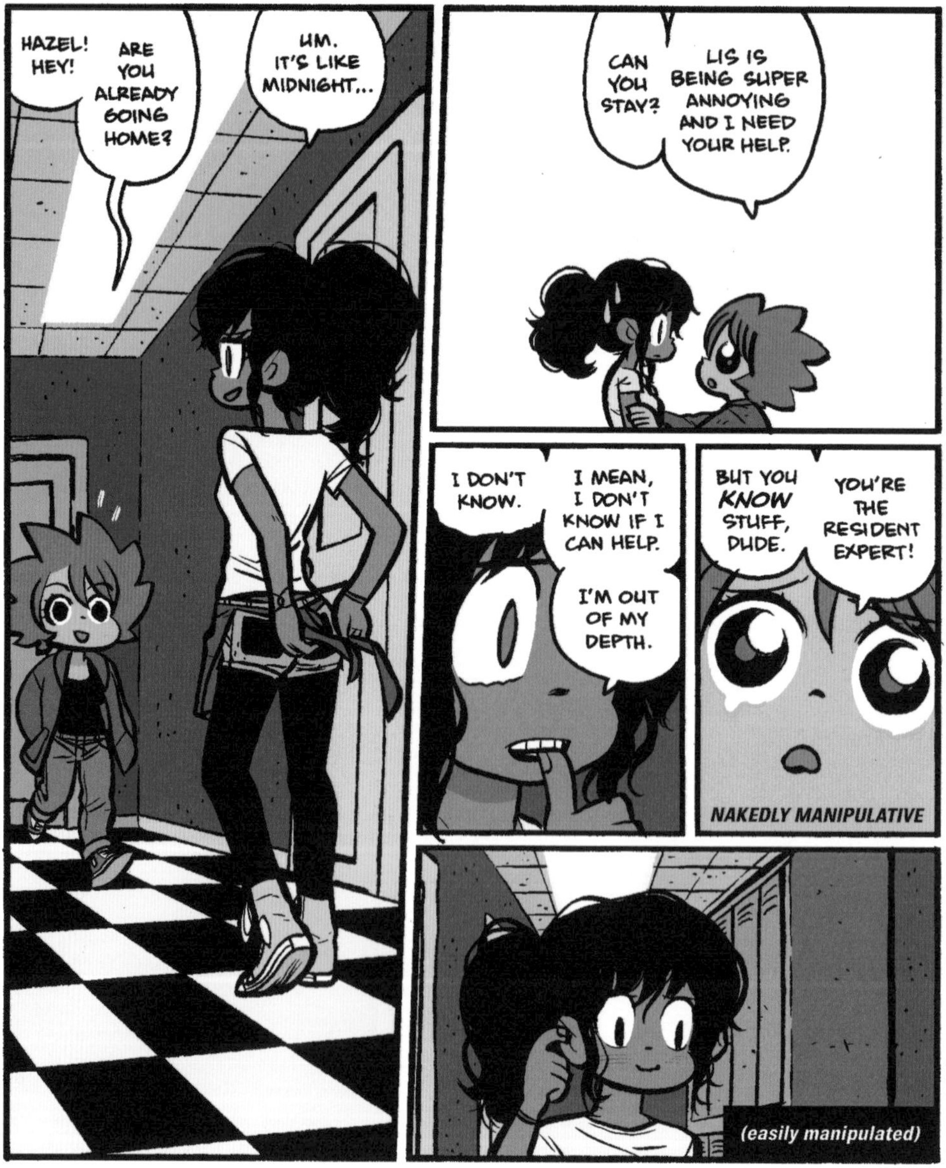
HAZEL! HEY!
ARE YOU ALREADY GOING HOME?
UM. IT'S LIKE MIDNIGHT...
CAN YOU STAY?
LIS IS BEING SUPER ANNOYING AND I NEED YOUR HELP.
I DON'T KNOW.
I MEAN, I DON'T KNOW IF I CAN HELP.
I'M OUT OF MY DEPTH.
BUT YOU KNOW STUFF, DUDE.
YOU'RE THE RESIDENT EXPERT!
NAKEDLY MANIPULATIVE
(easily manipulated)

OKAY, JUST DO YOUR THING.

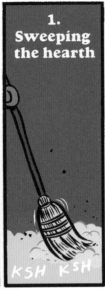

1. **Sweeping the hearth**

KSH KSH

2. **Feeding the fire**

THEY LIKE TO SLEEP BY THE FIRE, SO I KEEP IT NICE!

3. **Clothing drop**

I GOT HER A NEW COAT.

ANIMAL PRINT. I DUNNO.

I HOPE SHE LIKES IT.

4. **Bread on the rafters**

ALWAYS FRESH BREAD, NEVER DAY-OLDS.

PATRICK SAVES ENDS FOR ME.

PLEASE DON'T TELL HIM WHAT I DO WITH THEM...

YOU FEED HER BREAD EVERY DAY? JUST BREAD? WOW.

YEAH... WHY WOW?

I MEAN... UH... WILL SHE GET FAT?

WAIT,... BREAD MAKES YOU *FAT?*

SORRY...

135

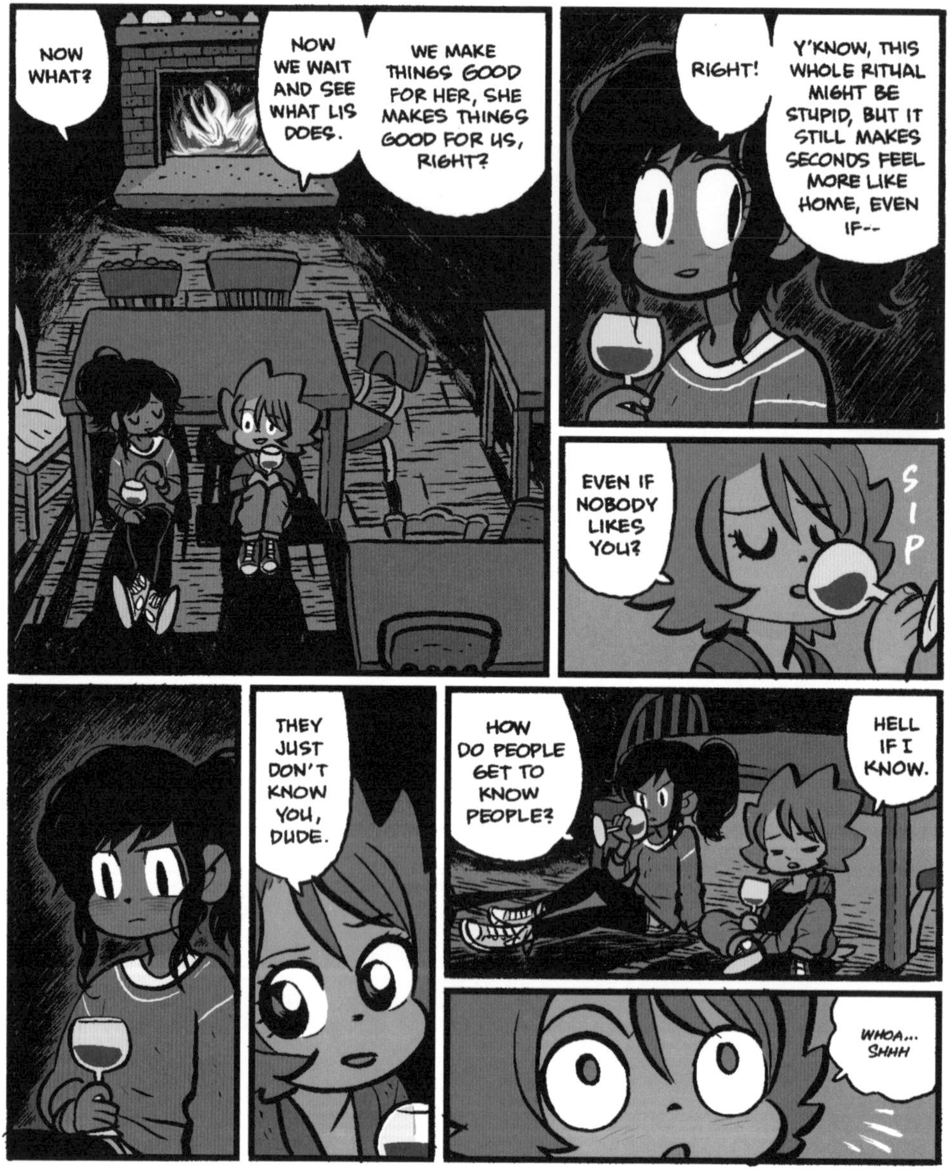
NOW WHAT?
NOW WE WAIT AND SEE WHAT LIS DOES.
WE MAKE THINGS GOOD FOR HER, SHE MAKES THINGS GOOD FOR US, RIGHT?
RIGHT!
Y'KNOW, THIS WHOLE RITUAL MIGHT BE STUPID, BUT IT STILL MAKES SECONDS FEEL MORE LIKE HOME, EVEN IF--
EVEN IF NOBODY LIKES YOU?
SIP
THEY JUST DON'T KNOW YOU, DUDE.
HOW DO PEOPLE GET TO KNOW PEOPLE?
HELL IF I KNOW.
WHOA... SHHH

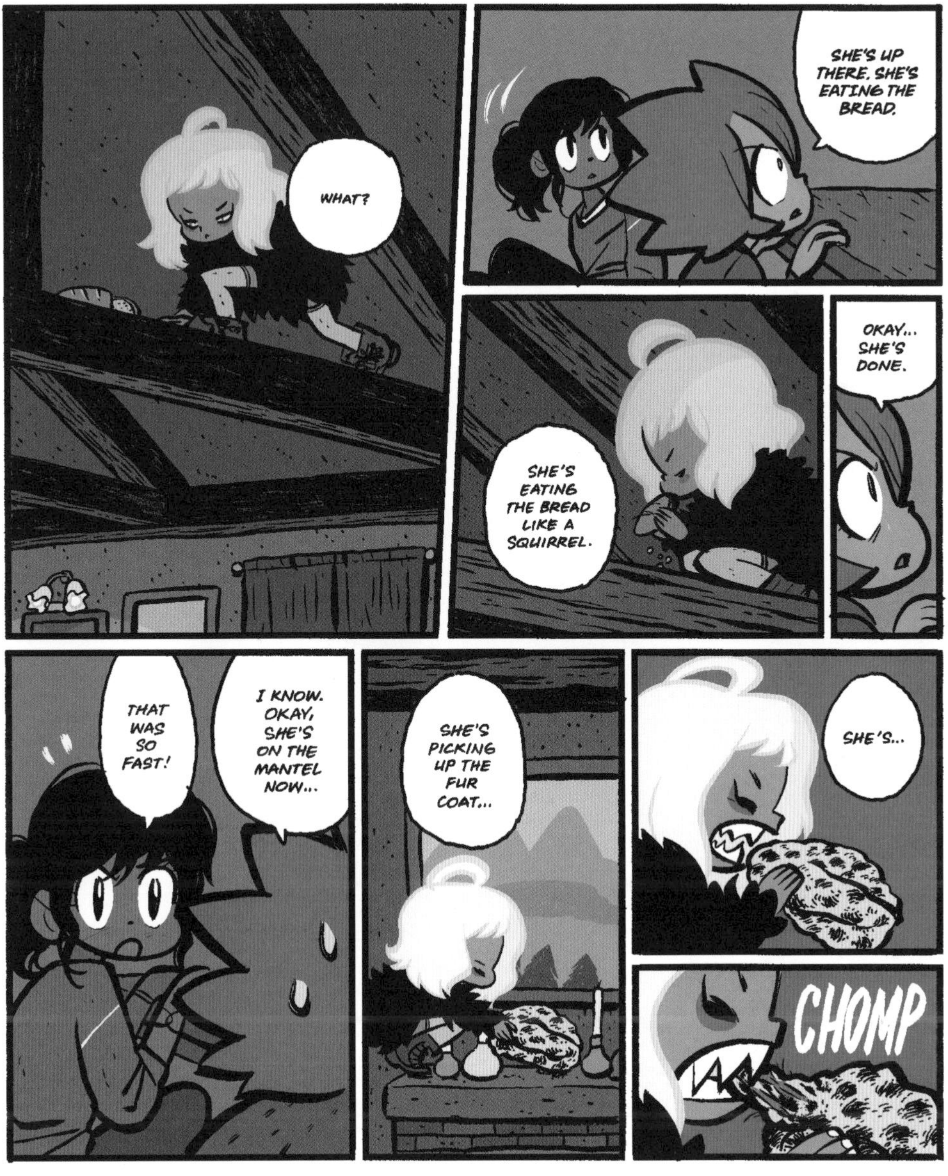
WHAT?
SHE'S UP THERE. SHE'S EATING THE BREAD.
SHE'S EATING THE BREAD LIKE A SQUIRREL.
OKAY... SHE'S DONE.
THAT WAS SO FAST!
I KNOW. OKAY, SHE'S ON THE MANTEL NOW...
SHE'S PICKING UP THE FUR COAT...
SHE'S...
CHOMP

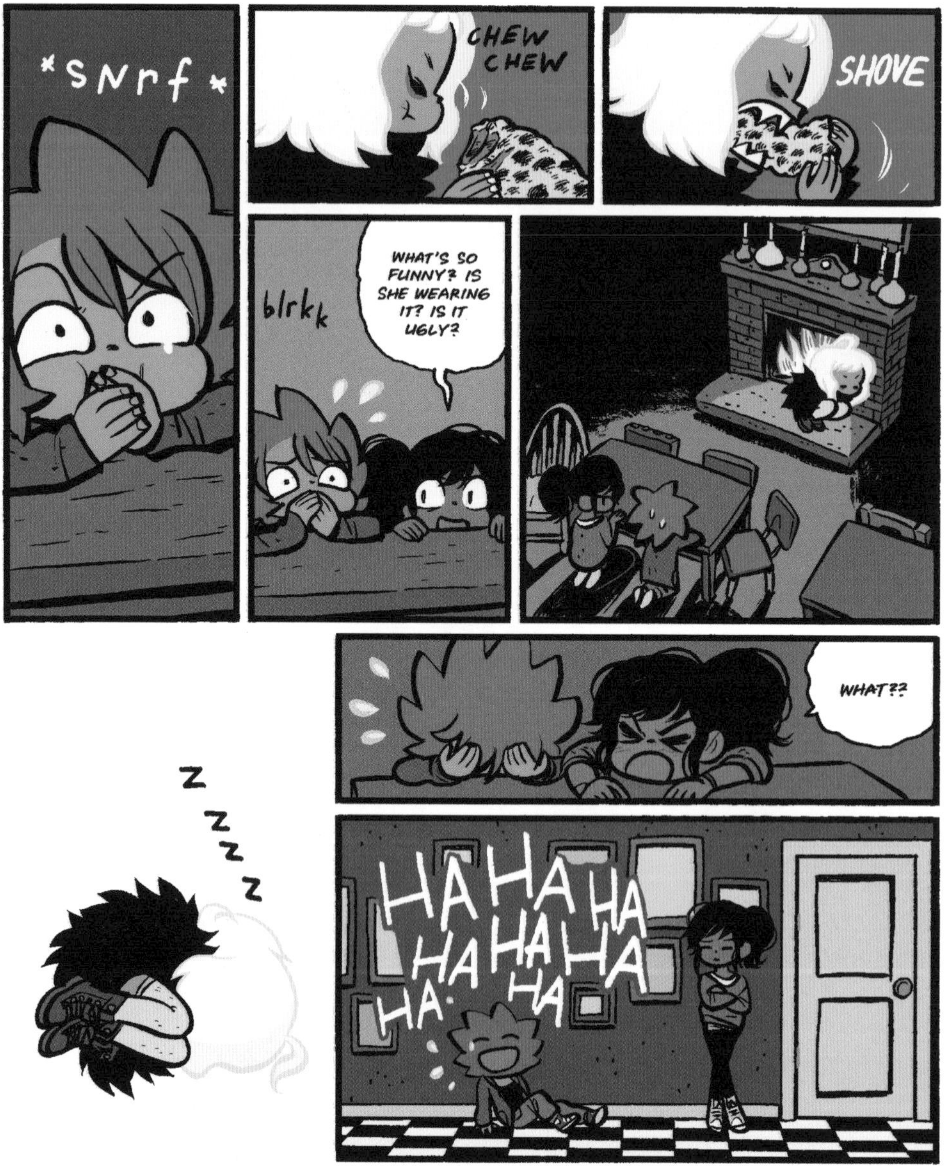

SNrf
CHEW CHEW
SHOVE
blrkk
WHAT'S SO FUNNY? IS SHE WEARING IT? IS IT UGLY?
WHAT??
HA HA HA HA HA HA HA HA HA HA
Z Z Z Z

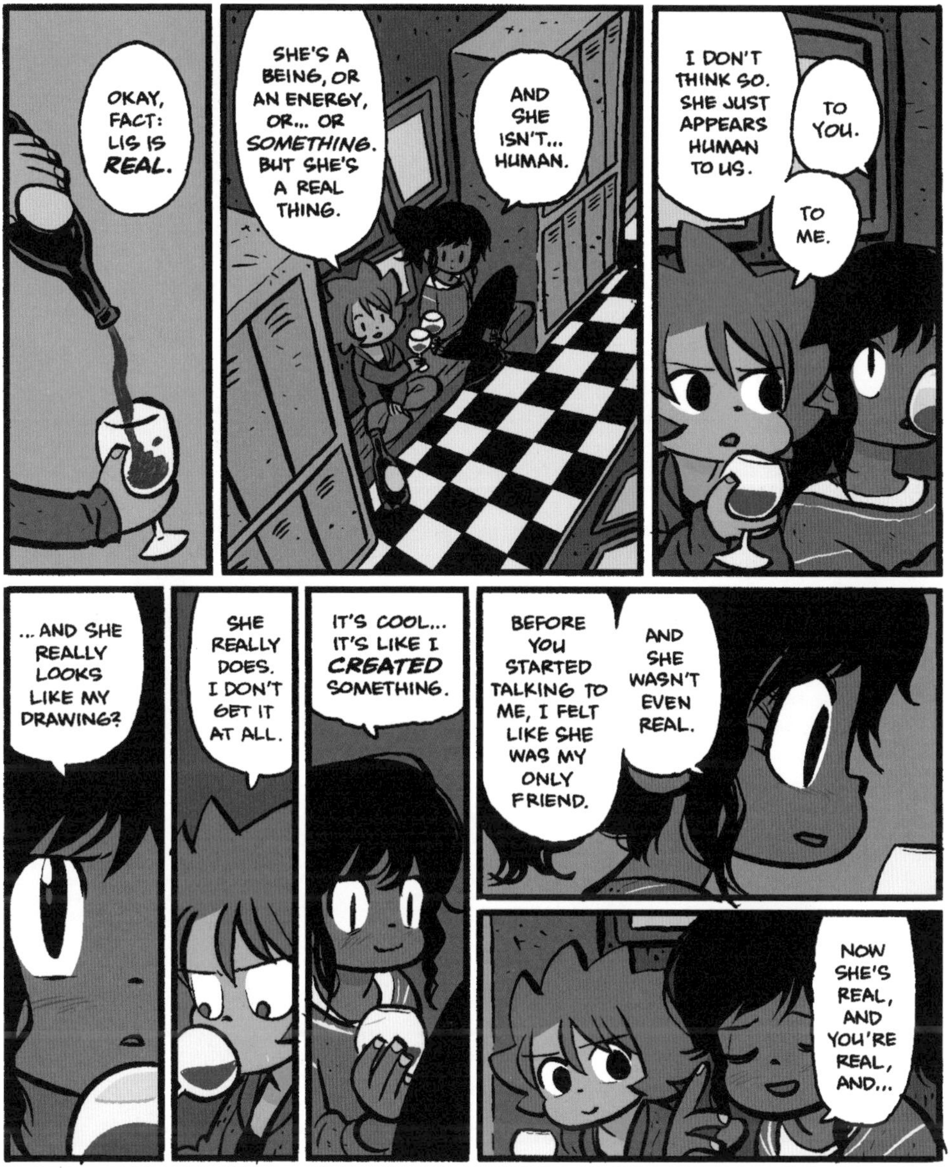

OKAY, FACT: LIS IS *REAL*.
SHE'S A BEING, OR AN ENERGY, OR... OR *SOMETHING*. BUT SHE'S A REAL THING.
AND SHE ISN'T... HUMAN.
I DON'T THINK SO. SHE JUST APPEARS HUMAN TO US.
TO YOU.
TO ME.
... AND SHE REALLY LOOKS LIKE MY DRAWING?
SHE REALLY DOES. I DON'T GET IT AT ALL.
IT'S COOL... IT'S LIKE I *CREATED* SOMETHING.
BEFORE YOU STARTED TALKING TO ME, I FELT LIKE SHE WAS MY ONLY FRIEND.
AND SHE WASN'T EVEN REAL.
NOW SHE'S REAL, AND YOU'RE REAL, AND...

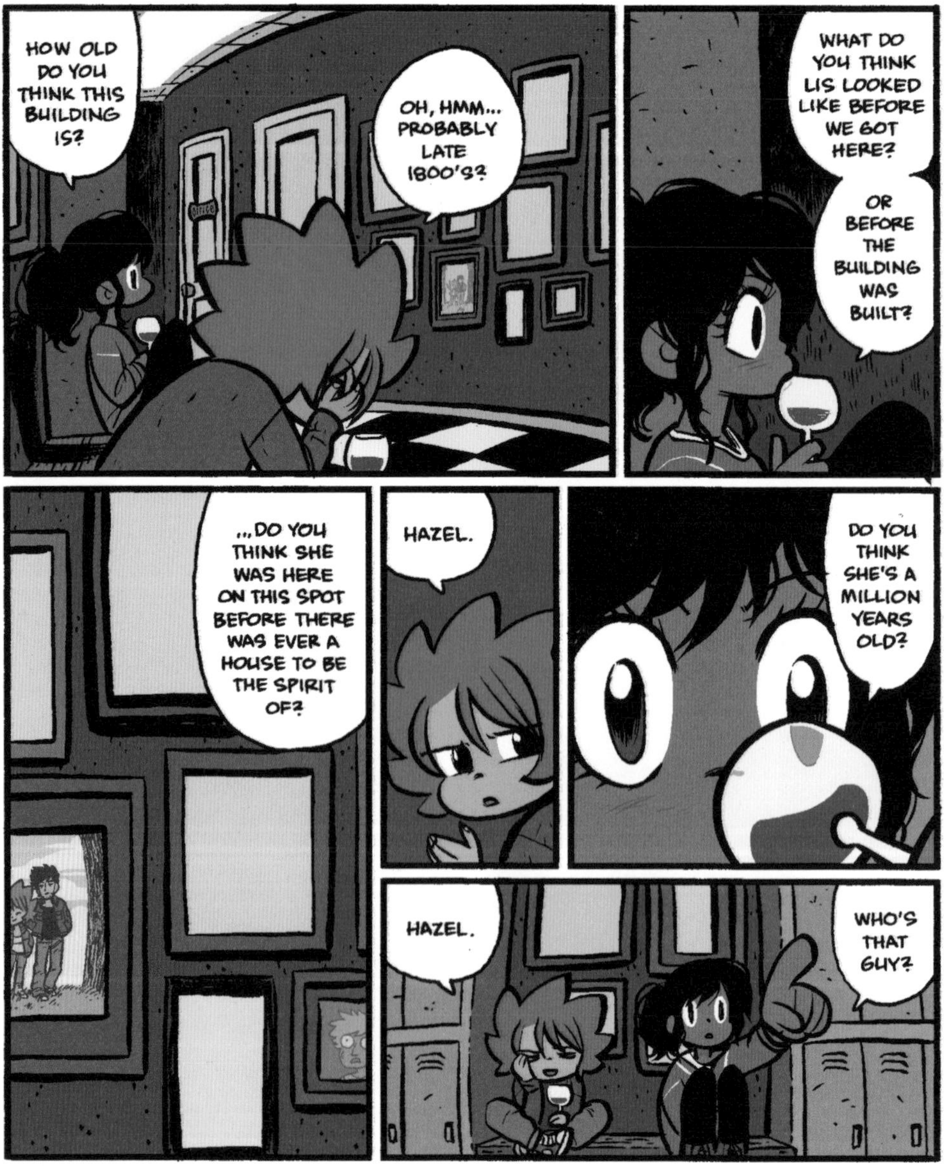
HOW OLD DO YOU THINK THIS BUILDING IS?
OH, HMM... PROBABLY LATE 1800'S?
WHAT DO YOU THINK US LOOKED LIKE BEFORE WE GOT HERE?
OR BEFORE THE BUILDING WAS BUILT?
...DO YOU THINK SHE WAS HERE ON THIS SPOT BEFORE THERE WAS EVER A HOUSE TO BE THE SPIRIT OF?
HAZEL.
DO YOU THINK SHE'S A MILLION YEARS OLD?
HAZEL.
WHO'S THAT GUY?

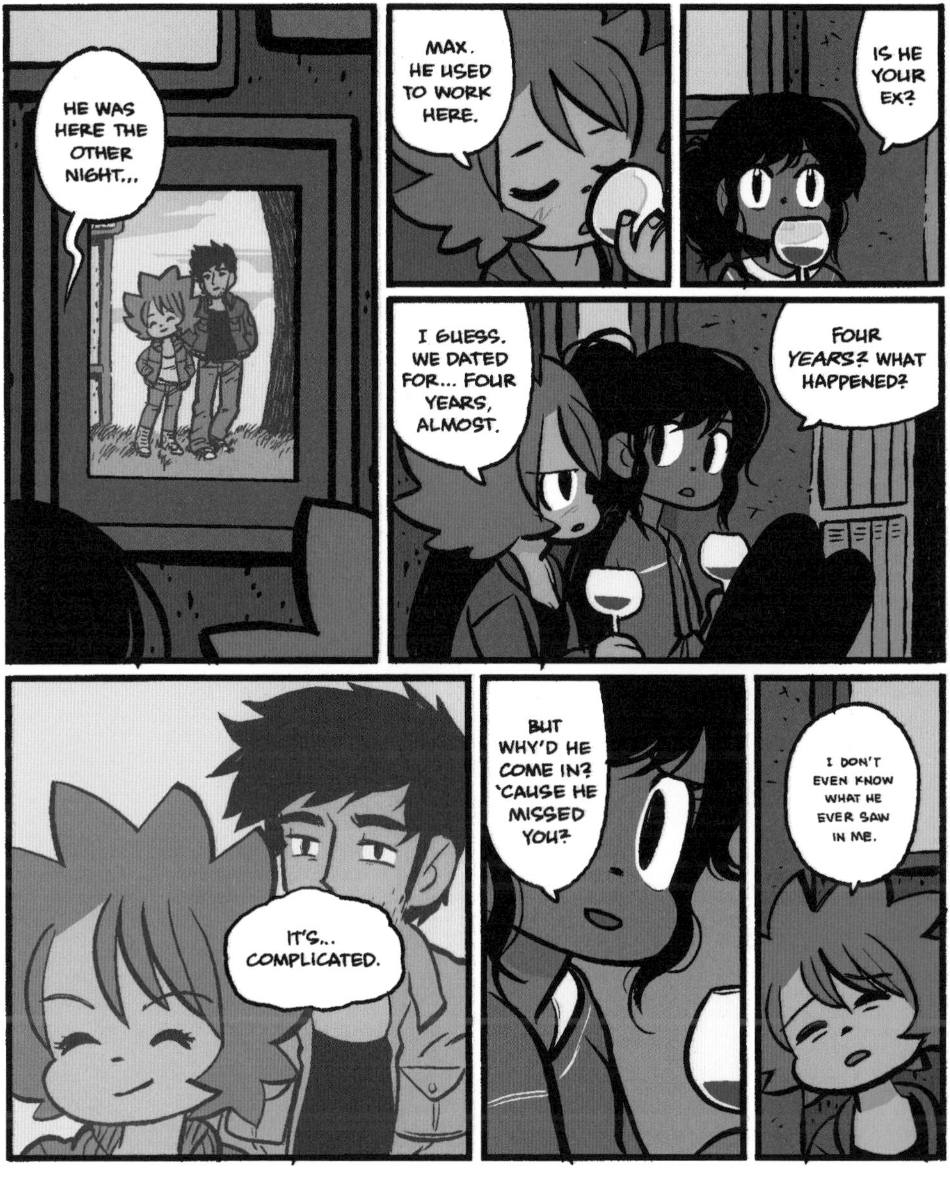
HE WAS HERE THE OTHER NIGHT...
MAX. HE USED TO WORK HERE.
IS HE YOUR EX?
I GUESS. WE DATED FOR... FOUR YEARS, ALMOST.
FOUR YEARS? WHAT HAPPENED?
IT'S... COMPLICATED.
BUT WHY'D HE COME IN? 'CAUSE HE MISSED YOU?
I DON'T EVEN KNOW WHAT HE EVER SAW IN ME.

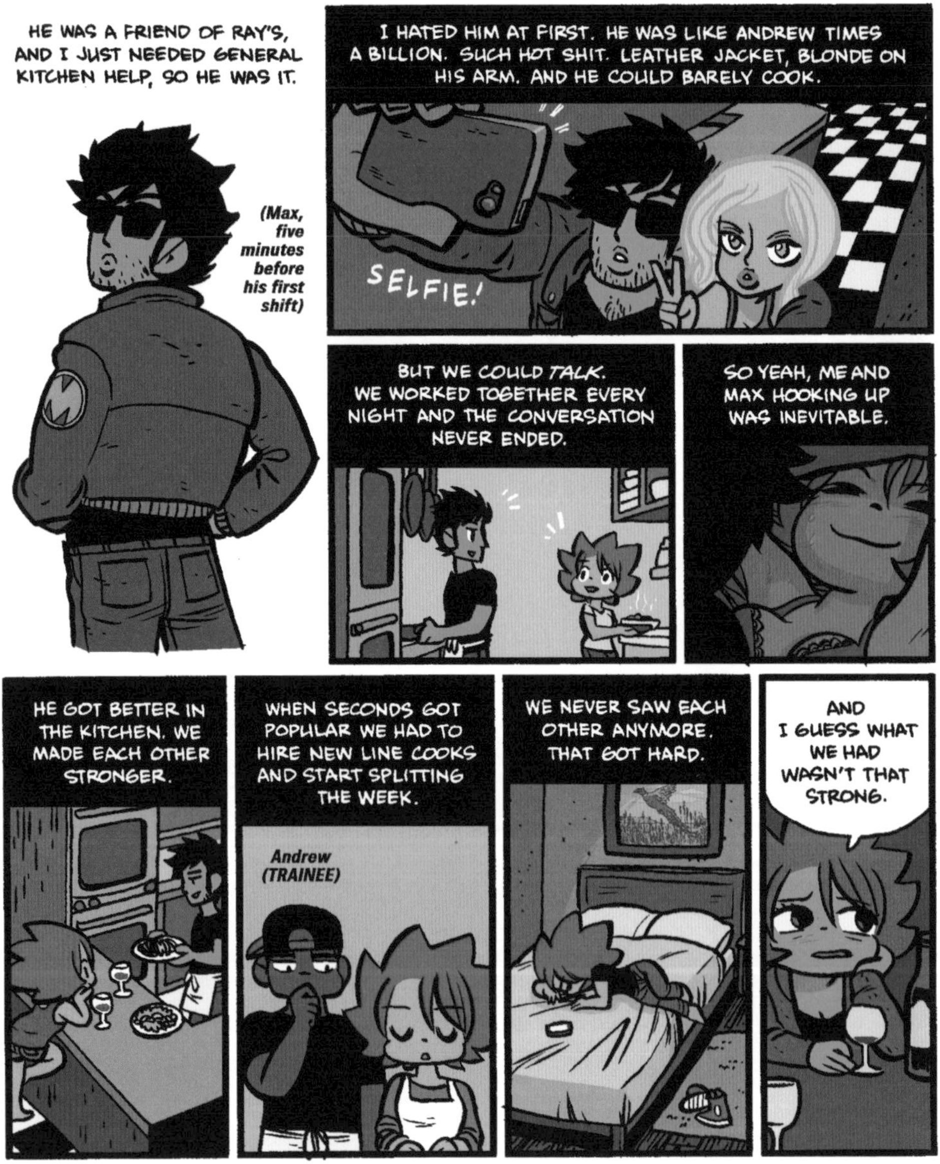
HE WAS A FRIEND OF RAY'S, AND I JUST NEEDED GENERAL KITCHEN HELP, SO HE WAS IT.
(Max, five minutes before his first shift)
I HATED HIM AT FIRST. HE WAS LIKE ANDREW TIMES A BILLION. SUCH HOT SHIT. LEATHER JACKET, BLONDE ON HIS ARM. AND HE COULD BARELY COOK.
SELFIE!
BUT WE COULD TALK. WE WORKED TOGETHER EVERY NIGHT AND THE CONVERSATION NEVER ENDED.
SO YEAH, ME AND MAX HOOKING UP WAS INEVITABLE.
HE GOT BETTER IN THE KITCHEN. WE MADE EACH OTHER STRONGER.
WHEN SECONDS GOT POPULAR WE HAD TO HIRE NEW LINE COOKS AND START SPLITTING THE WEEK.
Andrew (TRAINEE)
WE NEVER SAW EACH OTHER ANYMORE. THAT GOT HARD.
AND I GUESS WHAT WE HAD WASN'T THAT STRONG.

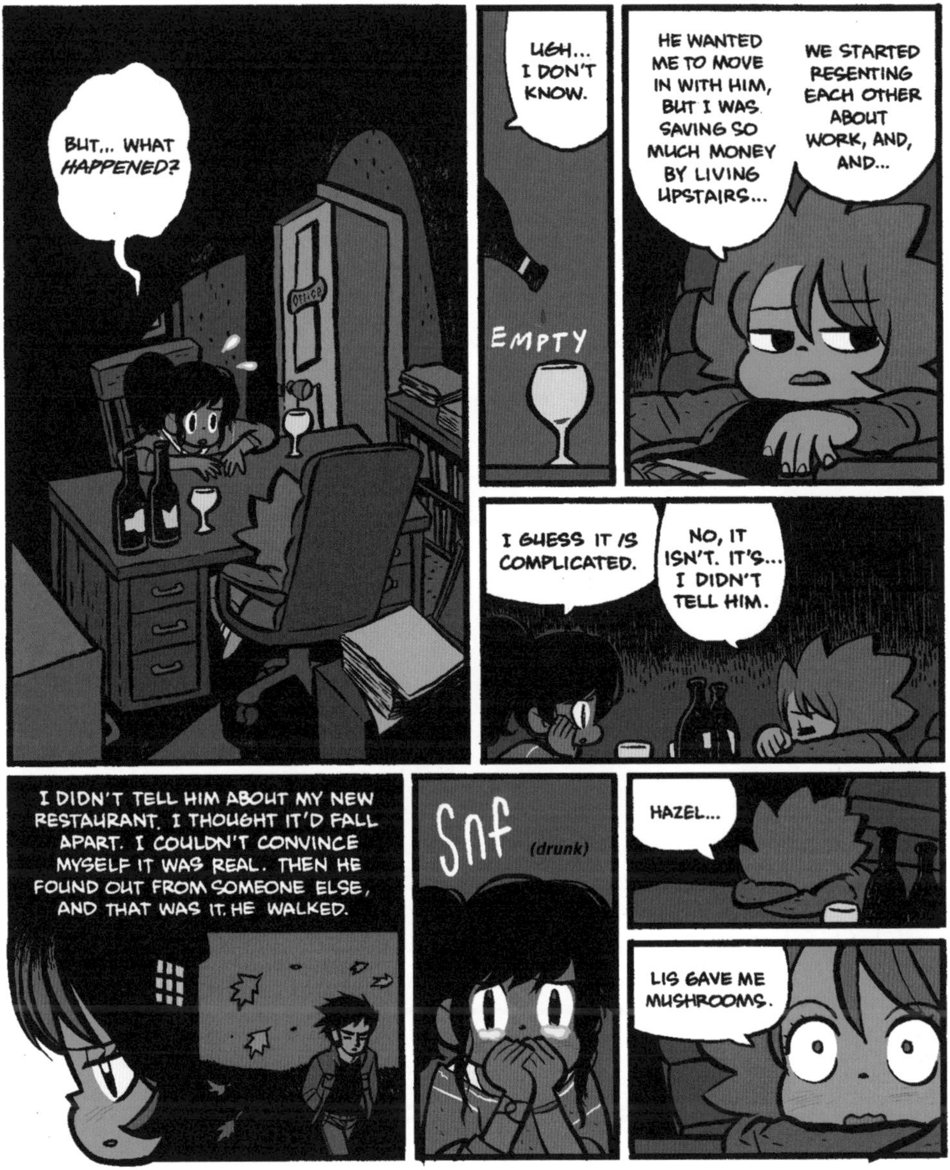
BUT... WHAT *HAPPENED?*
UGH... I DON'T KNOW.
EMPTY
HE WANTED ME TO MOVE IN WITH HIM, BUT I WAS SAVING SO MUCH MONEY BY LIVING UPSTAIRS...
WE STARTED RESENTING EACH OTHER ABOUT WORK, AND, AND...
I GUESS IT *IS* COMPLICATED.
NO, IT ISN'T. IT'S... I DIDN'T TELL HIM.
I DIDN'T TELL HIM ABOUT MY NEW RESTAURANT. I THOUGHT IT'D FALL APART. I COULDN'T CONVINCE MYSELF IT WAS REAL. THEN HE FOUND OUT FROM SOMEONE ELSE, AND THAT WAS IT. HE WALKED.
Snf
(drunk)
HAZEL...
LIS GAVE ME MUSHROOMS.

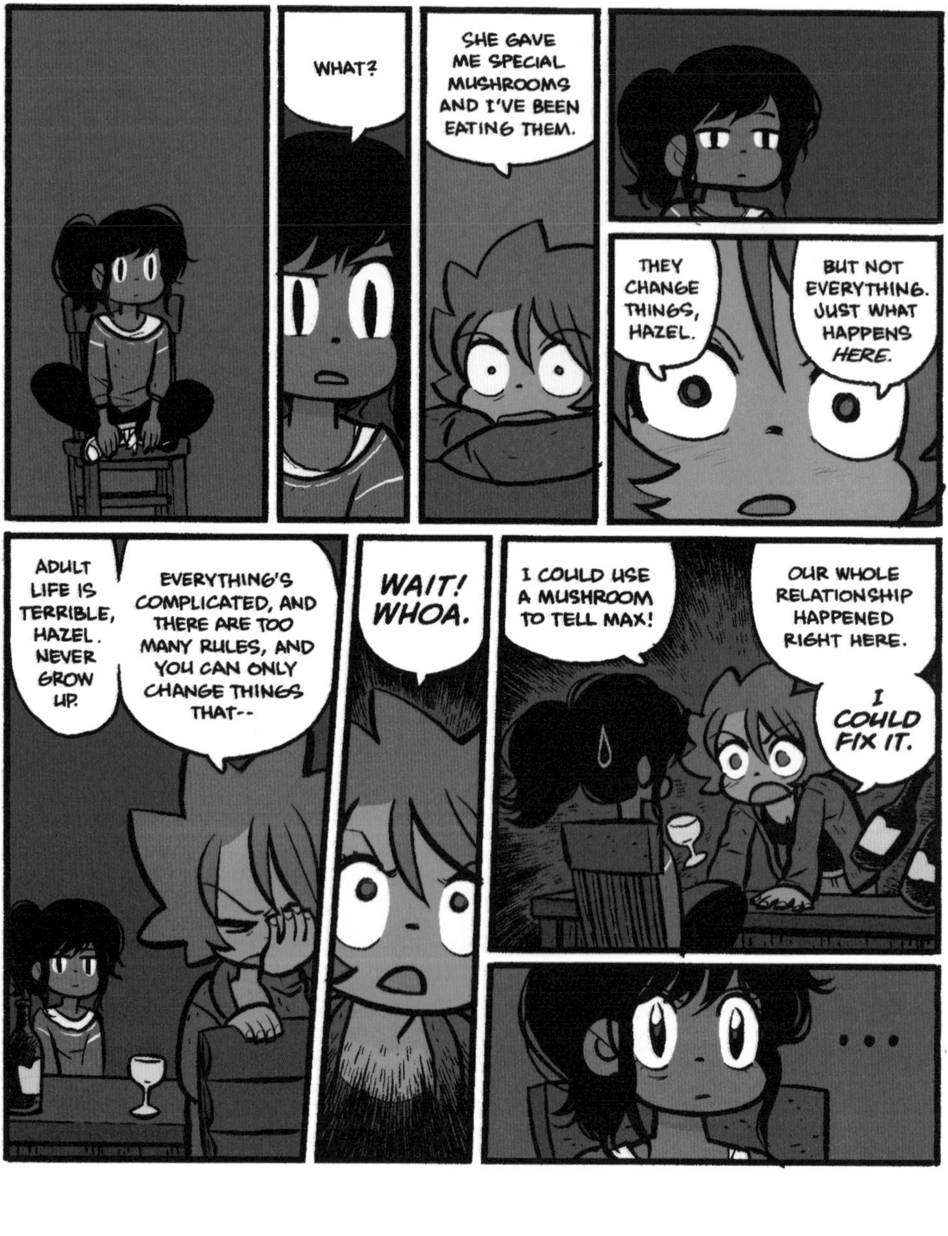
WHAT?
SHE GAVE ME SPECIAL MUSHROOMS AND I'VE BEEN EATING THEM.
THEY CHANGE THINGS, HAZEL.
BUT NOT EVERYTHING. JUST WHAT HAPPENS *HERE.*
ADULT LIFE IS TERRIBLE, HAZEL. NEVER GROW UP.
EVERYTHING'S COMPLICATED, AND THERE ARE TOO MANY RULES, AND YOU CAN ONLY CHANGE THINGS THAT--
WAIT! WHOA.
I COULD USE A MUSHROOM TO TELL MAX!
OUR WHOLE RELATIONSHIP HAPPENED RIGHT HERE.
I COULD FIX IT.
...

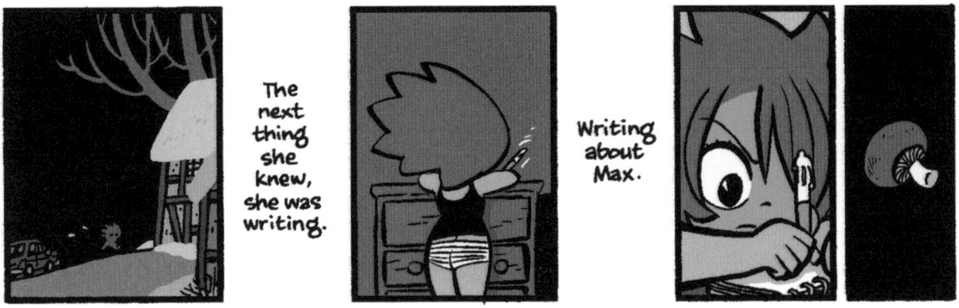
The next thing she knew, she was writing.
Writing about Max.

REVISION #6

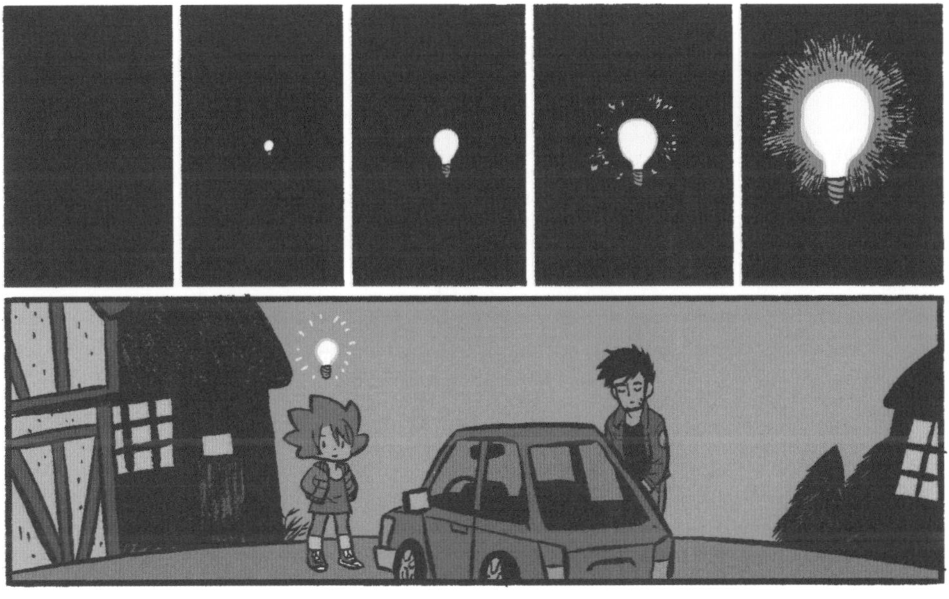

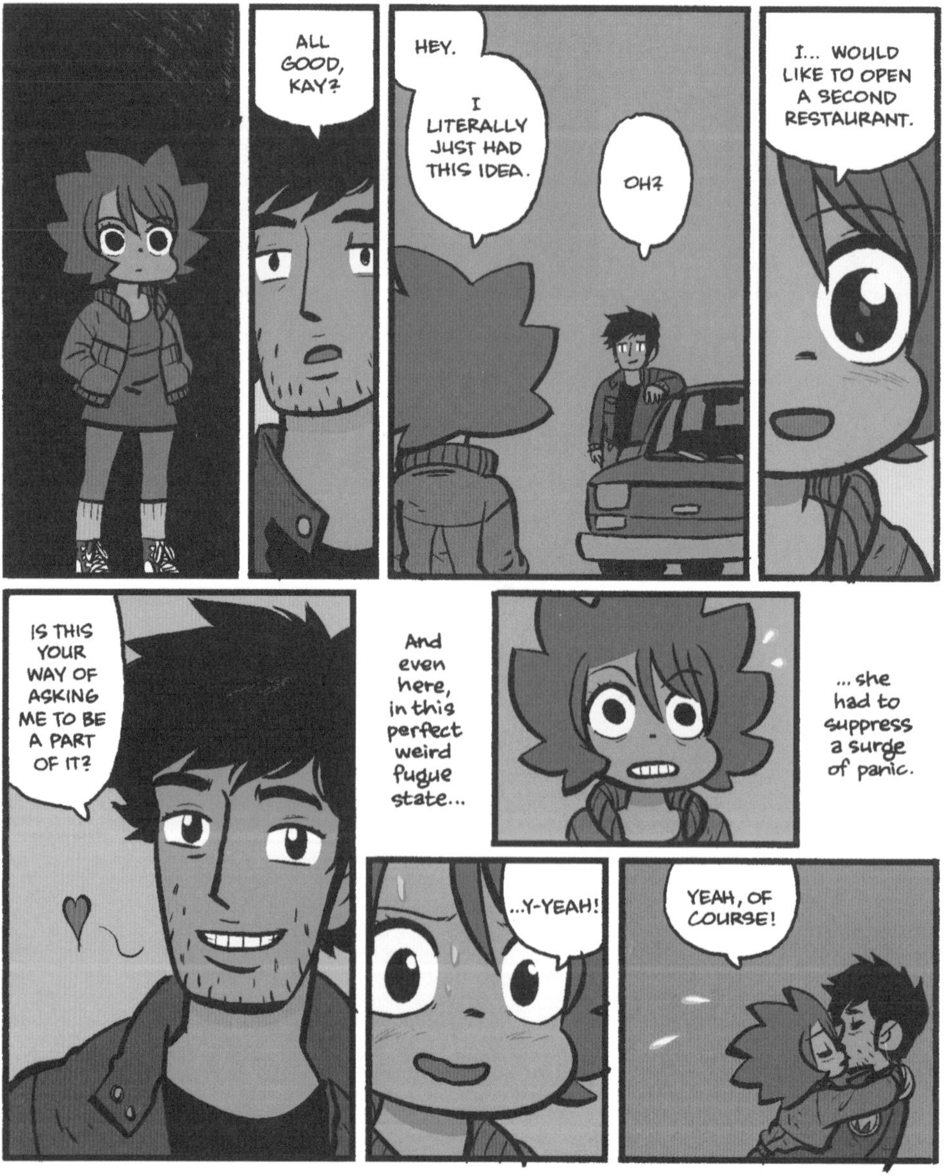
ALL GOOD, KAY?
HEY.
I LITERALLY JUST HAD THIS IDEA.
OH?
I... WOULD LIKE TO OPEN A SECOND RESTAURANT.
IS THIS YOUR WAY OF ASKING ME TO BE A PART OF IT?
And even here, in this perfect weird fugue state...
...she had to suppress a surge of panic.
...Y-YEAH!
YEAH, OF COURSE!

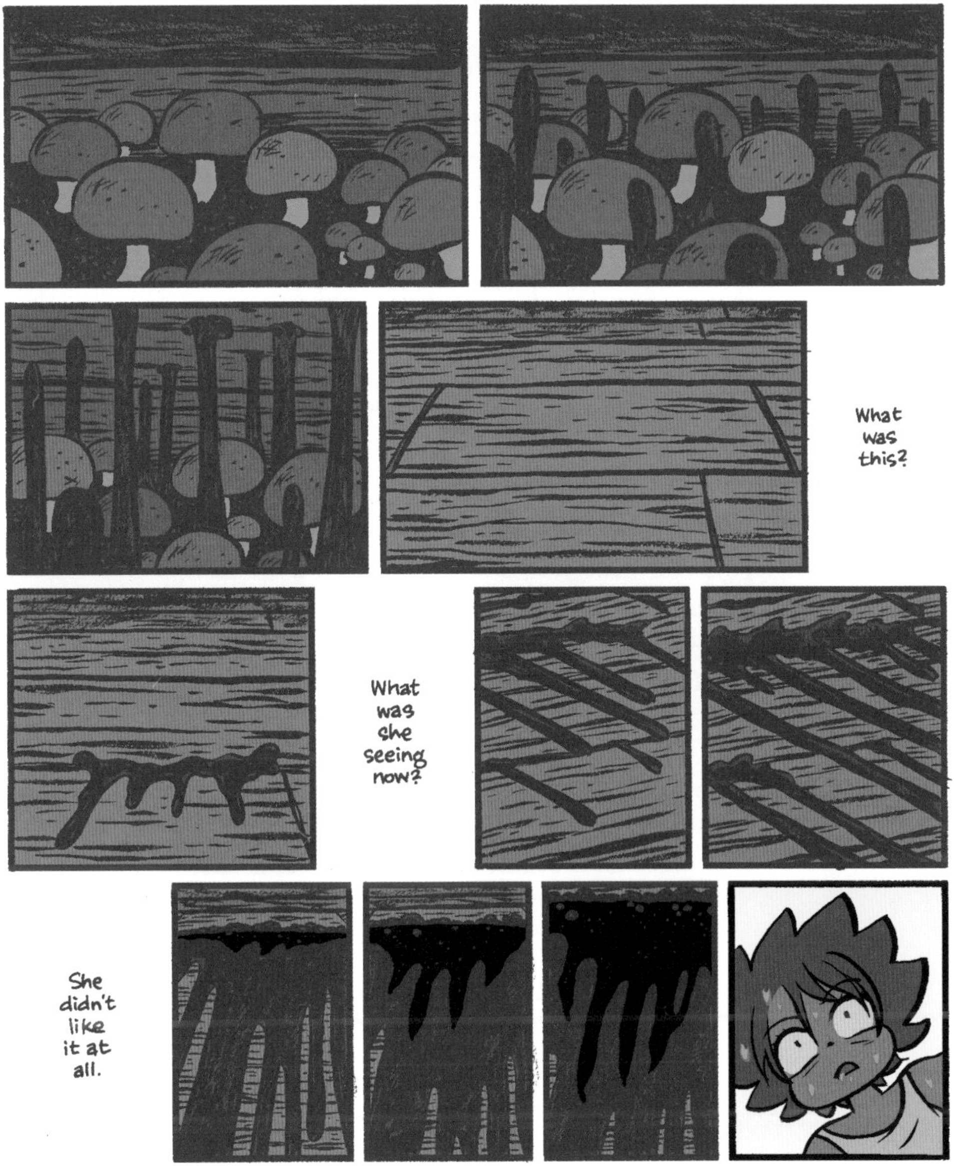
What was this?
What was she seeing now?
She didn't like it at all.

And when she woke up,

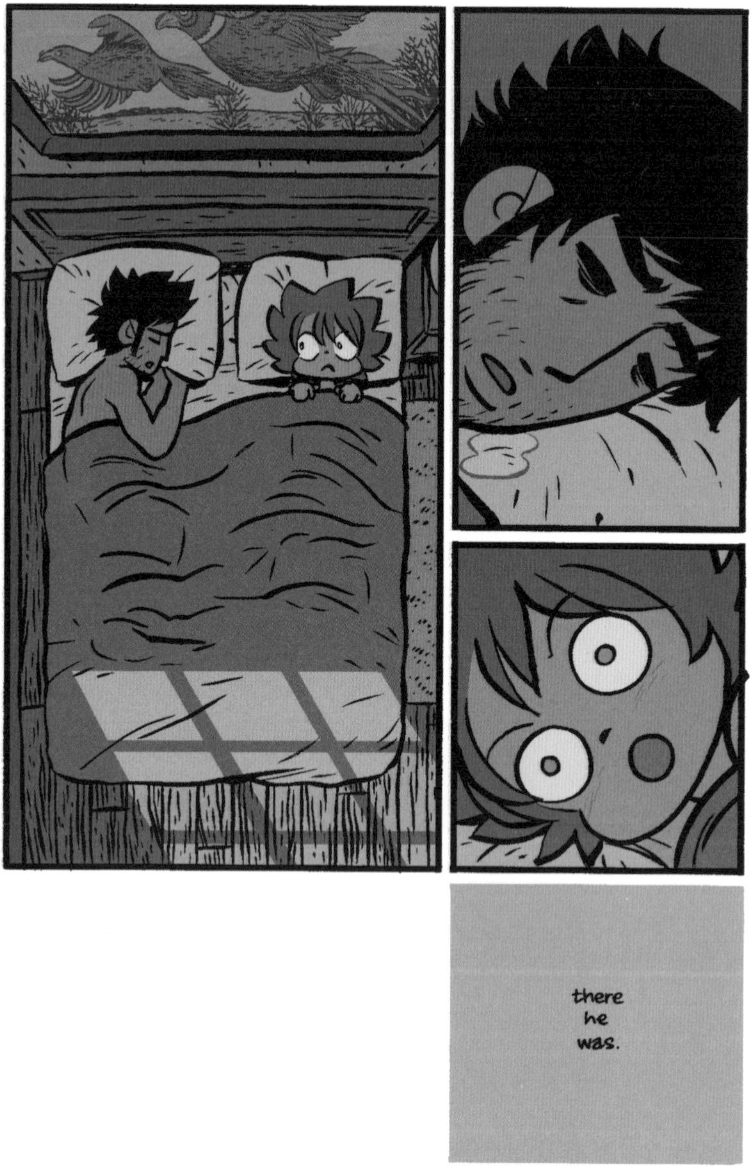
there he was.

5
Max

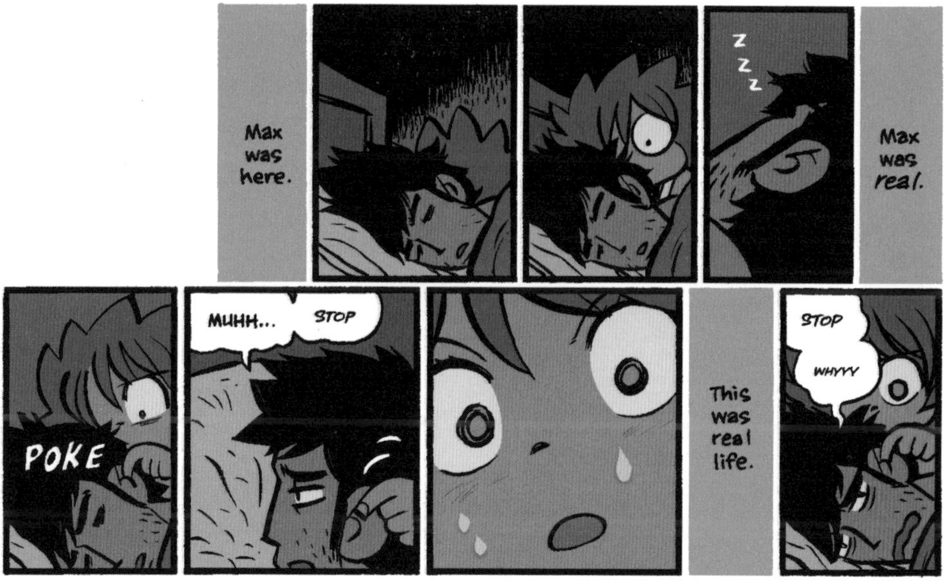

Max was here.
Z Z Z
Max was real.
POKE
MUHH...
STOP
This was real life.
STOP
WHYYY

KATIE

WHAT'S

YOUR

PROBLEM

She woke him up the rest of the way.

Afterward, he took a long shower in her tub.

(Which was weird.)

150

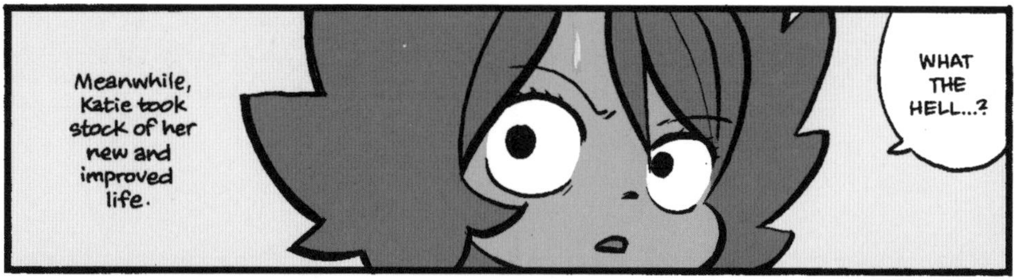
Meanwhile, Katie took stock of her new and improved life.
WHAT THE HELL...?

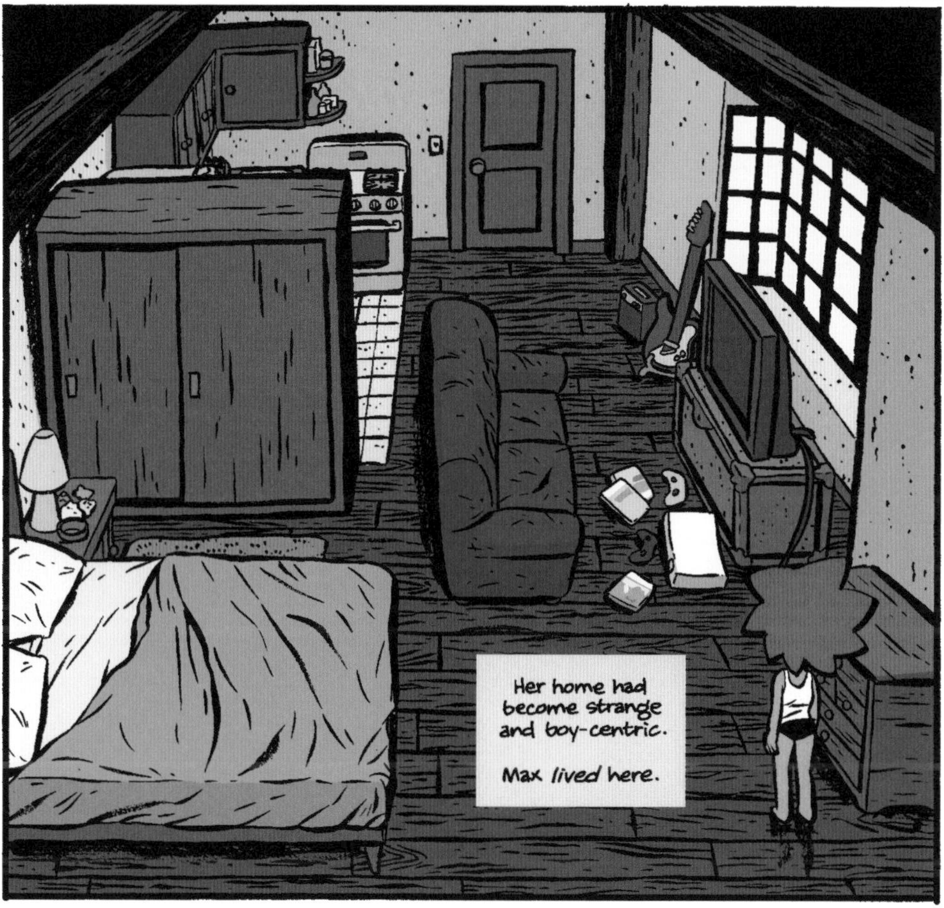
Her home had become strange and boy-centric.
Max lived here.

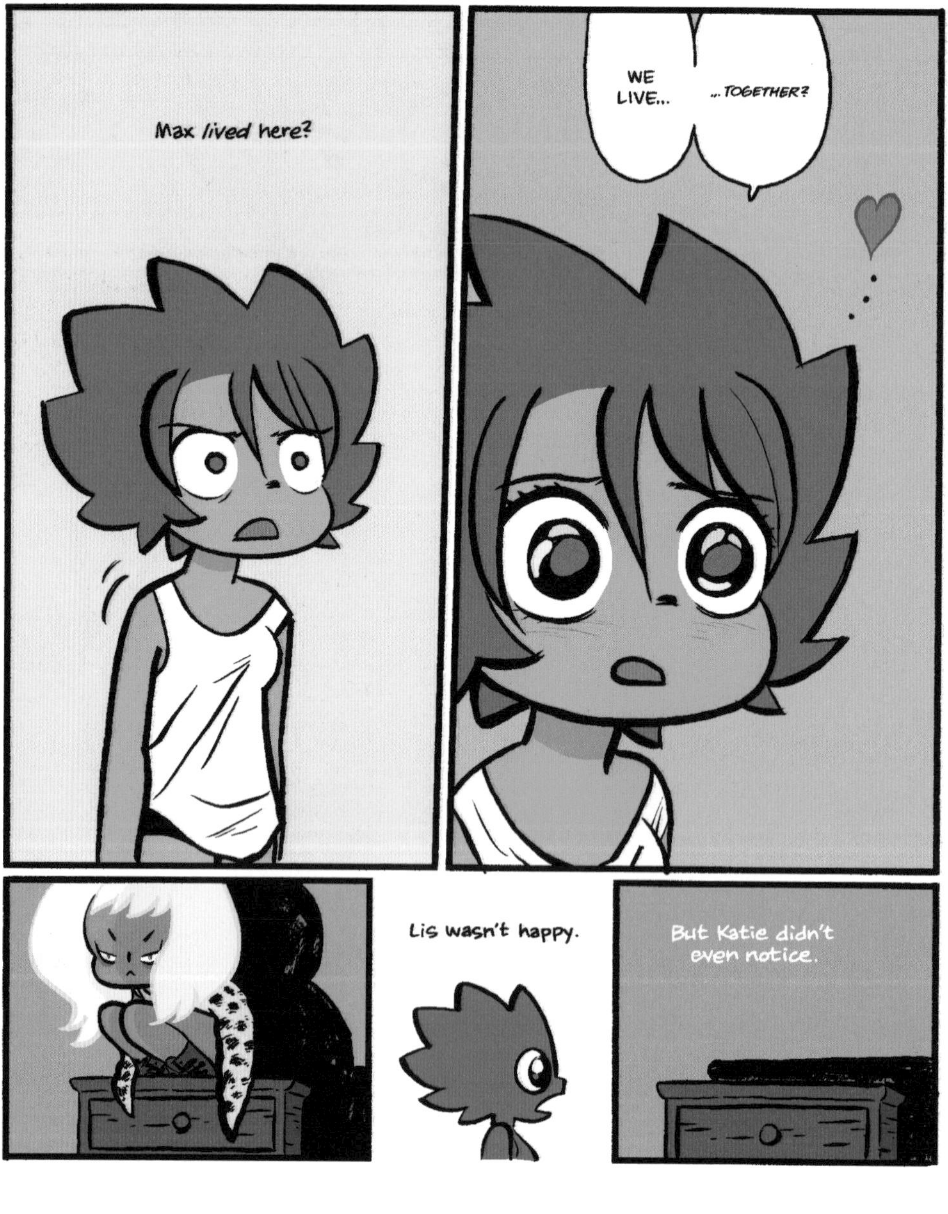
Max lived here?
WE LIVE...
...TOGETHER?
Lis wasn't happy.
But Katie didn't even notice.

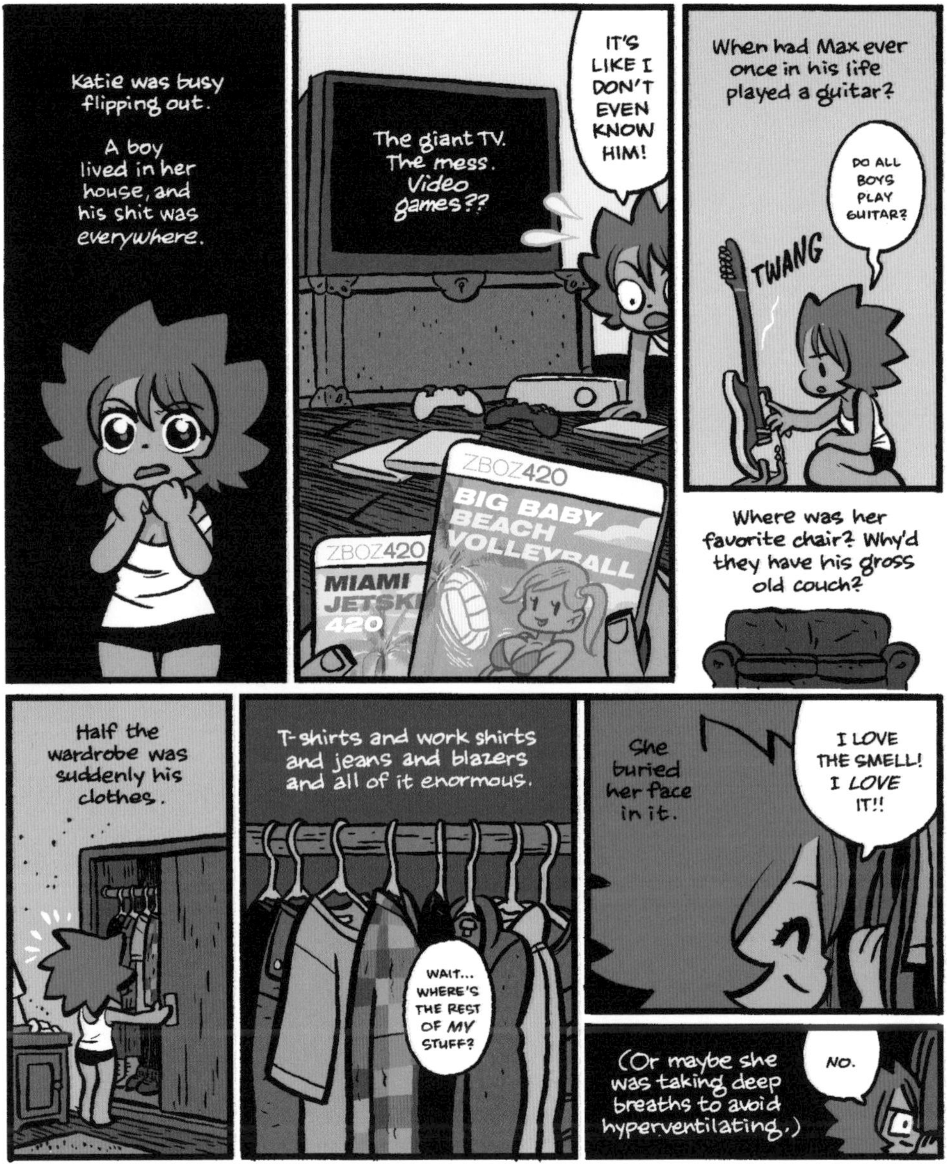
Katie was busy flipping out.
A boy lived in her house, and his shit was everywhere.
The giant TV. The mess. Video games??
IT'S LIKE I DON'T EVEN KNOW HIM!
ZBOZ420
BIG BABY BEACH VOLLEYBALL
ZBOZ420
MIAMI JETSKI 420
When had Max ever once in his life played a guitar?
DO ALL BOYS PLAY GUITAR?
TWANG
Where was her favorite chair? Why'd they have his gross old couch?
Half the wardrobe was suddenly his clothes.
T-shirts and work shirts and jeans and blazers and all of it enormous.
WAIT... WHERE'S THE REST OF MY STUFF?
She buried her face in it.
I LOVE THE SMELL! I LOVE IT!!
(Or maybe she was taking deep breaths to avoid hyperventilating.)
NO.

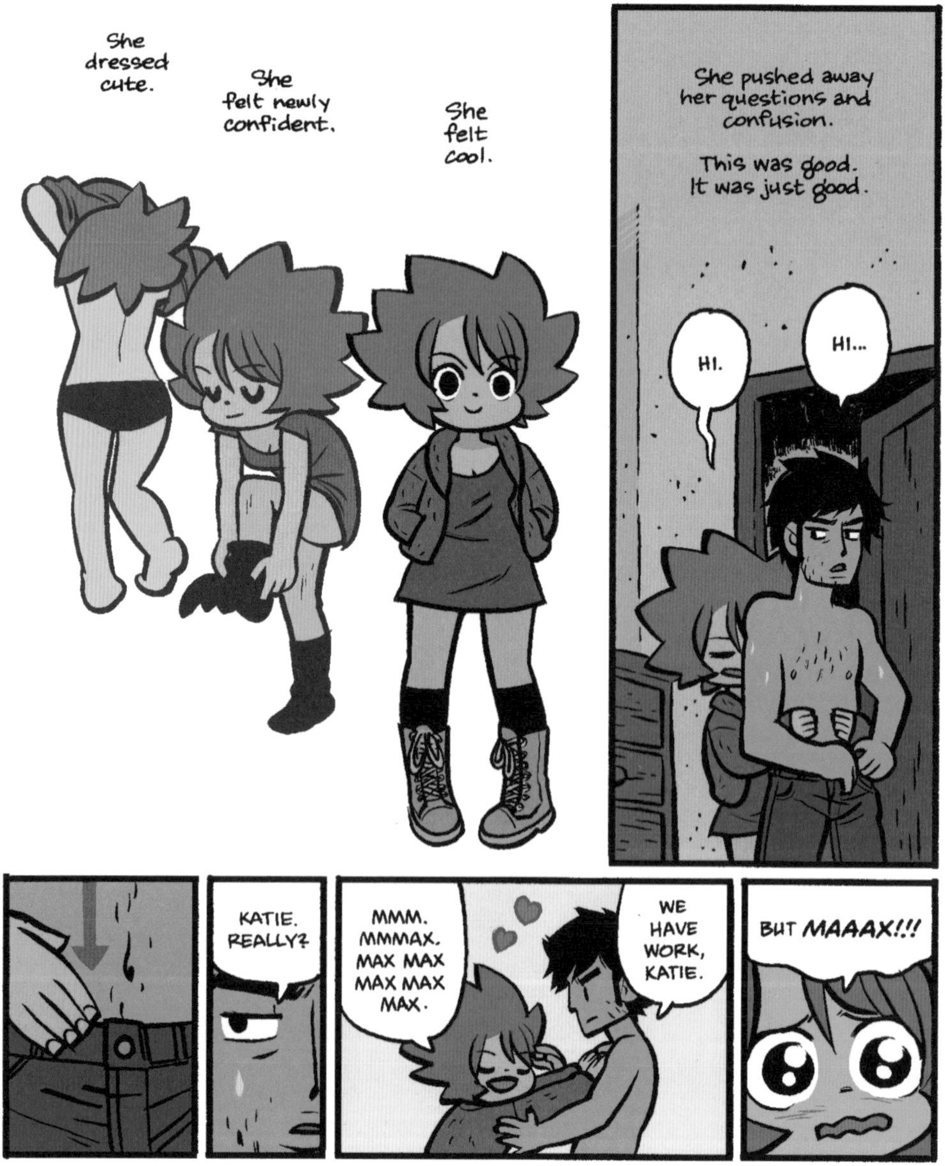
She dressed cute.
She felt newly confident.
She felt cool.
She pushed away her questions and confusion.
This was good. It was just good.
HI.
HI...
KATIE. REALLY?
MMM. MMMAX. MAX MAX MAX MAX MAX.
WE HAVE WORK, KATIE.
BUT MAAAX!!!

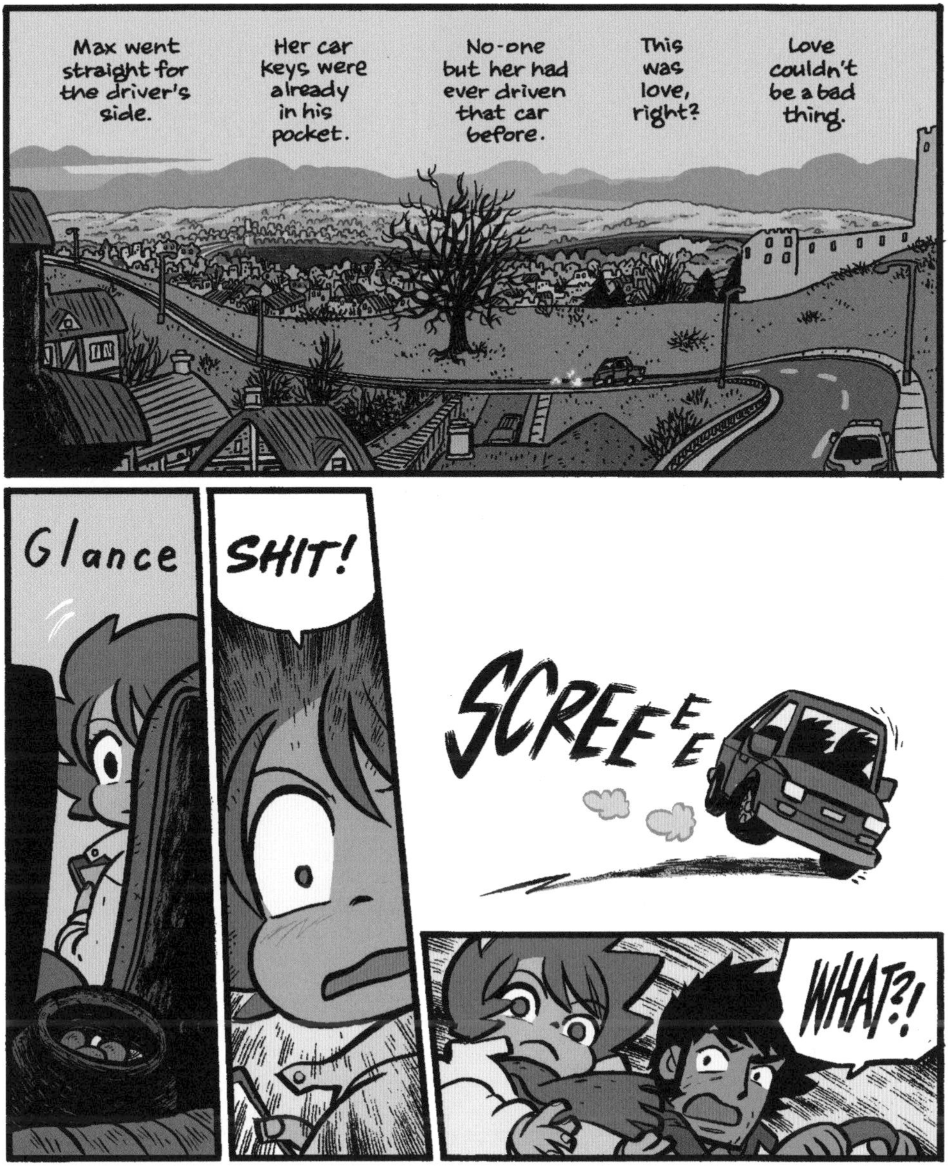

Max went straight for the driver's side.
Her car keys were already in his pocket.
No-one but her had ever driven that car before.
This was love, right?
Love couldn't be a bad thing.
Glance
SHIT!
SCREEEE
WHAT?!

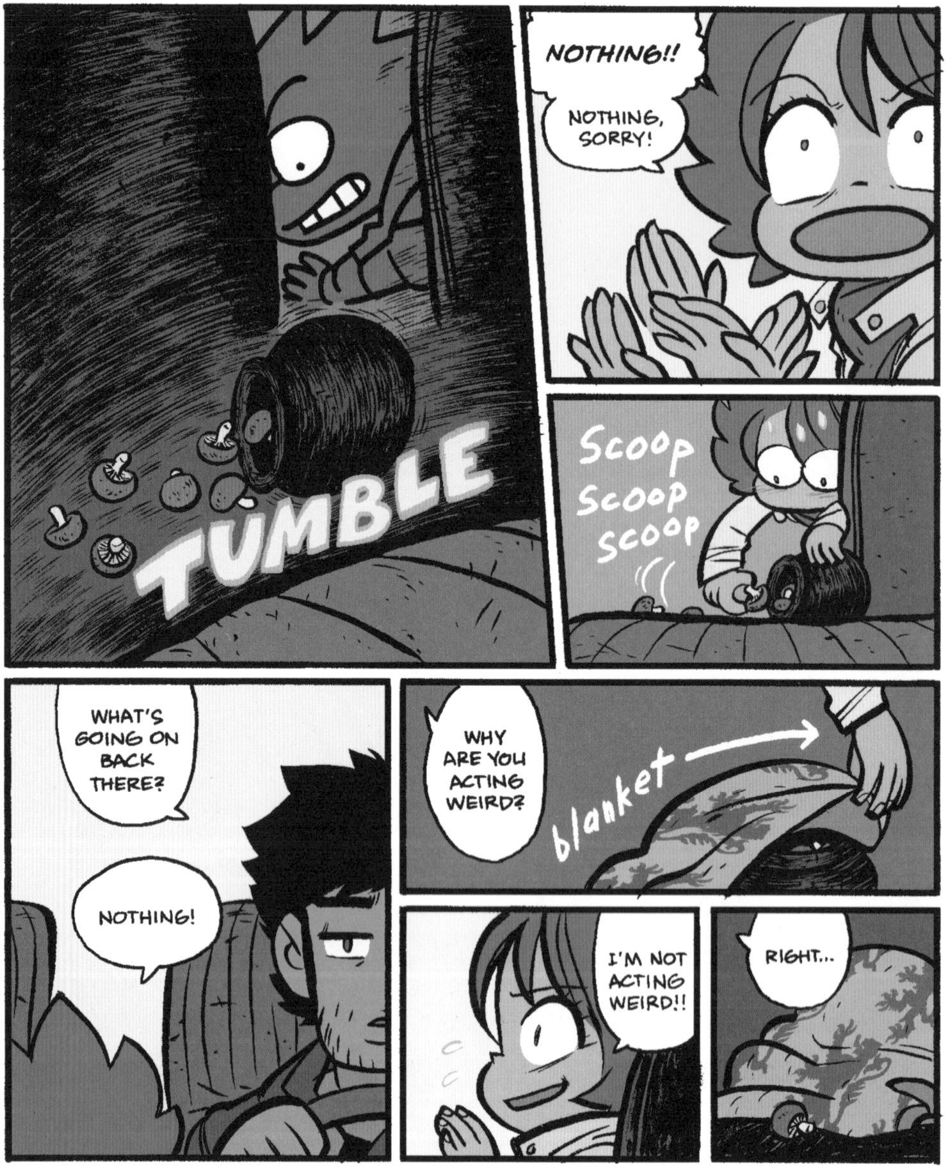
NOTHING!!
NOTHING, SORRY!
TUMBLE
Scoop
Scoop
scoop
WHAT'S GOING ON BACK THERE?
NOTHING!
WHY ARE YOU ACTING WEIRD?
blanket
I'M NOT ACTING WEIRD!!
RIGHT...

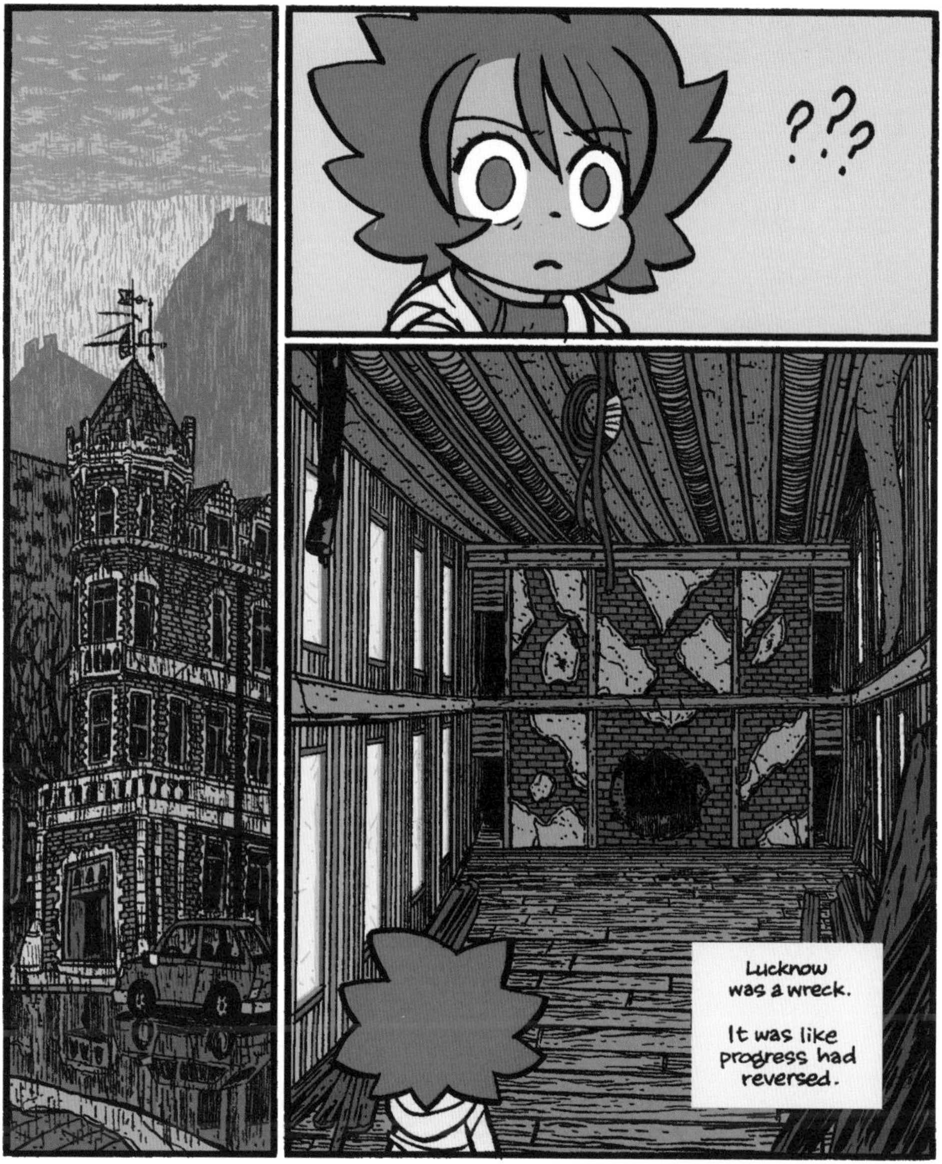
???
Lucknow was a wreck.
It was like progress had reversed.

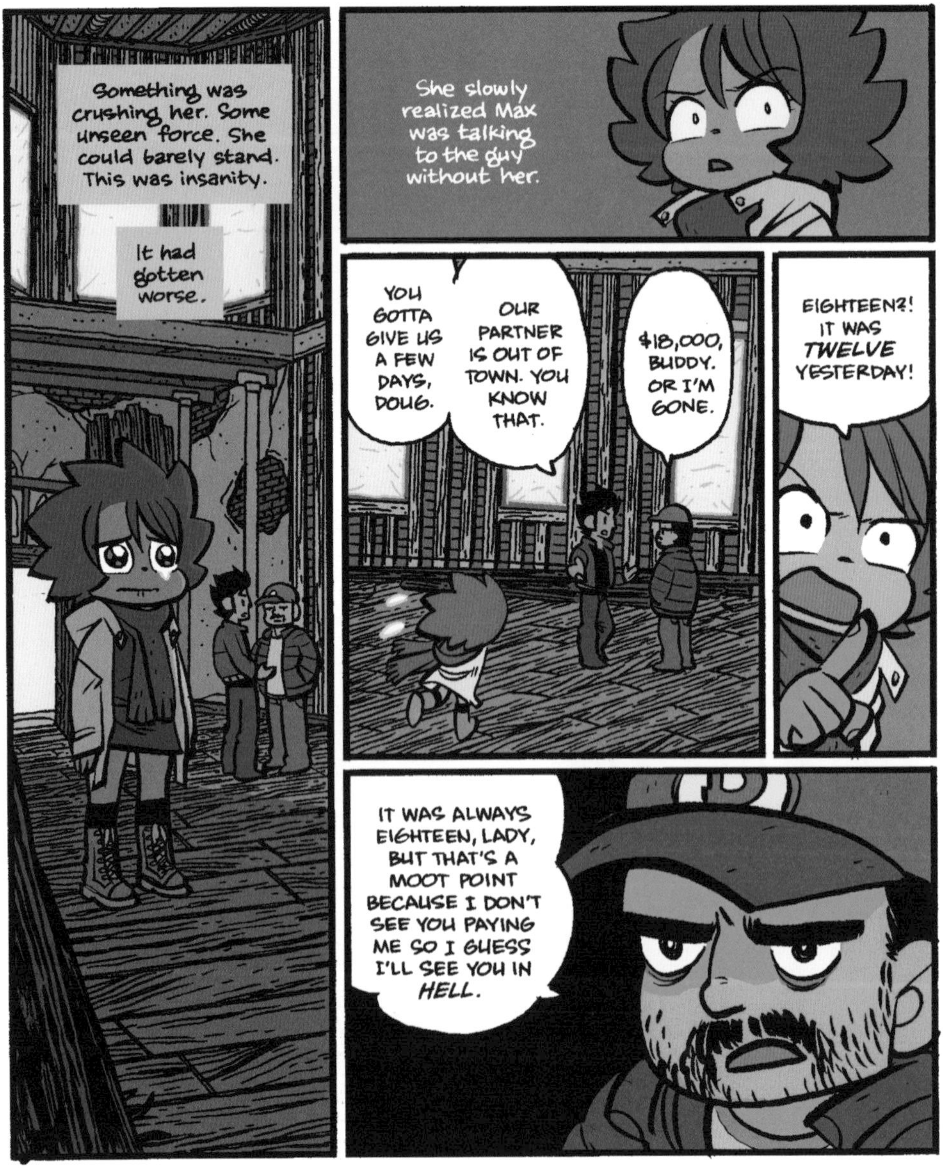
Something was crushing her. Some unseen force. She could barely stand. This was insanity.
It had gotten worse.
She slowly realized Max was talking to the guy without her.
YOU GOTTA GIVE US A FEW DAYS, DOUG.
OUR PARTNER IS OUT OF TOWN. YOU KNOW THAT.
$18,000, BUDDY. OR I'M GONE.
EIGHTEEN?! IT WAS TWELVE YESTERDAY!
IT WAS ALWAYS EIGHTEEN, LADY, BUT THAT'S A MOOT POINT BECAUSE I DON'T SEE YOU PAYING ME SO I GUESS I'LL SEE YOU IN HELL.

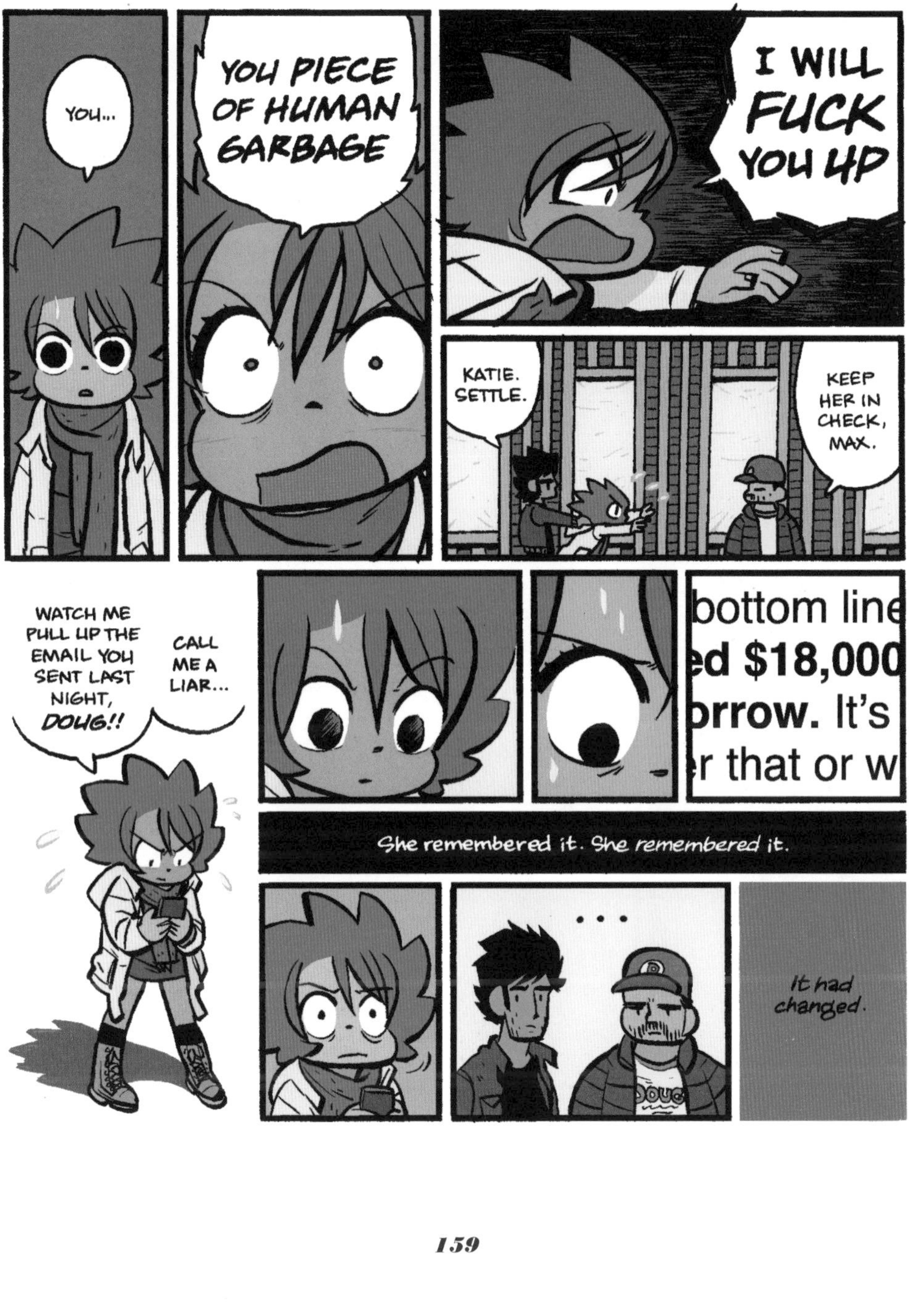
YOU...
YOU PIECE OF HUMAN GARBAGE
I WILL FUCK YOU UP
KATIE. SETTLE.
KEEP HER IN CHECK, MAX.
WATCH ME PULL UP THE EMAIL YOU SENT LAST NIGHT, DOUG!!
CALL ME A LIAR...
bottom line
ed $18,000
orrow. It's
r that or w
She remembered it. She remembered it.
...
It had changed.

What else had changed?

What was happening to her?

IF YOU GET THE FUNDS, GIVE ME A CALL.

YOU AND YOUR WIFE HAVE A NICE DAY.

WIFE?! EXCUSE ME, YOU SEXIST DICK--

WE'RE MARRIED NOW?!

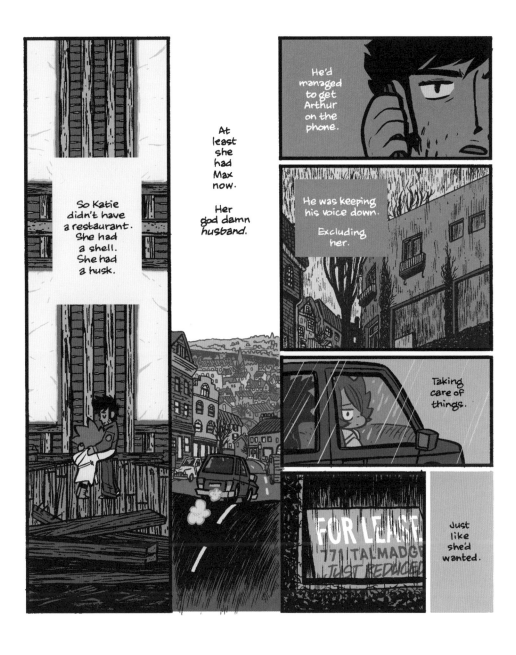

So Katie didn't have a restaurant. She had a shell. She had a husk.

At least she had Max now.

Her god damn husband.

He'd managed to get Arthur on the phone.

He was keeping his voice down.

Excluding her.

Taking care of things.

Just like she'd wanted.

FOR LEASE
771 TALMADGE
JUST REDUCED

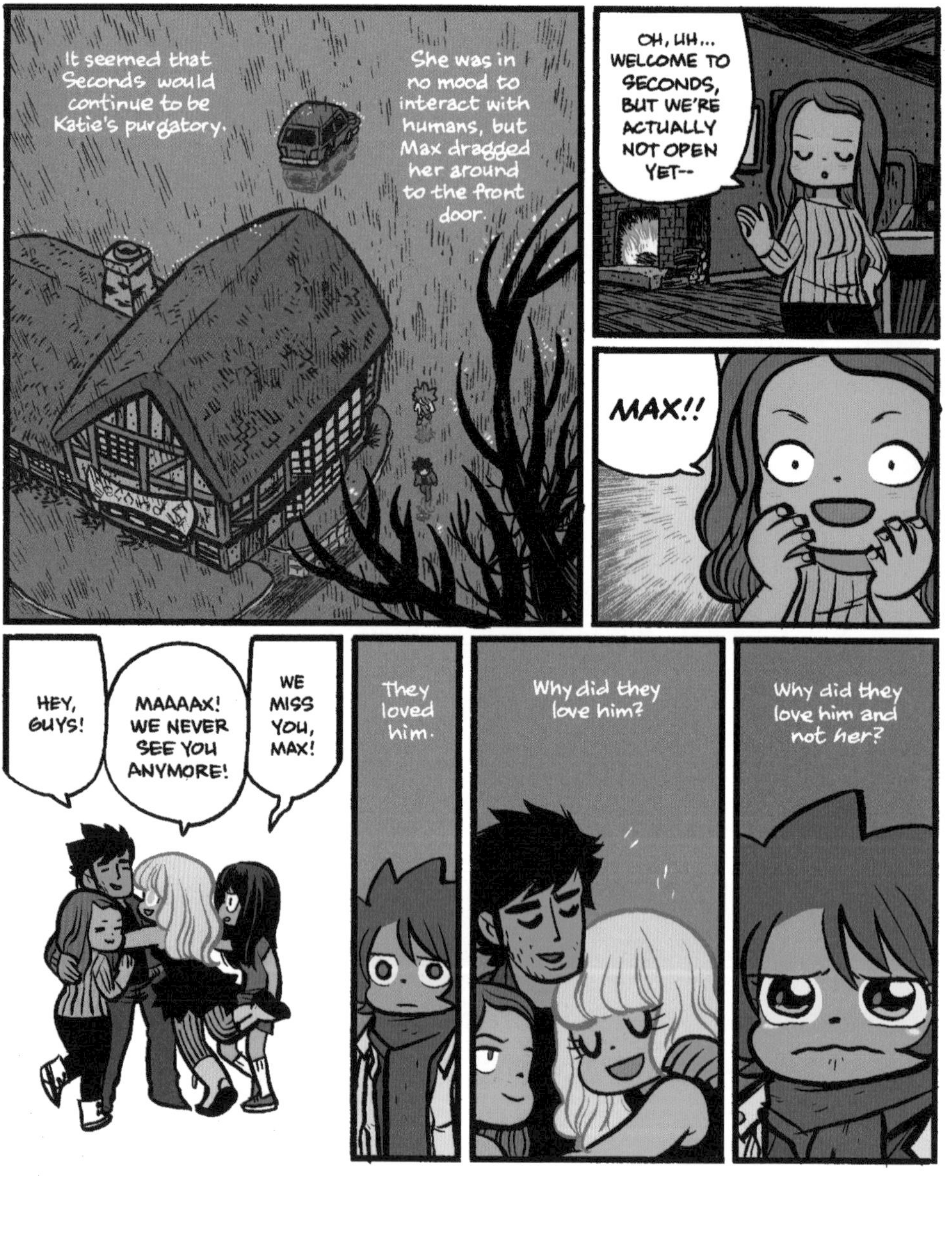
It seemed that Seconds would continue to be Katie's purgatory.
She was in no mood to interact with humans, but Max dragged her around to the front door.
OH, UH... WELCOME TO SECONDS, BUT WE'RE ACTUALLY NOT OPEN YET--
MAX!!
HEY, GUYS!
MAAAAX! WE NEVER SEE YOU ANYMORE!
WE MISS YOU, MAX!
They loved him.
Why did they love him?
Why did they love him and not *her*?

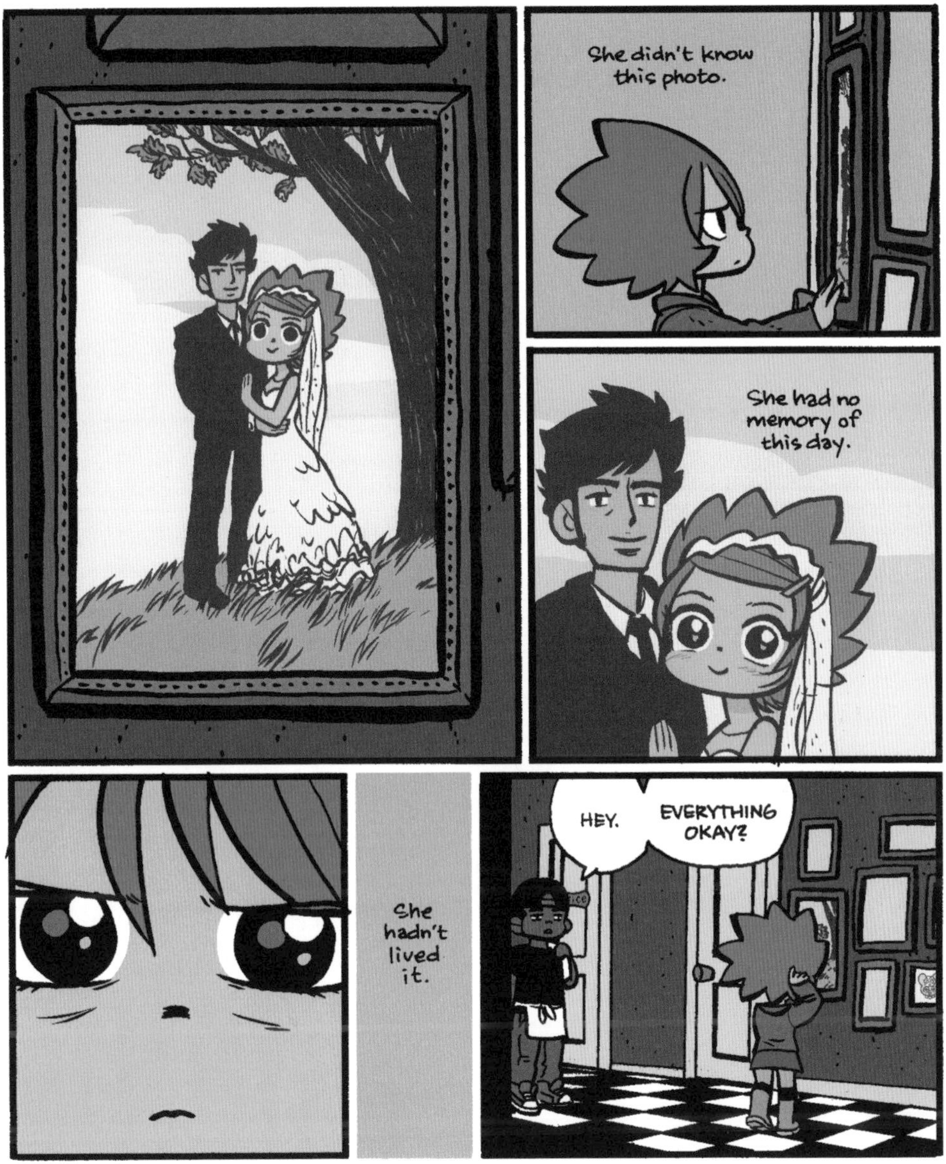
She didn't know this photo.
She had no memory of this day.
She hadn't lived it.
HEY.
EVERYTHING OKAY?

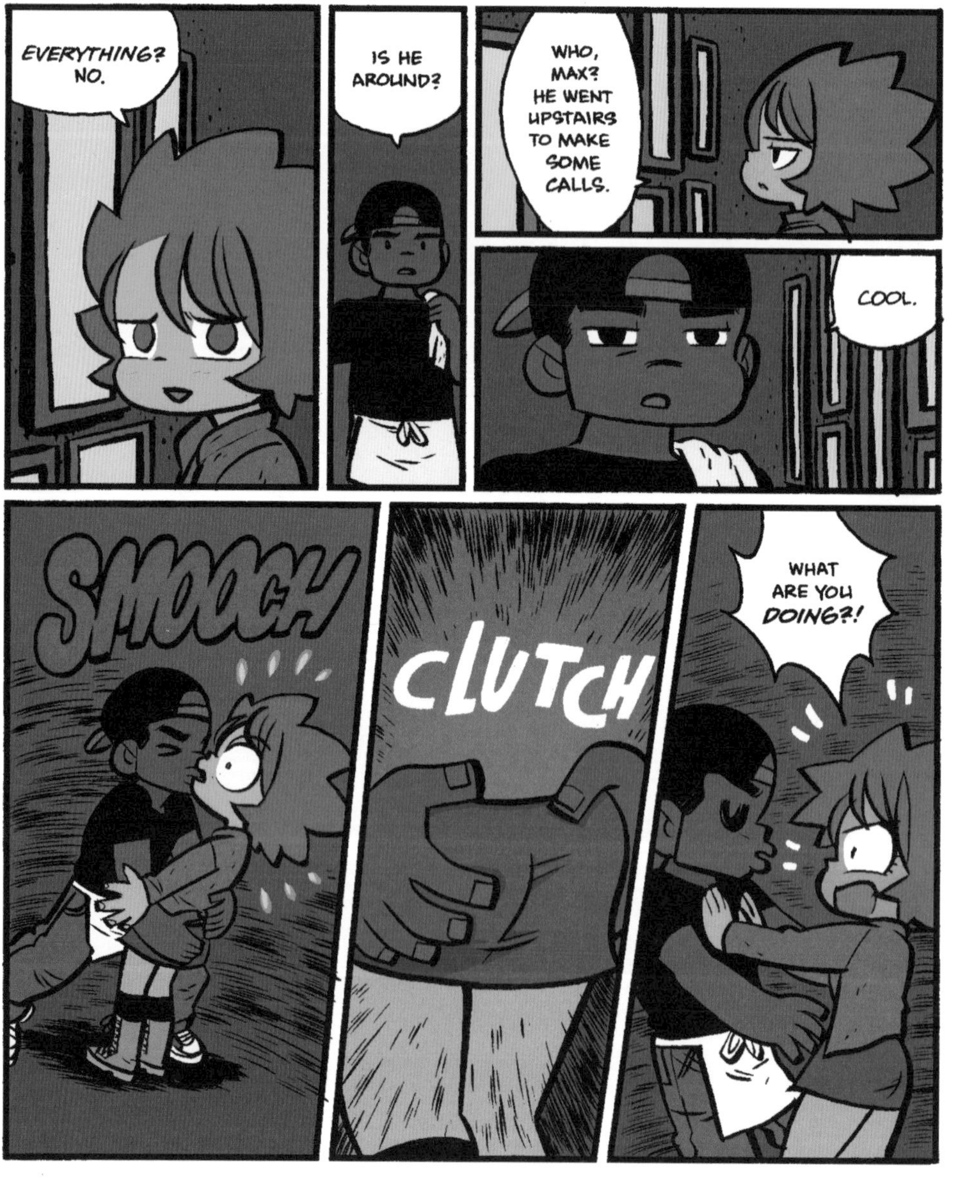
EVERYTHING? NO.
IS HE AROUND?
WHO, MAX? HE WENT UPSTAIRS TO MAKE SOME CALLS.
COOL.
SMOOCH
CLUTCH
WHAT ARE YOU *DOING?!*

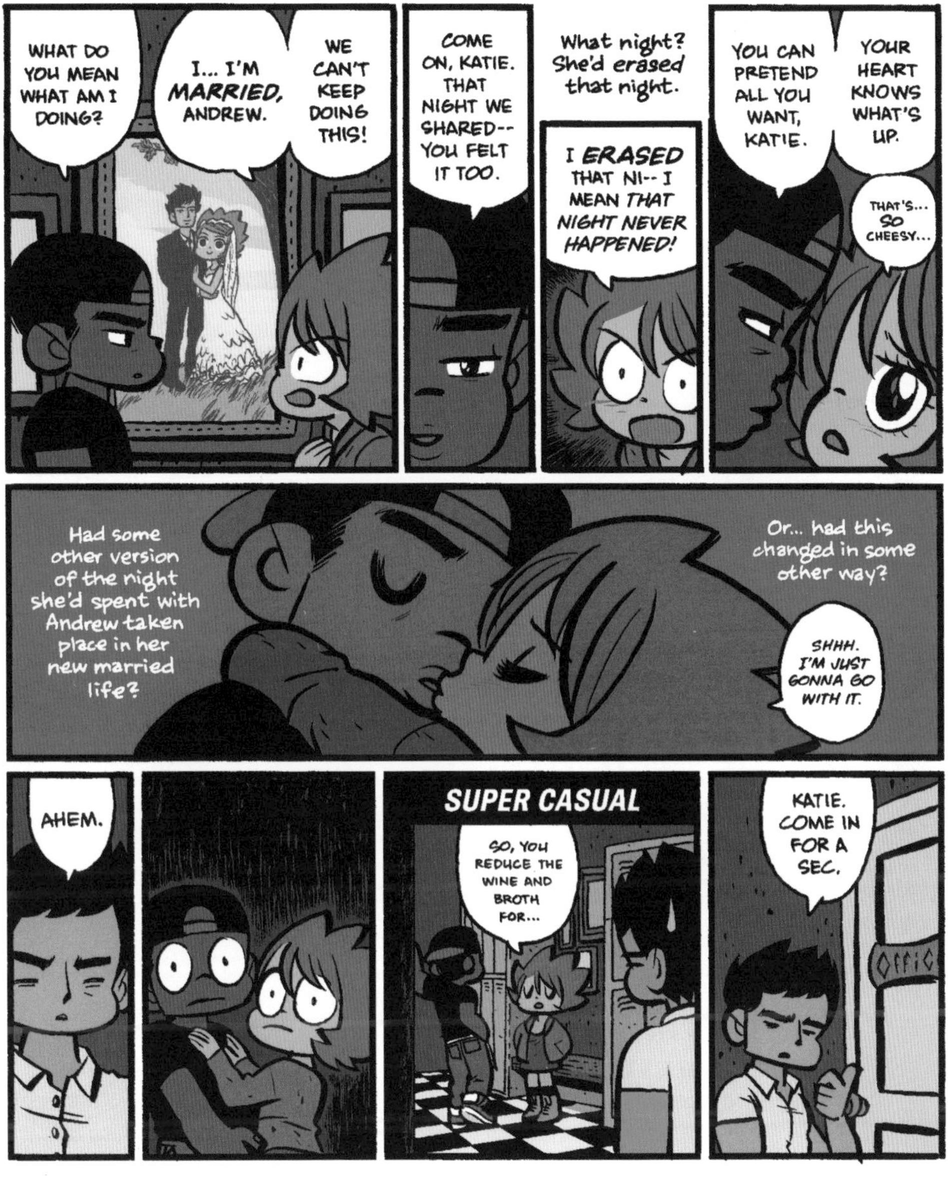
WHAT DO YOU MEAN WHAT AM I DOING?
I... I'M MARRIED, ANDREW.
WE CAN'T KEEP DOING THIS!
COME ON, KATIE. THAT NIGHT WE SHARED-- YOU FELT IT TOO.
What night? She'd erased that night.
I ERASED THAT NI-- I MEAN THAT NIGHT NEVER HAPPENED!
YOU CAN PRETEND ALL YOU WANT, KATIE.
YOUR HEART KNOWS WHAT'S UP.
THAT'S... SO CHEESY...
Had some other version of the night she'd spent with Andrew taken place in her new married life?
Or... had this changed in some other way?
SHHH. I'M JUST GONNA GO WITH IT.
AHEM.
SUPER CASUAL
SO, YOU REDUCE THE WINE AND BROTH FOR...
KATIE. COME IN FOR A SEC.
OFFIC

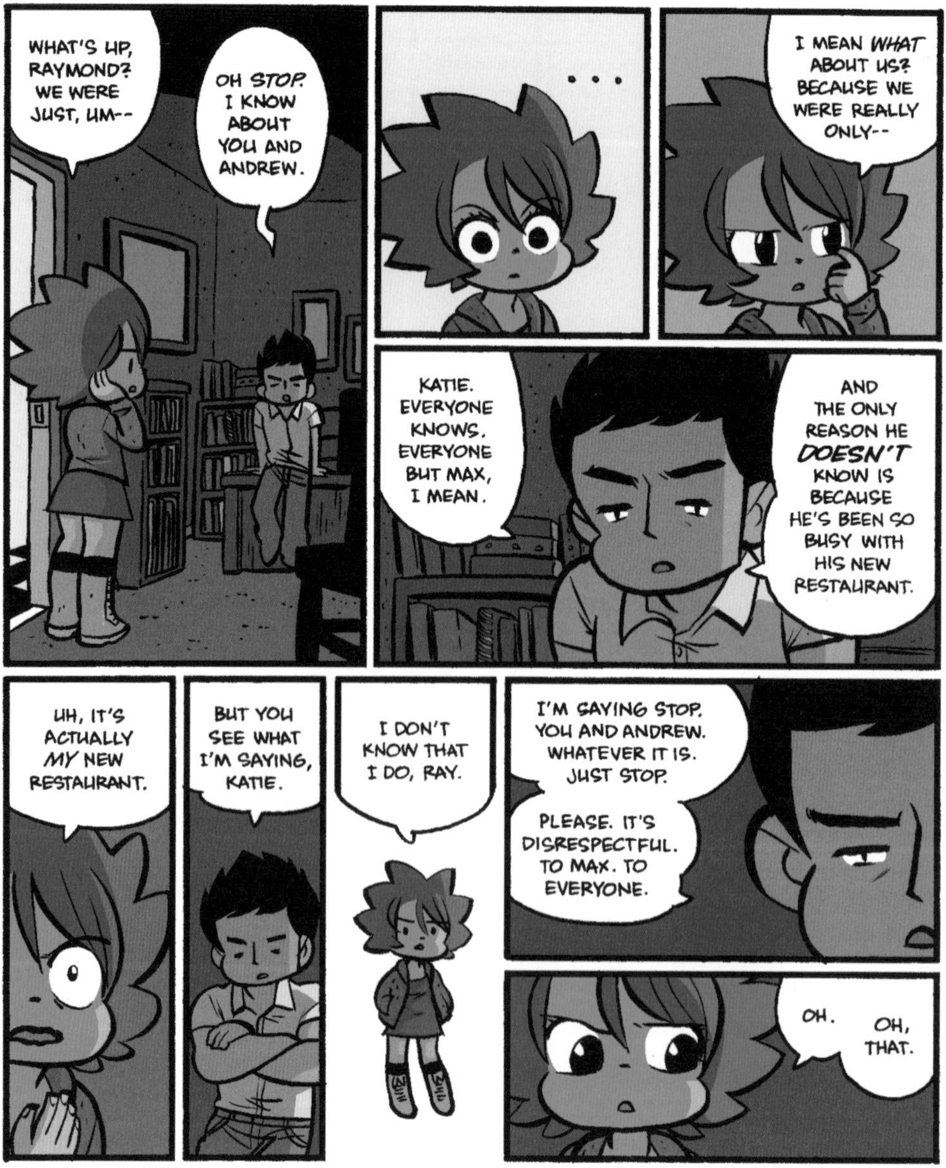
WHAT'S UP, RAYMOND? WE WERE JUST, UM--
OH STOP. I KNOW ABOUT YOU AND ANDREW.
...
I MEAN WHAT ABOUT US? BECAUSE WE WERE REALLY ONLY--
KATIE. EVERYONE KNOWS. EVERYONE BUT MAX, I MEAN.
AND THE ONLY REASON HE DOESN'T KNOW IS BECAUSE HE'S BEEN SO BUSY WITH HIS NEW RESTAURANT.
UH, IT'S ACTUALLY MY NEW RESTAURANT.
BUT YOU SEE WHAT I'M SAYING, KATIE.
I DON'T KNOW THAT I DO, RAY.
I'M SAYING STOP. YOU AND ANDREW. WHATEVER IT IS. JUST STOP.
PLEASE. IT'S DISRESPECTFUL. TO MAX. TO EVERYONE.
OH.
OH, THAT.

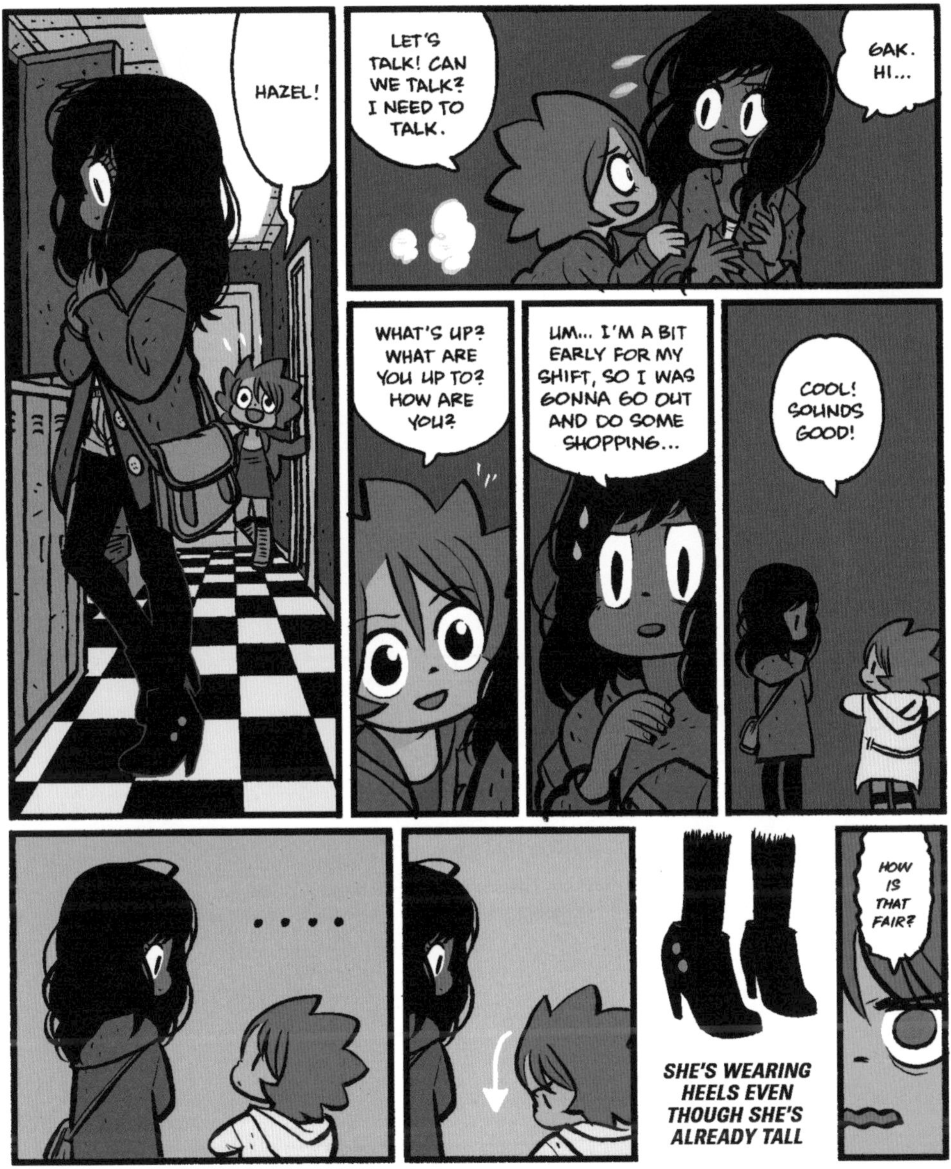
HAZEL!
LET'S TALK! CAN WE TALK? I NEED TO TALK.
GAK. HI...
WHAT'S UP? WHAT ARE YOU UP TO? HOW ARE YOU?
UM... I'M A BIT EARLY FOR MY SHIFT, SO I WAS GONNA GO OUT AND DO SOME SHOPPING...
COOL! SOUNDS GOOD!
....
SHE'S WEARING HEELS EVEN THOUGH SHE'S ALREADY TALL
HOW IS THAT FAIR?

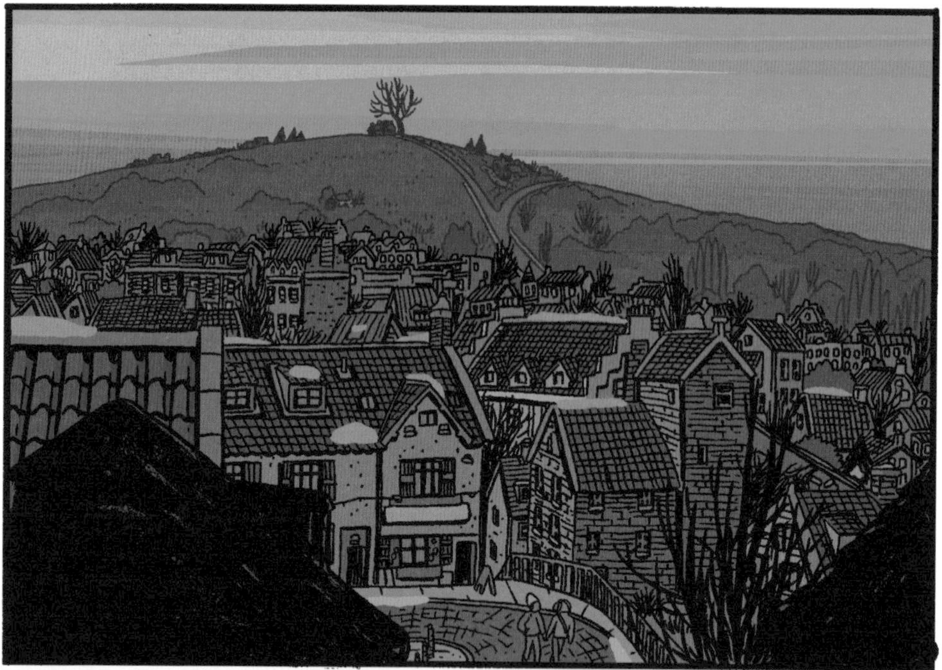

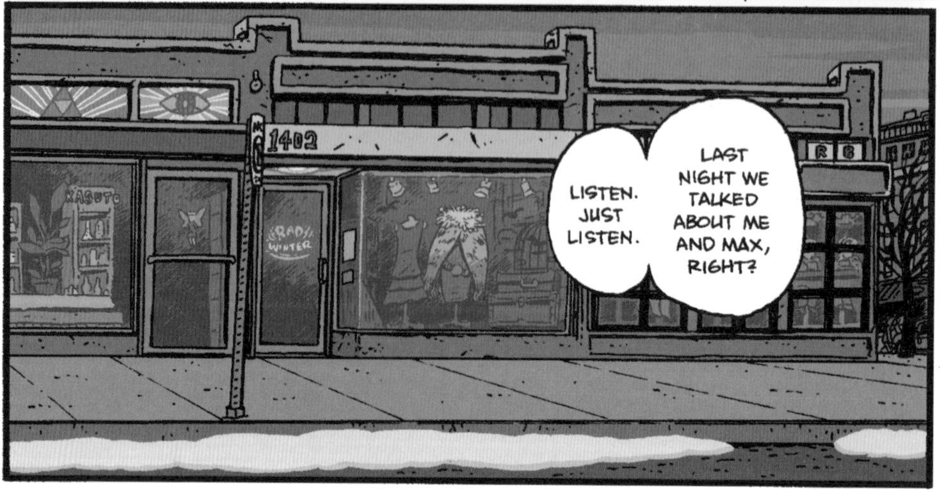
1402
LISTEN. JUST LISTEN.
LAST NIGHT WE TALKED ABOUT ME AND MAX, RIGHT?

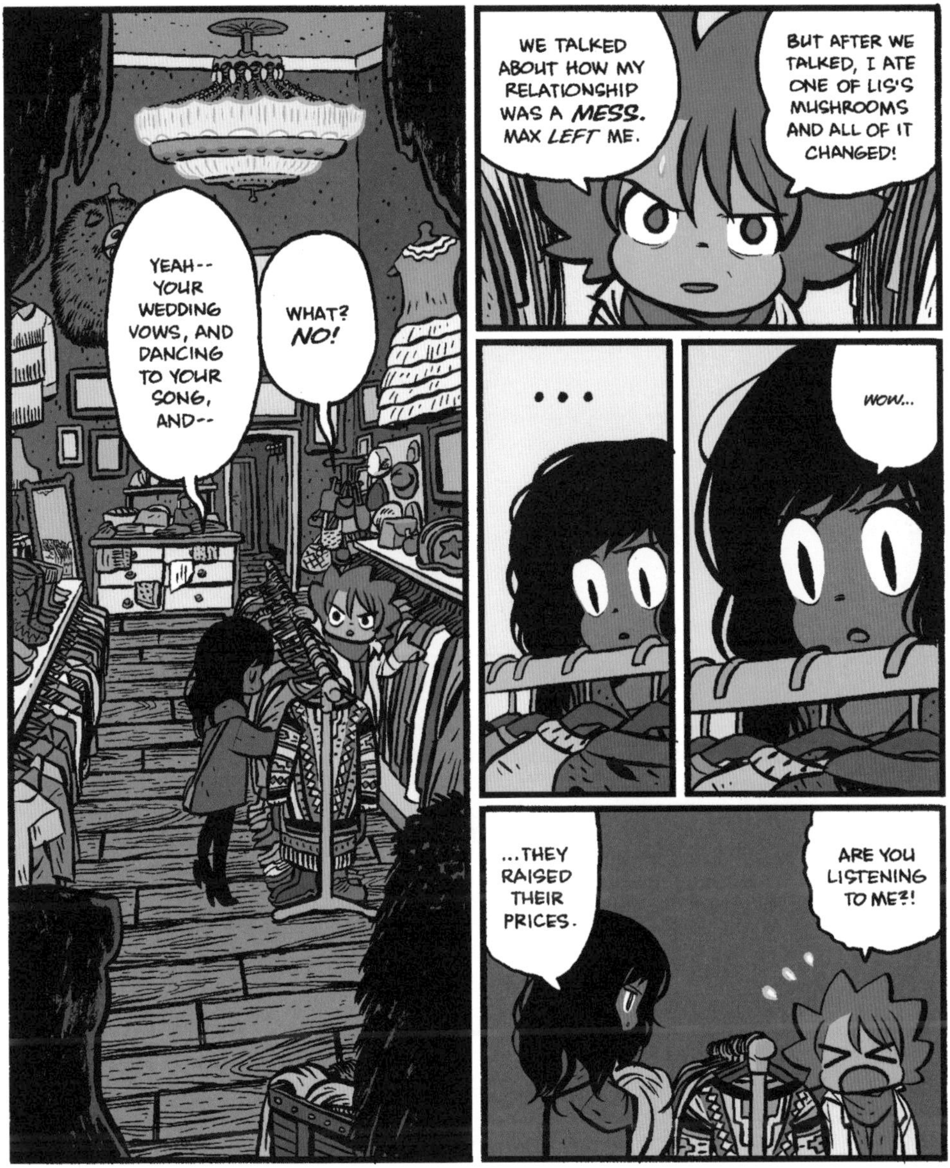
YEAH-- YOUR WEDDING VOWS, AND DANCING TO YOUR SONG, AND--
WHAT? NO!
WE TALKED ABOUT HOW MY RELATIONSHIP WAS A MESS. MAX LEFT ME.
BUT AFTER WE TALKED, I ATE ONE OF LIS'S MUSHROOMS AND ALL OF IT CHANGED!
...
WOW...
...THEY RAISED THEIR PRICES.
ARE YOU LISTENING TO ME?!

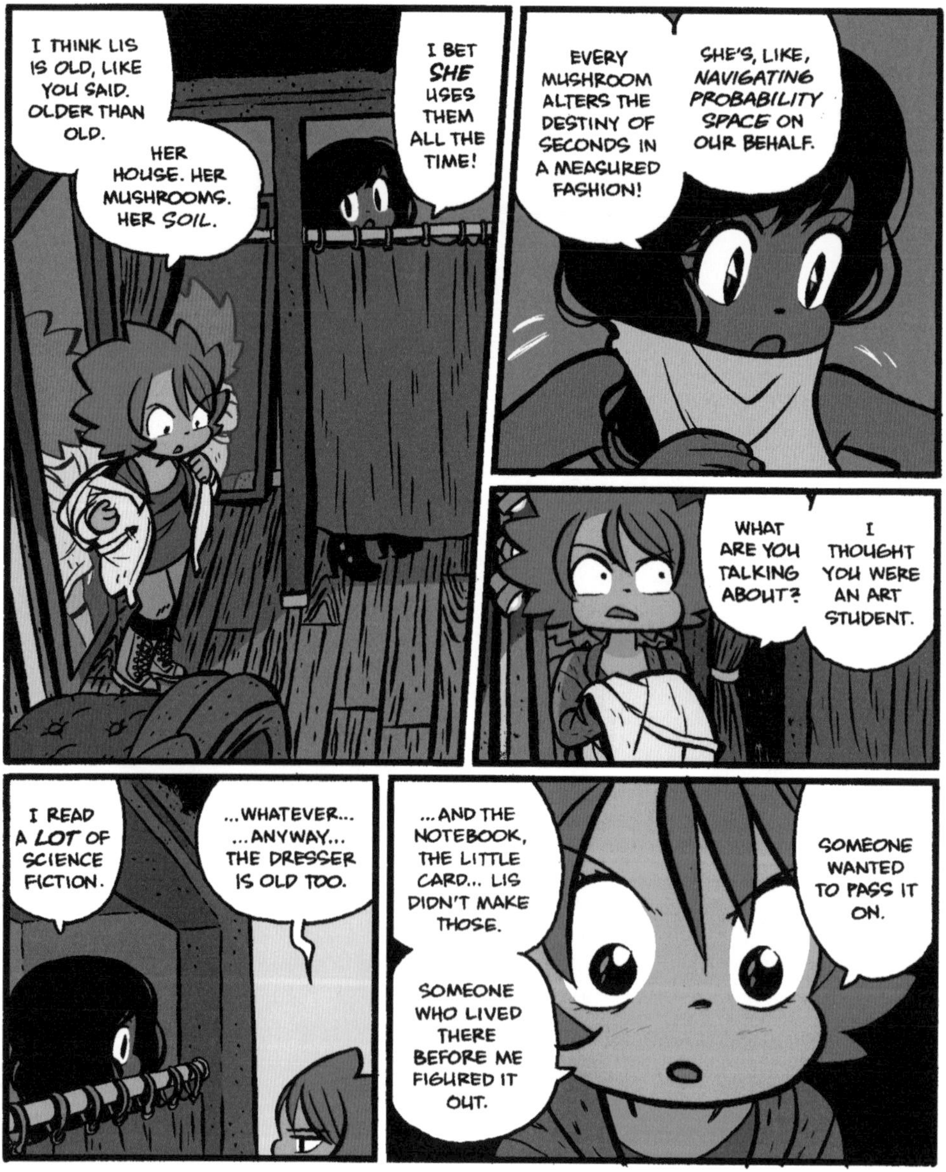
I THINK LIS IS OLD, LIKE YOU SAID. OLDER THAN OLD.
HER HOUSE. HER MUSHROOMS. HER SOIL.
I BET SHE USES THEM ALL THE TIME!
EVERY MUSHROOM ALTERS THE DESTINY OF SECONDS IN A MEASURED FASHION!
SHE'S, LIKE, NAVIGATING PROBABILITY SPACE ON OUR BEHALF.
WHAT ARE YOU TALKING ABOUT?
I THOUGHT YOU WERE AN ART STUDENT.
I READ A LOT OF SCIENCE FICTION.
...WHATEVER... ...ANYWAY... THE DRESSER IS OLD TOO.
...AND THE NOTEBOOK, THE LITTLE CARD... LIS DIDN'T MAKE THOSE.
SOMEONE WHO LIVED THERE BEFORE ME FIGURED IT OUT.
SOMEONE WANTED TO PASS IT ON.

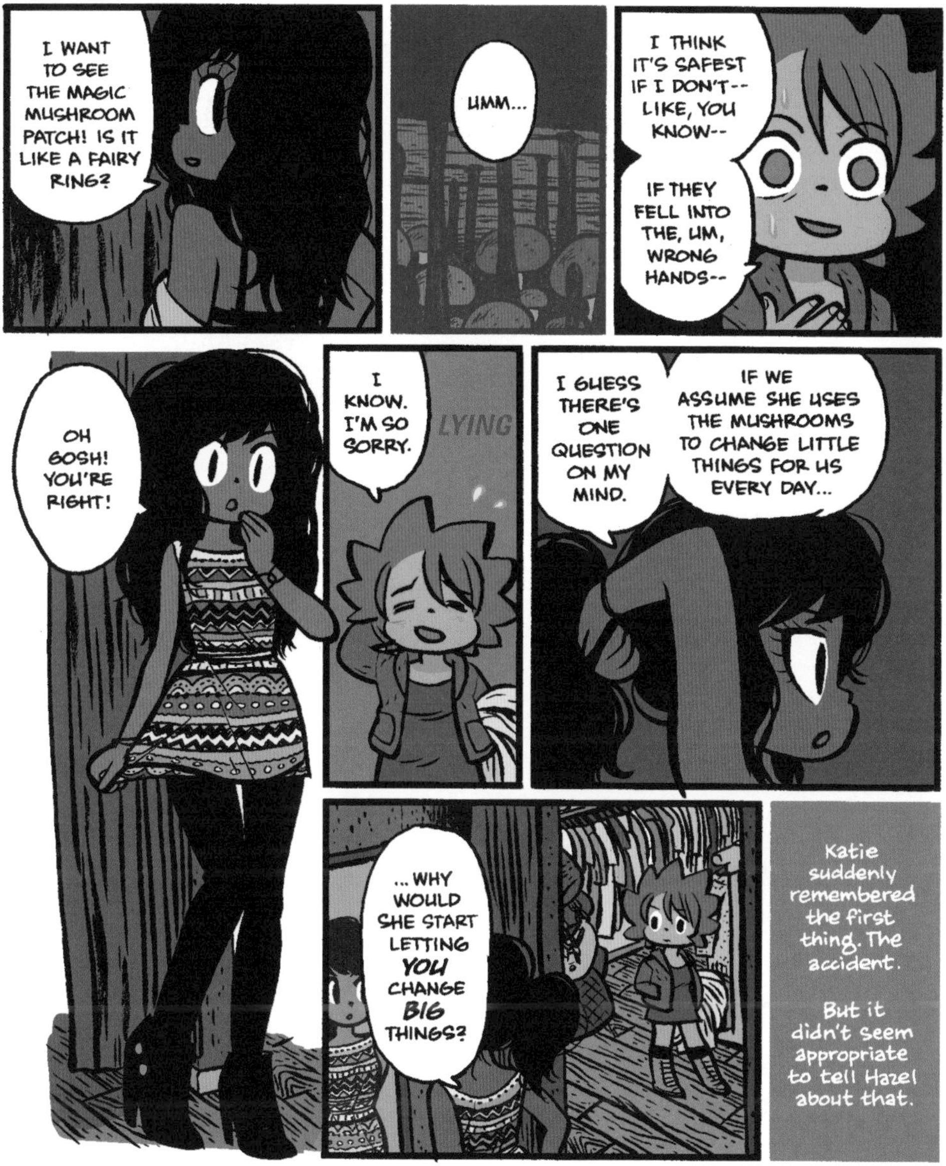
I WANT TO SEE THE MAGIC MUSHROOM PATCH! IS IT LIKE A FAIRY RING?
UMM...
I THINK IT'S SAFEST IF I DON'T-- LIKE, YOU KNOW--
IF THEY FELL INTO THE, UM, WRONG HANDS--
OH GOSH! YOU'RE RIGHT!
I KNOW. I'M SO SORRY.
LYING
I GUESS THERE'S ONE QUESTION ON MY MIND.
IF WE ASSUME SHE USES THE MUSHROOMS TO CHANGE LITTLE THINGS FOR US EVERY DAY...
...WHY WOULD SHE START LETTING *YOU* CHANGE *BIG* THINGS?
Katie suddenly remembered the first thing. The accident.
But it didn't seem appropriate to tell Hazel about that.

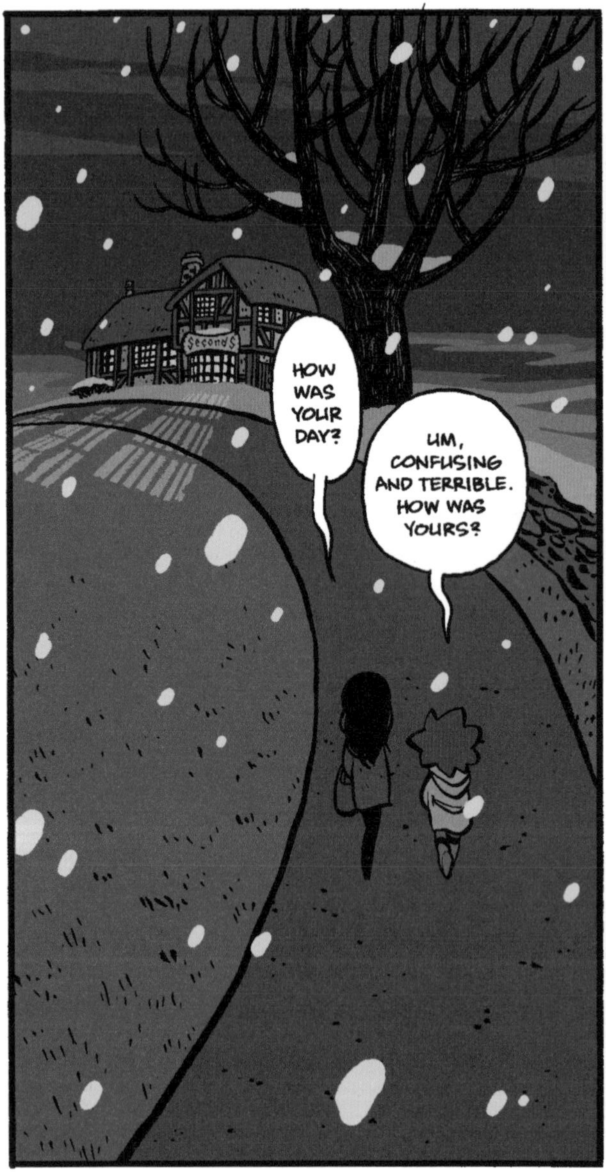
Seconds
HOW WAS YOUR DAY?
UM, CONFUSING AND TERRIBLE. HOW WAS YOURS?

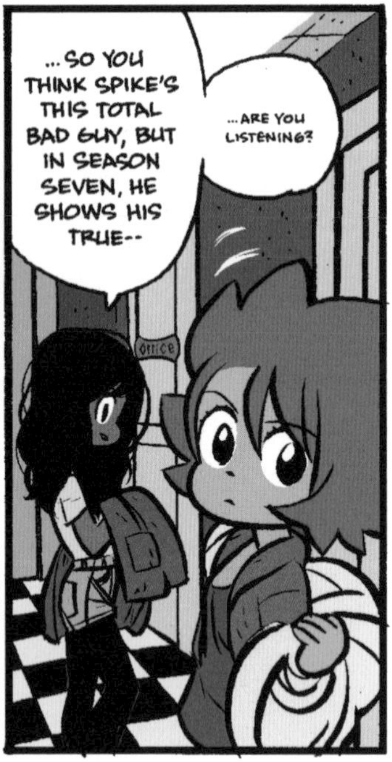
...SO YOU THINK SPIKE'S THIS TOTAL BAD GUY, BUT IN SEASON SEVEN, HE SHOWS HIS TRUE--
...ARE YOU LISTENING?
office

Back in the basement, Katie noticed that the office door was ajar...

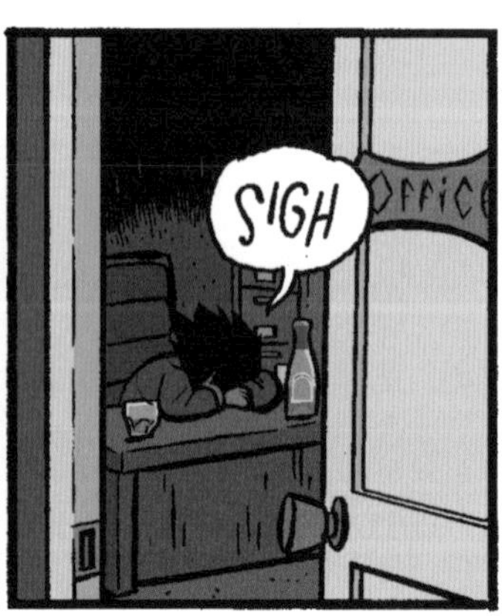
SIGH

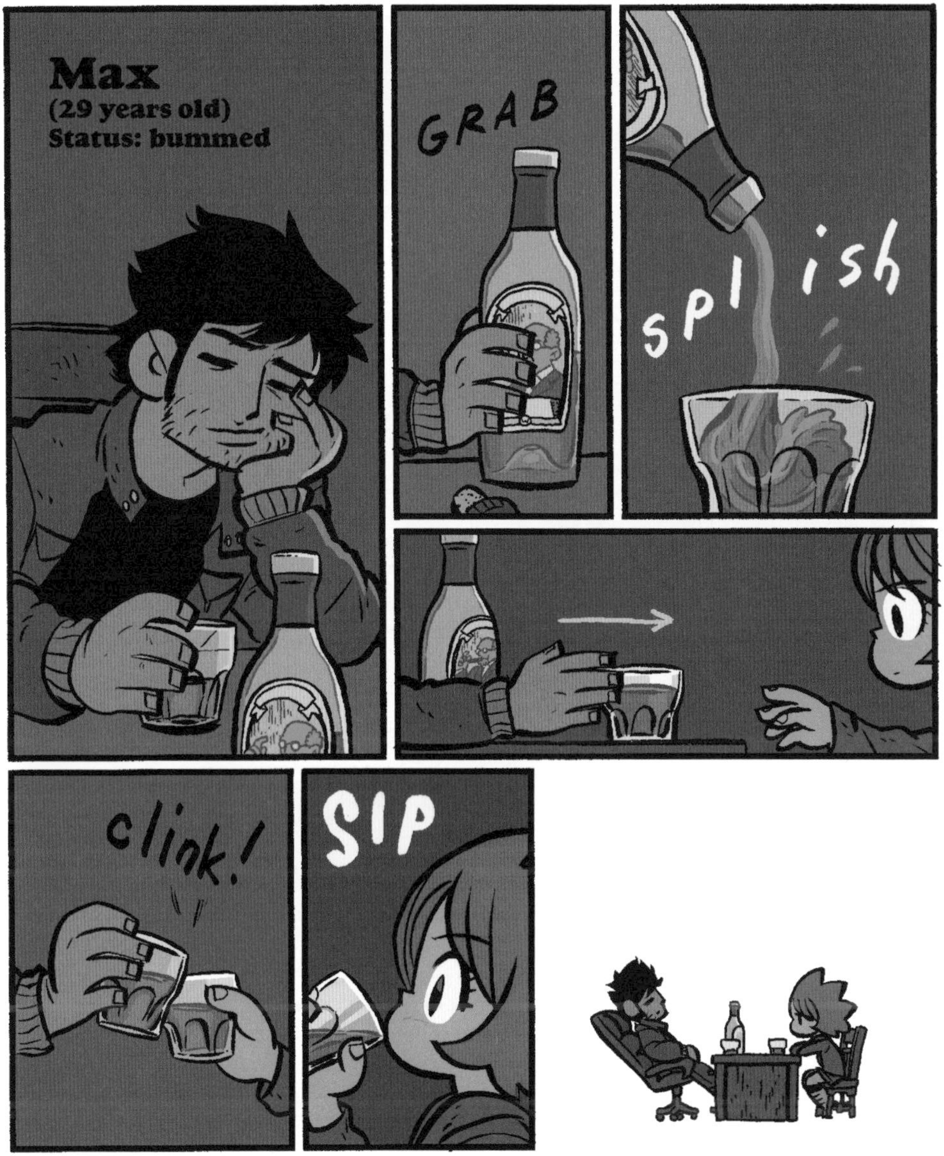
Max
(29 years old)
Status: bummed
GRAB
splish
clink!
SIP

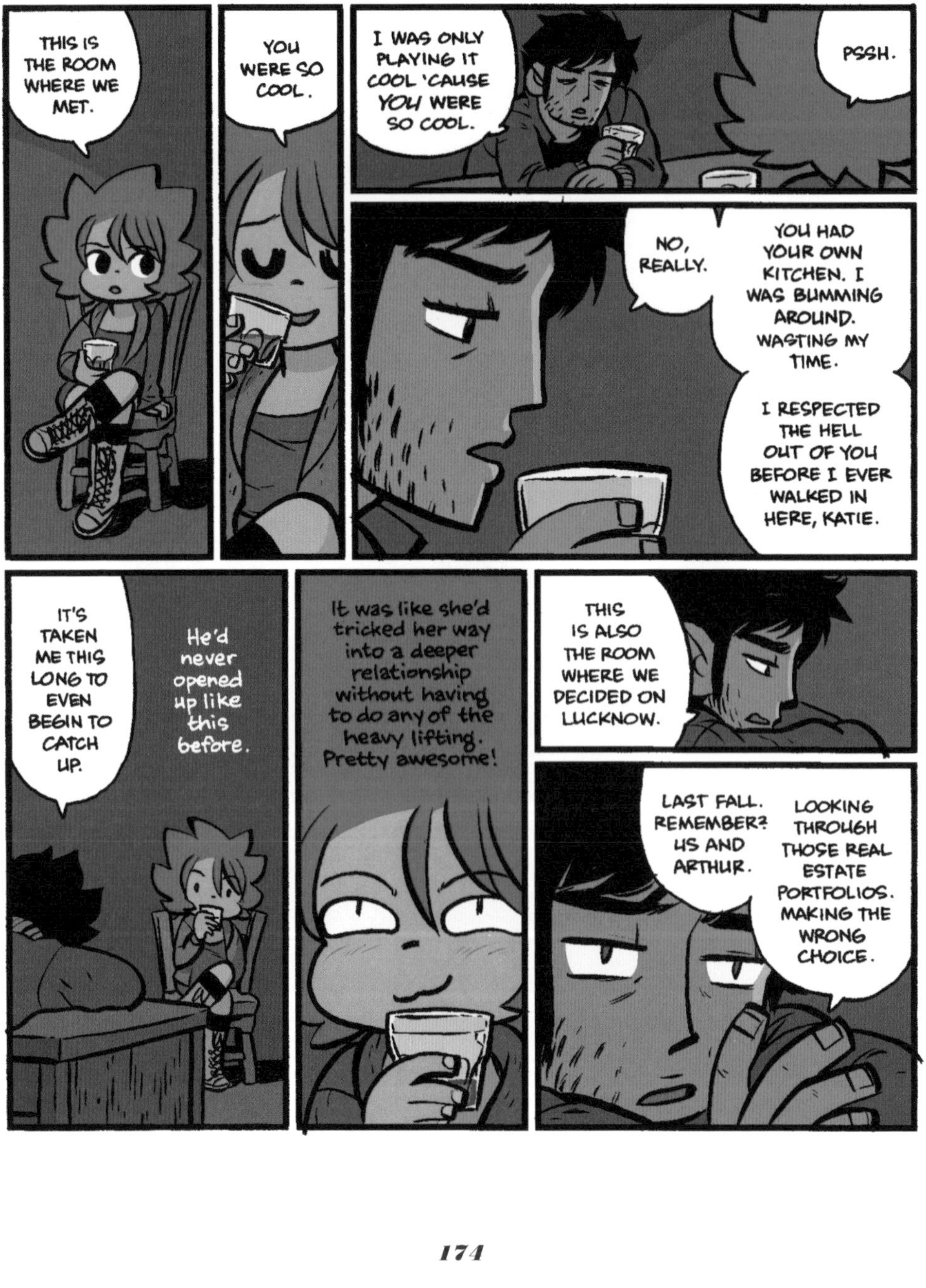
THIS IS THE ROOM WHERE WE MET.
YOU WERE SO COOL.
I WAS ONLY PLAYING IT COOL 'CAUSE YOU WERE SO COOL.
PSSH.
NO, REALLY.
YOU HAD YOUR OWN KITCHEN. I WAS BUMMING AROUND. WASTING MY TIME.
I RESPECTED THE HELL OUT OF YOU BEFORE I EVER WALKED IN HERE, KATIE.
IT'S TAKEN ME THIS LONG TO EVEN BEGIN TO CATCH UP.
He'd never opened up like this before.
It was like she'd tricked her way into a deeper relationship without having to do any of the heavy lifting. Pretty awesome!
THIS IS ALSO THE ROOM WHERE WE DECIDED ON LUCKNOW.
LAST FALL. REMEMBER? US AND ARTHUR.
LOOKING THROUGH THOSE REAL ESTATE PORTFOLIOS. MAKING THE WRONG CHOICE.

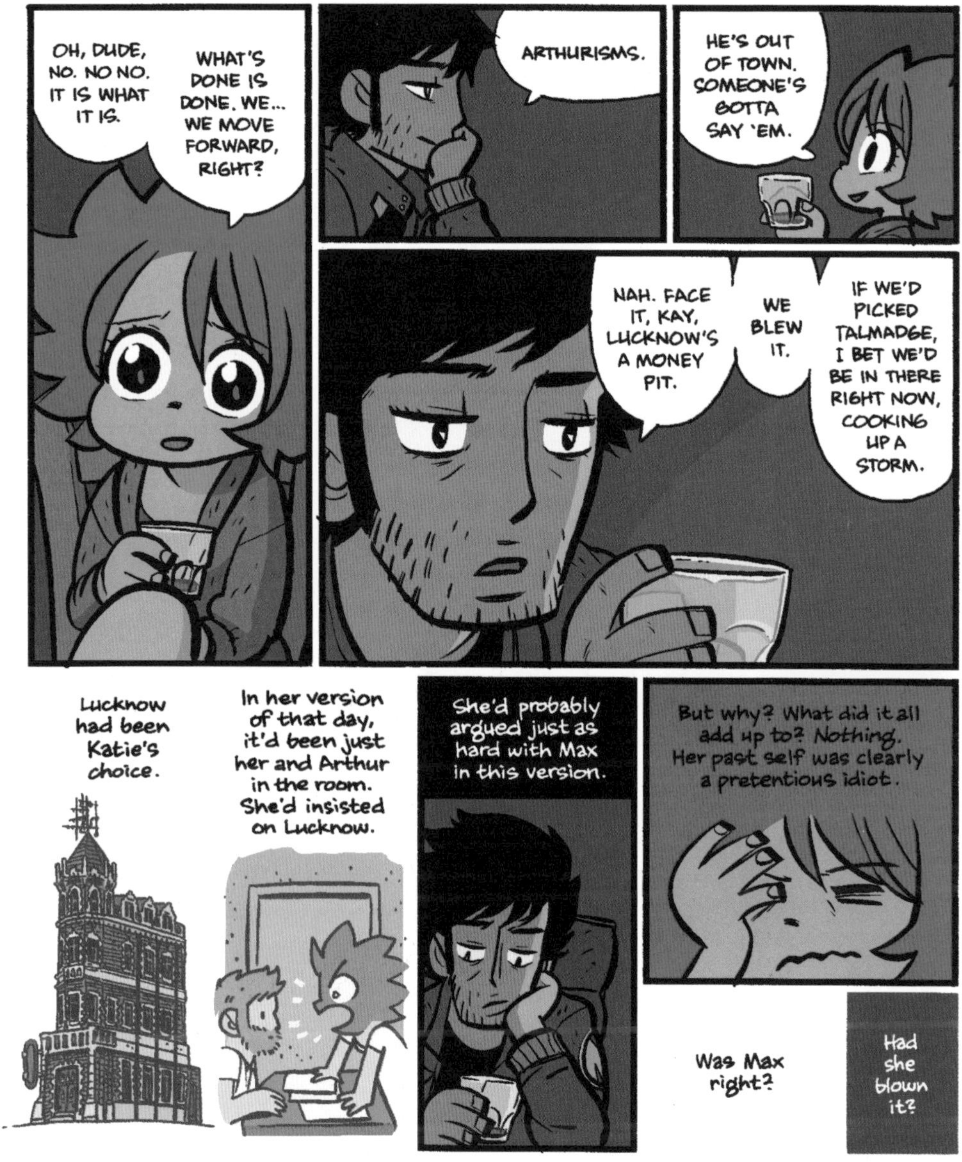
OH, DUDE, NO. NO NO. IT IS WHAT IT IS.
WHAT'S DONE IS DONE. WE... WE MOVE FORWARD, RIGHT?
ARTHURISMS.
HE'S OUT OF TOWN. SOMEONE'S GOTTA SAY 'EM.
NAH. FACE IT, KAY, LUCKNOW'S A MONEY PIT.
WE BLEW IT.
IF WE'D PICKED TALMADGE, I BET WE'D BE IN THERE RIGHT NOW, COOKING UP A STORM.
Lucknow had been Katie's choice.
In her version of that day, it'd been just her and Arthur in the room. She'd insisted on Lucknow.
She'd probably argued just as hard with Max in this version.
But why? What did it all add up to? Nothing. Her past self was clearly a pretentious idiot.
Was Max right?
Had she blown it?

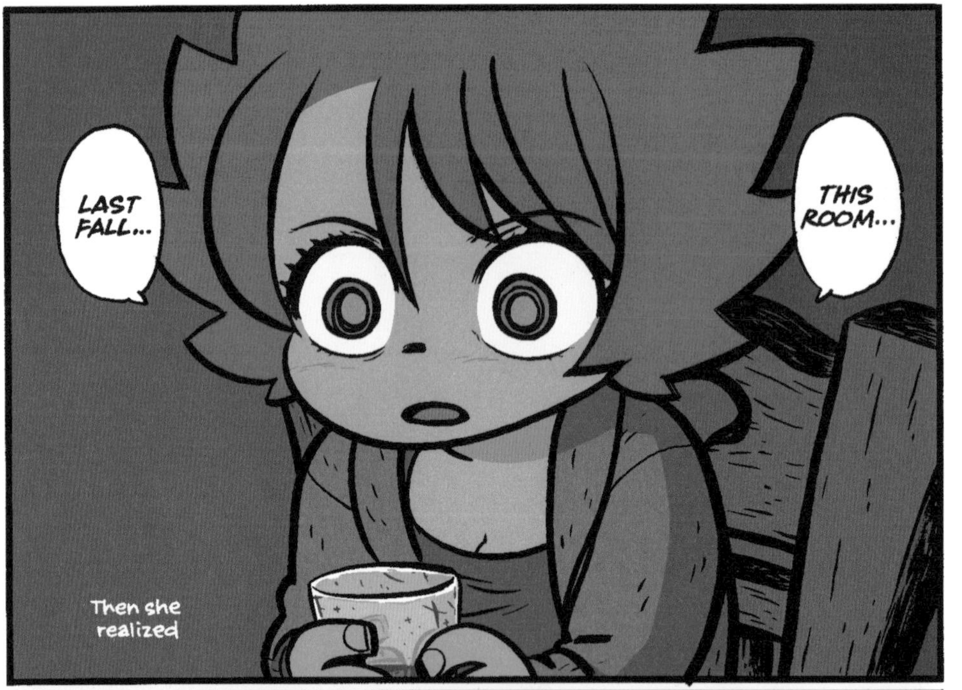
LAST FALL...
THIS ROOM...
Then she realized

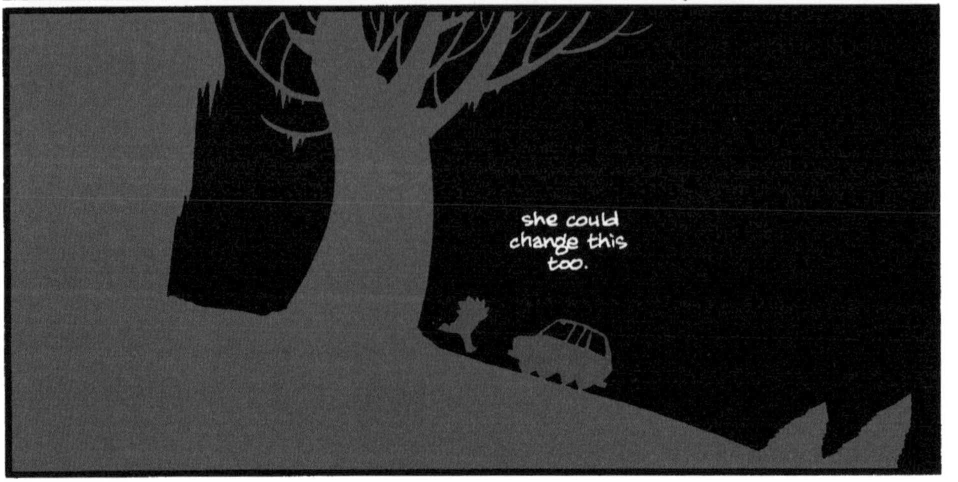
she could change this too.

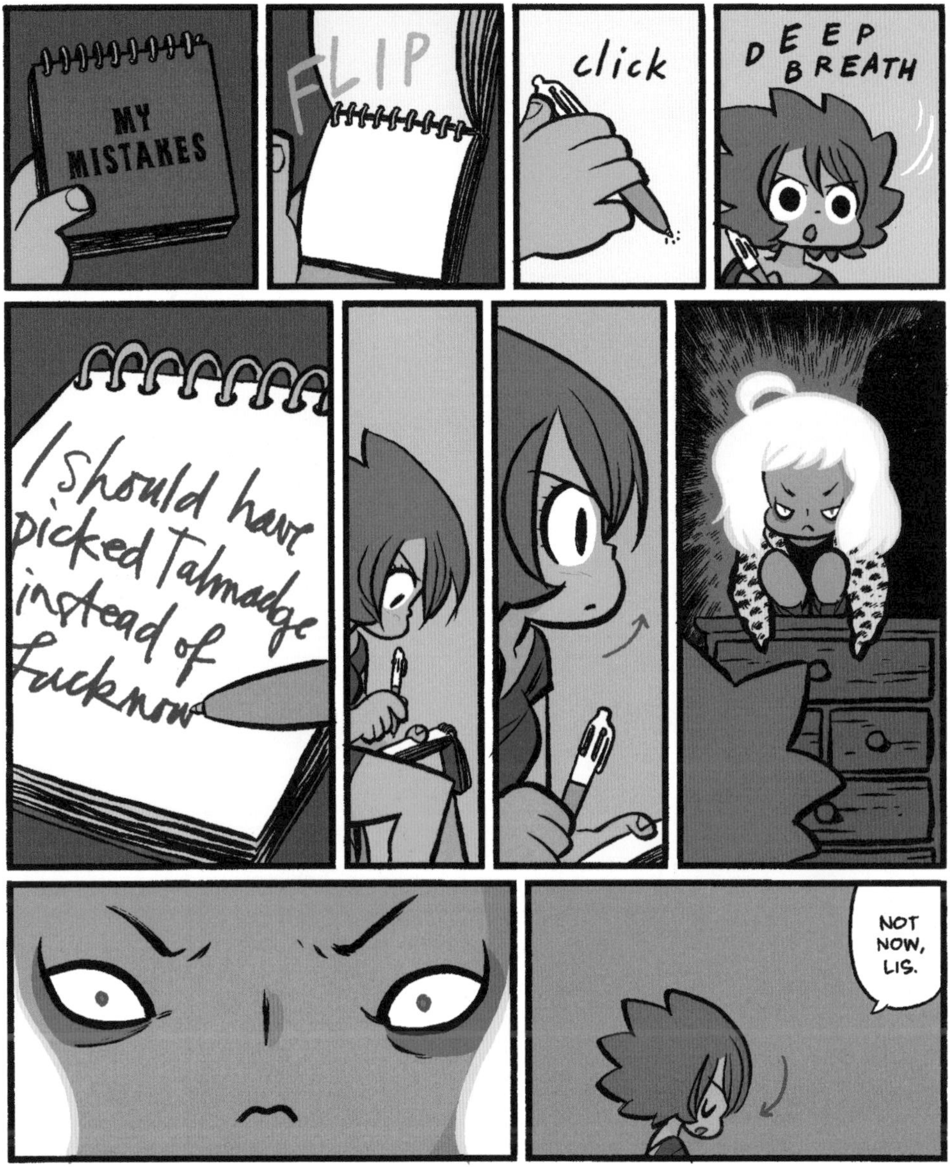
MY MISTAKES
FLIP
click
DEEP BREATH
I should have picked Talmadge instead of Fucknow
NOT NOW, LIS.

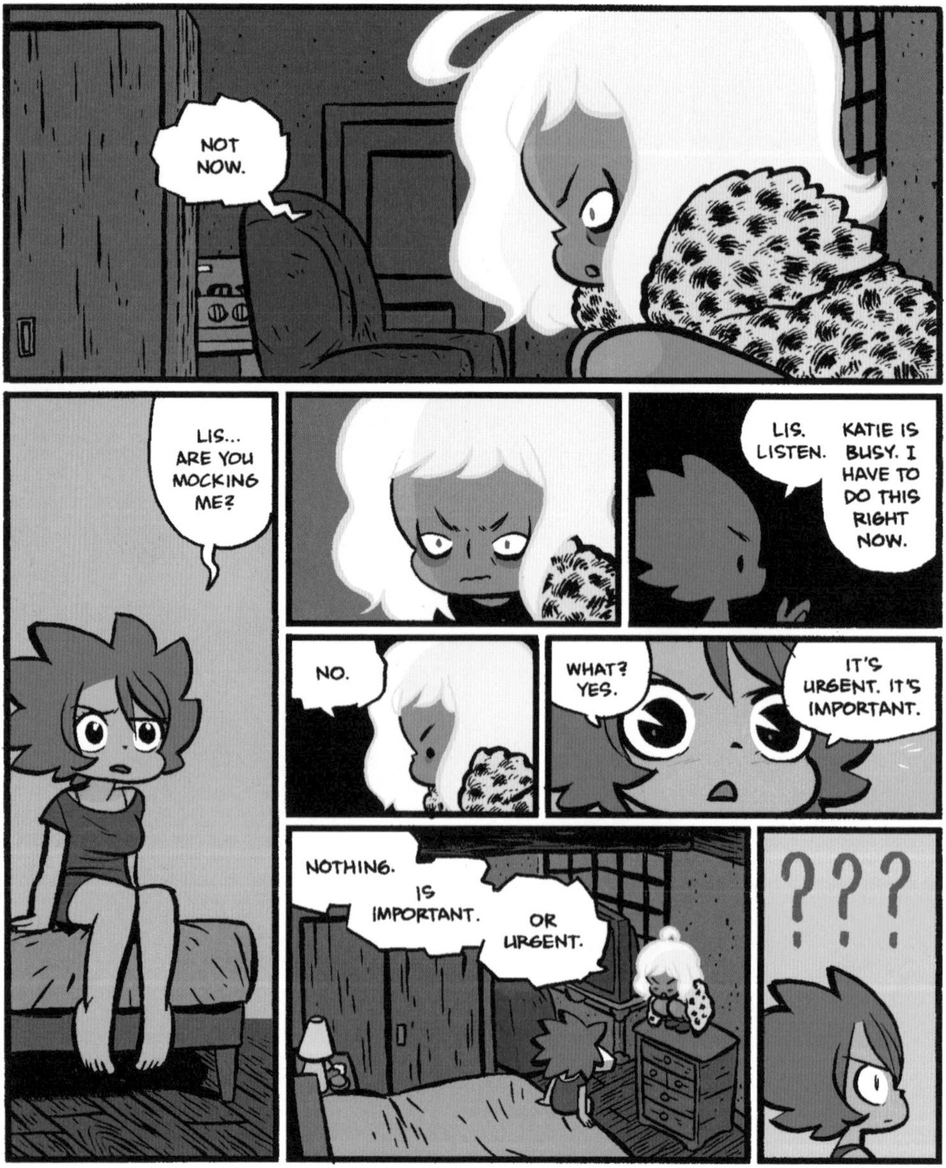
NOT NOW.
LIS... ARE YOU MOCKING ME?
LIS. LISTEN.
KATIE IS BUSY. I HAVE TO DO THIS RIGHT NOW.
NO.
WHAT? YES.
IT'S URGENT. IT'S IMPORTANT.
NOTHING.
IS IMPORTANT.
OR URGENT.
???

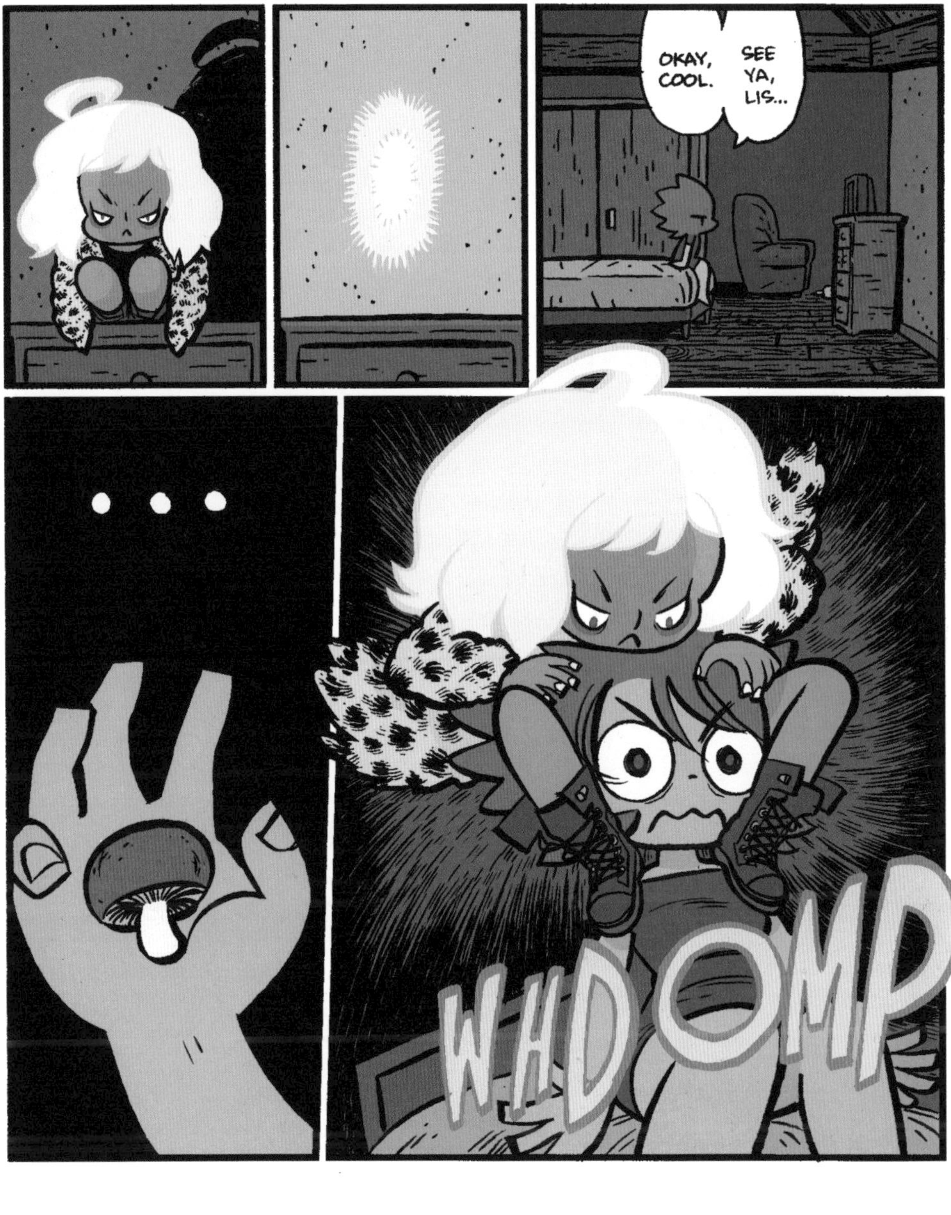
OKAY, COOL.
SEE YA, LIS...
• • •
WHDOOMP

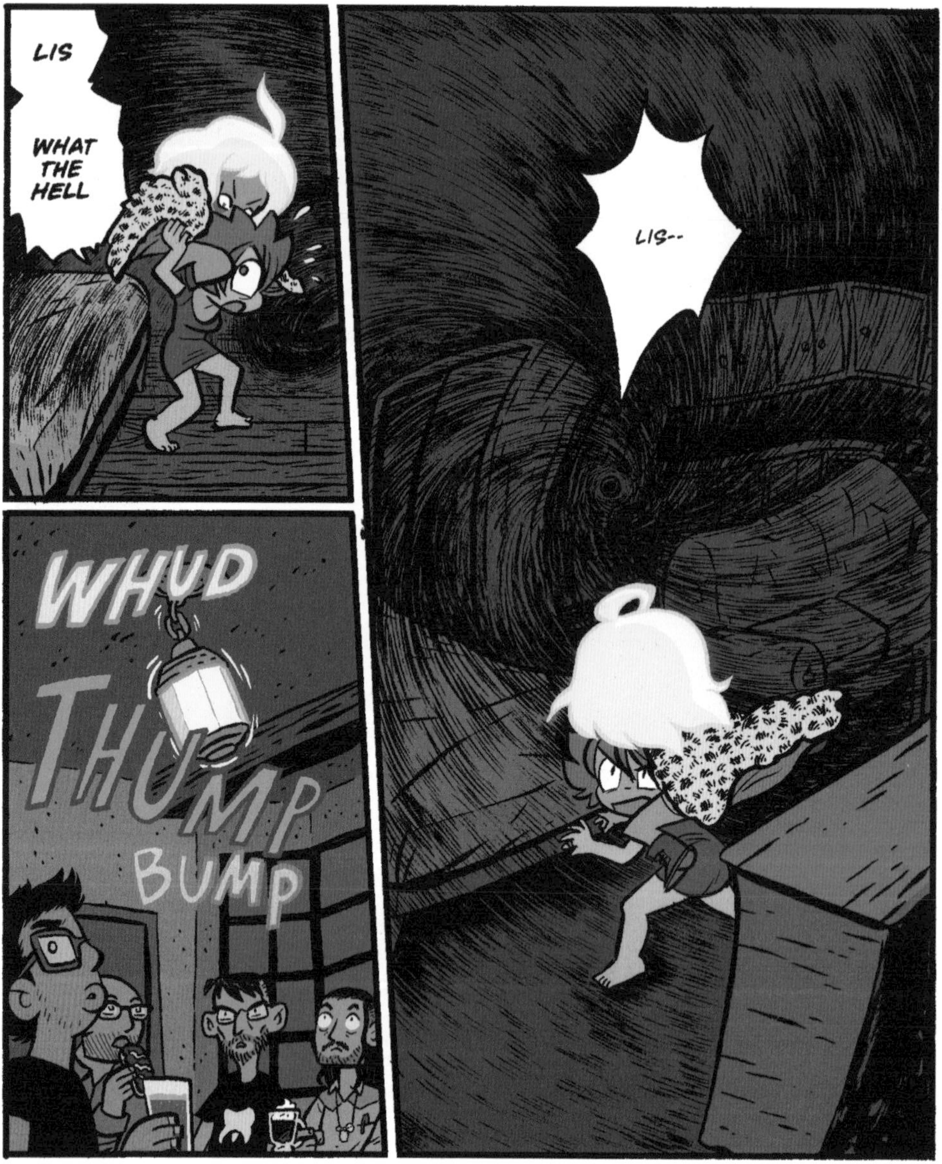
LIS
WHAT THE HELL
LIS--
WHUD
THUMP
BUMP

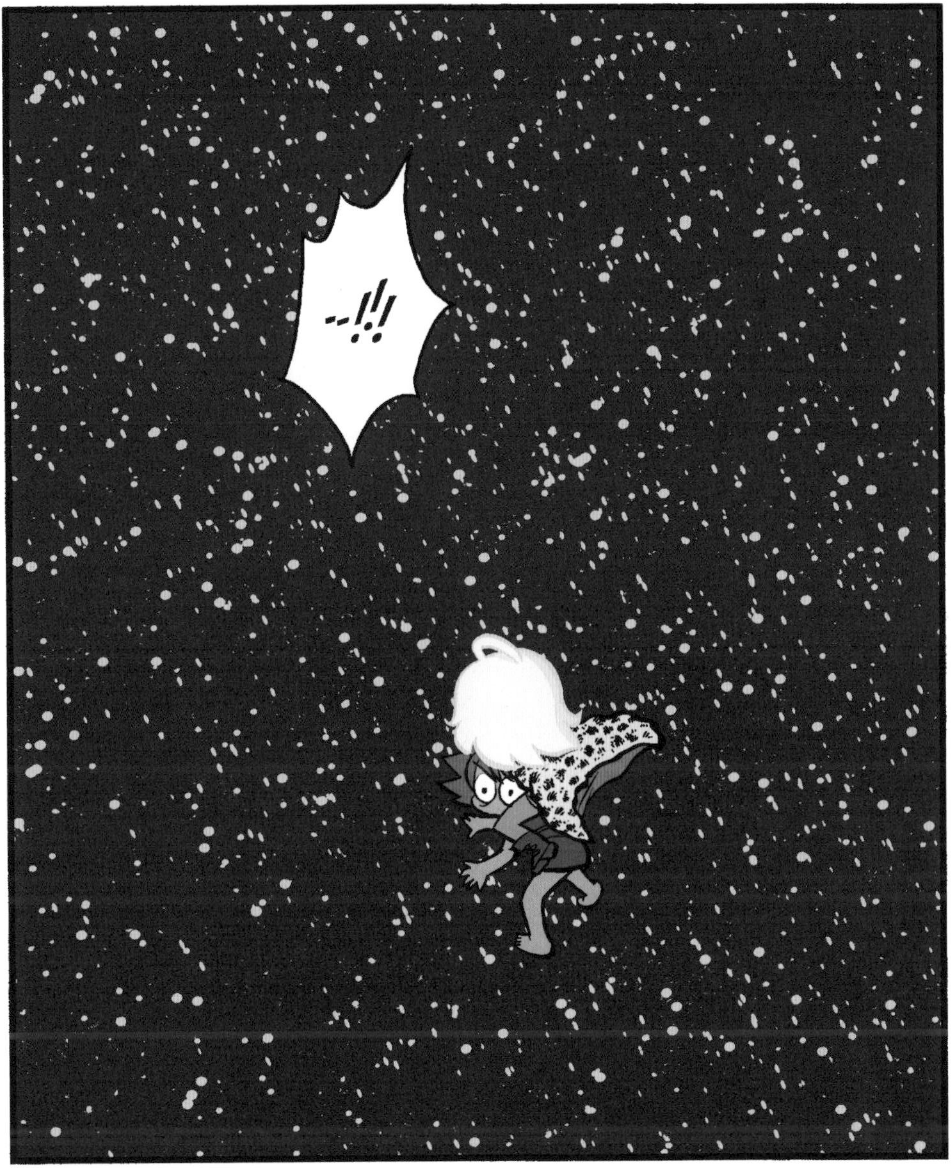
--!!!

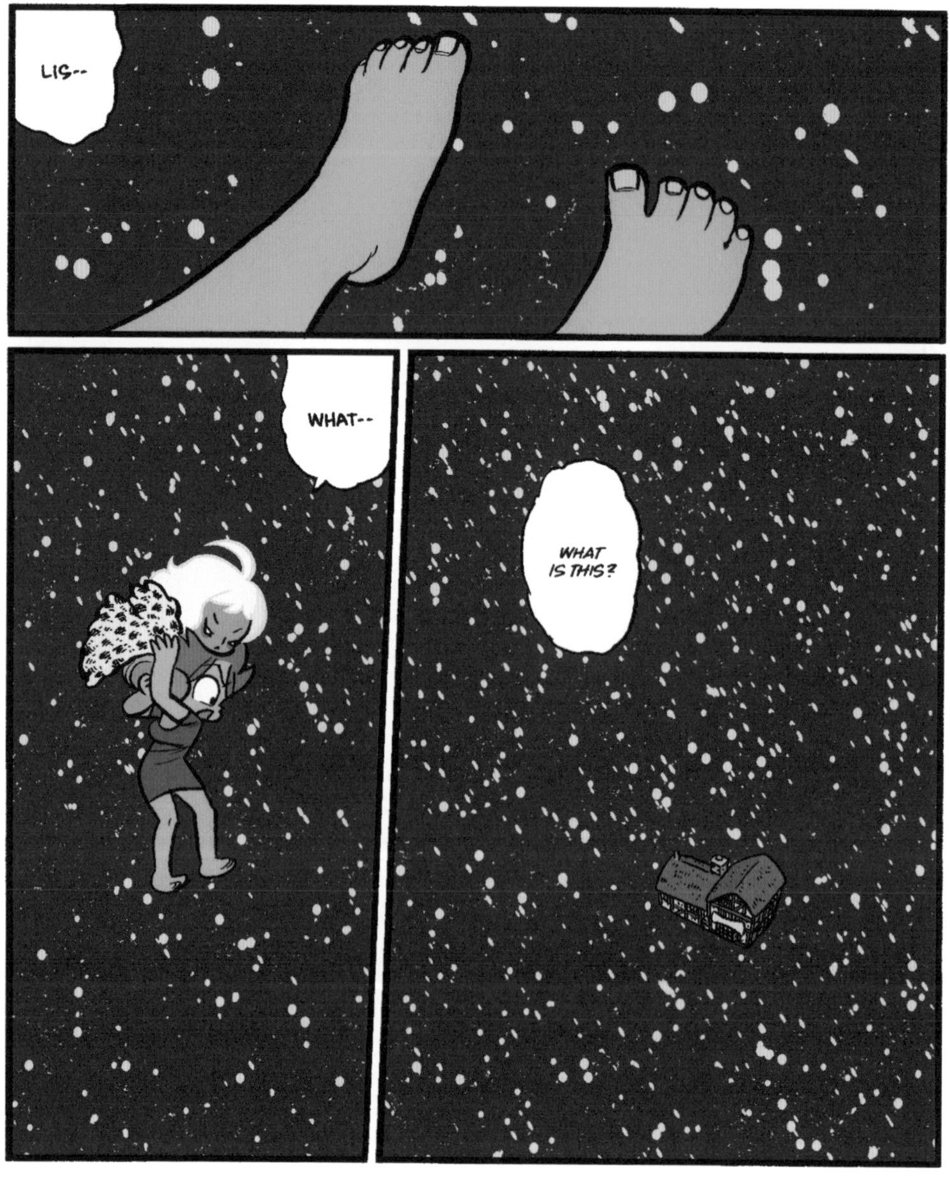
LIS--
WHAT--
WHAT IS THIS?

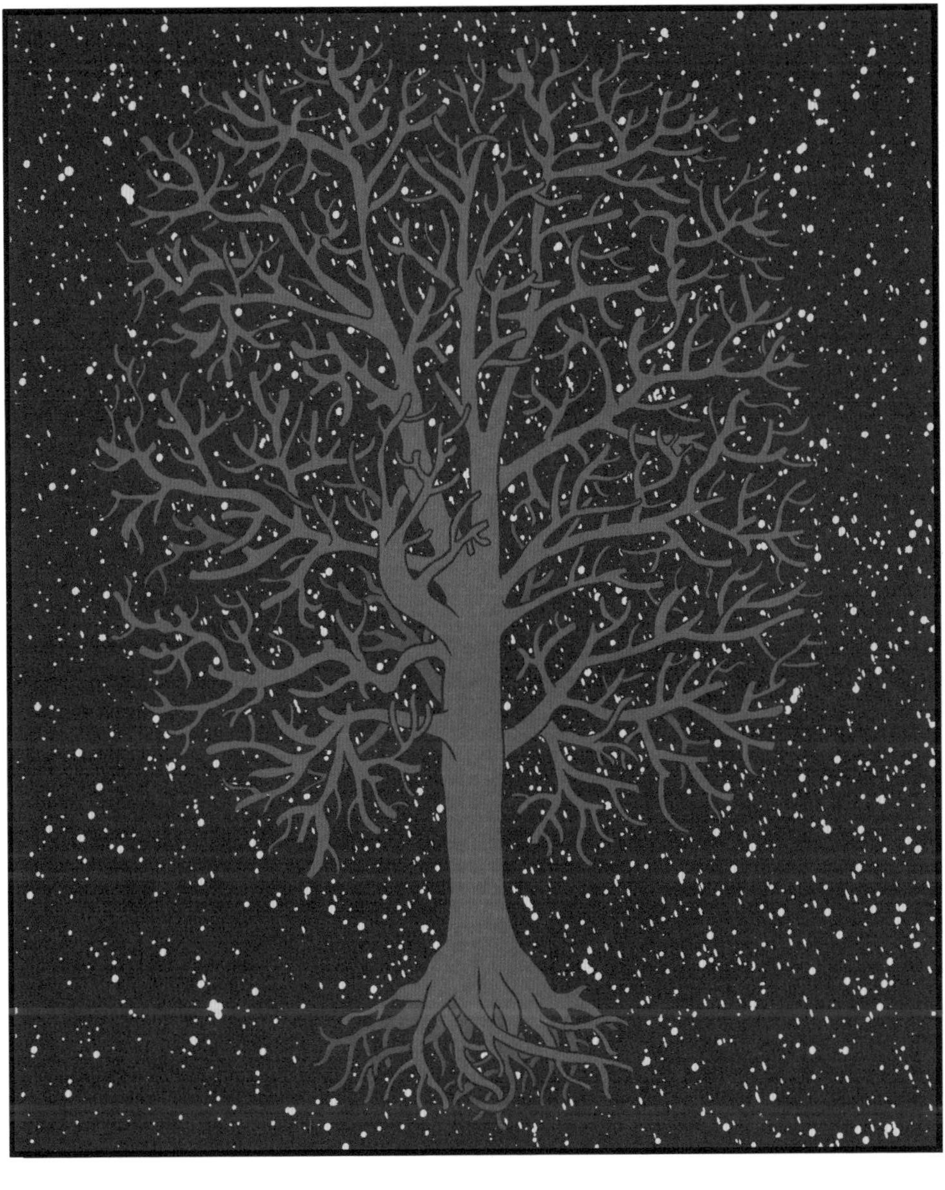

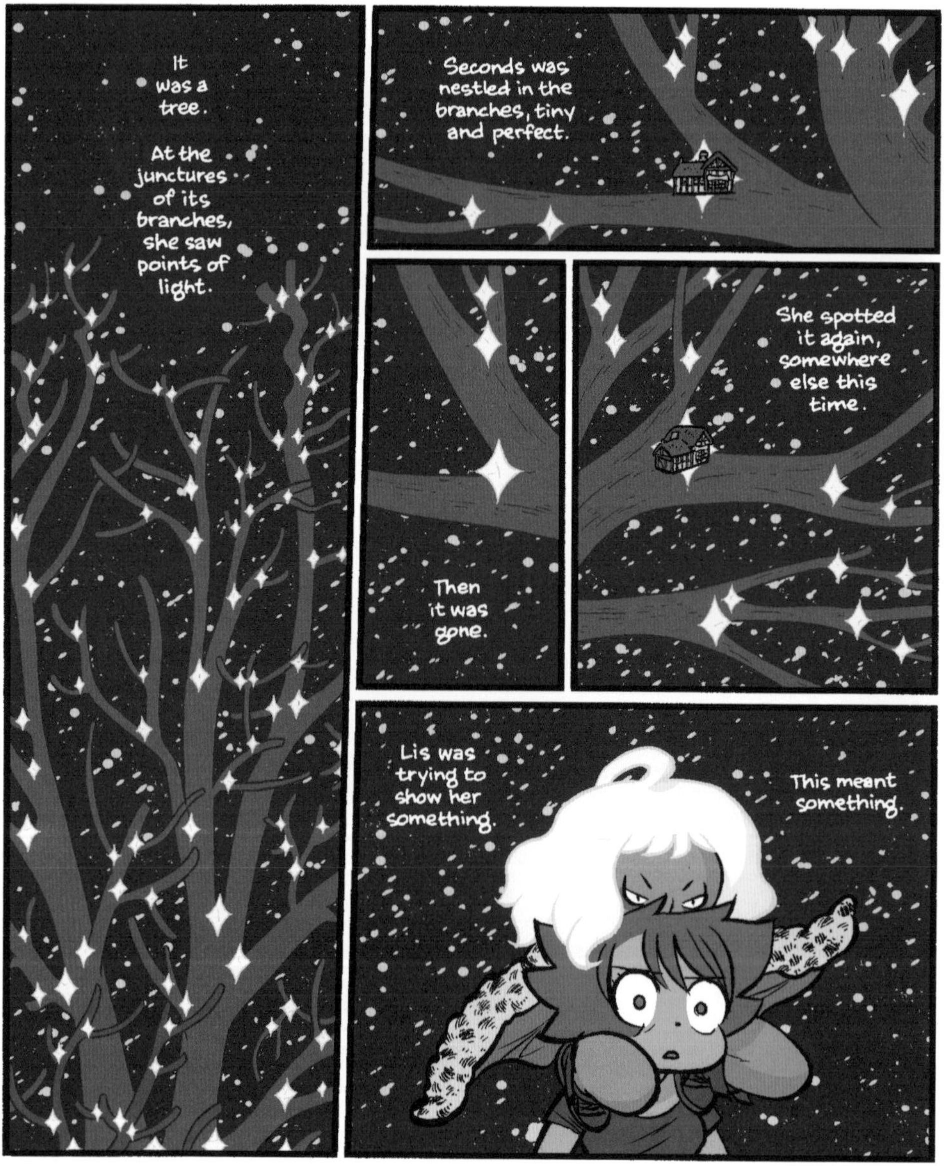
It was a tree.
At the junctures of its branches, she saw points of light.
Seconds was nestled in the branches, tiny and perfect.
Then it was gone.
She spotted it again, somewhere else this time.
Lis was trying to show her something.
This meant something.

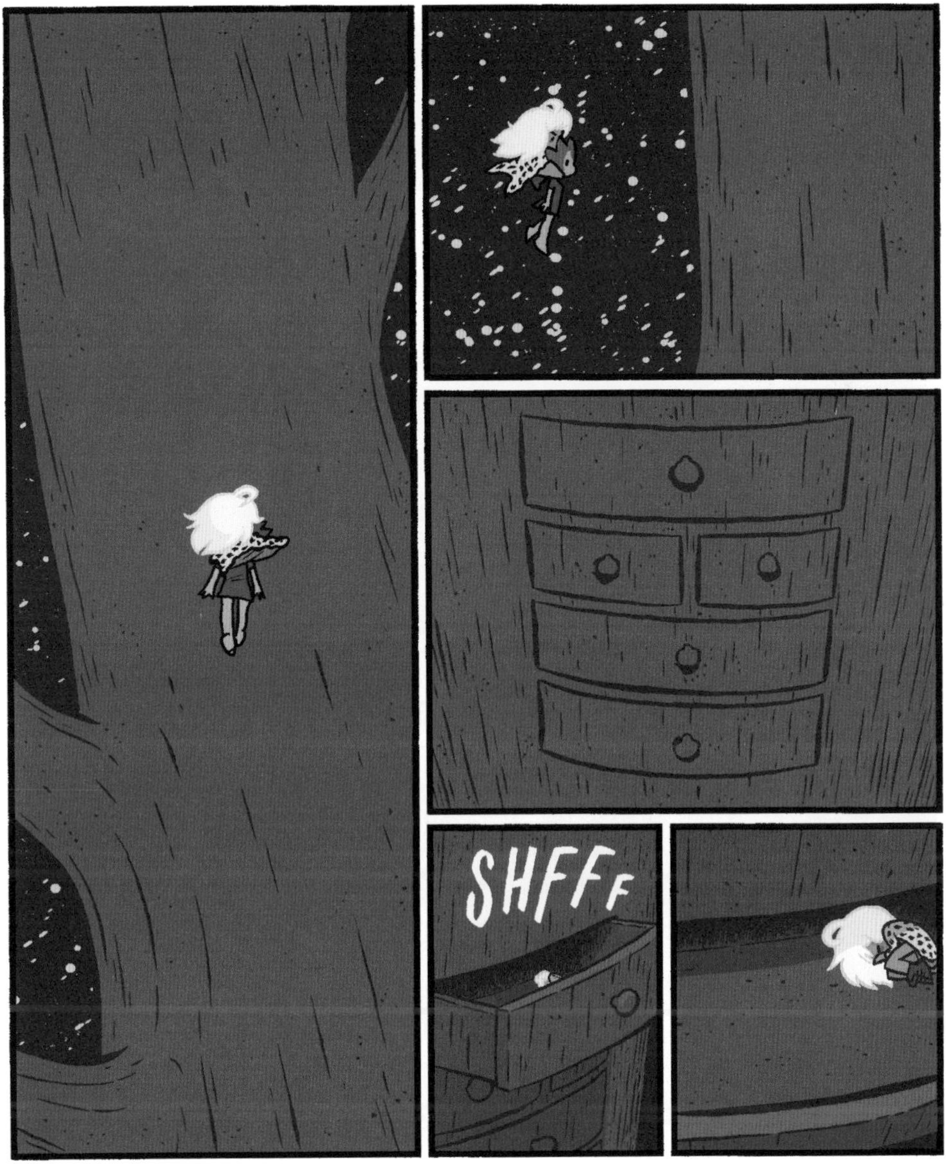
SHFFF

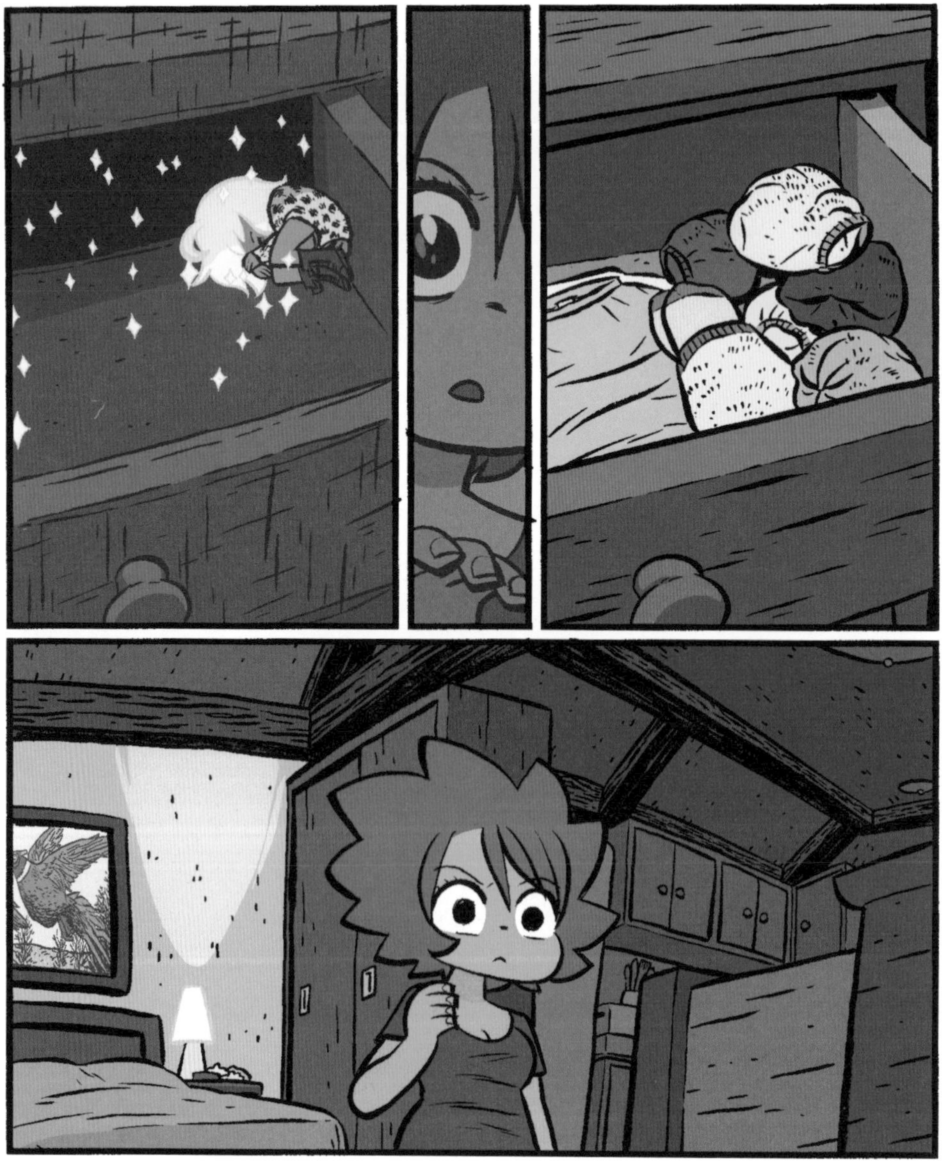

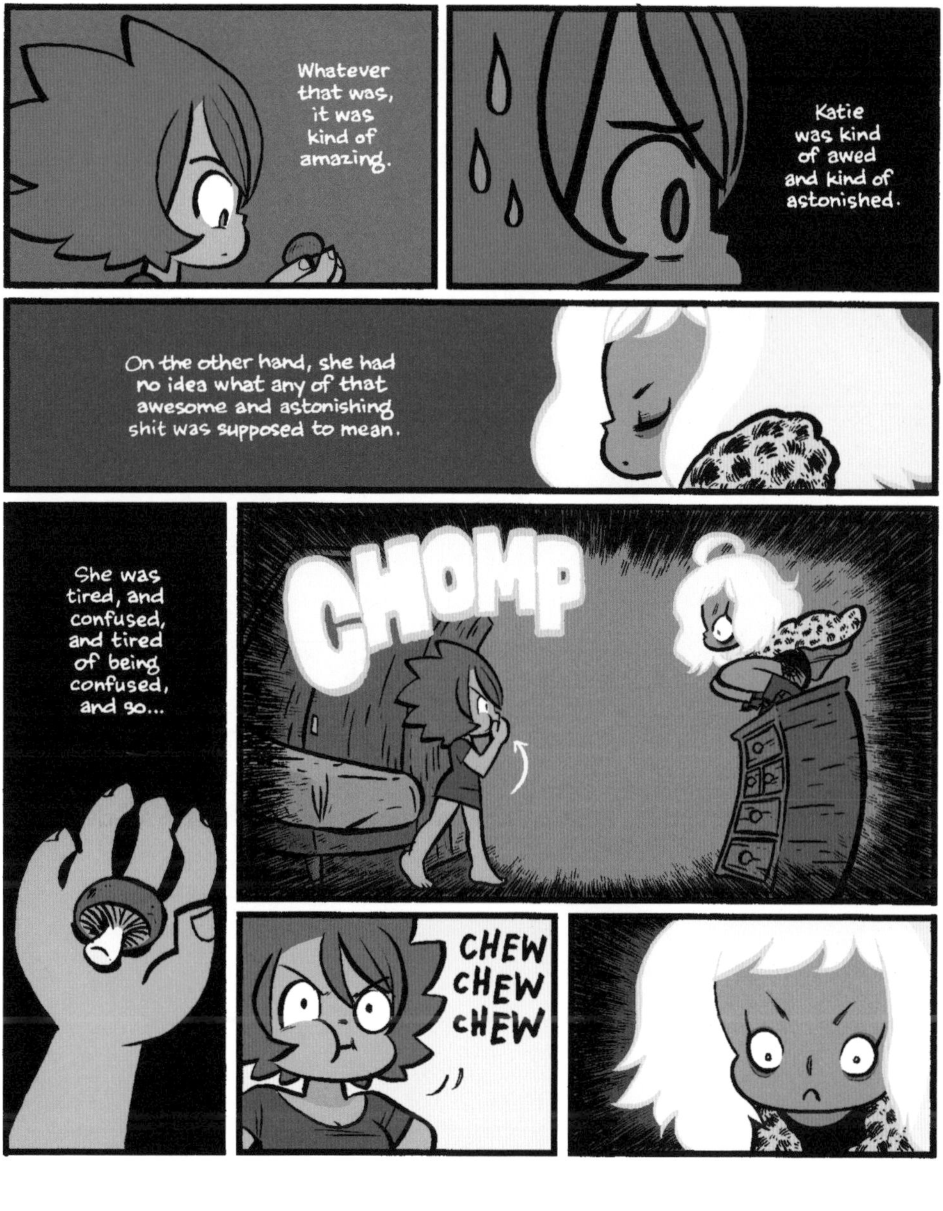
Whatever that was, it was kind of amazing.
Katie was kind of awed and kind of astonished.
On the other hand, she had no idea what any of that awesome and astonishing shit was supposed to mean.
She was tired, and confused, and tired of being confused, and so...
CHOMP
CHEW CHEW CHEW

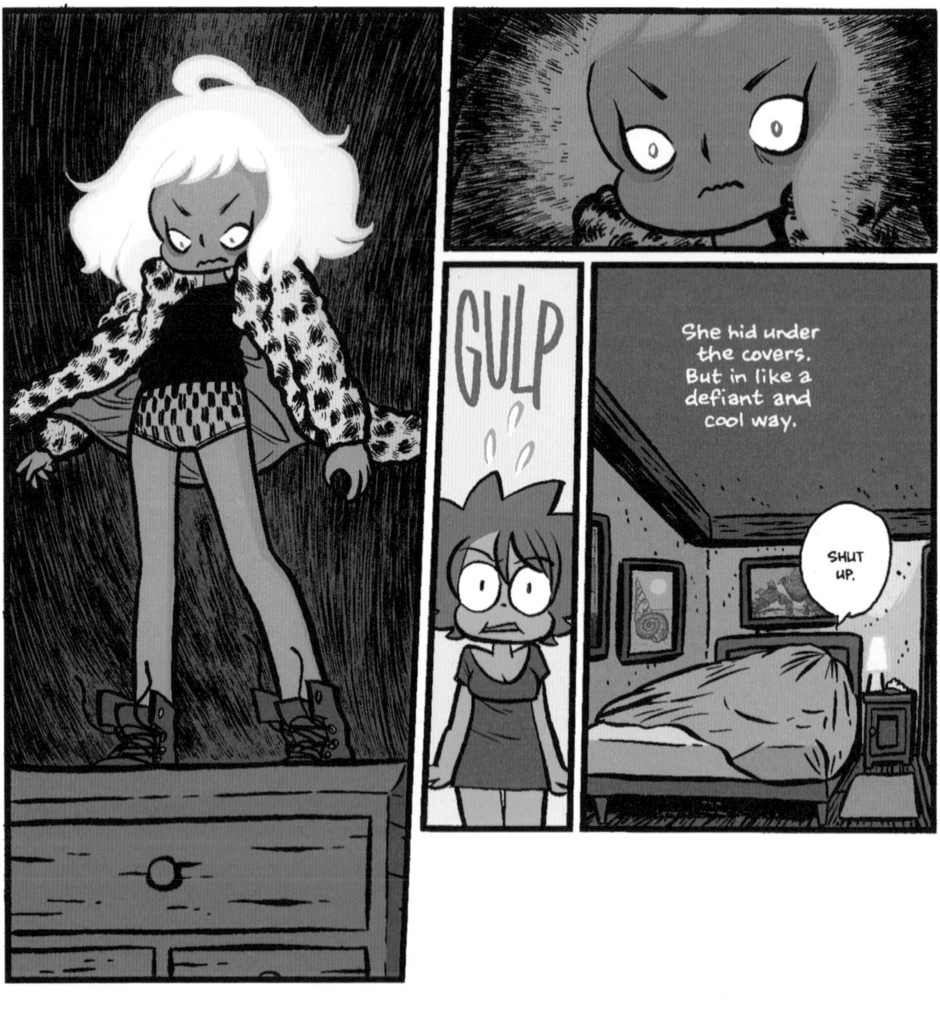
GULP
She hid under the covers. But in like a defiant and cool way.
SHUT UP.

REVISION #7

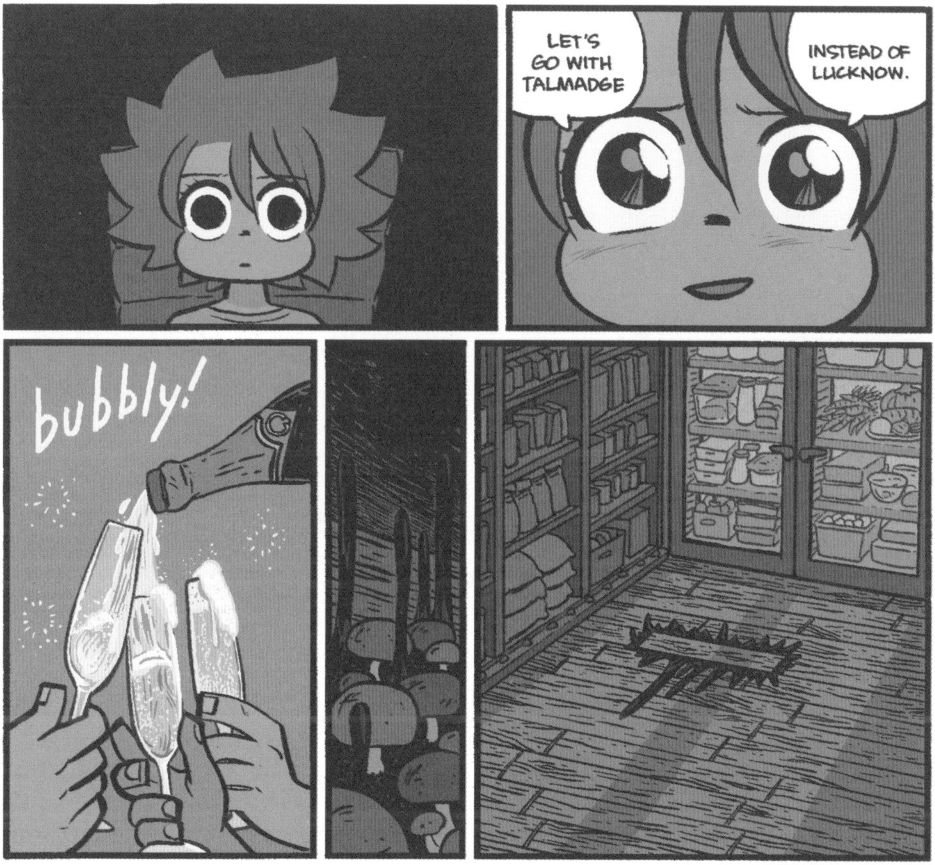
LET'S GO WITH TALMADGE
INSTEAD OF LUCKNOW.
bubbly!

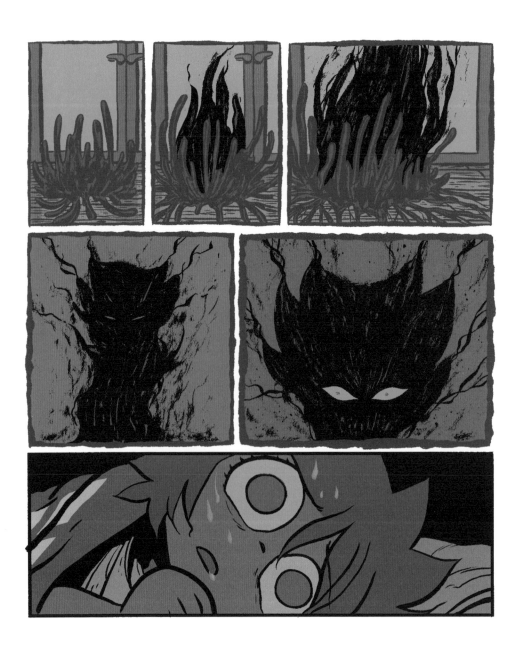

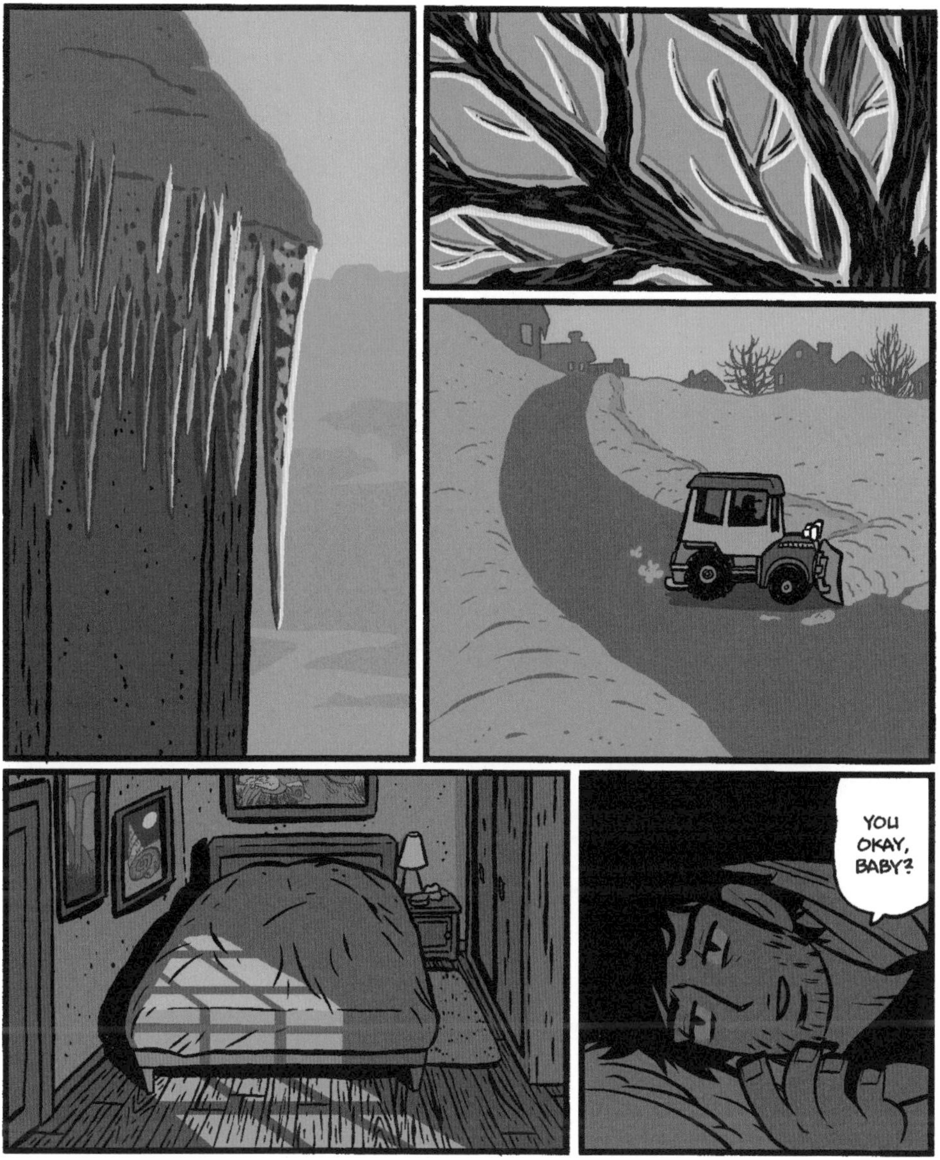
YOU OKAY, BABY?

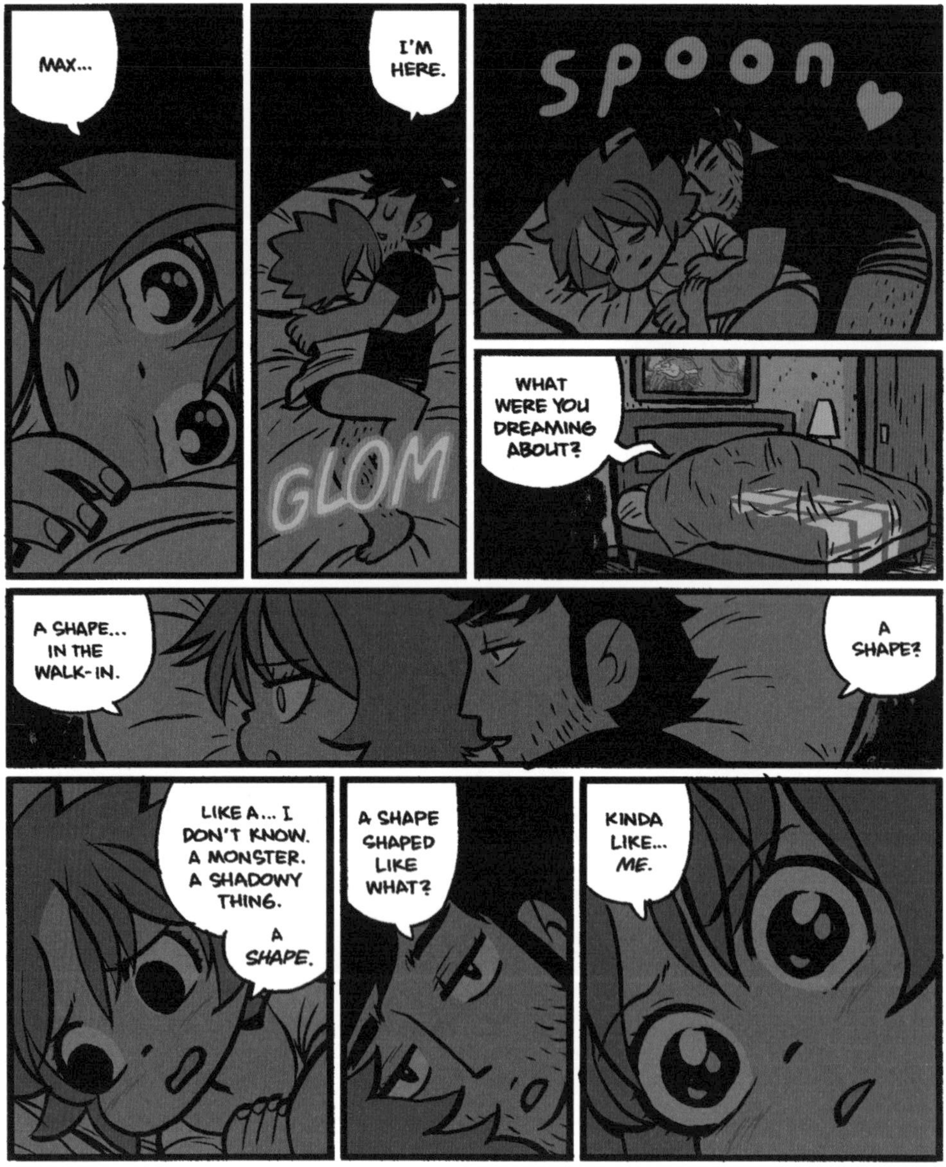
MAX...
I'M HERE.
SPOON
GLOM
WHAT WERE YOU DREAMING ABOUT?
A SHAPE... IN THE WALK-IN.
A SHAPE?
LIKE A... I DON'T KNOW. A MONSTER. A SHADOWY THING.
A SHAPE.
A SHAPE SHAPED LIKE WHAT?
KINDA LIKE... ME.

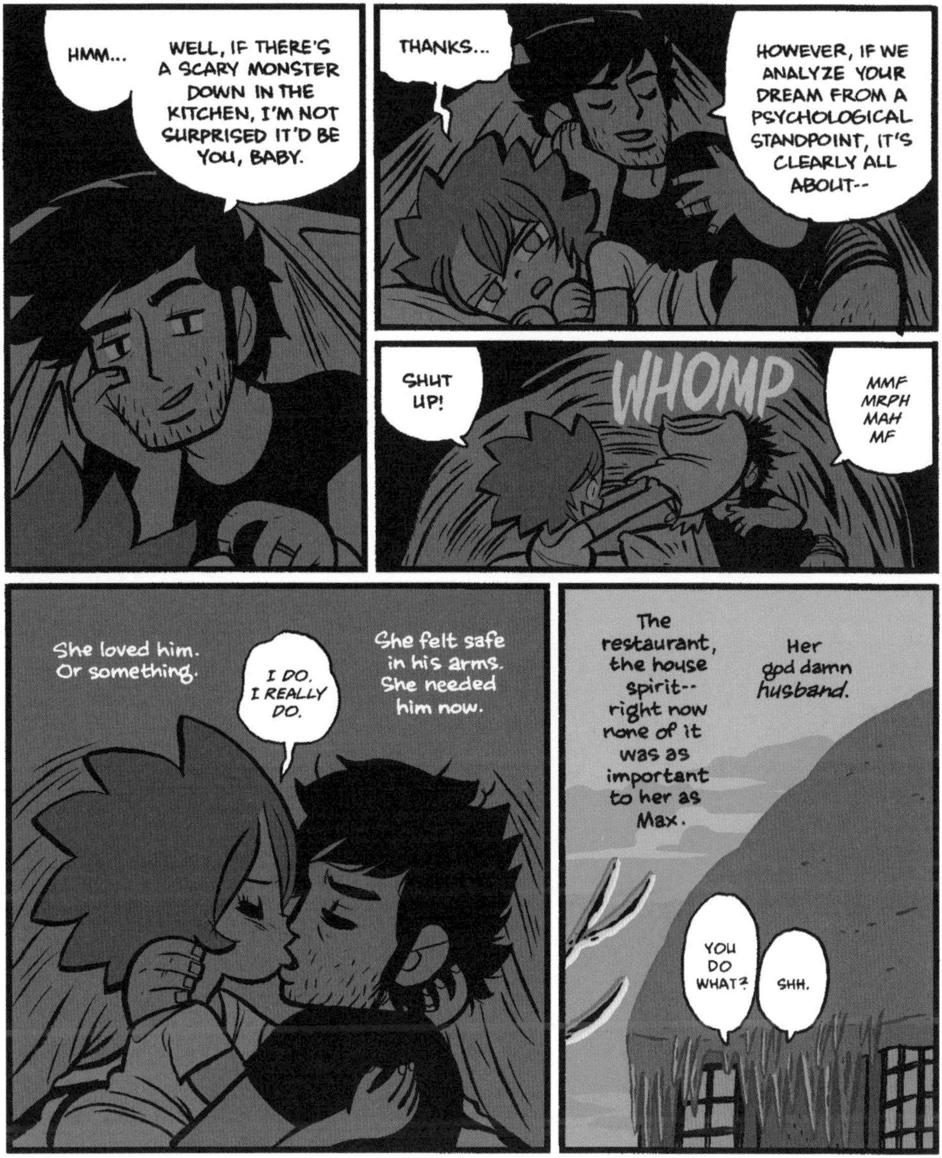
HMM...
WELL, IF THERE'S A SCARY MONSTER DOWN IN THE KITCHEN, I'M NOT SURPRISED IT'D BE YOU, BABY.
THANKS...
HOWEVER, IF WE ANALYZE YOUR DREAM FROM A PSYCHOLOGICAL STANDPOINT, IT'S CLEARLY ALL ABOUT--
SHUT UP!
WHOMP
MMF MRPH MAH MF
She loved him. Or something.
I DO. I REALLY DO.
She felt safe in his arms. She needed him now.
The restaurant, the house spirit-- right now none of it was as important to her as Max.
Her god damn *husband*.
YOU DO WHAT?
SHH.

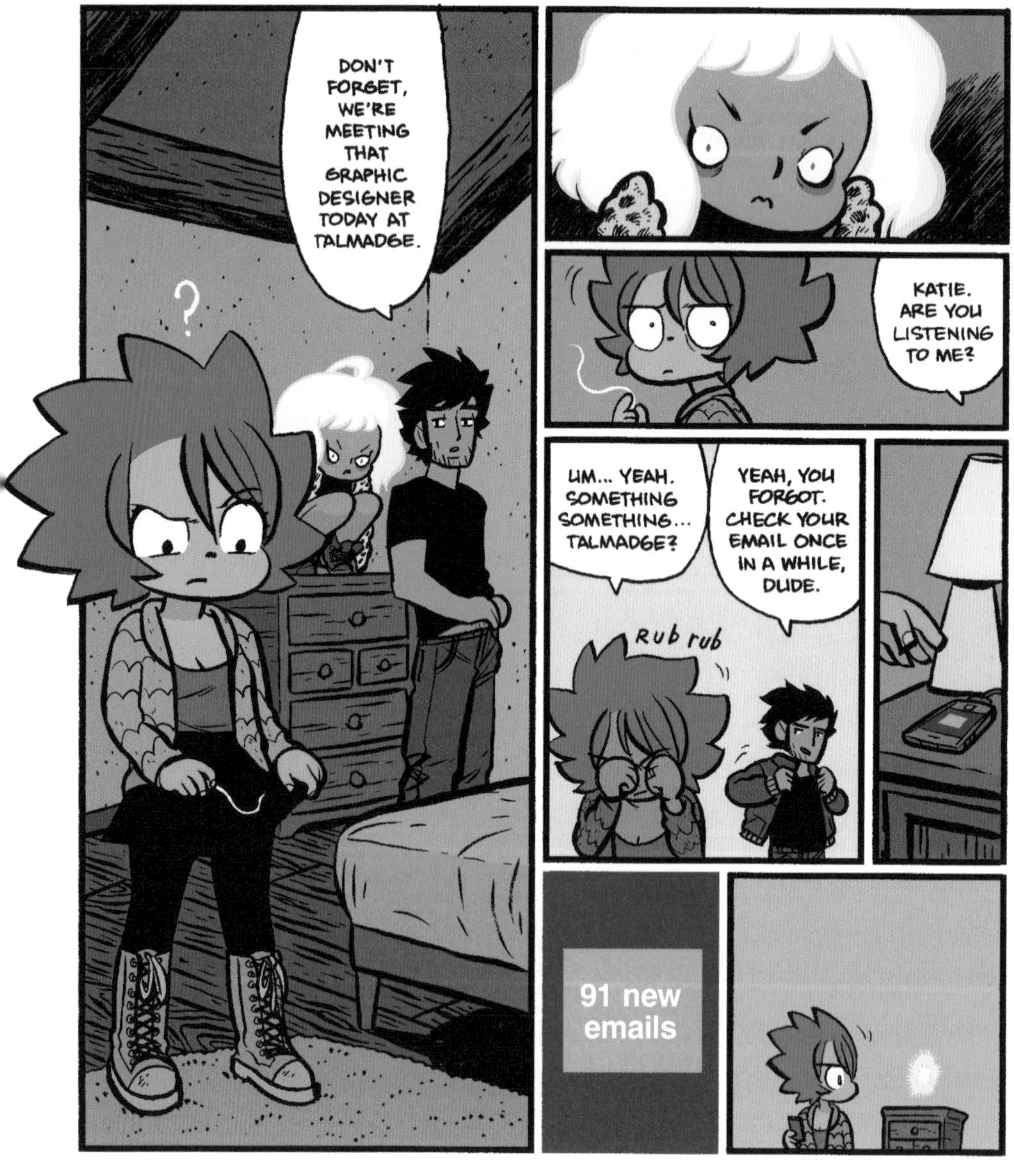

DON'T FORGET, WE'RE MEETING THAT GRAPHIC DESIGNER TODAY AT TALMADGE.
?
KATIE. ARE YOU LISTENING TO ME?
UM... YEAH. SOMETHING SOMETHING... TALMADGE?
YEAH, YOU FORGOT. CHECK YOUR EMAIL ONCE IN A WHILE, DUDE.
Rub rub
91 new emails

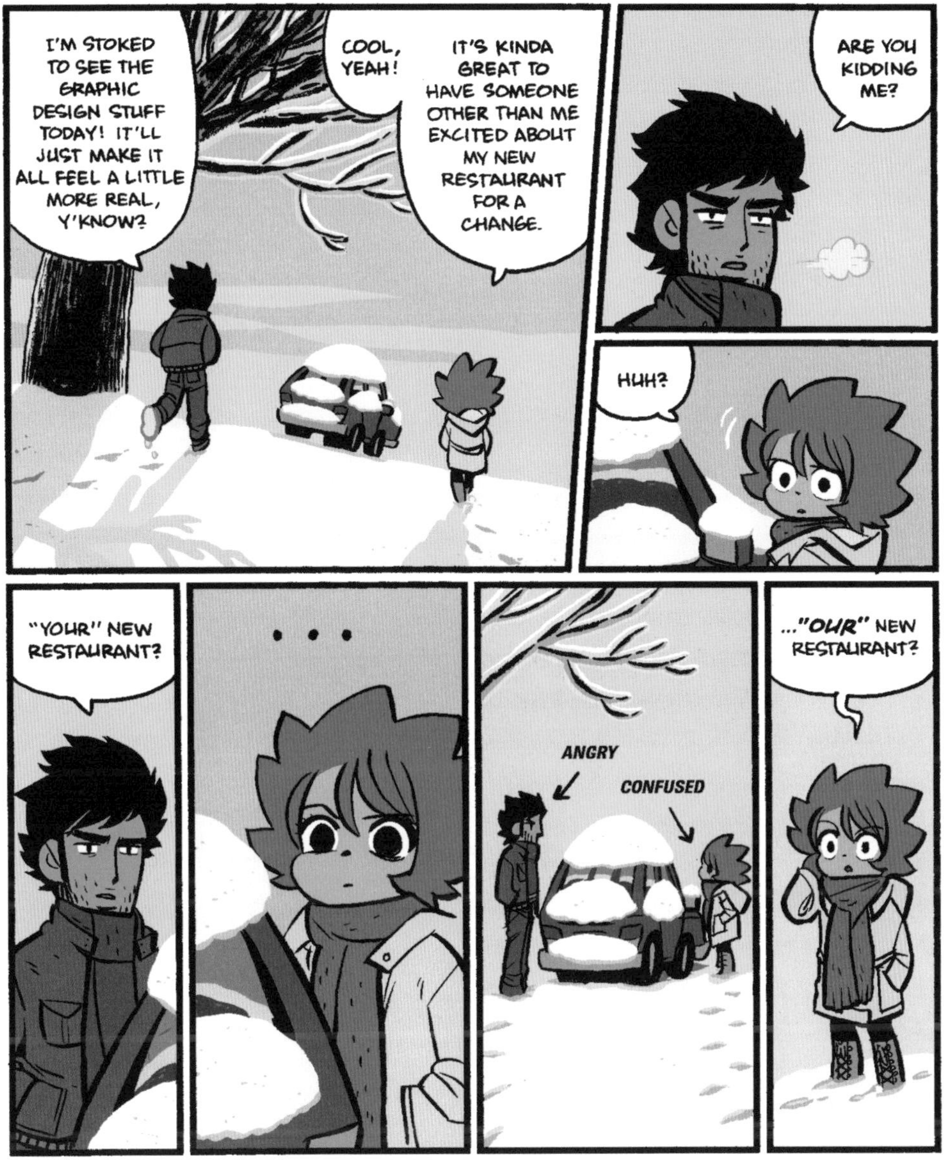
I'M STOKED TO SEE THE GRAPHIC DESIGN STUFF TODAY! IT'LL JUST MAKE IT ALL FEEL A LITTLE MORE REAL, Y'KNOW?
COOL, YEAH!
IT'S KINDA GREAT TO HAVE SOMEONE OTHER THAN ME EXCITED ABOUT MY NEW RESTAURANT FOR A CHANGE.
ARE YOU KIDDING ME?
HUH?
"YOUR" NEW RESTAURANT?
. . .
ANGRY
CONFUSED
..."OUR" NEW RESTAURANT?

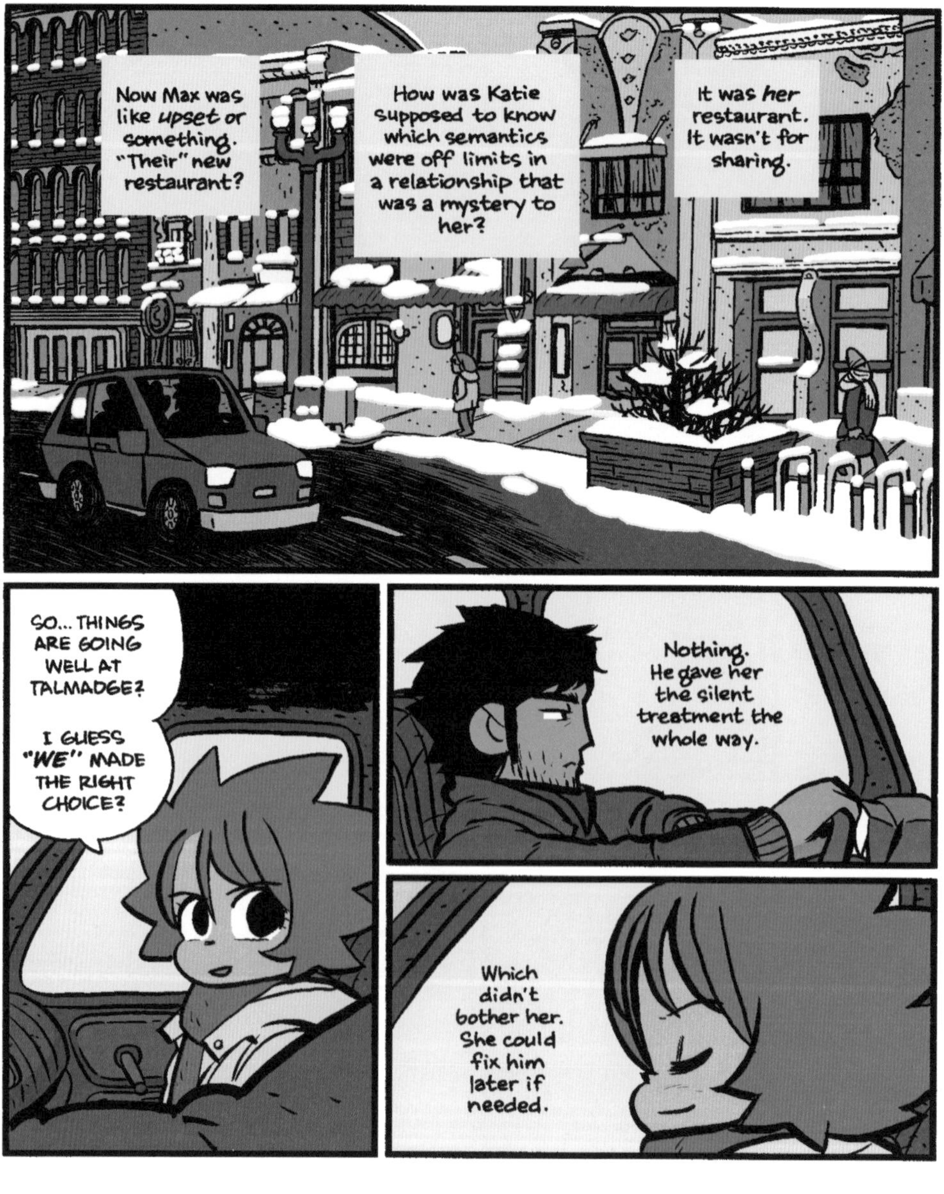
Now Max was like *upset* or something. "Their" new restaurant?
How was Katie supposed to know which semantics were off limits in a relationship that was a mystery to her?
It was *her* restaurant. It wasn't for sharing.
SO... THINGS ARE GOING WELL AT TALMADGE?
I GUESS "*WE*" MADE THE RIGHT CHOICE?
Nothing. He gave her the silent treatment the whole way.
Which didn't bother her. She could fix him later if needed.

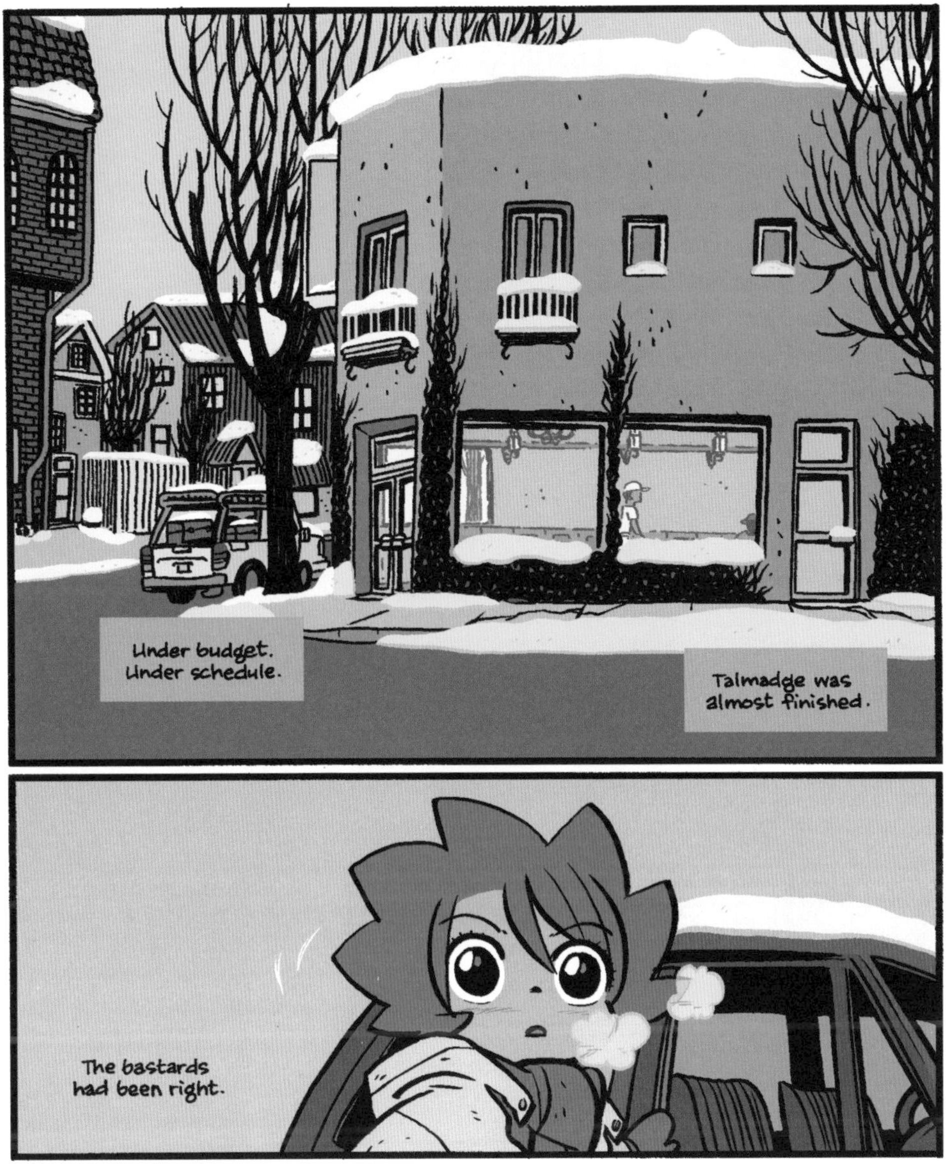
Under budget.
Under schedule.
Talmadge was almost finished.
The bastards had been right.

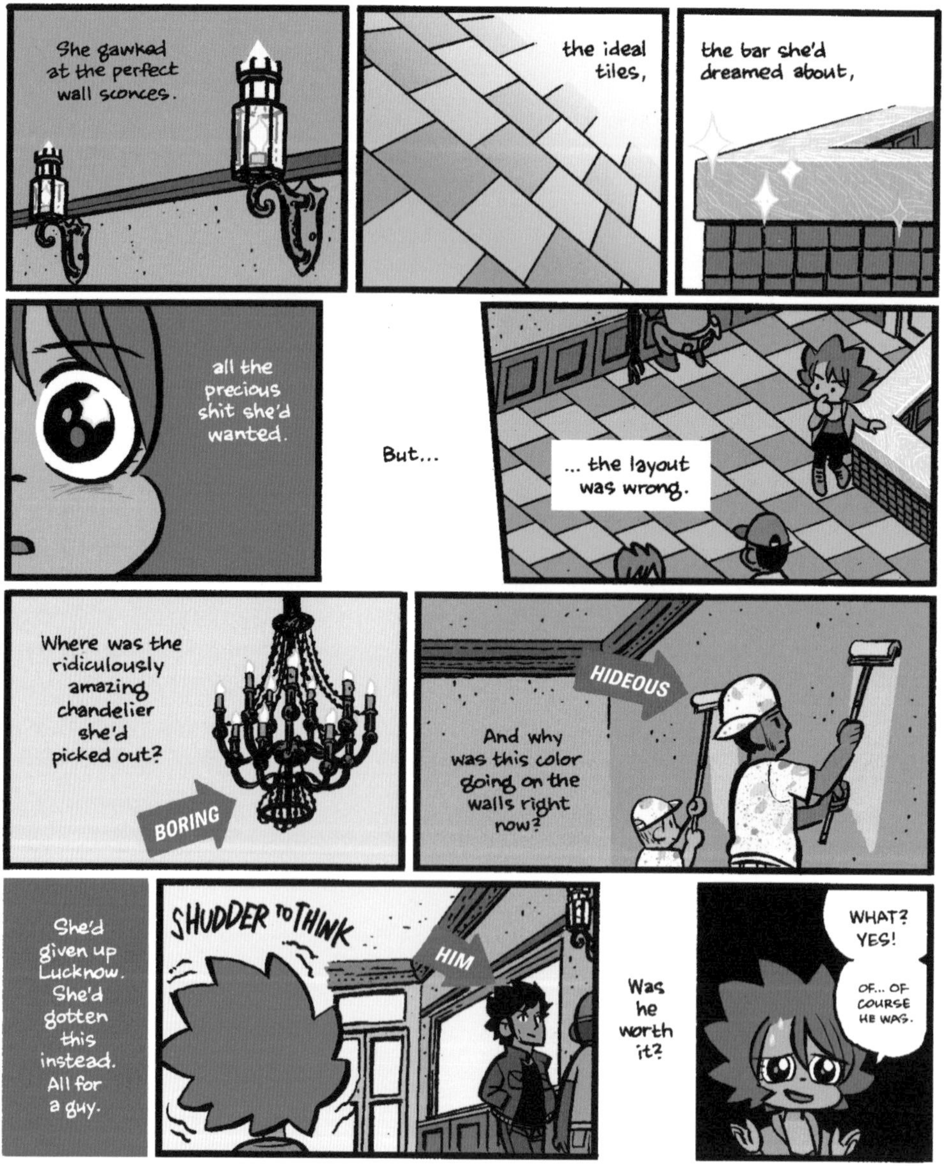
She gawked at the perfect wall sconces.
the ideal tiles,
the bar she'd dreamed about,
all the precious shit she'd wanted.
But...
... the layout was wrong.
Where was the ridiculously amazing chandelier she'd picked out?
BORING
HIDEOUS
And why was this color going on the walls right now?
She'd given up Lucknow. She'd gotten this instead. All for a guy.
SHUDDER TO THINK
HIM
Was he worth it?
WHAT? YES!
OF... OF COURSE HE WAS.

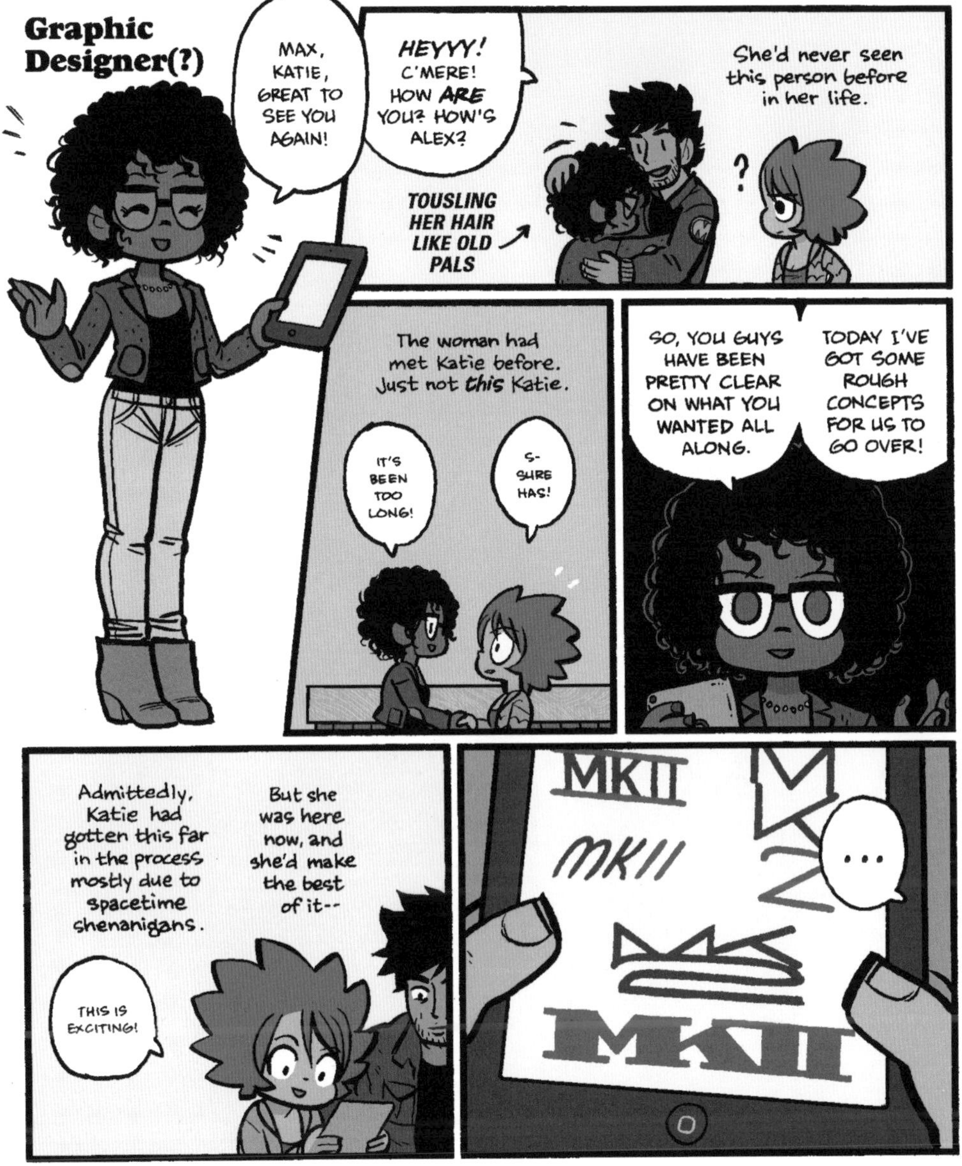
Graphic Designer(?)
MAX, KATIE, GREAT TO SEE YOU AGAIN!
HEYYY! C'MERE! HOW ARE YOU? HOW'S ALEX?
She'd never seen this person before in her life.
?
TOUSLING HER HAIR LIKE OLD PALS
The woman had met Katie before. Just not this Katie.
IT'S BEEN TOO LONG!
S-SURE HAS!
SO, YOU GUYS HAVE BEEN PRETTY CLEAR ON WHAT YOU WANTED ALL ALONG.
TODAY I'VE GOT SOME ROUGH CONCEPTS FOR US TO GO OVER!
Admittedly, Katie had gotten this far in the process mostly due to spacetime shenanigans.
But she was here now, and she'd make the best of it--
THIS IS EXCITING!
MKII
MKII
...
MKII

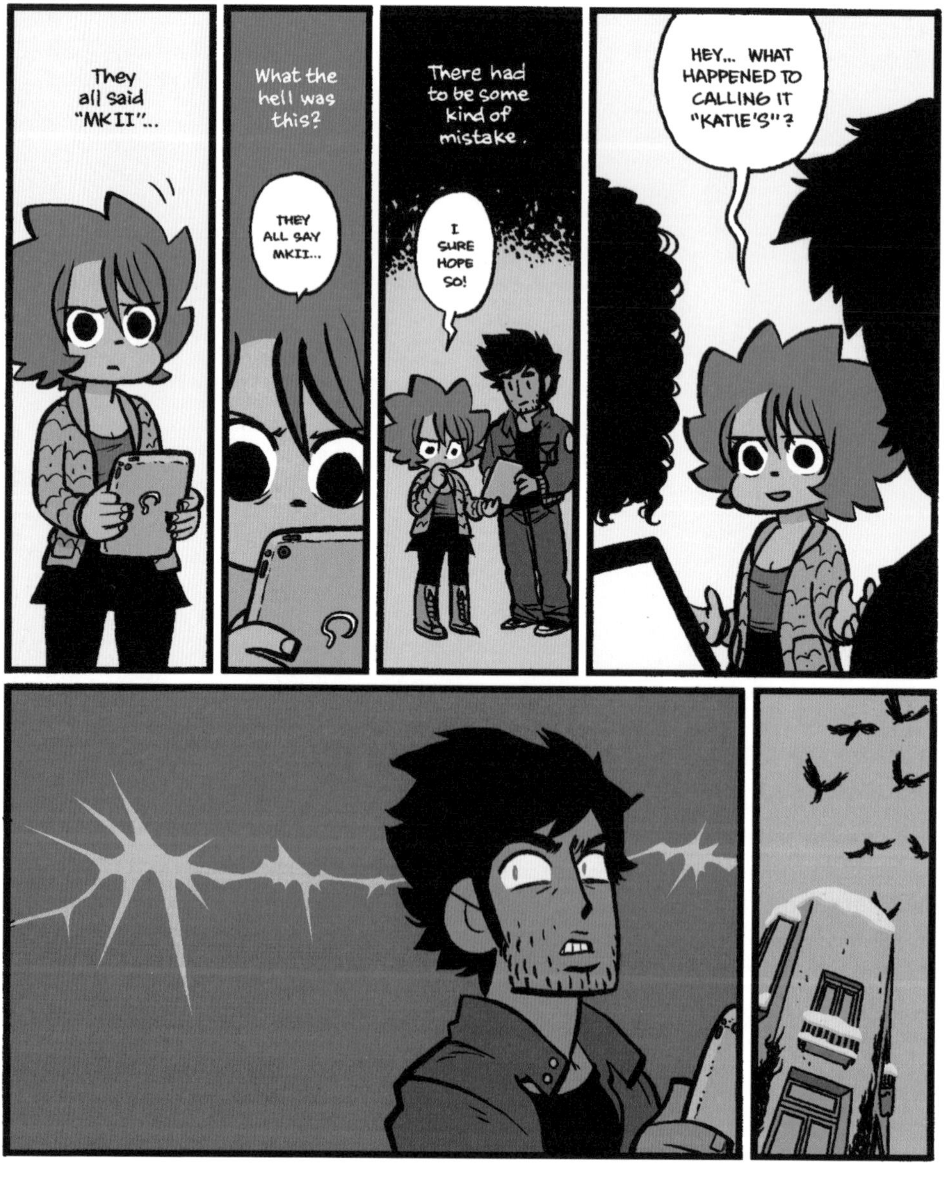
They all said "MKII"...
What the hell was this?
THEY ALL SAY MKII...
There had to be some kind of mistake.
I SURE HOPE SO!
HEY... WHAT HAPPENED TO CALLING IT "KATIE'S"?

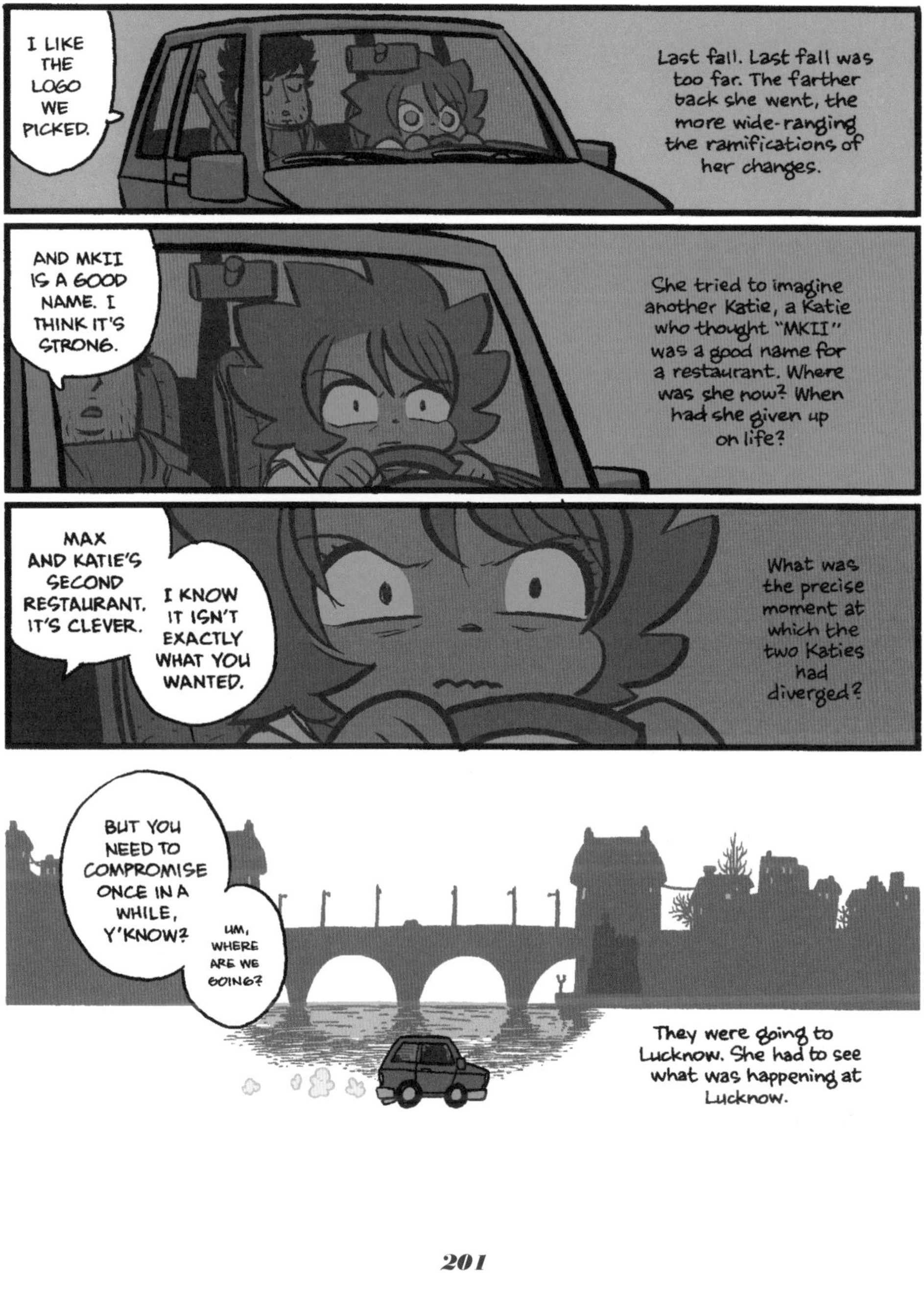
I LIKE THE LOGO WE PICKED.
Last fall. Last fall was too far. The farther back she went, the more wide-ranging the ramifications of her changes.
AND MKII IS A GOOD NAME. I THINK IT'S STRONG.
She tried to imagine another Katie, a Katie who thought "MKII" was a good name for a restaurant. Where was she now? When had she given up on life?
MAX AND KATIE'S SECOND RESTAURANT. IT'S CLEVER.
I KNOW IT ISN'T EXACTLY WHAT YOU WANTED.
What was the precise moment at which the two Katies had diverged?
BUT YOU NEED TO COMPROMISE ONCE IN A WHILE, Y'KNOW?
UM, WHERE ARE WE GOING?
They were going to Lucknow. She had to see what was happening at Lucknow.

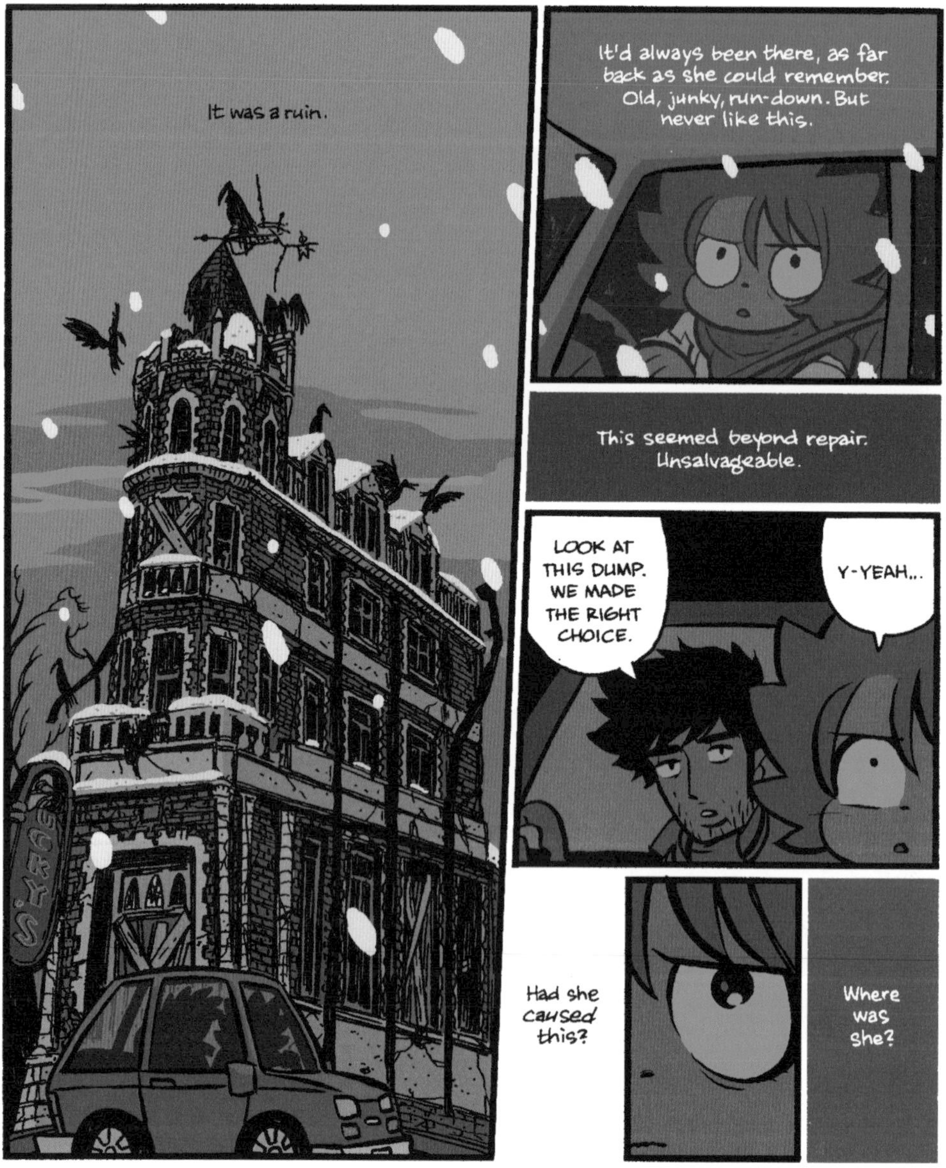

It was a ruin.
It'd always been there, as far back as she could remember. Old, junky, run-down. But never like this.
This seemed beyond repair. Unsalvageable.
LOOK AT THIS DUMP. WE MADE THE RIGHT CHOICE.
Y-YEAH...
Had she caused this?
Where was she?

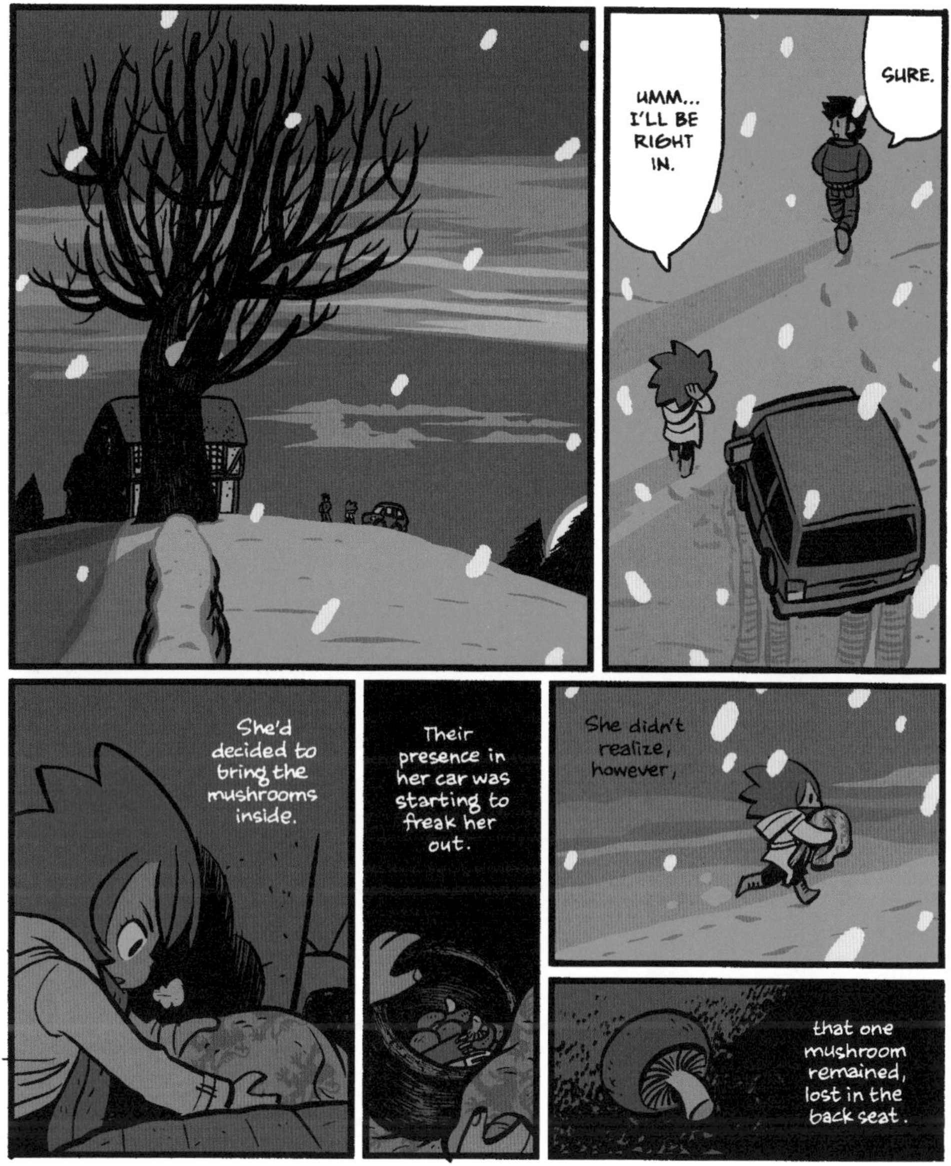
UMM... I'LL BE RIGHT IN.
SURE.
She'd decided to bring the mushrooms inside.
Their presence in her car was starting to freak her out.
She didn't realize, however,
that one mushroom remained, lost in the back seat.

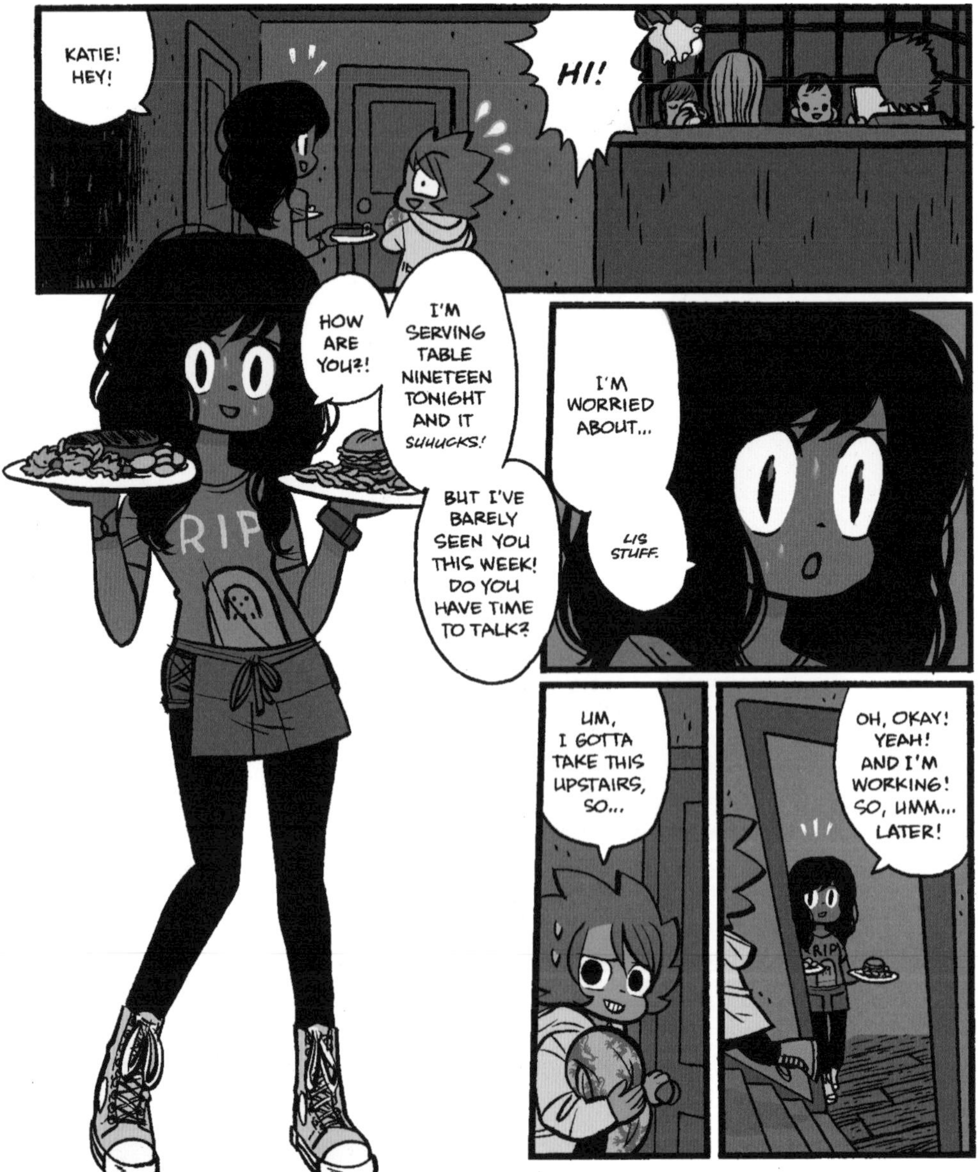
KATIE! HEY!
HI!
HOW ARE YOU?!
I'M SERVING TABLE NINETEEN TONIGHT AND IT SUUUCKS!
BUT I'VE BARELY SEEN YOU THIS WEEK! DO YOU HAVE TIME TO TALK?
I'M WORRIED ABOUT...
US STUFF.
UM, I GOTTA TAKE THIS UPSTAIRS, SO...
OH, OKAY! YEAH! AND I'M WORKING! SO, UMM... LATER!

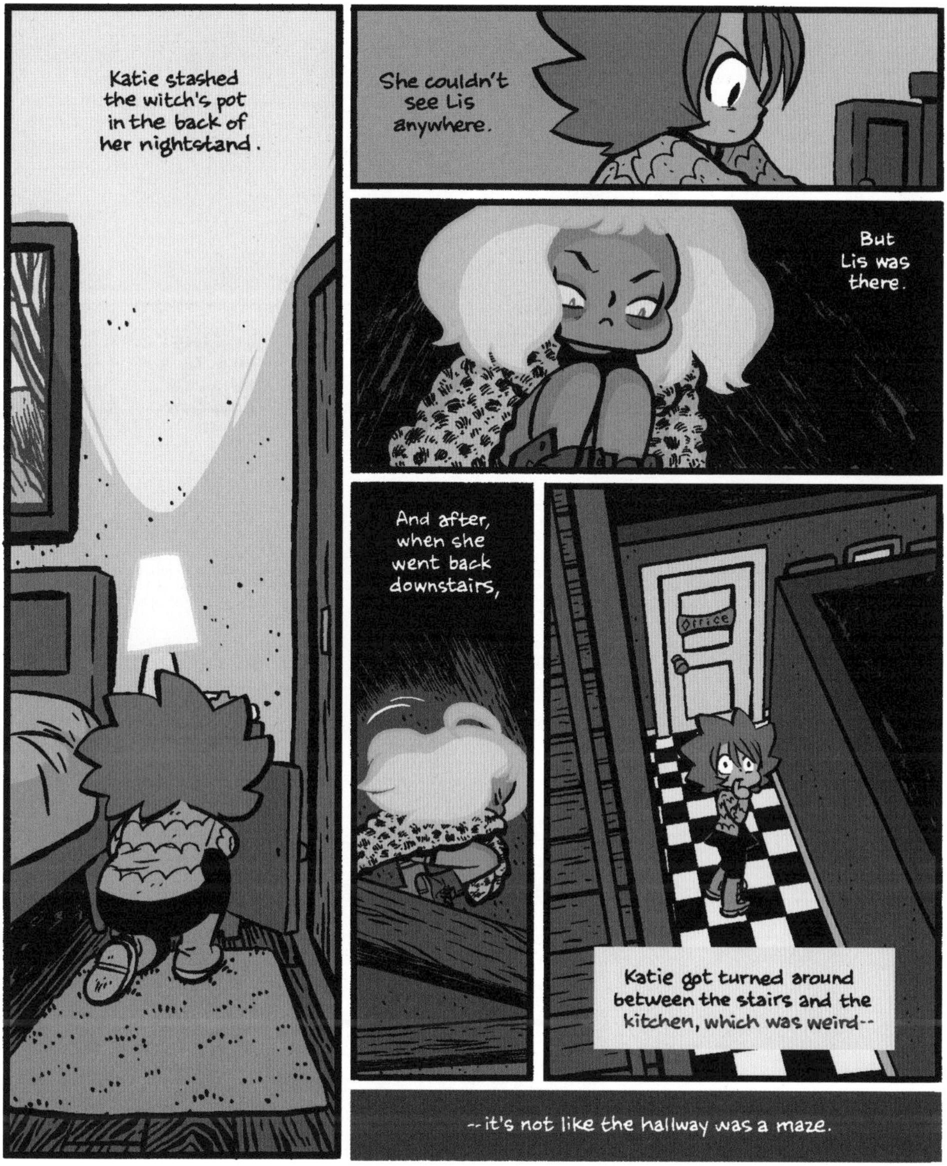
Katie stashed the witch's pot in the back of her nightstand.
She couldn't see Lis anywhere.
But Lis was there.
And after, when she went back downstairs,
Office
Katie got turned around between the stairs and the kitchen, which was weird--
--it's not like the hallway was a maze.

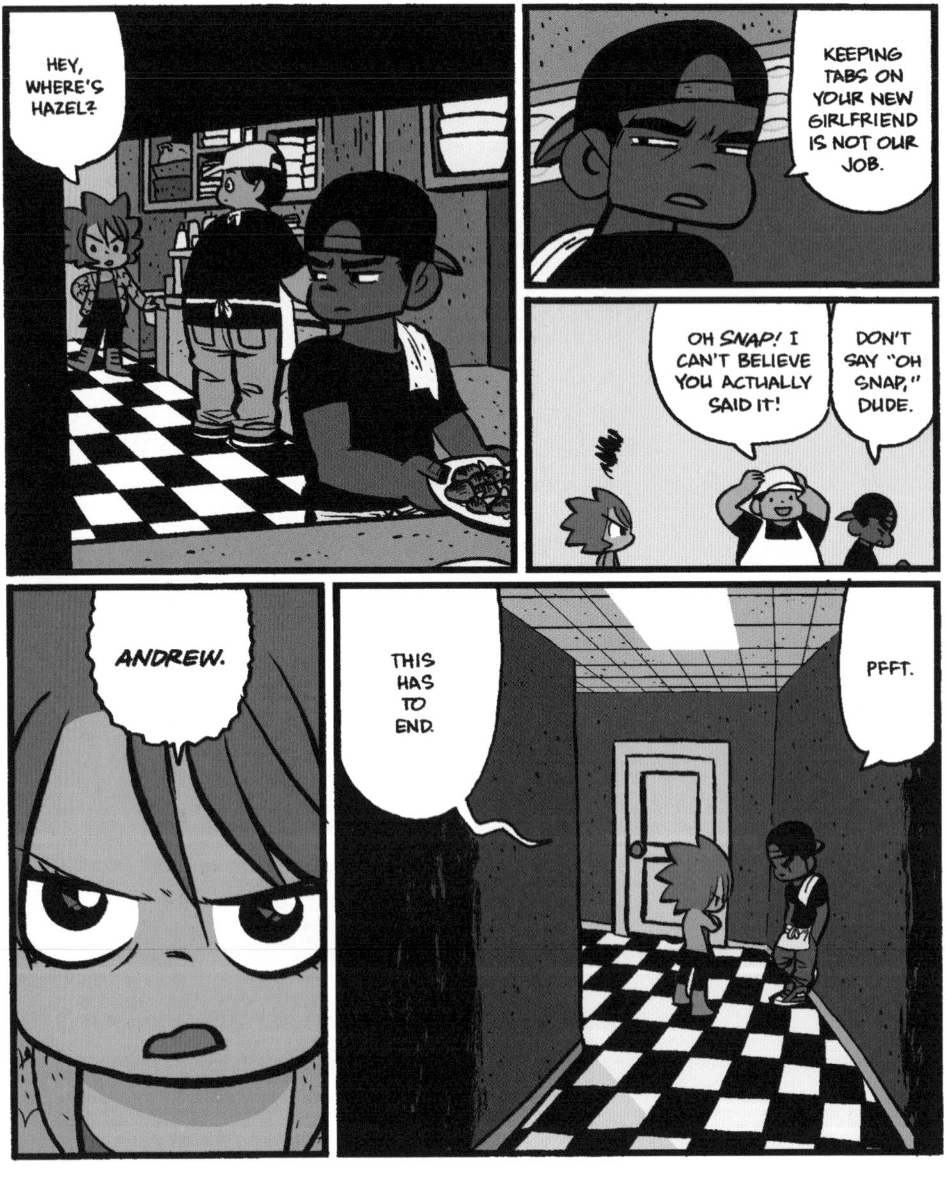
HEY, WHERE'S HAZEL?
KEEPING TABS ON YOUR NEW GIRLFRIEND IS NOT OUR JOB.
OH SNAP! I CAN'T BELIEVE YOU ACTUALLY SAID IT!
DON'T SAY "OH SNAP," DUDE.
ANDREW.
THIS HAS TO END.
PFFT.

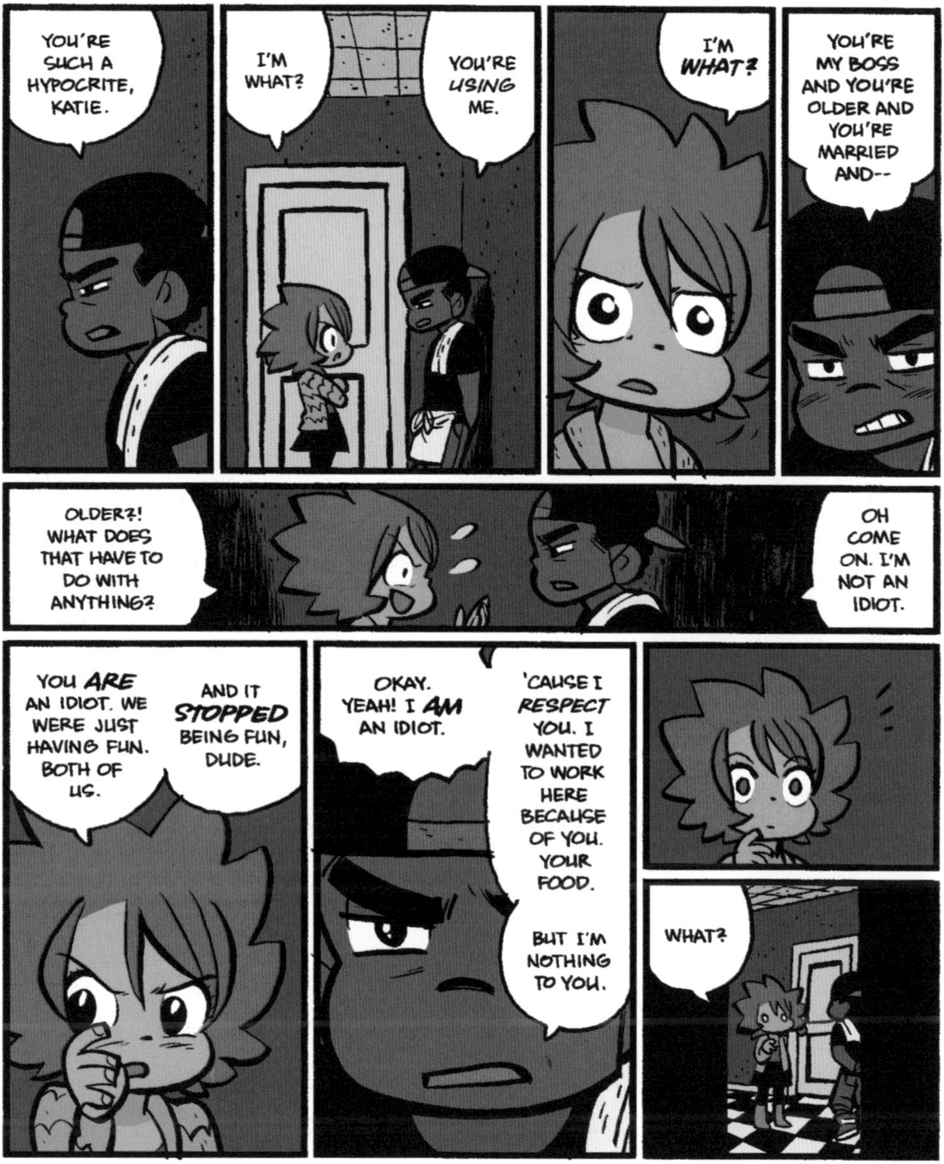
YOU'RE SUCH A HYPOCRITE, KATIE.
I'M WHAT?
YOU'RE USING ME.
I'M WHAT?
YOU'RE MY BOSS AND YOU'RE OLDER AND YOU'RE MARRIED AND--
OLDER?! WHAT DOES THAT HAVE TO DO WITH ANYTHING?
OH COME ON. I'M NOT AN IDIOT.
YOU ARE AN IDIOT. WE WERE JUST HAVING FUN. BOTH OF US.
AND IT STOPPED BEING FUN, DUDE.
OKAY. YEAH! I AM AN IDIOT.
'CAUSE I RESPECT YOU. I WANTED TO WORK HERE BECAUSE OF YOU. YOUR FOOD.
BUT I'M NOTHING TO YOU.
WHAT?

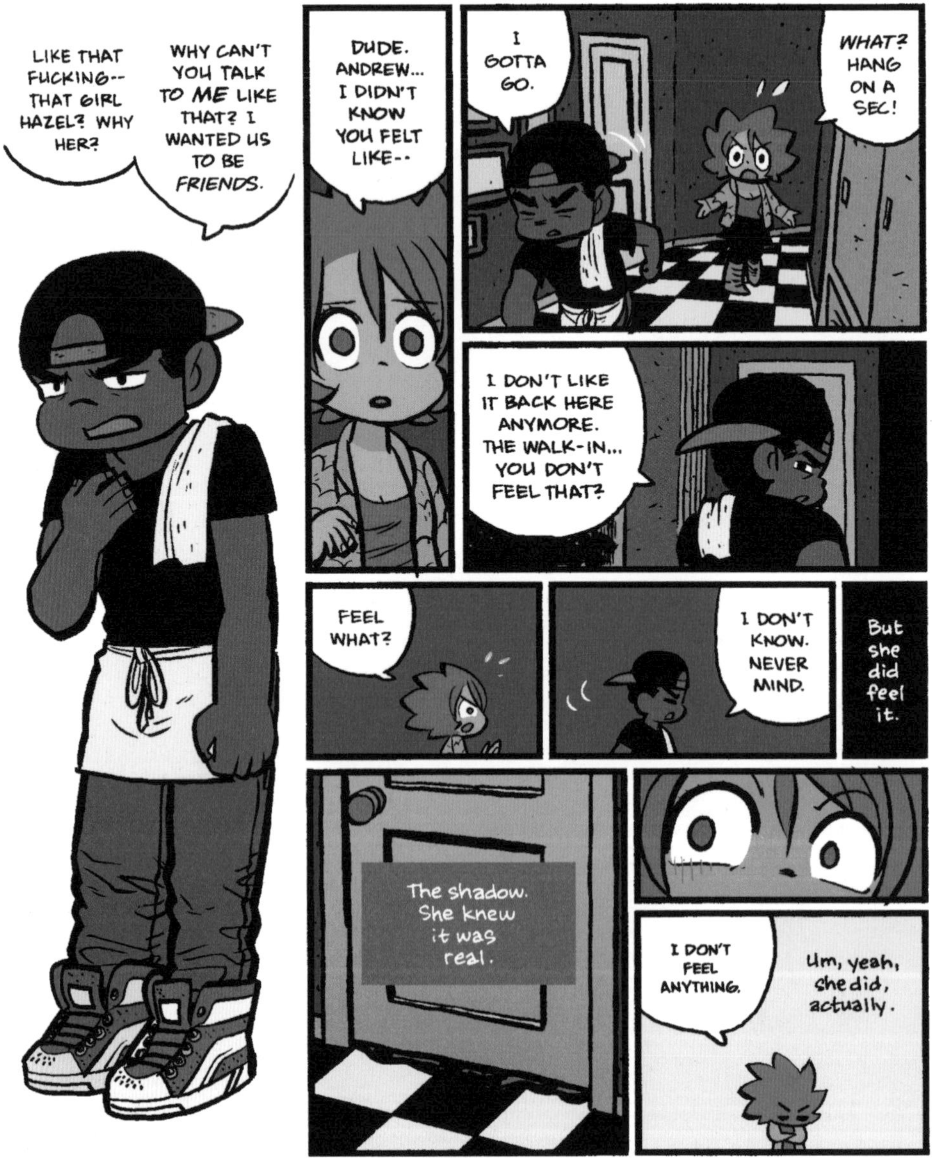

LIKE THAT FUCKING-- THAT GIRL HAZEL? WHY HER?
WHY CAN'T YOU TALK TO ME LIKE THAT? I WANTED US TO BE FRIENDS.
DUDE. ANDREW... I DIDN'T KNOW YOU FELT LIKE--
I GOTTA GO.
WHAT? HANG ON A SEC!
I DON'T LIKE IT BACK HERE ANYMORE. THE WALK-IN... YOU DON'T FEEL THAT?
FEEL WHAT?
I DON'T KNOW. NEVER MIND.
But she did feel it.
The shadow. She knew it was real.
I DON'T FEEL ANYTHING.
Um, yeah, she did, actually.

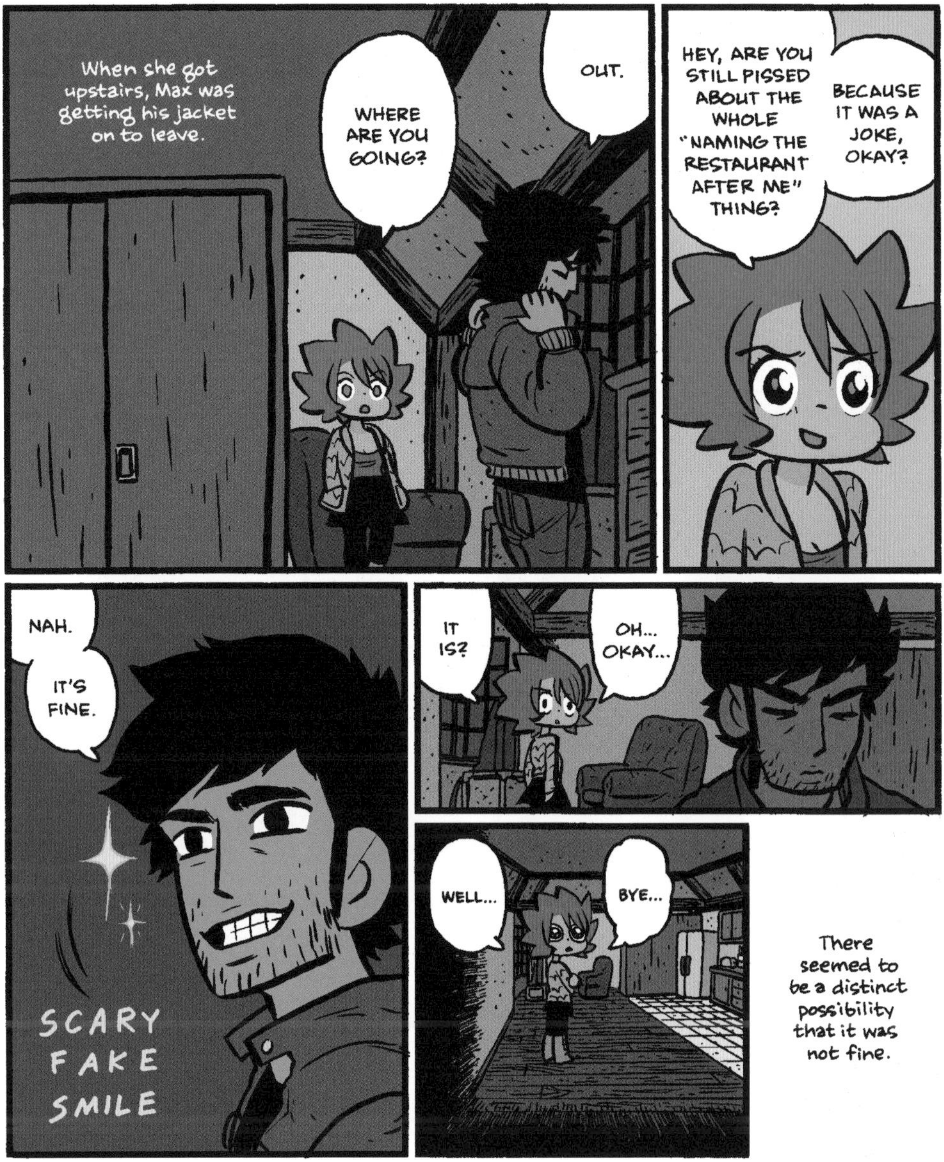
When she got upstairs, Max was getting his jacket on to leave.
WHERE ARE YOU GOING?
OUT.
HEY, ARE YOU STILL PISSED ABOUT THE WHOLE "NAMING THE RESTAURANT AFTER ME" THING?
BECAUSE IT WAS A JOKE, OKAY?
NAH.
IT'S FINE.
SCARY FAKE SMILE
IT IS?
OH... OKAY...
WELL...
BYE...
There seemed to be a distinct possibility that it was not fine.

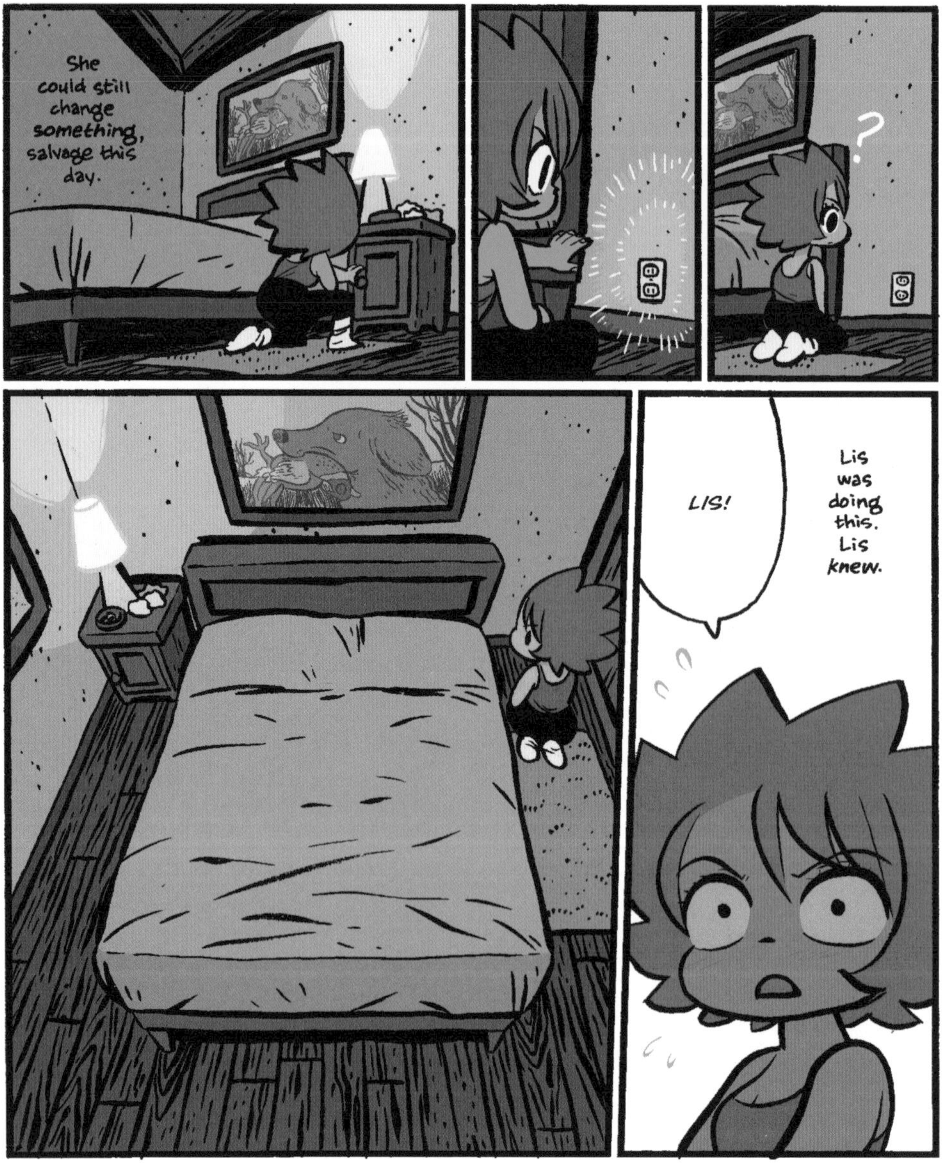
She could still change something, salvage this day.
?
LIS!
Lis was doing this. Lis knew.

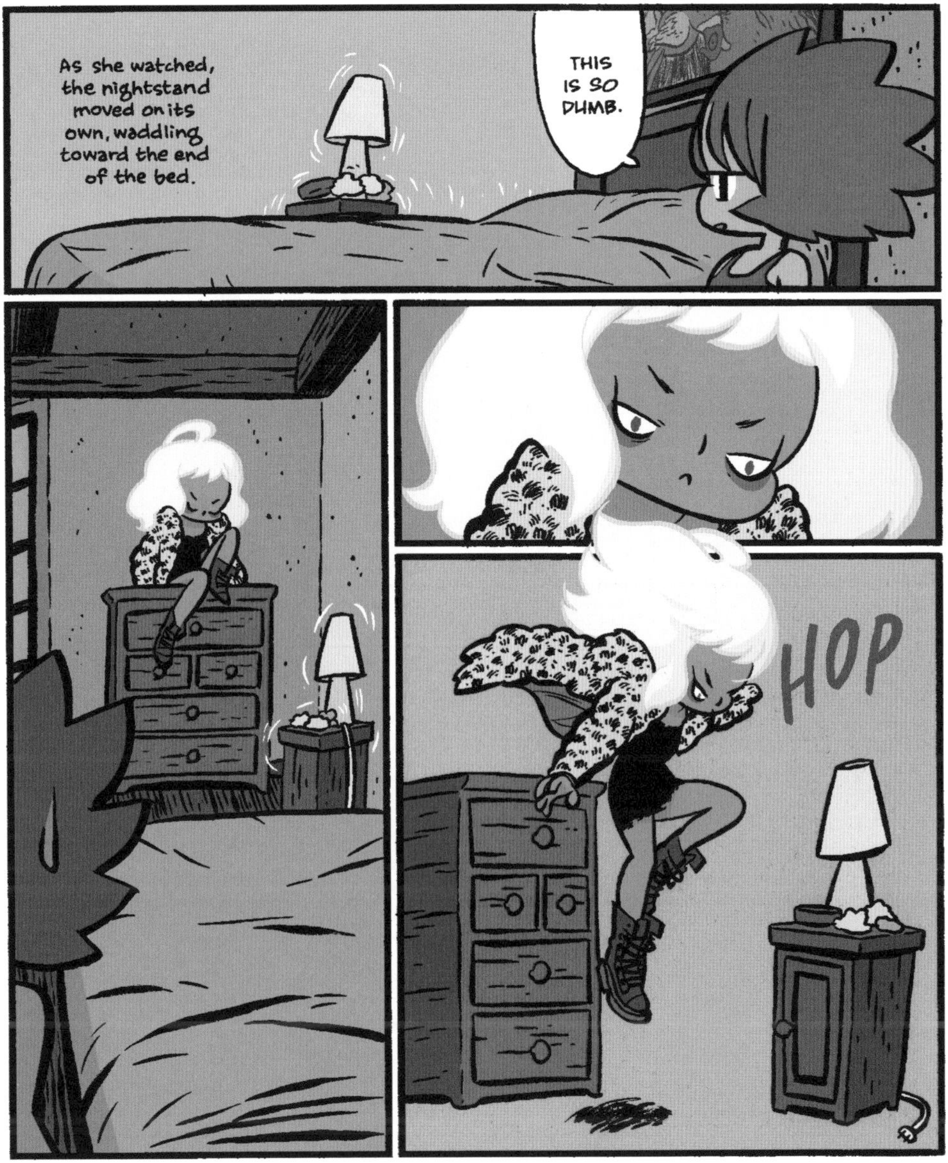
As she watched, the nightstand moved on its own, waddling toward the end of the bed.
THIS IS SO DUMB.
HOP

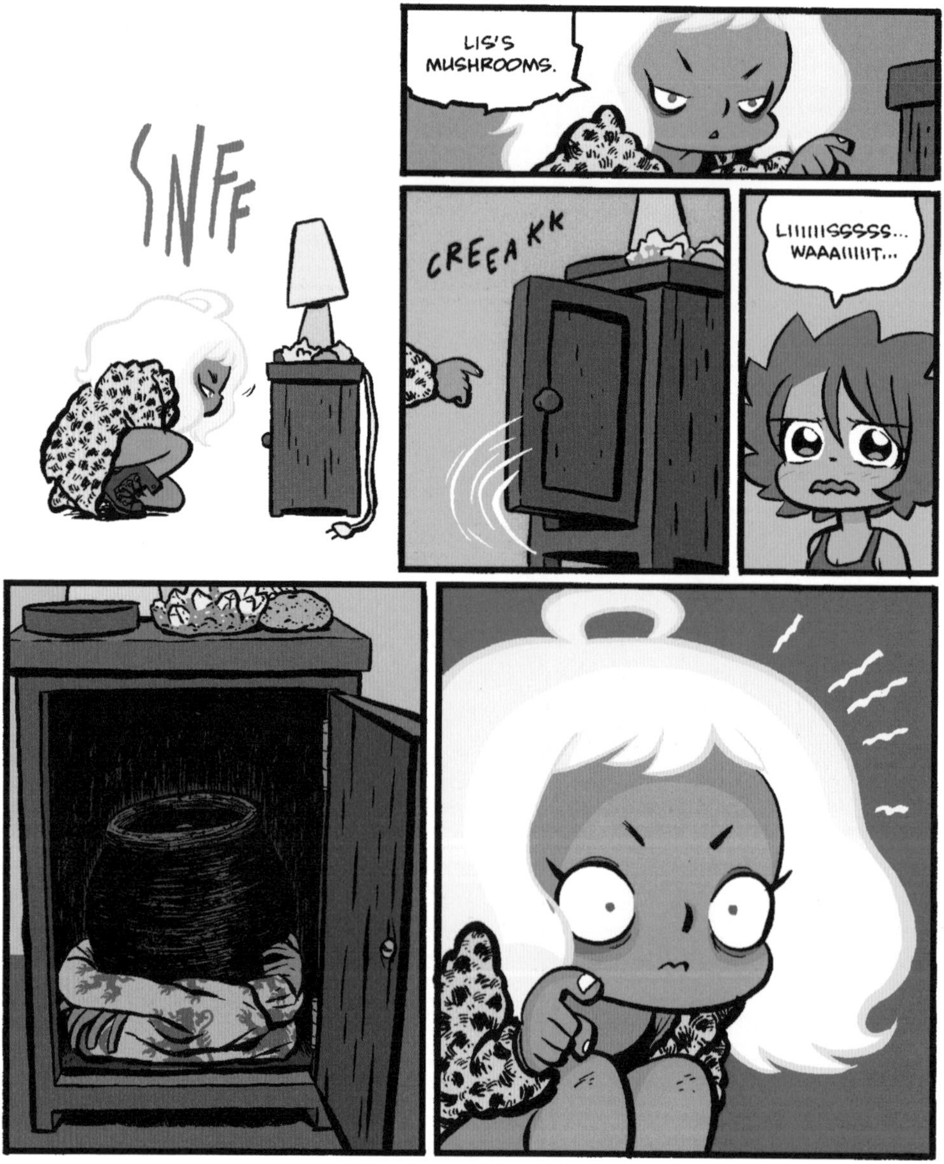
SNFF
LIS'S MUSHROOMS.
CREEAKK
LIIIIIISSSSS... WAAAIIIIIT...

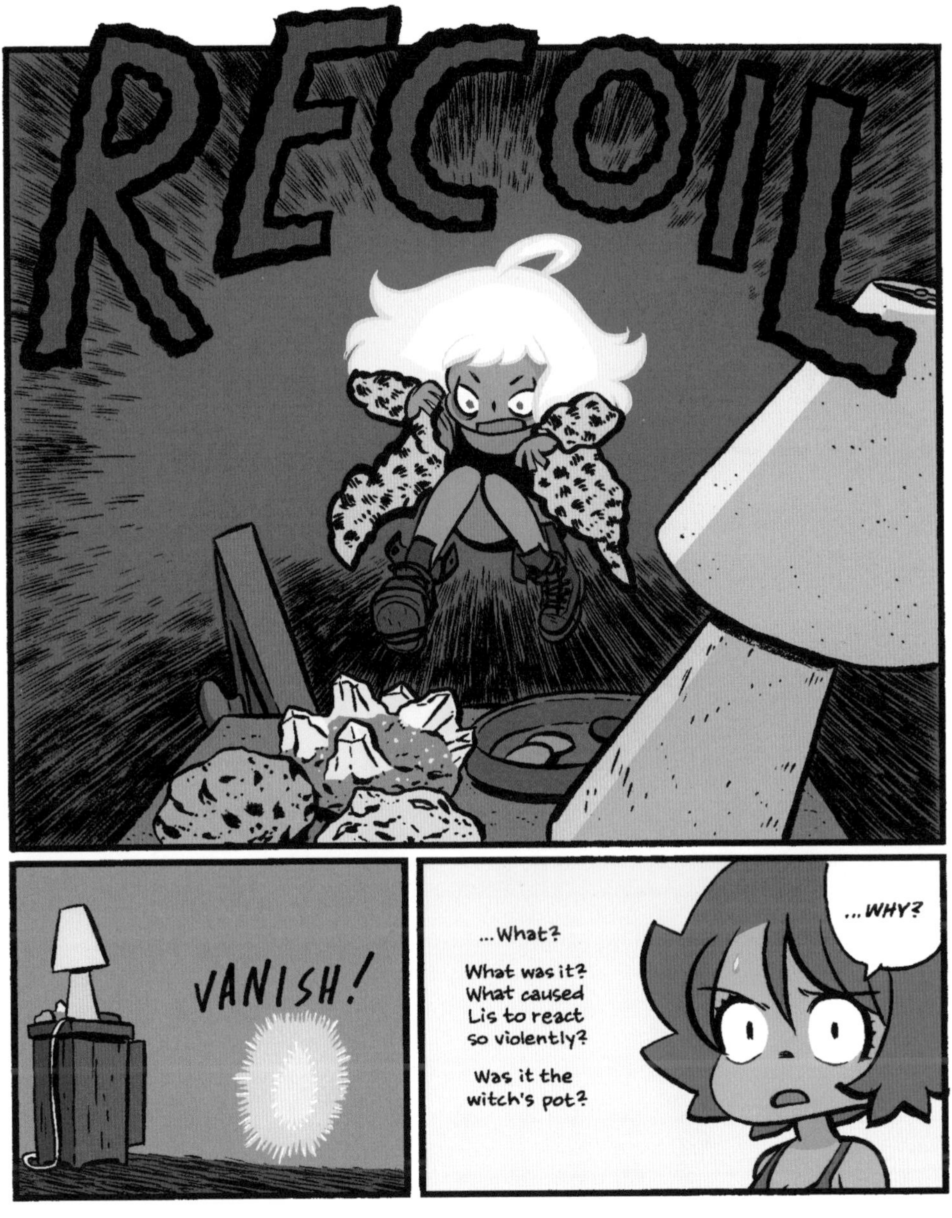
RECOIL
VANISH!
...What?
What was it? What caused Lis to react so violently?
Was it the witch's pot?
...WHY?

There were six mushrooms in the pot.

How many changes had she made now?

She tried to do the math, but immediately gave up.

toss

REVISION #8

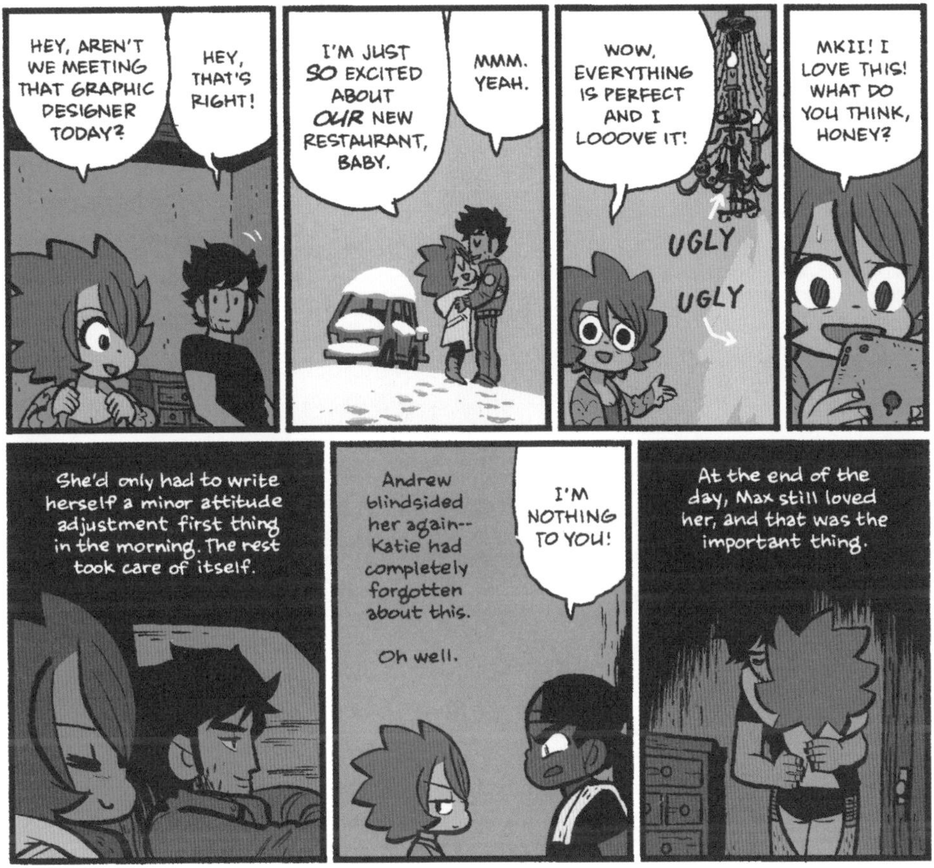

HEY, AREN'T WE MEETING THAT GRAPHIC DESIGNER TODAY?
HEY, THAT'S RIGHT!
I'M JUST SO EXCITED ABOUT OUR NEW RESTAURANT, BABY.
MMM. YEAH.
WOW, EVERYTHING IS PERFECT AND I LOOOVE IT!
UGLY
UGLY
MKII! I LOVE THIS! WHAT DO YOU THINK, HONEY?
She'd only had to write herself a minor attitude adjustment first thing in the morning. The rest took care of itself.
Andrew blindsided her again-- Katie had completely forgotten about this.
Oh well.
I'M NOTHING TO YOU!
At the end of the day, Max still loved her, and that was the important thing.

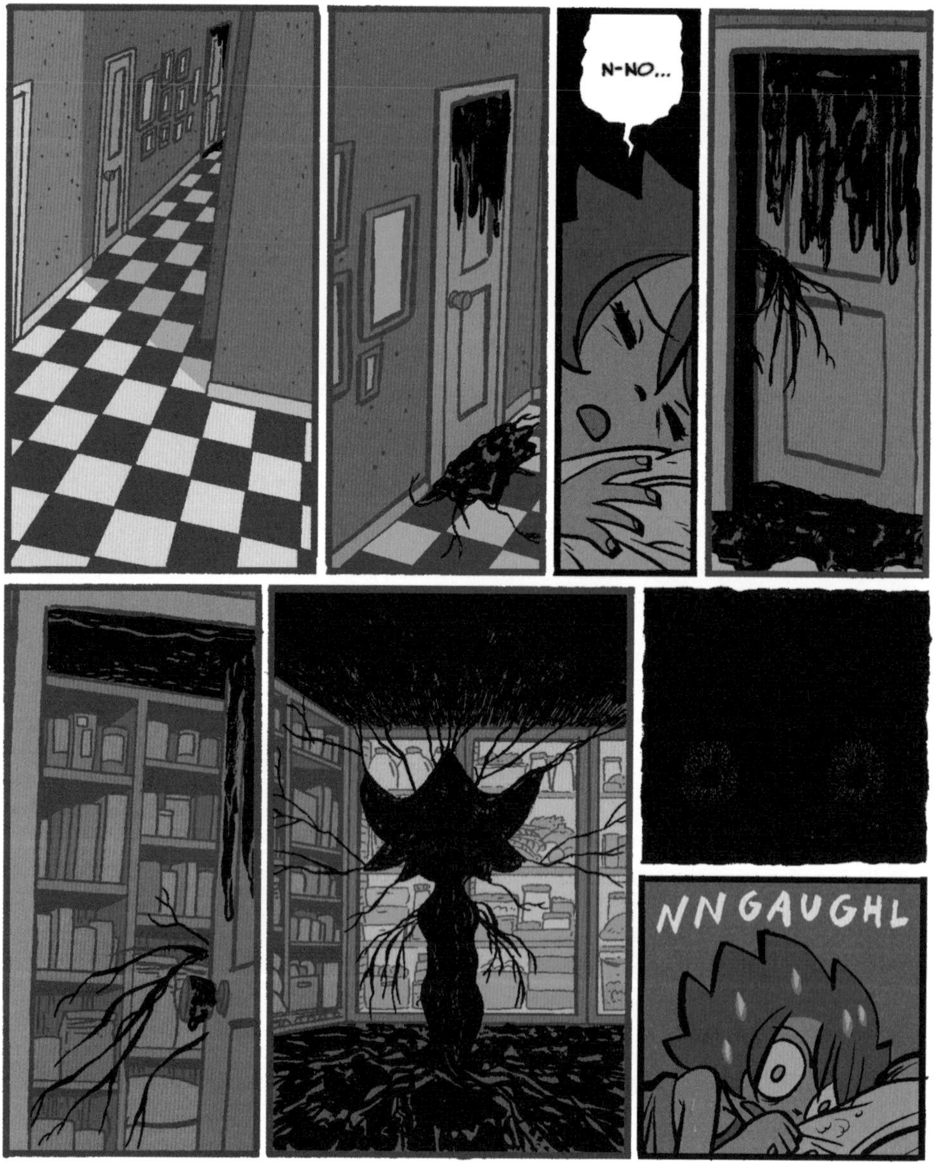
N-NO...
NNGAUGHL

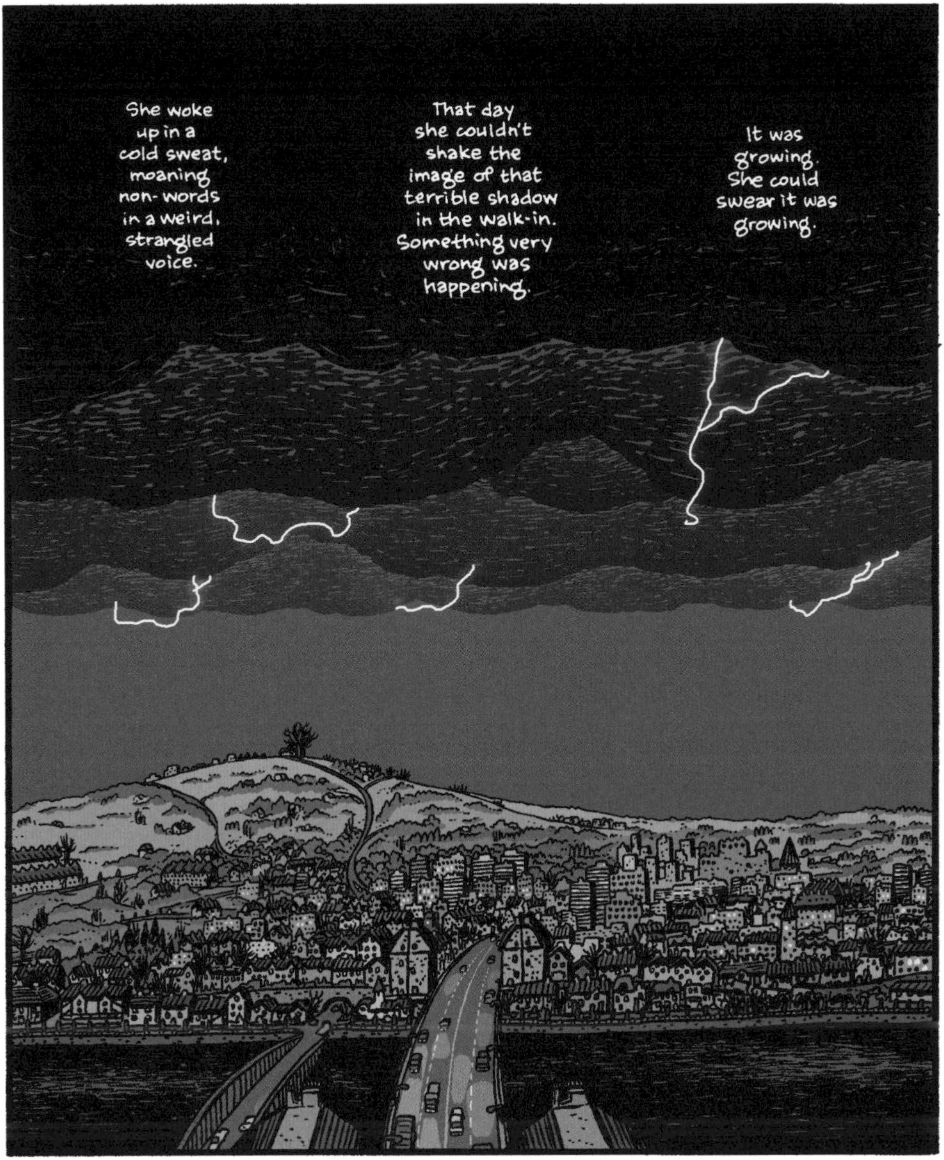
She woke up in a cold sweat, moaning non-words in a weird, strangled voice.
That day she couldn't shake the image of that terrible shadow in the walk-in. Something very wrong was happening.
It was growing. She could swear it was growing.

REVISION #9

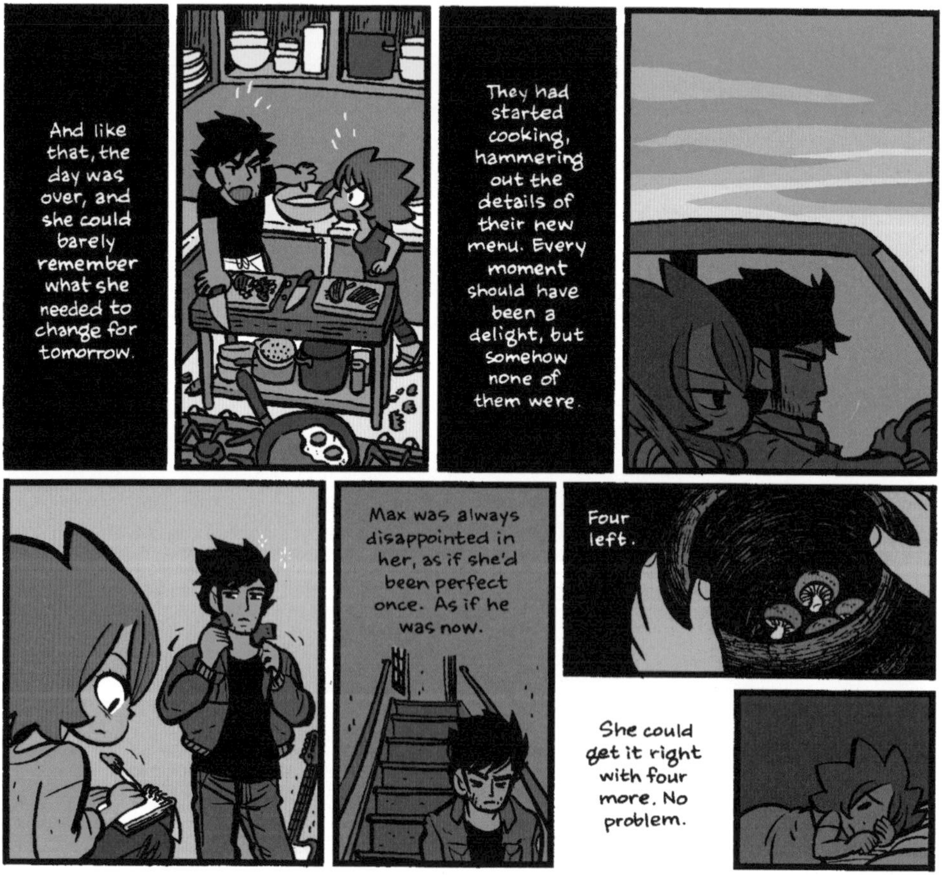
And like that, the day was over, and she could barely remember what she needed to change for tomorrow.
They had started cooking, hammering out the details of their new menu. Every moment should have been a delight, but somehow none of them were.
Max was always disappointed in her, as if she'd been perfect once. As if he was now.
Four left.
She could get it right with four more. No problem.

REVISION #10

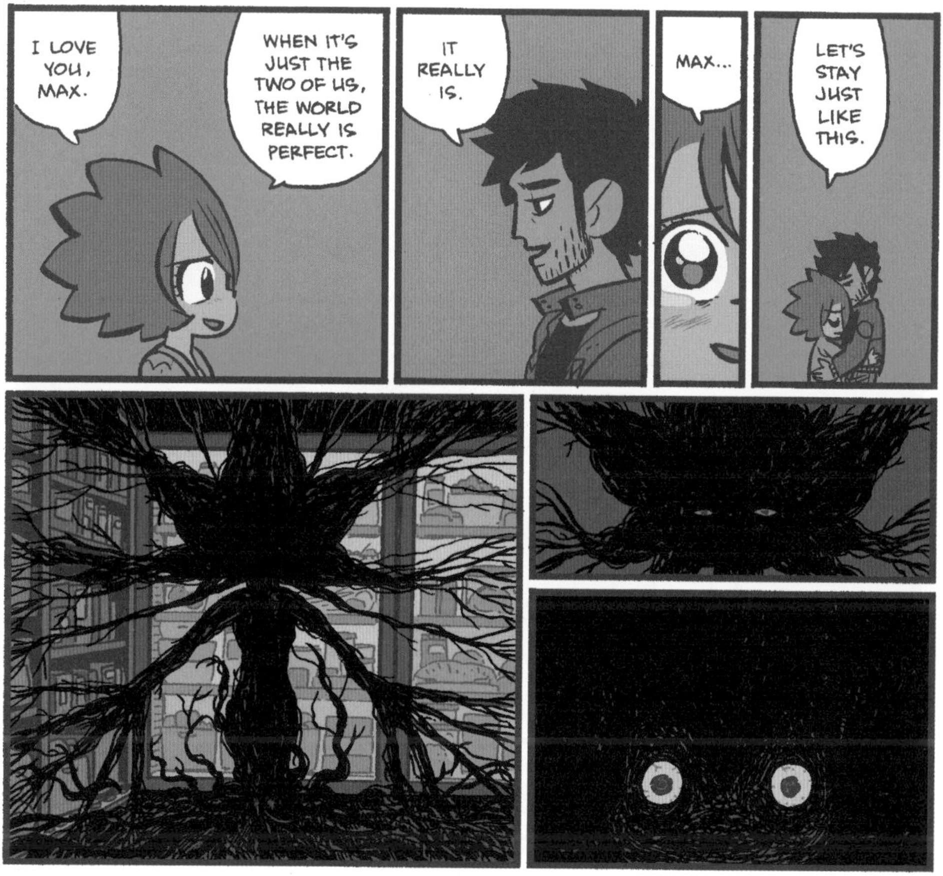
I LOVE YOU, MAX.
WHEN IT'S JUST THE TWO OF US, THE WORLD REALLY IS PERFECT.
IT REALLY IS.
MAX...
LET'S STAY JUST LIKE THIS.

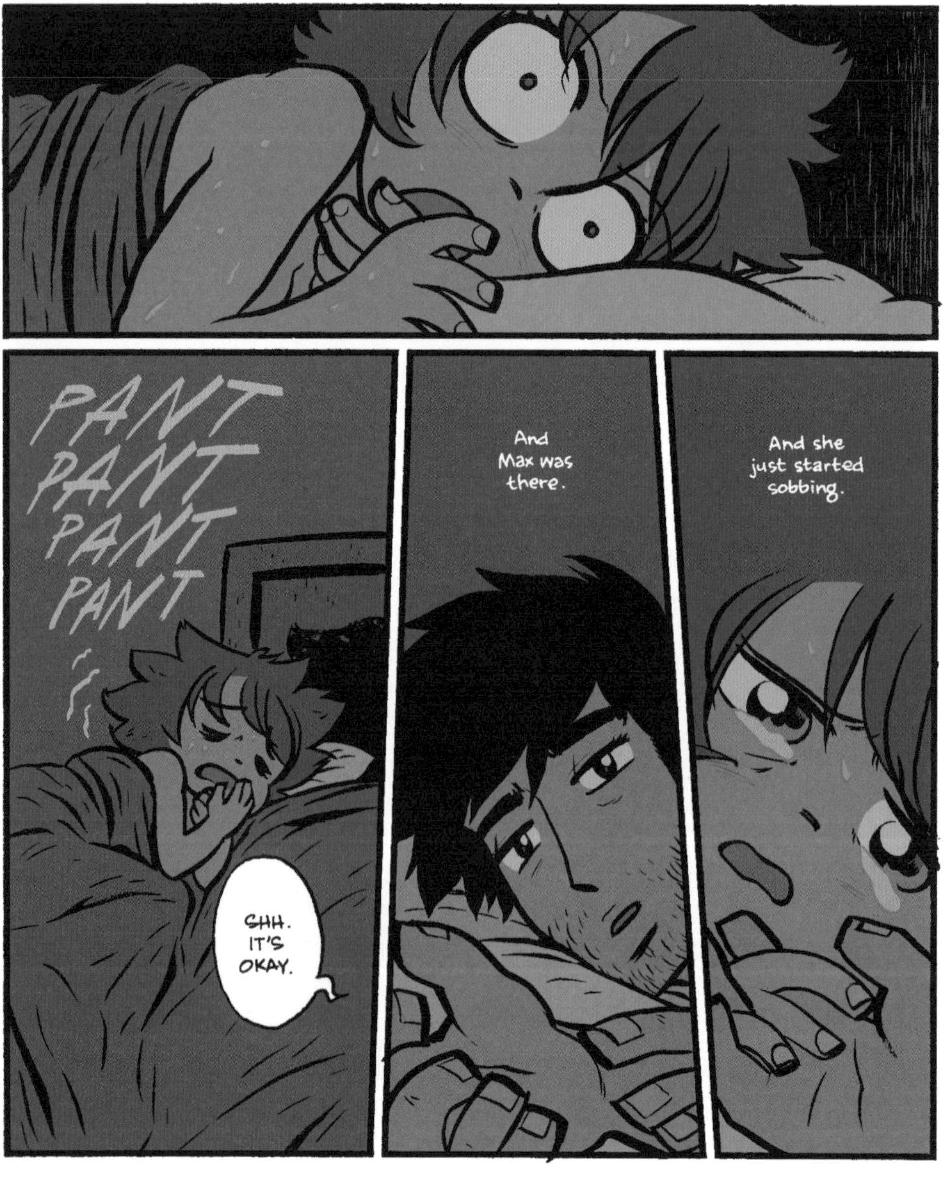
PANT
PANT
PANT
PANT
SHH. IT'S OKAY.
And Max was there.
And she just started sobbing.

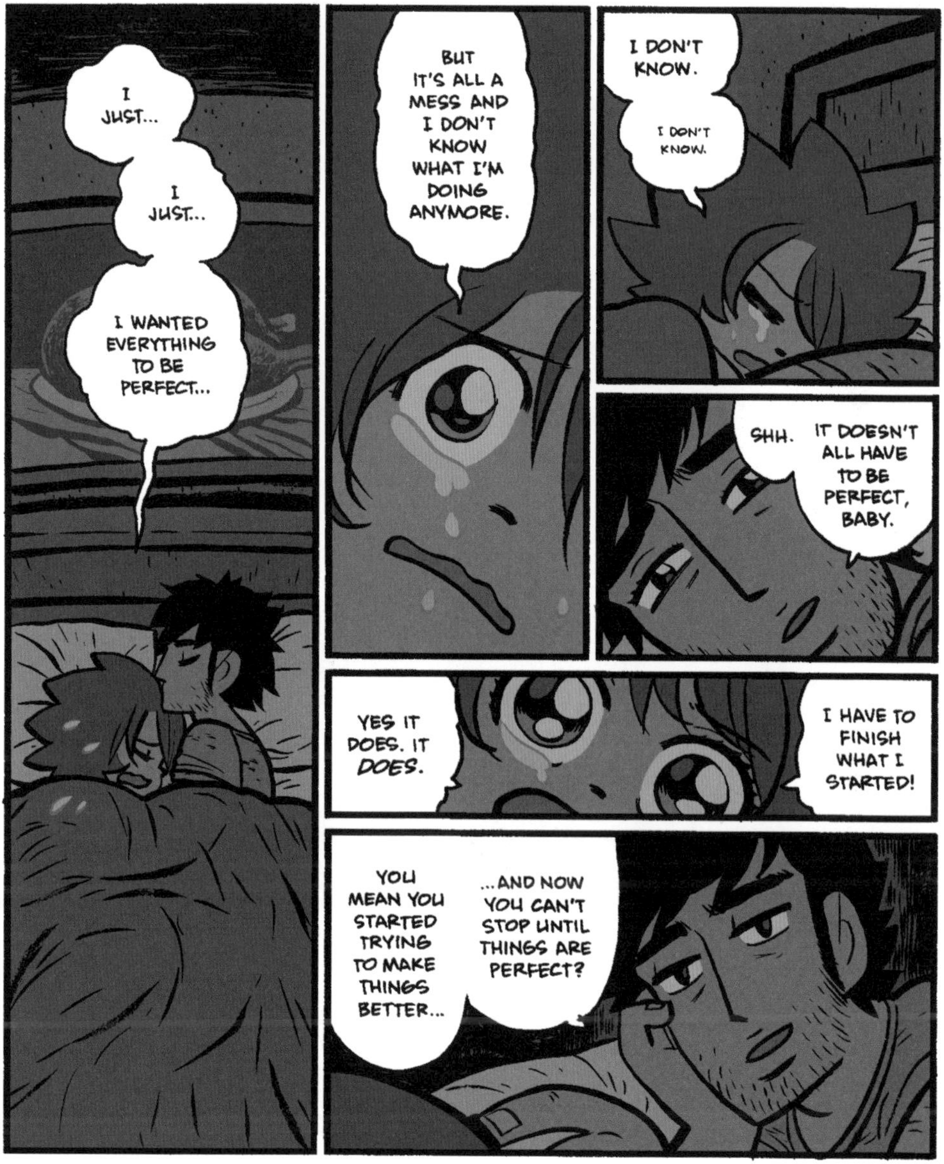
I JUST...
I JUST...
I WANTED EVERYTHING TO BE PERFECT...
BUT IT'S ALL A MESS AND I DON'T KNOW WHAT I'M DOING ANYMORE.
I DON'T KNOW.
I DON'T KNOW.
SHH.
IT DOESN'T ALL HAVE TO BE PERFECT, BABY.
YES IT DOES. IT *DOES*.
I HAVE TO FINISH WHAT I STARTED!
YOU MEAN YOU STARTED TRYING TO MAKE THINGS BETTER...
...AND NOW YOU CAN'T STOP UNTIL THINGS ARE PERFECT?

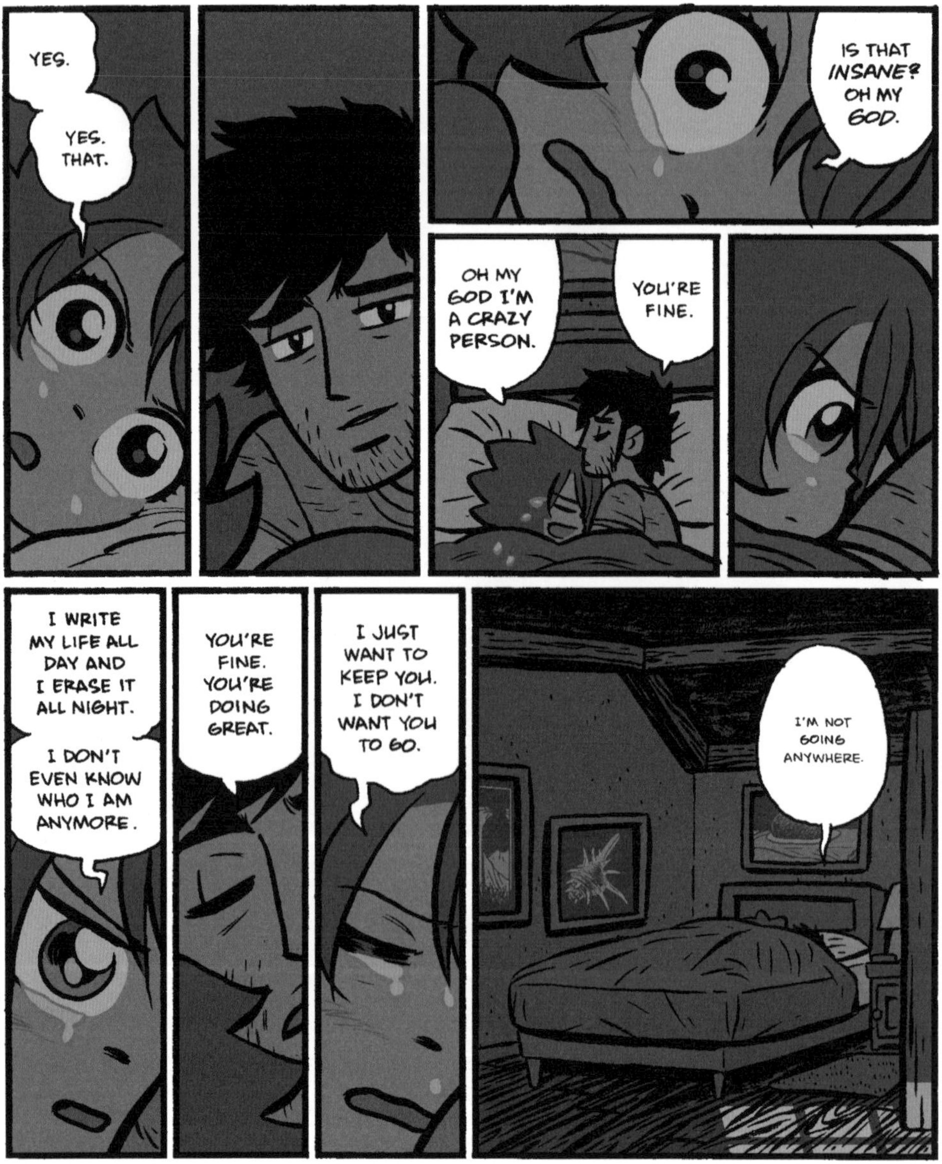
YES.
YES. THAT.
IS THAT INSANE? OH MY GOD.
OH MY GOD I'M A CRAZY PERSON.
YOU'RE FINE.
I WRITE MY LIFE ALL DAY AND I ERASE IT ALL NIGHT.
I DON'T EVEN KNOW WHO I AM ANYMORE.
YOU'RE FINE. YOU'RE DOING GREAT.
I JUST WANT TO KEEP YOU. I DON'T WANT YOU TO GO.
I'M NOT GOING ANYWHERE.

Katie
fell
asleep
again.

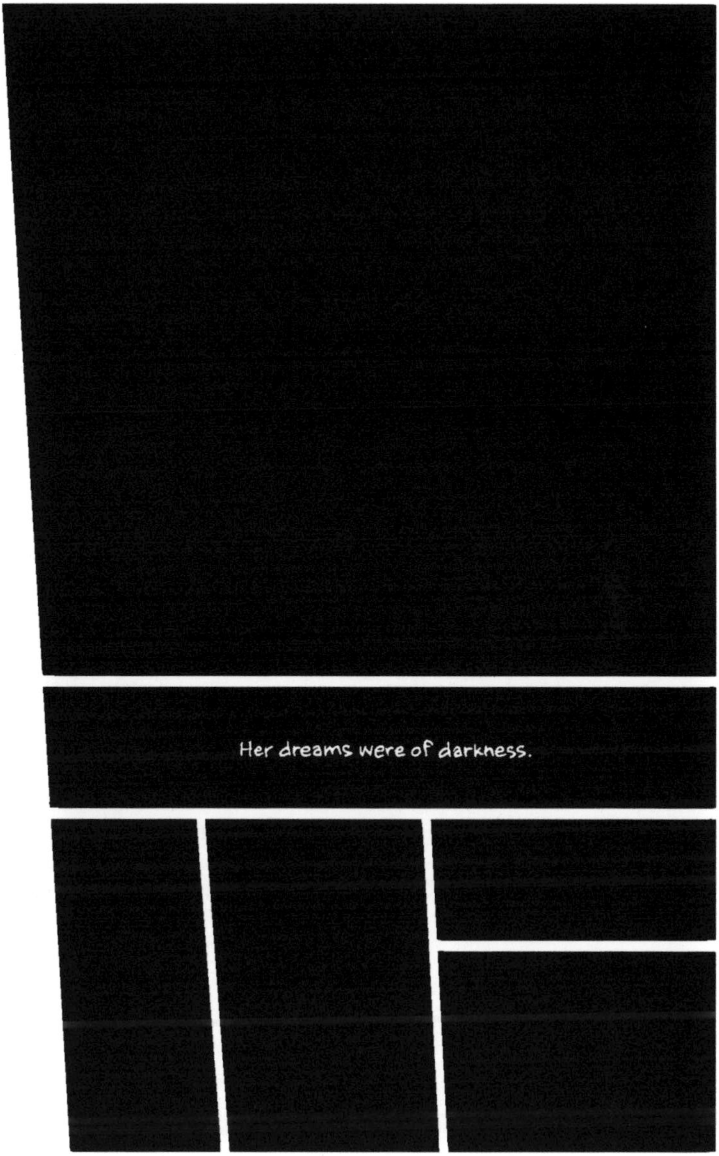
Her dreams were of darkness.

She woke up,

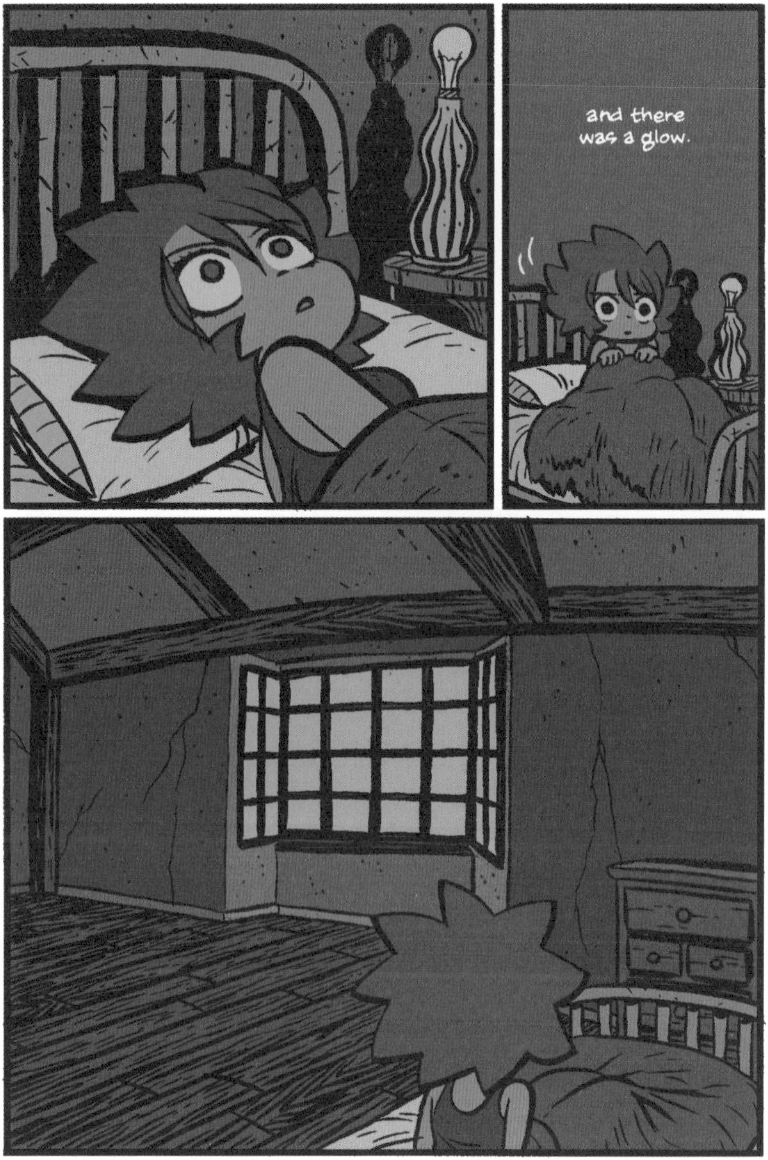
and there was a glow.

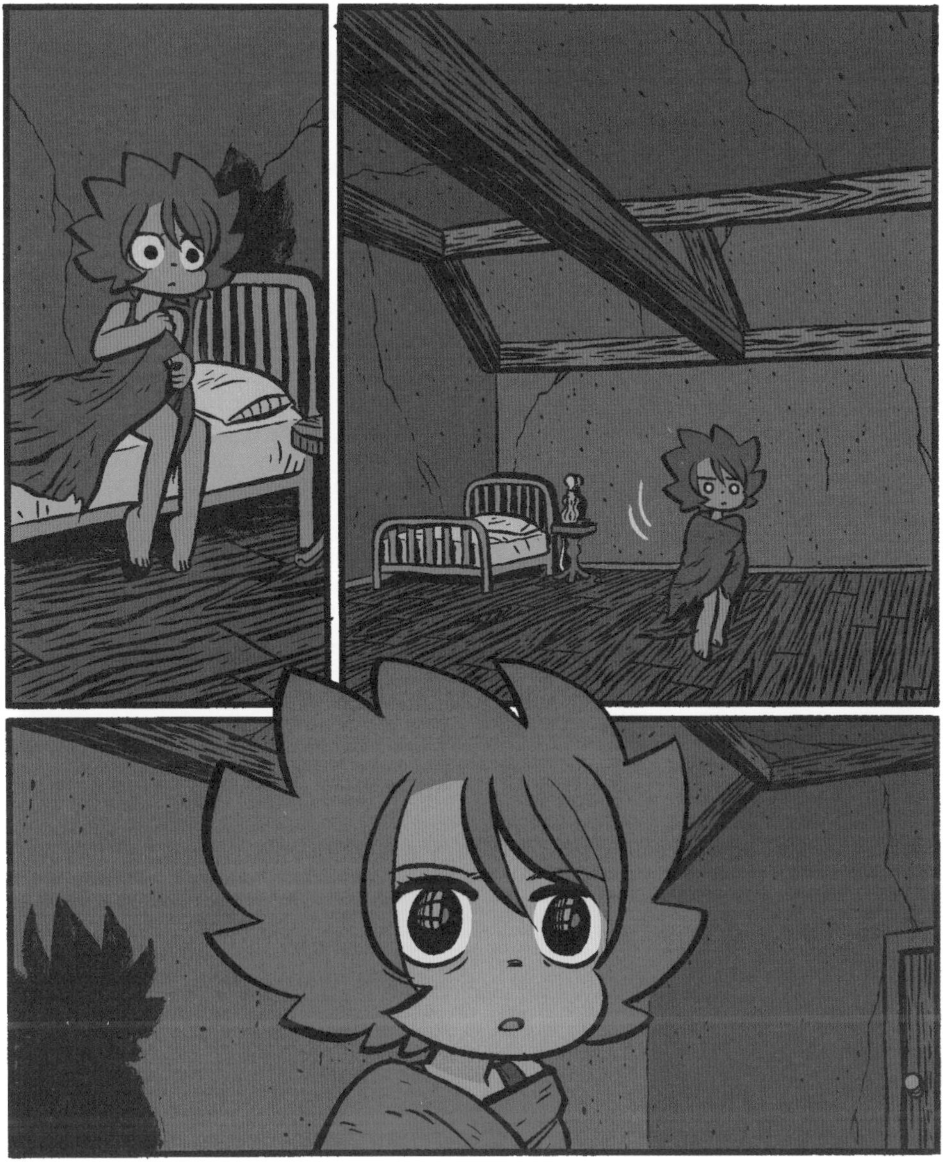

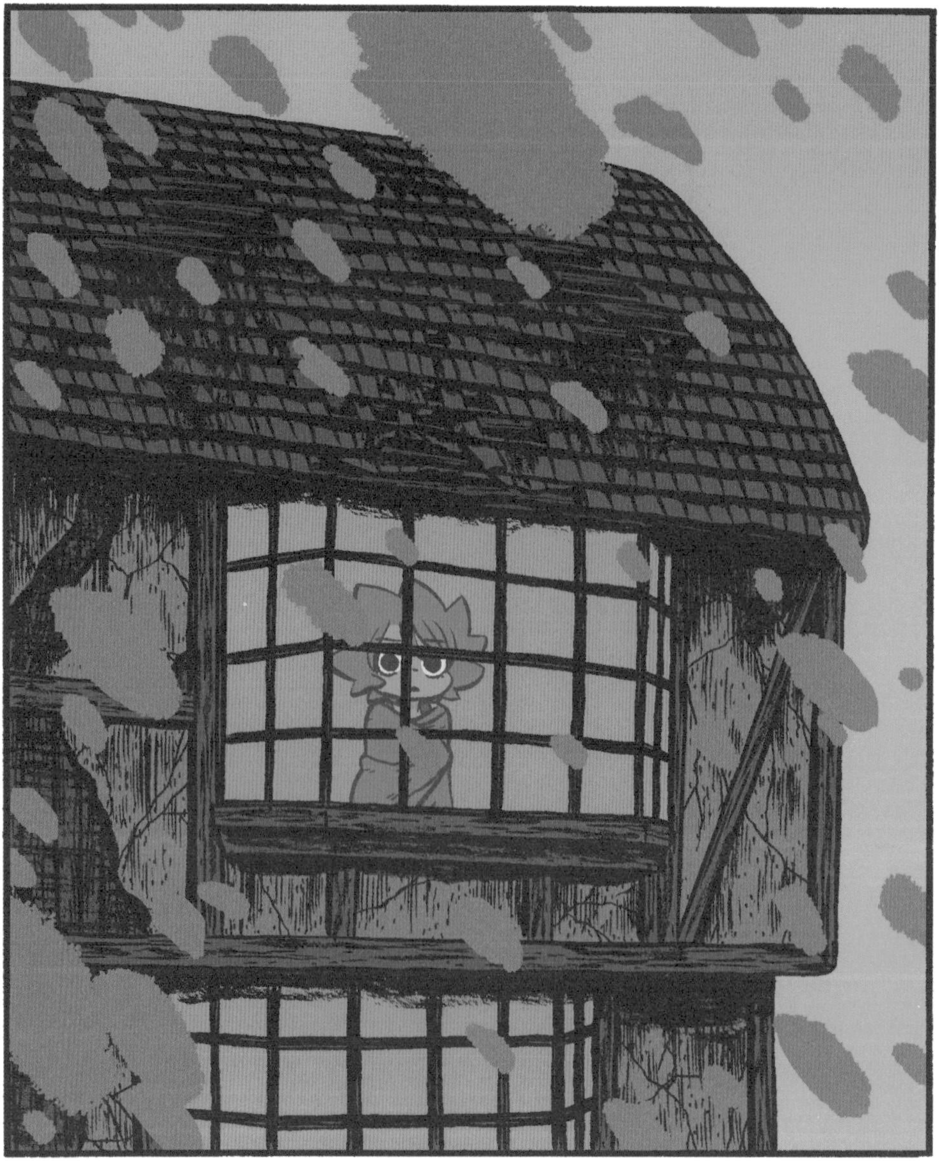

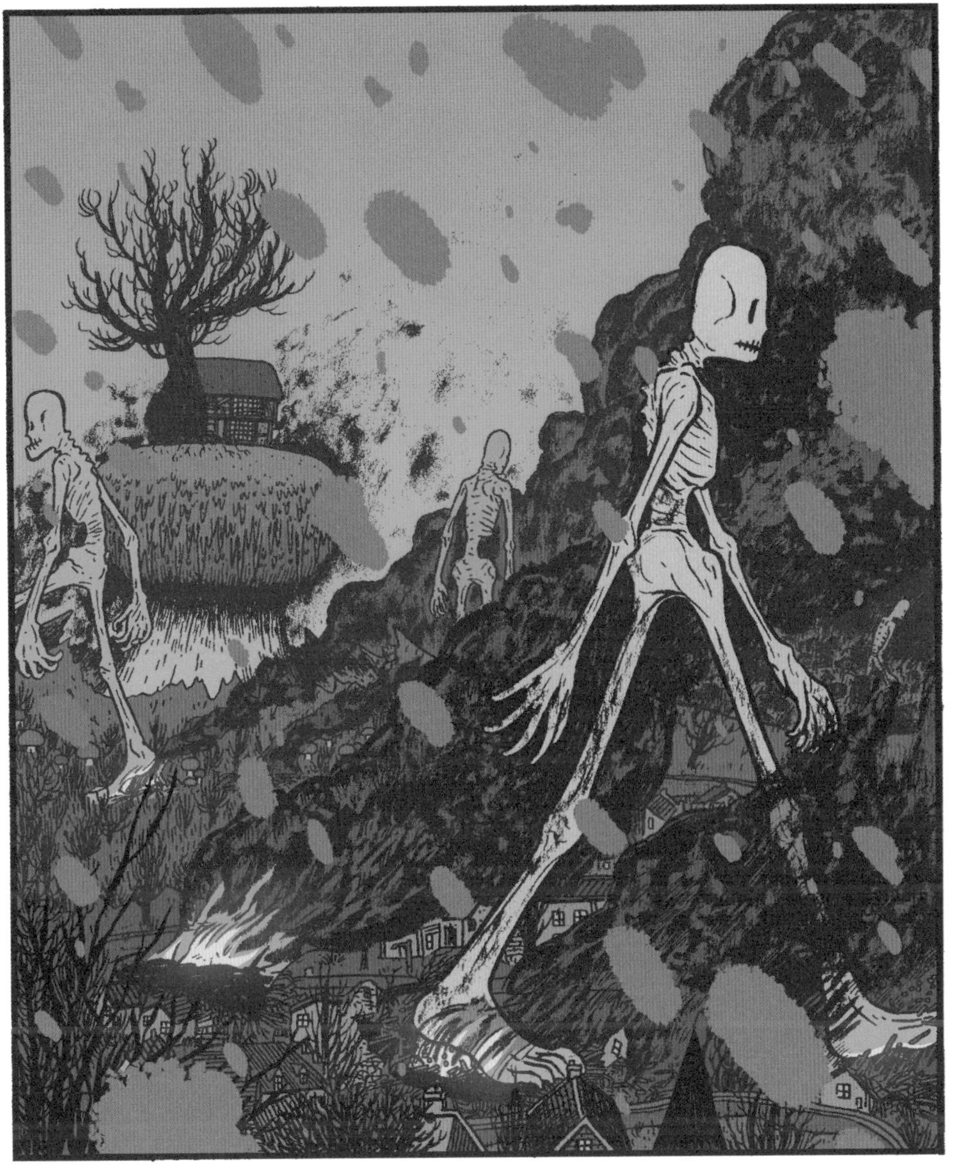

6
Control

When Katie woke up, she was back in her normal bedroom with Max asleep beside her.

She decided to take an early-morning drive. Away from here.

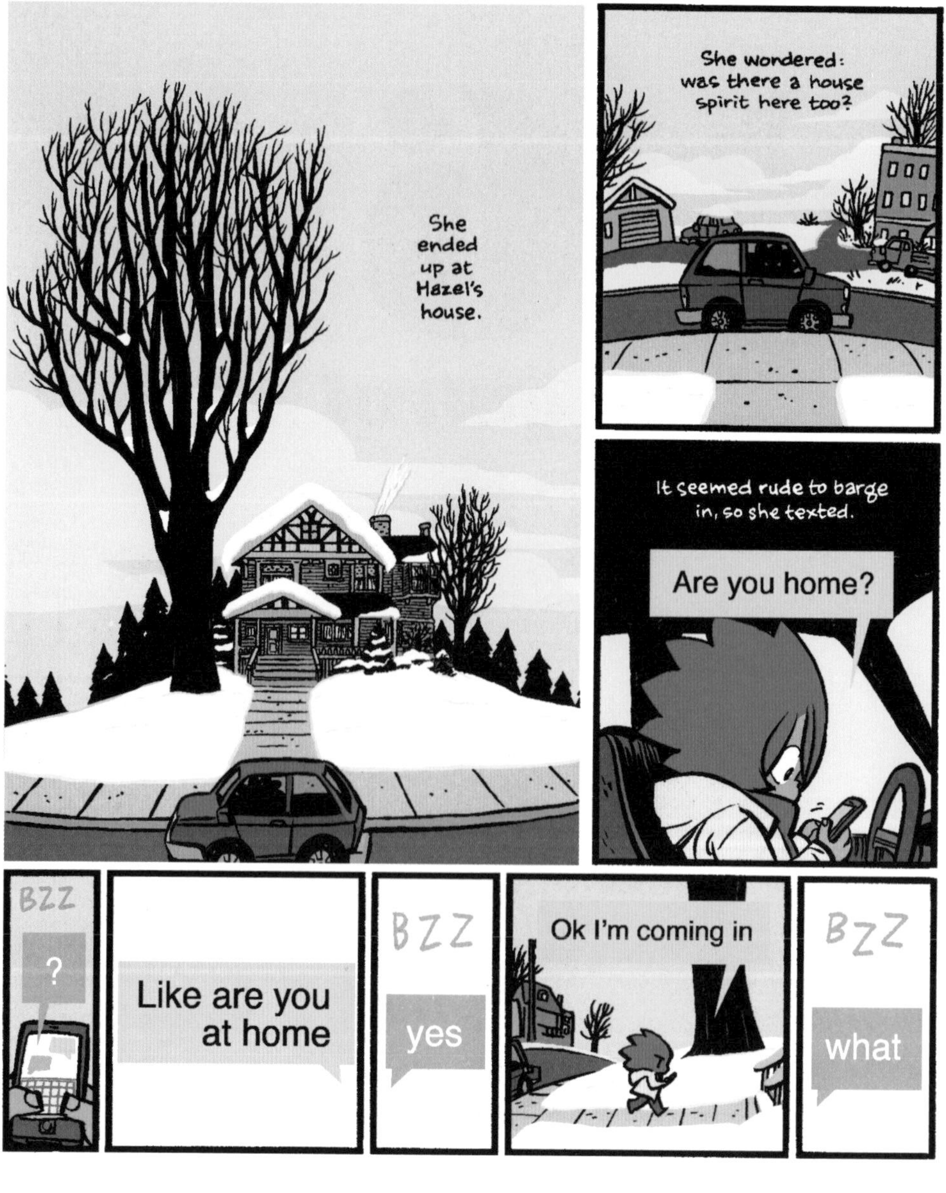
She ended up at Hazel's house.
She wondered: was there a house spirit here too?
It seemed rude to barge in, so she texted.
Are you home?
BZZ
?
Like are you at home
BZZ
yes
Ok I'm coming in
BZZ
what

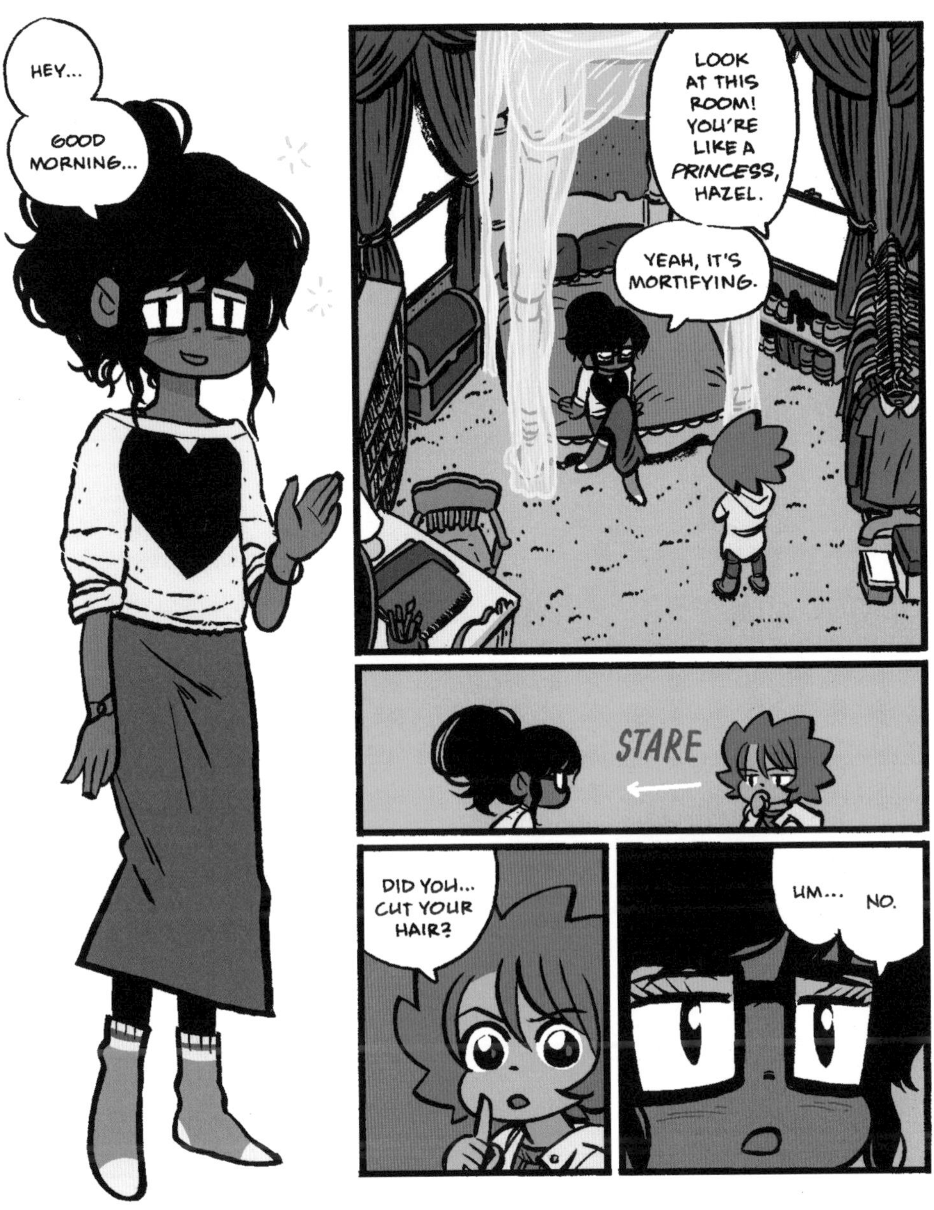
HEY...
GOOD MORNING...
LOOK AT THIS ROOM! YOU'RE LIKE A *PRINCESS*, HAZEL.
YEAH, IT'S MORTIFYING.
STARE
DID YOU... CUT YOUR HAIR?
UM...
NO.

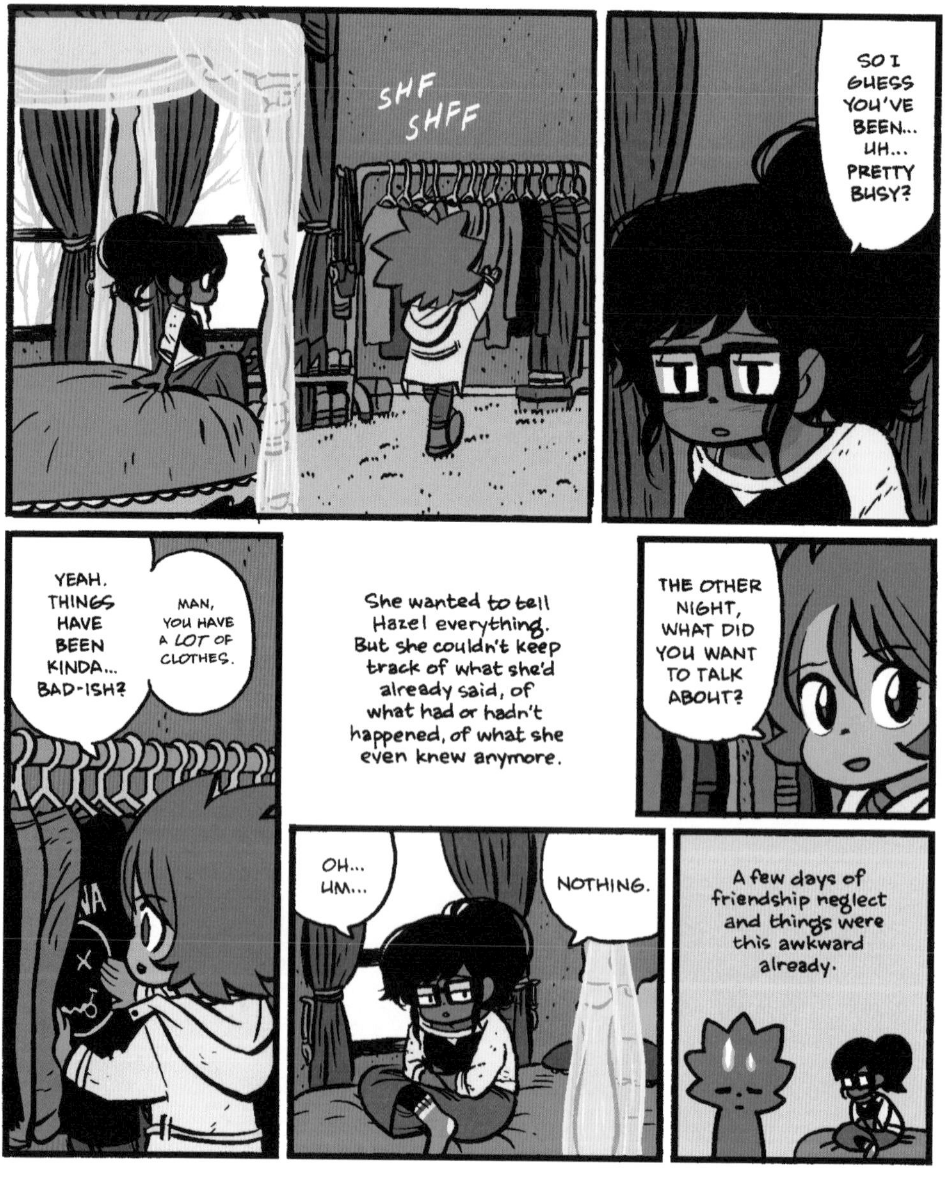
SHF
SHFF
SO I GUESS YOU'VE BEEN... UH... PRETTY BUSY?
YEAH. THINGS HAVE BEEN KINDA... BAD-ISH?
MAN, YOU HAVE A *LOT* OF CLOTHES.
She wanted to tell Hazel everything. But she couldn't keep track of what she'd already said, of what had or hadn't happened, of what she even knew anymore.
THE OTHER NIGHT, WHAT DID YOU WANT TO TALK ABOUT?
OH... UM...
NOTHING.
A few days of friendship neglect and things were this awkward already.

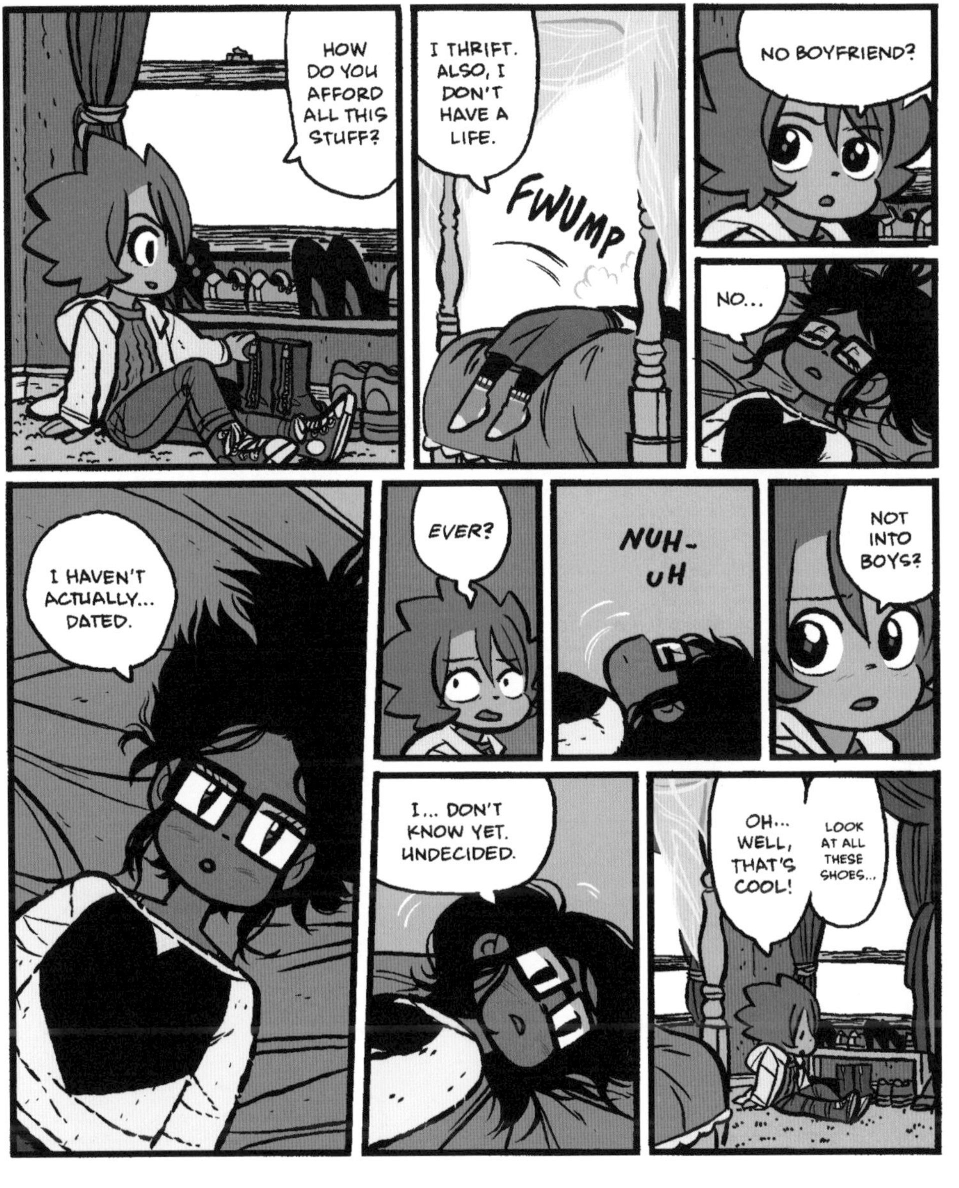
HOW DO YOU AFFORD ALL THIS STUFF?
I THRIFT. ALSO, I DON'T HAVE A LIFE.
FWUMP
NO BOYFRIEND?
NO...
I HAVEN'T ACTUALLY... DATED.
EVER?
NUH-UH
NOT INTO BOYS?
I... DON'T KNOW YET. UNDECIDED.
OH... WELL, THAT'S COOL!
LOOK AT ALL THESE SHOES...

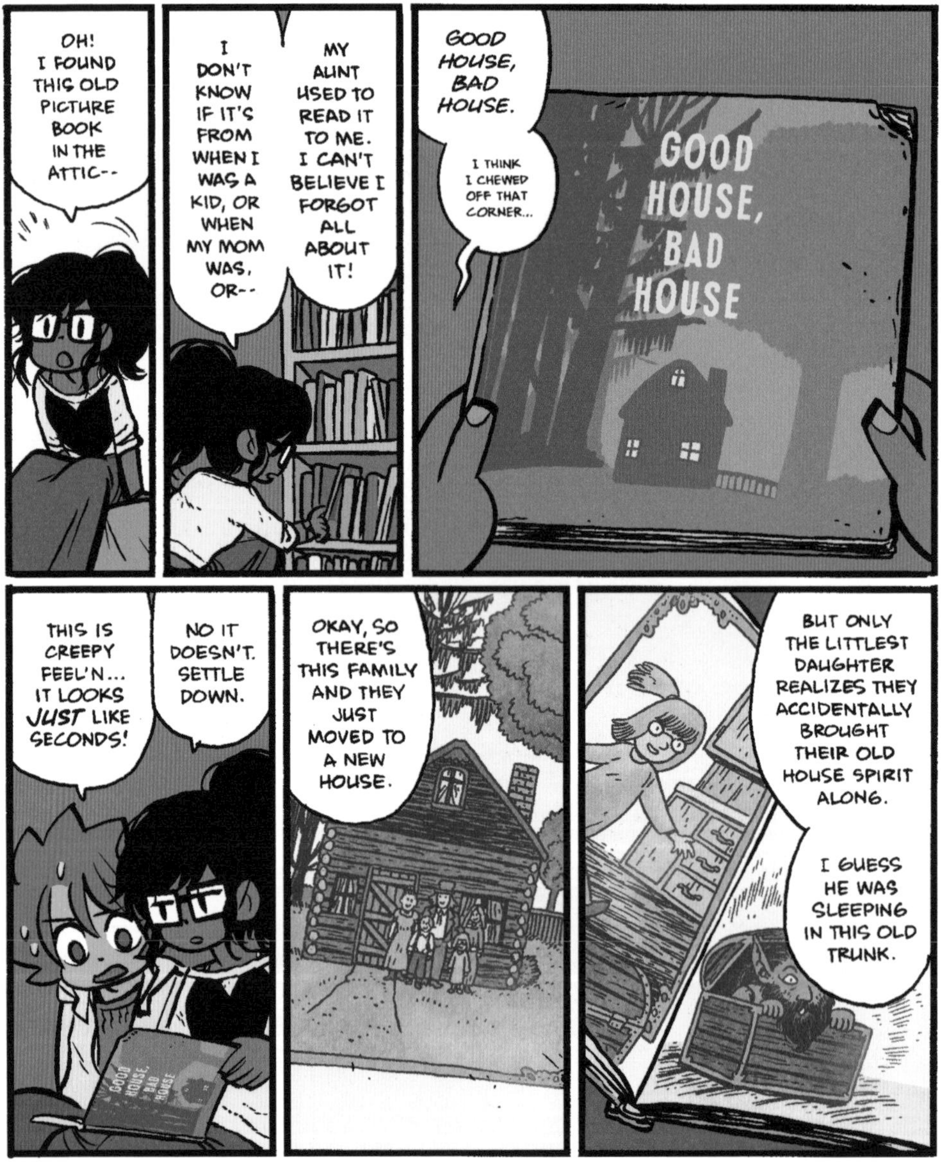
OH! I FOUND THIS OLD PICTURE BOOK IN THE ATTIC--
I DON'T KNOW IF IT'S FROM WHEN I WAS A KID, OR WHEN MY MOM WAS, OR--
MY AUNT USED TO READ IT TO ME. I CAN'T BELIEVE I FORGOT ALL ABOUT IT!
GOOD HOUSE, BAD HOUSE.
I THINK I CHEWED OFF THAT CORNER...
GOOD HOUSE, BAD HOUSE
THIS IS CREEPY FEEL'N... IT LOOKS JUST LIKE SECONDS!
NO IT DOESN'T. SETTLE DOWN.
OKAY, SO THERE'S THIS FAMILY AND THEY JUST MOVED TO A NEW HOUSE.
BUT ONLY THE LITTLEST DAUGHTER REALIZES THEY ACCIDENTALLY BROUGHT THEIR OLD HOUSE SPIRIT ALONG.
I GUESS HE WAS SLEEPING IN THIS OLD TRUNK.

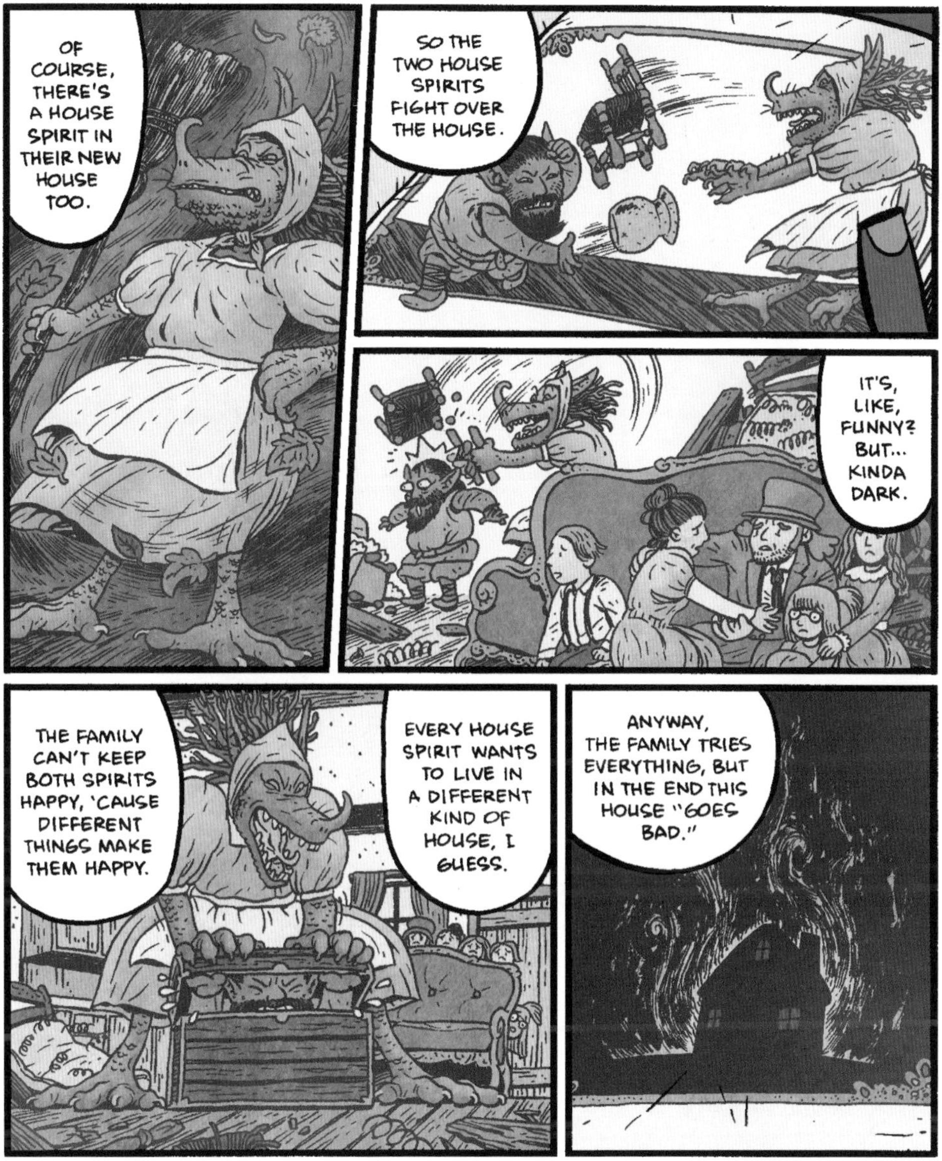
OF COURSE, THERE'S A HOUSE SPIRIT IN THEIR NEW HOUSE TOO.
SO THE TWO HOUSE SPIRITS FIGHT OVER THE HOUSE.
IT'S, LIKE, FUNNY? BUT... KINDA DARK.
THE FAMILY CAN'T KEEP BOTH SPIRITS HAPPY, 'CAUSE DIFFERENT THINGS MAKE THEM HAPPY.
EVERY HOUSE SPIRIT WANTS TO LIVE IN A DIFFERENT KIND OF HOUSE, I GUESS.
ANYWAY, THE FAMILY TRIES EVERYTHING, BUT IN THE END THIS HOUSE "GOES BAD."

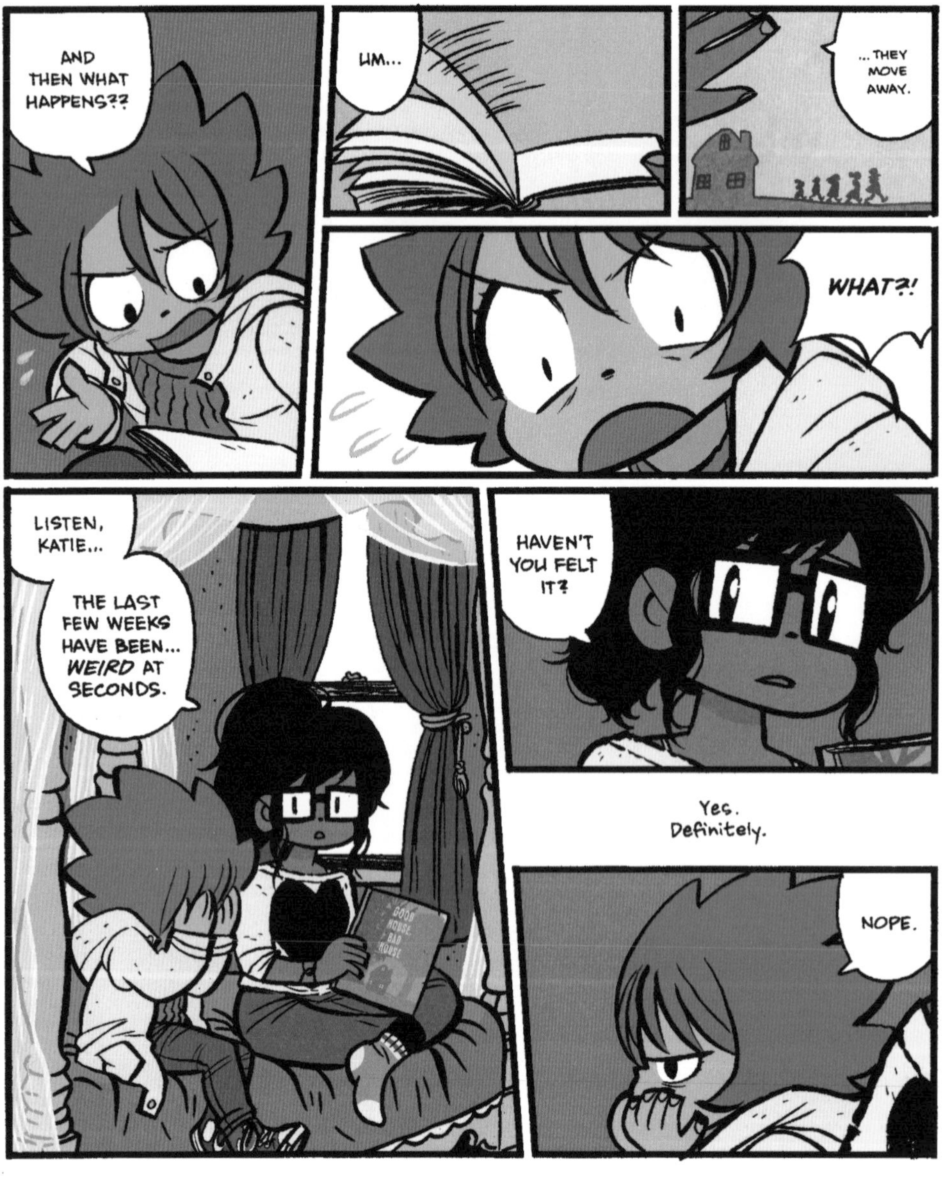
AND THEN WHAT HAPPENS??
UM...
...THEY MOVE AWAY.
WHAT?!
LISTEN, KATIE...
THE LAST FEW WEEKS HAVE BEEN... WEIRD AT SECONDS.
GOOD HOUSE, BAD HOUSE
HAVEN'T YOU FELT IT?
Yes. Definitely.
NOPE.

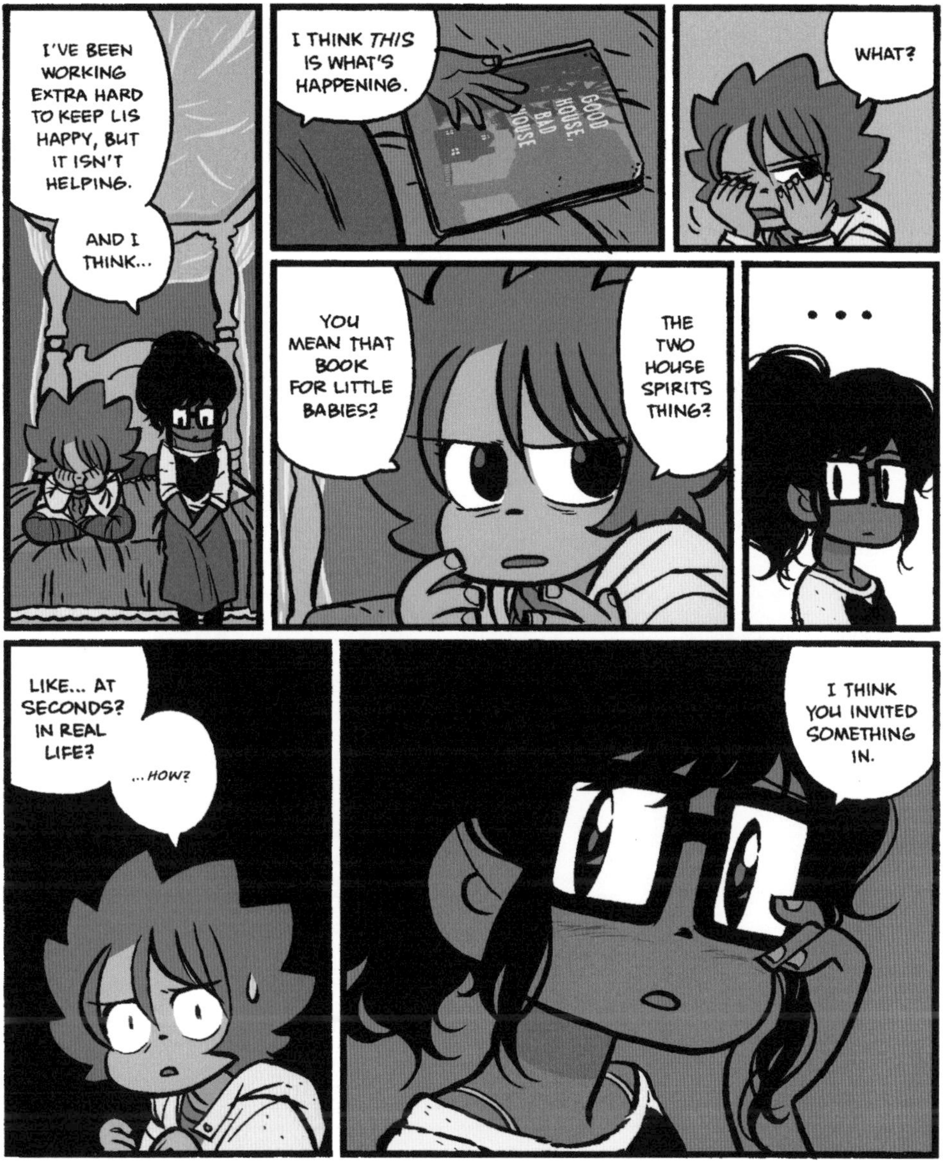
I'VE BEEN WORKING EXTRA HARD TO KEEP LIS HAPPY, BUT IT ISN'T HELPING.
AND I THINK...
I THINK *THIS* IS WHAT'S HAPPENING.
GOOD HOUSE, BAD HOUSE
WHAT?
YOU MEAN THAT BOOK FOR LITTLE BABIES?
THE TWO HOUSE SPIRITS THING?
• • •
LIKE... AT SECONDS? IN REAL LIFE?
...HOW?
I THINK YOU INVITED SOMETHING IN.

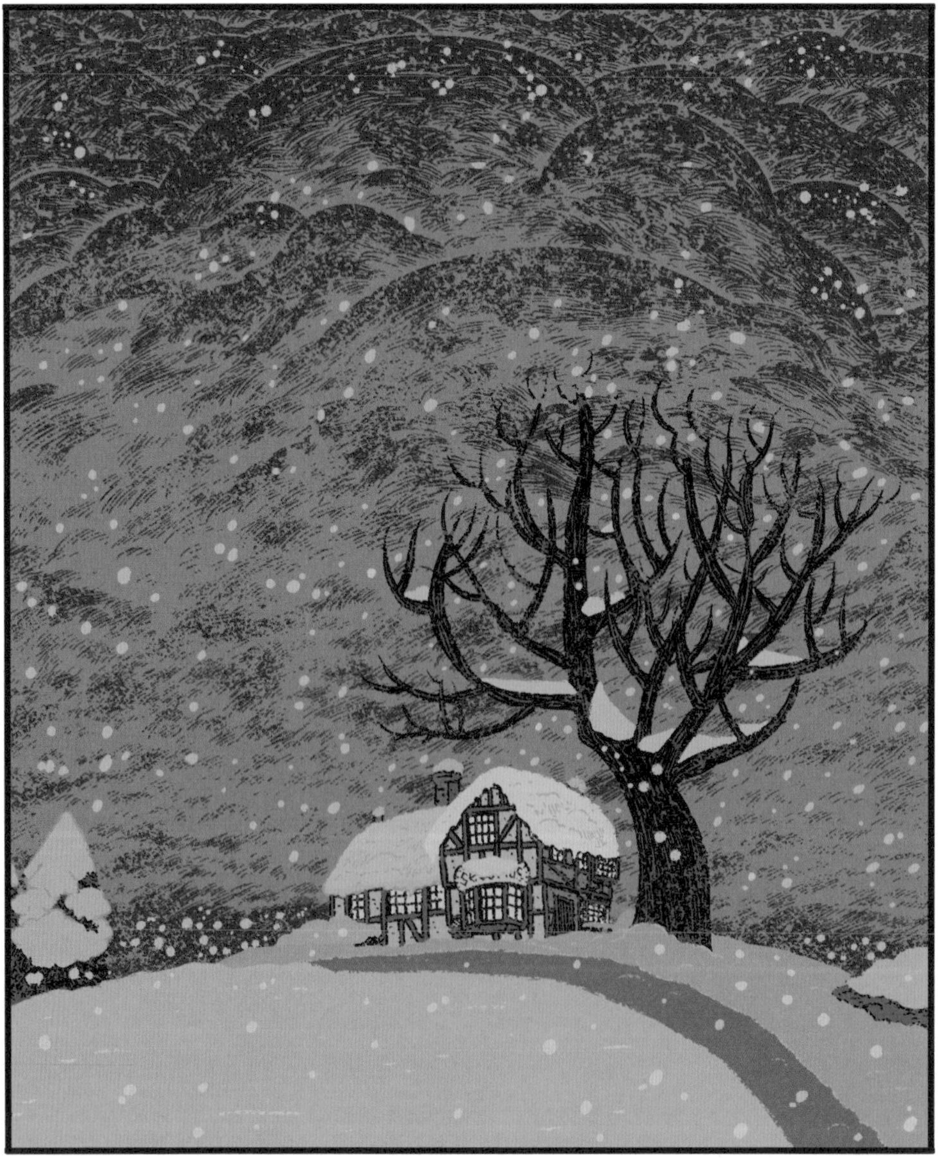

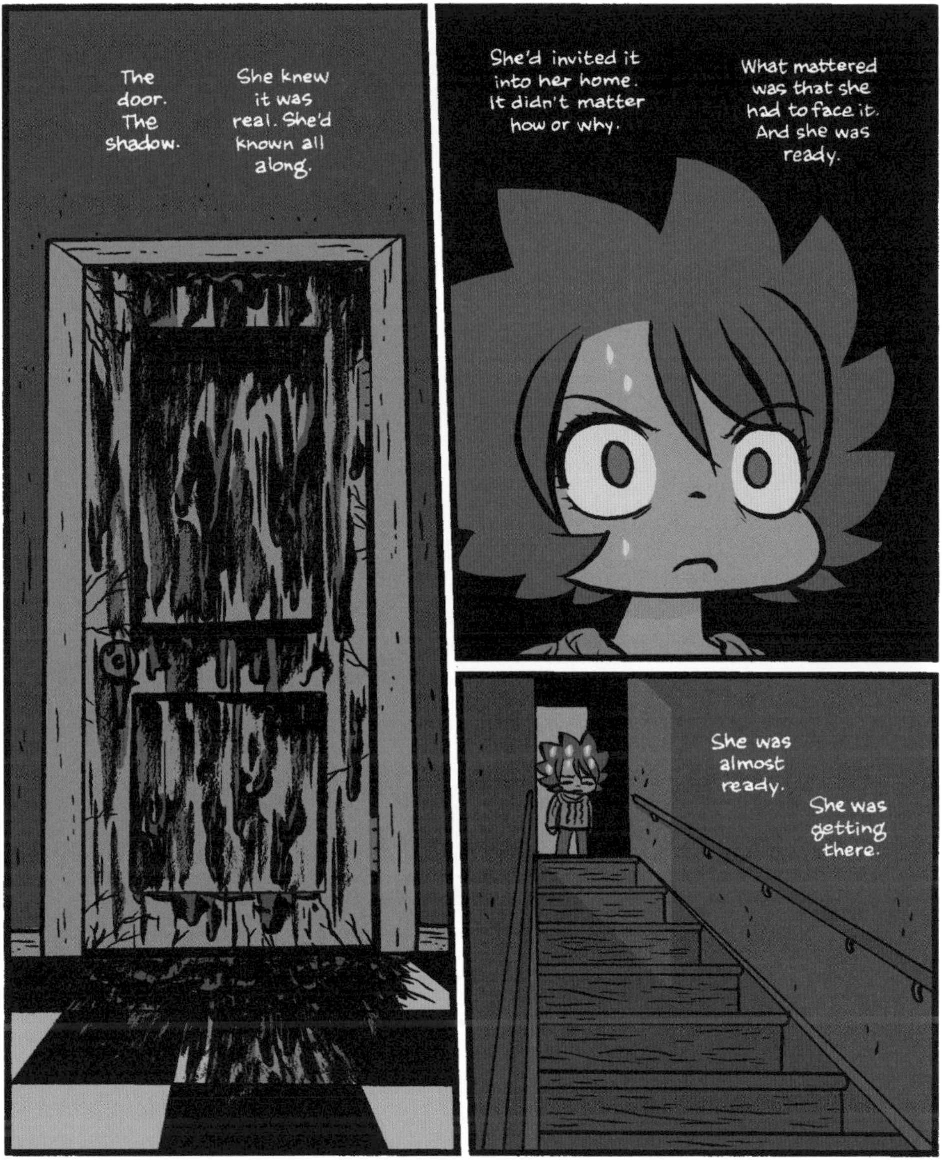
The door. The shadow.
She knew it was real. She'd known all along.
She'd invited it into her home. It didn't matter how or why.
What mattered was that she had to face it. And she was ready.
She was almost ready.
She was getting there.

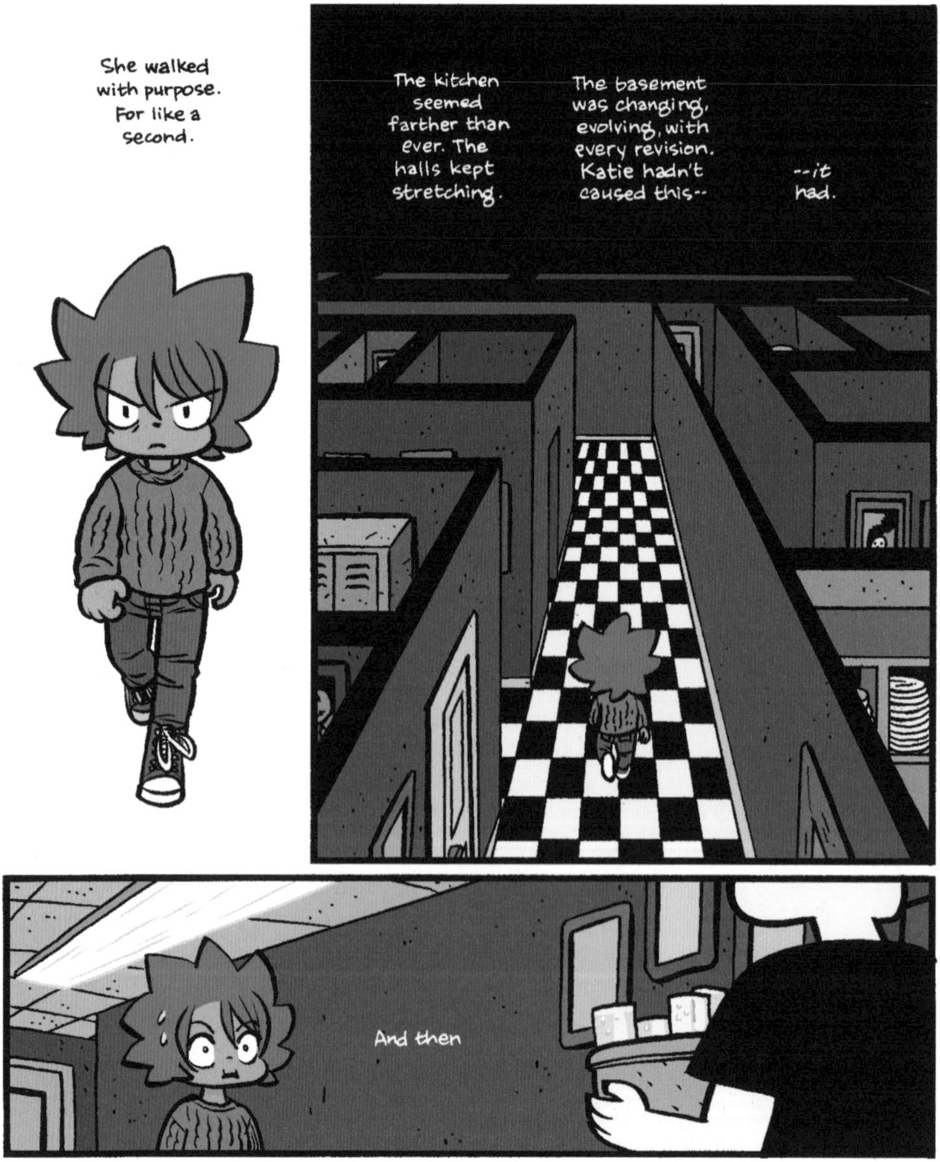
She walked with purpose. For like a second.
The kitchen seemed farther than ever. The halls kept stretching.
The basement was changing, evolving, with every revision. Katie hadn't caused this--
--it had.
And then

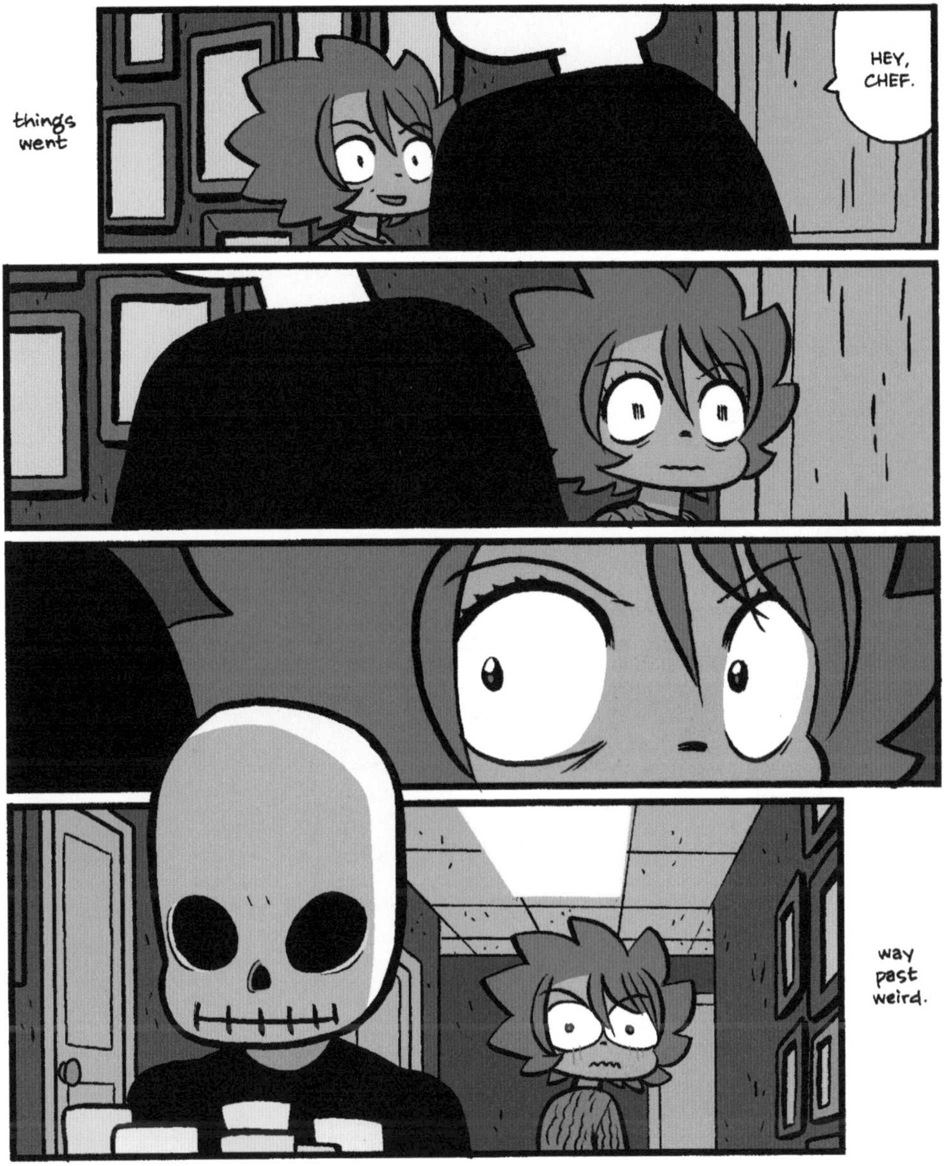
things went
HEY, CHEF.
way past weird.

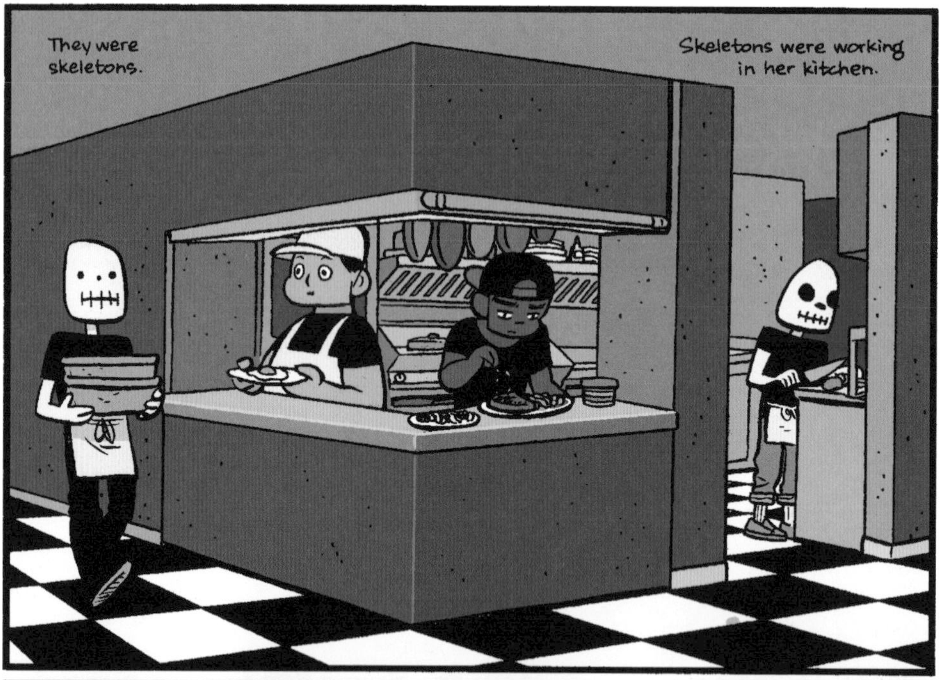
They were skeletons.
Skeletons were working in her kitchen.

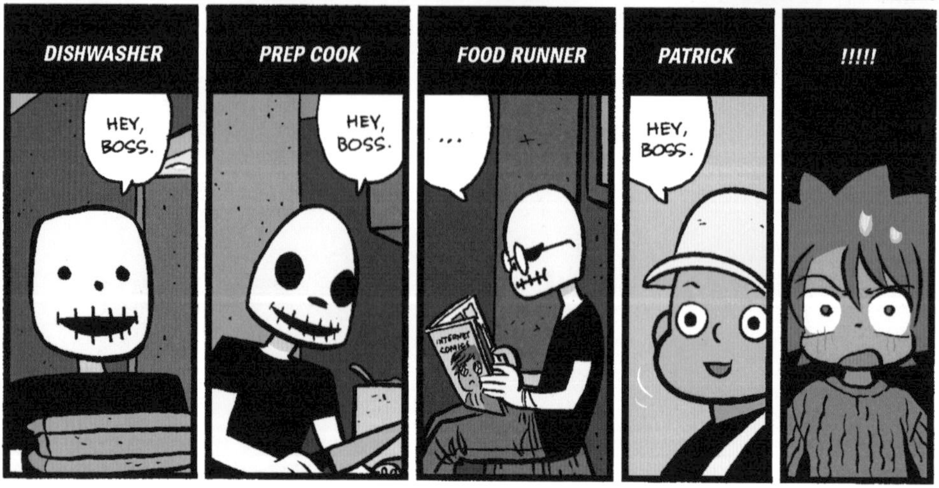
DISHWASHER
HEY, BOSS.
PREP COOK
HEY, BOSS.
FOOD RUNNER
...
INTERNET COMICS
PATRICK
HEY, BOSS.
!!!!!

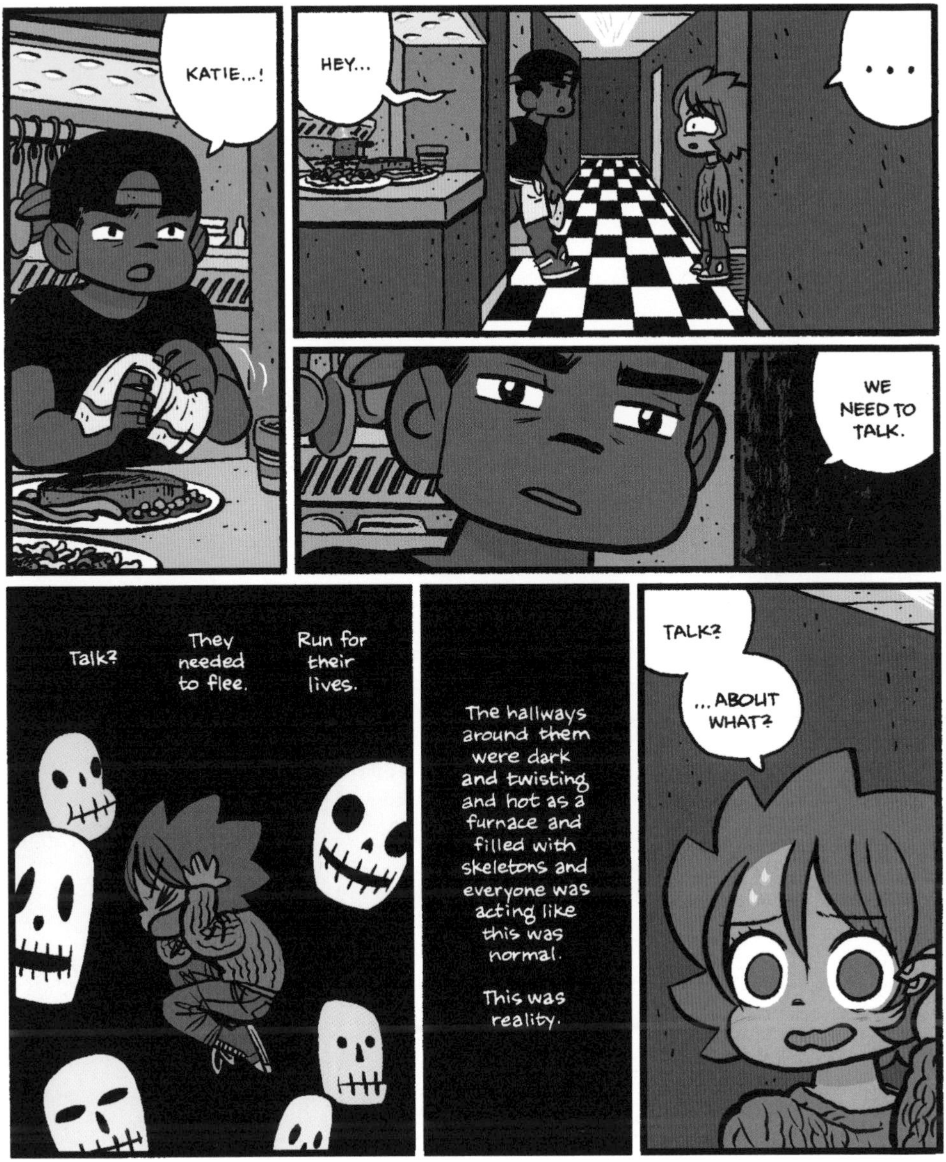

KATIE...!
HEY...
...
WE NEED TO TALK.
Talk?
They needed to flee.
Run for their lives.
The hallways around them were dark and twisting and hot as a furnace and filled with skeletons and everyone was acting like this was normal.
This was reality.
TALK?
...ABOUT WHAT?

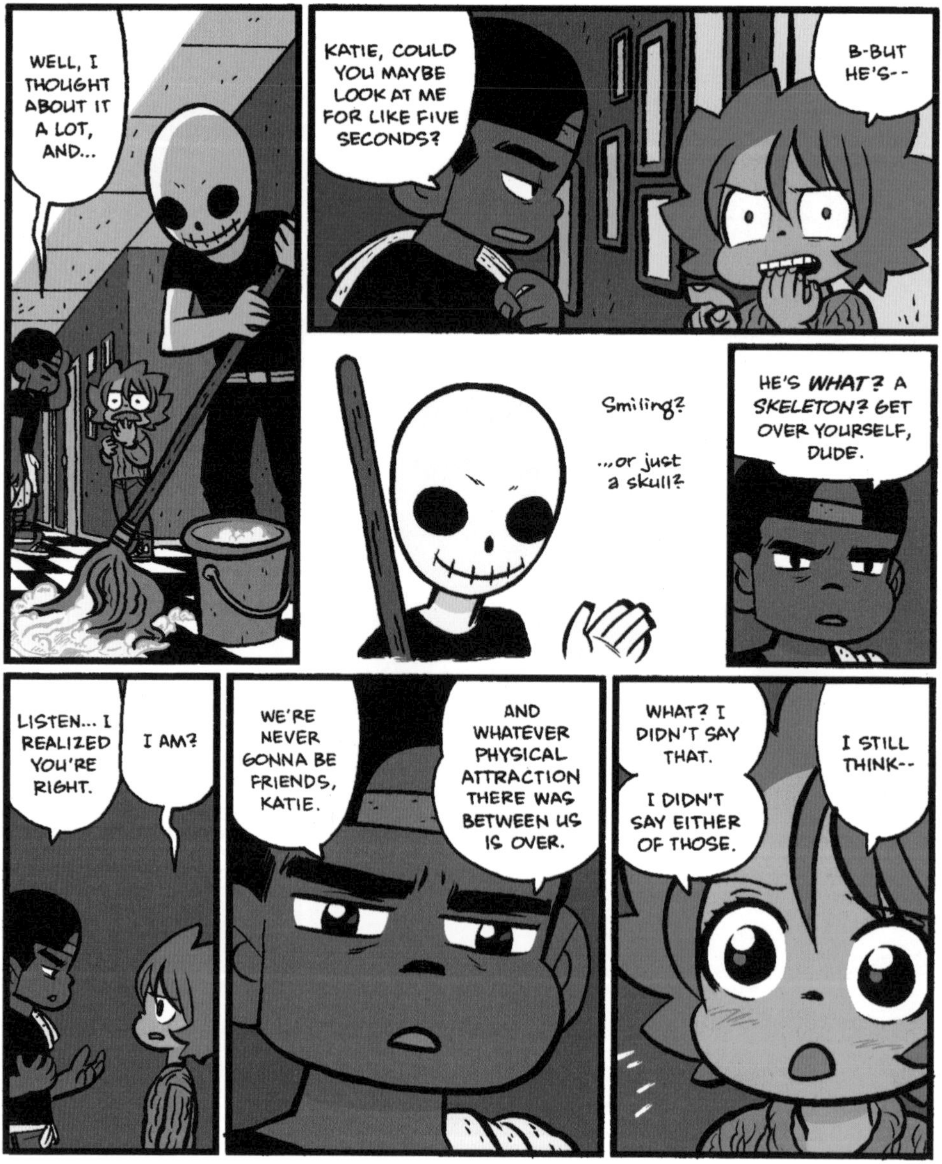
WELL, I THOUGHT ABOUT IT A LOT, AND...
KATIE, COULD YOU MAYBE LOOK AT ME FOR LIKE FIVE SECONDS?
B-BUT HE'S--
Smiling?
...or just a skull?
HE'S WHAT? A SKELETON? GET OVER YOURSELF, DUDE.
LISTEN... I REALIZED YOU'RE RIGHT.
I AM?
WE'RE NEVER GONNA BE FRIENDS, KATIE.
AND WHATEVER PHYSICAL ATTRACTION THERE WAS BETWEEN US IS OVER.
WHAT? I DIDN'T SAY THAT.
I DIDN'T SAY EITHER OF THOSE.
I STILL THINK--

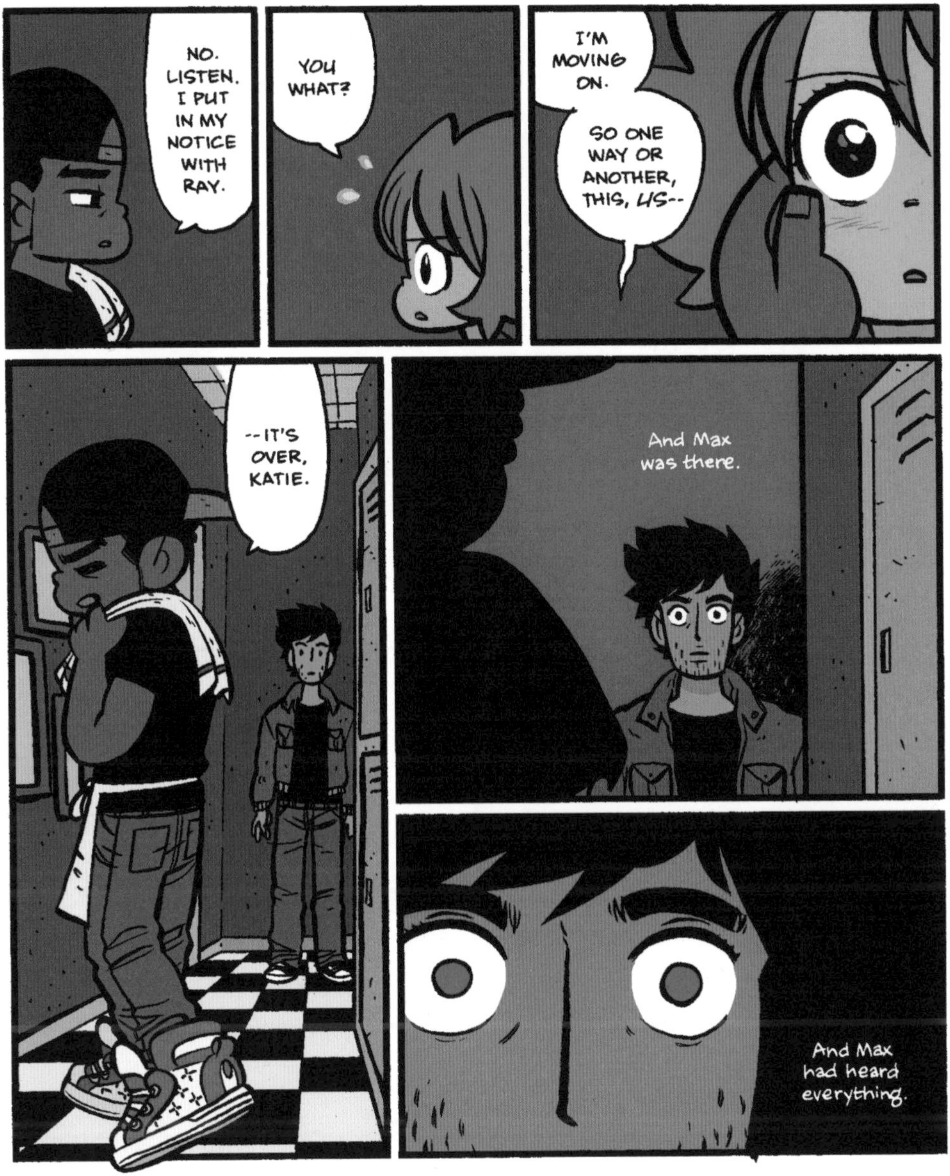
NO. LISTEN. I PUT IN MY NOTICE WITH RAY.
YOU WHAT?
I'M MOVING ON.
SO ONE WAY OR ANOTHER, THIS, US--
--IT'S OVER, KATIE.
And Max was there.
And Max had heard everything.

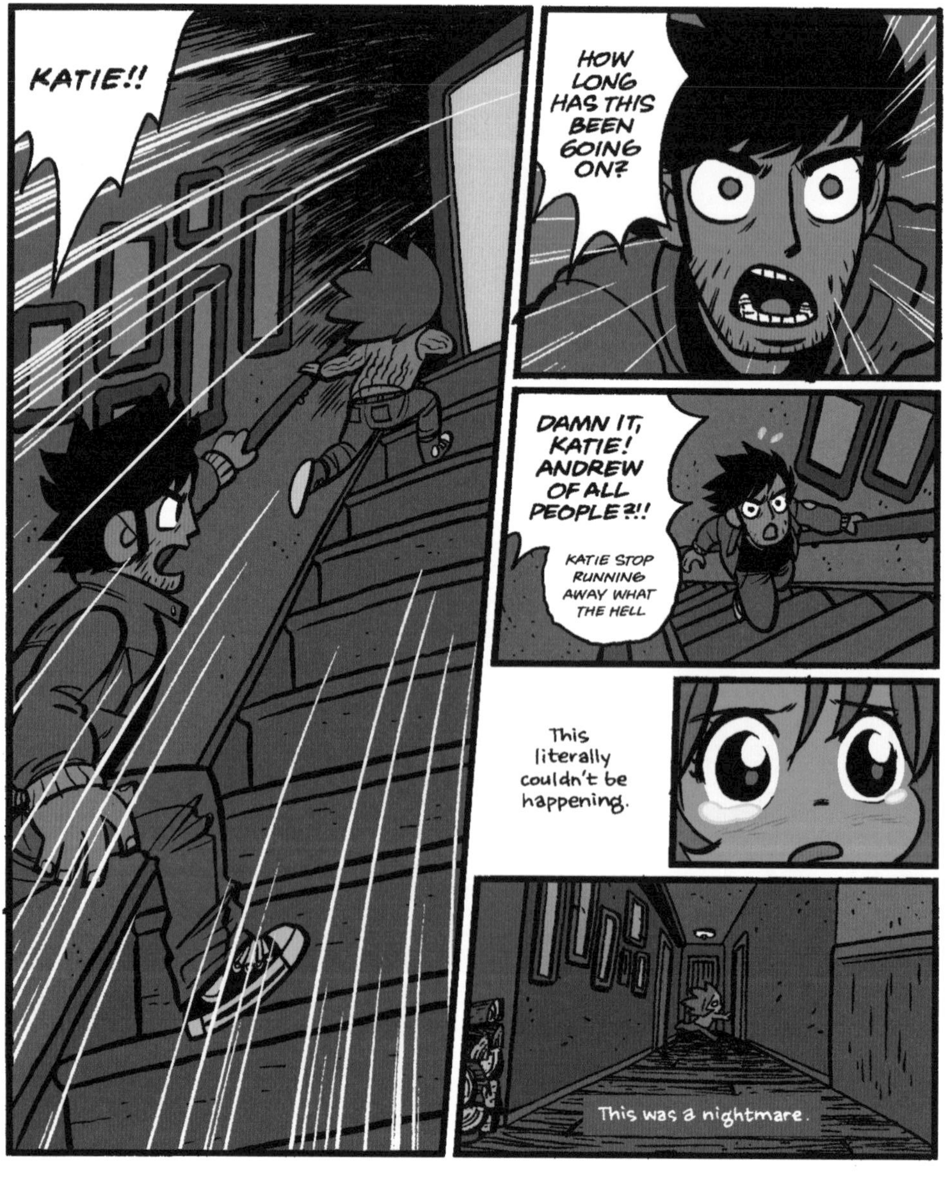
KATIE!!
HOW LONG HAS THIS BEEN GOING ON?
DAMN IT, KATIE! ANDREW OF ALL PEOPLE?!!
KATIE STOP RUNNING AWAY WHAT THE HELL
This literally couldn't be happening.
This was a nightmare.

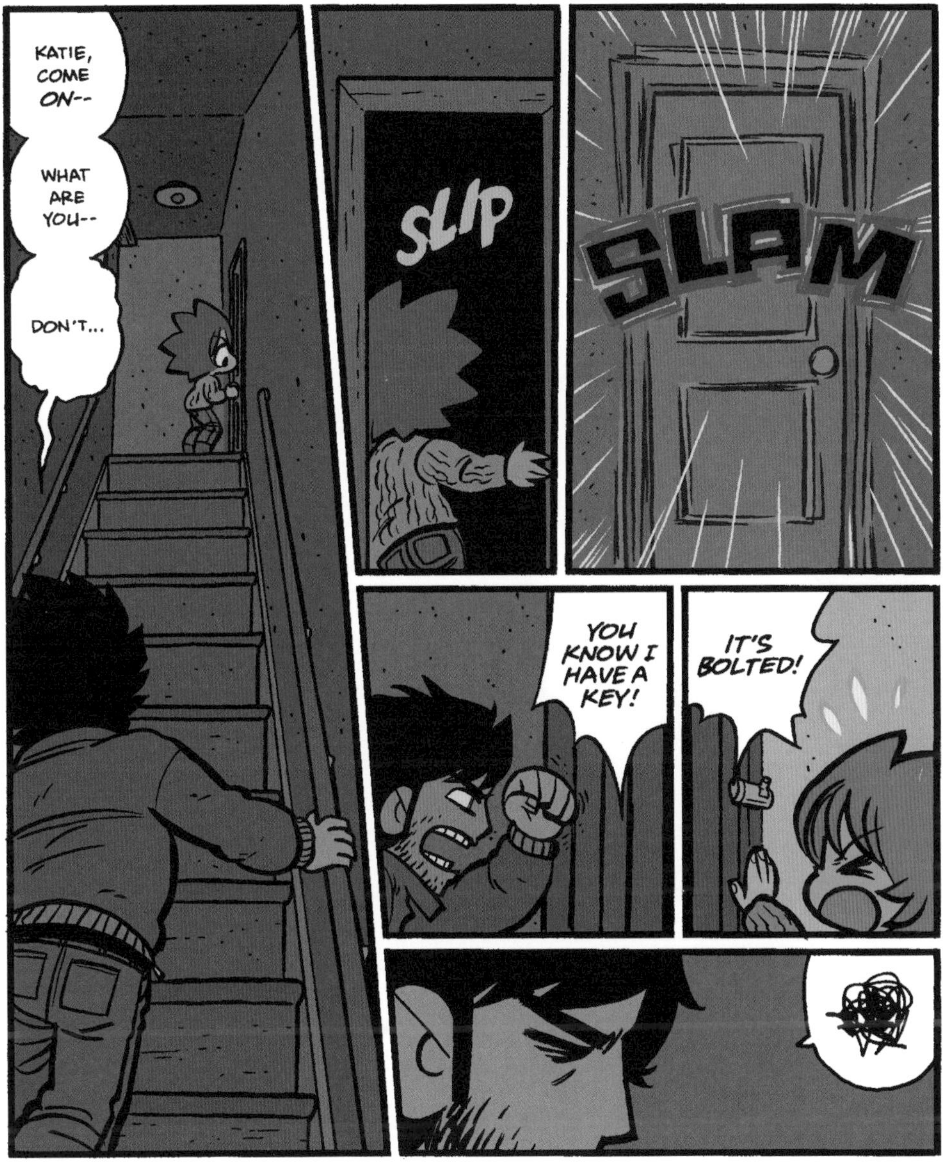
KATIE, COME ON--
WHAT ARE YOU--
DON'T...
SLIP
SLAM
YOU KNOW I HAVE A KEY!
IT'S BOLTED!

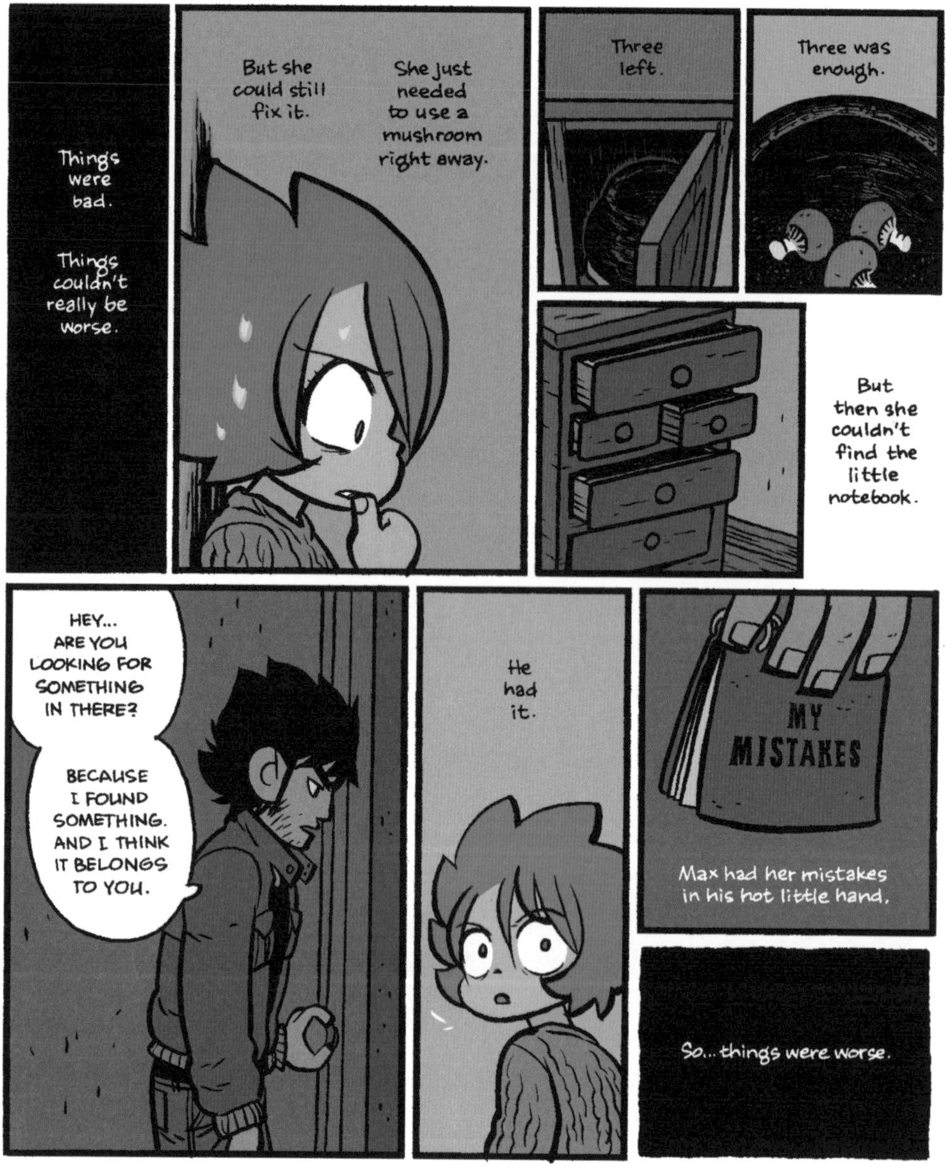
Things were bad.
Things couldn't really be worse.
But she could still fix it.
She just needed to use a mushroom right away.
Three left.
Three was enough.
But then she couldn't find the little notebook.
HEY... ARE YOU LOOKING FOR SOMETHING IN THERE?
BECAUSE I FOUND SOMETHING. AND I THINK IT BELONGS TO YOU.
He had it.
MY MISTAKES
Max had her mistakes in his hot little hand.
So... things were worse.

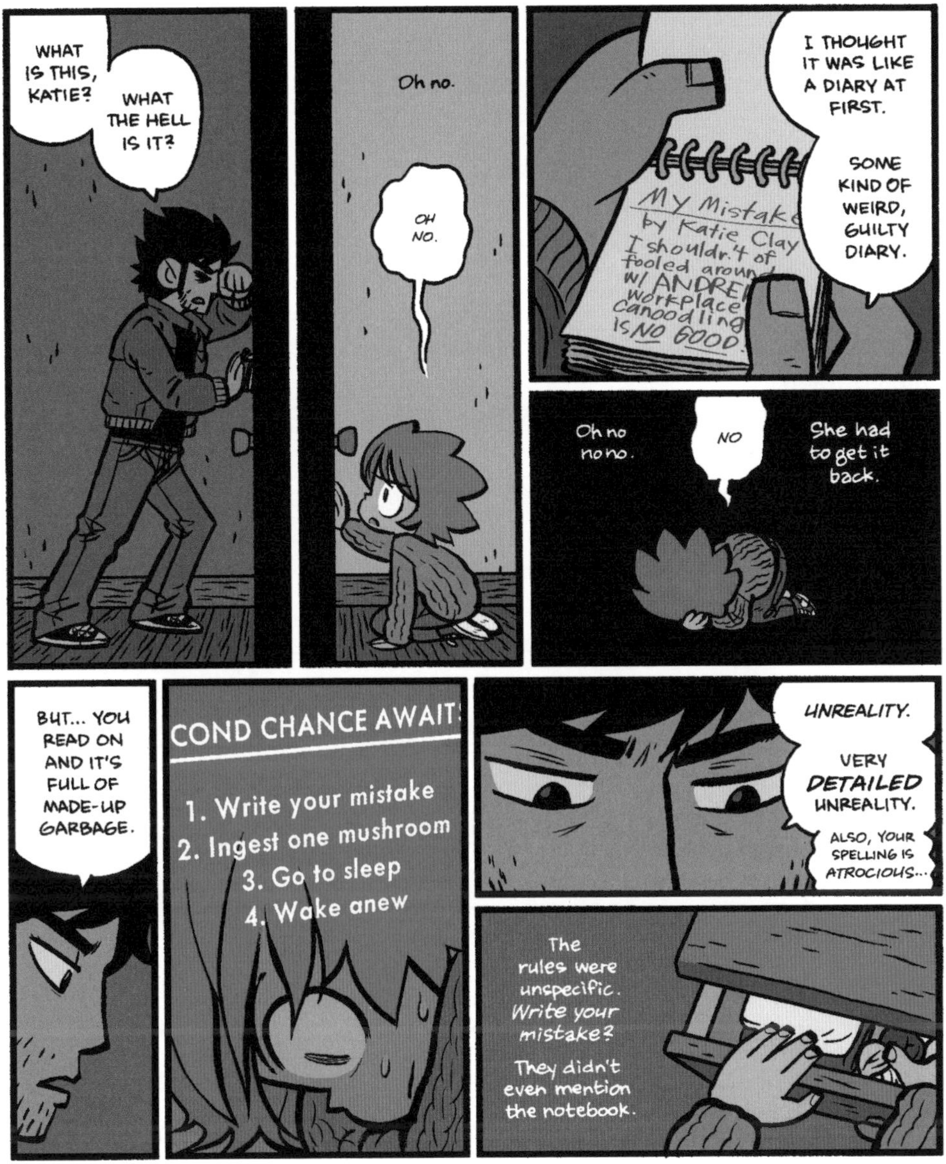

WHAT IS THIS, KATIE?
WHAT THE HELL IS IT?
Oh no.
OH NO.
I THOUGHT IT WAS LIKE A DIARY AT FIRST.
SOME KIND OF WEIRD, GUILTY DIARY.
My Mistake
by Katie Clay
I shouldn't of fooled around w/ ANDRE
workplace canoodling is NO GOOD
Oh no nono.
NO
She had to get it back.
BUT... YOU READ ON AND IT'S FULL OF MADE-UP GARBAGE.
COND CHANCE AWAIT
1. Write your mistake
2. Ingest one mushroom
3. Go to sleep
4. Wake anew
UNREALITY.
VERY DETAILED UNREALITY.
ALSO, YOUR SPELLING IS ATROCIOUS...
The rules were unspecific. Write your mistake?
They didn't even mention the notebook.

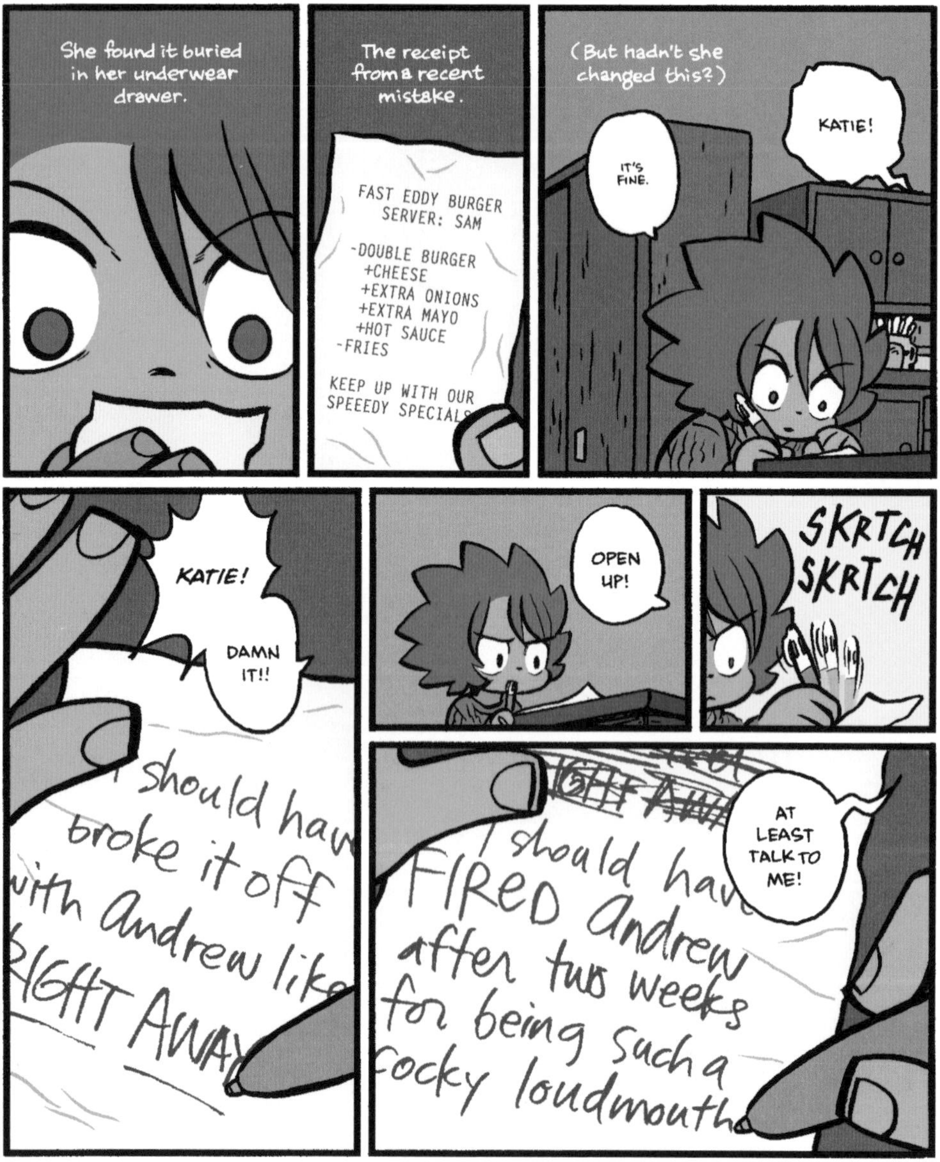
She found it buried in her underwear drawer.
The receipt from a recent mistake.
FAST EDDY BURGER
SERVER: SAM
-DOUBLE BURGER
+CHEESE
+EXTRA ONIONS
+EXTRA MAYO
+HOT SAUCE
-FRIES
KEEP UP WITH OUR
SPEEEDY SPECIALS
(But hadn't she changed this?)
KATIE!
IT'S FINE.
KATIE!
DAMN IT!!
I should have broke it off with andrew like RIGHT AWAY
OPEN UP!
SKRTCH SKRTCH
AT LEAST TALK TO ME!
I should have FIRED andrew after two weeks for being such a cocky loudmouth

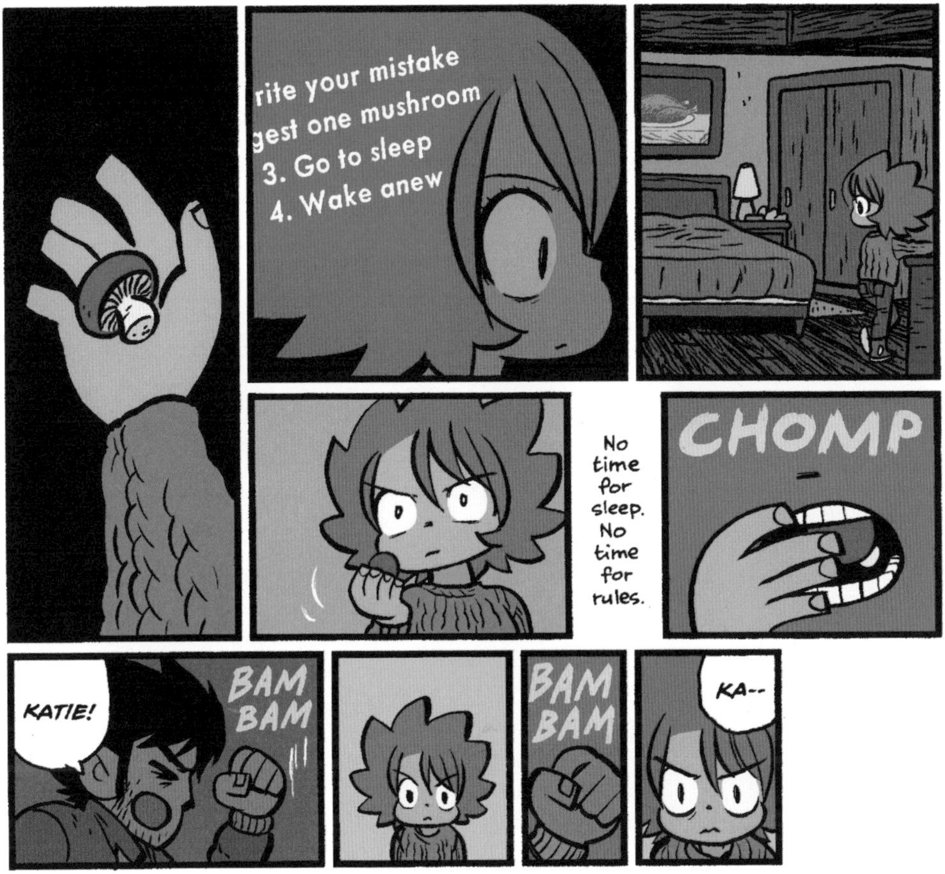
rite your mistake
gest one mushroom
3. Go to sleep
4. Wake anew
No time for sleep. No time for rules.
CHOMP
KATIE!
BAM BAM
BAM BAM
KA--

REVISION #11

She felt it.

The world shuddered and changed.

She felt it.

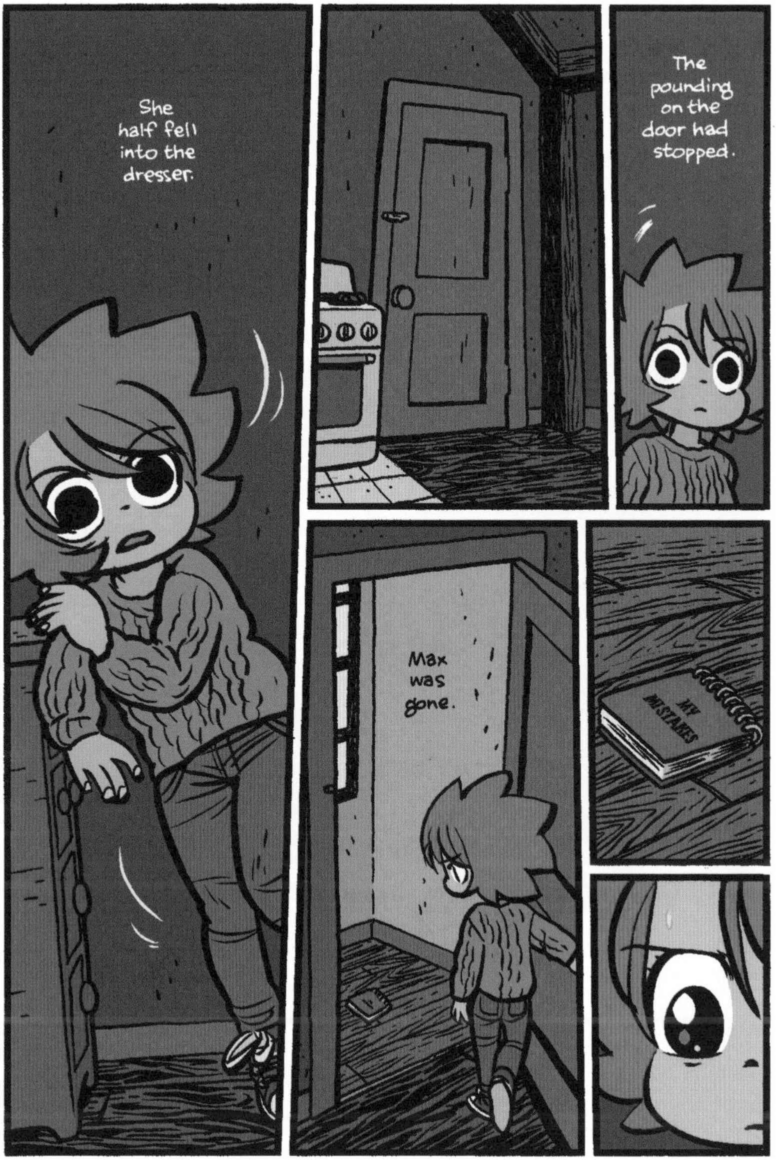
She half fell into the dresser.
The pounding on the door had stopped.
Max was gone.
MY MISTAKES

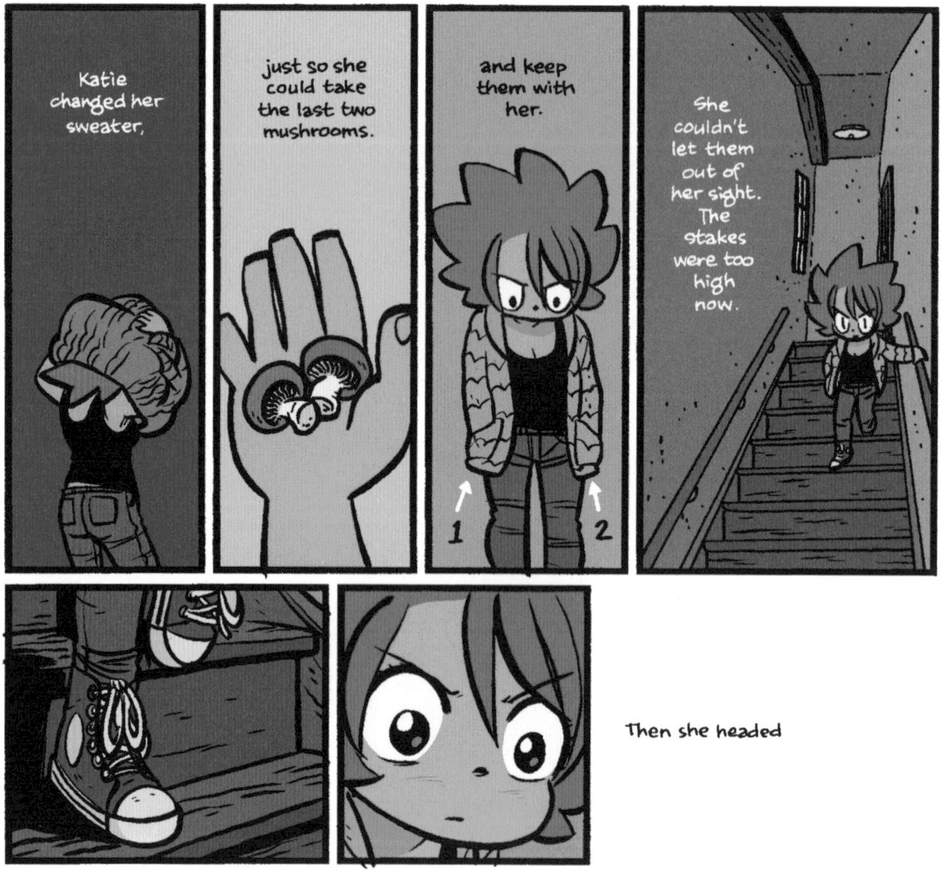
Katie changed her sweater,
just so she could take the last two mushrooms.
and keep them with her.
1
2
She couldn't let them out of her sight. The stakes were too high now.

Then she headed

???????

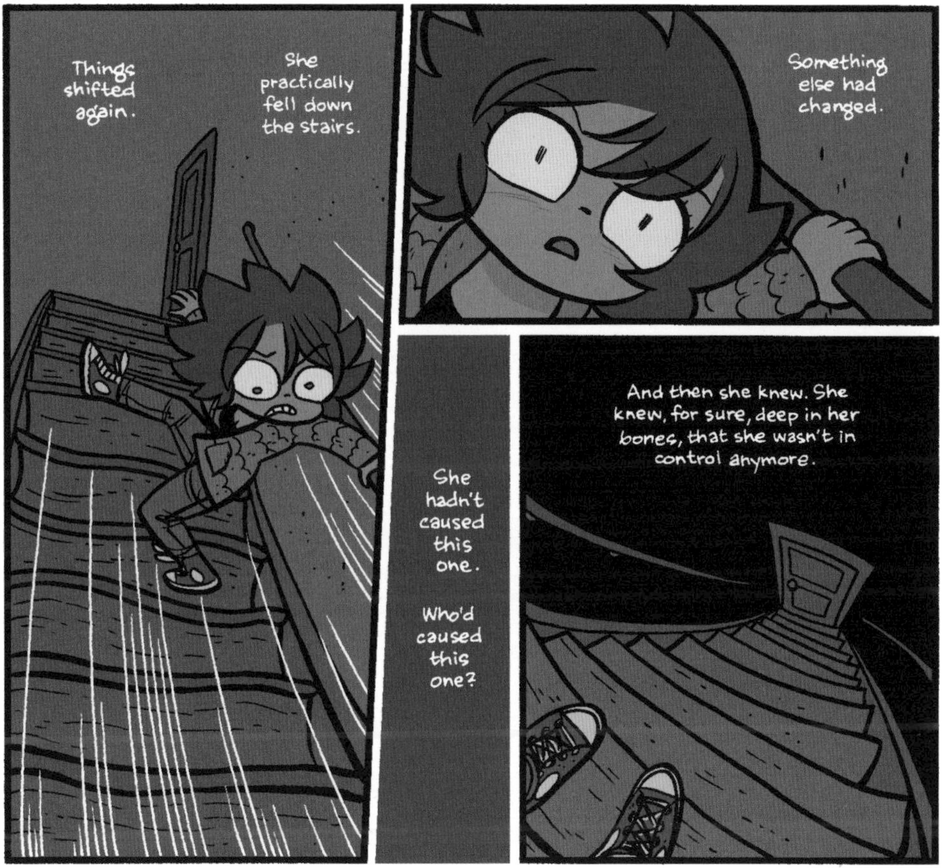
Things shifted again.
She practically fell down the stairs.
Something else had changed.
She hadn't caused this one.
Who'd caused this one?
And then she knew. She knew, for sure, deep in her bones, that she wasn't in control anymore.

The state of the dining room did not dispel this notion.

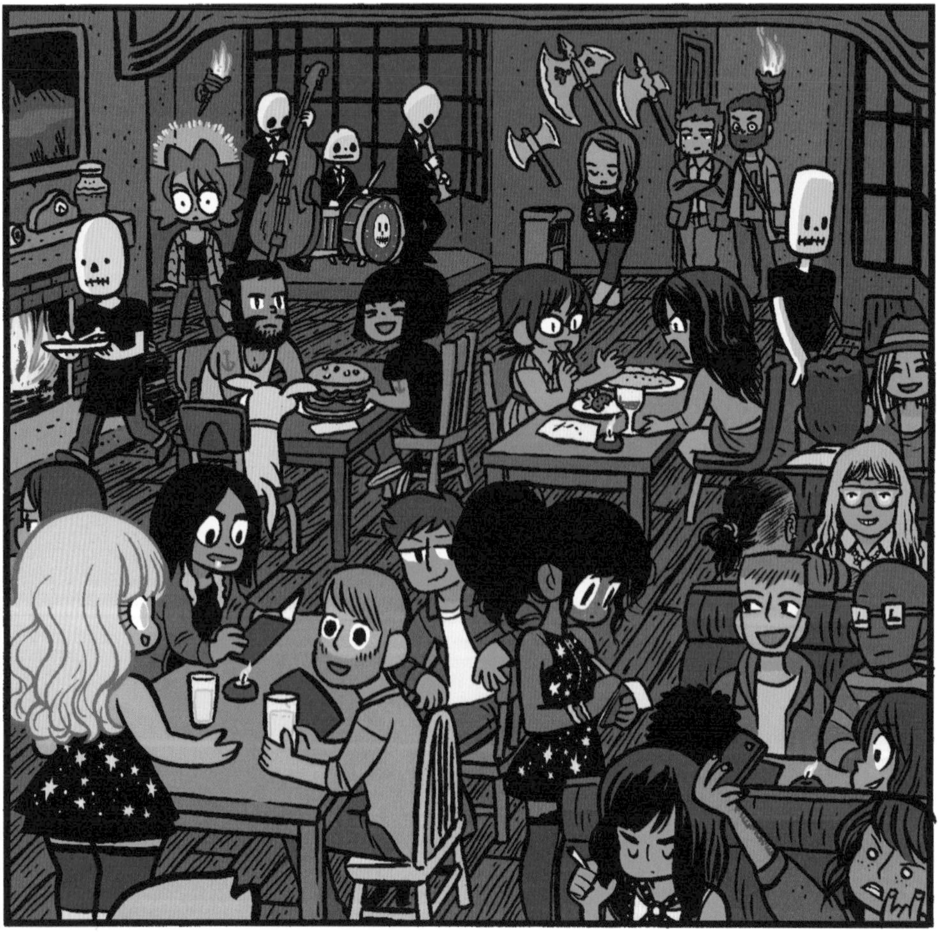

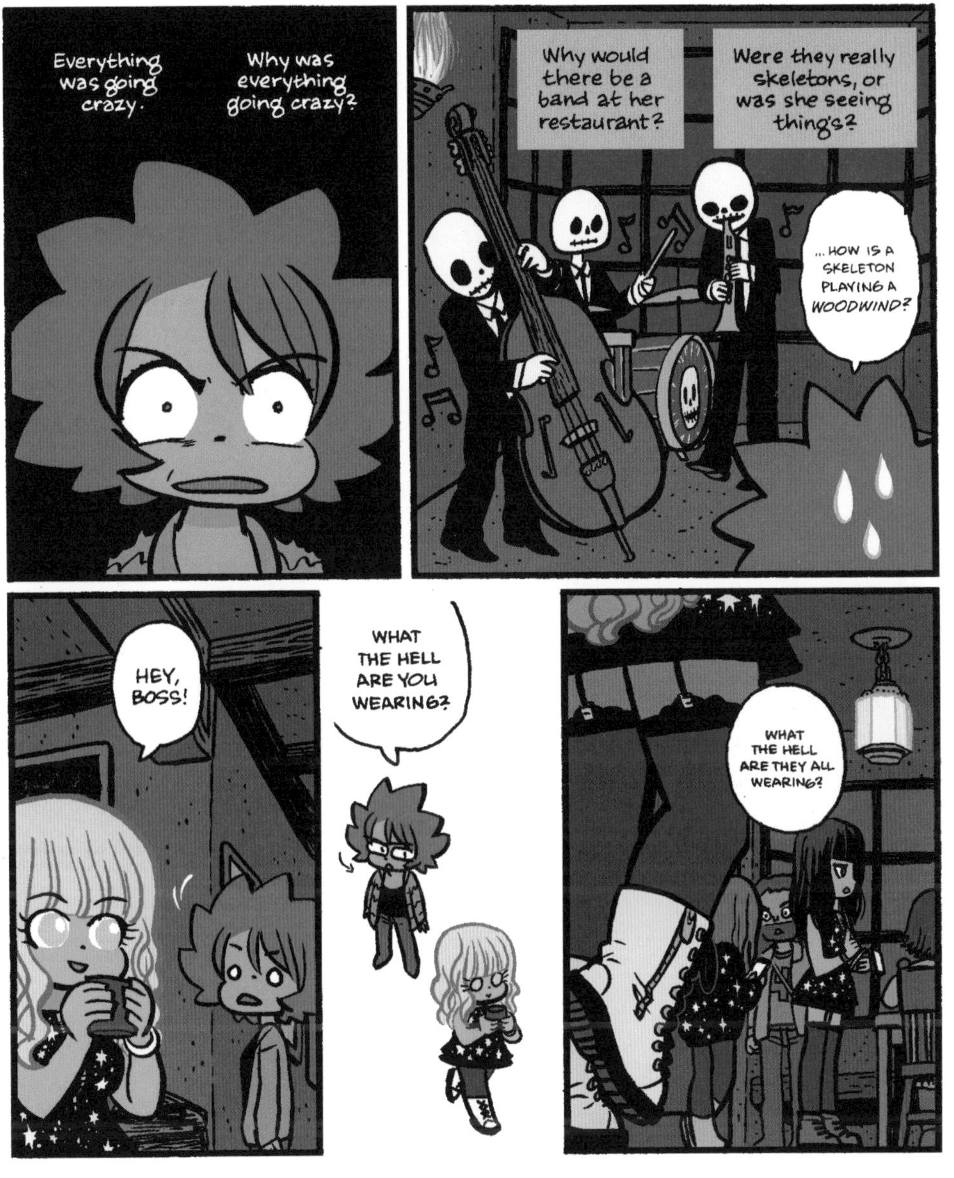
Everything was going crazy.
Why was everything going crazy?
Why would there be a band at her restaurant?
Were they really skeletons, or was she seeing things?
...HOW IS A SKELETON PLAYING A WOODWIND?
HEY, BOSS!
WHAT THE HELL ARE YOU WEARING?
WHAT THE HELL ARE THEY ALL WEARING?

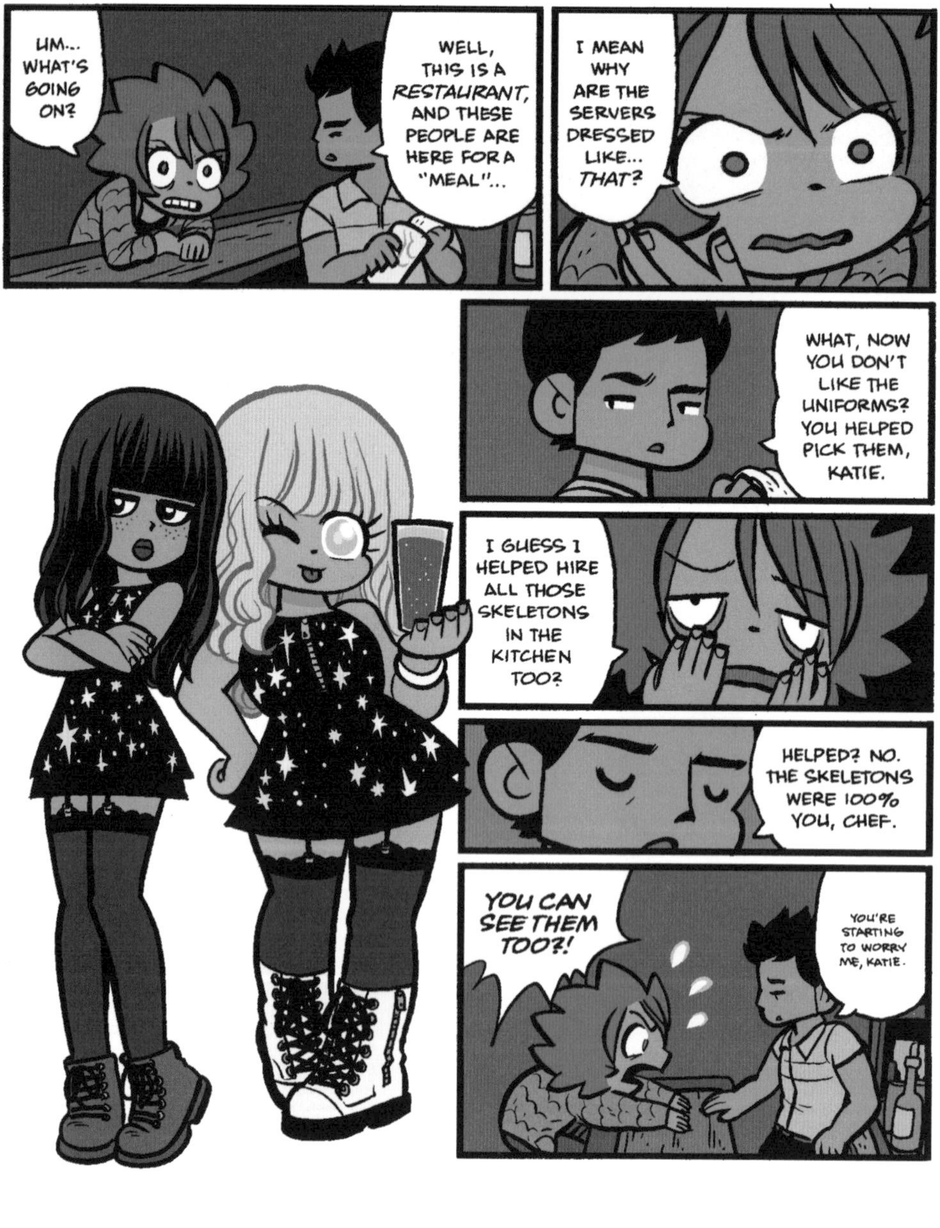
UM... WHAT'S GOING ON?
WELL, THIS IS A RESTAURANT, AND THESE PEOPLE ARE HERE FOR A "MEAL"...
I MEAN WHY ARE THE SERVERS DRESSED LIKE... THAT?
WHAT, NOW YOU DON'T LIKE THE UNIFORMS? YOU HELPED PICK THEM, KATIE.
I GUESS I HELPED HIRE ALL THOSE SKELETONS IN THE KITCHEN TOO?
HELPED? NO. THE SKELETONS WERE 100% YOU, CHEF.
YOU CAN SEE THEM TOO?!
YOU'RE STARTING TO WORRY ME, KATIE.

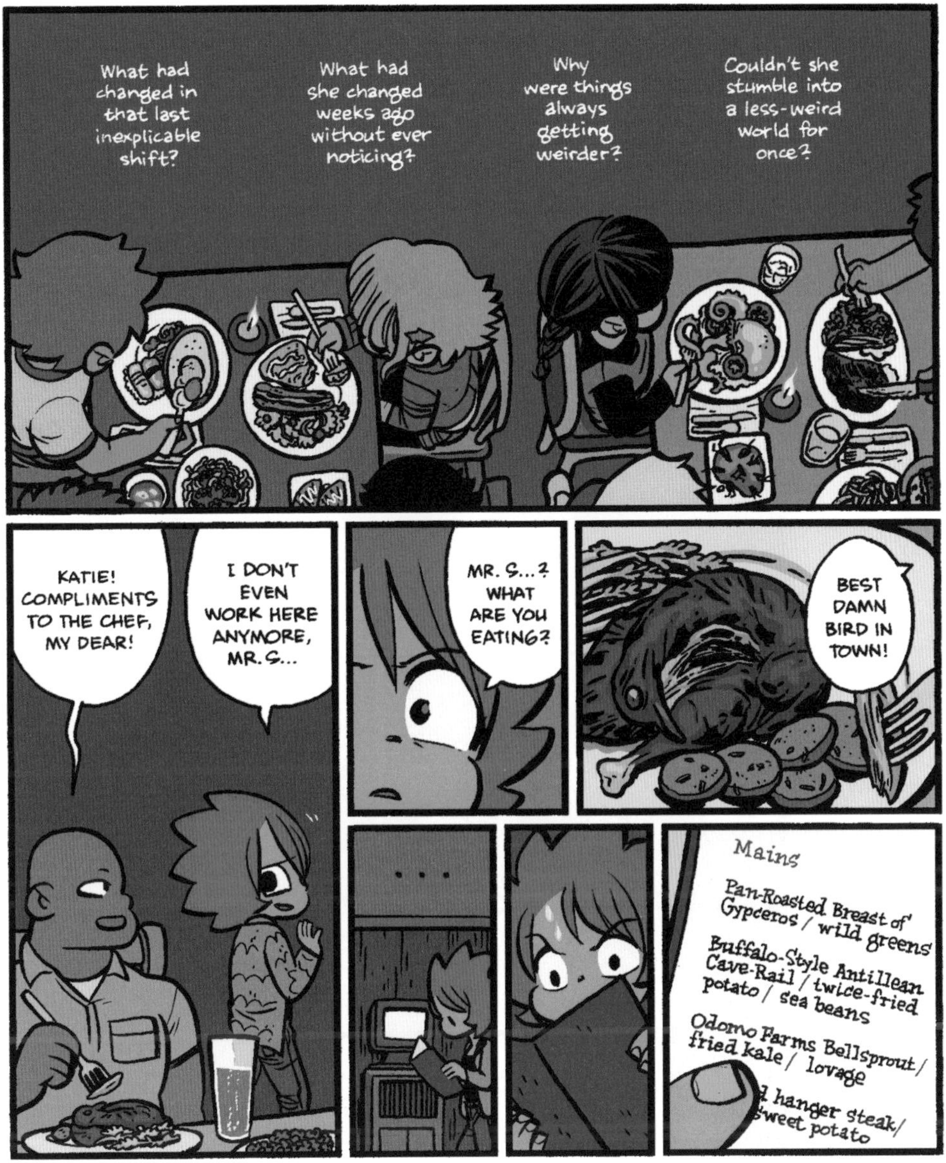
What had changed in that last inexplicable shift?
What had she changed weeks ago without ever noticing?
Why were things always getting weirder?
Couldn't she stumble into a less-weird world for once?
KATIE! COMPLIMENTS TO THE CHEF, MY DEAR!
I DON'T EVEN WORK HERE ANYMORE, MR. S...
MR. S...? WHAT ARE YOU EATING?
BEST DAMN BIRD IN TOWN!
...
Mains
Pan-Roasted Breast of Gypceros / wild greens
Buffalo-Style Antillean Cave-Rail / twice-fried potato / sea beans
Odomo Farms Bellsprout / fried kale / lovage
hanger steak / sweet potato

The kitchen was hot and dark and impossibly far from the stairs.

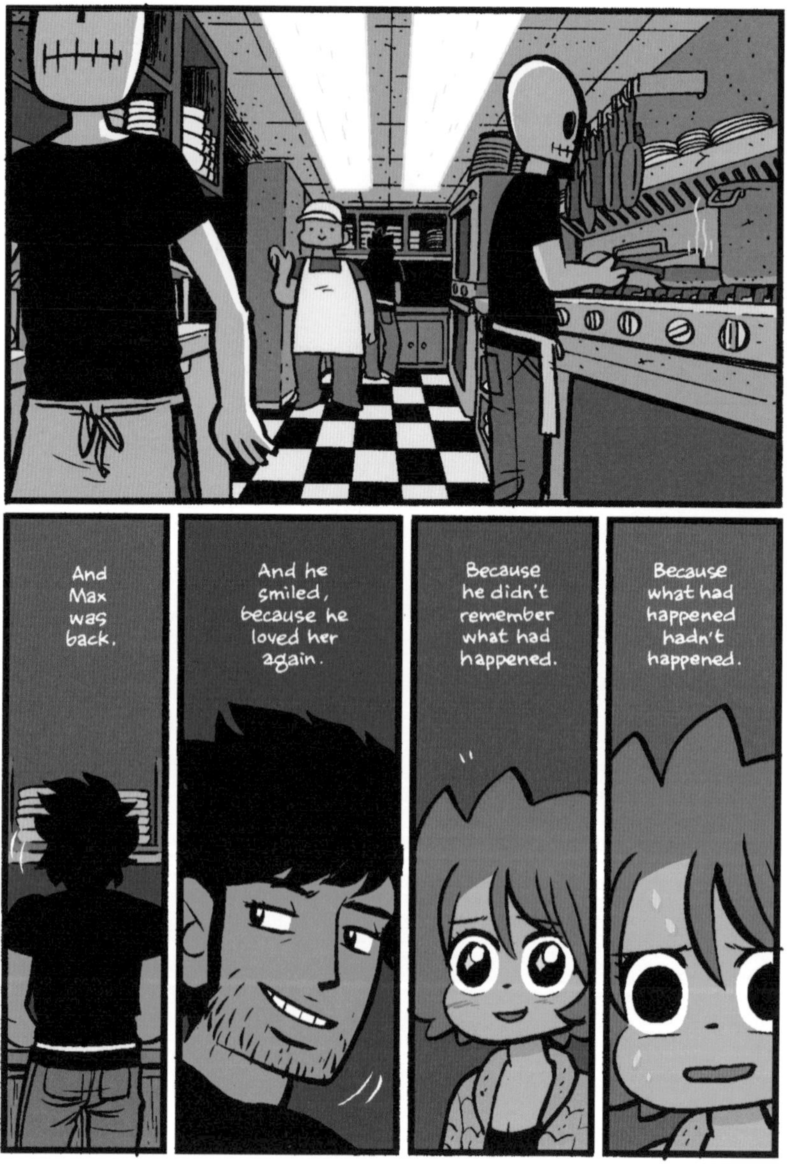
And Max was back.
And he smiled, because he loved her again.
Because he didn't remember what had happened.
Because what had happened hadn't happened.

MAX...
I LOVE YOU.
I LOVE YOU TOO.
AND I'M SEARING THREE STEAKS RIGHT NOW. I AM SO TALENTED.
MAX.

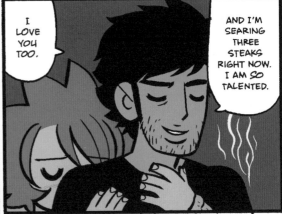

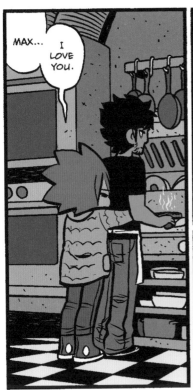

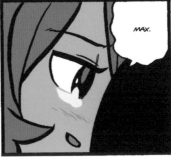

She loved him, and he loved her, and that was all that mattered now.

The other stuff was--

[redacted]

[redacted]

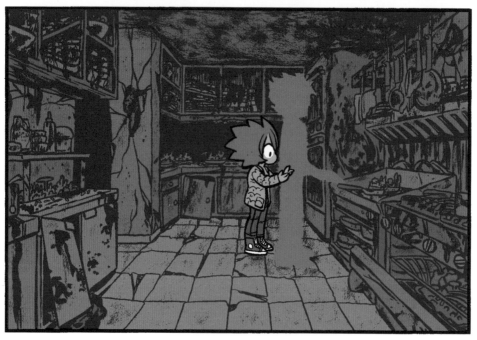

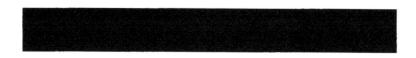

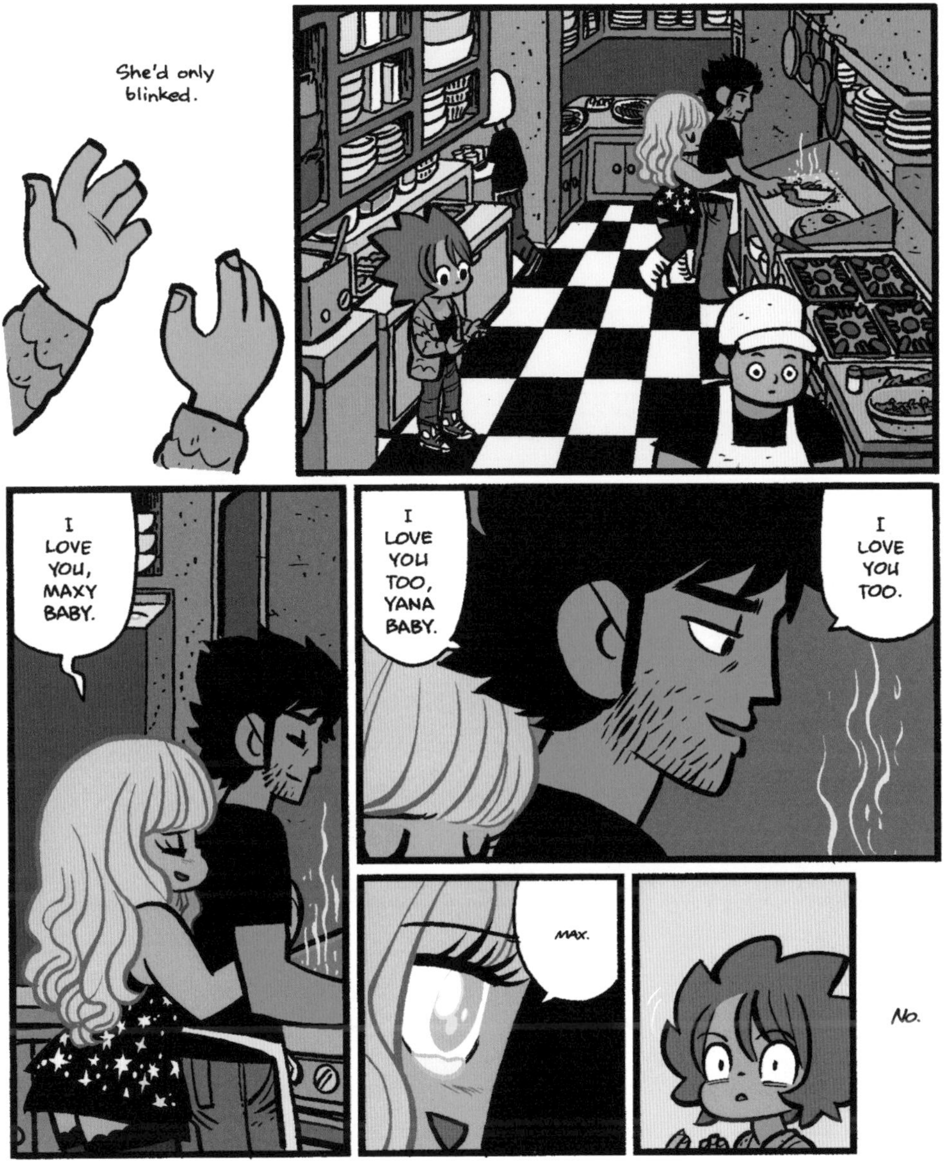
She'd only blinked.
I LOVE YOU, MAXY BABY.
I LOVE YOU TOO, YANA BABY.
I LOVE YOU TOO.
MAX.
No.

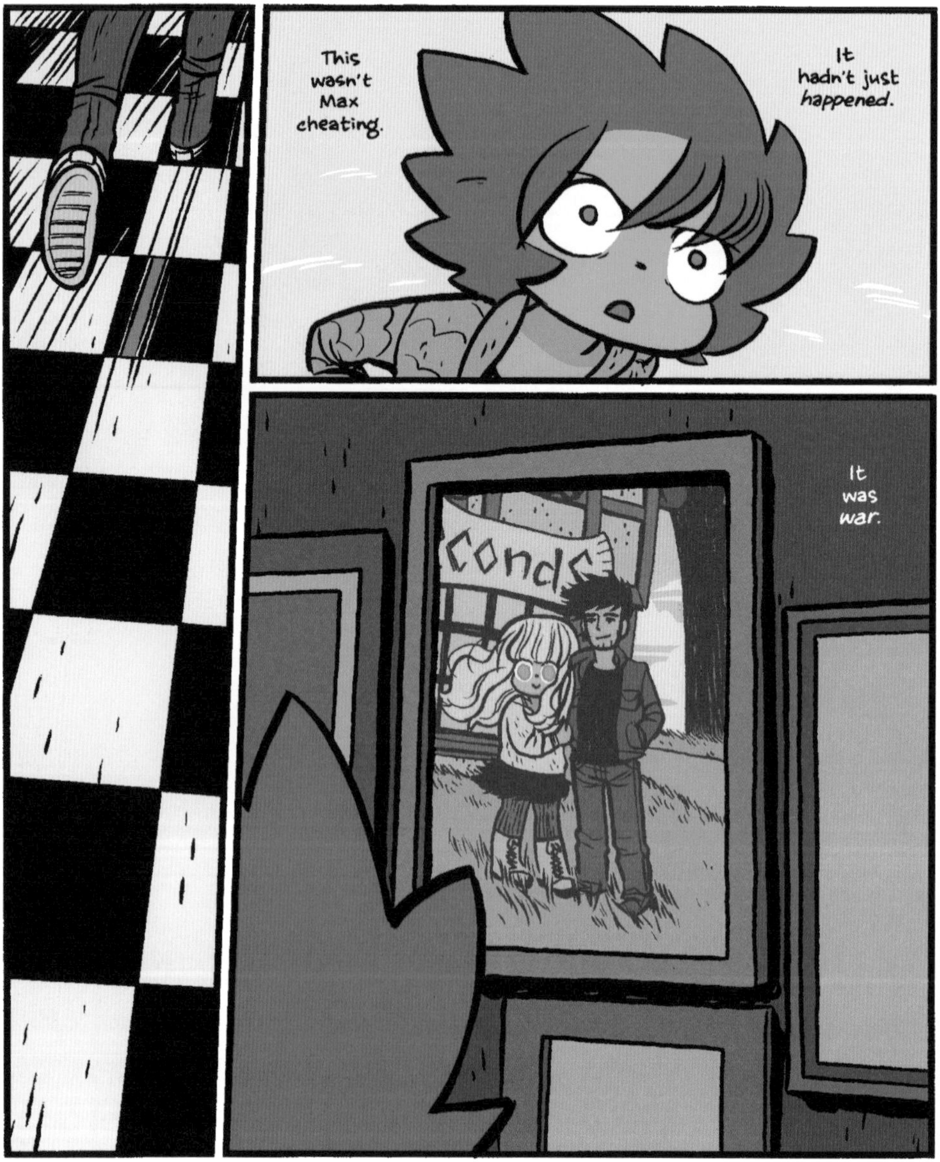
This wasn't Max cheating.
It hadn't just *happened*.
It was *war*.
conds

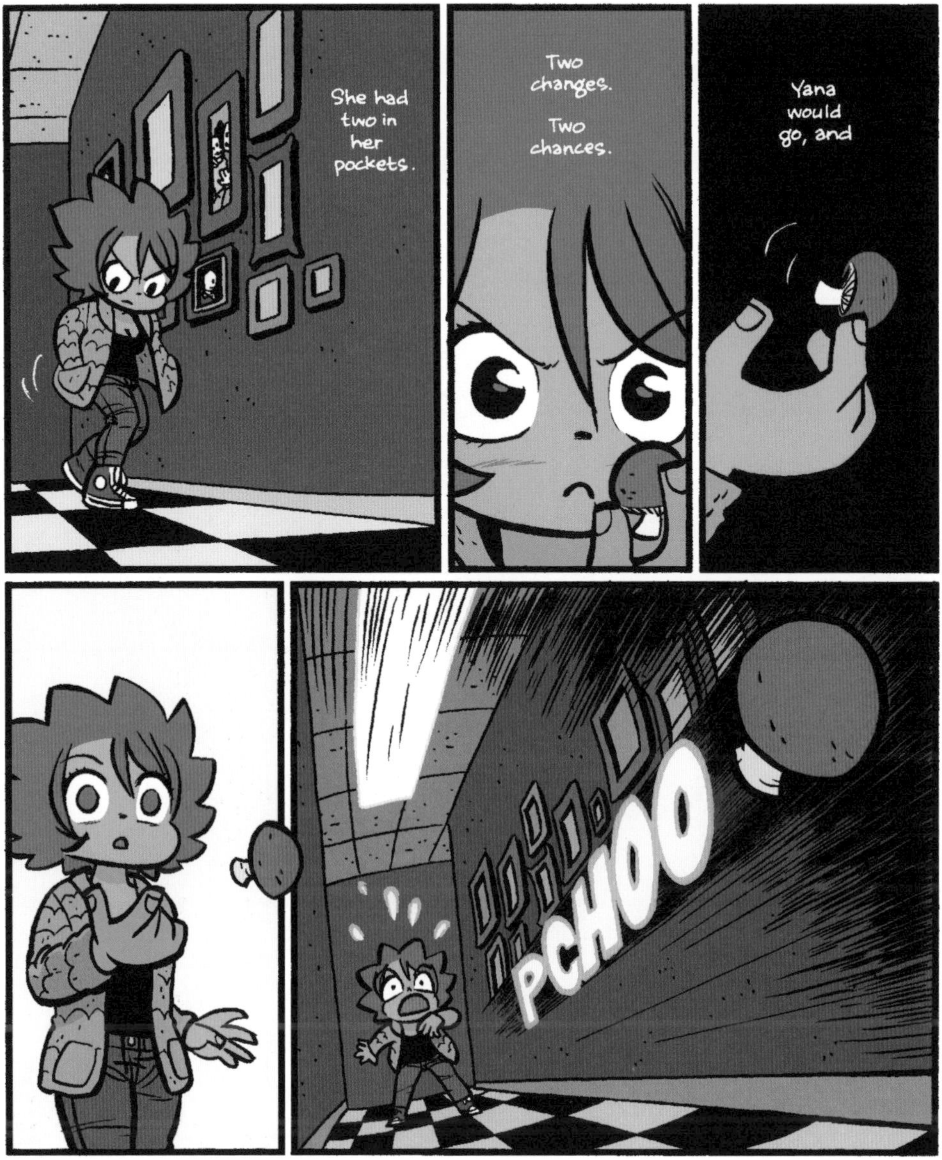
She had two in her pockets.
Two changes.
Two chances.
Yana would go, and
PCHOO

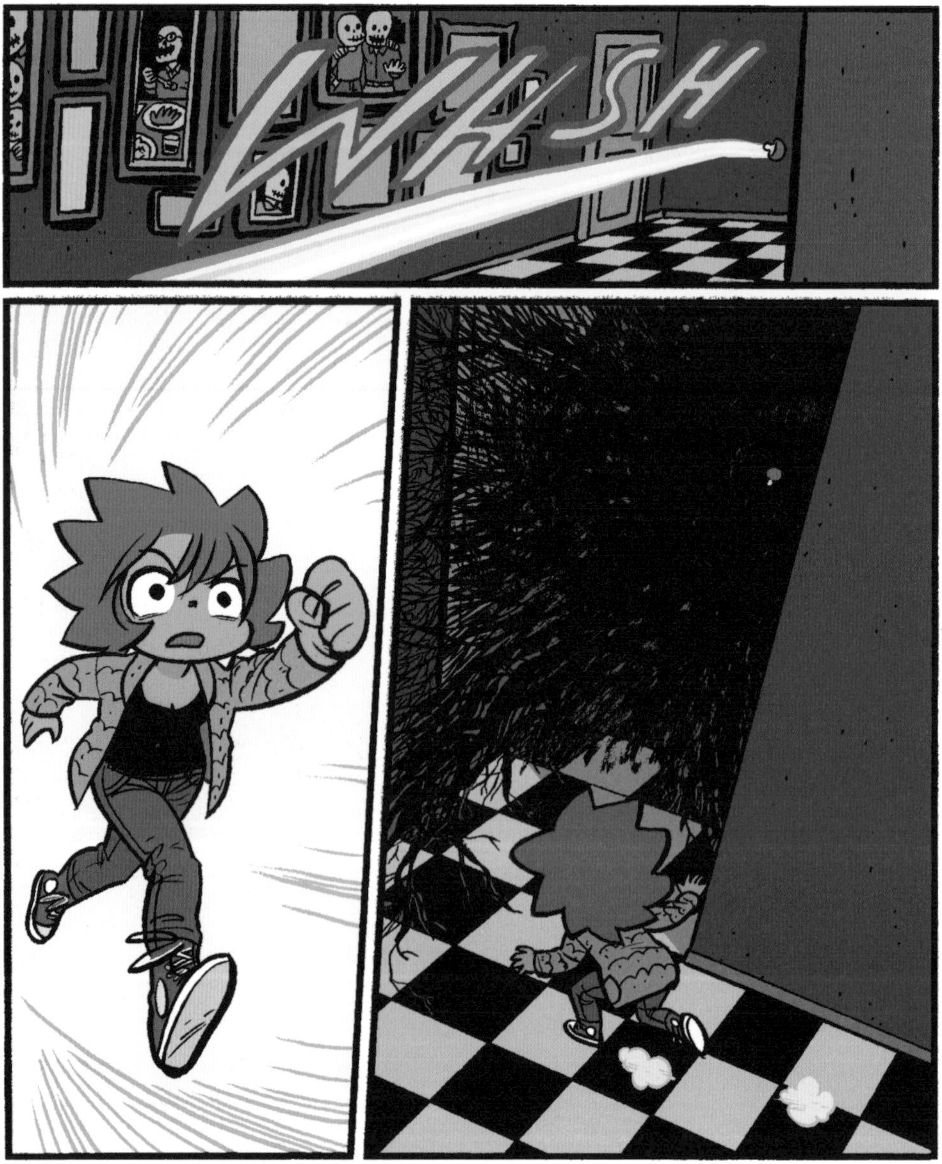
WHSH

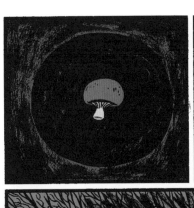

267

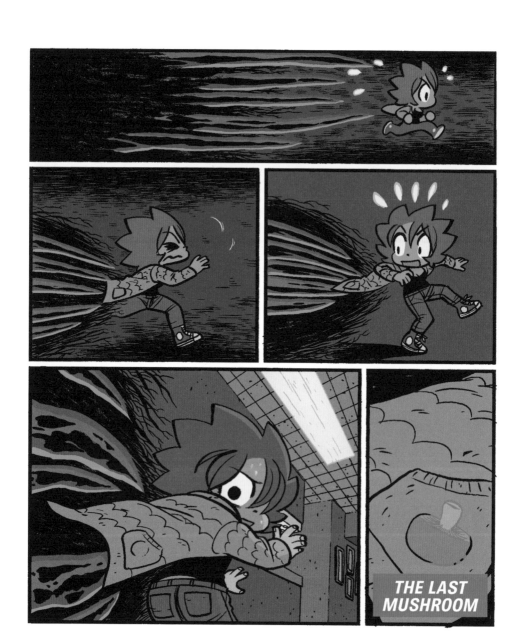

THE LAST MUSHROOM

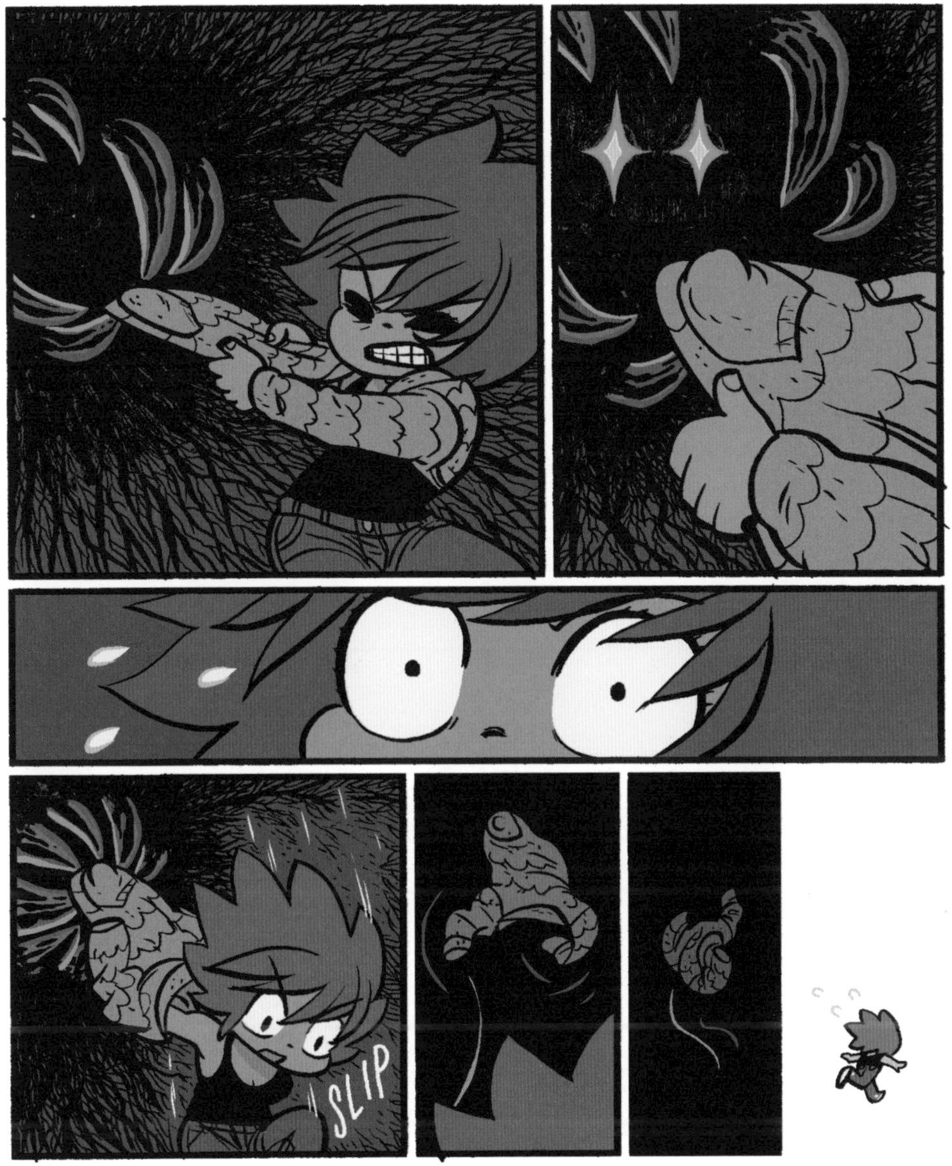
SLIP

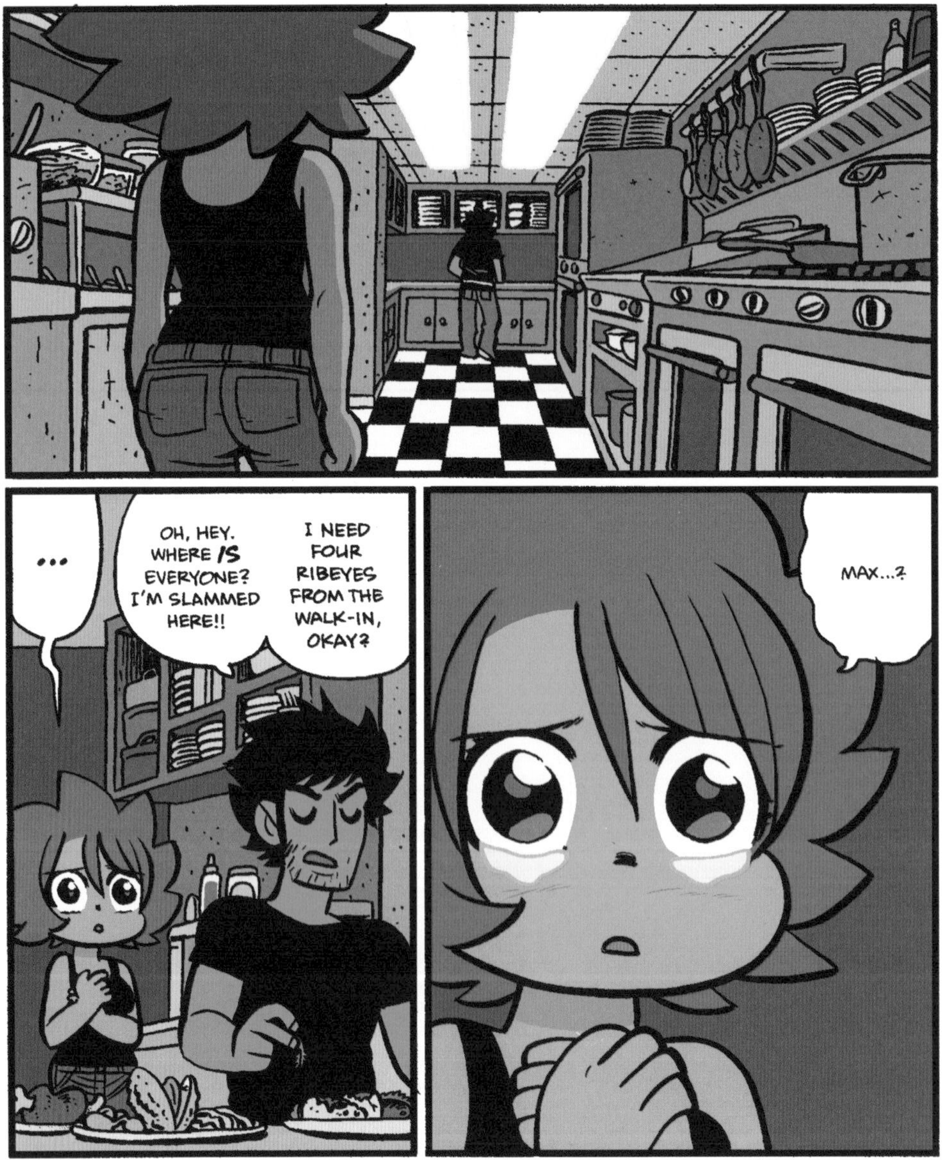
...
OH, HEY. WHERE IS EVERYONE? I'M SLAMMED HERE!!
I NEED FOUR RIBEYES FROM THE WALK-IN, OKAY?
MAX...?

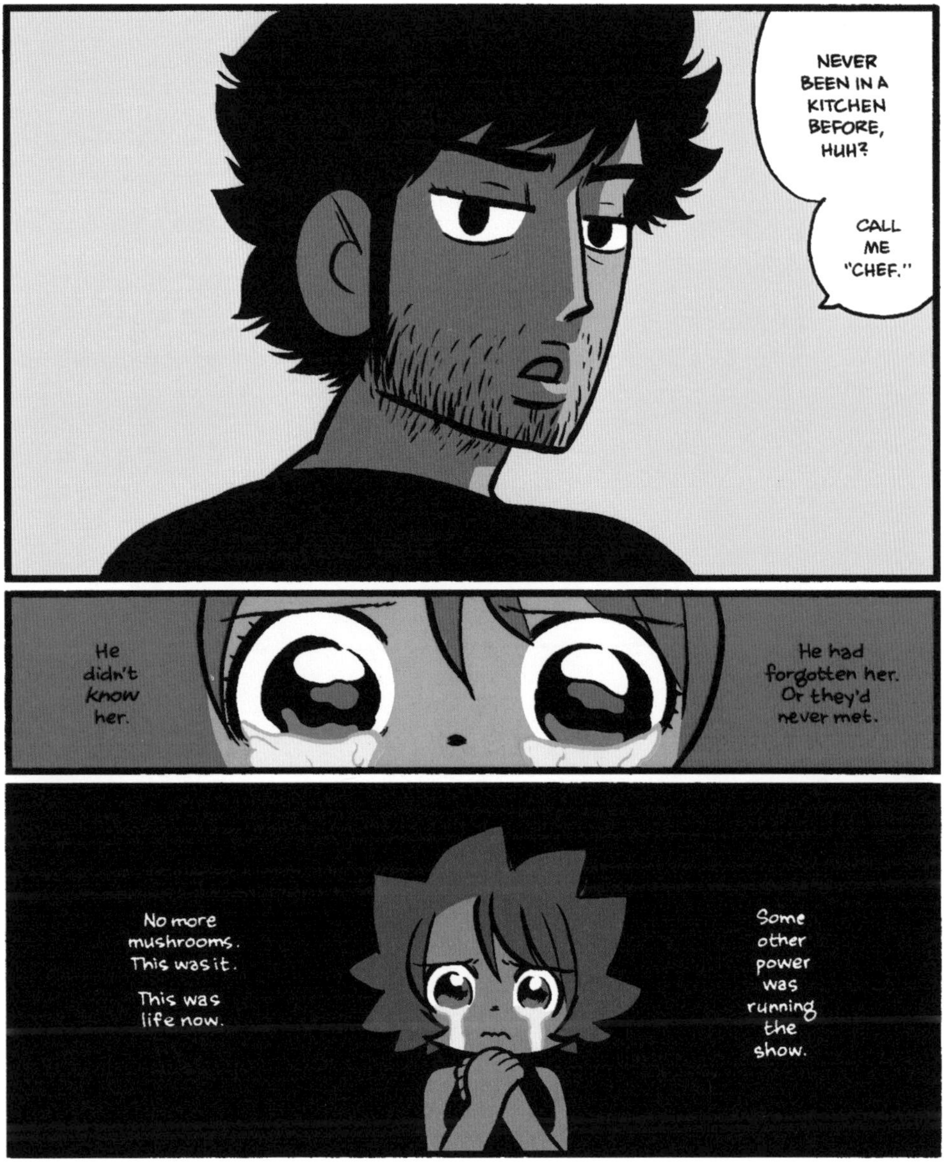
NEVER BEEN IN A KITCHEN BEFORE, HUH?
CALL ME "CHEF."
He didn't *know* her.
He had forgotten her. Or they'd never met.
No more mushrooms. This was it.
This was life now.
Some other power was running the show.

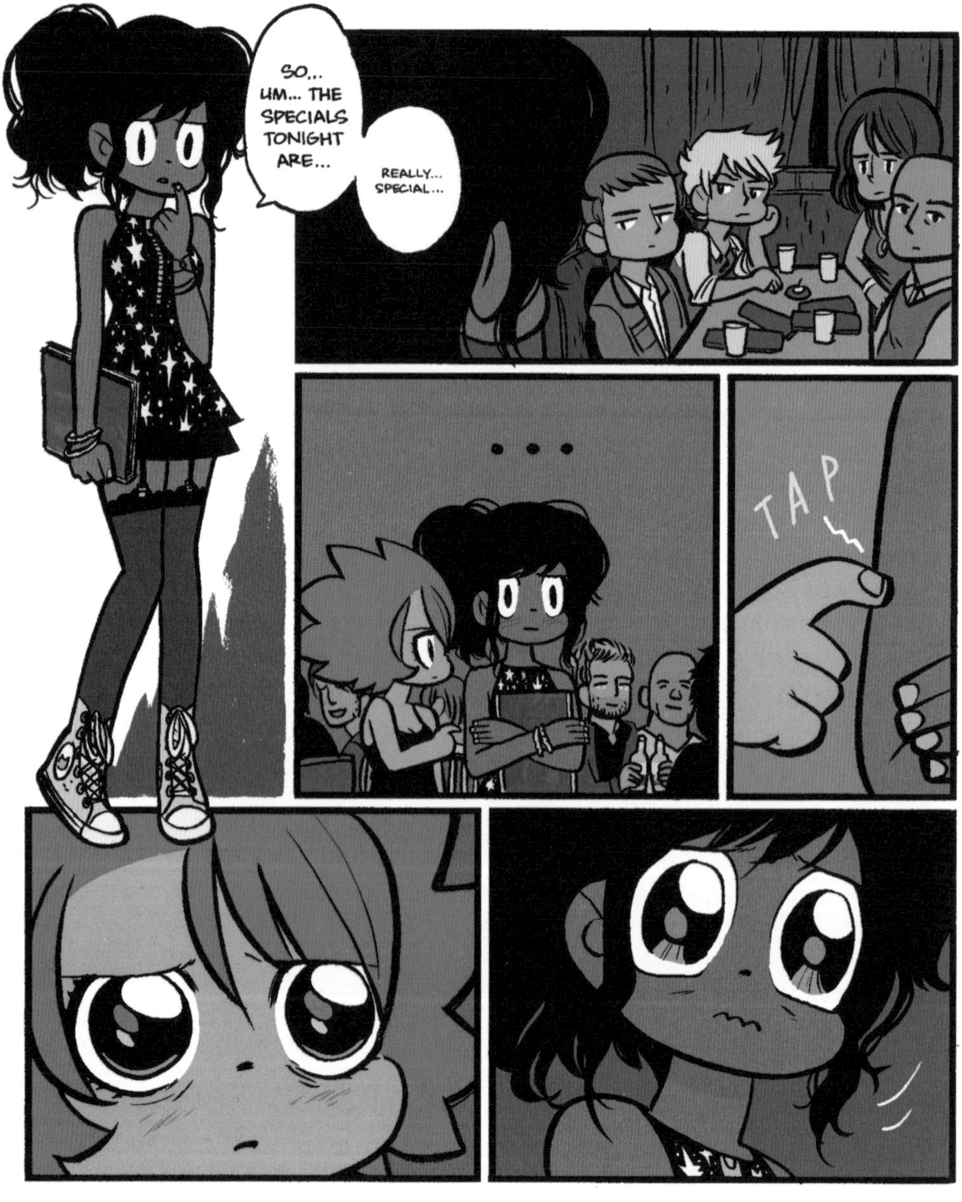
SO... UM... THE SPECIALS TONIGHT ARE...
REALLY... SPECIAL...
• • •
TAP

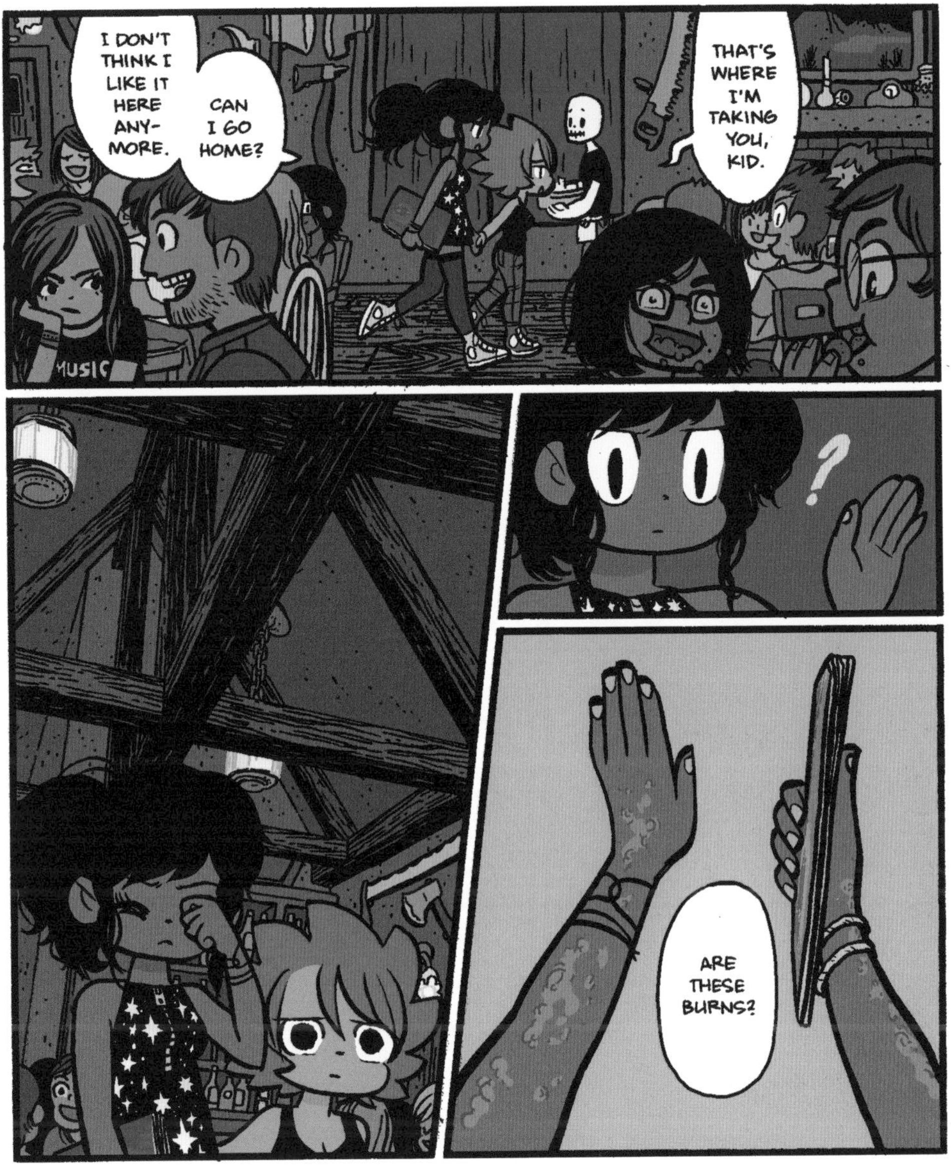
I DON'T THINK I LIKE IT HERE ANY-MORE.
CAN I GO HOME?
THAT'S WHERE I'M TAKING YOU, KID.
MUSIC
?
ARE THESE BURNS?

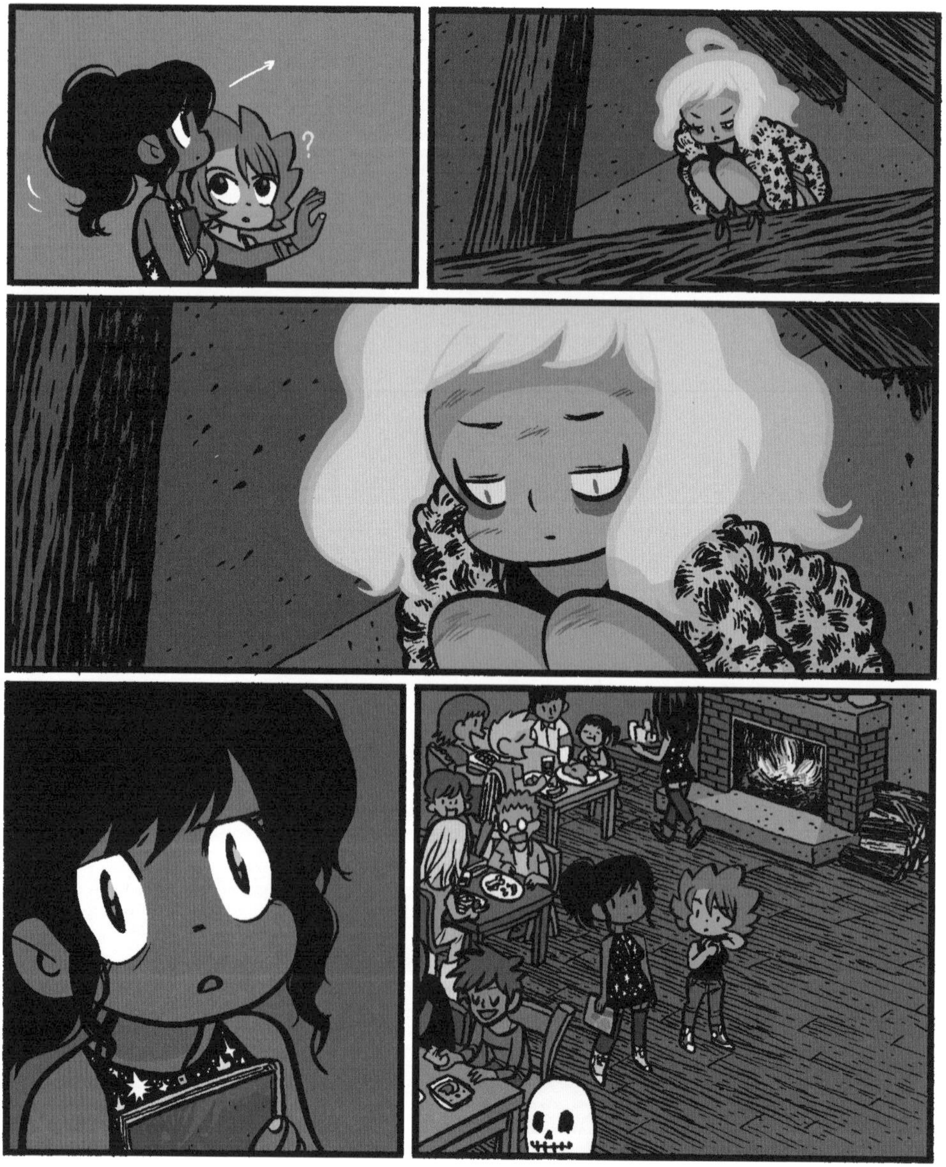
?

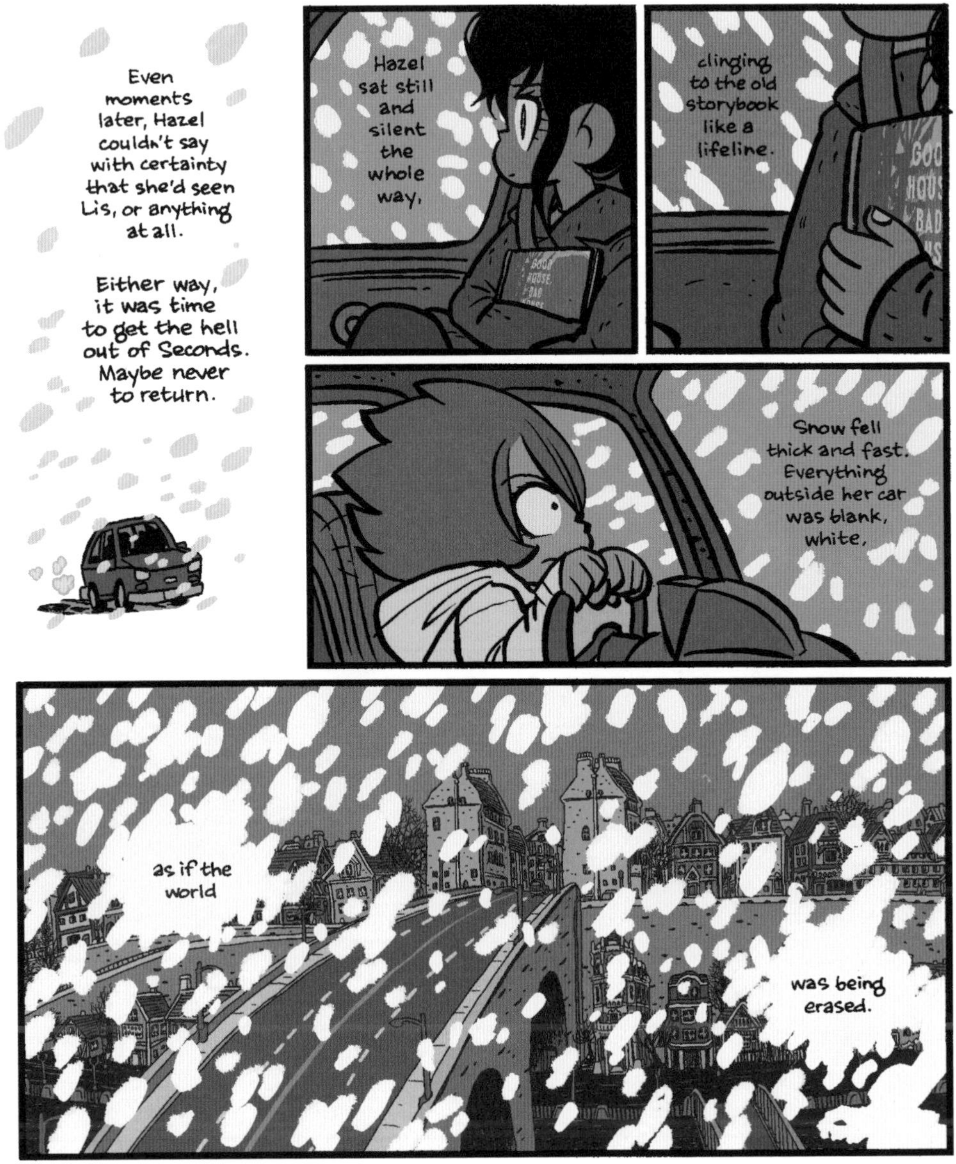
Even moments later, Hazel couldn't say with certainty that she'd seen Lis, or anything at all.
Either way, it was time to get the hell out of Seconds. Maybe never to return.
Hazel sat still and silent the whole way,
clinging to the old storybook like a lifeline.
Snow fell thick and fast. Everything outside her car was blank, white,
as if the world
was being erased.

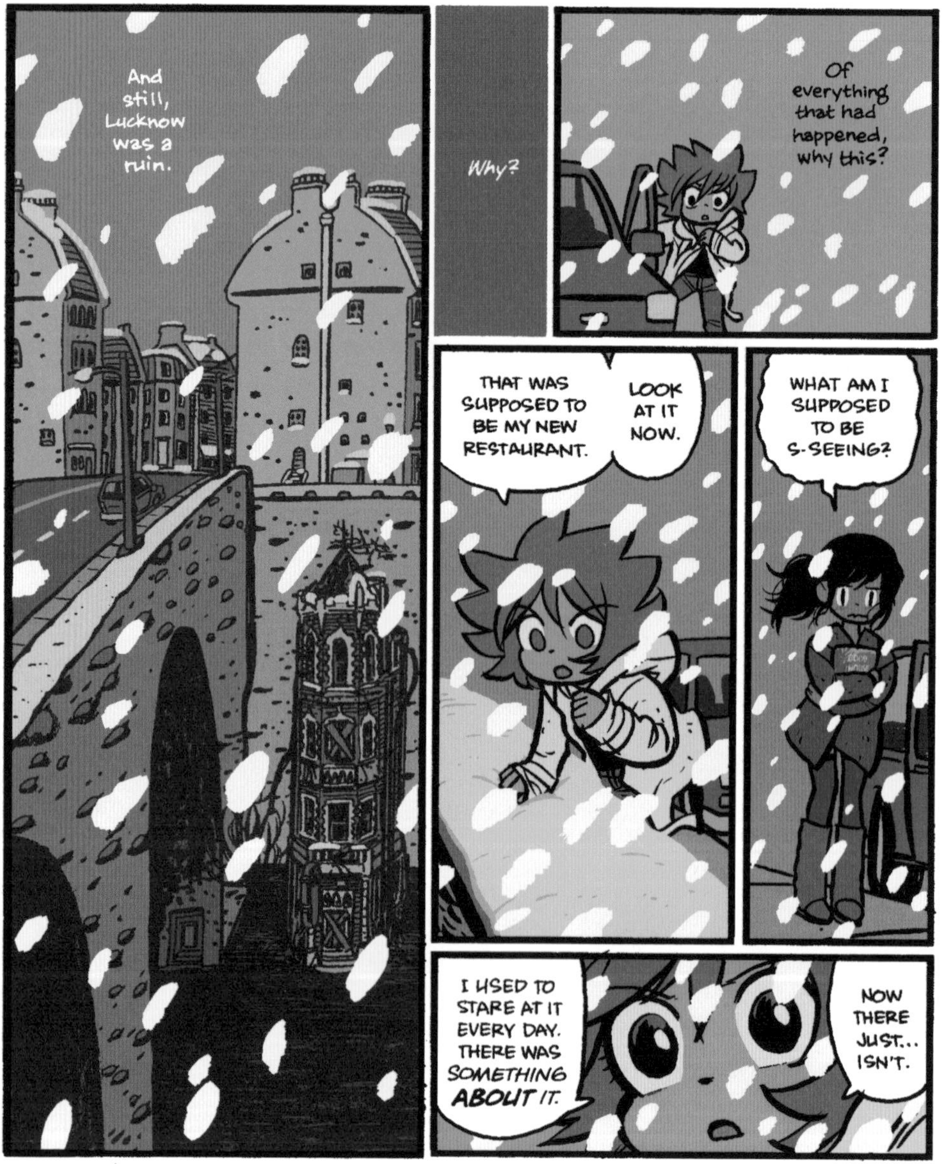

And still, Lucknow was a ruin.
Why?
Of everything that had happened, why this?
THAT WAS SUPPOSED TO BE MY NEW RESTAURANT.
LOOK AT IT NOW.
WHAT AM I SUPPOSED TO BE S-SEEING?
I USED TO STARE AT IT EVERY DAY. THERE WAS SOMETHING ABOUT IT.
NOW THERE JUST... ISN'T.

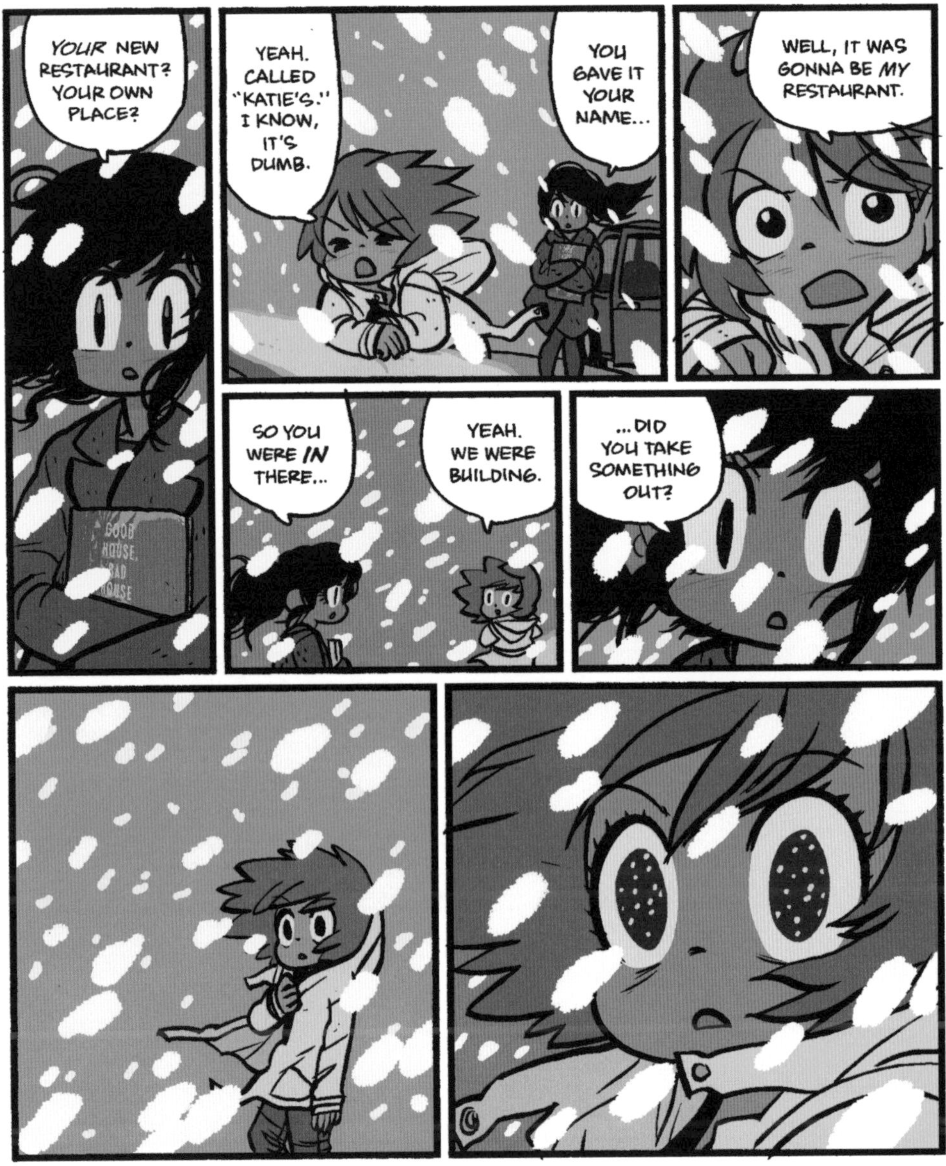
YOUR NEW RESTAURANT? YOUR OWN PLACE?
YEAH. CALLED "KATIE'S." I KNOW, IT'S DUMB.
YOU GAVE IT YOUR NAME...
WELL, IT WAS GONNA BE MY RESTAURANT.
SO YOU WERE IN THERE...
YEAH. WE WERE BUILDING.
...DID YOU TAKE SOMETHING OUT?

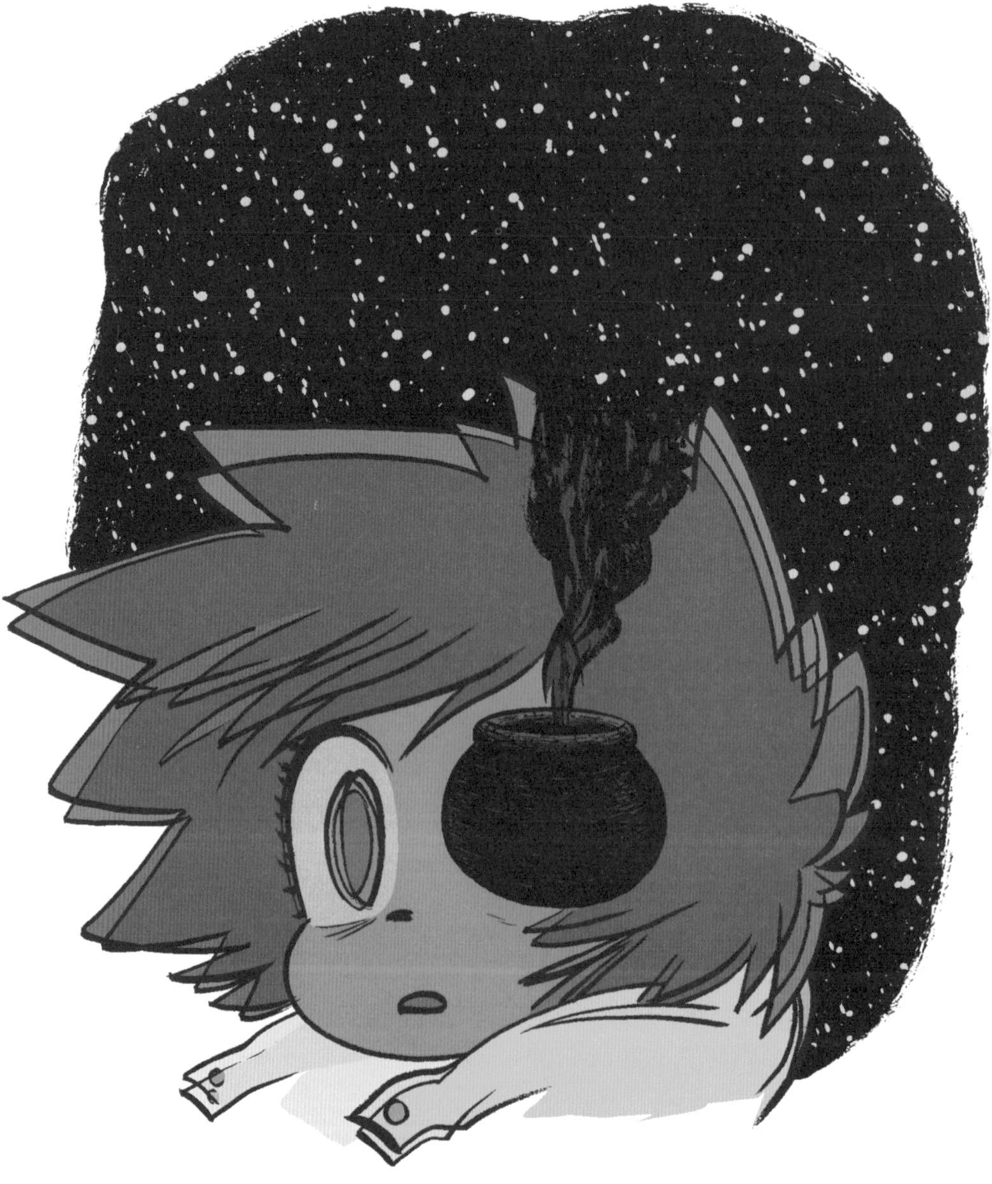

7
Can't Go Back

The witch's pot.

If she could find it, if she could bring it back--

IT'D FIX EVERYTHING!

...well... Maybe it'd help, anyway.

First of all, she had to get Hazel home safely.

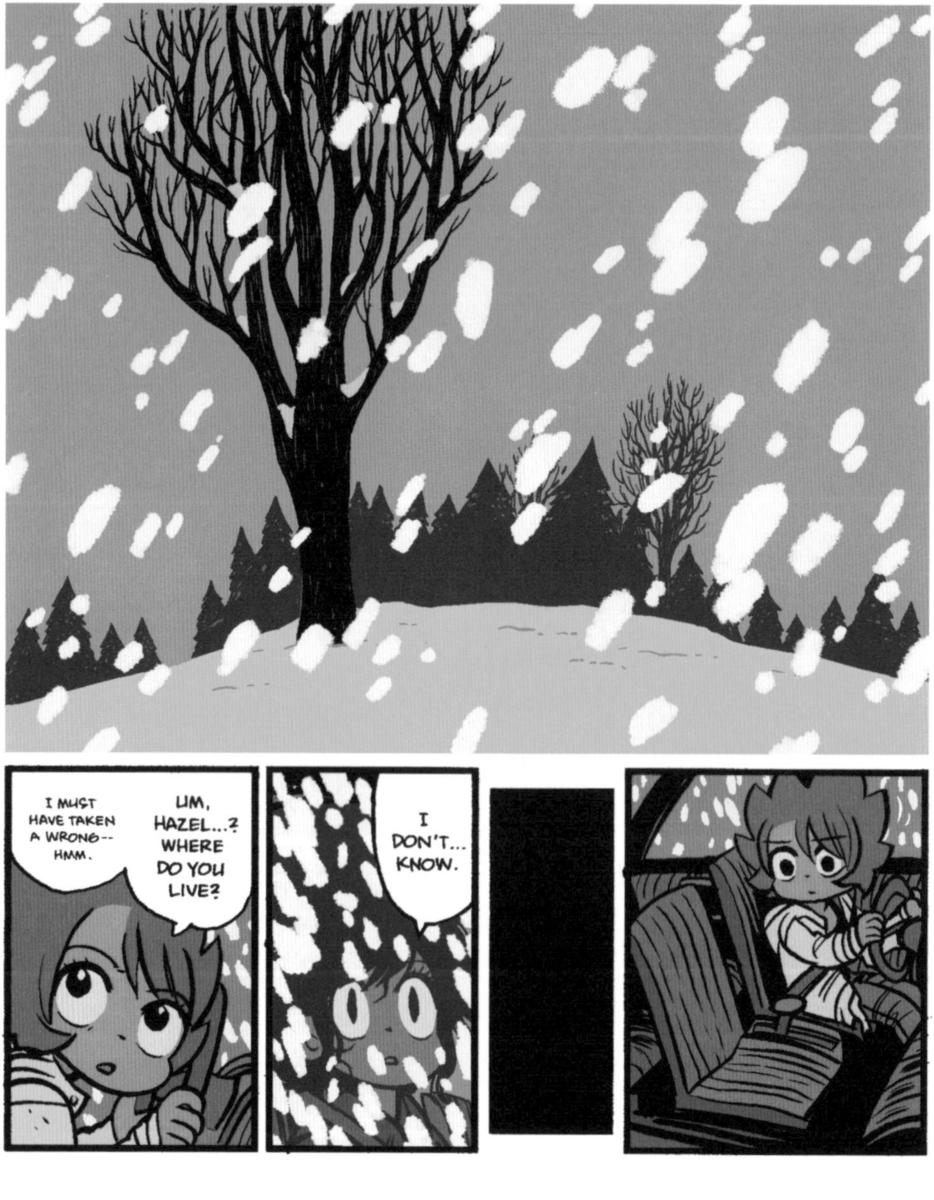
I MUST HAVE TAKEN A WRONG-- HMM.
UM, HAZEL...? WHERE DO YOU LIVE?
I DON'T... KNOW.

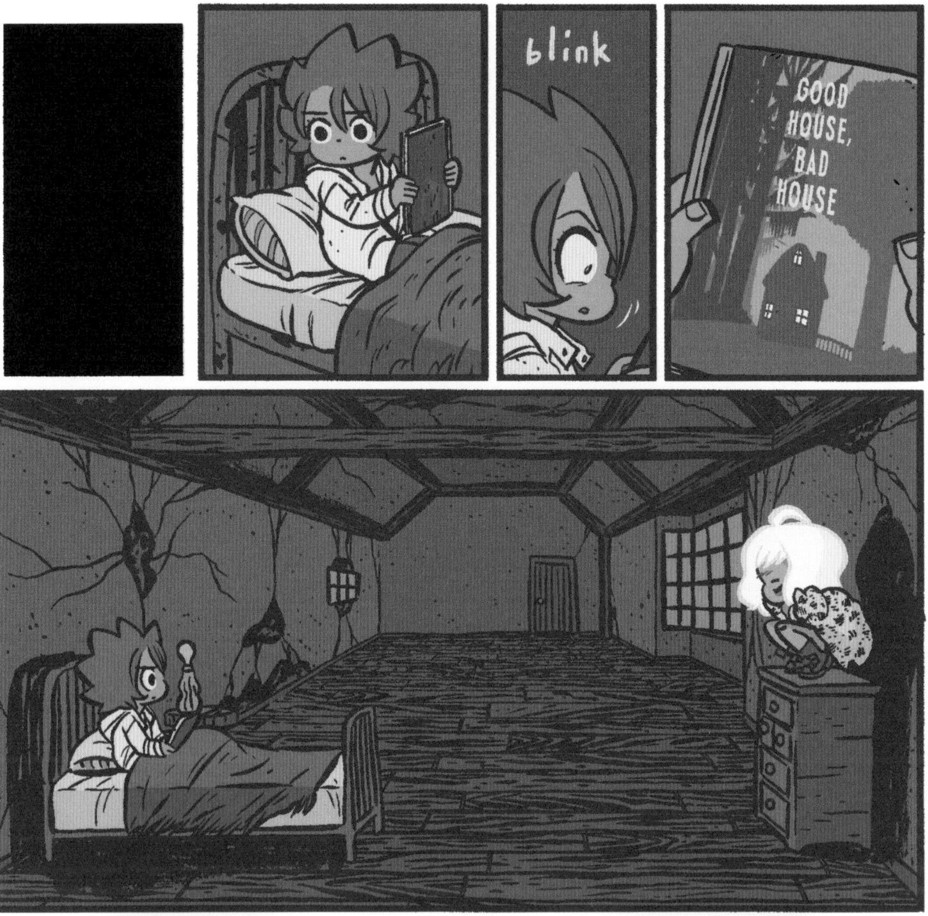
blink
GOOD HOUSE, BAD HOUSE

And like that, she was at the start again,

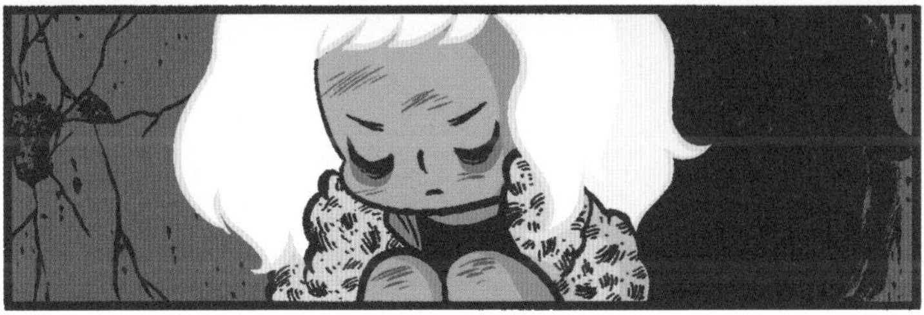

a little bit closer to the end.

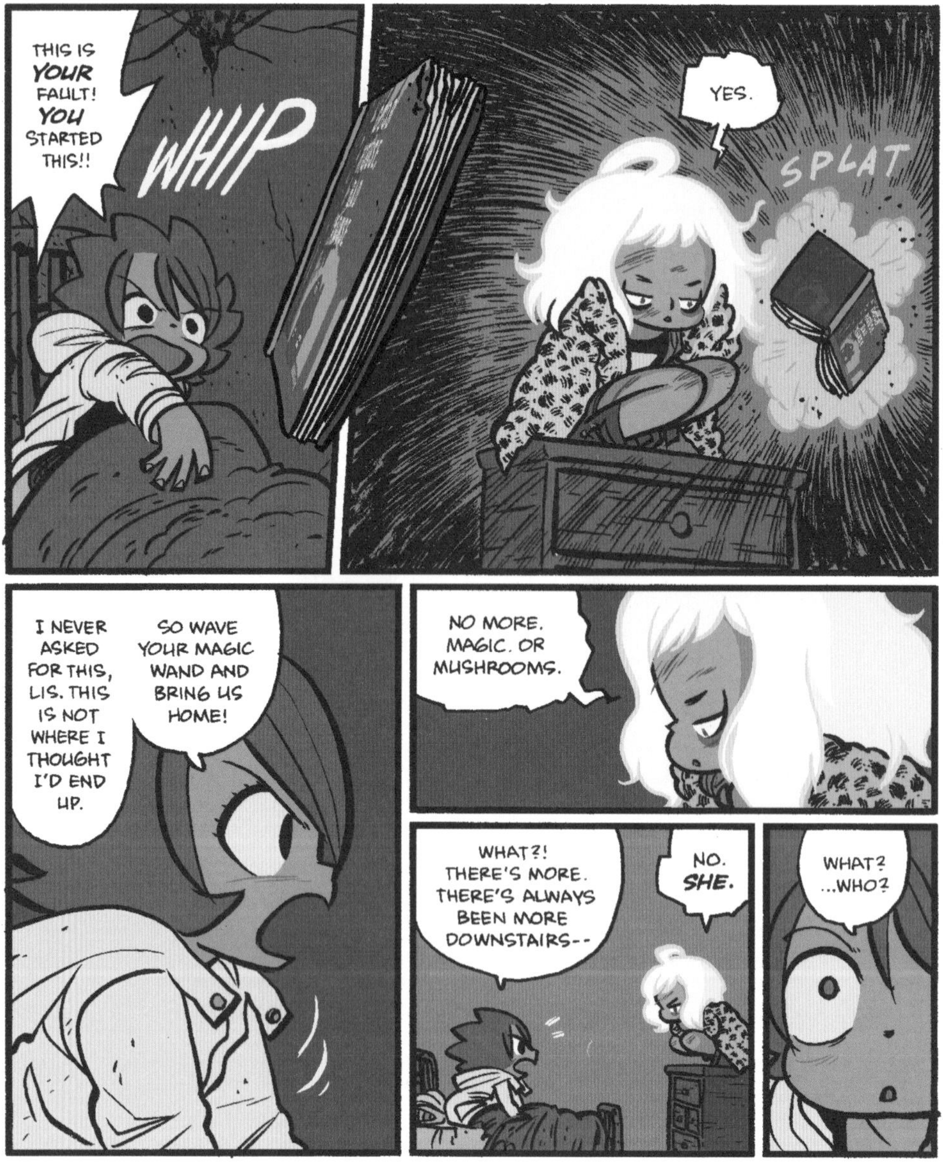
THIS IS **YOUR** FAULT! **YOU** STARTED THIS!!
WHIP
YES.
SPLAT
I NEVER ASKED FOR THIS, LIS. THIS IS NOT WHERE I THOUGHT I'D END UP.
SO WAVE YOUR MAGIC WAND AND BRING US HOME!
NO MORE. MAGIC. OR MUSHROOMS.
WHAT?! THERE'S MORE. THERE'S ALWAYS BEEN MORE DOWNSTAIRS--
NO. **SHE.**
WHAT? ...WHO?

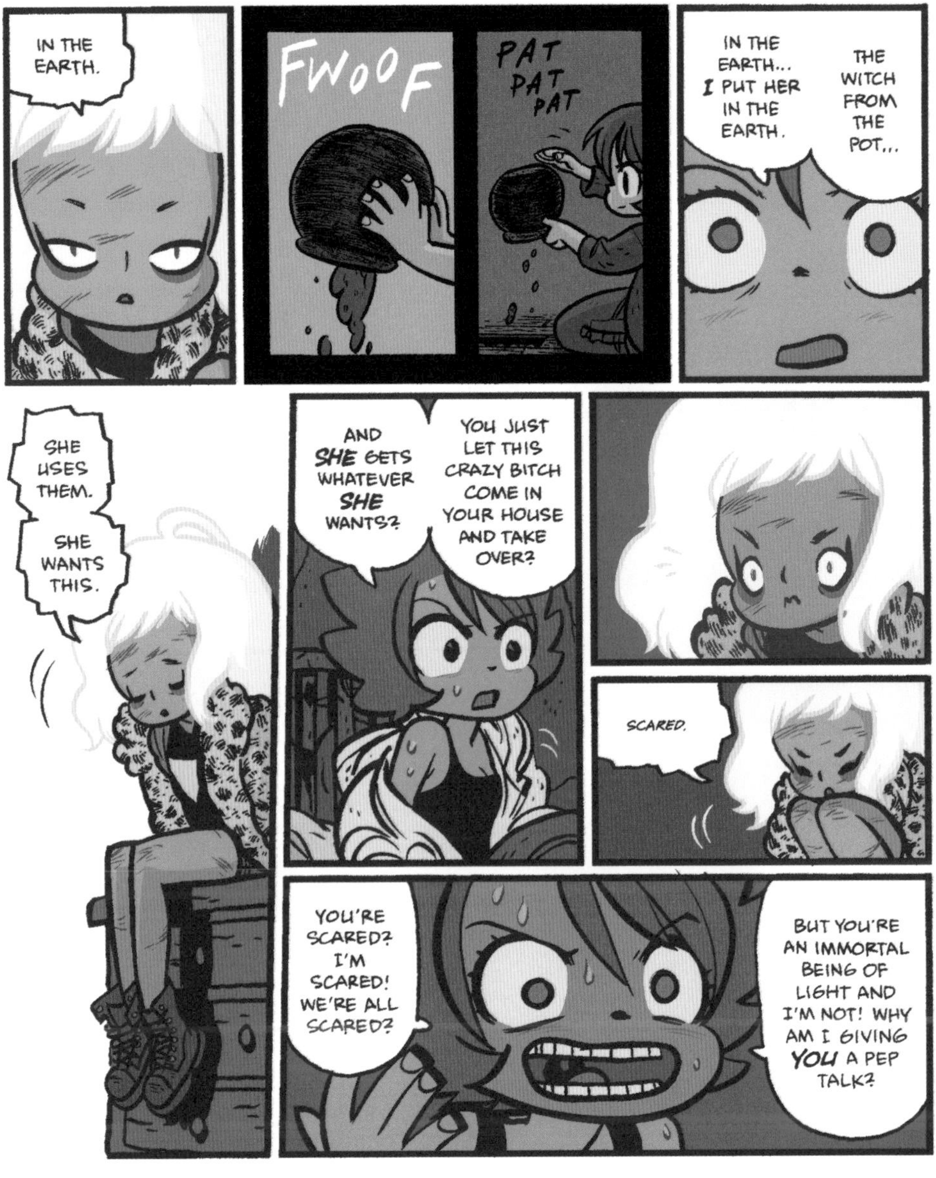
IN THE EARTH.
FWOOF
PAT PAT PAT
IN THE EARTH... I PUT HER IN THE EARTH.
THE WITCH FROM THE POT...
SHE USES THEM.
SHE WANTS THIS.
AND SHE GETS WHATEVER SHE WANTS?
YOU JUST LET THIS CRAZY BITCH COME IN YOUR HOUSE AND TAKE OVER?
SCARED.
YOU'RE SCARED? I'M SCARED! WE'RE ALL SCARED?
BUT YOU'RE AN IMMORTAL BEING OF LIGHT AND I'M NOT! WHY AM I GIVING YOU A PEP TALK?

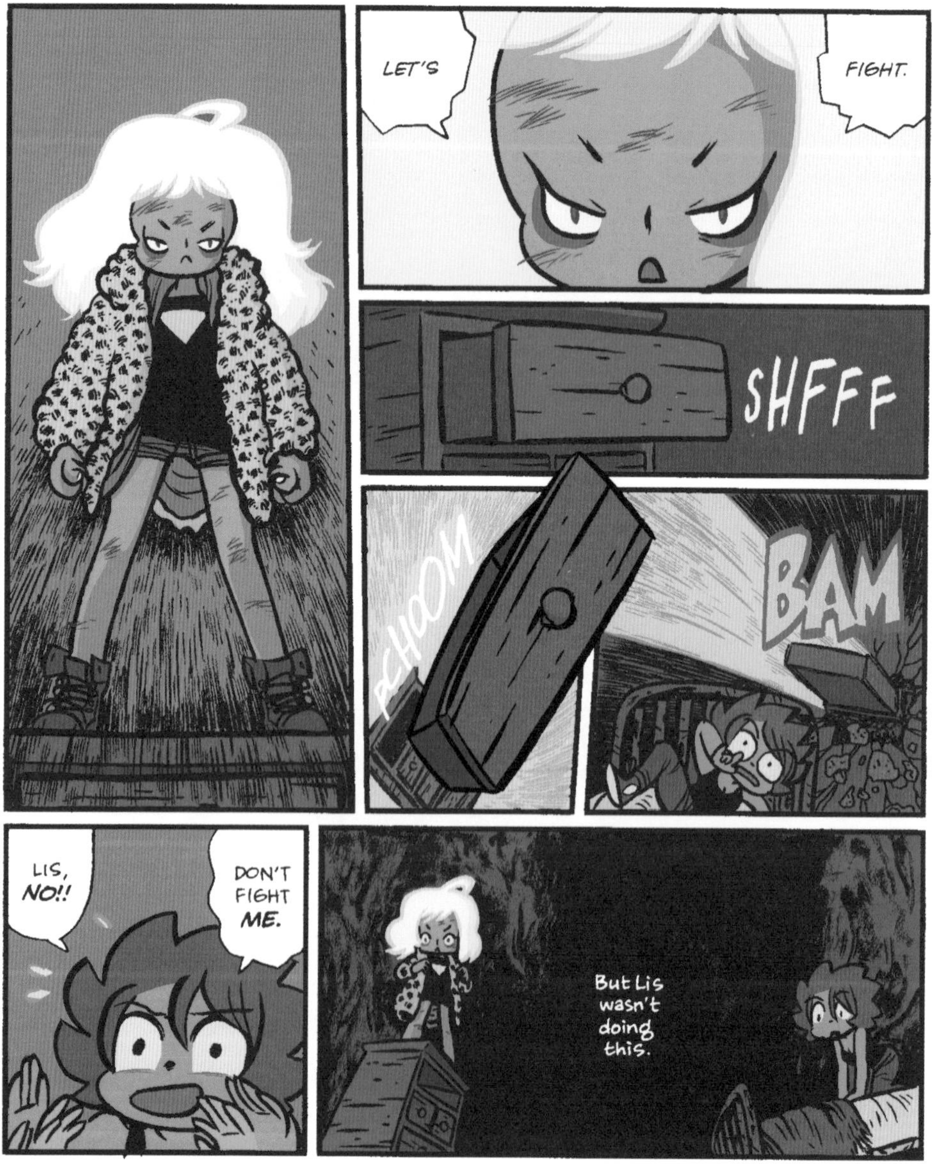
LET'S
FIGHT.
SHFFF
PCHOOM
BAM
LIS, NO!!
DON'T FIGHT ME.
But Lis wasn't doing this.

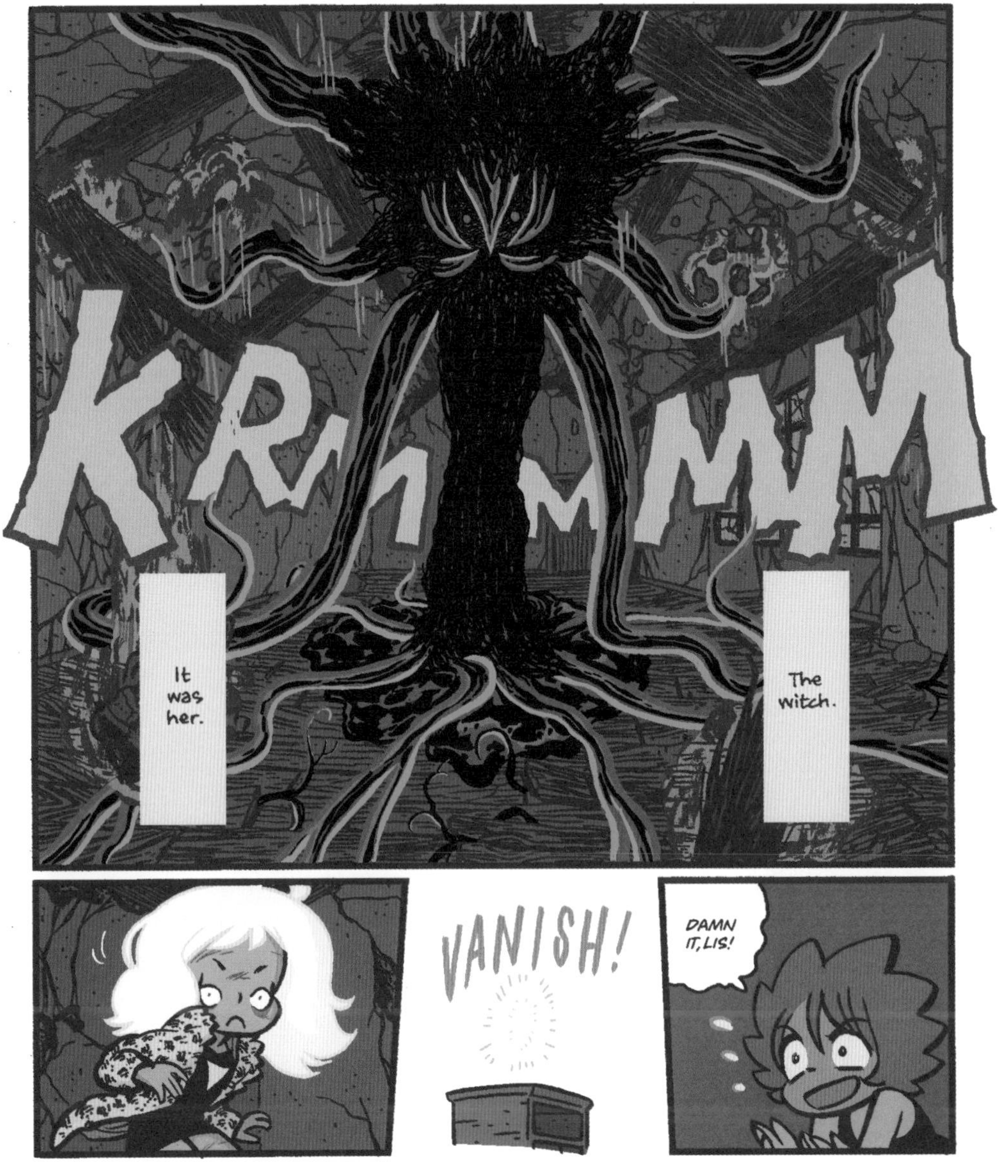
KRMMMM
It was her.
The witch.
VANISH!
DAMN IT, LIS!

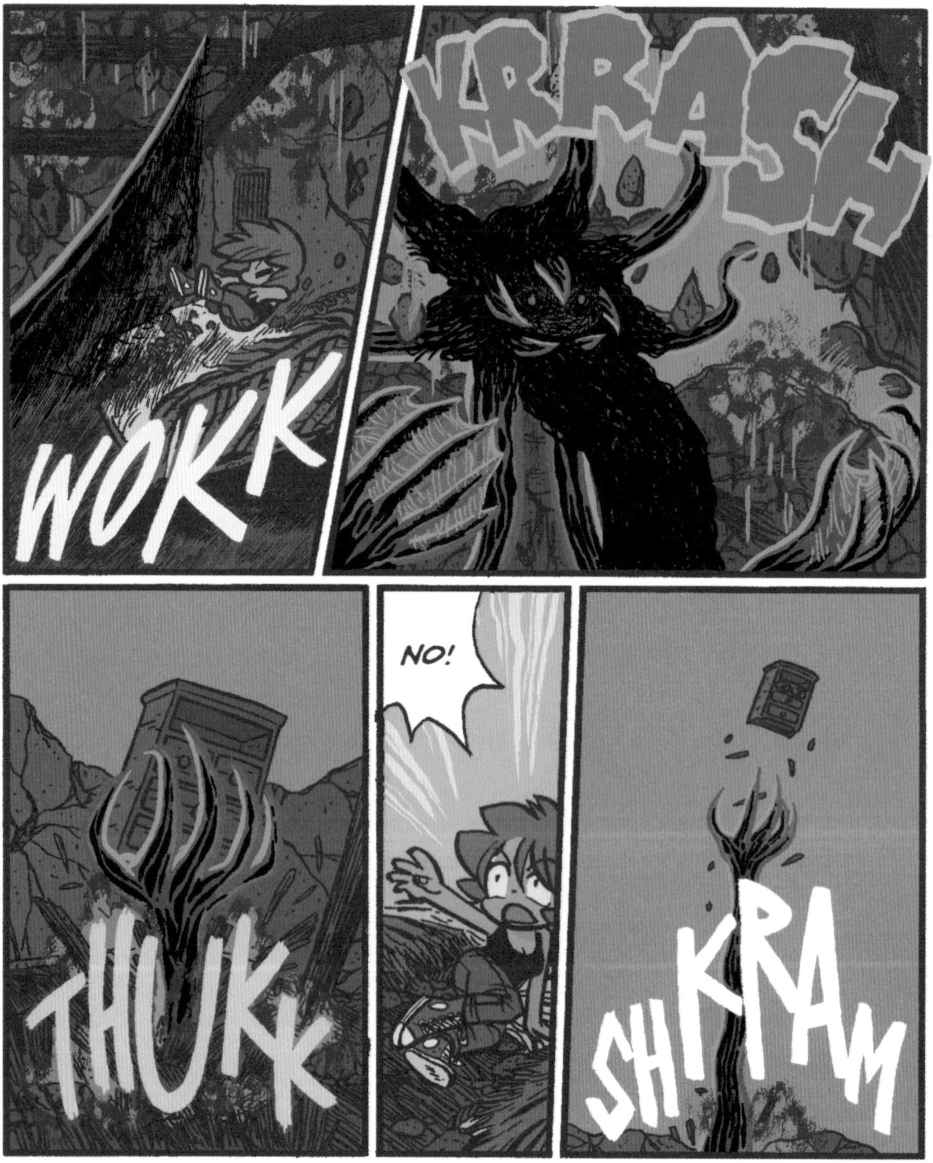
WOKK
KRRASH
THUKK
NO!
SHKRAM

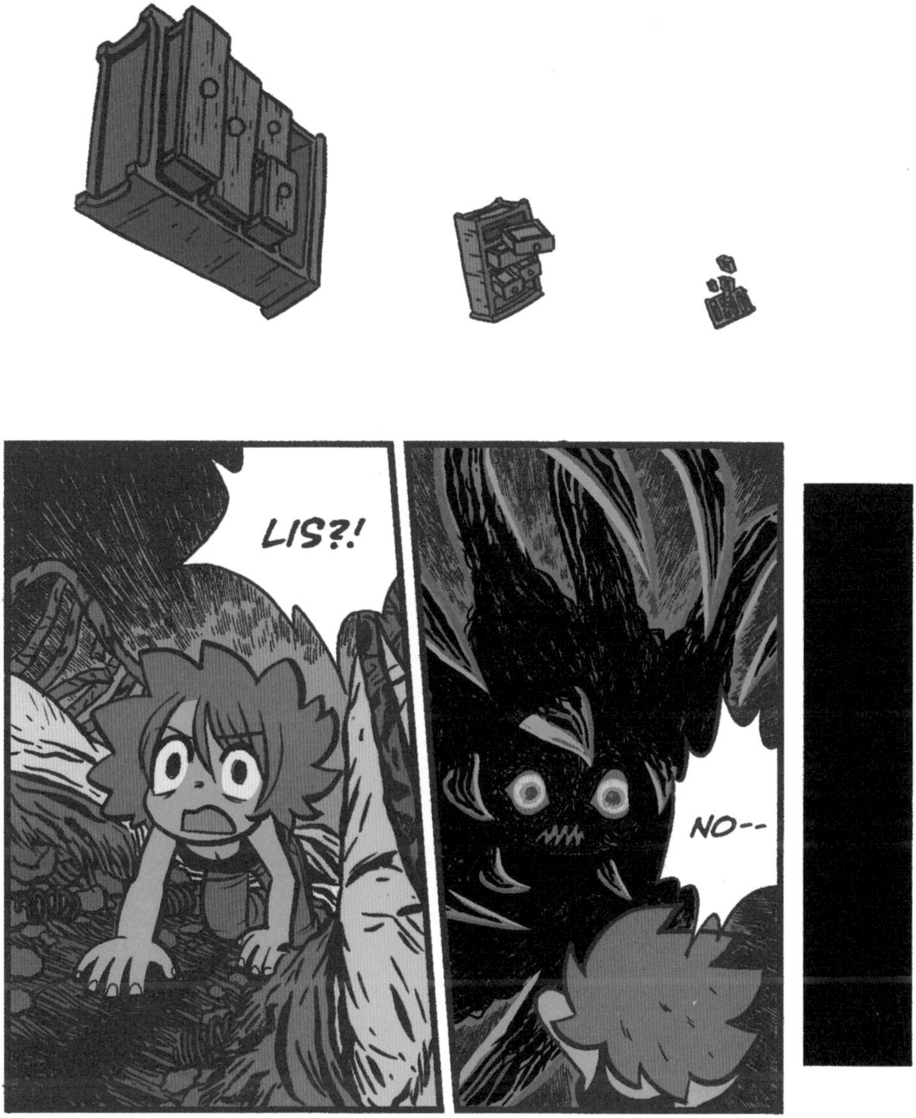
LIS?!
NO--

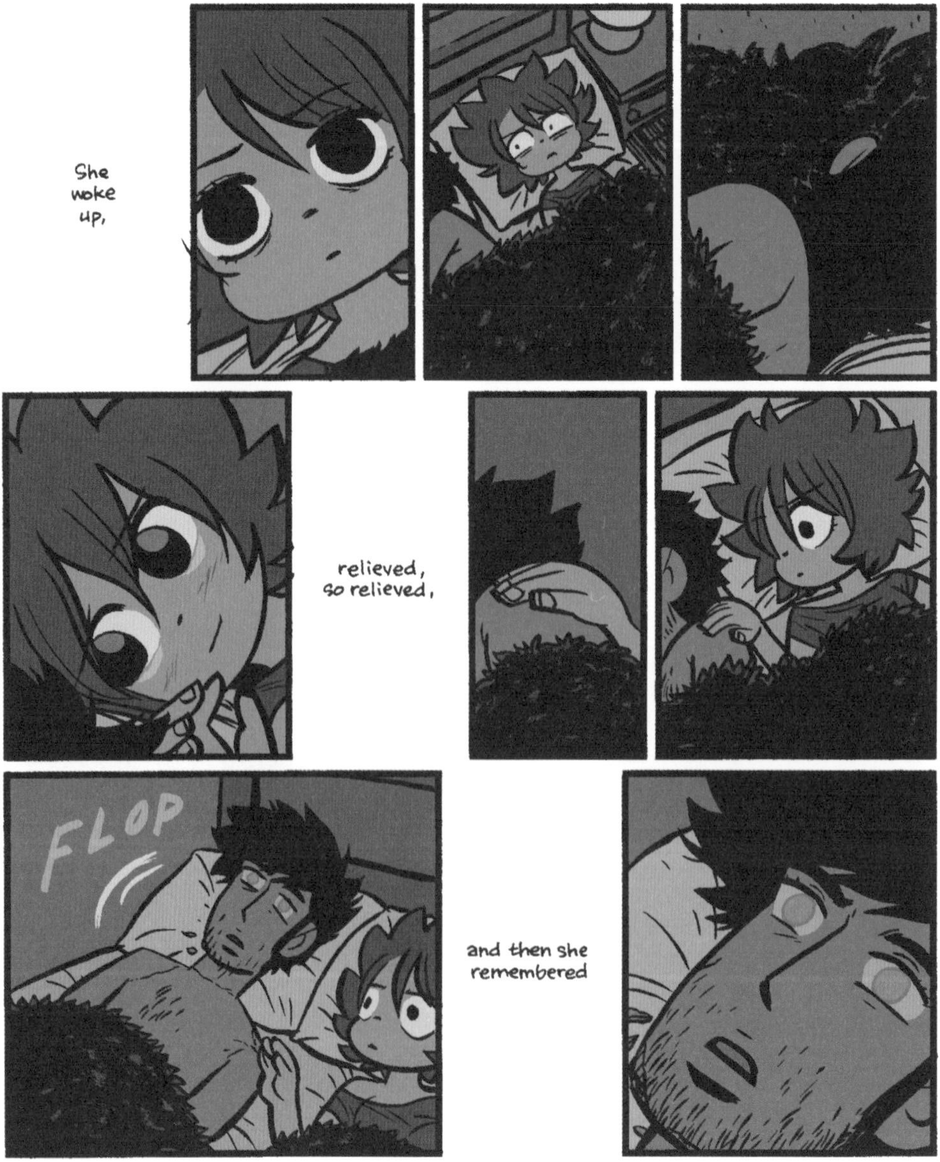
She woke up,
relieved, so relieved,
FLOP
and then she remembered

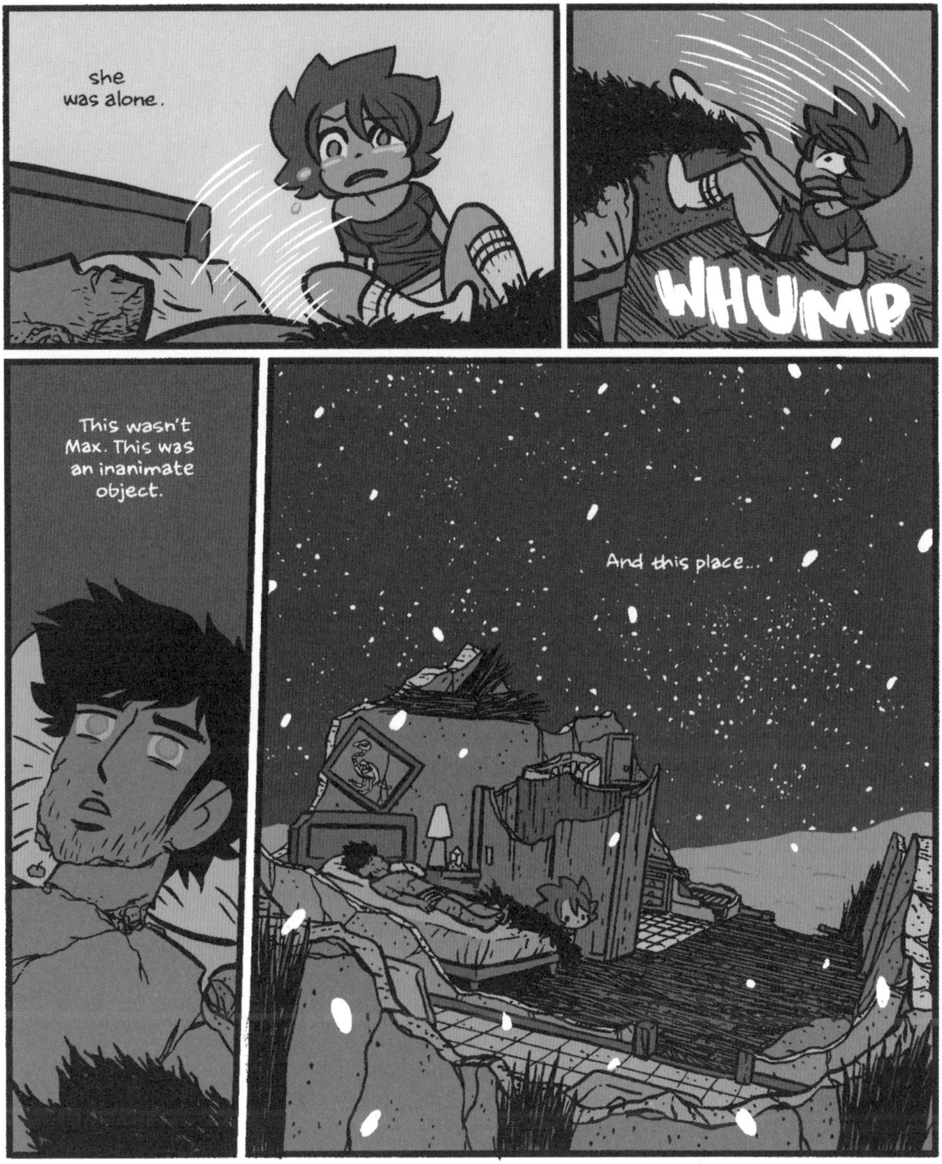
she was alone.
WHUMP
This wasn't Max. This was an inanimate object.
And this place...

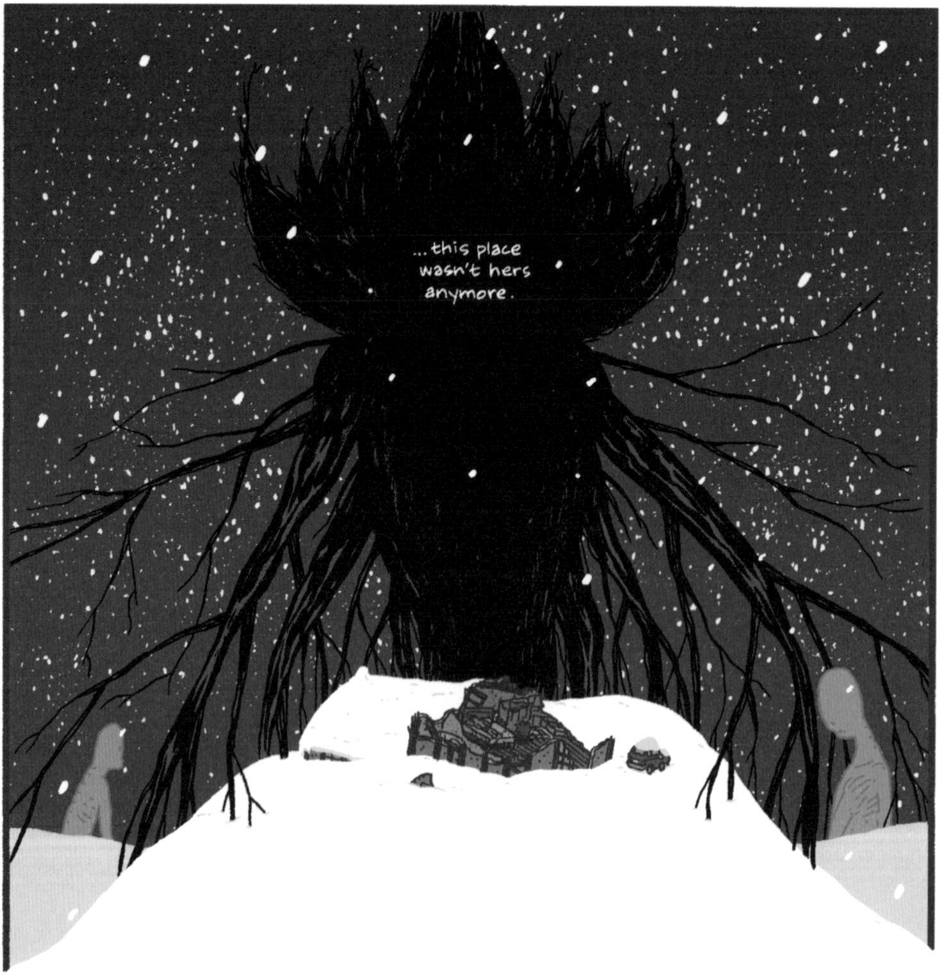
...this place wasn't hers anymore.

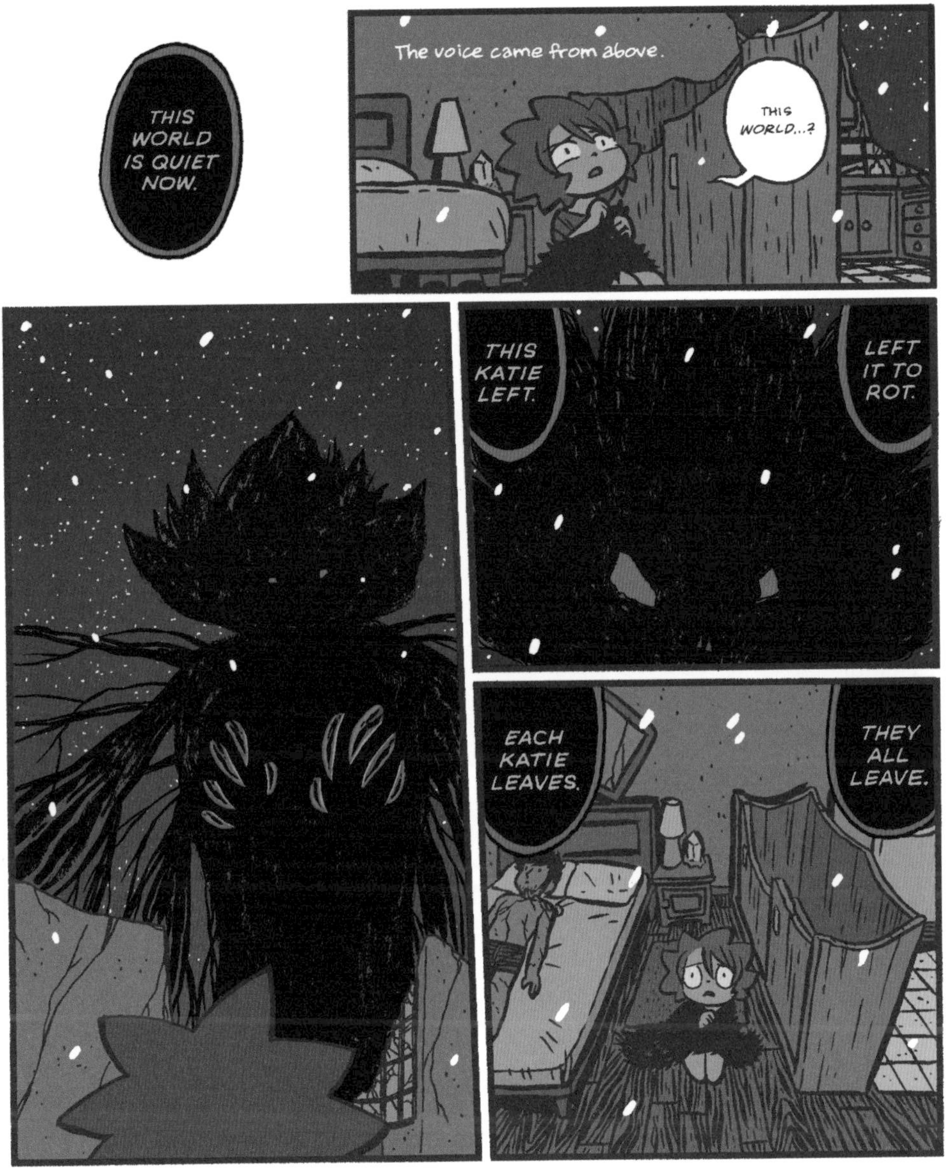
THIS WORLD IS QUIET NOW.
The voice came from above.
THIS WORLD...?
THIS KATIE LEFT.
LEFT IT TO ROT.
EACH KATIE LEAVES.
THEY ALL LEAVE.

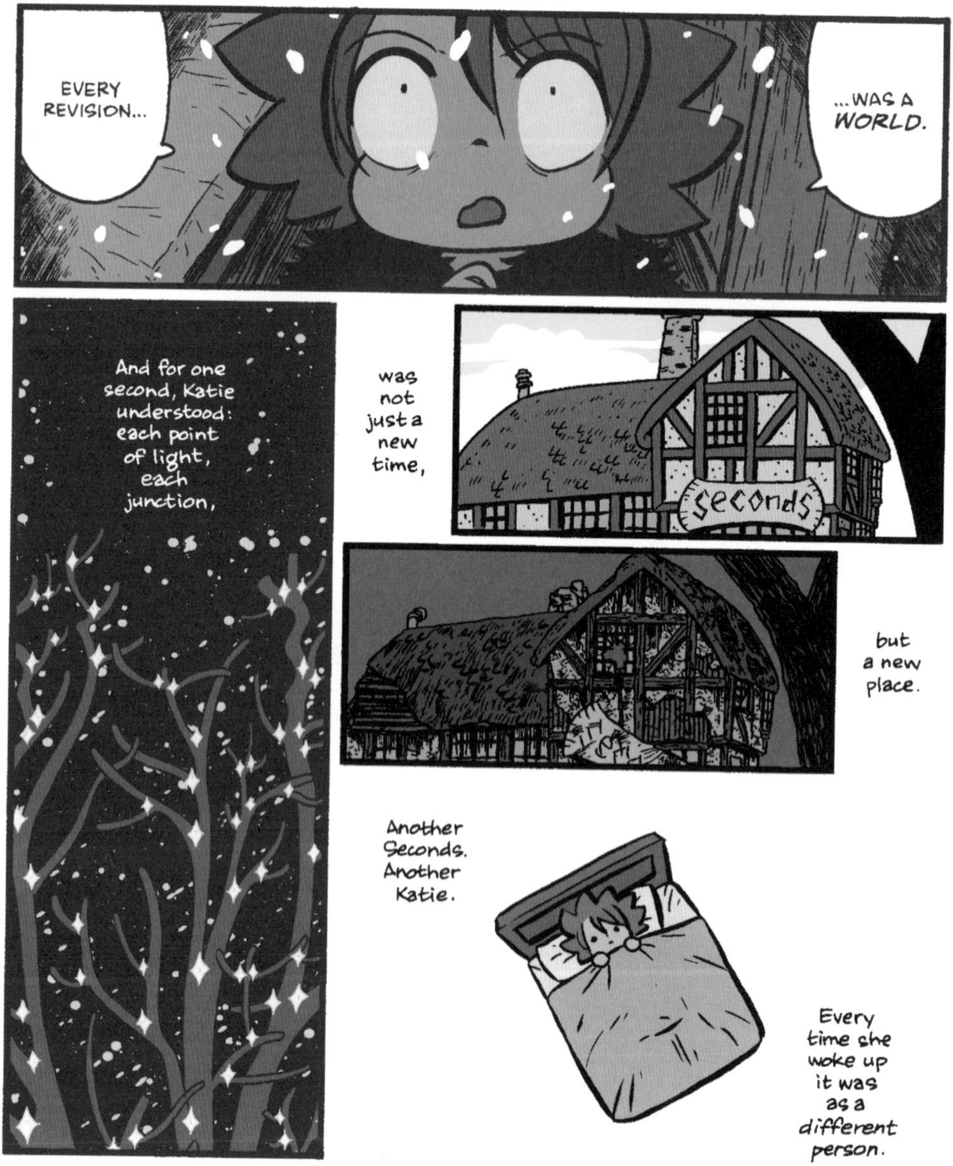
EVERY REVISION...
...WAS A WORLD.
And for one second, Katie understood: each point of light, each junction,
was not just a new time,
SECONDS
but a new place.
Another Seconds. Another Katie.
Every time she woke up it was as a different person.

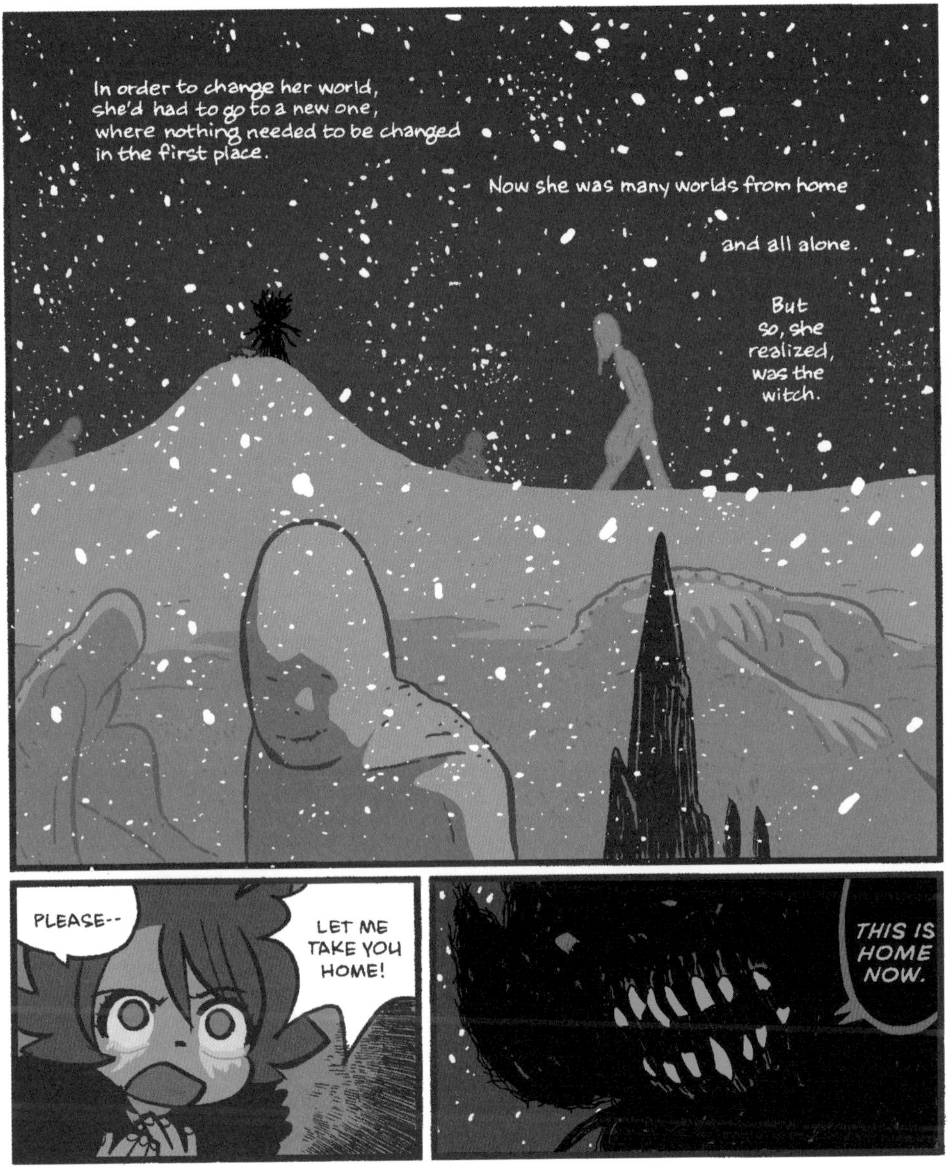
In order to change her world, she'd had to go to a new one, where nothing needed to be changed in the first place.
Now she was many worlds from home
and all alone.
But so, she realized, was the witch.
PLEASE--
LET ME TAKE YOU HOME!
THIS IS HOME NOW.

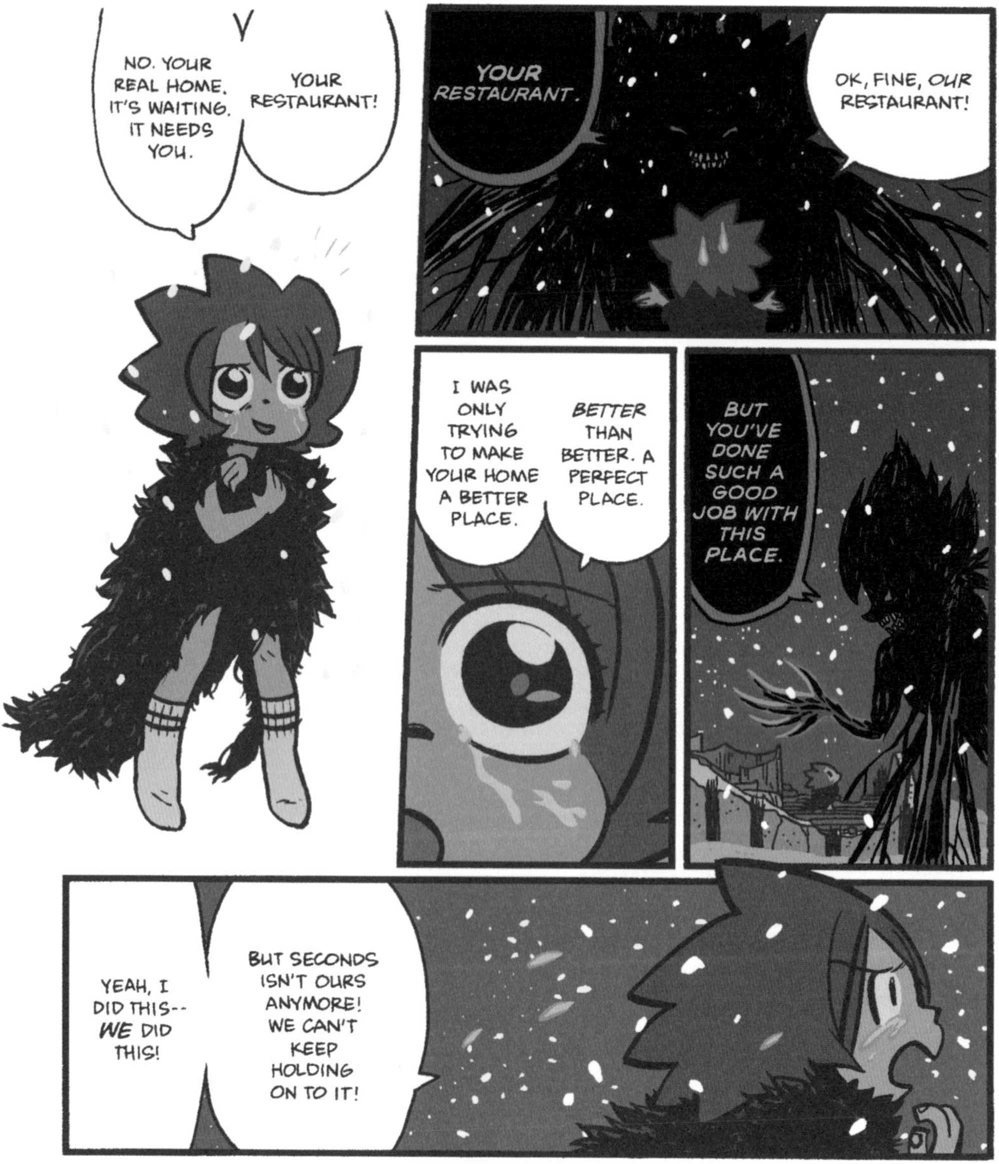
NO. YOUR REAL HOME. IT'S WAITING. IT NEEDS YOU.
YOUR RESTAURANT!
YOUR RESTAURANT.
OK, FINE, OUR RESTAURANT!
I WAS ONLY TRYING TO MAKE YOUR HOME A BETTER PLACE.
BETTER THAN BETTER. A PERFECT PLACE.
BUT YOU'VE DONE SUCH A GOOD JOB WITH THIS PLACE.
YEAH, I DID THIS-- WE DID THIS!
BUT SECONDS ISN'T OURS ANYMORE! WE CAN'T KEEP HOLDING ON TO IT!

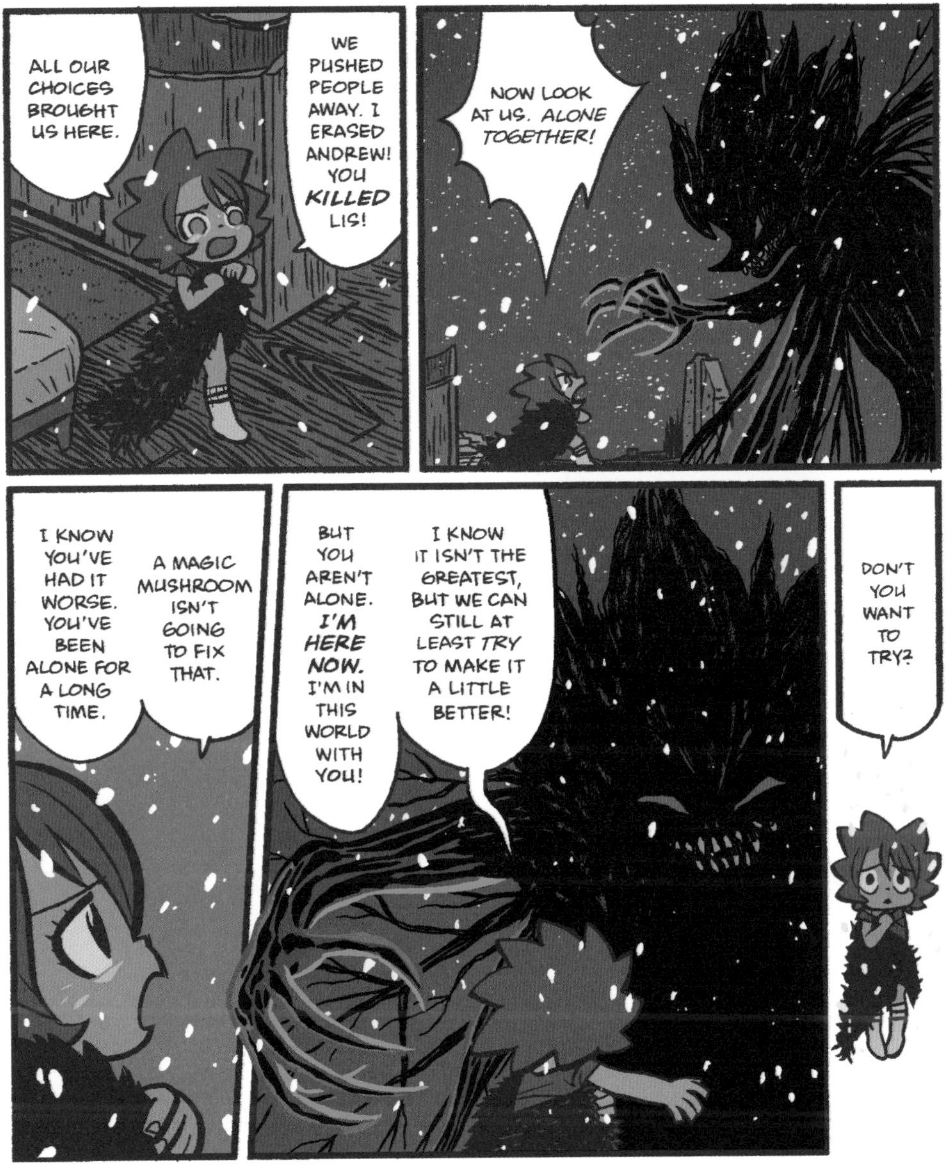
ALL OUR CHOICES BROUGHT US HERE.
WE PUSHED PEOPLE AWAY. I ERASED ANDREW! YOU KILLED LIS!
NOW LOOK AT US. ALONE TOGETHER!
I KNOW YOU'VE HAD IT WORSE. YOU'VE BEEN ALONE FOR A LONG TIME.
A MAGIC MUSHROOM ISN'T GOING TO FIX THAT.
BUT YOU AREN'T ALONE. I'M HERE NOW. I'M IN THIS WORLD WITH YOU!
I KNOW IT ISN'T THE GREATEST, BUT WE CAN STILL AT LEAST TRY TO MAKE IT A LITTLE BETTER!
DON'T YOU WANT TO TRY?

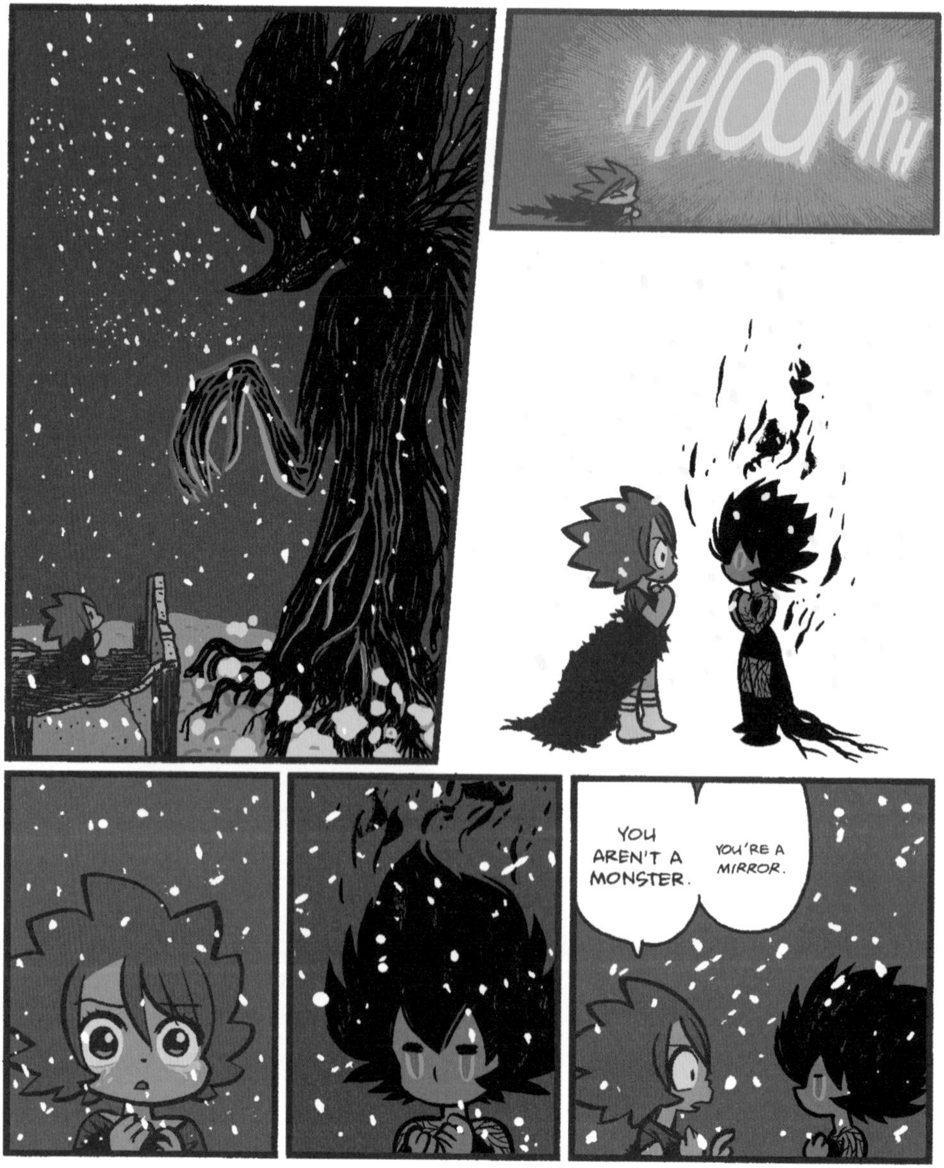
WHOOMPH
YOU AREN'T A MONSTER.
YOU'RE A MIRROR.

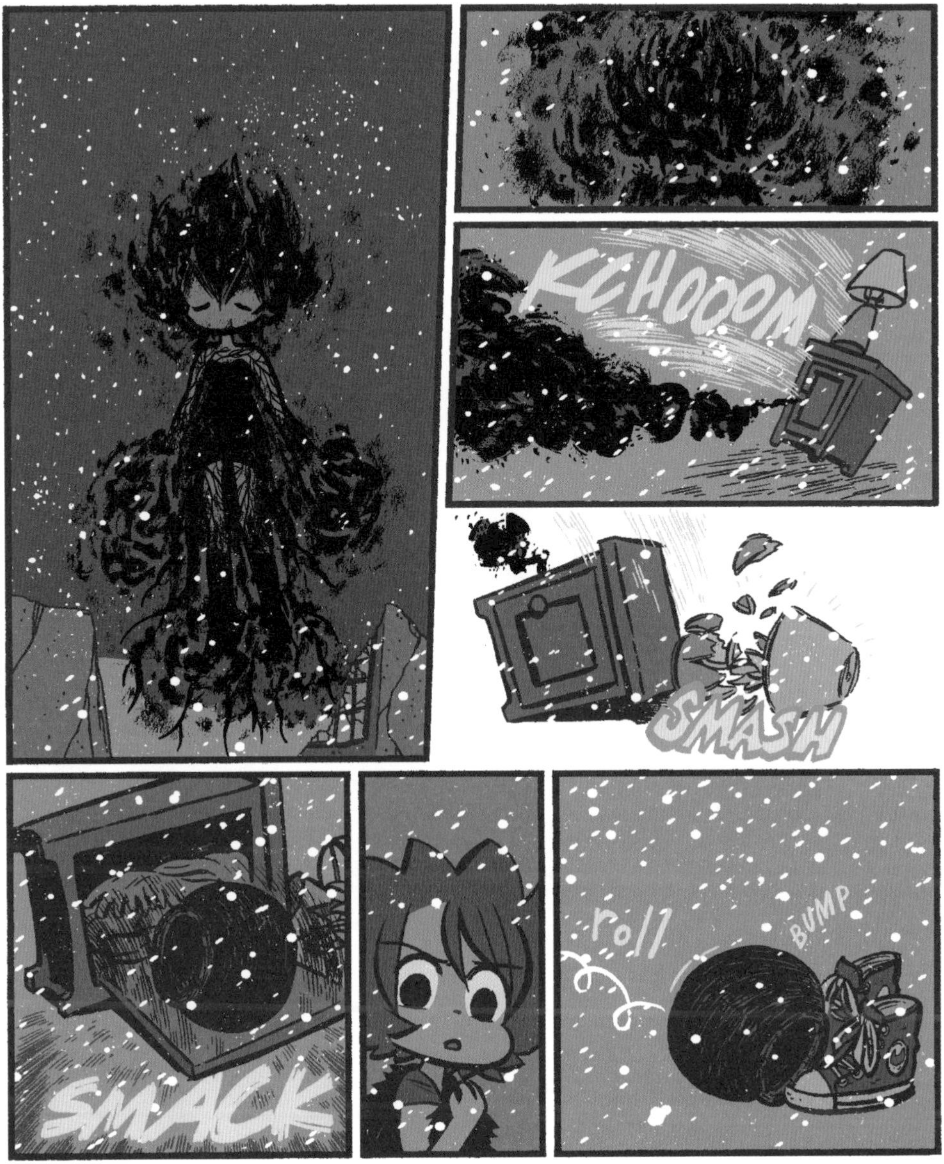
KCHOOOM
SMASH
SMACK
roll
BUMP

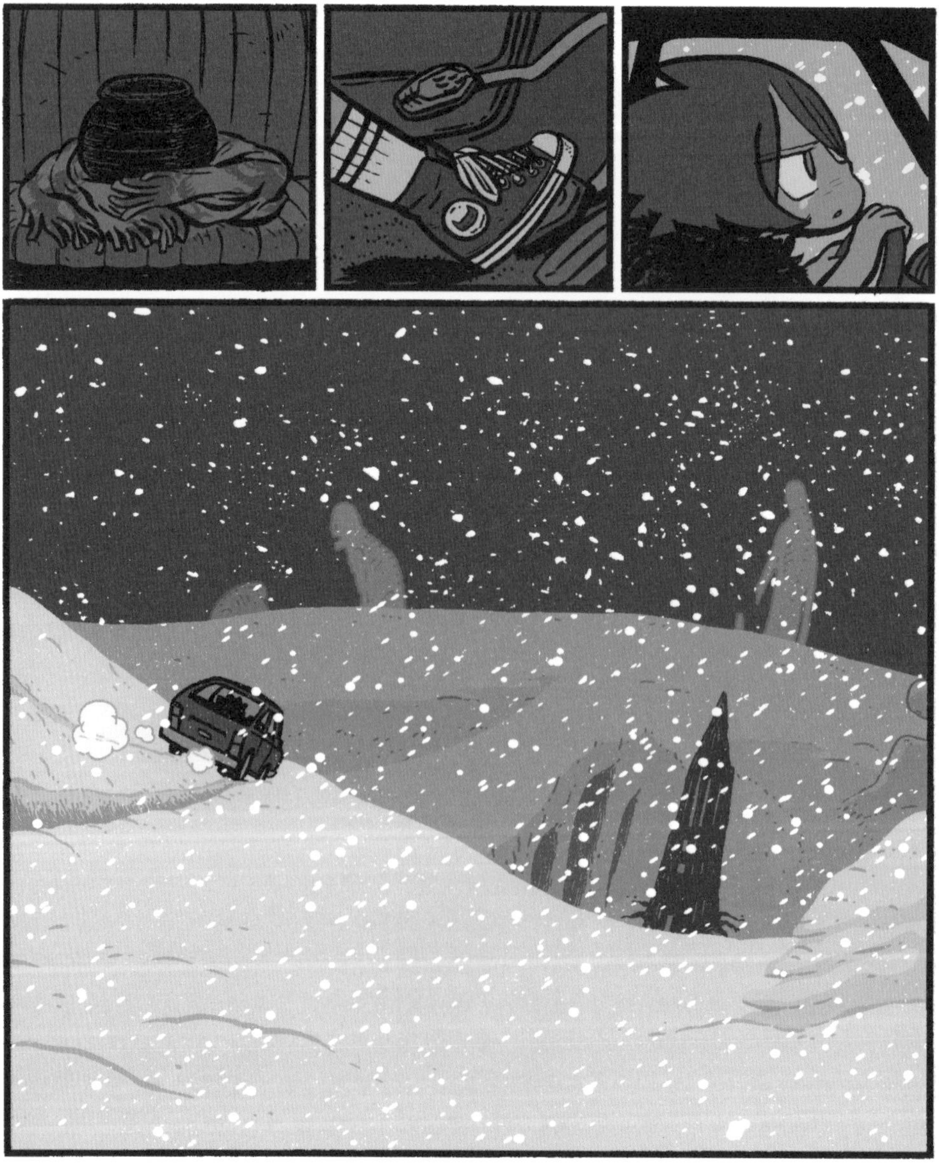

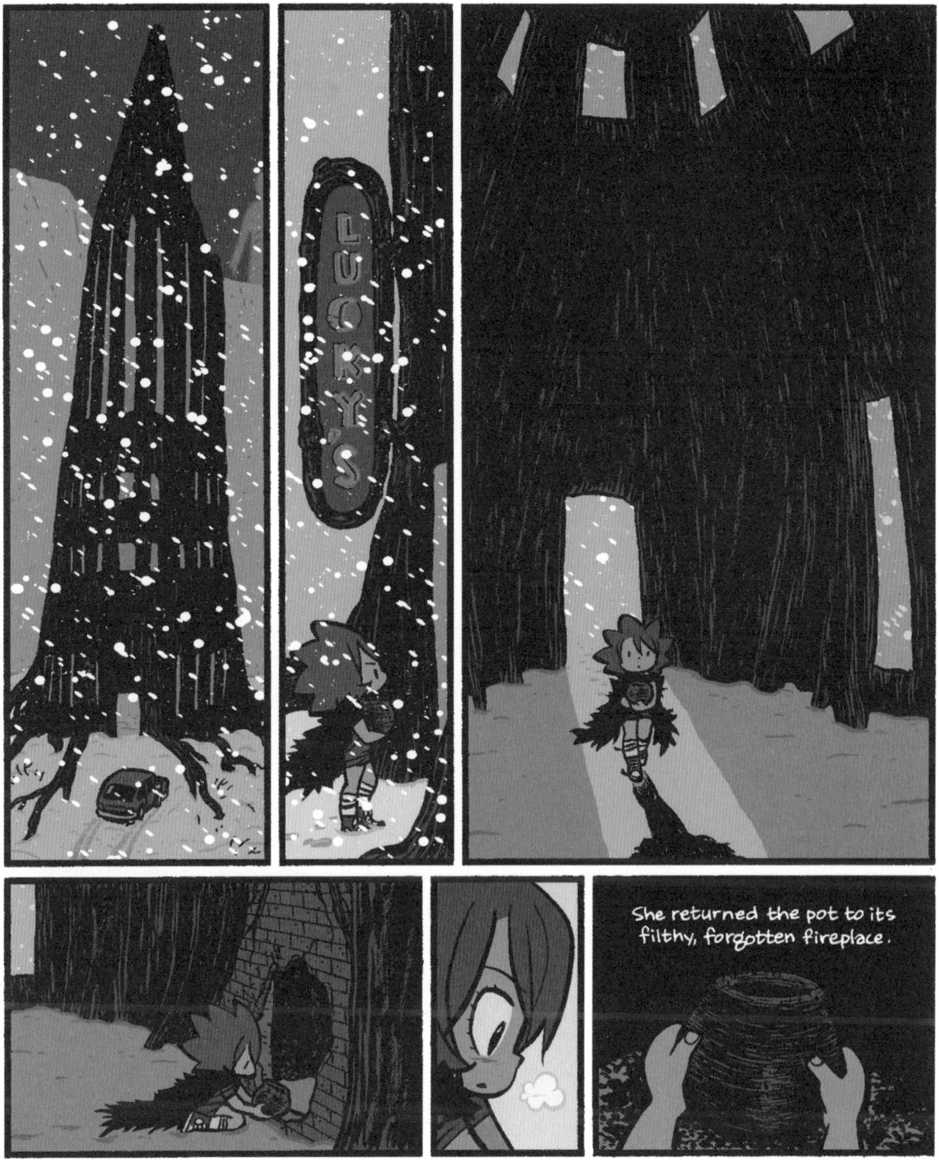
LUCKY'S
She returned the pot to its filthy, forgotten fireplace.

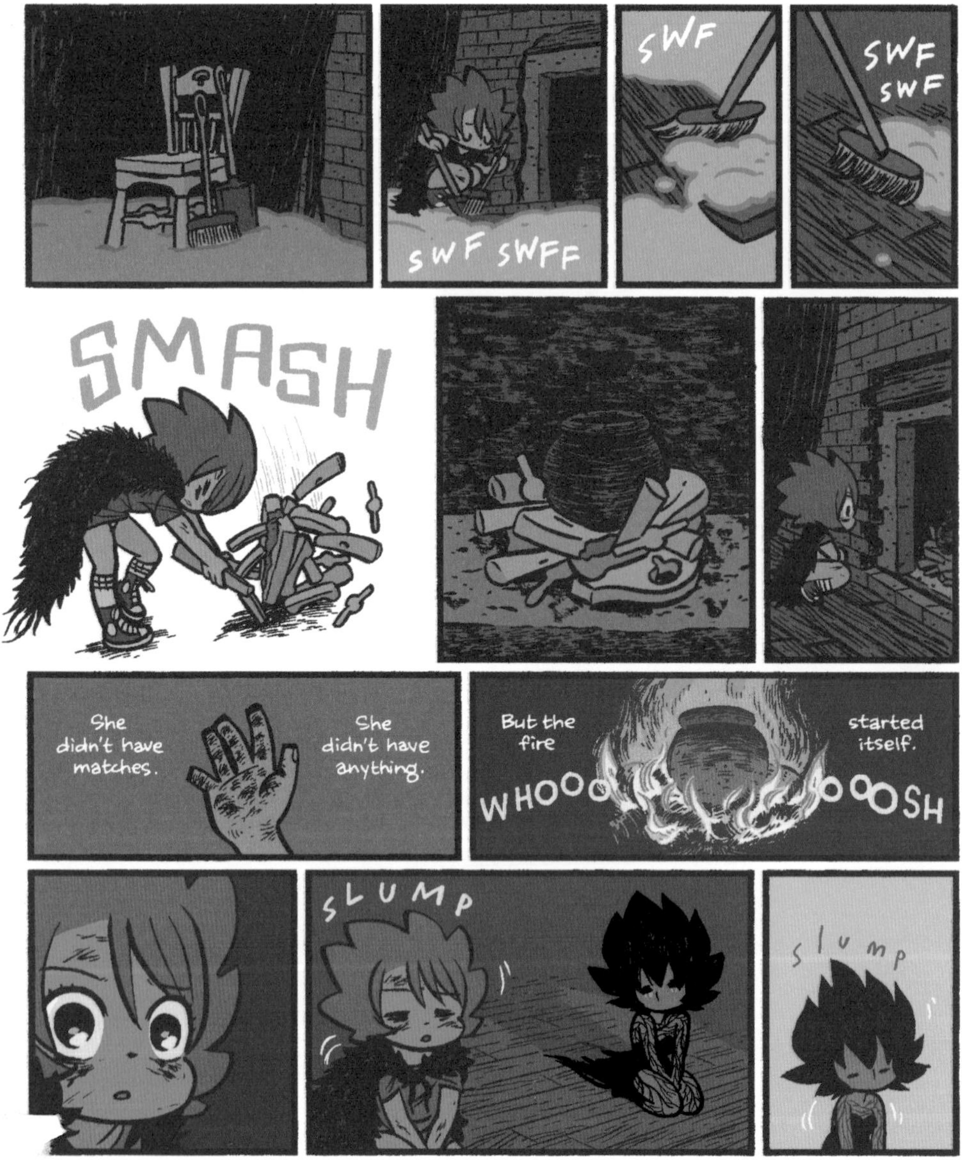
SWF SWFF
SWF
SWF SWF
SMASH
She didn't have matches.
She didn't have anything.
But the fire
started itself.
WHOOOOOOOOSH
SLUMP
slump

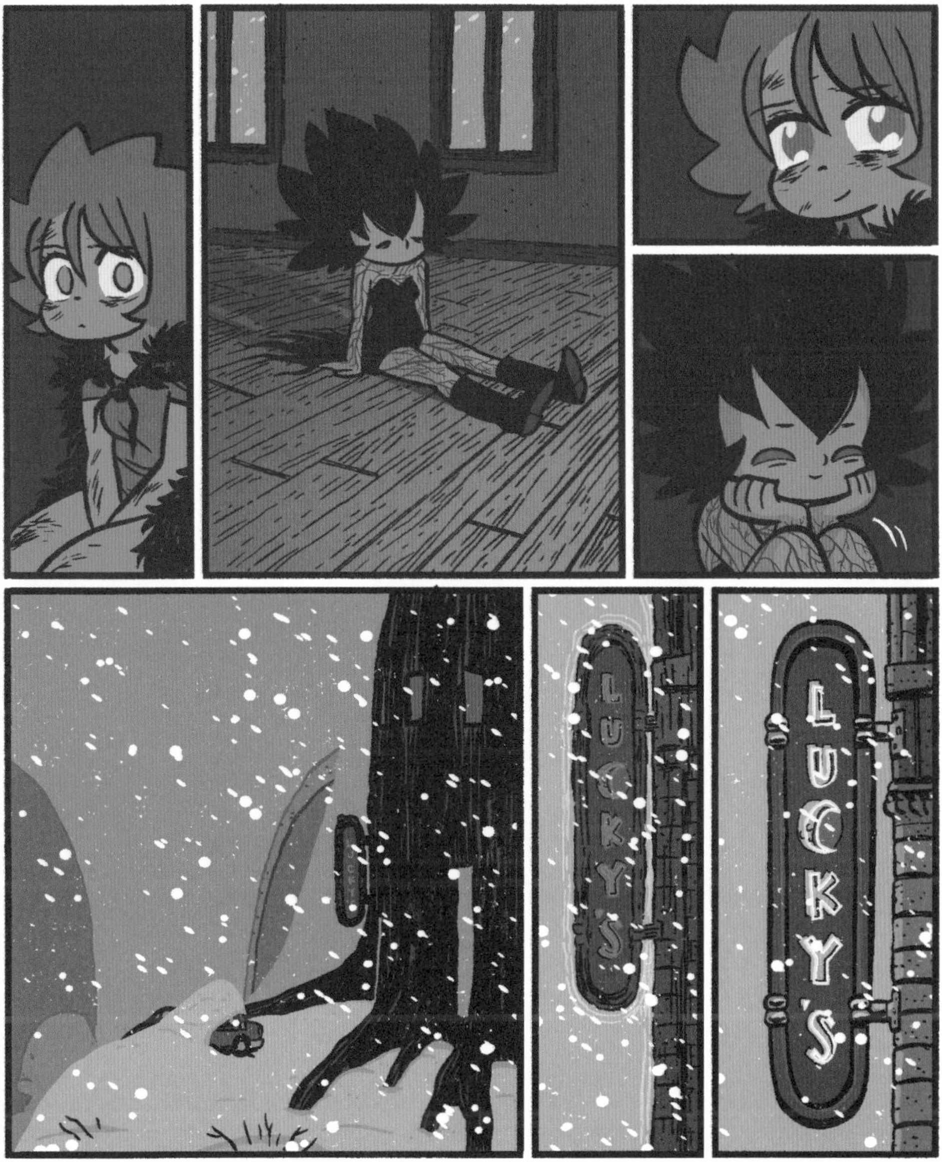
LUCKY'S
LUCKY'S

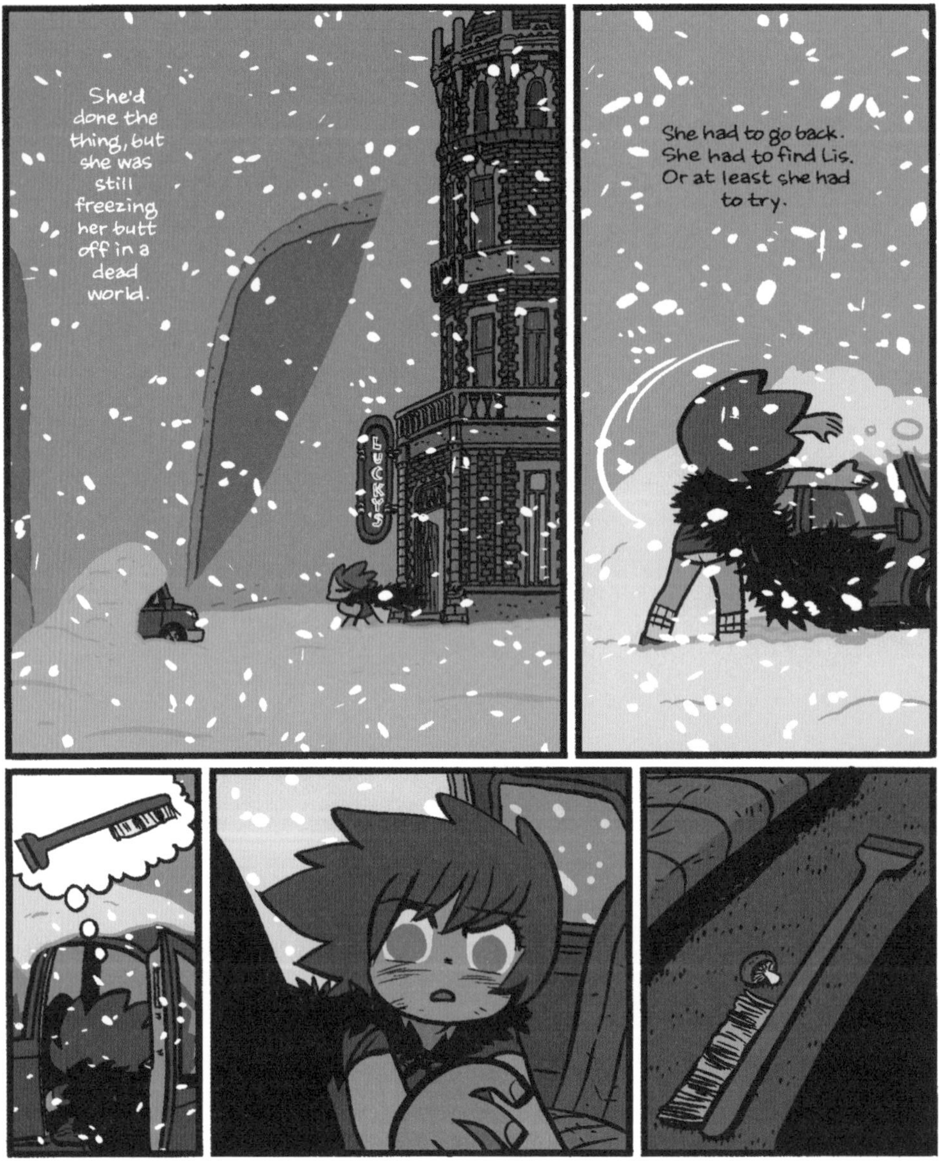
She'd done the thing, but she was still freezing her butt off in a dead world.
LUCKY'S
She had to go back. She had to find Lis. Or at least she had to try.

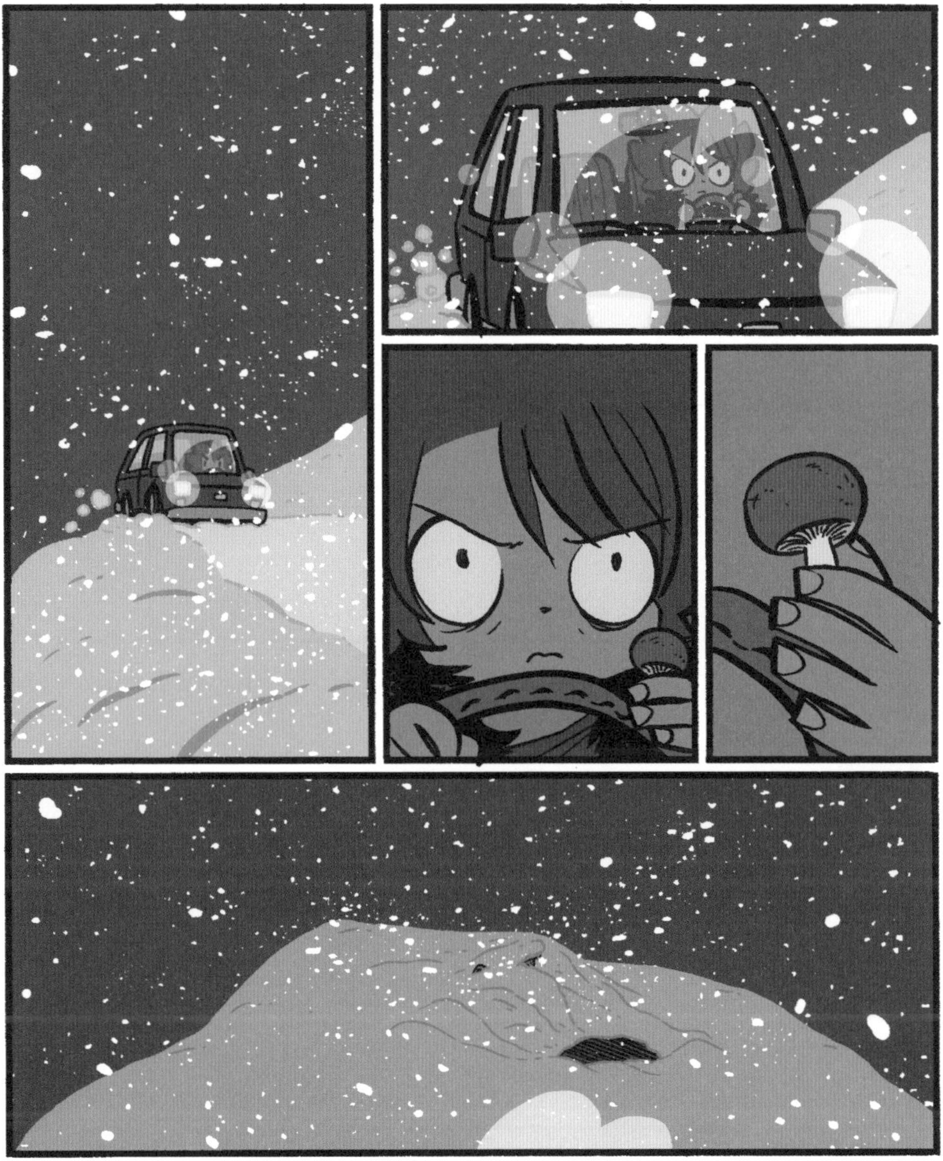

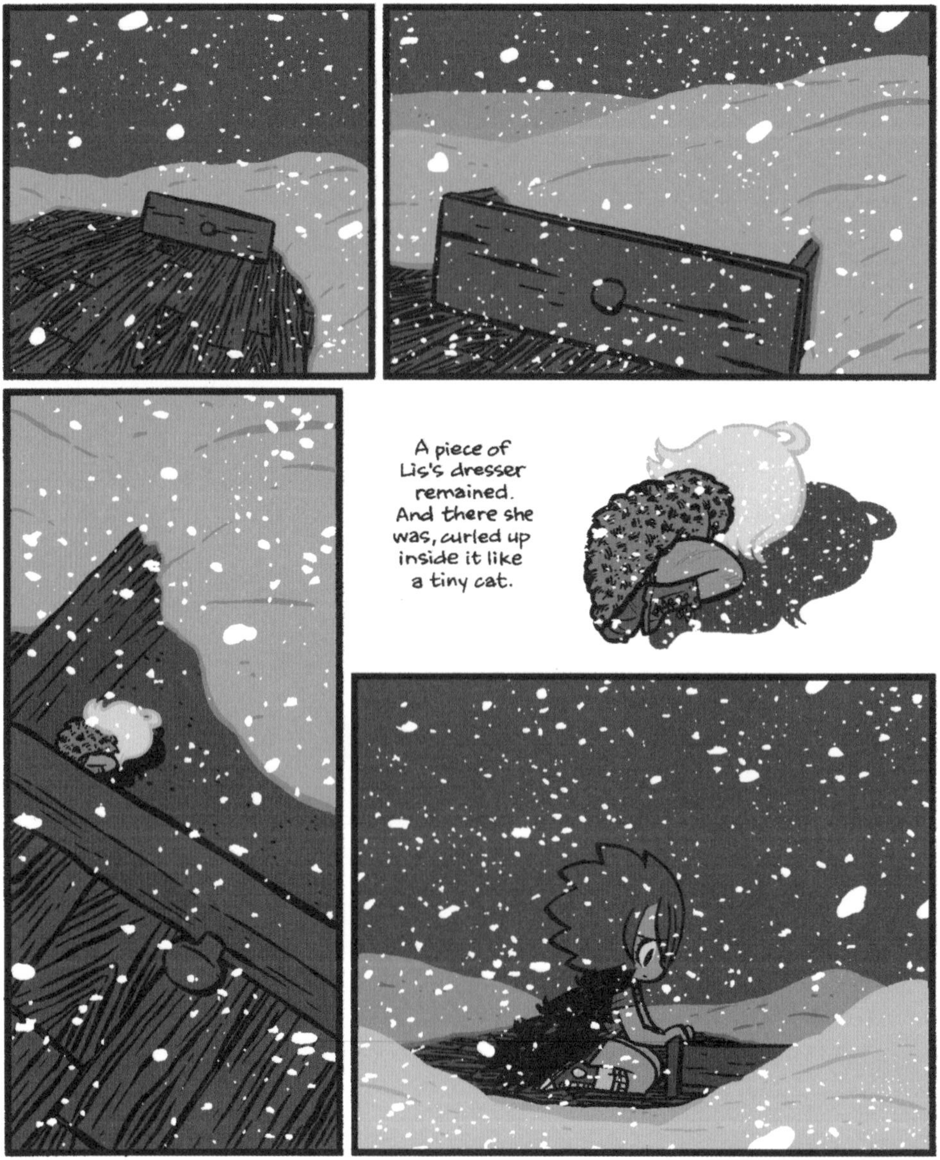
A piece of Lis's dresser remained. And there she was, curled up inside it like a tiny cat.

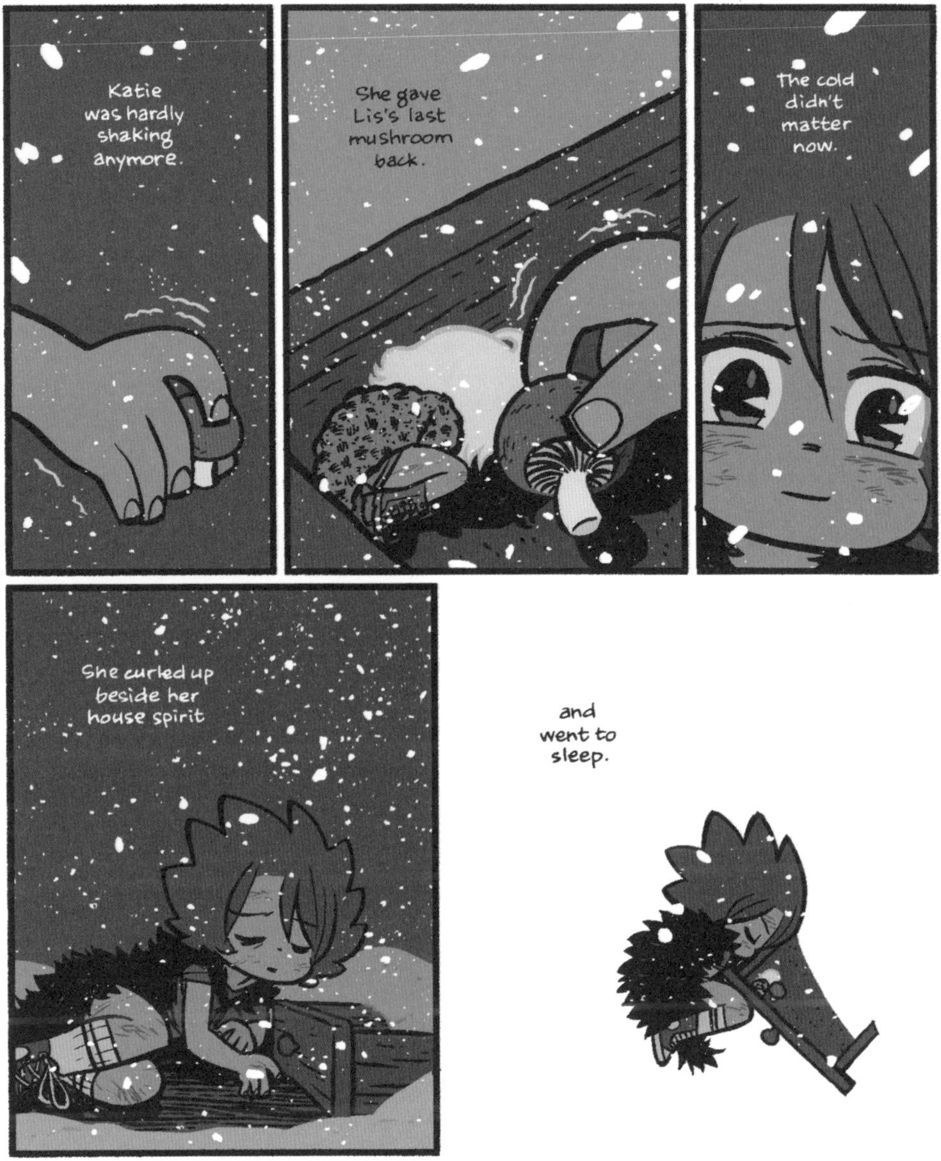
Katie was hardly shaking anymore.
She gave Lis's last mushroom back.
The cold didn't matter now.
She curled up beside her house spirit
and went to sleep.

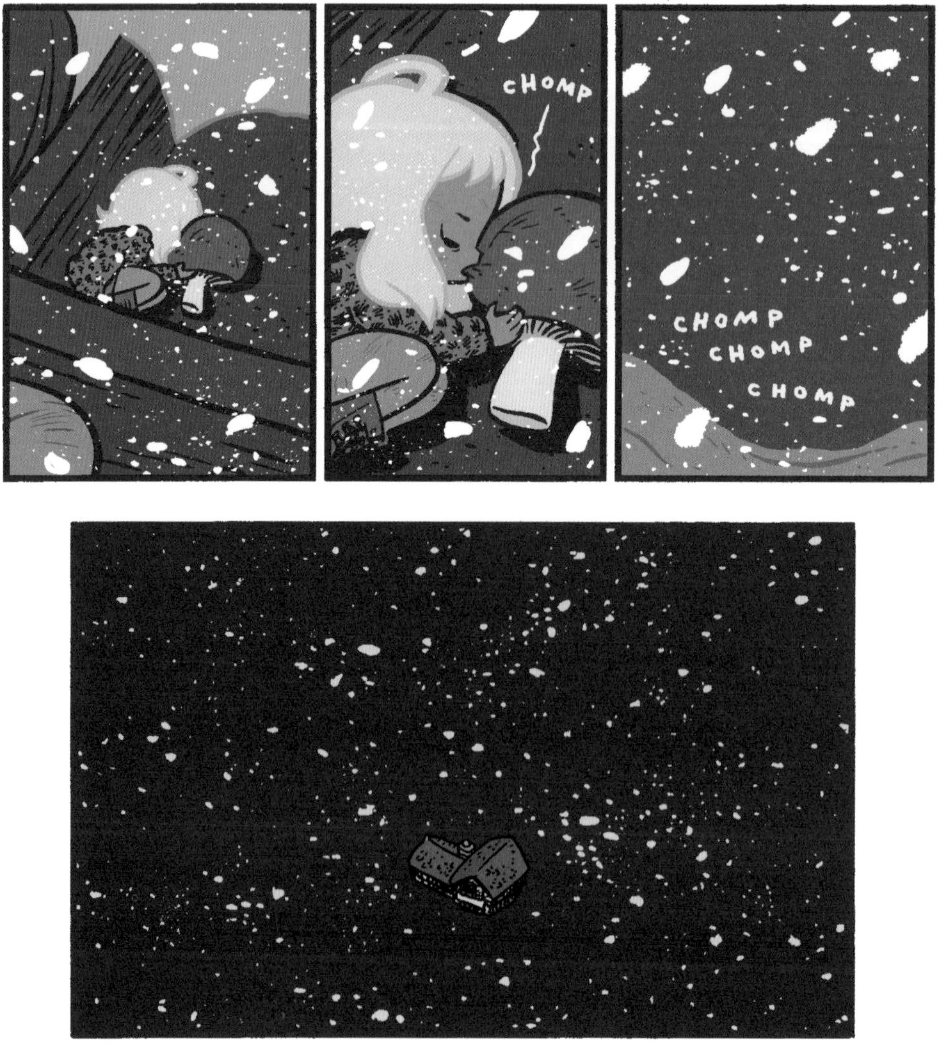
CHOMP
CHOMP
CHOMP
CHOMP

She
woke
up.

W--

WHERE
AM I?

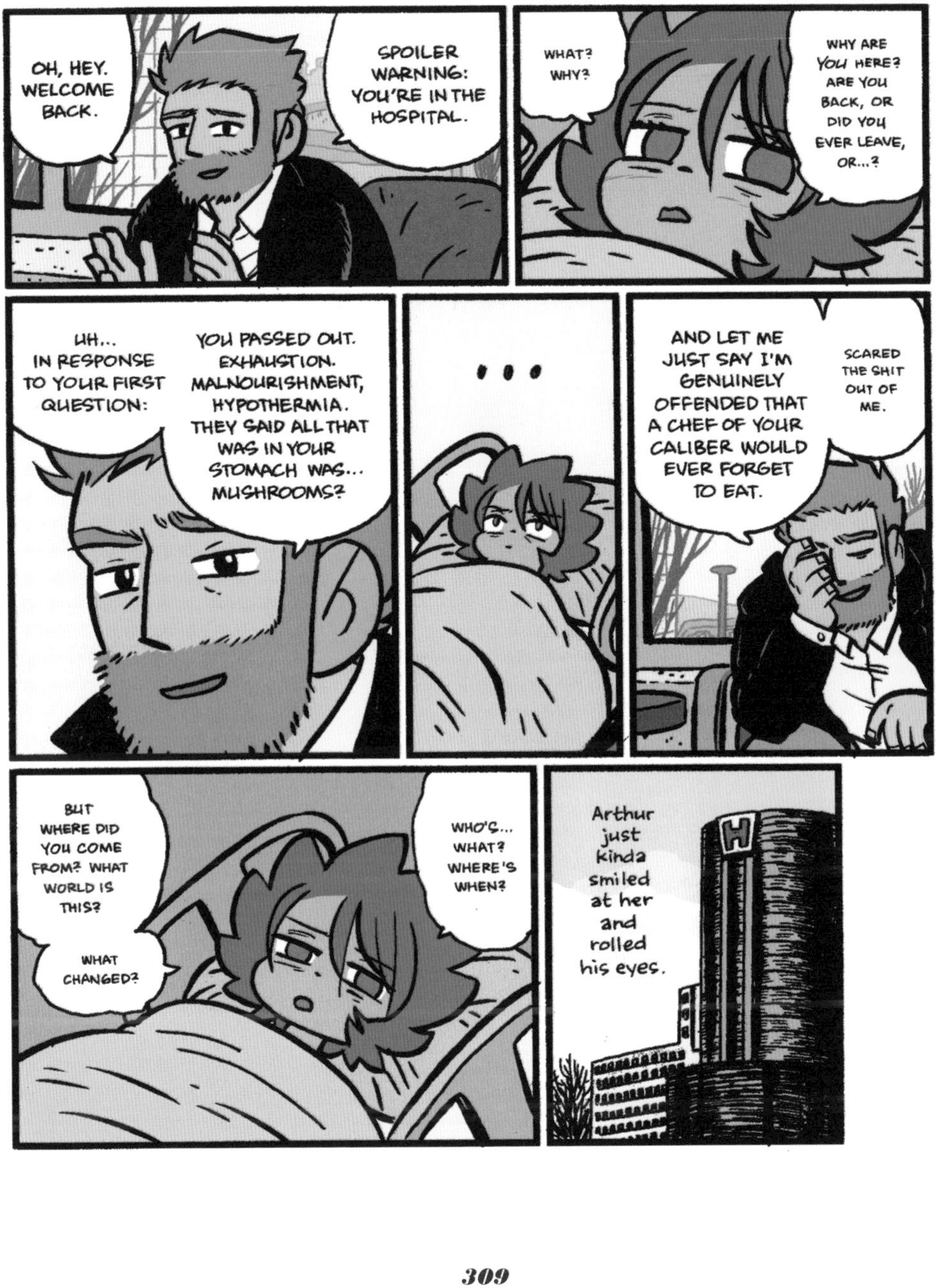
OH, HEY. WELCOME BACK.
SPOILER WARNING: YOU'RE IN THE HOSPITAL.
WHAT? WHY?
WHY ARE YOU HERE? ARE YOU BACK, OR DID YOU EVER LEAVE, OR...?
UH... IN RESPONSE TO YOUR FIRST QUESTION:
YOU PASSED OUT. EXHAUSTION. MALNOURISHMENT, HYPOTHERMIA. THEY SAID ALL THAT WAS IN YOUR STOMACH WAS... MUSHROOMS?
...
AND LET ME JUST SAY I'M GENUINELY OFFENDED THAT A CHEF OF YOUR CALIBER WOULD EVER FORGET TO EAT.
SCARED THE SHIT OUT OF ME.
BUT WHERE DID YOU COME FROM? WHAT WORLD IS THIS?
WHAT CHANGED?
WHO'S... WHAT? WHERE'S WHEN?
Arthur just kinda smiled at her and rolled his eyes.
H

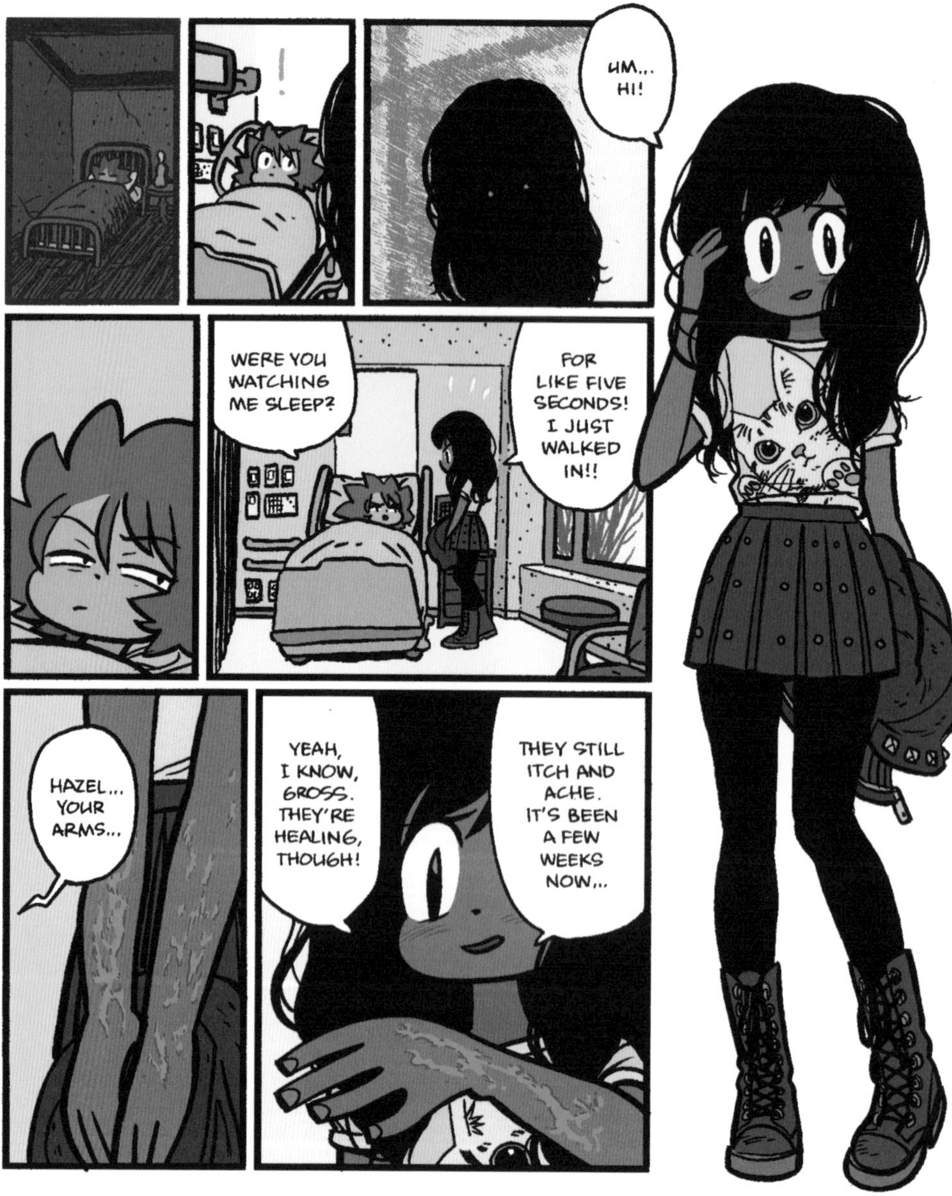
UM...
HI!
!
WERE YOU WATCHING ME SLEEP?
FOR LIKE FIVE SECONDS! I JUST WALKED IN!!
HAZEL... YOUR ARMS...
YEAH, I KNOW, GROSS. THEY'RE HEALING, THOUGH!
THEY STILL ITCH AND ACHE. IT'S BEEN A FEW WEEKS NOW...

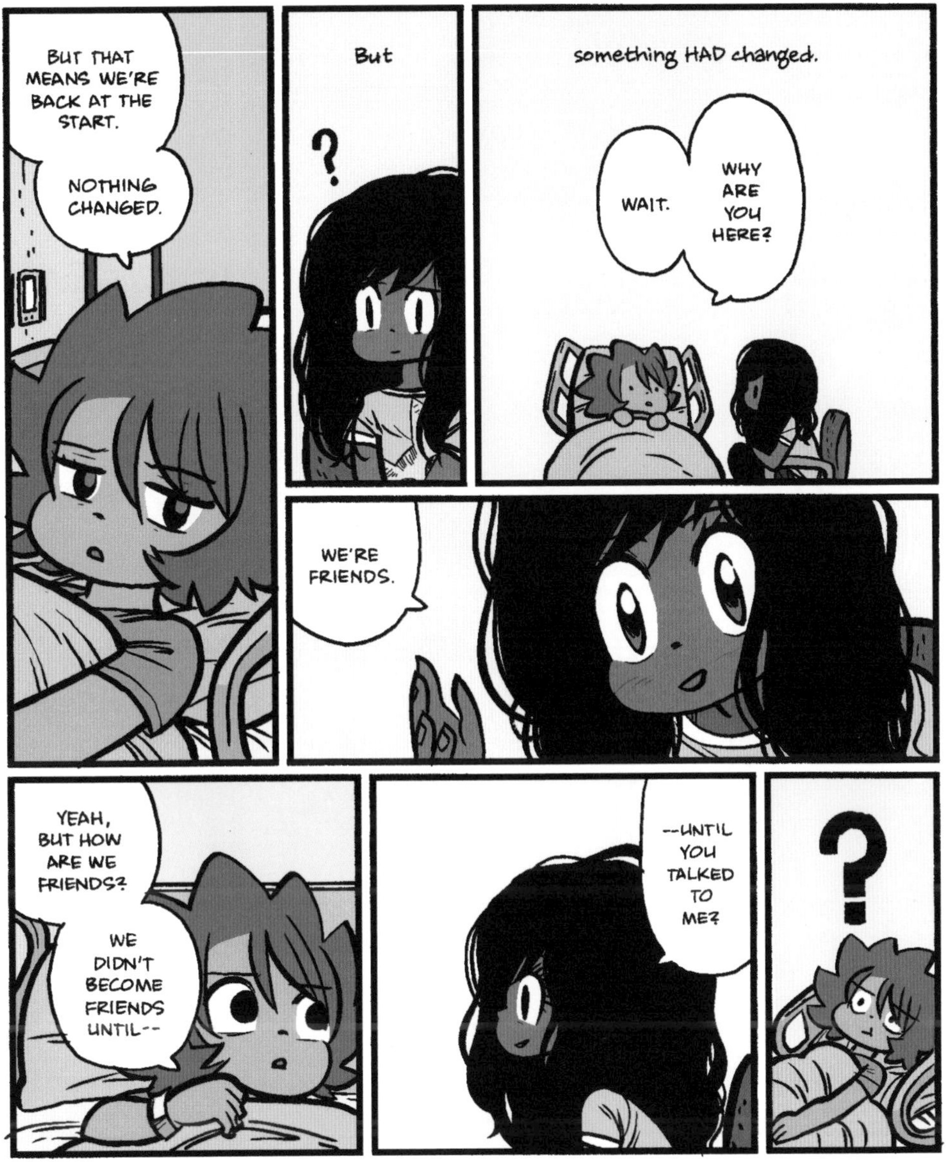

BUT THAT MEANS WE'RE BACK AT THE START.
NOTHING CHANGED.
But
?
something HAD changed.
WAIT.
WHY ARE YOU HERE?
WE'RE FRIENDS.
YEAH, BUT HOW ARE WE FRIENDS?
WE DIDN'T BECOME FRIENDS UNTIL--
--UNTIL YOU TALKED TO ME?
?

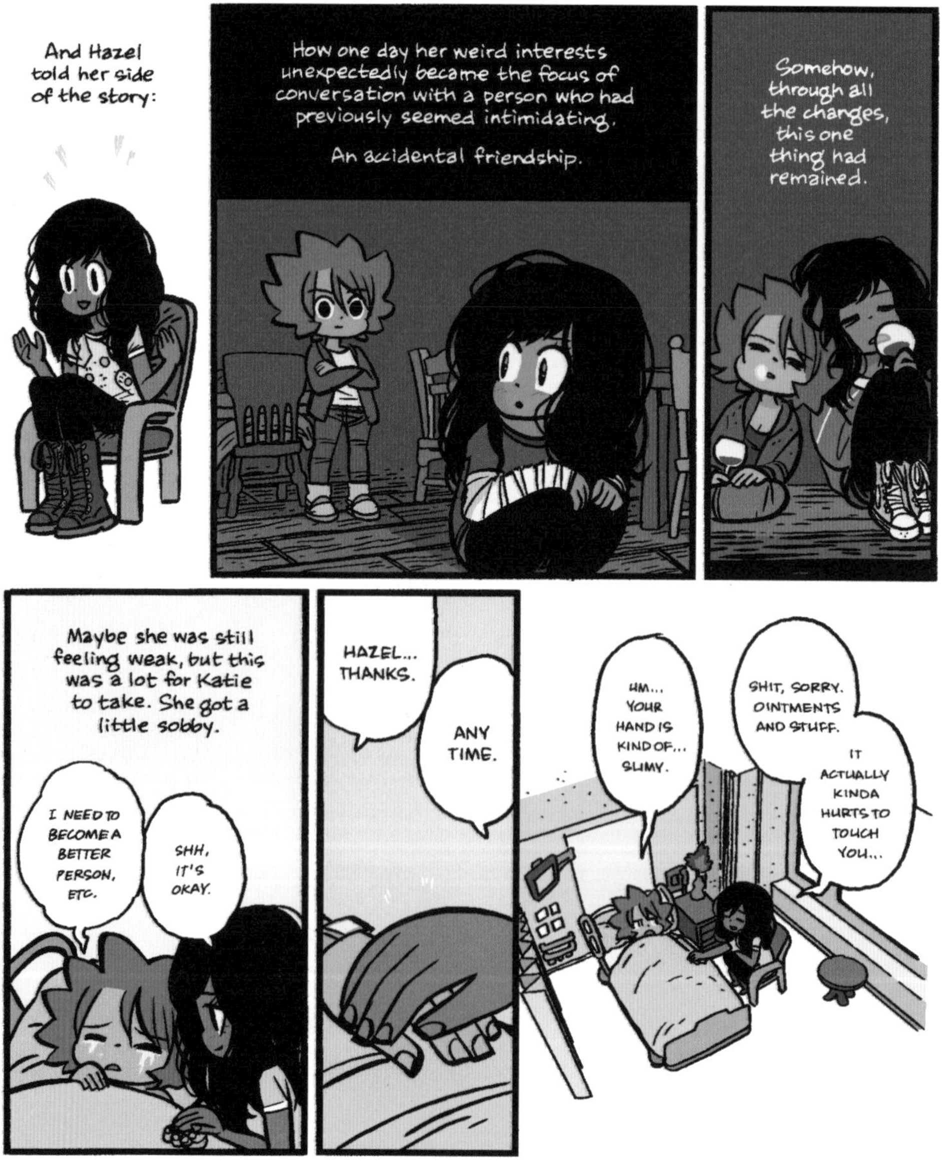
And Hazel told her side of the story:
How one day her weird interests unexpectedly became the focus of conversation with a person who had previously seemed intimidating.
An accidental friendship.
Somehow, through all the changes, this one thing had remained.
Maybe she was still feeling weak, but this was a lot for Katie to take. She got a little sobby.
I NEED TO BECOME A BETTER PERSON, ETC.
SHH, IT'S OKAY.
HAZEL... THANKS.
ANY TIME.
UM... YOUR HAND IS KIND OF... SLIMY.
SHIT, SORRY. OINTMENTS AND STUFF.
IT ACTUALLY KINDA HURTS TO TOUCH YOU...

Where was she now?

How many empty worlds had she left behind?

When Arthur drove her home, she wasn't sure what would be waiting for her.

But it was him.

And Katie's life was perfect for just one moment.

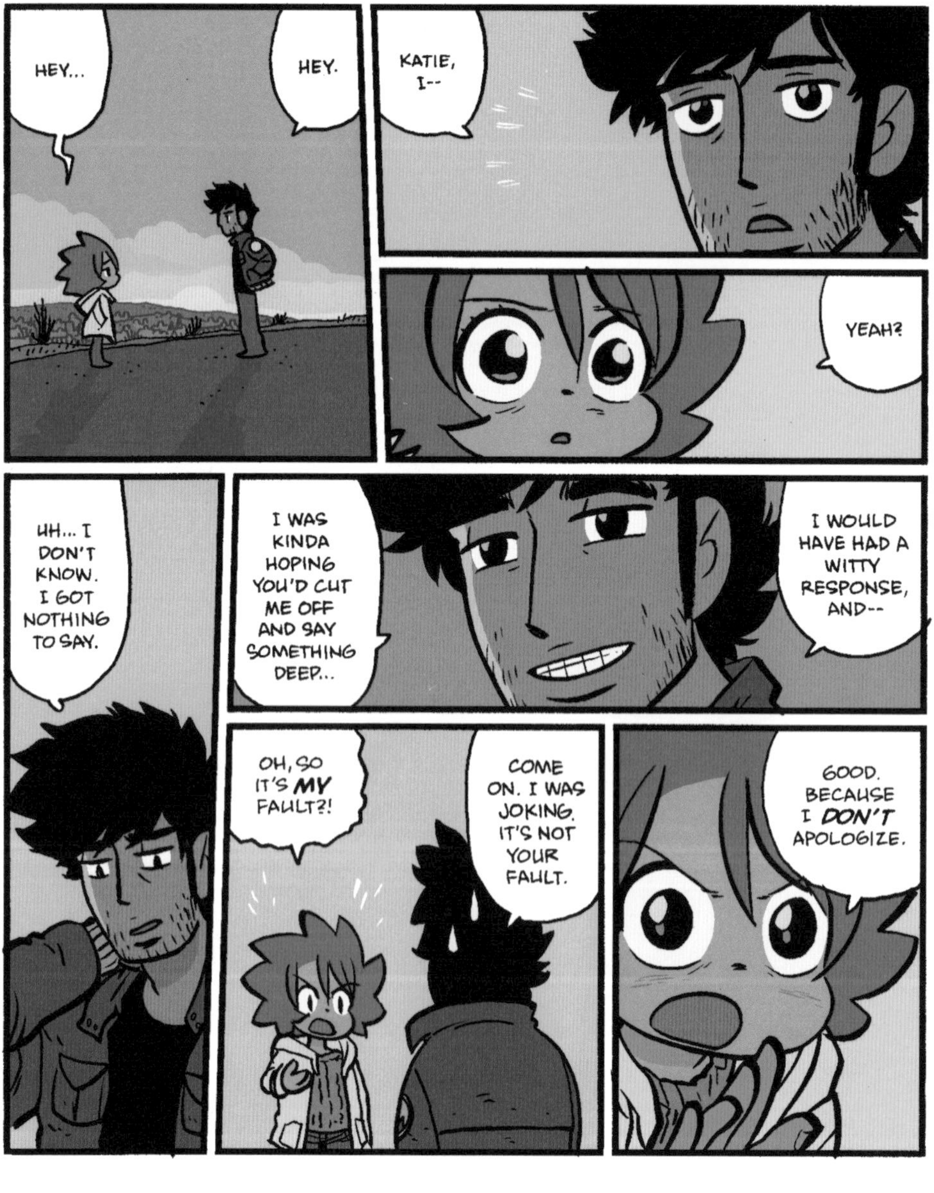
HEY...
HEY.
KATIE, I--
YEAH?
UH... I DON'T KNOW. I GOT NOTHING TO SAY.
I WAS KINDA HOPING YOU'D CUT ME OFF AND SAY SOMETHING DEEP...
I WOULD HAVE HAD A WITTY RESPONSE, AND--
OH, SO IT'S **MY** FAULT?!
COME ON. I WAS JOKING. IT'S NOT YOUR FAULT.
GOOD. BECAUSE I ***DON'T*** APOLOGIZE.

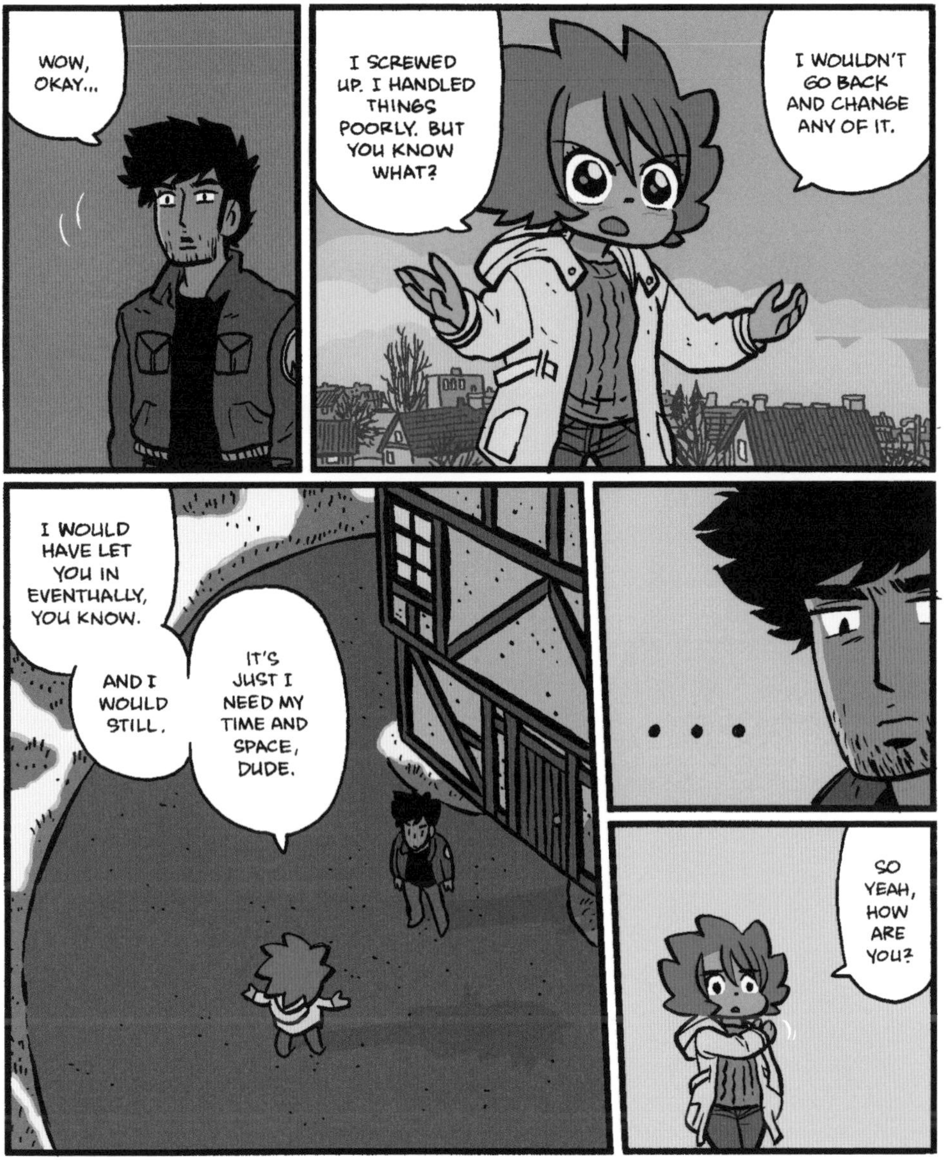
WOW, OKAY...
I SCREWED UP. I HANDLED THINGS POORLY. BUT YOU KNOW WHAT?
I WOULDN'T GO BACK AND CHANGE ANY OF IT.
I WOULD HAVE LET YOU IN EVENTUALLY, YOU KNOW.
AND I WOULD STILL.
IT'S JUST I NEED MY TIME AND SPACE, DUDE.
• • •
SO YEAH, HOW ARE YOU?

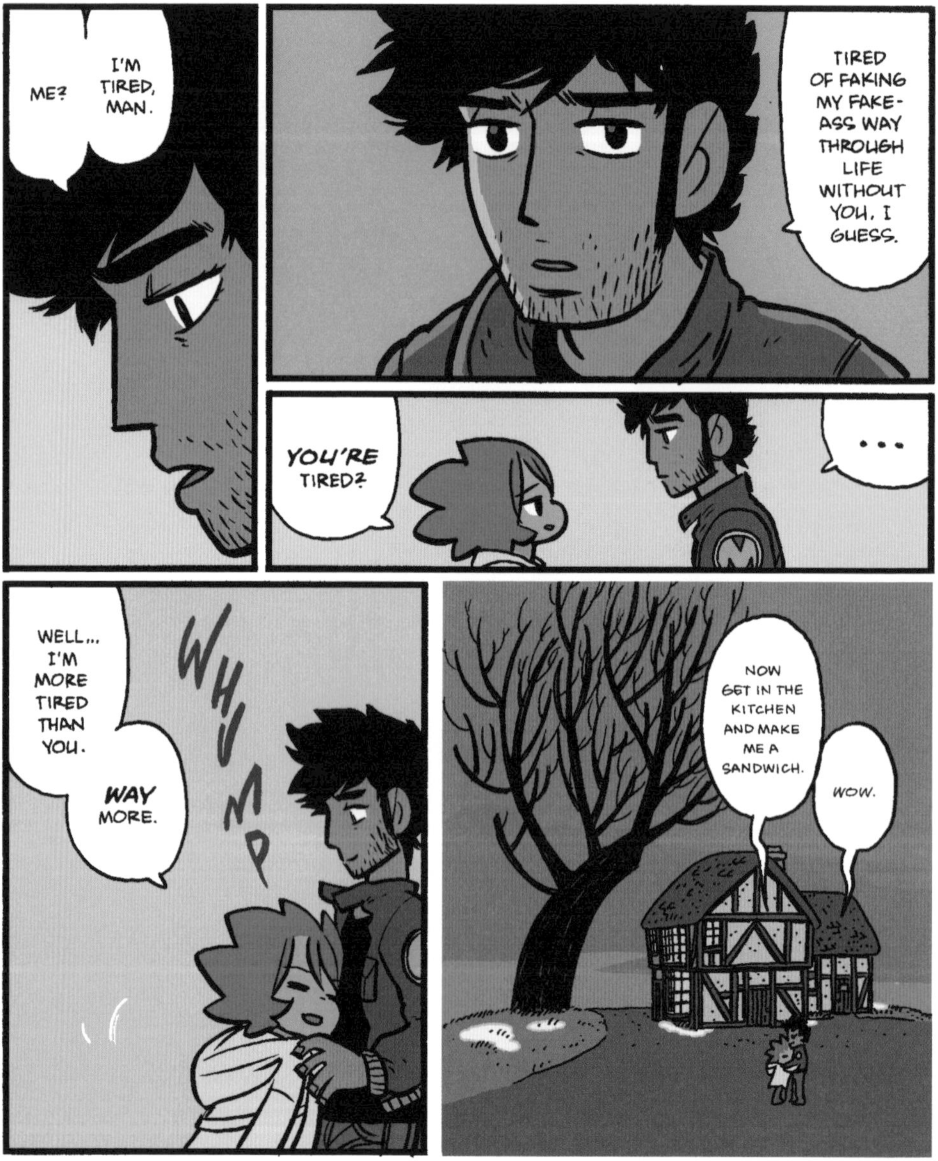
ME?
I'M TIRED, MAN.
TIRED OF FAKING MY FAKE-ASS WAY THROUGH LIFE WITHOUT YOU, I GUESS.
YOU'RE TIRED?
...
WELL... I'M MORE TIRED THAN YOU.
WAY MORE.
WHUMP
NOW GET IN THE KITCHEN AND MAKE ME A SANDWICH.
WOW.

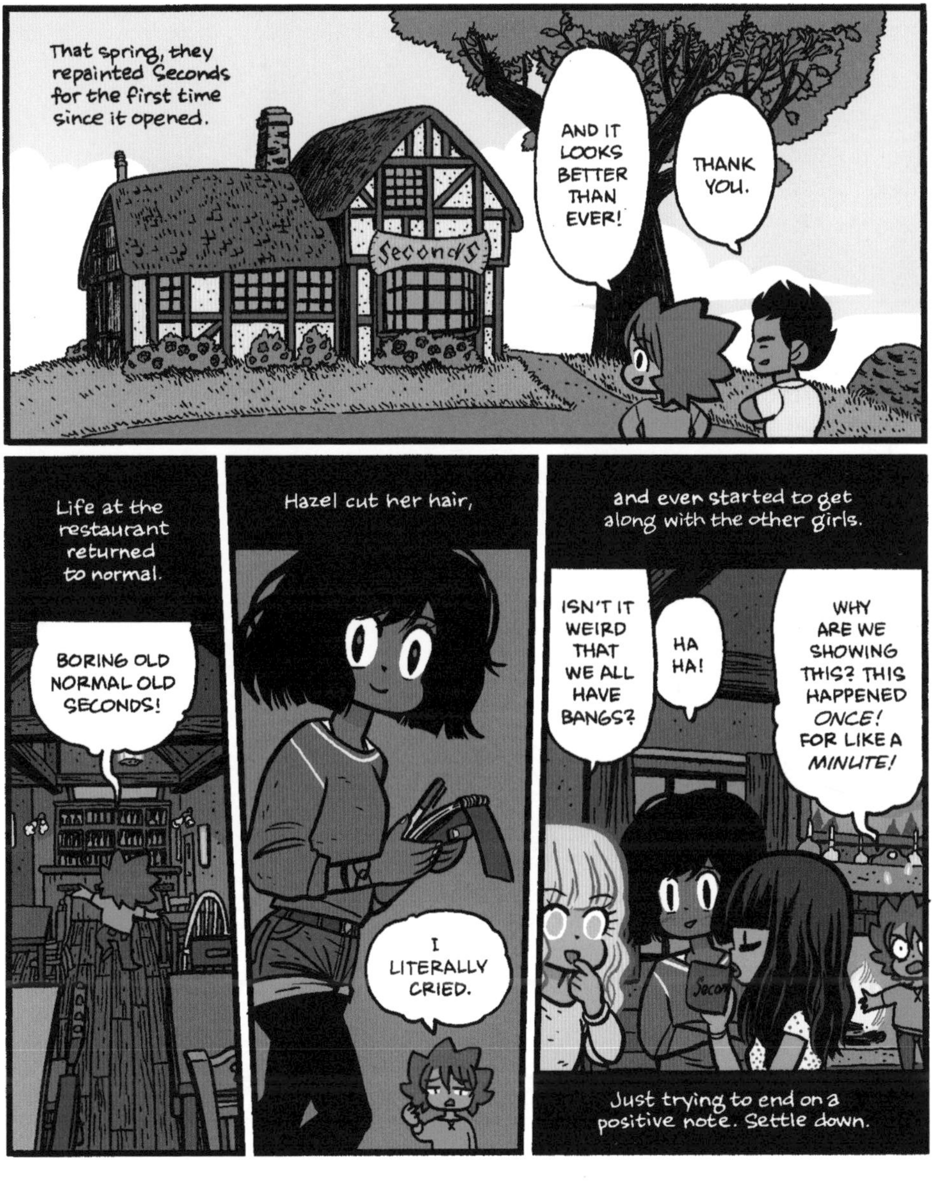
That spring, they repainted Seconds for the first time since it opened.
Seconds
AND IT LOOKS BETTER THAN EVER!
THANK YOU.
Life at the restaurant returned to normal.
BORING OLD NORMAL OLD SECONDS!
Hazel cut her hair,
I LITERALLY CRIED.
and even started to get along with the other girls.
ISN'T IT WEIRD THAT WE ALL HAVE BANGS?
HA HA!
WHY ARE WE SHOWING THIS? THIS HAPPENED ONCE! FOR LIKE A MINUTE!
Just trying to end on a positive note. Settle down.

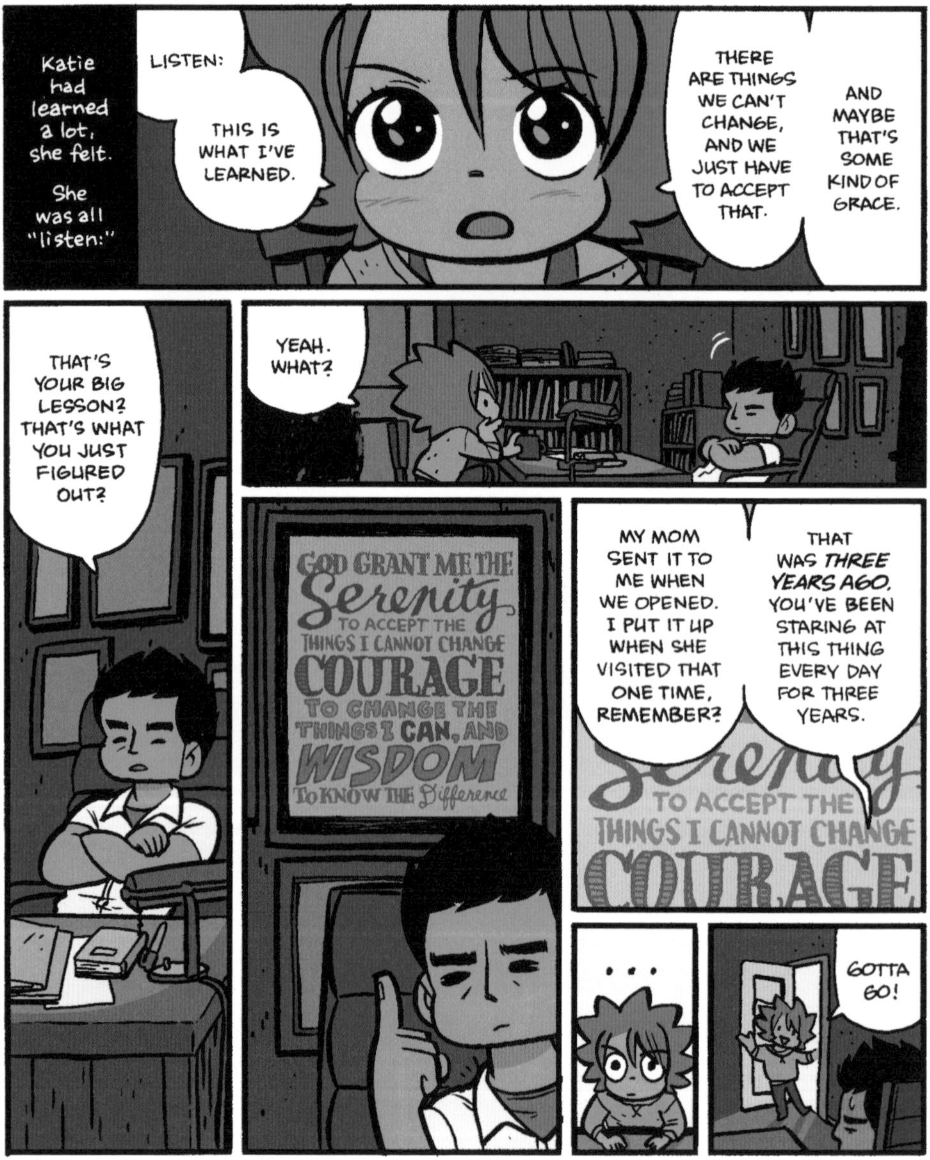
Katie had learned a lot, she felt.
She was all "listen:"
LISTEN:
THIS IS WHAT I'VE LEARNED.
THERE ARE THINGS WE CAN'T CHANGE, AND WE JUST HAVE TO ACCEPT THAT.
AND MAYBE THAT'S SOME KIND OF GRACE.
THAT'S YOUR BIG LESSON? THAT'S WHAT YOU JUST FIGURED OUT?
YEAH. WHAT?
GOD GRANT ME THE Serenity TO ACCEPT THE THINGS I CANNOT CHANGE COURAGE TO CHANGE THE THINGS I CAN, AND WISDOM TO KNOW THE Difference
MY MOM SENT IT TO ME WHEN WE OPENED. I PUT IT UP WHEN SHE VISITED THAT ONE TIME, REMEMBER?
THAT WAS *THREE YEARS AGO.* YOU'VE BEEN STARING AT THIS THING EVERY DAY FOR THREE YEARS.
TO ACCEPT THE THINGS I CANNOT CHANGE COURAGE
...
GOTTA GO!

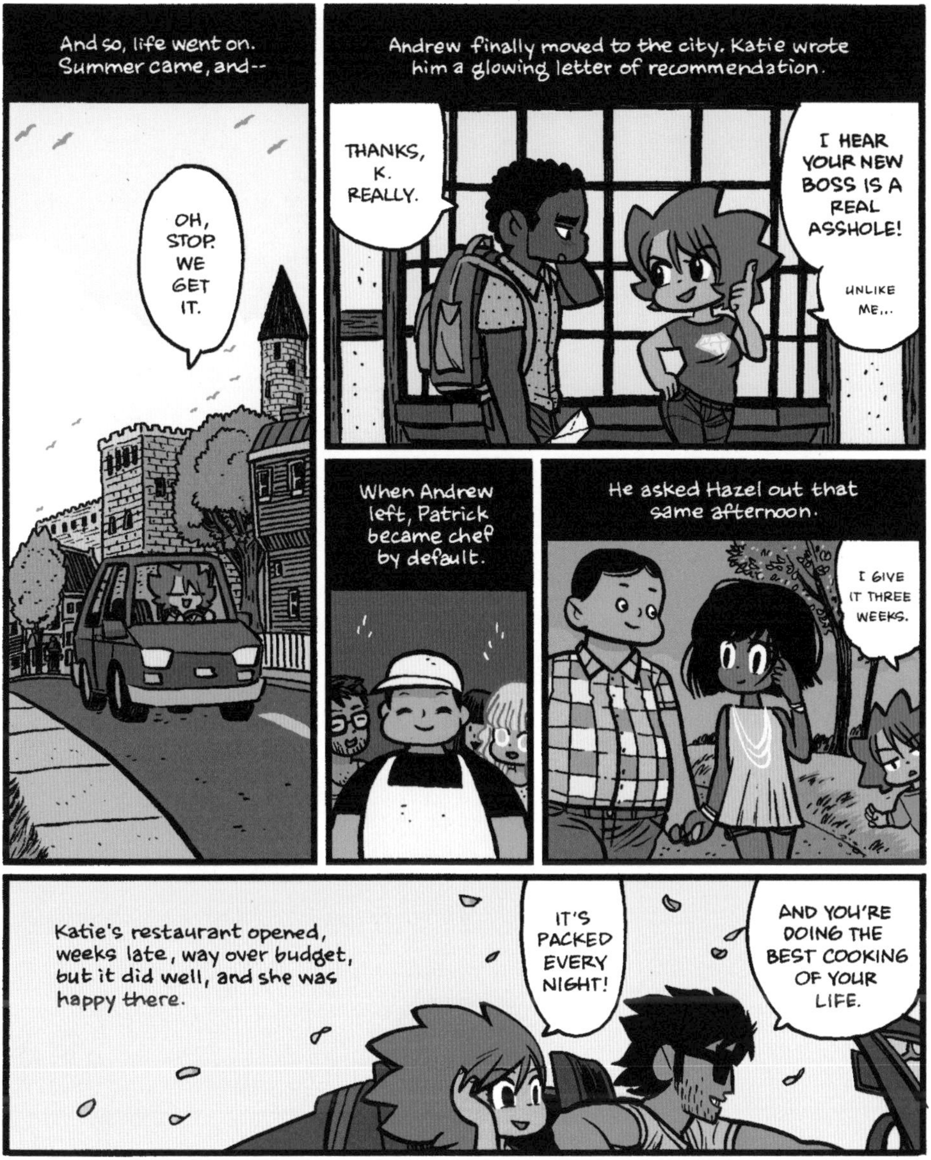
And so, life went on. Summer came, and--
OH, STOP. WE GET IT.
Andrew finally moved to the city. Katie wrote him a glowing letter of recommendation.
THANKS, K. REALLY.
I HEAR YOUR NEW BOSS IS A REAL ASSHOLE!
UNLIKE ME...
When Andrew left, Patrick became chef by default.
He asked Hazel out that same afternoon.
I GIVE IT THREE WEEKS.
Katie's restaurant opened, weeks late, way over budget, but it did well, and she was happy there.
IT'S PACKED EVERY NIGHT!
AND YOU'RE DOING THE BEST COOKING OF YOUR LIFE.

It was often said that Lucky's had a real energy to it, that there was something special about it.

And Katie? She was the same old Katie.

I'M STILL PRETTY YOUNG, BUT THANKS.

Still cooking. Still making people happy.

UH, YEAH: *MY FOOD.* DUH.

OR AT LEAST TRYING, EVERY DAY!

... still talking to herself.

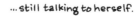

320

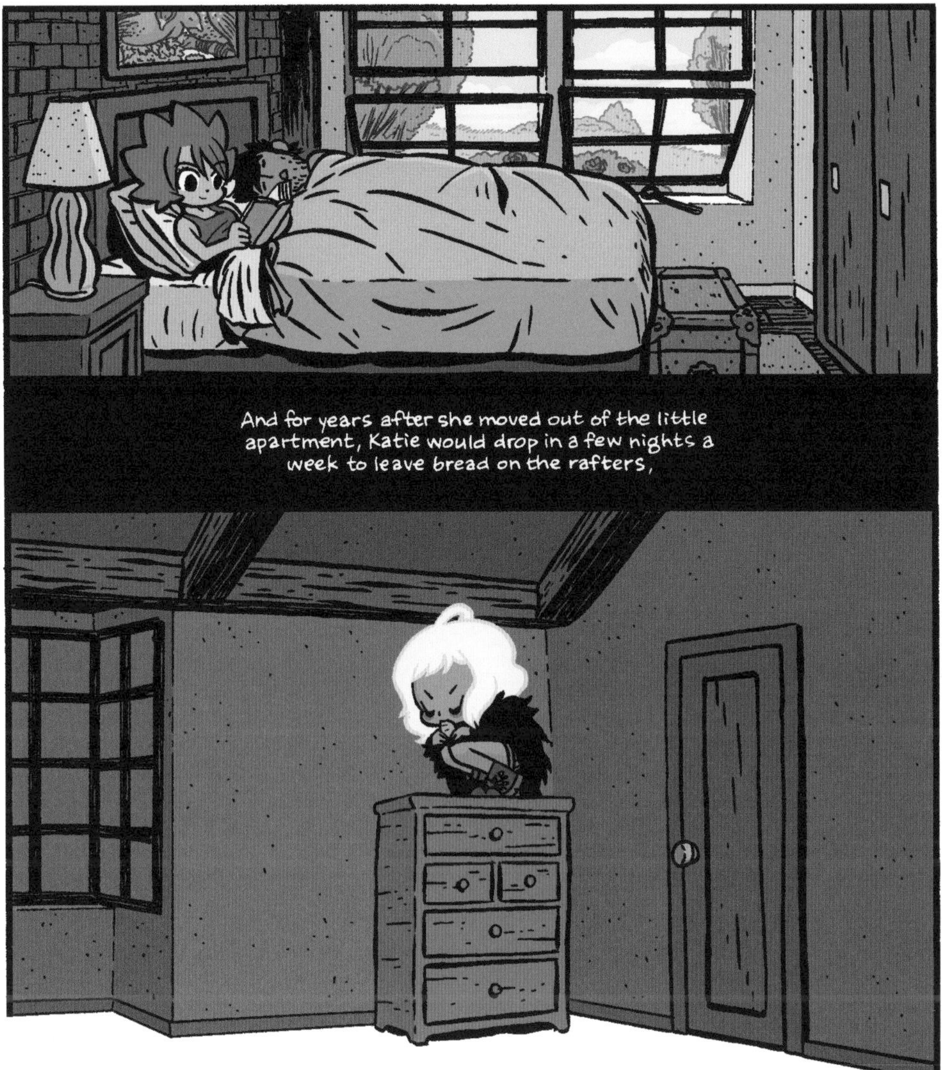
And for years after she moved out of the little apartment, Katie would drop in a few nights a week to leave bread on the rafters,

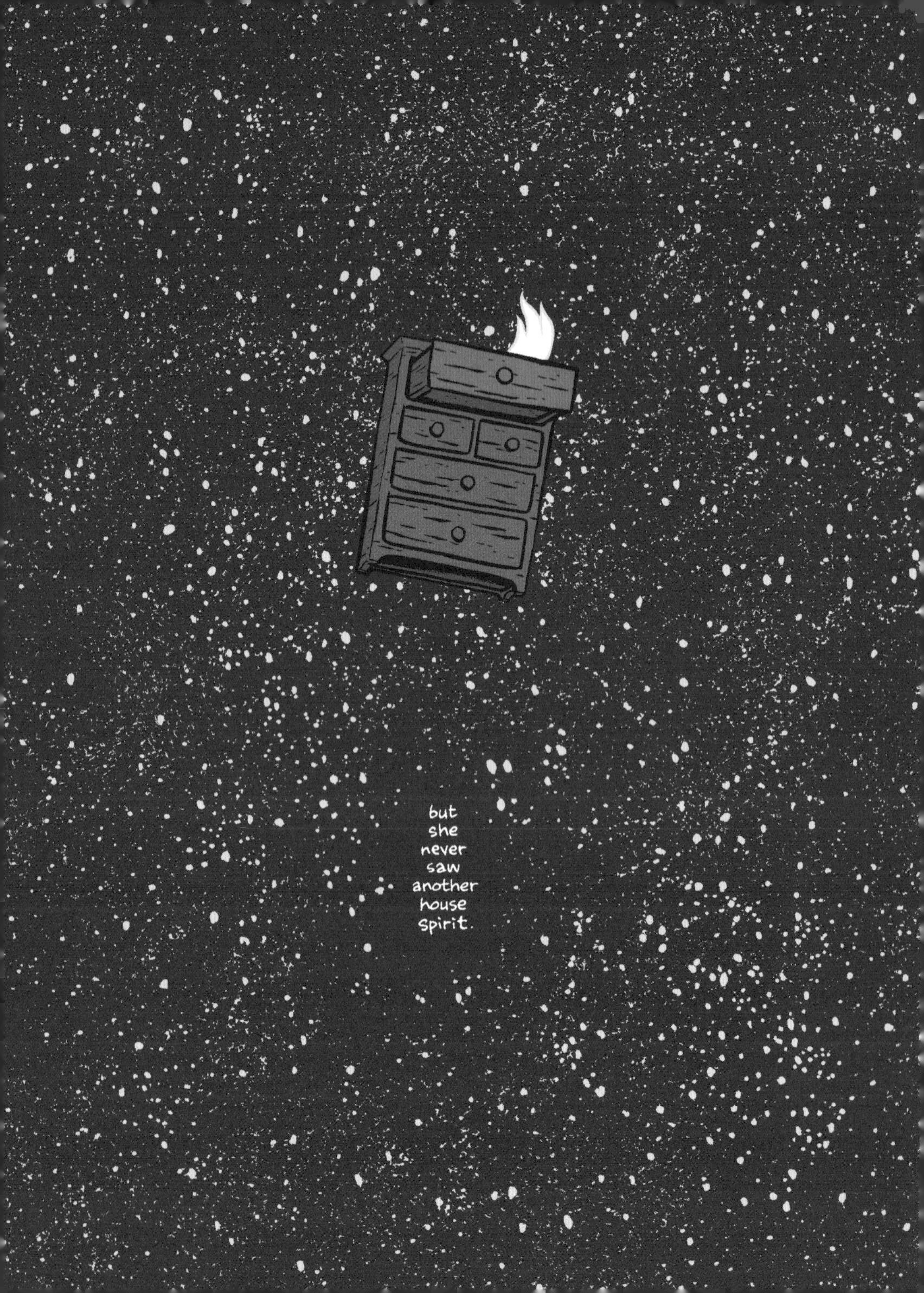
but she never saw another house spirit.

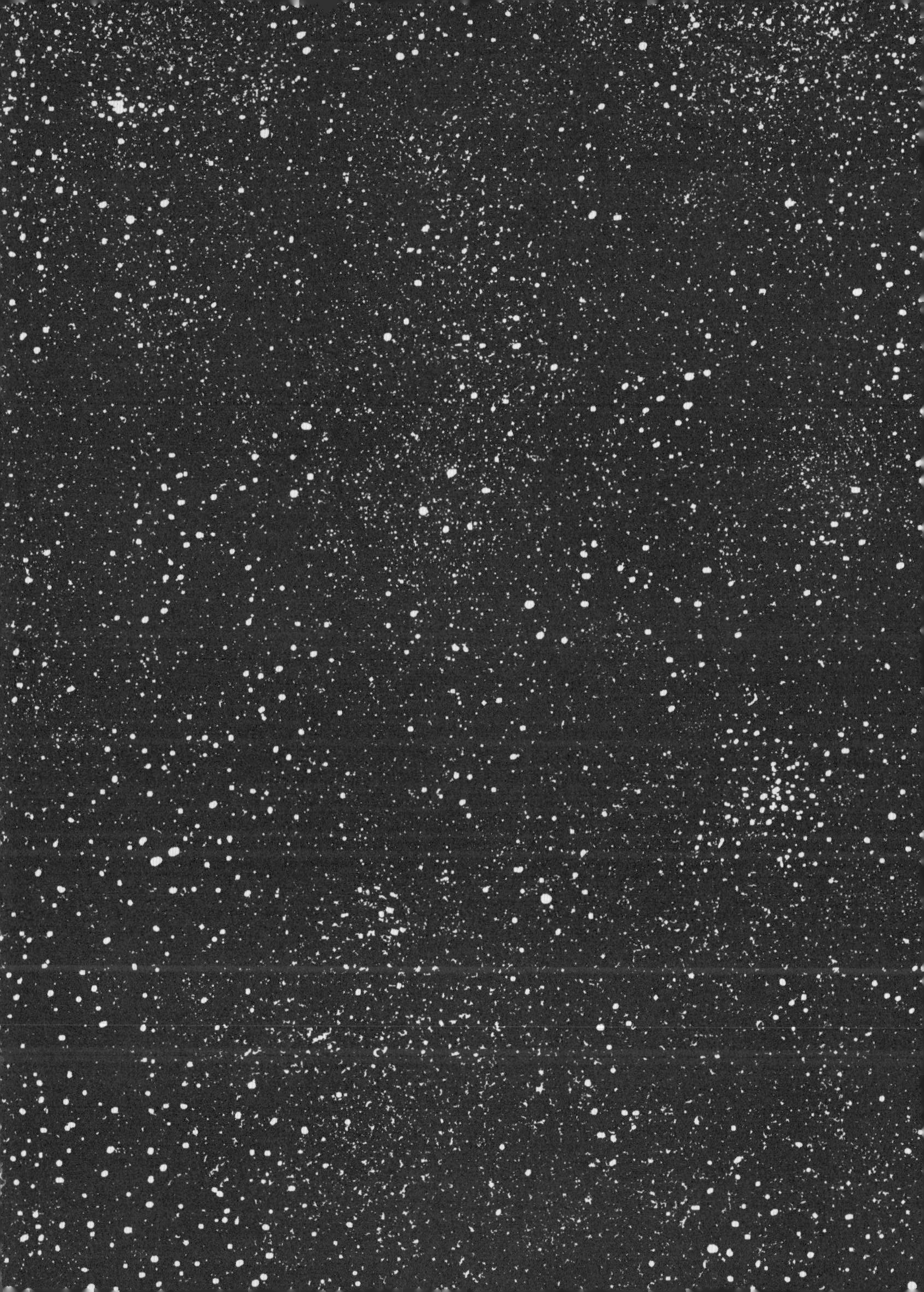

Acknowledgments

There would be no *Seconds* without my team of Jason, Nathan, and Dustin, and without the whole team at Random House/ Ballantine. I have been truly blessed to have all of you with me on this book. All love to my friends and family for all their support during these wild and crazy years. Thanks to Mike S. for providing the recipe in chapter 3—not only did he write it, he actually came to my house and cooked it in front of me, and then we ate it. Additional thanks to Joel and Cory, my food and restaurant consultants, and very special thanks to Heather, Julie, Rosanna, Vili, and Miguel, for helping me to not completely destroy my body during this process.

A Note about the Assistants

Jason Fischer (drawing assistant) is a cartoonist from Los Angeles now living in Portland, Oregon. He loves to draw monsters and food. He enjoys collecting rocks, Daruma dolls, knives, pressed pennies, and Playmobil people.

Nathan Fairbairn (color) is a colorist and writer of comics. He's also a pretty decent cook, despite what his kids might tell you. He lives in Vancouver, Canada.

Dustin Harbin (lettering) is a cartoonist who lives and works in Charlotte, North Carolina. He's too fussy to be a good cook but just fussy enough to be an okay baker.

Additional assistance provided by Megan Messina, Hannah Ayoubi, and Jeremy Arambulo. We love them.

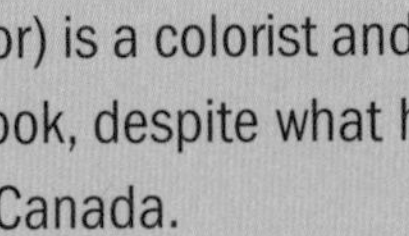
seconds

About the Author

Bryan Lee O'Malley is the creator of the bestselling Scott Pilgrim graphic novel series, which was adapted into a major motion picture, *Scott Pilgrim vs. the World,* in 2010. He lives in Los Angeles, where he continues to make comics.